One of the most unique and fascinating of all reference books, Wilstach's DICTIONARY OF SIMILES has proven an invaluable source book for writers and public speakers for more than three decades. Here you will find the most brilliant expressions of hundreds of the world's greatest authors, statesmen and public figures — the gems of thought and wisdom which have assured them lasting fame. Balzac, Chaucer, Shakespeare, Dickens and hundreds of other immortals contribute their store of similes, and such modern authors as George Bernard Shaw and Henry L. Mencken add wit and brightness to these pages.

From the many thousands of quotations — each carefully indexed by author and by subject — you can quickly find the simile which most closely expresses your meaning, the phrase which will add color and sparkle to your written or spoken words. And, for readers who like to browse, here are hundreds of pages of brilliant epigrams, clever couplets and quotations of lasting historical importance.

For everyone who works with the written or spoken language, here is an indispensable desk book for, as George Moore said, "It is hard to find a simile when one is seeking for one."

A DICTIONARY OF *SIMILES*

A DICTIONARY OF *SIMILES*

By FRANK J. WILSTACH

BONANZA BOOKS · NEW YORK

This edition published by Bonanza Books,
a division of Crown Publishers, Inc.,
by arrangement with Little, Brown and Company.
(A)

PRINTED IN THE UNITED STATES OF AMERICA

TO

FLORENCE WILSTACH

PREFACE TO THE SECOND EDITION

In the first edition of this dictionary, published in 1916, there were 17,000 similes, 1865 names in the index of authors, and 3465 subject headings. In this edition there have been added 2300 similes; 540 new authors have been added to the index, and there are 1200 new subject headings. The new matter will be found at the end of the volume.

The new index takes in all the old as well as the new matter, and the dates of birth and death of each author are given, together with dates of issue of anonymous poems, plays, and books. It will be noted that many of the ladies have stars after their names, indicating that no biographical data were available. It is necessary, it would appear, to catch an authoress young, else she refuses to divulge her age. One to whom I lately wrote for the date of her birth, replied: "Just write me down as 'twenty-nine-by-candle-light.'" A distinguished librarian of my acquaintance has suggested, when asking a lady author for her natal year, to threaten, if she refuses, to place after her name: "Ante-Civil War." Such means might fetch them; but such unkindness could not well be thought of outside of a Public Library.

It was pointed out in the preface to the first edition, that each event of world-wide interest, whether it be some invention, the introduction of some new style, a trend of thought or of manners, has usually led to the making of novel similes. The reader, so inclined, will discover in the added matter that there has been no change in this tendency. And it may be observed, furthermore, that much of the best wit and humor of the time finds its way into simile form.

Those who have had experience with type are aware of its satanic persistence towards error, and so the effort to provide approximate correctness in the text of this dictionary has been an arduous one. When it is said, ordinarily, that a line has been misquoted, it all depends upon which text has been accepted as final. One would imagine that the question of accuracy might be determined by consulting the first edition of an author's work. Considering that the first printing of any book is almost certain to be well sprinkled with mistakes, the frailty of this bland reliance will be apparent. And when it is taken into account that new errors are often made in correcting old ones and that authors have a habit of making changes from edition to edition, it will be seen that the maker of a Dictionary of Similes often has reason to be sorely perplexed.

But there are other curious and astonishing ways and means of providing annoyances. Take David Mallet's lovely couplet as an example:

"Her face was like the April morn
Clad in a wintry cloud."

These verses are to be found credited both to David Mallet and Vincent Bourne. The occasion for attributing them to Vincent Bourne is a curious one. The lines are to be found on page 212, in the 1743 edition of David Mallet's works. Along came Vincent Bourne, who translated the poem in which they appear into Latin, with the title "Thyrsis et Chloe." This Latin text is to be found on page

44 in the 1838 edition of Vincent Bourne's works. Some one then translated the Latin back into English, evidently overlooking the original authorship, and the deed was done.

There are, too, a number of similes to be met with, here and there, attributed to Shakespeare which are not to be found in his plays or his poems. The reason for this is not far to seek. Cibber, Tate, Garrick, and others, not entirely satisfied with the Bard as a dramatist, brought out revisions of the text and introduced new matter; and out of this came the spurious similes.

The correct spelling of names is still another occasion for lamentations. While the Elizabethans spelled their names with surprising variety — Shakespeare having spelled his name in a dozen or more different ways; Raleigh and others with equal diversity — these have finally been stabilized. Among modern writers, Gilbert Abbott À Beckett, the author of "The Comic History of England", for one, outdoes any of the Elizabethans. I have found his name in various books of reference, including the author's own published works, spelled in fourteen different ways. Moreover, writers other than the ladies have a way of changing their names that is often disconcerting, *vide:* Theodore Watts, who late in life affixed Dutton; and Ernest Seton Thompson, who turned his surname around and made it Ernest Thompson Seton.

Authors, too, whose names are identical are likely to get one into various temperatures of hot water. John Smith affixed to a quotation can mean little to a student without the date of birth and death, and for the reason that there has been a regiment of this name who have made their way into print. Then there have been three important Samuel Butlers; and as for John Browns, they are legion. Even Samuel Johnson without dates, after a name, may lead one far afield, for there were three in the eighteenth century: Doctor Samuel, the lexicographer; Samuel, commonly known as Maggoty or Fiddler, and quite a personage in his way; and that other Samuel, known as the doughty Whig. As in the first edition, where there could be any confusion on account of duplication, the date of birth and death has been given. It must be taken into account, also, that the ancients in this particular present some knotty problems. There were, for example, two Platos, one the philosopher, and the other a comic poet, both born the same year, 427 B.C. We are likewise confronted with two Senecas, one the orator and the other the philosopher, both living at Rome at the same time, and both with the same forename. One finds Bion affixed to quotations when, in point of fact there were Bion of Smyrna, Greek bucolic poet, *fl.* B.C. 280; Bion, Scythian philosopher, *fl.* B.C. 250; and Bion, Greek philosopher, *fl.* B.C. 241. It is pretty much a matter, as the saying goes, of paying your money and taking your choice.

I was greatly surprised on the publication of this dictionary to discover that so little was known of those renowned and prolific authors Anon and Ibid. Indeed, I had many letters saying that they could not be identified even after deep and plodding research. That such voluminous writers as Messrs. Anonymous and Ibidem should have so limited an acquaintanceship, despite their generally recognized talent, was indeed a matter for wonderment.

At the same time several reviewers expressed the fear that general use of this dictionary might incite the intellectual lacunæ to a slavish reliance. Such a contingency need not have been feared, nor has it been justified, except, possibly, in the case of musical comedy librettists. Certainly it was not my purpose to provide a grabbag out of which stencilled intellects might snatch tinselled phrases, scented sentiments, and jewelled periods.

Artists visit galleries, not for the purpose of making slavish copies of the masters, but rather to study technique. Collections of phrases, whether they be dictionaries of poetic or prose quotations, of proverbs, or of similes, may reasonably be regarded by literary artists as galleries where they may ramble, and possibly be tempted to originality. This dictionary, however, was not designed as a crutch for the dullard, but rather as a yeast for the platitudinarian.

It was noted in the first preface that I had not been able to discover, among other similes, the author of, "Noisy as a living skeleton having a fit on a hardwood floor." I have lately found that this simile appeared in an account of a baseball game, written by Leonard Washburn, in the eighties, for the since defunct Chicago *Inter-Ocean.* Washburn, who died in 1891, was one of the first of the baseball writers who injected humor into their reports. Another simile from his pen was of the sun-kissed Captain Anson: "His eyes were like twin daisies in a bucket of blood." It should not be overlooked, however, that Mark Twain had already pointed the way to sport writers. In describing a ball game, he wrote that one of the players "Threw himself on his stomach to slide to his base; it was like an iron-clad coming into port." One of the most picturesque baseball similes of late times was that by Heywood Broun — who, describing a heavy-footed base runner, in a so-called "World Series", wrote, "He ran the bases as if he was hauling William H. Taft in a rickshaw." Then a Philadelphia team was described by another sport writer as "Having about as much chance as a woodpecker making a nest in a concrete telephone pole." And a local hero of the diamond was said to have "a face like a jar of warts."

Not to be outdone, the scriveners of fisticuffs have not lagged far behind. Some unknown genius is quoted by Henry Seidel Canby, in his "English Composition in Theory and Practice", "As the exhausted prizefighter sat on his second's knee, his head dangled about like a poppy in a shower." Another pugilist was said, after a battle, to have "looked as though he had stuck his head into a bag full of cats, to see who was there." In Cincinnati a fighter was said to "have gone down like a letter in a mail chute." A champion was defeated, and his punishment was as "cruel as the pinch of a painless dentist."

It is very likely that never before in the history of sport has there been anything comparable to the rhetorical cataclysm that followed the historic meeting of Messrs. Willard and Dempsey at Toledo, Ohio, on July 4th, 1919. Mr. Frank Moran, the distinguished literary luminary of the "squared circle", also lent the charm of the simile to his compositions, for on the day before the famous Dempsey-Willard event he clicked off on his typewriter that "Willard showed a tenseness and a timorousness as well as a *qui vive* that was noticeable for its absence." Nor could any possible fault have been found with Mr. Tom O'Rourke's style, he having also remarked the day before the 1919 event that "Dempsey fighting Willard is like a bull trying to butt a locomotive off the track." This was a bad guess by Mr. O'Rourke, but a happy figure of speech. Mr. "Bugs" Bear said after the event, "Willard had about as much chance as a dishfaced chimpanzee in a beauty contest." Harry C. Witwer said that Dempsey "hits like an epileptic pile driver." According to Percy Hammond, when Dempsey started in on Willard's stomach and jaw, the sound thereof was "like rain dropping on a tin roof"; also, in a minute that "Willard looked like something the cat had brought in." Finally, Kerr N. Petrie reported that around the ringside there were many interesting personalities who "had ears like mangled doughnuts"; and the distinguished "Tad" discovered that Dempsey's brother at the ringside wore "a shirt that looked like a sea lion." The report that the contest between the gentlemen was a "frame-up" caused Mr. Witwer to remark, "If it was, so was the battle of the Marne."

One does not have to wander far afield, however, to find diverting and trenchant similes on almost any subject one might select, such, for example, as war and politics. Homer and Shakespeare have provided many memorable specimens, as one may easily discover. A famous simile has come down to us attributed to Frederick the Great: "An army, like a snake, goes upon its belly." And so also Marshal Saxe: "Soldiers are like cloaks, — one thinks of us only when it rains." Tom Brown had a like thought, stated in a different way: "Though a soldier in peace is like a chimney in summer, yet what wise man would pluck down his chimney because his almanac told him it was the middle of June." The late World War brought forth many picturesque similes. Coningsby Dawson said, "The guns begin to stamp like stallions." R. Hugh Knyvett, speaking of the gibbering of the various nationalities, said it was "like a gramophone-shop gone crazy." Describing a machine gun in action, Ian Hay Beath wrote that it made a noise "like a giant tearing calico." And Charles W. Baker said that "The German shells were coming down like rice at a wedding." Turning to politics, it will be found that the Democrats have been rather severely dealt with. "Brick" Pomeroy remarked that "It didn't last him as long as a ten dollar bill would a Democrat the night before election." And George W. Peck said that something came "down on him like a newly elected Republican President on a Democratic postmaster." "Bitter," writes Abe Martin, "as a disappointed Democrat." General Benjamin F. Butler declared that "The Democratic party is like a man riding backward in a carriage. It never sees a thing until it is gone by." Finally, Thomas Riley Marshall, while Vice-President of the United States, said his office was "like a man in a cataleptic state: he cannot speak; he cannot move; he suffers no pain, and yet he is perfectly conscious of everything that is going on about him."

It is matter of regret by the compiler, that since the first edition of this dictionary was published, he has not been able to enjoy a larger leisure for research, not only among the classics, but in modern literature. There has been no society of simile hunters to supplement his labors, so he has plodded on alone and, it is hoped, to some little purpose. It may here be said, also, that there has been as cordial a welcome for the colloquial simile as for those which were discovered in old and forgotten tomes. There is a disposition, however, among the long-haired contingent, who "hold high the banner of the ideal", to lament any contact with the present, — an attitude that looks upon whatever is old as golden and whatever is new as gilt. Such a state of mind is certain to lead to literary dry-rot. Because a simile has been discovered in an ephemeral contribution to the press, makes it none the less interesting. Witness a few that have lately come to hand:

Grave but satisfied, like a widower.

Flabbergasting as the amorous glances of a lady embalmer.

Surprised as a sardine that went to sleep in the ocean and woke up in a delicatessen store.

With nearly six hundred pages to select from, it is not necessary to multiply examples. Meanwhile, the making of similes goes on endlessly from day to day, — new ideas inviting novel and stimulating turns of thought.

Frank J. Wilstach

PREFACE

THE simile is one of the most ancient forms of speech. It is the handmaid of all early word records. It has proved itself essential to every form of human utterance.

If our first parents had had a Boswell, many similes which are now in general use would be known as having been current in the Garden of Eden. Undoubtedly, on many occasions, Father Adam, when addressing Mother Eve, made use of "Cold as ice", "Busy as a bee", "Proud as a peacock", "Weak as water", "Angry as a wasp", and "Bitter as gall." With reliable data, many a simile which is now marked Anon. would be credited to Adam.

In the absence of a Boswell, however, we have other authorities who testify that Father Adam and Mother Eve made frequent use of similes in their Garden conversation. As Moses, in his brief account of creation, failed to report the talks of our first parents, we are deprived of his testimony; but what Moses overlooked, John Milton and Elizabeth Barrett Browning have supplied.

Some of the most familiar similes in general use are to be found in the Old Testament. Among them are: "Multiply as the stars of heaven", "Unstable as water", "Still as a stone", "White as snow", "Swifter than a weaver's shuttle", "Boil like a pot", "Firm as a stone", "Melted like wax", "Sharp as a two-edged sword", and "Bitter as wormwood." The Songs of Solomon are a rich mine of similes; including, "Thy lips are like a thread of scarlet", "Thy neck is like the tower of David builded for an armoury", "Thy teeth are like a flock of sheep that are even shorn, which came up from the washing", and "Cruel as the grave."

From many other sources the antiquity of the simile is proved. In the time of Rameses II of Egypt, 1292–1225 B.C., according to Breasted's "History of Egypt", the Poem of Pentaur was written. The Heroic Theban poet's work was so highly prized that it was carved on the temple walls in hard stone. Pentaur was not ignorant of the simile. Thus he speaks of Pharaoh:

> "His heart is firm, his courage is like that of the god of war."
> "His courage is firm, like that of a bull."
> "The King is dreadful as the grim lion in the valley."
> "He appeared like the sun-god at his rising in the early morn."

Of Seti, the father of Rameses II, an unlocked inscription says: "He is as a jackal which rushed prowling through the land, as a grim lion that frequents hidden paths, as a powerful bull with sharpened horns." Now this Rameses, Ramses, or Ramessu, was that Pharaoh who oppressed the Israelites, the father of the princess who found the child Moses hid among the bulrushes.

Homer, Virgil, Horace, and all the ancient writers, abound in similes; but the first to confine his literary expression to the making of similes alone was a Pythagorean philosopher, Demophilus, whose history is little known. His work, "Life's Culture and Conduct", is extant only in portions which are in the form of selections called "Dialectic Similitudes." The first known edition of the work was printed in 1638. There were five editions in the seventeenth century, three in the eighteenth, and one in the nineteenth century. There is an interesting reference to Demophilus in "The Phoenix", described as "a collection of old and rare fragments", published by William Gowans, New York, 1835:

"Demophilus appears to have enjoyed the dignity of archon at Athens, where it was no unusual thing for the character of magistrate and philosopher to be united in the same person. Respecting the time when he lived, it is impossible to arrive at an absolute certainty. The most probable conjecture is that he flourished about the beginning of the Christian era, and prior to the reign of the Emperor Marcus Antoninus. Such of his writings as are extant have come down to us in company with the philosophical works of Maximus Tyrius. Whether they owe their preservation to the latter philosopher having, from his conviction of their excellence, appended them to his own writings, is, though not unlikely, impossible to determine."

Thus the making of similes has gone on from age to age. The New Testament is not so prolific in the use of this figure of speech as the Old; but the writers of the New had a way, not unknown to the Old, of repeating the same similes many times. Not only that, but many that are found in the Old reappear in the New Testament.

Since the very beginning of English literature, the simile has been a favorite figure of speech. This is particularly true of the English writings which obtained before the time of Elizabeth, and all of the great Elizabethans made happy use of it.

This volume, so far as I have been able to ascertain, is the first attempt to collect the best similes from English, as well as from all other literatures. It was not until the present collection was finished that I found Demophilus had several rivals. There was one collection of similes made in the sixteenth century, and three during the seventeenth. These books are:

(1) Certaine very proper and most profitable similes, also manie very notable virtues. Anthonie Fletcher, London, 1595.

(2) A treasurie or store-house of similies: both pleasant, delightful, and profitable, for all estates of men in generall. Newly collected into heades and common-places: by Robert Cawdray, London, 1600.

(3) A century of Similes, Thomas Shelton, London, 1640.

(4) Things new and old; or a store-house of Similes, John Spencer, 1658.

Of these four books, three, namely, Anthonie Fletcher's, Robert Cawdray's, and John Spencer's, are in the Library of Congress. Only one, John Spencer's, which is a reprint, is in the New York Public Library. All four are to be found in the British Museum. I have been able to examine three of the four books, missing that compiled by Thomas Shelton. The three I have seen are not, as the titles suggest, collections of similes, but are religious dissertations. Of the three, Robert Cawdray's is the only one with a savor of humor. There is, indeed, some justification for stating on his title page: "Similes: both pleasant, delightful, and profitable." By turning to the index, and examining some of the similes taken from his book, the reader will discover that while Robert Cawdray was an uncompromising "devil-chaser", he was possessed, at times, with a pungent wit. His statement, "Newly collected into heades", does not, as one might suppose, mean that he had collected the similes of the great writers of England up to his time; but merely that they are his own original efforts. His quotations are taken almost entirely from the scriptures. John Spencer appears to have known nothing of Chaucer, Spenser, Shakespeare, or Butler. In fact, his book shows that he was intimately acquainted only with the ecclesiastical writers of his time.

Perhaps some student of literature, — a hundred years hence, — will turn to this book to discover if I were acquainted in any degree with some writer now unknown to fame, but whose name will then be on everybody's lips! This, to me at least, is an interesting speculation. Who will then be remembered? Will it be George Ade or Henry James; O. Henry or Mrs. Humphry Ward; Joseph Conrad or George Meredith; Alfred Henry Lewis or Ambrose Bierce; Maurice Hewlett or Walter Pater; John Davidson or Rudyard Kipling? Robert Cawdray, in ignoring Shakespeare, — and indeed all the great Elizabethan writers, — thus missed his chance for a niche in the Temple of Fame.

The first to make a collection of similes was John Ray, botanist and miscellaneous writer. His "A Collection of English Proverbs" was published in 1670, and there have been many subsequent editions. It was not Ray's purpose to group together the proverbs and incidentally the similes to be found in English literature, but rather those in colloquial use by the people of England. The "Proverbial Similes" which he collected comprise but eight and a half pages of the two hundred and eighty, of the fifth edition of his book. Many of those gathered by Ray are of a character too gross for modern taste, while others are of a distinctly local character. Other collectors added many which came into general use after Ray's time; but all avoided making use of similes to be found in the works of the writers of preceding ages. The first to overcome this reluctance was Vincent Stuckey Lean, whose great work, "Lean's Collectanea", in five volumes, was published at Bristol, England, in 1903. A part of the second volume of this erudite compilation is given over to "A New Treasury of Similes." Lean not only embodied in his work all of the similes to be found in the various books of proverbs, but added very many from the old English writers. It is evident that he had a very considerable Elizabethan library to delve in; but, oddly enough, he made use of but three modern similes, — one each from Dickens, Tennyson, and George Eliot. Of the four simile books mentioned, Lean knew of but one, and that by Robert Cawdray.

I began this Dictionary of Similes in 1894. It did not occur to me at once that there might be any particular need for such a book, — nor had George Moore yet written: "It is hard to find a simile when one is seeking for one." One day in the spring of that year, when in Boston, I was looking over the morning papers and, being interested in some incident at the State House, read that "the news spread like wildfire." Having noted the coincidence of all the newspapers using this simile, and having observed its frequent use in the press, I asked a journalistic acquaintance if there was no substitute for "spread like wildfire." He replied that he had never heard of news spreading in any other way. My curiosity aroused, I stepped into the bookstore of Little, Brown & Company, then located in Washington Street, near the *Globe* newspaper office, and asked for a "Dictionary of Similes." The clerk looked in vain over the shelves; then, having fumbled through the leaves of a huge volume, returned with the information that such a book had never been published. As I was actively engaged at the time, I had then no intention of supplying the apparent omission. But from that day I began to copy into a large blank book the similes in every book I read. Finding this collection of use to others, as well as to myself, it occurred to me that as opportunity presented I would begin with Chaucer and gather all the useful and picturesque similes from all of the important poets and prose writers, down to the present time. It seemed an endless undertaking; but I pursued the work with growing interest and delight. As my occupation during the intervening years took me back and forth from New York to San Francisco and hither and thither to all parts of the country, much of the work was done on railroad trains, and many an evening hour was spent in the libraries of Boston, Washington, Chicago, Detroit, Cincinnati, New Orleans, St. Louis, and other cities.

Victor Hugo, in "Les Miserables", tells of an old man who never went out without a book, and who seldom came back without two. This has a humorous application to myself. Year after year I have carried about with me some volume or other on which I had set my covetous eyes, hoping during an idle moment in a busy day to rifle it of its similes. And often, like the character in "Les Miserables", I have ventured forth with a single volume and returned with a precious arm-load. So this work has been carried on through sheer love of the chase.

To shake all the similes, as leaves from the forest, of English Literature would be a task beyond the possibilities of one human life. Therefore, such a collection must necessarily be incomplete, except in so far as the great masters are concerned, and to have excluded the best from modern writers would have deprived such a collection of very much of its interest and charm. I have not been influenced by the reputation of any contemporary writer; but have selected those similes which seemed really worth while.

When I came to collate the similes under headings, — similes collected during nearly a quarter of a century, and from thousands of volumes, — I discovered that there were hundreds of duplicates. So, I credited the simile to that writer who was the one farthest back in point of time. When any simile was used by a group of authors of the same age, through necessity I have marked it anonymous.

In numerous instances, it will be discovered that I have given credit for many similes to authors far back in the reaches of time which are usually attributed to modern writers. There is no certainty, of course, that many of these similes were really original with the authors to whom they are credited. To have examined the writings of all authors would have been an impossibility. While I have been able to find many an apt simile as having been used hundreds of years before any collector has so far discovered them, I have no doubt I shall find, in time, that many similes in this Dictionary credited to a modern writer, have been "picked from the worm holes of old time."

Although I have drag-netted the ocean, as well as the numerous narrow streams and wide rivers of literature, for similes, many a rare and curious specimen has doubtless escaped me. Had all been secured this collection would be of too great a size for general use.

To discover the authorship of many curious similes has been a matter of long quest. Here are three examples: "Cold as an enthusiastic New England audience", "Noisy as a living skeleton having a fit on a hardwood floor", and "About as much privacy as a goldfish." The first of these I had from the lips of James Whitcomb Riley, in 1886. But when I lately wrote to the Hoosier poet and asked him if he were its father, he disclaimed ever having heard of the child. Years ago, I noted that Opie Read had been given credit for "Noisy as a living skeleton having a fit on a hardwood floor"; but Mr. Read, some years back, denied the authorship. On the other hand, Irvin S. Cobb informs me that he accepts all blame for having made merry with the privacy of the goldfish.

Much of an interesting nature might be said on the subjects chosen for similes during different periods. This will be apparent to any reader who has curiosity enough to examine this volume. Nature it will readily be observed, had well nigh the sole appeal for the ancients, — for Homer and Virgil particularly. As we come down to modern times, we find that new and novel inventions have been seized upon as means for comparison. Byron, shortly after the introduction of gas for illumination in the playhouse, wrote in "Don Juan":

"Grand a sight
As is a theatre lit up by gas."

Then came the adding machine, and Oliver Wendell Holmes made use of Mr. Babbage's calculating machine as a comparison for certainty; Morgan Robertson wrote "Faint as the voice of the telephone", and, lately, a play was advertised as "Crackling with wit like a Marconi." Then too, — "Sly as a submarine." The moving picture also furnishes interesting examples. Its first form was the magic lantern. Thomas Moore made use of it:

"But now 'a change came o'er my dream,'
Like the magic lantern's shifting slider."

The next invention was the diorama, and we have George Eliot saying: "Shifts its scenes like a diorama." Finally, when the moving picture was perfected, William Archer wrote: "Feverishly accelerate, like the movements we see in the cinematograph."

It would be unwise to credit a dramatist with a simile used in a play, for the reason that actors have, more especially in musical comedy, a way of introducing some happy phrase with or without the author's consent. It is astonishing how quickly a simile heard in a play will come into current use. Not long ago I overheard two persons talking in a street car, and one said: "It was as cruel as a barren stepmother's slap." I had no notion that this was an original phrase with the person in the street car. That night I went to see a play by Lady Gregory, and then discovered the source of the simile; the authoress, however, had written not "cruel", but "Hard as a barren stepmother's slap."

From earliest time poets have been remarkable for their intimate acquaintance with the solar system. Astronomers themselves could hardly have made so many observations on the sun, the moon, and the stars, — the moon particularly. Also, the bards, when in need of a simile, have been free in their use of the boundless ocean, and with the rippling brook as well. The flowers of the fields, the birds of the air, — of the latter the eagle being easily the favorite, — have graphically served their purpose. While the moon shows signs of waning popularity, the eagle retains an undiminished favor. Indeed, the poets have so delighted in similes that they have written whole poems, every line a simile. A small volume might easily be made of this species of poetistic ingenuity, — the most curious example being the one devised by John Gay.

Thomas Hood, in his poem "The Tale of the Trumpet", relates the adventures of an "old woman hard of hearing", in which he rings the changes on the simile "deaf as a post." By way of novelty, Sterne began the fifteenth chapter of "Tristram Shandy" with a simile, and added, — "I don't think the comparison a bad one:"

"An eye is, for all the world, exactly like a cannon, in this respect, That it is not so much the eye or the cannon, in themselves, as it is the carriage of the eye, and the carriage of the cannon; by which both the one and the other are enabled to do so much execution."

In the use of similes, Chaucer, Shakespeare, Spenser, Shelley and Swinburne were the most profuse. Of these, Swinburne, easily led the others in this form of expression. In fact there is hardly a page of his works that does not contain from one to three similes. The poet who made the smallest use of the simile was Walt Whitman.

I have taken the liberty, rather broadly, of including in this book, as an aid for reference, a number of comparisons from various sources which would not technically come under the definition of simile. There is, of course, a thin shade of difference, but one overlooked by many grammarians. However, when one can, without undue license, enlarge the usefulness of a book of reference there is no necessity of allowing research to be embarrassed by unimportant breaches of definition. The reader will find, I trust, the few comparisons in this dictionary quite as welcome as the out and out similes.

To achieve anything like correctness in quotation has proved, at times, a most perplexing matter, for the reason that the texts of many of the poets have undergone, from editor to editor, various alterations. With Shakespeare, because of the imperfect First Folio, this was necessary. But, in tampering with the text of the First Folio, there have been many curious revisions, or new readings, well known to students of the Bard. The most singular to come under my observation appears in the Blair edition of Shakespeare, which, according to its editor, J. Talfourd Blair, was "Carefully edited and compared with the best text." In this volume one may read:

"How sharper than a *servant's* tooth it is
To have a thankless child."

In this case we may well rely upon the First Folio, which has it "serpent's", not "servant's" tooth.

The ideal method would have been to select only those editions of the classics which have acquired authority. But this has been quite impossible, for I have had to accept whatever I have been able to lay hands on, for my purpose. In making verifications there have been disclosed many discrepancies. Take, for example, Thomas Campbell's verse:

"Like angel visits, few and far between."

The words "angel visits" are often printed as a compound word, but in Hoyt's "Cyclopedia of Practical Quotations", in one place they are printed as two words, and in another hyphenated.

Storms have raged around Robert Burns' best-known simile, beginning: "But pleasures are like poppies spread." These verses appeared first in Francis Grose's "Antiquities of Scotland", (London, 1791), volume 2, page 199–201, as follows:

"But pleasures are like poppies spread,
You seize the flower, its bloom is shed;
Or like the snow falls in the river,
A moment white — then melts for ever;

Or like the borealis race,
That flit ere you can point their place;
Or like the rainbow's lovely form,
Evanishing amid the storm."

Chambers printed the couplet:

"Or like the snowfall in the river,
A moment white — then melts for ever."

But it will be observed that Burns had it "snow falls", not "snowfall." The ever careful John Bartlett changed the third verse, making it read:

"Or, like the snow-fall in the river."

Several editors have arbitrarily made the line read "Like snow falls *on* the river." But Douglas says in his edition of 1877: "We suspect that Burns would have preferred: "Like snowflakes on the river."

In conclusion I would quote the final passage of Thomas Fuller's preface to John Spencer's "Things new and old, or a store-house of Similes": "But the reader will catch cold, by keeping him too long in the porch of the Preface, who now (the door being opened) may enter into the house itself."

Frank J. Wilstach.

INDEX

The * indicates that date has not been found.

SHEIL, RICHARD LALOR, 1791–1851: 157, 178, 246, 388, 499, 502, 507, 533
SHELLEY, PERCY BYSSHE, 1792–1822: 5, 9, 11, 14, 18, 21, 23, 25, 31, 35, 40, 43, 47, 54, 57, 62, 63, 64, 70, 77, 78, 80, 82, 85, 86, 87, 89, 95, 102, 120, 122, 125, 129, 134, 136, 137, 140, 141, 143, 144, 146, 148, 149, 150, 153, 154, 160, 166, 168, 171, 175, 181, 187, 189, 192, 201, 204, 205, 214, 218, 221, 222, 224, 228, 229, 230, 232, 236, 239, 242, 245, 257, 263, 267, 268, 276, 281, 284, 286, 289, 292, 298, 299, 303, 306, 307, 310, 311, 317, 325, 326, 327, 329, 336, 343, 344, 346, 352, 354, 356, 361, 363, 371, 377, 378, 381, 382, 384, 390, 394, 403, 404, 405, 409, 411, 413, 414, 422, 425, 429, 430, 433, 439, 445, 447, 449, 451, 454, 459, 462, 466, 473, 484, 500, 505, 519, 562, 576
SHELTON, THOMAS, "A CENTURY OF SIMILES", 1640–: 524, 548
SHENSTONE, WILLIAM, 1714–1763: 40, 111, 169, 230, 245, 260, 309, 371, 554
SHEPPARD, ELIZABETH S., 1830–1862: 413
SHERBURNE, SIR EDWARD, 1618–1702: 253, 366, 483
SHERIDAN, CAROLINE E. S. *See* NORTON, MRS.
SHERIDAN, HELEN SELINA, 1816–1903: 195
SHERIDAN, RICHARD BRINSLEY, 1751–1816: 10, 14, 27, 45, 48, 106, 112, 123, 196, 338, 350, 362, 414, 433
SHERMAN, ELLEN BURNS, 1867–: 449
SHERMAN, FRANK DEMPSTER, 1860–1916: 200, 292, 409, 427
SHERMAN, STUART P., 1881–: 535
SHILLABER, BENJAMIN P., 1814–1890: 327
SHIRLEY, JAMES, 1596–1666: 30, 165, 296
SHOEMAKER, BLANCHE, 1888–: 35
SHORTER, MRS. C. K. *See* SIGERSON, DORA
SIDNEY, SIR PHILIP, 1554–1586: 7, 49, 129, 185, 197, 228, 260, 366, 458, 497, 522, 569
SIENKIEWICZ, HENRYK, 1846–1916: 214, 383, 399
SIGERSON, DORA, 1866–1918: 5
SIGOURNEY, LYDIA HUNTLEY, 1791–1865: 120, 170, 434
SILL, EDWARD R., 1841–1887: 113, 154, 330
SILL, LOUISE MORGAN, *: 313
SIMONDS, FRANK H., 1878–: 500
SINCLAIR, CATHERINE, 1800–1864: 302
SINCLAIR, MAY, *: 512, 524, 559
SIRACH, fl. B.C. 190–170: 163
SITWELL, EDITH LOUISA, 1887–: 509
SITWELL, OSBERT, 1892–: 551
SKELTON, JOHN, 1460–1529: 7, 19, 41, 139, 146, 153, 171, 178, 187, 198, 201, 212, 229, 235, 248, 288, 324, 343, 377, 390, 436, 452, 478, 484
"SKETCH", LONDON, 1922: 540
SKETCHLEY, ARTHUR. *See* ROSE, GEORGE
SKIPSEY, JOSEPH, 1832–1903: 188
SLADEN, DOUGLAS B. W., 1856–: 160, 185
SLICK, SAM, 1796–1865: 85, 106, 166, 200, 239, 251, 402, 441, 478, 487, 505
SMART, CHRISTOPHER, 1722–1771: 35, 82, 226, 313, 452
SMEDLEY, MENELLA B., 1820–1877: 37
SMILES, SAMUEL, 1812–1904: 53, 203, 272, 307
SMITH, ABIGAIL A., 1765–1813: 67
SMITH, ALEXANDER, 1830–1867: 13, 37, 44, 54, 104, 121, 173, 175, 178, 193, 227, 240, 266, 267, 280, 290, 303, 328, 340, 354, 363, 366, 425, 426, 454, 462, 464, 466, 478, 517, 550, 552, 571, 573
SMITH, EDMUND, 1672–1710: 435
SMITH, ELIZABETH O., 1776–1806: 268, 358
SMITH, GORDON ARTHUR, *: 527
SMITH, F. BERKELEY, 1868–: 501, 526, 531, 546, 568
SMITH, F. HOPKINSON, 1838–1915: 529, 554
SMITH, CAPTAIN JOHN, 1580–1631: 511
SMITH, JOHN, 1662–1717: 558
SMITH, SIR JAMES E., 1759–1828: 501
SMITH, HARRY B., 1860–: 156, 286, 473, 509
SMITH, HORACE, 1779–1849; JAMES, 1775–1839: 229, 234
SMITH, HORACE, 1779–1849: 12, 69, 276, 338, 402, 468, 487
SMITH, HORATIO. *See* SMITH, HORACE
SMITH, J. RUSSELL, 1810–1894: 55
SMITH, JAMES, 1775–1839: 37, 41, 82, 229, 270, 294, 402
SMITH, SEBA, 1792–1868: 371
SMITH, STEPHEN, fl. 1872: 165, 235, 237, 470
SMITH, SYDNEY, 1771–1845: 46, 115, 253, 334, 450
SMOLLETT, TOBIAS, 1721–1771: 27, 105, 131, 178, 213, 226, 274, 291, 312, 350, 357, 366, 385, 390, 392, 396, 409, 444, 445, 452, 480, 484, 521, 539, 520, 522
SMOLLEY, GEORGE W., 1833–1916: 73
SOCRATES, B.C. 430–399: 145
SOMERVILLE, WILLIAM, 1675–1742: 37, 143, 157, 333, 366, 442
SOPHOCLES, B.C. 496–406: 147, 234
SOTHEBY, WILLIAM, 1757–1833: 346
SOUTH, ROBERT, 1634–1716: 216, 229, 314, 355, 491, 537, 561
SOUTHERNE, THOMAS, 1660–1746: 521
SOUTHGATE, "MANY THOUGHTS ON MANY THINGS", 1858: 566
SOUTHESK, EARL OF. *See* CARNEGIE, SIR WILLIAM
SOUTHEY, ROBERT, 1774–1843: 3, 18, 21, 22, 24, 30, 31, 35, 43, 47, 52, 79, 89, 95,

A DICTIONARY OF
SIMILES

A DICTIONARY OF SIMILES

A

Abandon.

Abandoned, like the waves we leave behind us. — DONALD G. MITCHELL.

Abate.

Abate, like a flame grown moderate. — ROBERT HERRICK.

Abide.

The sweet-laden thoughts come, like bees, to abide in his heart as a hive. — D. F. MCCARTHY.

Ability.

Native ability without education is like a tree without fruit. — ARISTIPPUS.

Natural abilities are like natural plants, that need pruning by study. — BACON.

The abilities of man must fall short on one side or the other, like too scanty a blanket when you are abed. — SIR WILLIAM TEMPLE.

Ablaze.

All ablaze like poppies in the sun. — OUIDA.

Abortive.

Abortive as the first-born bloom of spring. — MILTON.

Abound.

Abound, like blades of grass which clothe the pregnant ground. — GEORGE SANDYS.

Abrupt.

Abruptly as string that snaps beneath the bow. — E. W. HORNUNG.

Abrupt as a sultry little thunder shower. — AMY LESLIE.

Absence.

Absence, like death, sets a seal on the image of those we have loved. — GOLDSMITH.

Absolute.

Absolute, sure, as the sun-dial's gnomon, compassing all the world's fate. — A. H. BEESLY.

Absolute as the art which built the Parthenon. — BULWER-LYTTON.

Absolute as the Sultan of Turkey. — MACAULAY.

Abstemious.

Abstemious at the banquet as a hermit. — C. C. COLTON.

Absurd.

Absurd as an excuse. — ANON.

Absurd as to ask a man if he'll have salt on his ice cream. — IBID.

Absurd as to ask if the flowers love the dew. — IBID.

Absurd as to expect a beauty to search for her likeness in the back of a looking-glass. — IBID.

How absurd you must have looked with your legs and arms in the air, like a shipwrecked tea-table. — DION BOUCICAULT.

As absurd as for an epic poet to disdain the composition of a perfect epigram, or a consummate musician the melody of a faultless song. — BULWER-LYTTON.

Absurd as if you took a divorce petition to a chemist's. — ANTON TCHEKHOV.

Absurd — *continued.*

Absurd as giving bread-pills for a broken leg. — KIPLING.

Absurd as to imagine that the hair-lip or carbuncled nose a man sees in the glass, belongs to the figure in the mirror, and not to his own face. — BONNELL THORNTON.

Abundant.

Abundant as air and water. — ANON.

Abundant as the light of the sun. — CARLYLE.

As the sycamore trees are in the vale for abundance. — OLD TESTAMENT.

Abuse.

If abuse, like a weed, be cut down by the scythe of neglect, it will die of itself. — THOMAS BRYDSON.

Accelerate.

Feverishly accelerated like the movements we see in a cinematograph. — WILLIAM ARCHER.

Accounted.

We are accounted as sheep for the slaughter. — NEW TESTAMENT.

Accumulate.

Accumulate . . . like acorns beneath the trees of a modern forest. — THOMAS H. HUXLEY.

Accurate.

Could tell the hour by his movements as accurately as by a sun-dial. — WASHINGTON IRVING.

As accurately as a bugler knows the notes of the reveille. — OUIDA.

Ache.

His full heart ached with love's sweet pain
Like a sealed fountain, charged with rain,
That longs to sing in the summer air,
Yet faints in the caverns of despair.
— T. BUCHANAN READ.

Acrobats.

A troupe of acrobats is like a combination to a safe: both have tumblers. — ANON.

Action.

Like a squirrel in a cage, always in action. — APHRA BEHN.

Actions of the last age are like almanacs of the last year. — SIR JOHN DENHAM.

A good action like a ring on the finger, the relief of a man of wit, the patronization of a clergyman. — HUGO.

Reprehensible actions are like overstrong brandies; you cannot swallow them at a draught. — IBID.

Our actions are like the termination of verses, which we rhyme as we please. — ROCHEFOUCAULD.

No more action than a stalled hearse in a snow storm. — WILLIAM WINTER.

Active.

Active as a boy climbing a crab-apple tree for a cargo of cramp-generators. — ANON.

Active as a fire department during a conflagration. — IBID.

Active as a pea in a bladder. — IBID.

Active as a pea on a griddle. — IBID.

Active as quicksilver. — IBID.

As active as the roe. — NATHANIEL COTTON.

Active as some mind that turns a sphere. — COWLEY.

Active as an ape. — SIR A. CONAN DOYLE.

Active as a griffin. — HOOD.

Active as light. — HENRY VAUGHAN.

Active as the sun. — ISAAC WATTS.

Actor.

An actor is like a cigar; the more you puff him the smaller he gets. — ANON.

Actor — *continued.*

Actors are like pet birds. When a pet bird dies, there may be, to those who knew it in the day of its song and its ruffling plumage, some poor comfort in the sight of its stuffed body. For others, there is only a sense of depression. — MAX BEERBOHM.

Actors are like burglars: they always change their names for business purposes. — FRANK RICHARDSON.

Acute.

Acute like the glow of hope. — THOMAS TURNLEY.

Addition.

Additional, like the cipher on the left. — OSMANLI PROVERB.

Adhere.

Adhere like burrs.— ANON.

Adhering . . . like shipwrecked mariners on a rock. — J. M. BARRIE.

Adhere like ticks to a sheep's back. — MAURICE HEWLETT.

Adhesive.

Adhesive as a postage stamp. — ANON.

Adhesive as fly-paper. — IBID.

Admonition.

The admonition of a true friend should be like the practice of a wise physician, who wrappeth his sharp pills in fine sugar; or the cunning Chirurgeon, who lancing a wound with an iron, immediately applieth to it soft lint; or as mothers deal with their children for worms, who put their bitter seeds into sweet raisins. If this order had been observed in thy discourse, that interlacing sour taunts with sugared counsel, bearing as well a gentle rein as using a hard snaffle, thou mightest have done more with the whisk of a wand, than now thou canst with the pick of the spur, and avoid that which now thou mayest not, extreme unkindness. But thou art like that kind of judge which Propertius noeth, who condemning his friend, cause him for the more ease to be hanged with a silken twist. And thou, like a friend, cuttest my throat with a razor, not with a hatchet, for my more honour. — LYLY.

Adorable.

Adorable as a dazzling and innocent creature who walks along, holding in her hand the key to paradise without being conscious of it. — HUGO.

Adorable as is nothing save a child. — SWINBURNE.

Adrift.

Adrift as a pinnace in peril. — SWINBURNE.

Adrift as a spirit in doubt that dissembles
Still with itself, being sick of division and dimmed by dismay. — IBID.

Advance.

Where like a fire to heather set,
Bauld Thomas did advance. — ANON.

Advancing, as the chorus to the footlights. — ANON.

Advancing like the shadow of death. — RUSKIN.

Advance, like sheep before the wolf. — SOUTHEY.

Advanced, like Atalanta's star,
But rarely seen, and seen from far.
— SWIFT.

Adventure.

Adventurous as a paladin of romance. — WILLIAM H. PRESCOTT.

Adventures are like leaps in hunting, — they bring you into the chase sooner, but may chance to cost you a fall. — JAMES PUCKLE.

Adventurous as a bee. — WORDSWORTH.

Adversity.

The storms of adversity, like those of the ocean, rouse the faculties, and excite the invention, prudence, skill and fortitude of the voyager. — Captain Marryatt.

Sweet are the uses of adversity,
Which, like the toad, ugly and venomous,
Wears yet a precious jewel in his head.
— Shakespeare.

Advertising.

Doing business without advertising is like winking at a girl in the dark. You know what you are doing, but nobody else does. — Anon.

Advice.

Advice after mischief is like medicine after death. — Anon.

Advice is like kissing: it costs nothing and is a pleasant thing to do. — Josh Billings.

Advice is like snow; the softer it falls, and the longer it dwells upon, the deeper it sinks into the mind. — Coleridge.

To listen to the advice of a treacherous friend, is like drinking poison from a golden cup. — Demophilus.

Advice all the world over is like wind in a cage. In the case of lovers, like water in a sieve. — Pilpay.

Affable.

Affable as a wet dog. — Alfred Henry Lewis.

Affairs.

Affairs, like a salt fish, ought to be a good while a-soaking. — Anon.

Affectation.

Affectation is as necessary to the mind as dress is to the body. — William Hazlitt.

Affection.

Affection, like spring flowers, breaks through the most frozen ground at last, and the heart which asks but for another heart to make it happy, will never seek in vain. — Bentham.

Affection, like the nut within the shell, wants freedom. — Dion Boucicault.

The affections, like conscience, are rather to be led than driven. Those who marry where they do not love, will be likely to love where they do not marry. — Thomas Fuller.

The human affections, like the solar heat, lose their intensity as they depart from the centre, and become languid in proportion to the expansion of the circle on which they act. — Alexander Hamilton.

Affection, like melancholy, magnifies trifles; but the magnifying of the one is like looking through a telescope at heavenly objects; that of the other, like enlarging monsters with a telescope. — Leigh Hunt.

Affinity.

No more affinity for each other than a robin for a goldfish. — Eleanor Kirk.

Affliction.

Affliction, like the iron-smith, shapes as it smites. — C. N. Bovée.

Afflictions are like lightning: you can not tell where they will strike until they have fallen. — Lacordaire.

Afraid.

Afraid as a grasshopper. — Old Testament.

Age.

Age, like a double-fronted Janus, looks all ways, and ponders wisely on the past. — Barry Cornwall.

The age of man resembles a book; infancy and old age are the blank leaves, youth the preface, and man the body or most important portion of life's volume. — E. P. Day.

Age — *continued.*

Age, like woman, requires fit surroundings. — EMERSON.

Like mist upon the lea,
And like night upon the plain,
Old age comes o'er the heart.
— ROBERT NICOL.

Age like winter bare. — SHAKESPEARE.

Ageless.

Ageless as the sun. — SWINBURNE.

Aghast.

Aghast, like beaten hounds that dare not whine. — ANON.

Agile.

Agile as a cat. — ANON.

Agile as a monkey. — DUMAS, PÈRE.

Agitated.

Agitated with delight like a waving sea. — ARABIAN NIGHTS.

Aglow.

Aglow, like fruit when it colors. — WILLIAM CANTON.

Thy lips are aglow
As a lover's that kindle with kissing.
— SWINBURNE.

Agony.

Blind agony, like a scorpion, stung by his own rage. — SHELLEY.

Agree.

Agree like pikes in a pond, ready to eat up one another. — THOMAS ADAMS.

Agree like finger and thumb. — ANON.

Agree like the hare and the hound. — IBID.

Agree together as harp and harrow. — THOMAS BECON.

Agree like a bell and its clapper. — BULWER-LYTTON.

Agrees like the note with its measure. — DANTE.

Agree like Dogges and Cattes. — STEPHEN GOSSON.

Agree together like bells. — "A KNACKE TO KNOWE A KNAVE," 1584.

Agree as Lent and fishmongers. — JOHN MARSTON.

Agreement is like the uniting of two halves of a seal. — MENCIUS.

Agree like the wax and the wick of the candle. — RICHARD PERCIVAL.

Agree like pickpockets in a fair. — JOHN RAY'S "HANDBOOK OF PROVERBS," 1670.

Agree like married music in Love's answering air. — C. G. ROSSETTI.

Agree as wasp doth with bee. — THOMAS TUSSER.

Agree as Angels do above. — EDMUND WALLER.

Aimless.

Aimless as an autumn leaf
Borne in November's idle winds afar.
— P. H. HAYNE.

Alacrity.

Expressed their alacrity, like horses full of fire and neighing for the race. — PLUTARCH.

Alarm.

Full of alarm
She stood, like a young bird quitting its nest. — DORA SIGERSON.

Alert.

Alert as a chamois. — ANON.

Alert as a bird in the springtime. — GEORGE MOORE.

Alike.

Alike as two peas.— ANON.

Alike as my fingers is to my fingers. — SHAKESPEARE.

Alive.

Alive as a vision of life to be. — SWINBURNE.

Allure.

One of those beautiful, brilliant enigmas, which irresistibly allure every one like a sphinx. — GUY DE MAUPASSANT.

Alluring as a ripe peach. — IBID.

Allured all hearts as ocean lures the land. — BAYARD TAYLOR.

Alone.

Like to the moon am I, that cannot
shine
Alone. — MICHELANGELO.

Alone, like a leper. — ANON.

The old man proceeded alone into the waste, like a bold vessel leaving its haven to enter on the trackless field of the ocean. — J. FENIMORE COOPER.

Alone, like Crusoe. — EDWARD S. MARTIN.

Stands alone like a rock in a sandy vale. — OSSIAN.

Alone . . . like an owl in an ivy-bush. — J. R. PLANCHÉ.

I go alone
Like a lonely dragon, that his fen
Makes fear'd, and talk'd of more than
seen. — SHAKESPEARE.

Alone, like one that had the pestilence. — IBID.

Alone like some deserted world. — BAYARD TAYLOR.

Stand alone like a substantive. — SIR HENRY WOTTON.

Alter.

Altering, like one who waits for an ague fit. — DRYDEN.

Alteration of Religion is dangerous, because we know not where it will stay: 'tis like a Millstone that lies upon the top of a pair of Stairs; 'tis hard to remove it, but if once it be thrust off the first stair, it never stays till it comes to the bottom. — JOHN SELDEN.

Alternate.

But hope and fear alternate sway my soul, like light and shade upon a waving field. — JOHN HOME.

Alternate like the moon. — POPE.

Amazed.

Amazed, as one that unaware
Hath dropp'd a precious jewel in the
flood. — SHAKESPEARE.

Ambition.

Ambition is like choler, which is a humor that maketh men active, earnest, full of alacrity, and stirring, if it be not stopped: but if it be stopped, and cannot have its way, it becometh a dust (hot and fiery) and thereby malign and venomous. — BACON.

Ambitious as the devil. — BEAUMONT AND FLETCHER.

Ambition is like hunger; it obeys no law but its appetite. — JOSH BILLINGS.

To reach the height of our ambition is like trying to reach the rainbow; as we advance it recedes. — W. T. BURKE.

Like dogs in a wheel, birds in a cage or squirrels in a chain, ambitious men still climb and climb, with great labor and incessant anxiety, but never reach the top. — HENRY BURTON.

As a tree the higher it is, the greater force the winde hath of it, and euerie little blast will bee puffing at it, so that the sooner and greater is the fall thereof: So the Ambitious man, the higher he climeth, the greater is his fall. — ROBERT CAWDRAY'S "A TREASURIE OR STORE-HOUSE OF SIMILIES," 1600.

Ambition is like love, impatient both of delays and rivals. — SIR JOHN DENHAM.

Ambition — *continued.*

Ambition, like a seeled [blind] dove mounts upward,
Higher and higher still, to perch on clouds,
But tumbles headlong down with heavier ruin. — JOHN FORD.

As ambitious as Lady Macbeth. — JAMES HUNEKER.

Ambition, like a torrent, never looks back. — BEN JONSON.

Ambition, like love, can abide no lingering; and ever urgeth on his own successes, hating nothing but what may stop them. — SIR PHILIP SIDNEY.

Ambition
Is like the sea wave, which the more you drink
The more you thirst — yea — drink too much, as men
Have done on rafts of wreck — it drives you mad. — TENNYSON.

Amiable.

Amiable as the surface of parchment. — GEORGE MEREDITH.

Amorous.

Amorous as a pair of love-birds.— ANON.

Amorous as a parrakeet. — IBID.

Amorous as an Arcadian. — GEORGE COLMAN, THE YOUNGER.

Ample.

Ample as the largest winding-sheet. — KEATS.

Ample as the wants of man. — LONGFELLOW.

Amused.

Unbending their minds, and amused with every trifle; like birds, which, after the serious and important business of preparing nests for their young, fly sportfully about, free and disengaged, as if to relieve themselves from their toils. — CICERO.

Amusements.

Amusements are to religion like breezes of air to the flame, — gentle ones will fan it, but strong ones will put it out. — DAVID THOMAS.

Ancestors.

The man who has not anything to boast of but his illustrious ancestors is like a potato, — the only good belonging to him is under ground. — SIR THOMAS OVERBURY.

Ancient.

Ancient as the sun. — WILLIAM CULLEN BRYANT.

Ancient as the spot on which the bricks of Babylon are found. — J. FENIMORE COOPER.

Ancient as the stings of death. — DE QUINCEY.

As ancient as the world. — GEORGE GRANVILLE.

Ancient as the stars. — VOLTAIRE.

Ancient as the sea. — WALLER.

Angel.

Like angel visits, few and far between. — CAMPBELL.

Anger.

Anger in our mirth is like poison in a perfume. — ADDISON.

Like fragile ice, anger passes away in time. — ANON.

A fit of anger is as fatal to dignity as a dose of arsenic to life. — J. G. HOLLAND.

Watch against anger; neither speak of it nor act in it; for, like drunkenness, it makes a man a beast, and throws people into desperate inconvenience. — WILLIAM PENN.

Anger is like rain which breaks itself whereon it falls. — SENECA.

Anger is like a full-hot horse, who being allowed his way, self-mettle tires him. — SHAKESPEARE.

Angry as a waspe. — JOHN SKELTON.

Angling.

Our Angles are like money put to usury; they may thrive, though we sit still and do nothing but talk and enjoy one another. — IZAAK WALTON.

Angling is somewhat like Poetry, men are to be born so. — IBID.

Angling may be said to be so like the Mathematics that it can never be fully learnt; at least not so fully but that there will still be more new experiments left for the trial of other men that succeed us. — IBID.

Answer.

Answer like a book.— ANON.

Answer like a parrot.— IBID.

Answered like a sail taking a breeze. — IBID.

Antique.

Antiquity is like fame . . . her head is muffled from our sight. — BACON.

Antique as the statues of the Greeks. — BULWER-LYTTON.

Antique as if I had been preserved in the ark. — MRS. CENTLIVRE.

Anxious.

Anxious as hind towards her hidden fawn. — KEATS.

As anxious as a maid
To show a decent dress.
— GEORGE MEREDITH.

Apart.

Far apart as the earth and the arch above. — ANON.

Far apart as the poles.— IBID.

Blown apart
Like a rose that ready is
For the sun's perfecting kiss.
— CHARLES L. MOORE.

Lips apart,
Like monument of Grecian art.
— SIR WALTER SCOTT.

Sat apart, as one forbid. — WHITTIER.

Apathy.

Full of apathy as a territorial delegate during the chaplain's prayer. — O. HENRY.

Aphorism.

Aphorism, like vinegar, should be used with discretion. — ANON.

The aphorisms of wise and excellent men are of great value, like the dust of gold, or the least sparkle of diamonds. — DR. JOHNSON.

Appalled.

Appall'd;
As children discover'd bugbears.
— BYRON.

Appetite.

Appetite and reason are commonly like two buckets; when one is at the top, the other is at the bottom. — JEREMY COLLIER.

Appreciate.

Poorly appreciated — like a fine landscape in dull weather — or in the reflection of a bad camera obscura. — SCHOPENHAUER.

Approach.

Approaches his lighter topics as a humming bird approaches flowers. — DONALD G. MITCHELL.

April.

April is like a child that smiles in waking. — HUGO.

Apt.

As apt as new-fall'n snow takes any dint. — SHAKESPEARE.

Arch.

Arching, like a fish-hook. — ANON.

Arched, like a horn. — IBID.

Arched like a mule's back in a hail storm. — IBID.

Arch'd like the crescent moon. — EDWIN ATHERSTONE.

Arch — *continued.*

Arches like a giant's bow. — E. B. Browning.

Arched like the leaf of a peach-tree. — Edward Heron-Allen.

Arched like the bow of Cupid. — Lewis Morris.

Ardent.

Ardent as a boy. — Anon.

Ardent as the lips of love. — P. H. Hayne.

Ardent in the search as the Argonauts of forty-nine. — Brander Matthews.

Ardent as the sun. — C. J. Wells.

Argument.

Argument is like an arrow from a crossbow, which has equal force though drawn by a child. — Robert Boyle.

Arguments, like children, should be like
The subject that begets them.
— Thomas Dekker.

Arid.

Arid as the sands of Sahara, without restful shade, without refreshing water. — Joseph Conrad.

Arise.

Arise like Farianata from his fiery tomb. — Longfellow.

Arise as the spring out of tempest and snow. — Swinburne.

Saw the moon arise like Venus from the sea. — Robert K. Weeks.

Arm.

Behold mine arm
Is like a blasted sapling, withered up.
— Shakespeare.

Army.

An army, like a serpent, goes upon its belly. — Frederick the Great.

Aromatic.

Aromatic, like the perfume of faded leaves in a china jar. — Alfred Ainger.

Around.

She walked in flowers around my fields
As June herself around the sphere.
— Emerson.

Around him like a sun of a system. — Washington Irving.

Arrogant.

An arrogant person, is like unto a goodly tall tree, that groweth and mounteth very high, but bringeth forth no fruit. — Anthonie Fletcher's "Certain Very Proper and Profitable Similies", 1595.

Art.

Without favor, art is like a wind-mill without wind. — Juvenal.

Oaks, like arts, a length of years demand. — William Whitehead.

Arteries.

Pulseless arteries
Are like the fibres of a cloud instinct
With light. — Shelley.

Artful.

Artful as the most dexterous cast of the best trout-killing rod. — Donald G. Mitchell.

Artifice.

Shallow artifice begets suspicion,
And, like a cobweb veil, but thinly shades
The face of thy design.
— Congreve.

Artificial.

Artificial as clockwork. — Anon.

Artificial as made ice. — Alan Dale.

Artificial as a trellis. — Lowell.

Artless.

Artless, as Eve yet unbeguiled. — C. S. Calverley.

Artless as Nature's notes in birds untaught. — Congreve.

Artless . . . like a lammie. — John Imlāh.

Artless as the air. — Francis Thompson.

Ascend.

Ascends like the hoof of a camel. — Arabic.

Ascend, like angels beautiful, a shining Jacob's ladder of the mind. — P. H. Hayne.

Ascended as the smoke of a furnace. — Old Testament.

Ashamed.

Ashamed, like Elisha before the entreaties of Elijah's disciples. — Kingsley.

She that maketh you ashamed is as a rottenness in the bones. — Old Testament.

Ashamed, like a guilty thing. — Theodore Watts-Dunton.

Askew.

Askew, like sheep through a hurdle. — R. D. Blackmore.

Aslant.

Aslant, like the angels in Jacob's dream. — Dickens.

Asleep.

Asleep,
As Cerberus at Thracian poet's feet.
— Shakespeare.

Lay asleep like green waves on the sea. — R. B. Sheridan.

Aspire

Aspire, as all the sea's life toward the sun. — Swinburne.

Aspires as a flame. — Ibid.

Assault.

I advance to attack, I climb to assault,
Like a choir of young worms at a corpse in a vault.
— Charles Baudelaire.

Astray.

Gone astray like a lost sheep. — Old Testament.

Asunder.

Asunder like the arches of a bridge. — Robert Burton.

Attend.

Attending,
As if their lives were on his words depending.
— Tasso.

Attention.

Attracted about as much attention in the artistic world as the advent of another fly in a slaughter house. — James L. Ford.

Audacious.

Audacious as the day. — Charles L. Moore.

Austere.

Austere as a tree full of owls. — Anon.

Austere as the dawn. — Bliss Carman.

Austere as so many weather-beaten ascetics from the desert. — Sir A. Conan Doyle.

Authority.

Authority without wisdom is like an axe without an edge, fitter to bruise than polish. — Anne Bradstreet.

Authors.

Authors, like privateers, are always fair game for one another. — Dr. Johnson.

Authors, like maids at fifteen years,
Are full of wishes, full of fears.
— Robert Lloyd.

Authors — *continued.*

A pin has as much head as some authors and a great deal more point. — GEORGE D. PRENTICE.

Authors I have named are like certain workers in metal, who try a hundred different compounds to take the place of gold — the only metal which can never have any substitute. — SCHOPENHAUER.

Automatic.

He moved automatically, like a prisoner captured by the evil power of a masquerading skeleton out of the grave. — JOSEPH CONRAD.

Rose automatically as the sap in the twigs. — THOMAS HARDY.

Automobile.

Automobiles, gliding like phantoms with burning eyes. — LEONID ANDREYEF.

Avarice.

Avarice is like a graveyard; it takes all that it can get and gives nothing back. — JOSH BILLINGS.

Avaricious.

The avaricious man is like the barren, sandy ground of the desert, which sucks in all the rain and dews with eagerness, but yields no fruitful herbs or plants for the benefit of others. — ZENO.

Averse.

Averse to change as flesh. — ROBERT BROWNING.

Awake.

Awaken, like seas by a mighty tempest shaken. — BARRY CORNWALL.

Aware.

Aware as the air of the light that fills full all of its girth. — RICHARD HOVEY.

Away.

Away like a ghost at break of day. — ROBERT BROWNING.

Into the night away they go
Like a bolt that's launched from a steel crossbow.
— GOTTFRIED A. BURGER.

Away like a glance of thought. — JOSEPH R. DRAKE.

Away, like wild pigeons startled in the wood. — EURIPIDES.

Like two drops of dew
Exhaled to Phœbus' lips, away they are gone. — KEATS.

They fall away like the flower on which the sun looks in his strength, after the mildew has passed over it, and its head is heavy with the drops of night. — JAMES MACPHERSON.

Away, with never a look behind . . . like an eagle before the wind. — GEORGE H. MILES.

Away, like mists that flee from summer sea. — THOMAS MOORE.

Away, like mists when winds arise. — T. BUCHANAN READ.

Chased away as the vision of the night. — OLD TESTAMENT.

Away as with a whirlwind. — IBID.

Awful.

Awful as the negligence of woe. — ANON.

Awful as justice. — GEORGE H. BOKER.

Awful as the last trump that shall proclaim to mankind the end of the world. — ANATOLE FRANCE.

Awful as clouds that nurse the growing storm. — GOLDSMITH.

Awful as the thunder. — JOHN M. MASON.

Awful as a villain in a domestic melodrama. — CHARLES SELBY.

Awful as silence. — SHELLEY.

Awkward.

Awkward as a blind dog in a meat shop. — Anon.

Awkward as a bull in a China shop. — Ibid.

Awkward as a cow on ice.— Ibid.

Awkward as a pig in a parlor. — Ibid.

Awkward as a man in a bag. — John Burroughs.

Awkward . . . like jackanapes swallowing of pills. — Rabelais.

B

Babble.

Babble like one mad with wine. — Swinburne.

Bachelor.

The bachelor who passes through life without marrying, is like a fair mansion left by the builder unfinished; the half that is finished runs to decay from neglect, or becomes at best but a sorry tenement, wanting the addition of that which makes the whole both useful, comfortable, and ornamental. — A. P. Morris.

Back.

Back . . . with the instinct of homing pigeons. — Mary Austin.

Backward as the wind sweeps flame. — E. B. Browning.

Backward, like a witch's prayers. — Earl of Dorset.

Like the pace of a crab, backward. — Robert Greene.

Backward like the long wash of a wave. — Maurice Hewlett.

Spelling it backward, like a Hebrew book. — Longfellow.

Like a rope-maker's were his ways, for still one line upon another he spun, and, like his hempen brother, kept going backwards all his days. — Horace Smith.

Slideth back as a backsliding heifer. — Old Testament.

Bad.

Bad as the itch. — Anon.

Bad as a blight. — Hood.

As bad, as what is worst. — Lyly.

Bad as toothdrawing.—"Sir Thomas More" (Pseudo-Shakespearean).

Bad as marrying the devil's daughter and living with the old folks. — "Poor Robin's Almanack."

Bad as the fighting bull of Stamford. — English Proverb.

Bad as two kings of Brentford. — Ibid.

Bald.

Bald as a billiard ball. — Anon.

Bald as an egg. — Ibid.

Bald, as 'twere a scalp, reft of its hairs. — Arabian Nights.

His head was as bald as the palm of your hand. — R. H. Barham.

Bald as a Greek monk. — Richard Hovey.

Bald as is the winter tree. — William Morris.

Bald as a coot. — English Proverb.

Bald as a cannon ball. — Thackeray.

Baleful.

Baleful as the tomb-fire. — John Leyden.

Balmy.

Balmy, as after vernal rains. — William J. Mickle.

Baneful.

Baneful as the pride of handsome looks. — LUCIAN.

Barbarous.

Barbarous as a man who uses his finger for a paper knife. — ANON.

Bare.

Bare as a Scotchman's knee.—ANON.

Bare as a stone. — IBID.

Bare as January. — ROBERT ARMIN.

Bare as the back of my hand. — BALZAC.

Bare as a naked bairn. — ROBERT BUCHANAN.

Bare as winter. — BURNS.

Bare as beggary. — RICHARD CUMBERLAND.

As bare . . .
As the willow of leaves
When the bough-breaking wind
The warm day endeth.
— THE ELDER EDDA.

Bare as an Alpine precipice. — KINGSLEY.

Bare as a pig in a sty. — FRANCIS MAHONY.

Bare as lies the mirrored moon in silver sleeping seas. — GERALD MASSEY.

Bare as hop-stakes in November's mists. — GEORGE MEREDITH.

Bare as my nail. — THOMAS NASH.

Bare as a bird's tail. — ENGLISH PROVERB.

Bare as the birch at Yule. — IBID.

Bare, like a carcass picked by crows. — SWIFT.

Bare as a beggar. — SWINBURNE.

Bare as naked daylight. — IBID.

Bare as shame. — IBID.

As bare as a hornet's cell. — HENRY VAN DYKE.

Bare as an ape. — VOLTAIRE.

Bare as a goose-egg. — ARTEMUS WARD.

Bare as a school-boy's diary. — H. G. WELLS.

As bare
As winter trees.
— WORDSWORTH.

As bare as Egypt when the locusts got through with it. — RIDA JOHNSON YOUNG.

Barred.

Barred, like one infectious. — SHAKESPEARE.

Barren.

Barren as a New Hampshire granite hill. — ANON.

Barren as a South African veldt. — IBID.

Barren as winter rain. — ALFRED AUSTIN.

Barren as a continent of Brandenburg sand. — CARLYLE.

Barren as routine. — G. K. CHESTERTON.

Barren as the wind. — EBENEZER ELLIOTT.

A life as barren . . . as is the dust to which that life doth tend. — GEORGE HERBERT.

Barren as a desolate moor. — GERALD MASSEY.

Barren as a pelican-beach. — HERMAN MELVILLE.

Barren as a Pope's Bull. — SYDNEY MUNDEN.

Barren as death. — RUSKIN.

Brain as barren
As banks of Libya.
— SHAKESPEARE.

Barren as a rainy day. — ALEXANDER SMITH.

Barren as crime. — SWINBURNE.

Barren — *continued.*

Barren as a stock-fish. — JOHN TAYLOR.

Barren as the sea's bare sands. — SAMUEL WADDINGTON.

Base.

Baseless as the fabric of a vision. — ANON.

Base as spotted infamy. — COLERIDGE.

Bashful.

Bashful as a school-girl. — ANON.

Bashful as a maid. — BULWER-LYTTON.

Bashful as a Lenten lover. — SIR JOHN DENHAM.

Bashful as an egg at Easter. — IBID.

Bashful as a blooming bride. — SIR WILLIAM JONES.

Secluded bashful, like a shrine of love. — THOMAS MOORE.

Bawl.

Bawl like an auctioneer. — ANON.

Bawling like sailors in a tavern. — IBID.

Bawl like a boatswain of a man-of-war. — LEVER.

Beam.

Beaming like stars. — HANS CHRISTIAN ANDERSEN.

Beamed like the splendor of an eastern sky. — ANON.

His face beamed like a pearl with light. — ARABIAN NIGHTS.

Like ray-collecting mirrors, beams. — WALTER HARTE.

Beaming as the summer's morn. — O. W. HOLMES.

Slant yellow beam . . .
Like a lane into Heaven that leads
from a dream.
— SIDNEY LANIER.

Eyes beaming, like angel's looks. — DONALD G. MITCHELL.

Beamed like the rising sun. — MISS MULOCK.

Beaming like light on chaos. — THOMAS L. PEACOCK.

Beams like flowers. — SHELLEY.

Beard.

Long-bearded like kings of the Frankish race. — ARSÈNE HOUSSAYE.

His beard is cut like the spire of Grantham steeple. — THOMAS LODGE.

It was scarcely a beard at all, more like a deepening of the shadows in which his whole face seemed to lie. — JOHN ROLAND.

Bearded like the pard. — SHAKESPEARE.

A beard like an artichoke, with dry shrivelled jaws. — R. B. SHERIDAN.

Beard like foam swept off the broad blown sea. — SWINBURNE.

Beat.

Like the walnut tree,
The more he is beaten, the better he'll
be. — ANON.

Beaten as a road. — CHARLES COTTON.

My brain is beating like the heart of Haste. — SIDNEY LANIER.

Beaten like a Turco that pawns his musket. — OUIDA.

Beats like a maniac drummer in mid-battle. — T. BUCHANAN READ.

Each falling hoof
Beat like a flail beneath the thresher's
roof. — BAYARD TAYLOR.

Beat, like the pulse, perpetual. — ISAAC WATTS.

Beau.

A beau dressed out resembles the cinnamon tree, the bark is of greater value than the body. — H. PARR.

Beautiful.

Beautiful as a remembered single line of perfect poetry. — JOHN ALBEE.

Beautiful as a chemical blonde. — ANON.

Beautiful as Adonis. — IBID.

Beautiful as a sunset. — IBID.

Beautiful as the dawn. — IBID.

Beautiful as the face of a young Greek god. — IBID.

Beautiful as the seraph's dream. — IBID.

Beautiful as Zenobia. — IBID.

Beautiful as the bough of the myrobalan. — ARABIAN NIGHTS.

Darkly beautiful as death. — P. J. BAILEY.

Beautiful as a saint. — BALZAC.

Beautiful as the day. — IBID.

A note as beautiful as a thread of light. — GUSTAVO A. BECQUÉR.

Beautiful as the curtain of Soloman. — SAINT BERNARD.

Beautiful as fire. — AMBROSE BIERCE.

Beautiful as ever looked
From white clouds in a dream.
— BRYANT.

Beautiful as Absalom. — BULWER-LYTTON.

Beautiful as a feather in one's cap. — CARLYLE.

Beauteous as a summer's morn. — THOMAS CHATTERTON.

Beautiful as April rains. — COWPER.

Beautiful as heaven. — JOHN DAY.

Beautiful as noon-day. — DICKENS.

Beautiful as a rainbow. — DRYDEN.

Beautiful as a dying maid. — EBENEZER ELLIOTT.

Beautiful as is the rose in June. — EMERSON.

Beautiful . . . as childhood's dream. — F. W. FABER.

Beautiful as one of the swinging figures on a Greek vase. — FRANK HARRIS.

Beautiful as a fairy palace. — HAWTHORNE.

Beautiful as spring. — GERARD T. HOPKINS.

Beautiful as a Houri borne off from the Garden of the Seventh Heaven. — JĀMĪ.

Beautiful as the vernal willow. — DR. JOHNSON.

Beautiful, . . . like a fairy pageant floating for a pastime on the tide. — E. C. JONES.

Beautiful as angels. — J. J. JUSSERAND.

Beautiful as an oriole. — KEATS.

Beautiful as May. — LONGFELLOW.

Beautiful as morning. — IBID.

Beautiful as feet of friend
Coming with welcome at our journey's end.
— LOWELL.

Beautiful like the Moon. — MAHABHARATA.

Beautiful
As was bright Lucifer before his fall.
— MARLOWE.

Beautiful as dawn in Heaven. — GERALD MASSEY.

Beautiful as Dian's face. — JAMES MONTGOMERY.

As beautiful as sorceress. — OUIDA.

As beautiful as 'twere a dewy flower. — GEORGE D. PRENTICE.

Beautiful as youth. — MRS. D. RADFORD.

Beautiful as an Olympian divinity. — GEORGE ROSE.

Beautiful as a piece of chalk cliff — RUSKIN.

Beautiful — *continued.*

Beautiful as pine bridges over Alpine streams. — RUSKIN.

Her face as beautiful as though the rays of Paradise were there. — SADI.

Beautiful as sky and earth,
When Autumn's sun is downward going. — WHITTIER.

Beauteous as the silver moon. — WORDSWORTH.

Beautiful as heaven. — IBID.

Beauteous as the sun. — EDWARD YOUNG.

Beauty.

Beauty is like an almanac; if it lasts a year, it is well. — THOMAS ADAM.

Beauty without modesty is like a flower broken from its stem. — ANON.

Beauty is as summer fruits, which are easy to corrupt and that cannot last. — BACON.

Beauty, like truth and justice, lives within us; like virtue and like moral law, it is a companion of the soul. — GEORGE BANCROFT.

As amber attracts a straw, so does beauty admiration, which only lasts while the warmth continues; but virtue, wisdom, goodness, and real worth, like the loadstone, never lose their power. — ROBERT BURTON.

Beauty in a modest woman is like fire or a sharp sword at a distance; neither doth the one burn, nor the other wound, those that come not too near them. — CERVANTES.

Beauty, like ice, our footing does betray:
Who can tread sure in the smooth slippery way?
Pleased with the passage, we slide swiftly on,
And see the dangers which we cannot shun. — DRYDEN.

We cannot get at beauty. Its nature is like opaline doves'-neck lustres, hovering and evanescent. — EMERSON.

Thy beauty lies
Veiled like a violet nestling in the moss. — CLAYTON HAMILTON.

The made-up beauties we commonly meet, like artificial flowers, are all show, and no fragrance. — THOMAS HOLCROFT.

Beauty's a slipp'ry good, which decreaseth Whilst it is increasing resembling the Medler, which, in the moment of its full Ripeness, is known to be in a rottenness. — LYLY.

Beautie is like the blackberry, which seemeth red, when it is not ripe, resembling precious stones that are polished with honie, which the smoother they looke, the sooner they breake. — IBID.

Beauty, — like a beacon burns above the dark of strife. — GERALD MASSEY.

Beauty, like the fair Hesperian tree,
Laden with blooming gold, hath need the guard
Of dragon watch with unenchanted eye,
To save her blossoms and defend her fruit
From the rash hand of bold incontinence. — MILTON.

A chaste beauty is like the bellows, whose breath is cold, yet makes others burn. — SIR THOMAS OVERBURY.

Her beauties were like sunlit snows,
Flush'd but not warm'd with my desire. — COVENTRY PATMORE.

Beauties, like tyrants, old and friendless grown,
Yet hate repose, and dread to be alone. — POPE.

Ah! yet doth beauty like a dial-hand,
Steal from his figure and no pace perceived. — SHAKESPEARE.

Beauty — *continued.*

Beauty, like truth, never is so glorious as when it goes plainest. — STERNE.

Beauty, like supreme dominion,
Is best supported by opinion.
— SWIFT.

Beauty passes like a breath. — ALFRED TENNYSON.

A beauty masked, like the sun in eclipse, gathers together more gazers than if it shined out. — WYCHERLEY.

Bedraggled.

Bedraggled, like the flounce of a vulgar rich woman's dress that trails on the sidewalk. — O. W. HOLMES.

Beg.

Beg like a dog at a fair.— ANON.

Beg like a cripple at a cross. — WHITTINGTON'S "VULGARIA."

Behavior.

Men's behaviour should be like their apparel, not too straight or point device, but free for exercise or motion. — BACON.

Behind.

His tail extended all the while
Behind him like a rat-tail file.
— O. W. HOLMES.

See behind, as doth the hunted hare. — KEATS.

Always behind, like a donkey's tail. — ENGLISH PROVERB.

Belch.

Belch . . . as loud as a Musket. — APHRA BEHN.

Belching like a torn balloon. — ANGUS MCNEILL.

Belief.

Cherished beliefs are like those drinking glasses of the ancient pattern, that serve us all so long as we keep them in our hand, but spill all if we attempt to set them down. — O. W. HOLMES.

Bellow.

Bellows like the vagrant winds. — ANON.

Bellow, like a burst of thunder. — ARISTOPHANES.

Bellowing as if he was possessed of the devil. — BOCCACCIO.

Bellows as the sea does in a tempest, if by opposing winds 'tis combated. — DANTE.

Bellowed as a hunted ox. — HOOD.

Bellow like a rascal trooper strung up for the cat. — GEORGE MEREDITH.

Bellow as bulls. — OLD TESTAMENT.

Beloved.

Beloved . . . like a plant whose leaf and bud and blossom are all beautiful. — JOHN GAY.

Bend.

Bends like a willow in the wind. — ANON.

Bend on me thy tender eyes,
As stars look on the sea.
— BULWER-LYTTON.

Bend one way, like a field of corn in a hurricane. — WILLIAM CARTRIGHT.

Bending her form towards him, like a torch when it indicates a gentle draught of air. — HAWTHORNE.

Bend in the blast as blade of grass. — O. W. HOLMES.

Bends and sinks like a column of sand
In the whirlwind of his great despair.
— LONGFELLOW.

Bending like a wand of willow. — IBID.

Bends . . . like a wave near a rock. — OSSIAN.

Bending like corn on the upland lea. — JAMES G. PERCIVAL.

Bend — *continued.*

Bends like an angel softly through
The blue-pavilioned skies.
— MRS. A. B. WELBY.

Benefits.

Benefits, like flowers, please most when they are fresh. — ANON.

Benevolence.

That is fine benevolence, finely executed, which, like the Nile, comes from hidden sources. — C. C. COLTON.

Bent.

Bent down like violets after rain. — T. B. ALDRICH.

Bent . . . like some rapt poet o'er his rhyme. — IBID.

Bent like a drooping rose. — ANON.

Bent like a whip. — IBID.

Bent like an old bruised lantern. — R. D. BLACKMORE.

Bent-down like corbels of a building. — CARLYLE.

Bent . . . like a soldier at the approach of an assault. — HUGO.

Bent and trembled like the rushes. — LONGFELLOW.

Bent like some great bow unstrung. — JOAQUIN MILLER.

Bent, like a rainbow. — SOUTHEY.

Bequeath.

Bequeath, like sunset to the skies,
The splendor of its prime.
— SHELLEY.

Bereft.

Bereft,
As trees that suddenly have dropped
their leaves. — JEAN INGELOW.

Bereft as a man whom bitter time
bereaves
Of blossom at once and hope of
garnered sheaves,
Of April at once and August.
— SWINBURNE.

Bereft,
As when some tower doth fall,
With battlement, and wall,
And gate, and bridge, and all,
And nothing left.
— MARY A. TOWNSEND.

Besmear.

Besmeared like a gypsy or a chimney-sweeper. — ROBERT BURTON.

Betray.

Thou hast betrayed thy secret as a bird betrays her nest, by striving to conceal it. — LONGFELLOW.

Bewailing.

Bewailing and tolling within like a funeral bell. — LONGFELLOW.

Bewildering.

A sweet bewildering pain,
Like flowers in the wind and rain.
— THOMAS ASHE.

Bewitching.

Bewitching like the wanton mermaid's song. — SHAKESPEARE.

Bible.

Like the needle to the North Pole, the Bible points to heaven. — R. B. NICHOL.

The Bible among books is as a diamond among precious stones. — J. STOUGHTON.

Big.

Big as a church debt. — GEORGE ADE.

Big as an elephant. — ANON.

Big as a house. — IBID.

Big as a whale. — IBID.

Big as life and twice as natural. — IBID.

Big as all out of doors. — J. R. BARTLETT'S "DICTIONARY OF AMERICANISMS."

No bigger than an unobserved star. — KEATS.

Big — *continued.*

As big a liar as Tom Pepper who got licked out of hell for telling lies. — LEAN'S "COLLECTANEA."

As big as a parson's barn, — always ready for more. — IBID.

Looking as big as bull-beef. — ENGLISH PROVERB.

Another stain, as big as hell can hold,
Were there no more but it.
— SHAKESPEARE.

Bigot.

The bigot is like the pupil of the eye; the more light you put upon it, the more it will contract. — O. W. HOLMES.

Bill.

Bill as Doves. — ROBERT BURTON.

Billing,
Like Philip and Mary on a shilling.
— SAMUEL BUTLER.

Bind.

Binding as a wedding ring. — ANON.

Bind like an adamant-chain. — ARABIAN NIGHTS.

Nothing binds so fast as souls in pawn, and mortgage past. — SAMUEL BUTLER.

Bindeth me about as the collar of my coat. — OLD TESTAMENT.

Biography.

The biographies of great and good men, like Elijah's mantle, ought to be gathered up and preserved by their survivors. — MATTHEW HENRY.

Bite.

Bite like finches when they bill and kiss. — ROBERT BROWNING.

Bite like pepper. — JOHN GAY.

Biting like the east wind. — JOHN SKELTON.

Bites like fire. — SWINBURNE.

Bitter.

Bitter as the suffering of life. — ANON.

Bitter as gall. — IBID.

Bitter as chestnut husks. — BALZAC.

Bitter as self-sacrifice. — E. B. BROWNING.

Bitter, like a day of mourning. — JOSEPH CONRAD.

More bitter than the sea. — IBID.

Bitter as a nausea. — D'ANNUNZIO.

Their earthly days were bitter, like the oil-tree. — DE QUINCEY.

Love bitter as Despair. — LORD DE TABLEY.

Bitter as Penthea's curse. — JOHN FORD.

Bitter as truth. — HUGO.

Bitter in the mouth as a page torn out of Ecclesiastes. — JAMES HUNEKER.

Bitter as home-brewed ale. — LONGFELLOW.

Bitter as hemlock. — FITZ-JAMES O'BRIEN.

Bitter as coloquintida. — SHAKESPEARE.

Bitter to me as death. — IBID.

Bitter as fell. — SPENSER.

Bitter as a tear. — SWINBURNE.

Bitter as harsh-lipped spring. — IBID.

Bitter as the breaking down of love. — IBID.

Thy speech is bitterer than the sea. — IBID.

Bitter like blood. — IBID.

Her heart within
Burnt bitter like an aftertaste of sin
To one whose memory drinks and loathes the lee
Of shame or sorrow deeper than the sea.
— IBID.

Bitter — *continued.*

And I find more bitter than death the woman, whose heart is snares and nets, and her hands as bands. — OLD TESTAMENT.

Bitter as wormwood. — IBID.

Bitterer than Sardinian herbage. — VIRGIL.

Black.

Black as Alaskan sealskin. — ANON.

Black as a stack of black cats. — IBID.

Black as a thundercloud. — IBID.

Black as a tinker. — IBID.

Black as blindness. — IBID.

Black as Egypt's night. — IBID.

Black as a sloe. — IBID.

Black as snow in London. — IBID.

Black as the Duke of Hell's black riding boots. — IBID.

Black as the inside of a man who drank a bottle of ink. — IBID.

Black as the mantle that shrouds the blind. — IBID.

Black as Uncle Tom. — IBID.

Black as the bear on Iskardoo. — EDWIN ARNOLD.

Thoughts as black as hell, as hot and bloody. — BEAUMONT AND FLETCHER.

Black as a coal pit. — HENRY WARD BEECHER.

Black as the tents of Kedar. — SAINT BERNARD.

Black as a young rook. — DION BOUCICAULT.

Black, like plumes at funerals. — E. B. BROWNING.

Black as death. — BYRON.

Black as Gehenna and the Pit of Hell. — CARLYLE.

Black as a crow. — CHAUCER.

Blak as fende in helle. — IBID.

Black as a cave mouth. — IRVIN S. COBB.

Black as the devil. — GEORGE COLMAN, THE YOUNGER.

Black as Tophet. — JOSEPH CONRAD.

Black as the mine. — COWPER.

Black as if lightning-scarred or curst of God. — AUBREY DE VERE.

Black as thunder. — DICKENS.

Black as beads. — AUSTIN DOBSON.

Black as a wolf's mouth. — SIR A. CONAN DOYLE.

Black as ebony. — DUMAS, PÈRE.

Black as night when the tempests pass. — F. W. FABER.

Black as starless night. — PHINEAS FLETCHER.

Black as a cassock. — SAMUEL FOOTE.

Black as the pit. — W. E. HENLEY.

Blacker than a raven in a coal mine. — O. HENRY.

Black as stormy darkness. — THOMAS HEYWOOD.

Black as gunpowder. — HOOD.

Black as the fruit of the thorn. — IBID.

Black as your hat. — IBID.

Blackens like a thunder cloud. — IBID.

Black as the fleet from Aulis 'gainst doomed Troy. — R. H. HORNE.

Black as the wood of the gallows-tree. — HUGO.

As black as any Moor. — JACQUES JASMIN.

Black as the devil in a comedy. — THOMAS KILLIGREW.

Black as the sliding water over a mill-dam. — KIPLING.

Black — *continued.*

Black as the king of Ashantee. — LEVER.

Black as sightless eyes. — GEORGE CABOT LODGE.

As blacke as deepest dark. — LYLY.

Blacke as jeat. — IBID.

Blacke as the burnt coale. — IBID.

My Arab steed is black —
Black as the tempest cloud that flies
Across the dark and muttering skies.
— ADAM MICKIEWICZ.

Black as a [chimney] sweep. — F. P. NORTHALL.

Black and glossy as the raven's wing. — THOMAS L. PEACOCK.

Black as winter chimney. — JOHN PHILLIPS.

Black as despair. — IBID.

Black as autumn's sky. — W. M. PRAED.

Black as a burned stump. — OPIE READ.

As black as the steeds of night. — T. BUCHANAN READ.

Black as fiery Africa's slaves. — IBID.

Black as black iron. — C. G. ROSSETTI.

Black as pitch. — THOMAS SACKVILLE.

Black as the newly-pruned crow. — GEORGE SANDYS.

Black as a funeral pall. — JOHN G. SAXE.

Black as mourning weed. — SCOTTISH BALLAD ("PERCY'S RELIQUES").

Black as Acheron. — SHAKESPEARE.

Black
As if besmear'd in hell.
— IBID.

Black as incest. — IBID.

Black as ink. — IBID.

Black as Vulcan in the smoke of war. — IBID.

Black as a cormorant. — SHELLEY.

Black as Erebus and Night. — SOUTHEY.

Black as the womb of darkness. — SWINBURNE.

Black as crushed worms that sicken in the sense. — IBID.

Black as thunderous night. — IBID.

As midnight black. — IBID.

Black as flameless brand. — IBID.

Black as ashbuds in the front of March. — TENNYSON.

Black as sackcloth of hair. — NEW TESTAMENT.

Black as a raven. — OLD TESTAMENT.

Black like an oven. — IBID.

Blacker than a coal. — IBID.

Black as Hell.—WILLIAM THOMSON.

Black as winter sky. — WALTER THORNBURY.

Black as soot. — VOLTAIRE.

Black as a berry. — FRANÇOIS VILLON.

Black as with wrath. — ALARIC A. WATTS.

Black as black. — W. B. YEATS.

Blameless.

Blameless as the snow. — ERIC MACKAY.

Blanched.

Blanched like plants raised in cellars. — HUGO.

Bland.

Bland as a Jesuit. — W. E. HENLEY.

Bland
As ocean-breezes gathered from the flowers
That blossom in Elysium.
— THOMAS MOORE.

Blank.

Blank as an empty bottle. — ANON.

Hopelessly blank, like the face of a blind man. — JOSEPH CONRAD.

Look as blank as a pickpocket. — HENRY JAMES.

Blank as the eyeballs of the dead. — LONGFELLOW.

Blank as death. — TENNYSON.

Blast.

Like a mildewed ear,
Blasting his wholesome brother.
— SHAKESPEARE.

Blasts like a pestilence. — SOUTHEY.

Blaze.

Blaze like the eyes of a maniac. — ANON.

Blazed up like a beacon. — IBID.

Blaze like the fat in sacramental flame. — P. J. BAILEY.

Blaze like a couple of lamps on a yellow post-chaise. — R. H. BARHAM.

Blaze like a wyvern flying round the sun. — ROBERT BROWNING.

Blazed like a sun over the startled East. — BULWER-LYTTON.

Blaze like a box of matches. — JOSEPH CONRAD.

Blazing like a brace of suns. — DAUDET.

Blazed as if with inward fire. — D'ANNUNZIO.

Her heart blazed up like fire before the wind. — FIRDAUSI.

Blaze like a furnace. — FREDERICK TENNYSON.

Blazes like a mighty sword
Leaping to the fight.
— G. S. VIERECK.

Bleak.

Bleak as the ocean vast. — ANON.

Bleak and bare
Like furnace-chimneys in the air.
— LONGFELLOW.

Bleat.

Bleat like a lamb. — ANON.

Bleeding.

Bleeding as if he had been through a thicket of troubles. — DAUDET.

Blend.

Blending all in one long and delicious tremble like a chord. — P. J. BAILEY.

Blended
Like tints in an immortal gem.
— BYRON.

Inseparably blend
Like two bright dewdrops meeting in
a flower. — COLERIDGE.

Blended like the colors in the rainbow. — DICKENS.

Blent,
Like the soft aromatic gales
That meet the mariner, who sails
Through the Moluccas, and the seas
That wash the shores of Celebes.
— LONGFELLOW.

Blended, like the sea's phosphor lustre. — RUSKIN.

Bless.

Blesses, like the dews of Heaven. — JOHN GAY.

Blest.

Blest as the saint to his home above flying. — E. M. KELLY.

Blew.

Blew as if he had been to puff up a pig's bladder. — RABELAIS.

Blight

Blighted and forlorn, like Autumn waiting for the snow. — WHITTIER.

Blind.

Blind as a bank director. — ANON.

Blind as a bat. — IBID.

Blind — *continued.*

Blind as a white cat with a blue eye. — IBID.

Blind as Cupid. — IBID.

Blind as the blue skies after sunset. — P. J. BAILEY.

Blind as ignorance. — BEAUMONT AND FLETCHER.

Blind as moles. — IBID.

Blind as the fool's heart. — ROBERT BROWNING.

Blind
Ay, as a man would be inside the sun,
Delirious with the plentitude of light.
— IBID.

Blind as fortune. — BULWER-LYTTON.

Blind as the blindworm. — AUBREY DE VERE.

Blind as a brickbat. — DICKENS.

Blind as the Cyclop. — DRYDEN.

Blindness acts like a dam, sending the streams of thought backward along the already-traveled channels, and hindering the course onward. — GEORGE ELIOT.

Blind as death itself. — W. S. GILBERT.

His eye is blind as that of a potato. — HOOD.

Blind as inexperience. — HUGO.

Blind as a beetle. — BEN JONSON.

Blind as a woman in love. — NINON DE L'ENCLOS.

Blind as one that hath been found drunk a seven-night. — THOMAS MIDDLETON.

Blind as justice. — MISS MITFORD.

Blind as hooded falcons. — THOMAS MOORE.

Blind as he who closes
His eyes to the light and will not have
it shine. — LEWIS MORRIS.

Like fortune in her frenzy, blind. — SARAH W. MORTON.

Blind as the song of birds. — T. BUCHANAN READ.

Blind as love. — SHELLEY.

Blind as moonless night. — ROBERT LOUIS STEVENSON.

Blind and stark as though the snows made numb all sense within it. — SWINBURNE.

Blind as a pilot beaten blind with foam. — IBID.

Blind as glass. — IBID.

Blind as grief. — IBID.

Blind as the night. — IBID.

Blind and vain
As rain-stars blurred and marred by
rain
To wanderers on a moonless main
Where night and day seem dead.
— IBID.

Blind as any noonday owl. — TENNYSON.

Blind like tragic masks of stone. — JAMES THOMSON.

Blink.

Blinking like a toad in a sand heap. — ANON.

Blink my eyes like a whacked donkey. — ANTON TCHEKHOV.

Blinking like a disreputable, drunken owl. — O. HENRY.

Blissful.

Blissful as a leap to daylight out of a nightmare. — GEORGE MEREDITH.

Blissful, as if sin
Or more than gentlest grief had never
been. — BAYARD TAYLOR.

Blithe.

Blithe as a bird on a cherry bough. — ANON.

Blithe as a grig. — IBID.

Blithe — *continued.*

Danced as blithely and briskly as a lost red maple leaf fluttering madly in a keen October breeze. — ANON.

As blithe as the bird that rejoices. — A. H. BEESLY.

Blithe as a boblink. — ROBERT BROWNING.

Blithe as our kettle's boiling. — IBID.

Blithe as the lark that each day hails the dawn. — COLLINS.

Blithe as finches sing. — COWPER.

Blithe as shepherd at a wake. — IBID.

Blithe as a bird new risen from the corn. — AUSTIN DOBSON.

Blithe as the first blithe song of birds that waken. — IBID.

Blithe as a bird in the spring. —TOM DURFEY.

Blithe as May. — R. FLETCHER.

Blithe, as if on earth
Were no such thing as woe.
— JOHN KEBLE.

Blithe as the orchards and birds with the new coming of spring. — LOWELL.

Blithe as a blithe bird in air. — OWEN MEREDITH.

As blithe and sunny as the summer days. — JAMES WHITCOMB RILEY.

Blithe as swallows,
Wheeling in the summer sky at close of day. — SOUTHEY.

Blither than Spring's when her flowerful tresses
Shake forth sunlight and shine with rain. — SWINBURNE.

Blithe as the lark on sun-gilt wings
High poised, or as the wren that sings
In shady places to proclaim
Her modest gratitude.
— WORDSWORTH.

Bloated.

Bloated like a squeezed cat. — ANON.

Bloodless.

Lips as bloodless as lips of the slain — WHITTIER.

Bloody.

Bloody as the hunter. — SHAKESPEARE.

Bloom.

Blooming as health. — ANACREON.

Bloomed like a bridal-chamber. — ANON.

Blooming as a peach. — IBID.

Blooming with promise like an apple in the month of May. — IBID.

Her bloom was like the silver flower,
That sips the silver dew.
— VINCENT BOURNE.

Bloomed like smouldering lilies unconsumed. — JOHN DAVIDSON.

Blooming as a bridal maid. — WALTER HARTE.

Blooms like a bower in the garden of Bliss. — O. W. HOLMES.

Blooming as roses in the vale. — MRS. J. HUNTER.

Her bloom was like the springing flower,
That sips the silver dew;
The rose was budded in her cheeks,
Just opening to the view.
— DAVID MALLET.

Verses bloom like a flower. — JAMES WHITCOMB RILEY.

Bloom'd in the winter of his days,
Like Glastonbury thorn.
— SIR CHARLES SEDLEY.

Bloomed, as new life might in a bloodless face. — SWINBURNE.

Bloomed like a rose in a garden green. — DAVID VEDDER.

Blossom.

Blossomed like a rose. — HUGO.

Blossomed like a wreath. — D. G. ROSSETTI.

Blown.

Blown up like a tumor. — EMERSON.

Blowing like a blacksmith's bellows. — HUGO.

Blown like vapor on the summer air. — ROSSITER JOHNSON.

Blowing like a grampus. — KIPLING.

Puffing and blowing like a porpoise. — LOVER.

Blown like a leaf on the blast. — JOHN BOYLE O'REILLY.

Blown like leaves before the whirlwind's fury fleeing. — BAYARD TAYLOR.

Blubbered.

Blubbering like a seal. — C. S. CALVERLEY.

Blubbered like a child that's nursed. — HOOD.

Blue.

Blue as a whale. — ANON.

Blue as blue-bell bed. — IBID.

Blue as cobalt. — IBID.

Blue as forget-me-nots. — IBID.

Blue as indigo. — IBID.

Blue as melancholy. — IBID.

Blue as October skies. — IBID.

Blue as the soft azure surface of the southern sea. — IBID.

Blue as your nose on a cold day. — IBID.

Blue as the sky in spring. — R. D. BLACKMORE.

Blue as a vein o'er the Madonna's breast. — ROBERT BROWNING.

Blue as shimmering steel. — H. C. BUNNER.

Blue like the sea of a dream. — JOSEPH CONRAD.

Waters blue as violet banks. — AUBREY DE VERE.

A sky as blue as the enamel on the statuettes of Osiris. — GAUTIER.

Blue like a corpse. — NIKOLAI V. GOGOL.

Blue as lips of death. — EUGENE LEE-HAMILTON.

Blue as tint of maiden's eye. — JAMES HASKINS.

Blue each visage grew,
Just like a pullet's gizzard.
— HOOD.

Sky as blue as June. — R. G. INGERSOLL.

Blue were her eyes as fairy-flax. — LONGFELLOW.

Lips, as blue as salt-water. — MASSINGER.

Blue
And beautiful, like skies seen through
The sleeping wave.
— THOMAS MOORE.

Blue as blazes. — J. C. NEAL.

Blue as autumn's skies. — W. M. PRAED.

Blue . . . like a patch of fallen April sky. — WILLIAM M. REEDY.

Blue as the eyes of a saint. — FRANCIS S. SALTUS.

Blue as bilbery. — SHAKESPEARE.

Blue as the overhanging heaven. — SHELLEY.

Blue
As are the violets that hide
Our dewy earth from view.
— EVALEEN STEIN.

Blue as plague. — SWINBURNE.

Blue as heaven's cloudless canopy — ESAIAS TEGNÉR.

Blue like an ancient Briton. — THACKERAY.

Blue — *continued.*

Blue as with the cold. — ISRAEL ZANGWILL.

Blunder.

Blundyrst as a blynde buserde. — T. WRIGHT'S "POLITICAL POEMS AND SONGS."

Blunt.

Blunt as a hammer. — ANON.

Blunt as a meat-ax. — IBID.

Blunt as the back of a knife. — ROBERT HEATH.

Blunt as the fencer's foils, which hit, but hurt not. — SHAKESPEARE.

Blur.

The masthead light . . . blurred like a last star ready to dissolve. — JOSEPH CONRAD.

Blurred the air like blown sand. — HAMLIN GARLAND.

Blurred like a lamp's that when the
night drops dead
Dies. — SWINBURNE.

Blurt.

Blurted it out like a school-boy. — LONGFELLOW.

Blush.

Blush like an opal. — ANON.

Blush like the heart of flame. — HENRY W. AUSTIN.

Blushing like a wedding night. — BALZAC.

I blushed like any rose. — T. H. BAYLY.

Blushing like a Worcestershire orchard before harvest. — BEACONSFIELD.

Blushing like the skies to crimson
burning,
When Aurora Borealis fires her premises by night. — AMBROSE BIERCE.

Blushes, like the flushes upon high
When Aurora Borealis lights her circumpolar palace. — IBID.

Blush like rose when Roland speaks. — E. B. BROWNING.

Blushing like a sea-shell. — BULWER-LYTTON.

Blush'd like the waves of hell. — BYRON.

Blushing, like a bride. — COLERIDGE.

Blushes like a new-born flower. — BARRY CORNWALL.

Blush as hot as June. — IBID.

Blush'd and smiled like a clear and rosy eventide. — SIR JOHN DAVIES.

Blusheth like the Indian ivory which is with dip of Tyrian purple dy'd. — IBID.

Blushes as adorn the ruddy welkin or the purple morn. — DRYDEN.

Blushes like a red bull-calf. — A. B. EVANS' "LEICESTER WORDS, PHRASES AND PROVERBS."

Make us blush like copper. — JOHN FLETCHER.

Her cheek of beauty blushed like rose-bud in the rain. — JAMES HOGG.

Blushed like blood. — O. W. HOLMES.

A blush like sunrise o'er the rose. — MISS LANDON.

Blushes like the birds of spring. — IBID.

Blush as of opening flowers. — GEORGE P. LATHROP.

Blush like the backside of a chimney. — LEAN'S "COLLECTANEA."

Blush like a sunset. — ALFRED HENRY LEWIS.

Blushes like a virgin. — RICHARD LOVELACE.

Blush as lovely as the dawn. — LOVER.

Blush — *continued.*

Blushing like the dogwood crimson in October. — GEORGE MEREDITH.

Blushed like timid daybreak when the dawn
Looms crimson on the night, and then again is withdrawn.
— THOMAS MILLER.

Blushing like a summer morning. — BARON MUNCHAUSEN.

Blushed like a girl fresh from school. — SIR GILBERT PARKER.

Blushing as in vintage-hours. — THOMAS L. PEACOCK.

Blush'd like a carnation. — IBID.

Blush like a banner bathed in slaughter. — JAMES G. PERCIVAL.

Blush like lads of seventeen. — JAMES WHITCOMB RILEY.

Blushes bright pass o'er her cheek,
But pure and pale as is the glow of sunset on a mountain peak,
Robed in eternal snow. — RUSKIN.

Blushing, like some shy maid in convent bred. — SIR WALTER SCOTT.

Blush . . . like a black dog, as the saying is. — SHAKESPEARE.

Blushing like the perfumed morn. — R. B. SHERIDAN.

Blush like my waistcoat. — IBID.

Blushing like Aurora. — SMOLLETT.

Blushed as with bloodless passion, and its hue
Was as the life and love of hearts on flame. — SWINBURNE.

Blushes . . . as a young virgin on her wedding night. — BAYARD TAYLOR.

I blush as red as cochineal. — THACKERAY.

Blushin as red as the Baldinsville skool house when it was fust painted. — ARTEMUS WARD.

A faint blush melting through the light of thy transparent cheek like a rose-leaf bathed in dew. — WHITTIER.

Boast.

With all his tumid boasts, he's like the sword-fish, who only wears his weapon in his mouth. — SAMUEL MADDEN.

Whoso boasteth himself of a false gift is like clouds and wind without rain. — OLD TESTAMENT.

Bobbing.

Bobbing up and down like a duck in a mud puddle. — ANON.

Bob up like the hammers in a pianoforte. — DICKENS.

Bobbing like a quill-float with a "minnum" biting at the hook below. — O. W. HOLMES.

Body.

The body is like a piano, and happiness is like music. It is needful to have the instrument in good order. — HENRY WARD BEECHER.

Man's Body's like a *House:* His greater Bones
Are the maine *Timber;* And the lesser ones,
Are smaller *Splints:* His Ribs are *Laths,* daubed ore,
Plaister'd with *flesh* and *bloud:* His Mouth's the *Doore:*
His Throat's the narrow *Entry:* And his Heart
Is the *Great Chamber,* full of curious Art:
His Midreife is a large partition-*Wall,*
'Twixt the *Great Chamber,* and the spacious *Hall:*
His Stomacke is the *Kitchin,* where the Meate
Is often but half sod, for want of *Heate:*
His Spleen's a *Vessell,* Nature does allott
To take the *skimme,* that rises from the Pott:

Body — *continued.*

His Lungs are like the *Bellowes* that respire
In ev'ry office, quickning ev'ry Fire:
His Nose, the *Chimney* is, whereby are vented
Such Fumes, as with the *Bellowes* are augmented:
His Bowels are the *Sinke,* whose part's to dreine
All noysome filth, and keep the *Kitchin* cleane:
His Eyes like Christall *Windowes* cleare and bright
Lets in the *Object* and lets out the *Sight:*
And as the *Timber* is, or great or small,
Or strong or weake; 'tis apt to stand or fall. — FRANCIS QUARLES.

Boil.

He maketh the deep to boil like a pot. — OLD TESTAMENT.

Boisterous.

Boisterous as stormy sea-winds.— R. H. STODDARD.

Bold.

Bold as a blind man. — ANON.

Bold as Beauchamp. — IBID.

Bold as Joan of Arc. — IBID.

Boldly . . . like giants conquering in a noble cause. — IBID.

Bold as a petty provincial attorney. — BALZAC.

Bold as a bucket. — JOEL BARLOW.

As boldly as a brigadier
Tricked out with marks and signs all o'er
Of rank, brigade, division, corps,
To show by every means he can
An officer is not a man.
— AMBROSE BIERCE.

Boold as is Bayard the Blynde. — CHAUCER.

As bold as the blast. — BARRY CORNWALL.

Boldly, like eagles on the wing. — HUGO.

Bold as brass. — LEAN'S "COLLECTANEA."

He was bold as a hawk. — LOVER.

Bold as an embodied storm. — T. BUCHANAN READ.

Bold as the glare of the gold. — R. H. STODDARD.

As boldly as a sunflower faces the orb of day. — NEW YORK SUN.

Bold as a lion. — OLD TESTAMENT.

Bolde as a Knight. — "THE NUTBROWN MAID."

Bold as day. — WORDSWORTH.

Bones.

His bones are as strong pieces of brass; his bones are like bars of iron. — OLD TESTAMENT.

Bony.

Bony as an ossified shad. — ANON.

Books.

A house without books is like a room without windows. — HENRY WARD BEECHER.

Books, like invisible scouts, permeate the whole habitable globe, and Timbuctu itself is not safe from British Literature. — CARLYLE.

A book, like a grape-vine, should have good fruit among its leaves. — E. P. DAY.

As a thing on the eastern mountains shineth by the presence of the sun; so one of humble birth, even, may be enlightened by the allurements of good books. — HITOPADESA.

Be as careful of the books you read as of the company you keep, for your habits and character will be as much influenced by the former as the latter. — PAXTON HOOD.

It is with books as with women, — where a certain plainness of manner

Books — *continued.*

and of dress is more engaging than the glare of paint and airs and apparel, which may dazzle the eye, but reach not the affections. — David Hume.

Gentlemen vse bookes as Gentlewomen handle their flowers, who in the morning stick them in their heads, and at night strawe them at their heeles. — Lyly.

Books are as meats and viands are : some are good, some of evil substance. — Milton.

A book, like a person, has its fortunes with one ; is lucky or unlucky in the precise moment of its falling in our way, and often by some happy accident ranks with us for something more than its independent value. — Walter Pater.

We ought to regard books as we do sweetmeats, not wholly to aim at the pleasantest, but chiefly to respect the wholesomest ; not forbidding either, but approving the latter most. — Plutarch.

To buy books only because they were published by an eminent printer, is much as if a man should buy clothes that did not fit him, only because made by some famous tailor. — Pope.

Books, like men their authors, have no more than one way of coming into the world, but there are ten thousand to go out of it, and return no more. — Swift.

Books, like proverbs, receive their value from the stamp and esteem of ages through which they have passed. — Sir William Temple.

Boom.

Boomed like a split trombone. — O. Henry.

Boom, like the advance shout of battle. — Margaret E. Easter.

Bore.

Boring in and out . . . like a stubby needle going through a tuck. — Irvin S. Cobb.

Born.

Born like a momentary fly to flutter, buzz around, and die. — Robert Lloyd.

Borrowed.

Borrowed as beautifully as the moon
The fire of the sun.
— Stephen Phillips.

Bosom.

White her bosom, like two snowy dovelets. — Servian Ballad.

Bosom as white as ever
The foam-wreaths rise on the leaping river. — Whittier.

Bottom.

Go to the bottom of things, like a custom house officer. — Sydney Munden.

Bottomless.

Bottomless as the foundation of the Universe. — Carlyle.

Bounce.

Bounce, like corn poppin' in a shovel. — Harriet E. B. Stowe.

Bound (Adjective).

Bound,
Like doomsday prisoned underground.
— D. G. Rossetti.

Fast bound and free,
As all the world is girdled with the sea.
— Swinburne.

Fast bound as a frost-bound water. — Ibid.

Bound as the sun to the world's wheel. — Ibid.

Bound
Like as thralls with links of iron fast in bonds of doom. — Ibid.

Bound (Verb).

My heart bounds like an imprisoned bird against its wiry barrier. — JOHN BROUGHAM.

Bounds like deer from the hounds. — ELIZA COOK.

Bounding like nymphs in vales of Arcady. — WILLIAM HAZLITT.

Like an antelope he bounded. — LONGFELLOW.

Bounds, light as hind before the hound. — AMBROSE PHILIPS.

Bounded like a madman. — POE.

Bound like a stoned horse. — JAMES SHIRLEY.

My pulses bound like a stag at play. — JOHN STERLING.

Like a greyhound when slipped from the leash, he bounded. — BAYARD TAYLOR.

Boundless.

Boundless as the ocean. — BULWER-LYTTON.

Boundless as the glory of Texas. — ALFRED HENRY LEWIS.

Boundless as the sheeted sky. — GEORGE P. MORRIS.

Boundless as the sea. — SHAKESPEARE.

Boundless as the wind. — SWIFT.

Bounteous.

Bounteous as nature. — DRYDEN.

Bounteous as the Nile's dark waters. — JAMES MONTGOMERY.

Bounteous as the air which fed Israel. — SOUTHEY.

Bountiful.

Bountiful as April rains. — COWPER.

Bountiful
As mines of India.
— SHAKESPEARE.

Bountiful as the showers that fall
Into the Spring's green bosom.
— J. SHIRLEY.

Bounty.

Our bounty, like a drop of water, disappears when diffused too widely. — GOLDSMITH.

Bow.

Bow like a field of wheat before the rising wind. — ANON.

Bows like a reed in a tempest. — IBID.

Like a field of standing corn, that's moved with a stiff gale, their heads bow all one way. — BEAUMONT AND FLETCHER.

Bow'd like weeping willows. — CAMPBELL.

Arching bow'd, like color'd rainbows o'er a show'ry moon. — HOMER (POPE).

Bowed, like a man sawing marble. — HOOD.

Bow'd like a sleeping flower. — MISS LANDON.

Bowed like bondmen. — SHAKESPEARE.

A life bowed under its own wealth as the vine is bowed under its fruit. — SUDERMANN.

Bowed like a flowering weed when May's wind heaves the reed-bed the stream kisses. — SWINBURNE.

Bowed down as briars or palms
Even at the breathless blast as of a
breeze
Fulfilled with clamour and clangour
and storms of psalms. — IBID.

I bowed down heavily, as one that mourneth for his mother. — OLD TESTAMENT.

Bow down his head like a bulrush. — IBID.

Bowed to them like a tree in a storm — EDITH WHARTON.

Bracing.

Bracing as an Alpine breeze. — ISRAEL ZANGWILL.

Brag.

Brag boldly, like the cock beside his partlet. — ÆSCHYLUS.

Brain.

Brainless as chimpanzees. — C. S. CALVERLEY.

Great brains (like brightest glass), crack straight; while those of stone or wood hold out, and fear not blows. — BISHOP EARLE.

I suspect that there is in an Englishman's brain a valve that can be closed at pleasure, as an engineer shuts off steam. — EMERSON.

My brain, methinks, is like an hour-glass,
Wherein th' imaginations run to sands,
Filling up time; but there are turn'd and turn'd
So that I know not what to stay upon,
And less to put in act.
— BEN JONSON.

Brain like liquid lead. — SOUTHEY.

Brave.

Brave as a Barbary lion. — ANON.

Brave as Achilles. — IBID.

Brave as a mad bull. — IBID.

Brave as Launcelot. — IBID.

Brave as a falcon and as merciless. — WILFRID S. BLUNT.

Brave as a grenadier. — HUGO.

Is brave like unto the Lord of the Celestials. — MAHABHARATA.

Brave and stern as soldier's mother might be. — ROSA MULHOLLAND.

Brave as winds that brave the sea. — SWINBURNE.

Brave as bannered chivalry. — THOMAS WATSON.

Brawl.

Brawls
Like jarring steel on ruining walls.
— SWINBURNE.

Brazen.

Brazen as an image. — ANON.

Brazen as alabaster. — DICKENS.

Break.

Break him like a biscuit. — BEAUMONT AND FLETCHER.

Break like an o'er-bent bow. — SAMUEL BUTLER.

Break as a bubble o'er-blown in a dream. — SIDNEY LANIER.

Their ranks are breaking like thin clouds before a Biscay gale. — MACAULAY.

Breaking, like rosy clouds at even-tide
Around the rich pavilion of the sun.
— THOMAS MOORE.

The columns break, like shattered foam. — EDWARD PEPLE.

Breaking his oath and resolution, like
A twist of rotten silk.
— SHAKESPEARE.

Break like a bursting heart. — SHELLEY.

Break forth as laughter on lips that said nought till the pulse in them beat love's march. — SWINBURNE.

Breast.

Breasts as the buds of May. — LORD DE TABLEY.

His breast is like a gentlewoman's closet, which locks up every toy or trifle, or some bragging mountebank that makes every stinking thing a secret. — JOHN EARLE'S "MICROCOSMOGRAPHY; A PIECE OF THE WORLD DISCOVERED," 1628.

Her brest fairer than the vernal bloom of valley-lily, op'ning in a show'r. — JOHN LOGAN.

Breast — *continued.*

Breasts half-globed
Like folded lilies deepset in the stream.
— D. G. ROSSETTI.

Breasts like clusters dropping balm. — GEORGE SANDYS.

Her brest like to a bowl of creame uncurdded. — SPENSER.

Breasts like spring. — SWINBURNE.

Thy two breasts are like two young roes that are twins, which feed among the lilies. — OLD TESTAMENT.

Breath.

Her breath is like the fragrant breeze,
That gently stirs the blossom'd bean,
When Phœbus sinks beneath the seas.
— BURNS.

Breath like the sweets from the hawthorn tree. — BARRY CORNWALL.

Her breath
Like a soft western wind, when it glides o'er
Arabia, creating gums and spices.
— MASSINGER.

A breath,
Hot as the blasts that dried old seas.
— ISAAC R. PENNYPACKER.

Breath like morn's young breeze. — PILPAY.

Breathe.

Breathing like the Spring. — ANON.

Breathe like toads under ground. — IBID.

Breathed out, hard and still, as a statue might whisper. — JOSEPH CONRAD.

The young lips breathe like a dewy rose
Fanned by the fire-fly's wing.
— ELIZA COOK.

Breathing like the bellows of a forge. — LORD DE TABLEY.

Breathing like a second-hand bicycle pump. — O. HENRY.

Brethe as the damask Rose. — ROBERT HERRICK.

Breathing sweetness like a bridal bower. — O. W. HOLMES.

She breathes sweet serene as 'twere a gentle spirit from the skies. — PETRARCH.

Breathing like sanctified and pious bawds,
The better to beguile.
— SHAKESPEARE.

Breathe
As March breathes back the spirit of winter. — SWINBURNE.

Breathless as the deer
Driven hard to bay. — IBID.

Breed.

Bred like rats on a grain ship. — LI HUNG CHANG.

A breed, like a dialect of a language, can hardly be said to have a distinct origin. — DARWIN.

Breeds like a rabbit. — SWIFT.

Brief.

Briefer than the twinkling of an eye. — ANON.

Brief as the song
Of the wood dove.
— LORD DE TABLEY.

Brief
As sunset clouds in heaven.
— O. W. HOLMES.

Brief as sparkles from the flint. — HOOD.

Brief as time. — BEN JONSON.

As brief as a dragon-fly's repose. — LOWELL.

As brief as the wave's poise before it breaks in pearls. — IBID.

Brief, as the sunshine scattered over the plains. — MIMNERMUS.

Brief as a dream. — PTAH-HOTEP.

As the fading of a flower,
As the falling of a leaf,
So brief its day and its hour.
— C. G. ROSSETTI.

Brief — *continued.*

Brief as the lightning in the collied night. — SHAKESPEARE.

Brief like a signal. — ROBERT LOUIS STEVENSON.

Brief as the word strong sorrow saith. — IBID.

Brief as a broken song. — SWINBURNE.

Thou art brief as a glitter of sand 'twixt tide and tide. — WILLIAM WATSON.

Brief and tremulous as a passing shadow. — WILLIAM WINTER.

Bright.

Bright as fair sunshine after winter's storms. — ÆSCHYLUS.

Bright as a blister. — ANON.

Bright as a dollar. — IBID.

Bright as a new penny. — IBID.

Bright as a pewter pot. — IBID.

Bright as at Creation's day. — IBID.

Bright as fairies that in a sunbeam dance. — IBID.

Bright as Japanese bronze. — IBID.

Bright as new silver. — IBID.

Bright as saucepans. — IBID.

Bright as Sharon's rose. — IBID.

Bright as sunshine on the sea. — IBID.

Bright as the captain's cabin of a man-of-war. — IBID.

Bright was her soul as Dian's crest. — IBID.

Bright as fullest moon in blackest air. — ARABIAN NIGHTS.

Bright as though a moon of the fourteenth night. — IBID.

Bright as a beach in the moonlight. — ALFRED AUSTIN.

Bright as the great stream of stars which flows through heaven. — P. J. BAILEY.

Bright like night with stars. — IBID.

Bright, like river gold. — IBID.

Bright as midnight's brightest eyes. — T. L. BEDDOES.

Bright, as Moerice-Queens in June. — A. H. BEESLY.

Bright within
As when from the sky there shines
unclouded heaven's candle.
— "BEOWULF."

Bright as an iceberg. — R. D. BLACKMORE.

Brighter than the sun through wheat. — IBID.

As bright as the waves of a rill. — GEORGE H. BOKER.

Bright as the rippling ocean in sunshine. — ROBERT BRIDGES (English).

Bright as icicles about a laurel-tree. — MARIA G. BROOKS.

Bright as Paphia's eyes. — E. B. BROWNING.

Bright, like a flash of sunlight. — BULWER-LYTTON.

Bright as the bow that spans the storm. — CAMPBELL.

Bright as day. — CHAUCER.

Bright as stars in winter. — IBID.

As rody and bright as doth the yonge
sonne
That in the ram is foure degrees ronne.
— IBID.

Bright as joy. — HARTLEY COLERIDGE.

Bright as the moon she shone, with
silver light,
And charmed his sense with wonder
and delight. — CONGREVE.

Bright as truth. — BARRY CORNWALL.

Bright as orient morn. — COWPER.

Bright — *continued.*

Bright as innocence. — JOHN DAY.

Bright as a flame. — DANIEL DEFOE.

Bright as sunset. — LORD DE TABLEY.

Bright as Apollo's breastplate. — AUBREY DE VERE.

Bright as May-day's morn. — IBID.

Bright as the pastures of the sun. — IBID.

Shone as bright as sea-foam sparkling on a moonlit night. — IBID.

Bright as Heav'n. — WENTWORTH DILLON.

Bright and steady as a sunbeam. — DR. JOHN DORAN.

Bricht as chrysolite. — GAWAIN DOUGLAS.

Bright as goodness. — DRYDEN.

Bright as Lucifer. — WILLIAM DUNBAR.

Bright and barren as the sea,
Bare of sorrow, bare of glee.
— F. W. FABER.

Bright . . . as all the flowers of May. — FRANCIS FAWKES.

Bright as Phœbus. — IBID.

Bright as live coals in the gloom. — FLAUBERT.

Bright as the breaking east. — JOHN FLETCHER.

Bright as any star in heaven. — GOETHE.

Bright as at creation's day. — IBID.

Bright as before the day-star will appear. — JAMES HAMMOND.

Bright as the visions of youth. — T. K. HERVEY.

Bright as the jewels of the seven-starr'd crown. — O. W. HOLMES.

Bright
As the resplendent cactus of the night
That floods the gloom with fragrance
and with light. — IBID.

Bright as noon in a conservatory of smoked glass. — E. W. HORNUNG.

Bright as a beacon. — HUGO.

Bright,
Most like a fleet of stars that southing
go. — JEAN INGELOW.

Brycht as gold. — JAMES THE FIRST.

Bright as ruddy meteors through the sky. — ROBERT JEPHSON.

Bright as the lily of the vale. — SIR WILLIAM JONES.

Bright as the bow of Iris. — KEATS.

Bright as the humming-bird's green diadem. — IBID.

Bright as the gold-sparks that glisten and quiver at morning or eve, on the breast of the river. — E. M. KELLY.

Bright as an opium-eater's dream. — KINGSLEY.

Bright as Hope's first smile. — MISS LANDON.

Bright as autumn's fleecy clouds with golden glittering lightning decked. — "LAYS OF ANCIENT INDIA."

Bright as a button. — LEAN'S "COLLECTANEA."

Bright, like a fire-flash that crosses the depth of the night. — J. S. LE FANU.

Bright as living coal. — CAMILLE LEMONNIER.

Bright as the argent-horned mornes. — RICHARD LOVELACE.

Bright as the ruby's blaze. — LOVER.

As bright as glow-worms in the night. — LYLY.

Bright as the sunbeam of the morning. — EVAN MACCOLL.

Bright — *continued.*

Bright as musky moss-rose summer's sun. — George Mac-Henry.

Bright as the dimpled smiles that spring enwreath. — Ibid.

As bright as dewdrops in the sun. — Charles Mackay.

Bright like the moon when the stars are dimm'd with her blaze. —Ewen Maclachan.

Bright as the sunbeam's light. — D. F. McCarthy.

Bright as new pottery. — Maurice Maeterlinck.

Bright as the Burning Bush of Moses. — James C. Mangan.

Bright as beams of Paradise. — Mary E. Mannix.

Orange bright,
Like golden lamps in a green night.
— Andrew Marvell.

Bright as orb that gives the day. — William Mason.

Rose-bright as a star dipped in sunset. — Owen Meredith.

As bright as a spot of June day sunshine on the grass. — Donald G. Mitchell.

Bright as Minerva's yellow hair. — Thomas Moore.

Bright, like common things, glorified in love's light. — Miss Mulock.

Bright as an angel new dropt from the sky. — Thomas Parnell.

Bright, as from blessed place. — Stephen Phillips.

Bright as the star of morn. — Robert Pollok.

Bright as the rising sun, in summer's day. — Pope.

Bright as the star that fires autumnal skies. — Ibid.

Bright, as visions of expiring maids. — Ibid.

Bright
As golden morning's flashing light.
— W. H. Prideaux.

Bright as the sun. — Rabelais.

Bright as the crimson glow when love first sends a missive to a maiden. C. D. Raymer.

Bright as a cloud in the sunset air. — T. Buchanan Read.

Bright as an opening rose fresh with dew. — Charles Reade.

Bright as the sunset's glow. — Laura E. Richards.

Bright as the light of her glorious eyes. — James Whitcomb Riley.

His smile as bright as the midst of May when the truce-bird pipes. — Ibid.

As bright as the morning sun. — Ibid.

Bright as the golden poppy is that the beach breeds for the surf to kiss. — C. G. Rossetti.

Bright as a new bell. — W. C. Russell.

Bright as all between cloudless skies and windless streams. — Shelley.

Bright as Spring. — Ibid.

Bright as are the Heavens that lie
Illumed by stars at night.
— Blanche Shoemaker.

As bright . . . as the vestal fire. — Christopher Smart.

Bright as mountain snow. — Southey.

Bright as the summer lightning when it spreads its glory o'er the midnight heaven. — Ibid.

Bright as doth the morning starre appeare. — Spenser.

Bright, like twinckling starres. — Ibid.

Bright as a rose new blown. — T. D. Sullivan.

Bright — *continued.*

Bright as an angel. — SWIFT.

Bright as a dew-drop engilt of the sun on the sedge. — SWINBURNE.

Bright as all above. — IBID.

Bright as a warrior's belt. — IBID.

Bright as burns at sunrise, heaven's own. — IBID.

Song bright as heaven above the mounting bird. — IBID.

Bright as heaven's bare brow with hope of gifts withholden. — IBID.

Bright as hell-fire. — IBID.

Bright as hope. — IBID.

Bright as Maytime. — IBID.

Bright as mercy. — IBID.

Bright as the kindling dews when the dawn begins. — IBID.

Bright as the night is dark on the world. — IBID.

Bright as though death's dim sunrise thrilled it there and life re-risen took comfort. — IBID.

Bright like spring with flower-soft wealth of branching tracery. — IBID.

Brighter than joy's own tears. — IBID.

Bloom as bright as opening moon. — BAYARD TAYLOR.

Bright as light. — TENNYSON.

Bright and light as the crest of a peacock. — IBID.

Bright as the eyes of angels and as pure. — WILLIAM THOMSON.

Shine bright,
As sun-showers at the break of day.
— HENRY D. THOREAU.

Bright as a facet-cut diamond scattering light. — TUPPER.

Bright as the seraphim pointing to eternity. — JOSEPH TURNLEY.

Bright as the blessings of heaven. — MICHAEL VÖRÖSMARTY.

Bright as the promise of a cloudless day. — C. P. WILSON.

Bright as a sunbeam sleeping till a shower
Brush it away, or cloud pass over it.
— WORDSWORTH.

Bright as spring. — IBID.

Bright as the glimpses of eternity,
To saints according in their mortal hour. — IBID.

Bright as the dazzling snow. — IBID.

As a rainbow bright. — THEODORE WRATISLAW.

Bright as Phebüs' sphere. — SIR THOMAS WYATT.

Shining bright as a new lance. — WILLIAM B. YEATS.

Brighten

Brighten like a morning of young spring. — JOHN M. LEAVITT.

Brightened as in sunshine gleam the ripples
That the cold wind makes in rivers.
— LONGFELLOW.

Brighten, like a meadow when the sun comes out. — MISS MULOCK.

Brightened, like the full moon of heaven; when the clouds vanish away, and leave her calm and broad in the midst of the sky. — OSSIAN.

Brightens all my sorrow,
Like gleams of sunshine in a low'ring sky. — AMBROSE PHILIPS.

Brightened
As a forest with birds.
— SWINBURNE.

Brightened like the moon. — BAYARD TAYLOR.

Brightening like a star at eve. — N. P. WILLIS.

Brilliant

Brilliant as a dream. — ANON.

Brilliant as Indian summer. — IBID.

Brilliant — *continued.*

Brilliant as the colors of the rainbow. — Ibid.

Brilliant, like chrysophrase glowing
Was my beautiful Rosalie Lee.
— Thomas Holley Chivers.

Brilliant as a mirror. — Dumas, père.

Brilliant as altar fires. — Vedic Hymn.

Brilliant as rain-drops, when the western sun
Sees his own miniature of beams in each. — Montgomery.

Brilliant as stars. — Ouida.

Brilliant, like transparent plates of mother-of-pearl. — Saint-Pierre.

As brilliant as a spangled dancing girl. — Alexander Smith.

How brilliant and mirthful the light of her eye,
Like a star glancing out from the blue of the sky! — Whittier.

Brim.

Brims with bliss, as a valley brims with life in spring-tide hours. — Gerald Massey.

Brisk.

Brisk as a flea. — Anon.

Brisk as bees that settle on a summer rose's petal. — C. S. Calverley.

Brisk as a burger over a bottle. — Austin Dobson.

Brisk as a bottled ale.— John Gay.

Brisk as a cup of wine. — Robert Greene.

Brisk as a bird. — William Hazlitt.

Briskly as a revolving firework. — Brander Matthews.

Brisk as bank stock. — Thomas Morton.

As brisk as a bailiff. — James Smith.

Brisk as a snake in merry May. — William Somerville.

Brisk as a body louse. — Swift.

Bristle.

Bristles all over like a porcupine. — Anon.

Bristling . . . like some mad Earth-god's spiny hair. — Thomas Hardy.

Bristle like spears in battle ranks. — Jayadeva.

Bristly . . . like a hedgehog. — Leo Tolstoy.

Brittle.

Brittle as glass that breaks with a touch. — Swinburne.

Broad.

Broad as barn doors. — John Heywood.

Broad as Heaven's expanse. — Hugo.

Broad as the kingdoms and empires of old. — Charles Mackay.

Broad as a furred stomacher. — Thomas Nash.

Broad and general as the casing air. — Shakespeare.

Broadens like the summer morn. — Menella B. Smedley.

Broader than the sea. — Old Testament.

Broadcast.

Broadcast as the light. — George E. Woodbury.

Broke.

Broken up like baffled dreams. — F. W. Faber.

A gleam of hope through my black night broke,
Like a star's bright form
Through a whistling storm,
Or the moon through a midnight oak.
— D. F. McCarthy.

Broke like a sea-bubble on the sand. — James Montgomery.

Brood.

Brooding like a dove for its mate. — ANON.

Brooded . . . like a hen over a chalk egg. — BULWER-LYTTON.

Broods like an owl. — ERNEST DOWSON.

Brow.

Her brow . . . is like the young moon. — ANON.

Her brows like bended bows do stand,
Threatening with piercing frowns to kill
All that approach with eye or hand
These sacred cherries to come nigh.
— ENGLISH BALLAD.

Her browe was like the mountain snae
Gilt by the morning beam.
— SCOTTISH BALLAD.

His brow was like the deep when tempest toss'd. — BYRON.

Brows like cloudless day. — ELIZA COOK.

Her brow is like the snaw-drift. — WILLIAM DOUGLAS.

Brows — thin like the stroke of a pen. — DOUGLAS HYDE'S "LOVE SONGS OF CONNACHT."

Thy brow like smooth Bandhûka-leaves. — JAYADEVA.

Brown.

Brown as forest flood. — CACHULAINN.

Browne as the fylberte droppyng from the shelle. — THOMAS CHATTERTON.

Browne as the nappy ale at Hock tyde game. — IBID.

Broun as is a berye. — CHAUCER.

Brown,
As is the ribbed sea-sand.
— COLERIDGE.

Brown as a pineapple. — DAUDET.

Brown as the hearth of a kitchen fire. — JOHN GAY.

Brown as a bun. — HOOD.

Locks . . . as brown as mavis in May. — RICHARD LE GALLIENNE.

Brown as nut. — LONGFELLOW.

Brown as vesper gloamings. — WALTER MALONE.

Brown as buckeyes. — EDWIN D. SCHOONMAKER.

Brown in hue as hazel nuts. — SHAKESPEARE.

As twilight brown. — SWINBURNE.

Brutal.

Brutal as an unclean word. — VANCE THOMPSON.

Bubble.

Bubbled like a tea-kettle beginning to boil. — ANON.

Bubbling and overflowing, like a brazen cup beneath an ardent sun. — MAURICE MAETERLINCK.

Bubbles.

Bubbles,
Like man's vain glory, and his vainer troubles. — BYRON.

Budded.

Budded as a thorn to sting. — GEORGE MAC-HENRY.

Buffoon.

A buffoon is like a mad dog, that has a worm in his tongue, which makes him bite at all that light in his way. — SAMUEL BUTLER.

Build

Many a thought did I build up on thought,
As the wild bee hangs cell on cell.
— ROBERT BROWNING.

Bulged.

Bulged like pudding. — FITZ-JAMES O'BRIEN.

Bulged out in the sun like a pumpkin. — THACKERAY.

Bulk.

Huge bulk like a sea monster among the minnows of the Thames. — DICKENS.

Buoyant.

Buoyant as wings. — BYRON.

Buoyant as light. — ELIZA COOK.

Buoyant as the thistle-down. — HOOD.

Merry buoyancy, as of a boat. — ROBERT NOEL.

Buoyant as summer spray. — CHARLES TURNER.

Burly.

Burley as a Sunday beadle. — JAMES PILGRIM.

Burn.

Burn into your soul like a curse. — ANON.

Burned like a spilth of light
Out of the crashing of a myriad stars.
— ROBERT BROWNING.

Our wasted oil unprofitably burns,
Like hidden lamps in old sepulchral urns. — COWPER.

Burnt like caustic. — HOOD.

Burns, like some absent and impatient youth, to join the object of his warm desire. — SOAME JENYNS.

Burns like hate. — GEORGE MACDONALD.

Burn within me like an evil fire. — IBID.

Burn like the red light of the setting sun. — T. BUCHANAN READ.

Burn like black stars below the Orient moon. — FRANCIS S. SALTUS.

Burn like mines of sulphur. — SHAKESPEARE.

Burning like molten jewels. — W. W. STORY.

Burn and bleed
Like that pale princess-priest of Priam's seed. — SWINBURNE.

Burn as if all the fires of the earth and air
Had laid strong hold upon his flesh and stung
The soul behind it as with a serpent's tongue. — IBID.

Burn as that beamless fire which fills the skies
With troubled stars and travailing things of flame. — IBID.

Burning her like flame
That feeds on flowers in bloom.
— IBID.

Burns like joy. — IBID.

Burns low as fire wherein no firebrands glow. — IBID.

Burnt as a living fire of emeralds. — TENNYSON.

Burneth as a flaming fire. — OLD TESTAMENT.

Burning like the burning of a fire. — IBID.

Burns, like a fiery star in the upper air. — WHITTIER.

Burned like a heated opal. — OSCAR WILDE.

Burned like the ruby fire set
In the swinging lamp of a crimson shrine. — IBID.

Burrow.

Burrow like a weasel. — R. D. BLACKMORE.

Burst.

Burst like sand this brave embankment of the breast. — P. J. BAILEY.

Bursting like a bean-pod. — R. D. BLACKMORE.

Burst forth like the neighing of all Tattersall's. — CARLYLE.

Light burst on me as if a window of my memory had been suddenly flung open on a street in the city. — JOSEPH CONRAD.

Burst — *continued.*

Burst, like a morn lighted bubble of dew. — ELIZA COOK.

Like shallow ice-films 'neath a courser's hoof, burst. — AUBREY DE VERE.

Bursting like an overdone potato. — SIR A. CONAN DOYLE.

Burst like bellowing Ætna. — DRYDEN.

Burst into sound, like thunder with a shower. — FRANCIS FAWKES.

Burst like rockets into one wide blaze. — CHARLES HARPUR.

Burst frae their bounds like fiends of hell. — HOGG.

Burst like surf. — WESTLAND MARSTON.

Burst, like an enfranchised dove. — MISS MULOCK.

Bursts like the lightning's flash. — SCHILLER.

Burst like morning on dream, or like heaven on death. — SHELLEY.

Bursts like one sound from ten thousand streams
Of a tempestuous sea. — IBID.

Burst like a pimple from the vicious tide of acid blood. — WILLIAM SHENSTONE.

The banners burst,
Like buds of April breezes burst.
— BAYARD TAYLOR.

Burst, like a thunderbolt. — TENNYSON.

Burst like Heavenly Hope. — IBID.

Burst like new bottles. — OLD TESTAMENT.

Bury.

Burned, like Topeca beneath the bucklers of Sabines. — DUMAS, PÈRE.

Buried like a cauliflower. — WASHINGTON IRVING.

Bushy.

Bushy as the fleece of the ram. — ANON.

Business.

But certainly, some there are that know the resorts and falls of business that can not sink into the main of it; like a house that hath convenient stairs and entries, but never a fair room. — BACON.

Let business, like ill watches, go
Sometimes too fast, sometimes too slow. — SAMUEL BUTLER.

The tide of business, like the running stream,
Is sometimes high and sometimes low,
A quiet ebb, or a tempestuous flow,
And always in extreme.
Now with a noiseless gentle course,
It keeps within the middle bed,
Anon it lifts aloft the head,
And bears down all before it with impetuous force. — DRYDEN.

Bustle.

Bustled about like so many ants roused by the approach of a foe. — J. HAMPDEN PORTER.

Busy.

Busy as a beaver. — ANON.

Busy as a beehive attacked by a bear. — IBID.

Busy as a boy killing snakes. — IBID.

Busy as a good wife at an oven. — IBID.

Busy as a hen with one chick. — IBID.

Busy as a humming bird with two tails. — IBID.

Busy as a one-armed paperhanger with the hives. — IBID.

Busy as a pigeon at a shooting match. — IBID.

Busy as squirrels in a wheel. — IBID.

Busy — *continued.*

Busy as a ticking clock. — ANON.

Busy as a hen with fifteen chickens in a barnyard. — J. R. BARTLETT'S "DICTIONARY OF AMERICANISMS."

Busy as a cross-eyed boy at a three-ring circus. — REX BEACH.

Busy as a child at play. — SAMUEL BUTLER.

Busy as a cow's tail in fly time. — J. FENIMORE COOPER.

Busy as the devil in a gale of wind. — SIR JOHN DENHAM.

Busy as the day is long. — LEAN'S "COLLECTANEA."

Busie as a bee. — LYLY.

Busy as the day. — MACAULAY.

Death . . . was busy as on a battle field. — SKELTON.

As busy as bees in a glass hive. — JAMES SMITH.

Busy as the brooks. — THOREAU.

Busy as horses in a field of clover. — JOHN WOLCOTT.

Busy as a wren. — WORDSWORTH.

Busy as the lightning. — IBID.

Buzz.

Buzzing like a fly. — ANON.

Buzz in the ear like gnats. — ARLO BATES.

Buzzed like the bees when they swarm. — HOOD.

Buzz'd like bees
Fretting and swarming in the linden-trees. — W. S. LANDOR.

C

Calamity.

Domestic calamity is like the miniature of a friend, which we wear in our bosoms, and keep for secret looks and solitary enjoyment. — HENRY MACKENZIE.

Callous.

Callous as Comus to moral babble. — ANON.

Calm.

Calm as the Judge of Truth. — AKENSIDE.

Calm as a summer sea. — LOUISA M. ALCOTT.

Calm as a convent. — ANON.

Calm as a cradled child in Dreamland slumber. — IBID.

Calm as a June day. — IBID.

Calm as a midnight sea. — IBID.

Calm as a saint in Paradise. — IBID.

Calm as a soft summer eve. — IBID.

Calm as a virgin in her shroud. — IBID.

Calm as clam shells. — IBID.

Calm as the society column of a newspaper. — IBID.

Calm as deep rivers. — R. D. BLACKMORE.

Calm as glass. — CHARLOTTE BRONTË.

Features are as calm as marble. — JOHN BROUGHAM.

Calm, as one who, safe in heaven,
Shall tell a story of his lower life,
Unmoved by shame or anger.
— E. B. BROWNING.

Like the battle camp's fearful calm,
While the banners are spread, and the warriors arm. — IBID.

Calm as a babe new-born. — ROBERT BROWNING.

Calm — *continued.*

Calm as beauty. — ROBERT BROWNING.

A calm as out of just-quelled noise. — IBID.

Calm as Heaven's serenest deeps. — WILLIAM ALLEN BUTLER.

Calm as the fields of Heaven. — CAMPBELL.

Calm as a field of snow. — BLISS CARMAN.

Calm, unmoved as the very noon and centre of being. — IBID.

Calm like that when storm is done. — HELEN G. CONE.

Calm as the gliding moon. — COLERIDGE.

Calm as a discharged culverin. — CONGREVE.

Calm as infant-love. — CRABBE.

Calm as forgiven wits at the last hour. — SIR WILLIAM DAVENANT.

Calm as an autumn night. — LORD DE TABLEY.

Calm as Clapham. — DICKENS.

Calm as a mirror. — DUMAS, PÈRE.

Calm as a virgin who has never told a lie. — IBID.

As calm as evening when caressed
By twilight breezes from the west.
— SAM WALTER FOSS.

Calm as a statue-saint. — NORMAN GALE.

Calm as a lake in heaven. — W. S. GILBERT.

Calm as the child who, smiling, hears
The footsteps of advancing years.
— MRS. L. B. HALL.

Calmly, as to a night's repose, like flowers at set of sun. — FITZ-GREENE HALLECK.

Calm as ice. — HAWTHORNE.

Calm as the patient planet's gleam
That walks the clouded skies.
— O. W. HOLMES.

Calm as a Mandarin. — RICHARD HOVEY.

Calm as night. — HUGO.

Calm as the solitude between wide stars. — JEAN INGELOW.

Calm — as if she were always sitting for her portrait. — HENRY JAMES.

Calm as brooding clouds. — E. C. JONES.

Calm as a child in its soft slumber lying. — E. M. KELLY.

Calmly, like a soul at rest. — FRANCES ANNE KEMBLE.

Calm as a vestal. — WILLIAM LIVINGSTON.

Shone calm . . . like the moon in the midst of the night.
— D. F. MCCARTHY.

Calm as the calm that follows duty. — GEORGE MACDONALD.

Calm as the breast of the lake when the loud wind is laid. — JAMES MACPHERSON.

Calm as a statue of Memnon in prostrate Egypt.
— GEORGE MEREDITH.

A calmness like the calmness of a grave. — OWEN MEREDITH.

Calm as some lonely shepherd's song. — THOMAS MOORE.

Calm as an angel from the blessed land. — MISS MULOCK.

Calm as a spent day of peace ideal. — IBID.

Calm as a summer evening before the dark begins. — IBID.

Calm as under ground. — IBID.

Calm as the smoothest waters. — DANIEL O'CONNELL.

Calm as the breast of a lake when the loud wind is laid. — OSSIAN.

Calm — *continued.*

He is as calm as calm weather is wont to be. — PLAUTUS.

Calm like the sleep of a soul that is blest. — T. BUCHANAN READ.

Calm as Force. — D. G. ROSSETTI.

Calm as . . . a deeply sheltered mountain lake. — RUSKIN.

Calm, as in the days when all was right. — SCHILLER.

Calm as the clear evening after vernal rains. — JOHN SCOTT.

Calm as virtue. — SHAKESPEARE.

Calm as a cradled child in dreamless slumber bound. — SHELLEY.

Calm as a slumbering babe. — IBID.

Calm as an angel in the dragon's den. — IBID.

Calm as death. — IBID.

Calm, radiant, like the phantom of the dawn. — IBID.

Calm like duty. — SOUTHEY.

Calm as the blind who have not seen
the light,
The deaf who hear no precious voice.
— E. C. STEDMAN.

A forehead calm as fate. — IBID.

Calm as a Quaker. — THACKERAY.

Calm as that second summer which precedes the first fall of the snow. — HENRY TIMROD.

Calm as at Creation's dawn. — JOHN C. VAN DYKE.

Calm as the sky after a day of storm. — VOLTAIRE.

Calm as Neptune on the Halcyon seas. — WILLIAM WALSH.

Calm a conscience as ever blessed an anchorite. — THOMAS WATSON.

Serenely calm as summer evenings. — ISAAC WATTS.

Calm as the hermit in his grot. — CHARLES WESLEY.

Calm as dawn. — WALT WHITMAN.

Calm as a child to slumber soothed,
As if an Angel's hand had smoothed
The still, white features into rest.
— WHITTIER.

Calm as earliest morn. — OSCAR WILDE.

Calm and blessed . . . like a rich pearl beyond the diver's ken. — N. P. WILLIS.

Calm as a frozen lake when ruthless
winds
Blow fiercely. — WORDSWORTH.

Calm as the dew-drops. — IBID.

Calm as lakes that sleep.— IBID.

Calumniate.

The calumniator is like the dragon that pursued a woman, but, not being able to overtake her, opened his mouth and threw a flood after her to drown her. — EDWARD BLUNT.

Came.

He came down the road like hell beating tanbark. — ANON.

Came and went like the lighthouse gleam on a black night at sea. — ROBERT BUCHANAN.

Came out of his shell like the aurelia out of the grub. — WILLIAM HAZLITT.

Came from all sides like conspirators from a wood in a tragedy. — MAURICE HEWLETT.

Came, like a ray from Heaven, that shines and disappears. — JOHN HOME.

Candid.

Candid as a dove is white. — HUGO.

Candid as mirrors. — ROBERT G. INGERSOLL.

Candid as the skies. — FRANCIS THOMPSON.

Capacious.

Capacious like the storehouse of the rains. — EMERSON.

Capacious — *continued.*

Capacious as the sky. — JAMES A. HILLHOUSE.

Capacious as the mind of a boy. — DONALD G. MITCHELL.

Caper.

Caper like a dancing master. — THOMAS OTWAY.

Capers like a fly in a tar-box. — JOHN RAY'S "HANDBOOK OF PROVERBS."

Capricious.

Capricious as the vagrant wind. P. H. HAYNE.

Capricious, like the thinkings of a child. — GEORGE MACDONALD.

Capricious as a zephyr. — TUPPER.

Capture.

Captured the eyes as a sharp cry secures attention. — JOSEPH CONRAD.

Care.

Care is like a husbandman who doth guard our treasures:
And the while, all ways he can, spoils our harmless pleasures.
Loving hearts and laughing brows, most he seeks to plunder,
And each furrow that he ploughs turns the roses under. — ALICE CARY.

Second-hand cares, like second-hand clothes, come easily off and on. — DICKENS.

As much care as pilots of ships avoid the rocks of the sea. — RABELAIS.

As rust eats iron, so care eats the heart. — A. RICARD.

Careful.

Careful as the chief eunuch is of the Grand Seignior's favorite Sultana. — ANON.

Careless.

Carelessly as hurls the moth her wing
Against the light wherein she dies.
— BYRON.

Careless as the Salmon with its million young. — RICHARD LE GALLIENNE.

Careless as the wind. — WILLIAM J. LINTON.

Careless as a man in his first state. — E. V. LUCAS.

Careless as gods for who might live or die. — WILLIAM MORRIS.

Careless as the course of a meteor. — OSSIAN.

Careless as the young flower tossing on the summer breeze. — OUIDA.

Carelessly as the blossoming trees. — ALEXANDER SMITH.

Careless as are the brooks, or birds that sing,
Of any other song of brook or bird.
— JOHN T. TROWBRIDGE.

Careless . . . as Christians of their souls. — FRANCIS H. WILLIAMS.

Careless as the child at play. — WILLIAM WINTER.

Careless as if nothing were. — WORDSWORTH.

Caress.

Caressed him like a lap dog. — ANON.

Fast caressed,
Like living things that joyed or feared.
— ARTHUR HENRY HALLAM.

Caressing as a kiss. — GUY DE MAUPASSANT.

She bent thy pallor to caress, as snow that toucheth snow. — GEORGE STERLING.

Carnation.

Carnation'd like a sleeping infant's cheek. — BYRON.

Carol.

Carol like a bird in spring. — HOOD.

Carouse.

Carouse together
Like friends long lost.
— SHAKESPEARE.

Carry.

Carries it as badly as a callow youth in wine. — ANON.

Carve.

Carved like an apple-tart
Here's snip, and nip, and cut, and slish,
and slash,
Like a censer in a barber's shop.
— SHAKESPEARE.

Cast.

Casting, like a sower afield. — ANON.

Cast out of thy grave like an abominable branch, and as the raiment of those that are slain. — IBID.

Casual.

Casually, like John Drew counting up the house. — IRVIN S. COBB.

Catch.

Catching like fire in dry grass. — W. D. HOWELLS.

Catch at us, like strumpets. — SHAKESPEARE.

Caught.

Caught, like a bit of paper between the blades of a pair of shears. — ANON.

Caught, like vipers, with a bit of red cloth. — R. B. SHERIDAN.

Cautious.

Cautious as a fox. — ANON.

As cautious as a Scot. — IBID.

Cautious as a good housekeeper. — BALZAC.

Cautious as a cragsman. — G. K. CHESTERTON.

A vague caution, like that of a wild beast that is fierce but feeble — or like that of an insect whose little fragment of earth has given way, and made it pause in a palsy of distrust. — GEORGE ELIOT.

Cautious as a girl. — ARSÈNE HOUSSAYE.

As cautious as a burglar walking over a tin roof in cowhide boots. — WALLACE IRWIN.

Cease.

Ceased like an exquisite lyric
That dies on the breast of night.
— DON MARQUIS.

Ceaselessly,
Like delicate hands that are clapped in
glee. — T. BUCHANAN READ.

Celebrated.

Celebrated as the sun. — HENRI MURGER.

Celebrity.

Emile Augier . . . carried his celebrity not as a mantle but as a flower in his button-hole. — EDMONDO DE AMICIS.

Celerity.

Celerity : like the motion of a bullet in the air, which flieth so swift as it outruns the eye. — BACON.

Censure.

Censure is like the lightning which strikes the highest mountains. — BALTASAR GRACIAN.

Censorious . . . as a superannuated sinner. — WYCHERLEY.

Central.

One central mystery, as a darkness within a darkness. — DE QUINCEY.

Ceremony.

Ceremony keeps up all things : 'Tis like a Penny-Glass to a rich Spirit, or some excellent water ; without it the Water were spilt, the Spirit lost. — JOHN SELDEN.

Certain.

As certain as that a brook must have banks. — ANON.

As certain as that a squirrel will climb a tree. — IBID.

As certain as that your shadow will follow you. — IBID.

Certain — *continued.*

As certain as that the leaves will fall in autumn. — ANON.

Certain as gold. — IBID.

Certain as that a crooked tree will have a crooked shadow. — IBID.

Certain as that a person not guilty of his own death, shortens not his own life. — IBID.

Certain as that light and heat come and go with the sun. — IBID.

Certain as that no mill no meal. — IBID.

Certain as that plants and animals grow and die. — IBID.

Certain as that sticks burn away in the fire. — IBID.

Certain as the movements of heavenly bodies. — IBID.

Certain as the multiplication table. — IBID.

Certain as that the ocean is the meeting-place of all waters ; the skies, the meeting-place of all torches ; the tongue, of all tastes; the nose, of all smells ; the mind, of all precepts. — IBID.

Certain as the rising of the morning sun. — IBID.

Certain as that the Tweed runs from east to west. — IBID.

Certain as Christmas. — HAROLD BRIGHOUSE.

Certainly, as evening empties morning into night. — E. B. BROWNING.

Certain as a gun. — SAMUEL BUTLER.

As certain as a tail will follow a comet. — CARLYLE.

Certain to make his way there as a gimlet is to go through soft deal. — DICKENS.

A sound brain should always evolve the same fixed product with the certainty of Babbage's calculating machine. — O. W. HOLMES.

As certainly as the thunder-crash follows the lightning. — LEVER.

Certaine as wayes unto the blinde. — RICHARD LOVELACE.

Certain as bodies moved with greater impulse, progress more rapidly than those moved with less. — VOLTAIRE.

Certainly as day comes after day. — WILLIAM WATSON.

Chagrin.

His chagrin was like those newly invented furnaces which consume their own smoke. — HUGO.

Chambermaid.

Chambermaids are like lotteries : you may draw twenty, ere one worth anything. — SIR THOMAS OVERBURY.

Chance.

About as much chance as a lamb in Mr. Armour's slaughter house. — GEORGE ADE.

No more chance than a hen has of hatching a codfish from a fried egg. — ANON.

About as much chance as a man with a wooden leg in a forest fire. — GEORGE BROADHURST.

About as much chance as a Hamburg steak in front of a starving ironmoulder. — R. L. GOLDBERG.

Good a chance to win as a man learning to play poker on an ocean steamer. — O. HENRY.

As much chance as a dog with tallow legs chasing an asbestos cat in Hades. — ELBERT HUBBARD.

No more chance than a one-legged man in a football game. — IBID.

About as much chance as a fat June bug would have in the pathway of a road roller. — GRANTLAND RICE.

No more chance than a thaw in Zembla. — SYDNEY SMITH.

Chance — *continued.*

About as much chance as a prohibition candidate in a Democratic ward. — NEW YORK TIMES.

No more chance than a motorist's word has against a policeman's. — NEW YORK TRIBUNE.

Change.

Change as woman, wind and fortune. — ANON.

Change, like Proteus. — IBID.

Change, like women's thoughts and winter weather. — IBID.

Changeable as the moons. — IBID.

Changeful as the ocean bar. — IBID.

Quickly changed as are the winds. — BEAUMONT AND FLETCHER.

As changeful as the lights which flick and flash from off the facets of the diamond. — HEATHER BIGG.

Changest, as the wind upon the wave. — HUGH H. BRACKENRIDGE.

Changes like the moonlit cloud. — RICHARD H. DANA.

Changeable as a woman's whims. — FARQUHAR.

Thy song is changeful as yon starry frame,
End and beginning evermore the same.
— GOETHE.

Change . . . like unto the Camelion whiche upon every sondre hewe, that he behalt, he mote newe his colour. — JOHN GOWER.

Changeful as a child. — JOHN IMLAH.

Fortune changeth as the moon
To caravel and picaroon.
— KIPLING.

Changeful . . . as are the waves before the breath of winds. — SIGMUND KRASINSKI.

Changeful as the neck of dove
In colour.
— WALTER SAVAGE LANDOR.

Changeful . . . as windwaved flame. — LOWELL.

Changes color as a maid at sight of sword and shield. — MACAULAY.

In affection, as light and changeful as the gaudy fly which hastens to the rose with eager speed, and on its damask leaves, with fond embrace, flutters her painted wings a little while, but lift she but her eyes, and the first thistle flower that catches them catches her fancy too, and thither speeds she. — WILLIAM J. MICKLE.

But now a change came o'er my dream,
Like the magic lantern's shifting slider. — THOMAS MOORE.

As changeful as the spring. — LEWIS MORRIS.

Changed like one who knows his time must be
But short and bitter. — IBID.

Changeful as the lunar ray. — PETRARCH.

Like April, she may wear a changeful face
Of storm and sunshine.
— JAMES PILGRIM.

Changeful as a madman's dream. — WINTHROP M. PRAED.

Like leaves, as chance inclin'd,
Those wills were chang'd with every wind. — MATTHEW PRIOR.

Changeable, like the sparrow, who stops not on one twig. — OSMANLI PROVERB.

Like a chameleon, he changes. — IBID.

Changed me like a glove. — C. G. ROSSETTI.

Chang'd, like form in a dream. — SIR WALTER SCOTT.

Changes as a guilty dream. — IBID.

Ever changing, like a joyless eye
That finds no objects worth its constancy. — SHELLEY.

Change like the face of fortune. — SOUTHEY.

Change — *continued.*

Changed as a cloud in the night. — SWINBURNE.

Changeful as the sea. — BAYARD TAYLOR.

Change like a weathercock. — ROBERT TOFTE.

Changeful as a lover's hope. — FRANK WATERS.

Changeful as the April sky. — WILLIAM WINTER.

Changeless.

Changeless as truth. — KEATS.

Changeless as a ray of light. — SAINT-PIERRE.

Changeless as heaven. — WHITTIER.

Character.

Characterless as a china shepherdess. — ANON.

Character, like porcelain ware, must be painted before it is glazed. There can be no change after it is burned in. — HENRY WARD BEECHER.

A character is like an acrostic or Alexandrine stanza — read it forward, backward, or across, it spells the same thing. — EMERSON.

Some characters are like some bodies in chemistry; very good, perhaps, in themselves, yet fly off and refuse the least conjunction with each other. — FULKE GREVILLE.

Your character at present is like a person in a plethora, absolutely dying from too much health. — R. B. SHERIDAN.

Charitable.

Charitable as a whole convent. — PAUL BOURGET.

Charity.

Charity is like molasses, sweet and cheap. — ANNA CHAPIN RAY.

Charm.

Charms
Like new-mown meadows, when the grass exhales
Sweet fragrance to the foot that tramples it.
— D. A. ATTERBOM.

Charm, like beauty's goddess. — ENGLISH BALLAD.

Sheds a charm, like to the fabled Cytherea's zone, binding all things with beauty. — BYRON.

Charms, as resistless as the fascinating Egyptian, for which Anthony wisely paid the bauble of the world. — C. C. COLTON.

Charms like gleams of opening Heav'n. — JOHN GILBERT COOPER.

Charmed like an April rose. — W. H. HOLCOMBE.

Charming as a god. — OTWAY.

Chase.

Chase each other over the wind, as vagrant high-sweeping clouds chase over the sky. — DONALD G. MITCHELL.

Chase him as a tempest chases flame. — ORIENTAL PROVERB.

Chased as the chaff of the mountains before the wind, and like a rolling thing before the whirlwind. — OLD TESTAMENT.

Chased away as a vision of the night. — IBID.

Chased you, as bees do. — IBID.

Chasing like fire. — WHYTE-MELVILLE.

Chaste.

Chaste as marble. — ANON.

Chaste as Minerva. — IBID.

Chaste as the moon. — IBID.

Chaste as ice. — BEAUMONT AND FLETCHER.

Chaste as angels are. — APHRA BEHN.

Chaste as the thought of the maid on whose sight first shines the glow of love's planet. — LOUIS JAMES BLOCK.

Chaste — *continued.*

Chaste as Medicean Venus. — E. B. BROWNING.

As chaste as the silver-white beams of the moon. — JOHN GILBERT COOPER.

Chaste as innocent white souls. — JOHN DAY.

Chaste as Cynthia's breast. — THOMAS DEKKER.

Chaste as a lily. — JULIA C. R. DORR.

Chaste as nudity. — GEORGE DU MAURIER.

Chaste as though bathed in breaking day. — EDGAR FAWCETT.

Chaste as fate. — JOHN FORD.

Chaste as a veiled nun. — JOSEPH HALL.

Chaste . . . as an unfleshed sword. — HUGO.

Chaste . . . as the veil of a nun. — HENRY JAMES.

Chaste as a chyld. — LANGLAND.

Chaste as th' Arabian bird, who all the ayr denyes. — RICHARD LOVELACE.

Chaste as the air. — IBID.

Chaste as the pious rapture of the nun. — GEORGE MAC-HENRY.

As chaste as was Penelope. — MARLOWE.

Chaste as snow. — THOMAS MOORE.

Chaste as the virgin, and the cold pure saint. — LEWIS MORRIS.

Chaste as light. — JOHN POMFRET.

Chaste as cold Cynthia's virgin light. — POPE.

Chaste as Diana. — SHAKESPEARE.

Chaste as ice. — IBID.

Chaste as is the bud ere it be blown. — IBID.

Chaste as the icicle. — IBID.

Chaste as unsunned snow. — IBID.

Like faire Venus Chaste. — SIR PHILIP SIDNEY.

Chaste as purest vestals. — THEOBALD.

Like an unlighted taper, was cold and chaste. — CYRIL TOURNEUR.

Chaste . . . as April's mildest tear. — HENRY VAUGHAN.

Chaste as morning dew. — EDWARD YOUNG.

Chaste as the morning. — IBID.

Chastity.

Winter, like a cold, unapproachable beauty, retains her character until the lawful season of thaw has arrived. — IVAN GONCHAROV.

Chastity, like piety, is a uniform grace. — RICHARDSON.

Chatter.

Chattering like a flock of daws. — ANON.

Our teeth are all achatter like the clinking castanets. — ASHBY-STERRY.

Chatters like a jay. — ROBERT BROWNING.

Chatter like bone castanets. — LEWIS CARROLL.

Teeth chattering like a Morse sounder. — IRVIN COBB.

Chatter . . . Like silly school-girls in their silliest mood. — JEAN INGELOW.

Chatter like a mob of sparrows. — J. K. JEROME.

A constant chatter, like a magpie in the trees. — W. S. MCFETRIDGE.

Chattering like magpies.
— C. G. ROSSETTI.

Chatter like sick flies. — SWINBURNE.

Like a crane or a swallow, so did I chatter. — OLD TESTAMENT.

Hear him chatter, like a taught starling. — JOHN WEBSTER.

Cheap.

Cheap as dirt. — ANON.

Cheap as dog's meat. — IBID.

As cheap as pearls are costly. — ROBERT BROWNING.

Cheap as sunshine. — HOOD.

Cheap as the withered refuse of a blind-alley stall. — JAMES RALFE.

Cheap as lies. — SHAKESPEARE.

Cheap as stinking mackerel. — IBID.

Cheap as neck-beef. — SWIFT.

Cheap as old clothes. — HORACE WALPOLE.

Cheat.

Cheat like onie unhang'd blackguard. — BURNS.

Checked.

Checked its hand
Like Alpine cataracts frozen as they
leaped. — EMERSON.

Checked like a bondman. — SHAKESPEARE.

Cheek.

Cheeks as brown as oak leaves. — ANON.

Cheek as the blood of the dragon bright. — ARABIAN NIGHTS.

The down on his cheeks dispread like myrtles springing from the heart of a bright red rose. — IBID.

Cheeks like blood-red anemones. — IBID.

John Bull looked ruddy and plump, with a pair of cheeks like a trumpeter. — JOHN ARBUTHNOT.

Upon her tender cheek the mingled dye is scattered, of the lily and the rose. — ARIOSTO.

Cheeks, like men who live, and draw the vital air. — MATTHEW ARNOLD.

The blood within her crystal cheekes
did such a colour drive,
As though the lillye and the rose for
mastership did strive.
— ENGLISH BALLAD.

Her cheeks like living roses glow. — SCOTTISH BALLAD.

Cheeks as soft as July peaches. — W. C. BENNETT.

Her bright cheek, as soft and pure in its bloom as a wild rose. — EMILY BRONTË.

Cheeks full and swollen, like a ploughboy's. — BULWER-LYTTON.

Her cheek like the spray o' th' sea. — ALICE CARY.

Cheeks as brown as sun could kiss them. — IBID.

Her cheeks are like the blushing cloud that beautifies Aurora's face. — H. CONSTABLE.

There's a mantling flush that dwells in
his cheeks,
Like a roseleaf thrown on the snow.
— ELIZA COOK.

With a cheek like a burning rose. — BARRY CORNWALL.

Like a rose set in snow was the bloom on her cheek. — JOHN CRAWFORD.

Her glowing cheeks like youthful Hebe's fair. — JOHN CUNNINGHAM.

A blooming pair of vermeil cheeks, like Hebe's in her ruddiest hours. — GEORGE DARLEY.

Your cheeks of late are like bad
printed books,
So dimly charactered, I scarce can
spell
One line of love in them.
— THOMAS DEKKER.

Her cheeks were like the roses red. — MICHAEL DRAYTON.

The frighted blood
Scarce yet recalled to her pale cheeks,
Like the first streaks of light broke
loose from darkness,
And dawning into blushes.
— DRYDEN.

Cheeks pearly as those of Pallas of Virgil. — DUMAS, PÈRE.

Cheek — *continued.*

A cheek like an apple-blossom. — George Eliot.

Lovely her cheeks were, like berries red. — Ancient Erse.

Her cheeks are as red as the rose's sheen. — Sir Samuel Ferguson.

His cheek is like the rose of spring. — Firdausi.

Cheek crimsoned like the bloom of the pomegranate. — Ibid.

Her cheeks, as snowy apples sopt in wines. — Giles Fletcher.

Cheeks are as round and as red as a cherry. — David Garrick.

That human, humorous mouth ; those cheeks [Lincoln's] that hold
Like some harsh landscape all the summer's gold.
— Richard Watson Gilder.

Cheeks like the rose on a bed of snow. — A. P. Graves.

A cheek wherein for interchange of hue
A wrangling strife 'twixt lily and the rose. — Robert Greene.

Her cheeks, like rose and lily yield forth gleams. — Ibid.

Her cheeks like ripened lilies steeped in wine,
Or fair pomegranate kernels washed in milk,
Or snow-white threads in nests of crimson silk,
Or gorgeous clouds upon the sun's decline. — Ibid.

Cheeks that shamed the rose. — John Harrington.

Cheeks like creame enclairited. — Robert Herrick.

Cheeks like roses when they blow.— Ibid.

Cheeks as ripe as apples. — Leigh Hunt.

Her cheeks like winter apples red of hue. — Jean Ingelow.

Cheeks as pink as a seashell. — Mary Johnston.

Cheeks for all the world like a raspberry ice upon a ground of custard. — Hugh Kelly.

Her cheek was as a rainbow, it so changed,
As each emotion o'er its surface ranged. — Miss Landon.

Her cheeks are like the blushing cloud,
That beautifies Aurora's face;
Or like the silver crimson shroud,
That Phœbus' smiling looks doth grace. — Thomas Lodge.

Cheeks like the dawn of day. — Longfellow.

Your cheeks are roses fair yet pink. — Catulle Mendès.

Cheek was wan as clay. — William J. Mickle.

Her cheek was as white and cold as clay. — Winthrop M. Praed.

Cheeks like peaches. — Francis S. Saltus.

Cheeks like Punic apples are. — George Sandys.

The brightness of her cheek would shame those stars, As daylight doth a lamp. — Shakespeare.

Had wet their cheeks, like trees bedashed with rain. — Ibid.

Her cheekes lyke apples which the sun hath rudded. — Spenser.

His cheeks are as a bed of spices, as sweet flowers. — Old Testament.

His cheeks, as roses red, as lilies fair. — William Thompson.

Her cheeks are as the fading stain
Where the peach reddens to the south.
— Oscar Wilde.

Her cheek was like the moist heart of a rose. — N. P. Willis.

Cheek — *continued.*

Cheeks were red as ruddy clover. — WORDSWORTH.

Cheeky.

As cheeky as a young bantam cock.— SCOTTISH PROVERB.

Cheer.

Cheered her soul like dew a dusty flower. — PAUL LAURENCE DUNBAR.

Great cheare, like one unto a banquit bid. — EDMUND SPENSER.

Cheerful.

Cheerful as the birds. — ANON.

Cheerful as a mute at a funeral. — IBID.

Cheerful as the lively morn. — JOHN ARMSTRONG.

As cheerful . . . as singing lark. — COLERIDGE.

Cheerful as the day. — COWPER.

Cheerful as the summer's morn. — JOHN CUNNINGHAM.

Cheerful as the day was long. — DICKENS.

Cheerful as a prince. — MRS. GASKELL.

Cheered . . . like the bright eye of a friend. — JAMES HEDDERWICK.

Cheerfulness is like money well expended in charity; the more we dispense of it, the greater our possession. — HUGO.

Cheerful, as one who knows that he is redeemed. — KINGSLEY.

Cheering as a suburban London Sunday's promenade. — GEORGE MEREDITH.

Cheerful and yet profound like an October afternoon. — NIETZSCHE.

Cheerfulness opens, like spring, all the blossoms of the inward man. — J. P. RICHTER.

Cheerful . . . as the green winter of the holly-tree. — SOUTHEY.

Cheering as the hymn of "Hark from the Tombs." — THOMAS WATSON.

As cheerful as a grove in Spring. — WORDSWORTH.

Cheerless.

Cheerless as the grave. — ELIZA COOK.

Cheery.

Cheery as a June day in Georgia. — ANON.

Cheery as a sunbeam. — IBID.

As cheery as young day. — TYRONE POWER.

Chide.

Chide as loud
As thunder. — SHAKESPEARE.

Children.

Thou art not dead ; not even though thou didst die, for children are to the deceased reputation preserving ; and like corks they buoy up the net, upholding the twist of the flaxen cord from the deep. — ÆSCHYLUS.

Children . . .
Like bells rung backwards,
Nothing but noise and giddiness.
— BEAUMONT AND FLETCHER.

Children are like grown people ; the experience of others is never of any use to them. — DAUDET.

It is the case with children as with plants, that their future character is indicated by their early dispositions. — DEMOPHILUS.

Children are like beggars ; often coming without being called. — W. S. DOWNEY.

Childhood shows the man, as the morning shows the day. — MILTON.

Children are never too tender to be whipped; like tough beef-steaks, the more you beat them the more tender they become. — POE.

Children — *continued.*

The smallest children are nearest to God, as the smallest planets are nearest the sun. — J. P. RICHTER.

Childhood is like a mirror, which reflects in after life the images first presented to it. — SAMUEL SMILES.

Chill.

Chill as death. — ANON.

Chill as ice. — MATHILDE BLIND.

Chill me like dew damps of the unwholesome night. — COLERIDGE.

Chilly as a bottle of port in a hard frost. — GEORGE COLMAN. THE YOUNGER.

Chilly as a tomb. — HOOD.

Chilly as a dripping well. — KEATS.

Chill as the scent of a new-made grave. — KINGSLEY.

As chill and as green as the sea. — KIPLING.

Grew chill as an arctic landscape. — JACK LONDON.

Chill as aconite. — GEORGE MEREDITH.

Chill as a dull face frowning on a song. — IBID.

Chill as the Gryxabodill. — JAMES WHITCOMB RILEY.

Chime.

Death and Time, they chime and chime, like bells at sunset falling. — WILLIAM E. HENLEY.

We chime,
Like two soft lines when coupled into
rhyme. — CHRISTOPHER PITT.

Chimes, like silver hammers falling on silver anvils. — TENNYSON.

Chimerical.

Chimerical as the existence of the Brobdingnags or the Yahoos. — ANON.

Chimerical as the philosopher's stone. — VOLTAIRE.

Chirping.

Chirping like a cricket. — ANON.

Chirping like a gay Cicala in a sunny bower. — J. S. BLACKIE.

Chirp . . . like new-fledged linnet. — AUSTIN DOBSON.

Chirping as chirp the birds beneath the eaves. — HUGO.

Chirping, like the dry
High-elbow'd grigs that leap in summer grass. — TENNYSON.

Choleric.

Choleric as fire. — CHARLES READE.

Chorus.

He who makes use of a Chorus in Tragedy seems to me to do like a Physitian, who, prescribing a Dose for the evacuation of Peccant Humors, should afterwards order Restringents to be taken in the midst of its kind Operation. — JOHN DENNIS.

Christianity.

Christianity is like the neutrality of Belgium, which is guaranteed by all the nations and inviolate in times of peace, but which must not be allowed to stand in the way of the interests of a people on the road to great things. — SIMEON STRUNSKY.

Chubby.

Chubby as a cherub.— ANON.

Chubby as the Diana of Jordaens. — ARSÈNE HOUSSAYE.

Chuckle.

Chuckles, like the opening of a bottle of some effervescent beverage. — DICKENS.

Chuckling like a setting hen. — HUGO.

Cigar.

A cigar is like a wife !
Put it up to your lips, and light it ;
When you've learned to do it right, it
Adds a certain zest to life.
Mind you keep on puffing it,
Or it's out, and can't be lit.
Ah, the aroma !
Ah, the glow !
Will I have one ?
Thank you, No. — ALEISTER CROWLEY.

Circle.

Circular like Plato's year. — ALEXANDER BROME.

Circle, like a bear at stake. — SAMUEL BUTLER.

Circling like a gin-horse. — CARLYLE.

Circled . . . like flight of doves. — GEORGE MEREDITH.

Circling like an eddy. — CHARLES L. MOORE.

Circles around it, like the clouds that swim
Round the high moon in a bright sea of air. — SHELLEY.

Circles round,
Like the soft waving wings of noonday dreams. — IBID.

Circulate.

Circulate like oil. — BEN JONSON.

Circumstances.

Happy circumstances in life are like certain groups of trees. Seen from the distance they look very well; but go up to them and among them, and the beauty vanishes; you don't know where it can be; it is only trees you see. And so it is that we often envy the lot of others. — SCHOPENHAUER.

City.

Cities, like forests, have their dens in which hide all their vilest and most dangerous monsters. — HUGO.

I love the city as dearly as a brown thrasher loves the green tree sheltering its young. — CHARLES MATHEWS.

Civilization.

Civilization is like a soldier's stock ; it makes you carry your head a good deal higher, makes the angels weep a little more at your fantastic tricks, and half suffocates you the while. — ALEXANDER SMITH.

Clairvoyant.

Clairvoyant as the X-Ray. — ANON.

Clambering.

Clamb'ring, like a runaway lunatic. — COLERIDGE.

Clammy.

Clammy as death. — OWEN MEREDITH.

Clamor.

As clamorous as Hecuba. — ROBERT BURTON.

As when two vultures on the mountain's height
Stoop with resounding pinions to the fight;
They cuff, they tear, they raise a screaming cry;
The desert echoes, and the rocks reply :
The warriors thus oppos'd in arms, engage
With equal clamours, and with equal rage. — HOMER (POPE).

Clamored . . . as though a besieging foe was in the house. — DOUGLAS JERROLD.

Clamouring like a brazen bell. — GEORGE MEREDITH.

Clamorous . . . like croaking daws. — PINDAR.

Clamorous like mill-waters, at wild play. — D. G. ROSSETTI.

More clamorous than a parrot against rain. — SHAKESPEARE.

Clamor — *continued.*

Clamorous like as wave to wave at sea. — SWINBURNE.

Clamorous as a horn
Re-echoed by a naked rock.
— WORDSWORTH.

Clang.

Clash and clang like glaives at . . . Stiklastad. — WILLIAM ARCHER.

Clanging like a gong. — HOOD.

Clanging like a smithy-shop. — KIPLING.

Clapped.

Clapped his hands like the clapping of wings. — HUGO.

Clash.

Clashing in a frenzy as of a resounding battle. — PAUL BOURGET.

Clasp.

Clasp like ivy. — DONNE.

Clasp'd like a missal where swart Paynims pray. — KEATS.

Clasped her like a lover. — TENNYSON.

Clasped like some strange book of sorcery. — G. S. VIERECK.

Classic.

A good classic is as full of ancient myths, as that of a servant-girl of ghost stories. — HERBERT SPENCER.

Clatter.

Clatter like a churn-dasher dabbling in buttermilk. — O. HENRY.

Clatter like armor. — RABELAIS.

Clatter like a loose casement in the wind. — WORDSWORTH.

Claw.

Clawed like a parrot. — SHAKESPEARE.

Clean.

Clean as a die. — ANON.

Clean as a Dutch oven. — IBID.

Clean as a new pin. — IBID.

Clean as a pebble. — IBID.

Clean as crystal. — IBID.

Clean as light. — IBID.

Cleaner than our sister the water. — IBID.

Clean as virgin silver. — ARABIAN NIGHTS.

Clean as sifted corn. — ARISTOPHANES.

As clean as a Flemish interior. — BALZAC.

Clean as a maiden's honor. — BJÖRNSTJERNE BJÖRNSON.

Clean as a whistle. — JOHN BYROM.

Clean as a [new] penny. — JOHN GAY.

Clean as a beaver. — BRET HARTE.

Clean as a maid from guile and fleshy sin. — R. S. HAWKER.

Clean,
As if o'erwashed with Hippocrene.
— ROBERT HERRICK.

Clean as running water in a cress-fringed brook. — EDWIN LEIBFREED.

Clean as a red-hot poker. — GEORGE MEREDITH.

Clean as the bright from the black. — IBID.

His work is as clean as silver lace. — OSMANLI PROVERB.

As clean as a leek. — SCOTTISH PROVERB.

Clean as a rose is after rain. — JAMES WHITCOMB RILEY.

Clean as a hound's tooth. — THEODORE ROOSEVELT.

Clean as a sound sheep's heart.— SHAKESPEARE.

Clean as a sponge wipes a chalk problem from a blackboard. — J. RUSSELL SMITH.

Clean — *continued.*

Clean of cloud
As though day's heart were proud
And heaven's were glad.
— SWINBURNE.

Clean as blood of babes. — TENNYSON.

Clean as the carving knife chops the carrot. — THACKERAY.

Clear.

Clear as a midsummer sky. — FRANKLIN P. ADAMS.

Clear as a cube of solid sunshine. — ANON.

Clear as a die. — IBID.

About as clear as a misty morning on the Thames. — IBID.

Clear as daylight. — IBID.

Traced as clearly as currents upon a marble chart. — IBID.

A voice as clear as forest bird. — IBID.

Clear as mountain stream. — IBID.

Clear as paint. — IBID.

Clear as the notes of a cavalry bugle. — IBID.

Clear as the skin of a child. — IBID.

Clear as pearls and diaphanous gems. — ARABIAN NIGHTS.

Clear as day. — ROBERT ARMIN.

Clear at one glance, as two drops of rain in air might look into each other had they life. — P. J. BAILEY.

Clear, cold, and icy-blue, like a sea eagle's eye. — IBID.

Clear was her look,
Like an open book.
— WILLIAM F. BARNARD.

Clear as the skylark's earliest greeting in the morning of the year. — H. H. BOYESEN.

Clear as heaven's stars. — JAMES BEATTIE.

Her mind, as cleare as aire. — FRANCIS BEAUMONT.

Clear as the challenge ov a perlice officer. — JOSH BILLINGS.

Clear as virtue. — S. LAMAN BLANCHARD.

Clear, as God sees through the earth. — E. B. BROWNING.

Clear as flint. — ROBERT BROWNING.

Clear as noon. — IBID.

Clear as a commonplace. — BULWER-LYTTON.

His projects are clear to my eyes; clear as if he dwelt in glass. — IBID.

Clear as if no dirt had been cast thereat. — BUNYAN.

As clear and as manifest as the nose on a man's face. — ROBERT BURTON.

Clear as a whistle. — JOHN BYROM.

Clear as a bell. — CHAUCER.

Clear as lake. — COLERIDGE.

Clear as the morning. — IBID.

Clear as Spring. — THOMAS DAVIS.

Clear as the note of doom. — LORD DE TABLEY.

Cleared like a doubtful morning when it gives place to a bright noon. — DICKENS.

Clear as stars in frosty night. — WILLIAM DUNBAR.

His eye is as clear as the heavens. — EMERSON.

Clear as the conscious moon. — JAMES GRAEME.

Clear as noonday. — ANTHONY HAMILTON.

Clear as the pure River of Life shown to the Evangelist. — THOMAS HARDY.

Clear as the mid-day sunshine. — HAWTHORNE.

Clear as the water in trout pools. — O. HENRY.

Clear — *continued.*

Clear . . . as spring water in the high rocks. — MAURICE HEWLETT.

Loving eyes that gleam
Clear as a starlit mountain stream.
— O. W. HOLMES.

Clear as the glisten of dew on the brier. — RICHARD HOVEY.

As clear as rock-water. — JAMES HOWELL.

Clear as if an angel had washed it. — HUGO.

Clear like crystal beams. — ALEXANDER HUME.

Clear as the flame of sacrifice. — JEAN INGELOW.

Clear as infant's eyes. — KEATS.

Clear as summer-lightning flare. — KIPLING.

Ran clear as the light of heaven ere autumn closed. — W. S. LANDOR.

Clear as the finest porcelain. — RICHARD LE GALLIENNE.

Clear as running waters are. — LONGFELLOW.

Clear as a race course. — GEORGE MEREDITH.

Clear as widowed sky. — IBID.

As clear as the classics. — DONALD G. MITCHELL.

Clear as the blue, sublime, o'er-arching sky. — JAMES MONTGOMERY.

Clear as well water. — GEORGE MOORE.

Clear as the rosy dawn. — HENRY MORLEY.

The Spirit spake, clear as in Israel. — J. H. NEWMAN.

Thoughts as clear as limpid springs. — ORIENTAL.

Clear as glass. — OVID.

Clear, like the mysteries of divine science in the bosom of the pious. — PILPAY.

As clear as strains by sun-kissed Memnon given. — MARY ELIZABETH POWELL.

Clear as a brook's chuckle to the ear. — JAMES WHITCOMB RILEY.

Clear as the Autumn atmosphere. — IBID.

As clear as the twitter of birds. — IBID.

Light as clear as that which fills eternity. — A. J. RYAN.

As purely clear
As crystal drops on vernal grasses.
— MARGARET E. SANGSTER.

Clear as a mirror. — SCHILLER.

Clear
As morning roses newly washed with dew. — SHAKESPEARE.

Clear as is the summer's sun. — IBID.

Clear
As yonder Venus in her glimmering sphere. — IBID.

Countenance as clear as friendship wears at feasts. — IBID.

Clear as founts in July. — IBID.

As clear as when a veil of light is drawn o'er evening hills. — SHELLEY.

Cleare as the skye withouten blame or blot. — SPENSER.

Clear and fair as sunlight and the flowerful air. — SWINBURNE.

Clear as a child's own laughter. — IBID.

Clear as heaven of the toils of time. — IBID.

As clear as love. — IBID.

Clear as mirth. — IBID.

Clear as night beholds her crowning seven. — IBID.

Clear — *continued.*

Clear as righteousness.—SWINBURNE.

Soul as clear as sunlit dew. — IBID.

Clear as the closest seen and kindly star
That marries morn and even and winter and spring with one love's golden ring. — IBID.

Clear as the cloudless hour. — IBID.

Clear as the flame from the pyres of the dead. — IBID.

Clear as the plume of a bright black bird. — IBID.

Clear as the tocsin from the steeple. — IBID.

Clear as thy song's words or the live sun's light. — IBID.

Clear, as ever fell from angel's tongue. — PAULUS SYLLOGUS.

Clear as the blast of horn. — BAYARD TAYLOR.

Clear as wind. — TENNYSON.

Clear as crystal. — NEW TESTAMENT.

Clear as the sun. — OLD TESTAMENT.

Clear as a silver bell. — VANCE THOMPSON.

Clear as heaven's unclouded brow. — HENRY VAUGHAN.

Singers, that troll clear as bells of gold. — FRANÇOIS VILLON.

Clearly as two and two make four. — VOLTAIRE.

Clear as the crystal brooks. — IZAAK WALTON.

Words clear as the sun in its meridian brightness. — GEORGE WASHINGTON.

Clear as diamonds. — THEODORE WATTS-DUNTON.

Clear as the unsoil'd mountain-rill. — WHITTIER.

Clear as the crystal flood. — ELLA WHEELER WILCOX.

Clear as the profiles of goddesses. — C. N. AND A. M. WILLIAMSON.

A mirror, clear as 'twere a door of air. — N. P. WILLIS.

Clear as the crystal brooks or the pure azur'd heaven. — SIR HENRY WOTTON.

Clear as daylight. — ISRAEL ZANGWILL.

Cleave.

Cleave to you as a soul to its freedom cleaves. — BLISS CARMAN.

Cleaving it like a ploughshare. — DUMAS, PÈRE.

Cleave to me like the skin to my flesh. — JOHN WESLEY.

Clench.

His heart clenched the idea as a diver grasps a gem. — BEACONSFIELD.

Cleft.

Cleft like a narrow harvest swath,
O'ernodded by the plumes of wheat.
— CHARLES L. MOORE.

Cleft, as wax before the fire, and as the waters that are poured down a steep place. — OLD TESTAMENT.

Clever.

Clever as paint. — ANON.

Clever as sin. — KIPLING.

Clever as Chat-Noir impromptu. — AMY LESLIE.

Click.

Clicked like a spring lock. — ANON.

Climax.

Climax like a breaking wave. — MISS MULOCK.

Climbs.

She climbs her family tree like a squirrel. — PAUL KESTER.

Cling.

Cling around the soul, as the sky clings round the mute earth forever beautiful. — ANON.

Clinging . . . as ivy clings about an oak ; as tuft-hunters with buzz and purr about a fellow-commoner. — IBID.

Cling like a forlorn hope. — IBID.

Clinging like a wet towel to a nail. — IBID.

Cling like moss to a damp wall. — IBID.

Clung . . . like a damp dish-cloth around a stove pipe. — IBID.

Clung like a drowning man. — IBID.

Clings like the wicked stench of the harlot's room. — JOHN ANTROBUS.

Clung like a beast's hide to his fleshless bones. — EDWIN ARNOLD.

Clung to the merry music of her words, like a bird on a bough, high swaying in the wind. — P. J. BAILEY.

Clings fast as the clinging vine. — E. B. BROWNING.

Clings like an octopus. — ROBERT BROWNING.

Clinging . . . as friend with friend, or husband with wife,
Makes hand in hand the passage of life.
— WILLIAM CULLEN BRYANT.

Cling like Death's embrace. — H. C. BUNNER.

Cling like Ivy. — ROBERT BURTON.

Clung like a cuirass to his breast. — BYRON.

Clinging like a faint odor. — HENRY A. CLAPP.

Cling to the memory as tenaciously as the fragrance of lavender clings to glove or lace. — IBID.

Clung to the soil like Caliban. — DICKENS.

Cling to the old house as barnacles to a wrecked and stranded vessel. — SIR A. CONAN DOYLE.

Clinging . . . like pigeons on a roof-slope. — THOMAS HARDY.

Clung . . . like ivy to a tree. — MAURICE HEWLETT.

Cling . . . like the spokes of a wheel. — O. W. HOLMES.

Clings . . . like the weed in the face of the cliff. — HOOD.

Clings cruelly to us, like the gnawing sloth
On the deer's tender haunches.
— KEATS.

Cling like the sloth. — KIPLING.

Clings about thee close, like moss to stones. — WALTER S. LANDOR.

Cling, like bees about a flower's wine-cup. — GERALD MASSEY.

Cling
Like flies to the sheer precipice.
— LEWIS MORRIS.

Clung like a spectral snow. — JOHN G. NEIHARDT.

Clung . . . like magnet to steel. — T. BUCHANAN READ.

Clung like drowning men beneath the wave. — BAYARD TAYLOR.

Clung
Like serpent eggs together.
— TENNYSON.

Her kisses burn where they close and cling
Like pain of longing or fire of hell.
— G. S. VIERECK.

Clinging like sentry to his post. — VIRGIL.

Clings . . . like pitch. — IBID.

Cling, as clings the tufted moss,
To bear the winter's lightning chills.
— WHITTIER.

Clog.

Clogged like honey. — R. D. BLACKMORE.

Clog. — *continued.*

Clogged like a dripping pan. — THOMAS HARDY.

Close.

Close as clapboards on a house. — ANON.

Close as one second is to another. — IBID.

Close as heat to fire. — IBID.

Close as lovers sitting upon the sofa. — IBID.

Close as Noah in the ark. — IBID.

Close-mouthed as a clam. — IBID.

Close as a cockle. — BEAUMONT AND FLETCHER.

Close as wax. — IBID.

Close as brother leans to brother
When they press beneath the eyes
Of some father praying blessings
From the gifts of paradise.
— E. B. BROWNING.

Fitting as close as fits the dented spine
Its flexible ivory outside-flesh.
— ROBERT BROWNING.

Close as an oyster. — ROBERT BURTON.

Close as the finger nail and the quick. — HUGH CLIFFORD.

Close as a new cut yew-hedge. — GEORGE COLMAN, THE ELDER.

Close as your jacket. — GEORGE COLMAN, THE YOUNGER.

Close as a pill-box. — IBID.

Close as a nut. — GEORGE ELIOT.

Close as hand and glove. — "FOUNDLING HOSPITAL FOR WIT, 1743."

Close as night. — THOMAS HEYWOOD.

Close as thorn is to the rose. — ROBERT LLOYD.

I will sticke as close to thee, as the soale doth to the shoe. — LYLY.

Hide closer than Rachel did her father's images. — JAMES PUCKLE.

Close as oak and ivy stand.
— C. G. ROSSETTI.

Close as the young wheat.
— D. G. ROSSETTI.

Stick closer than a bump on your head. — AUSTIN STRONG.

Close as a jail. — THOMAS TUSSER.

Close as a lover in his hour of bliss. — N. P. WILLIS.

Close as a flea in a blanket. — "YEA AND NAY ALMANACK," 1680.

Closed.

Closed as a shrine. — ANON.

Then saw in death his eyelids close
Calmly, as to a night's repose,
Like flowers at set of sun.
— FITZ-GREENE HALLECK.

Closed his eyes, like a priest who at evening service closes the gold tabernacle after Benediction. — GUY DE MAUPASSANT.

Closed over their trail as the waves of the ocean close in the wake of a ship. — THEODORE ROOSEVELT.

Crept to the gate, and open'd it, and closed,
As lightly as a sick man's chamber-door. — TENNYSON.

Clothes.

A simple fellow in gay clothes is like a cinnamon-tree, the bark is of more value than the body. — ANON.

He wears his *Clotths* like a Hide, and shifts them no oftener than a Beast does his Hair. — SAMUEL BUTLER.

Cloud.

Cloudless as eternity. — ANON.

The hooded clouds, like friars,
Tell their beads in drops of rain.
— LONGFELLOW.

Clove.

Clove as Ruth unto Naomi. — Anon.

Clove as a ploughshare cleaves the field. — Swinburne.

Cloyed.

Cloyed like a quenched and satisfied lust. — Anon.

Clumsy.

Clumsy as a bear. — Anon.

Clumsy as a June-bug.— Ibid.

Clumsy as the antics of a leviathan. — Ibid.

Clumsy as a vine-press. — Charles Reade.

Cluster.

Clustering like bees around their commander. — Aristotle.

Clustering like bee-hives on the low flat strand of Oxus. — Matthew Arnold.

Clutch.

Your clutch is like the grasping of a wave. — T. L. Beddoes.

Clutches . . . like as a cog-wheel seizes whatever comes too near the machine. — Alexander Kielland.

Coarse.

Coarse as fustian. — Anon.

Coarse as hemp. — Ibid.

Coarse in grain as the bark of an oak. — Dickens.

Coiled.

Coiled like a snake. — W. S. Blunt.

Cold.

Cold as loveless duty done. — Mary Louisa Anderson.

Cold as a dog's nose. — Anon.

Cold as a frog. — Ibid.

Cold as a hot-water bag in the morning. — Ibid.

Cold as an enthusiastic New England audience. — Ibid.

Cold as a ramrod. — Ibid.

Cold as a tomb. — Ibid.

Cold as Greenland's icy mountains. — Ibid.

Cold as charity. — Ibid.

Cold as iron. — Ibid.

Cold as the heart of a courtesan. — Ibid.

Cold as the grave. — Matthew Arnold.

Icy cold as a crypt. — Balzac.

Tears as cold as the stones on which sorrowing hearts had caused to be carved their regrets. — Ibid.

Cold as the north side of a January gravestone by moonlight. — J. R. Bartlett's "Dictionary of Americanisms."

As cold as cucumbers. — Beaumont and Fletcher.

Cold . . . As a young nun the day she is envested. — Aphra Behn.

Cold like a corpse. — Charlotte Brontë.

Cold . . . as graveyard stones from which the lichen's scraped. — E. B. Browning.

Cold as the rocks on Torneo's hoary brow. — Campbell.

As colde as eny froste. — Chaucer.

Colde as ston. — Ibid.

Cold as the ice on northern sea. — Ella D. Clymer.

Cold as clay. — Coleridge.

Cold as a turtle. — Richard Cumberland.

Cauld as the drifting snow. — Allan Cunningham.

Cauld as the marble stone. — Ibid.

Cold as the clod. — Aubrey T. De Vere.

Cold as one who waits for burial mould. — Julia C. R. Dorr.

Cold. — *continued.*

Cold as a leaf long pillowed on a stone. — ARTHUR D. FISKE.

Cold as the coiling water-snake. — O. W. HOLMES.

Cold, just like a summer grate. — HOOD.

Cold as salt. — JAMES HUNEKER.

Cold as the mountain stream. — MRS. INGLIS.

Cold as a bubbling well. — KEATS.

Cold as a skeleton. — AMY LESLIE.

Cold as the breath of winds that blow
To silver shot descending snow.
— RICHARD LOVELACE.

As cold as an earthworm. — MAURICE MAETERLINCK.

Cold as the night-dews on the world. — GERALD MASSEY.

Cold as a fireless hearth. — IBID.

Cold as a fish. — GEORGE MEREDITH.

Cold as a mountain in its star-pitched tent. — IBID.

Cold as Death's chill hand. — WILLIAM J. MICKLE.

Cold as the snows of Rhodope. — HANNAH MORE.

Cold as a dead maid's cheek. — MISS MULOCK.

Cold as the Cloyster'd Nun. — "THE MUSES RECREATION," 1656.

Cold as marble. — PETRARCH.

Cold as Diana's Crescent. — JANE PORTER.

Cold as the world's heart. — CHARLES READE.

Cold as when death's foot shall pass. — D. G. ROSSETTI.

Cold as a dead man's nose.
— SHAKESPEARE.

Cold as a snowball. — IBID.

My belly is as cold as if I had swallowed snowballs for pills to cool the reins. — IBID.

Cold as dew to drooping leaves.
— SHELLEY.

Cold, like a frozen chaos. — IBID.

Cold as blight of dew. — SWINBURNE.

Cold as . . . dawn. — IBID.

Cold as the cast-off garb that is cold as clay. — IBID.

Grew cold as a winter wave
In the wind from a wide-mouthed
grave,
As a gulf wide open to swallow
The light that the world held dear.
— IBID.

Cold as fears. — IBID.

Cold as rains in autumn. — IBID.

Cold as winter's sky. — J. A. SYMONDS.

Cold as the moon. — JOHN B. TABB.

As the night-mists . . . cold. — BAYARD TAYLOR.

Cold, like a star. — WILLIAM WATSON.

Cold as the rank and wasting weeds, which lie in the pool's dark bed. WHITTIER.

Collapse.

Collapsed like a house of cards. — ANON.

Collapse, like the Apostle in the pictures of the Conversion of St. Paul. — WILLIAM DE MORGAN.

Like a dissolving palace of snow, it collapsed. — DE QUINCEY.

Collapse like the cheeks of a starved man. — DICKENS.

Collapses like a pricked bladder. — G. B. SHAW.

Color.

Colorless as a statue. — BULWER-LYTTON.

Colorless as an etching. — JOHN DENNIS.

Colorless as lead. — JOHN RUSKIN.

Coloured as the moon. — SWINBURNE.

Colorless as equal quantity of air. — HENRY D. THOREAU.

Colossal.

Colossal as the face of Big Ben. — ANON.

Come.

Where the dreams come in from the
rush and the din
Like sheep from the rains and the
thunder.
— W. S. BRAITHWAITE.

As the birds come in the Spring,
We know not from where;
As the stars come at evening
From depths of the air;

As the rain comes from the cloud,
And the brook from the ground;
As suddenly, low or loud,
Out of silence a sound;

As the grape comes to the vine,
The fruit to the tree;
As the wind comes to the pine,
And the tide to the sea;

As come the white sails of ships
O'er the ocean's verge;
As comes the smile to the lips,
The foam to the surge;

So come to the Poet his songs,
All hitherward blown
From the misty realm, that belongs
To the vast Unknown.
— LONGFELLOW.

Airy tinklings come and go,
Like chimings from far off tower,
Or prattling of an April shower,
That makes the daisies grow.
— MRS. AGNES E. MITCHELL.

Cometh forth like a flower, and is cut down. — OLD TESTAMENT.

Comely.

Comely as a bride. — ANON.

Comely as is a cow in a cage. — JOHN HEYWOOD.

Comely as Apollo. — ARSÈNE HOUSSAYE.

Comfort.

Comfortable as coin. — ANON.

Comfortable as an annuity. — IBID.

Comfortable as matrimony, — to an old woman. — IBID.

Comfortable as an anvil. — IRVIN S. COBB.

Comfortable as the hungry pig was, when he was shut up by mistake in the grain department of a brewery. — DICKENS.

Comforting as April air
After the snow. — JEAN INGELOW.

Love comforteth like sunshine after rain. — SHAKESPEARE.

That comfort comes too late;
'Tis like a pardon after execution.
— IBID.

Comfortless.

Comfortless as a truss of straw. — OUIDA.

Comfortless
As frozen water to a starved snake.
— SHAKESPEARE.

Comfortless,
As silent lightning leaves the starless
night. — SHELLEY.

Command.

Commands like a full soldier.
— SHAKESPEARE.

Comments.

Harsh comments have no effect: they are like hammers which are always repulsed by an anvil. — HELVETIUS.

Commit.

Commit as many absurdities as a clown in eating of an egg. — JOHN RAY'S "HANDBOOK OF PROVERBS," 1670.

Common.

Common as the stones in our streets. — THOMAS ADAMS.

Common as a convenient saying. — ANON.

Common as backfence cats. — IBID.

Common as boiled cabbage. — IBID.

Common as coals from Newcastle. — IBID.

Common as daisies. — IBID.

Common as lying. — IBID.

Common as pig tracks in wet weather. — IBID.

Common as pins. — IBID.

Common as pug noses in Pittsburgh. — IBID.

Common as sawdust around a saw-mill. — IBID.

Common as the town sewer. — IBID.

Common as the air. — APHRA BEHN.

Common as Robin Adair on a full brass band. — ARNOLD BENNETT.

Common as rain. — PIERCE EGAN.

Common as poverty. — MRS. GASKELL.

Friendship as common as a prostitute's favors. — GOLDSMITH.

Common as a barber's chair. — STEPHEN GOSSON.

As common as the power of moving the ears voluntarily, which is a moderately rare endowment. — O. W. HOLMES.

Common as a mart. — BEN JONSON.

Comune as the cart-wey to knaves and to alle. — LANGLAND.

Common as Get-out. — LEAN'S "COLLECTANEA."

Common as delirium tremens in New York. — ALFRED HENRY LEWIS.

Common as scolding at Billingsgate. — LYLY.

Common as the highway. — RAY'S "HANDBOOK OF PROVERBS," 1670.

Common as dirt. — CHARLES READE.

Common as the stairs
That mount the Capitol.
— SHAKESPEARE.

Common as any tavern door. — EDWARD SHARPHAM.

Common as light is love, and its familiar voice wearies not ever. — SHELLEY.

Common as bribery. — JOHN WEBSTER.

Common as sickness. — IBID.

Common as dew and sunshine. — WHITTIER.

Commonplace.

Commonplace as mud. — ANON.

Commonplace as a street pavement. — FLAUBERT.

Companionless.

Companionless as a prisoner in his dungeon. — CHARLOTTE BRONTË.

Companionless as the last cloud of an expiring storm. — SHELLEY.

Company.

Bad company is like a dog that dirts those most he loves the best.
— SWIFT.

Compare.

Compares with — as the glow-worm compares with the eagle. — ANON.

Compasseth.

Compasseth them about as a chain. — OLD TESTAMENT.

Compassionate.

If he be compassionate towards the afflictions of others, it shows that his heart is like the noble tree that is wounded itself when it gives the balm. — BACON.

Complacent.

Complacent as a cat. — KEATS.

Complex.

Complex as the Iliad. — HUGO.

Complex as a mathematician's schedule of the Zodiac. — AMY LESLIE.

Complexion.

Complexion like a pink rose's. — MAURICE HEWLETT.

Complexion clear and warm, like rose-cordial. — O. W. HOLMES.

Her complexion like the jasmine. — "VIKRAM AND THE VAMPIRE."

A complexion like the red glow of evening upon snow. — HEINRICH ZSCHOKKE.

Compliment.

A compliment is something like a kiss through a veil. — HUGO.

Composed.

Composed as heaven. — WILLIAM LIVINGSTON.

Concave.

Concave as a covered goblet, or a worm-eaten nut. — SHAKESPEARE.

Conceal.

Conceal, like cosmetics. — OSMAN EDWARDS.

Concealed,
Like some fair bud close folded in its sheath,
Gives not to view the blooming of its beauty. — KALIDASA.

Sorrow concealed, like an oven stopped,
Doth burn the heart to cinders.
— SHAKESPEARE.

Conceit.

Strong conceit is a kind of mental rudder which reason should hold for the purpose of steering the mind into its right courses. — ANON.

Deep conceits, like maggots, breed in carrion. — EARL OF DORSET.

Talk about conceit as much as you like, it is to human character what salt is to the ocean ; it keeps it sweet and renders it endurable. Say rather it is like natural unguent of the sea fowl's plumage, which enables him to shed the rain that falls on him and the waves in which he dips. When one has had all his conceit taken out of him, when he has lost all his illusions, his feathers will soon soak through, and he will fly no more. — O. W. HOLMES.

Conceit is just as natural a thing to human minds as a centre is to a circle. — IBID.

Concession.

Individual concessions are like political, when you once begin, there is no saying where you will stop. — BULWER-LYTTON.

Confident.

As confident as a bird committing itself to the air or a great fish to the deep. — ANON.

Confident as justice. — GEORGE COLMAN, THE YOUNGER.

Confident as Hercules. — WILLIAM PRYNNE.

Confident as of your own fingers. — RABELAIS.

Confident, as is the falcon's flight. — SHAKESPEARE.

Confidence in an unfaithful man in time of trouble is like a broken tooth, and a foot out of joint. — OLD TESTAMENT.

Confining.

Confining it to such limits as paintings are confined in by their frames. — W. S. Landor.

Conform.

Conform your temper to that of each friend. Be like the polypus, which looks like the rock it has twisted its arms around. — Theognis.

Confound.

Confounds thy fame as whirlwinds shake fair buds. — Shakespeare.

Confounded, as corn blasted before it is grown up. — Old Testament.

Confused.

Confused as in a dream. — Anon.

Confused, like the roaring of waves. — Ibid.

Confusion of voices, like the chirping of young birds when the brood is just hatched under the down. — Dumas, père.

Confusedly, like a flight of dark shadows. — Hugo.

Confused as a soul heavy-laden with trouble that will not depart. — Swinburne.

Speaks to confuse, like speech by age o'ertaken. — Bayard Taylor.

Conscience.

Many men carry their conscience like a drawn sword, cutting this way and that, in the world, but sheath it and keep it very soft and quiet, when it is turned within, thinking that a sword should not be allowed to cut its own scabbard. — Henry Ward Beecher.

A fly or dust shows itself at once in milk; so in a pure conscience, any, the smallest stain, cannot be hid. And, as a fly is quickly cast forth by any one who is drinking milk, so the busy fly of impure thought is cast from the pure conscience. — St. Bonaventura.

He that has a scrupulous conscience is like a horse that is not well wayed, he starts at every bird that flies out of the hedge. A knowing man will do that which a tender-conscience man dares not do by reason of his ignorance, the other knows there is no hurt: as a child is afraid to go into the dark when a man is not because he knows there is no danger. — Selden.

Conscientious.

Conscientious as a dog. — Robert Louis Stevenson.

Consistent.

Simple and consistent as a plant. — Anon.

Consoling.

Consoling as night. — Francis S. Saltus.

Conspicuous.

Conspicuous as pyramids. — Anon.

Conspicuous as the brightness of a star. — Cowper.

Conspicuous like a cathedral. — Robert Louis Stevenson.

Conspirator.

Conspirators and traitors are like moths, which eat the cloth in which they are bred ; like vipers, that gnaw the bowels where they are born ; like worms, which consume the wood in which they were engendered. — Agesilaus.

Constant.

Constant as a shadow in the sun. — Anon.

Constant in motion as the spheres. — Ibid.

Constantly in my thoughts, like the lost voice of his victim in those of the murderer. — Ibid.

More constant than the evening star,
Which mildly beams above. — Ibid.

Constant as the dove. — Mrs. J Hunter.

Constant — *continued.*

Constancy is like vnto the Storke, who wheresoeuer she flye commeth into no neast but hir owne, or the Lapwinge, whom nothing can driue from hir young ones, but death. — LYLY.

Constant as the years are rolled. — MARTIAL.

Her constancy, that, like a rock,
Beats off temptation, as that mocks the fury
Of the proud waves. — MASSINGER.

Constant in intercommunication as are the sun and earth. — GEORGE MEREDITH.

Constant as the day and night from east to west. — JAMES MONTGOMERY.

Constant as the stars that never move. — OTWAY.

Constant as the sun. — CHARLES READE.

Constant as the constant hours. — MARGARET E. EASTER.

But I am as constant as the northern star
Of whose true-fix'd and resting quality
There is no fellow in the firmament.
— SHAKESPEARE.

Constantly as the week passes. — ABIGAIL A. SMITH.

Constant as a soaring lark. — WORDSWORTH.

Constant as the motion of the day. — IBID.

Consume.

Consume as snow against the sun. — ANON.

Consumed her . . . like a flame. — MATTHEW ARNOLD.

Consume, like a devouring fire. — GEORGE SANDYS.

Consumeth, as a garment that is moth eaten. — OLD TESTAMENT.

Consume away like a moth ; surely every man is vanity. — IBID.

Consumed like smoke. — IBID.

Consumed them as stubble. — IBID.

Consuming like a vapor. — WHITTIER.

Contagious.

Contagious as activity. — ANON.

Contagious as a yawn. — IBID.

Contagious, like the gladness of a happy child. — BULWER-LYTTON.

Contagious as the smile of a keeper showing you through the wards of a madhouse. — J. H. GARDINER.

Contagious, like silliness. — ARSÈNE HOUSSAYE.

Contempt.

Contempt is like the hot iron that brands criminals : its imprint is almost always indelible. — ALIBERT.

Contemptible.

Contemptible as pebbles to an admirer of diamonds. — BALZAC.

Contemptible as habitual contempt. — E. L. MAGOON.

As contemptible as any man who breaks open a lock, or as any rascal on the lookout for a house left defenseless and without protection, or as any adventurer looking for some easy and profitable stroke of business. — GUY DE MAUPASSANT.

Contend.

Contended, like gales of spring. — OSSIAN.

Content.

Content as infant smiling through its dreams. — WILLIAM ALLINGHAM.

Content as the males of Adrianus. — ANON.

A contented man is like a good tennis-player, who never fatigues and confounds himself running eternally after the ball, but stays till it comes to him. — POPE.

Content — *continued.*

Contented as a Fox when the Hounds were drawn off and gone home from him. — COLLEY CIBBER.

Her sweet content is like a flattering glass to make my face seem fairer to mine eye. — THOMAS HEYWOOD.

Mutual content is like a river, which must have its banks on either side. — LE SAGE.

Contention.

Contention is like fire; for both burn so long as there is any exhaustible matter to contend with. — THOMAS ADAMS.

Contention, like a horse full of high feeding, madly hath broke loose, and bears down all before him. — SHAKESPEARE.

Contentious.

As coals are to burning coals, and wood to fire; so is a contentious man to kindle strife. — OLD TESTAMENT.

Continually.

As the bees come forth continually in fresh numbers, so fresh bands of Greeks keep continually coming forth from the ships and tents. — HOMER.

Continue.

Continuous, like the brook. — ANON.

Continued as long as the sun. — OLD TESTAMENT.

Continuous as the stars that shine
And twinkle on the milky way.
— WORDSWORTH.

Contract.

Her face contracted like the petals of a flower in the sultry heat that precedes a storm. — ALESSANDRO MANZONI.

Contract and purse thy brow together
As if thou then hadst shut up in thy brain
Some horrible conceit.
— SHAKESPEARE.

Contrary.

As contrary as Dick's hatband. — ANON.

Contrary, like wind and tide meeting. — IBID.

Contrary as light and darkness. — SIR RICHARD STEELE.

Contrast.

Contrast like twin sparks of fire. — AGNES REPPLIER.

Conversation.

Jeffrey, in conversation, was like a skilful swordsman flourishing his weapon in the air; while Mackintosh, with a thin sharp rapier, in the middle of his evolutions, ran him through the body. — SIR A. ALISON.

Our conversation with the ladies, like whip syllabub, was very pretty, but had nothing in it. — WILLIAM BYRD.

I have sometimes compared conversations to the Italian game of Mora, in which one player lifts his hand with so many fingers extended, and the other matches or misses the number, as the case may be, with his own. I show my thought, another his; if they agree, well; if they differ, we find the largest common factor, if we can, but at any rate avoid disputing about remainders and fractions, which is to real talk what tuning an instrument is to playing on it. — O. W. HOLMES.

A transition from an author's book to his conversation, is too often like an entrance into a large city, after distant prospect. Remotely, we see nothing but spires of temples and turrets of palaces, and imagine it the residence of splendor, grandeur, and magnificence; but, when we have passed the gates, we find it perplexed with narrow passages, disgraced with despicable cottages, embarrassed with obstructions and clouded with smoke. — DR. JOHNSON.

Conversation — *continued.*

The conversation of a man resembles a piece of embroidered tapestry, which, when spread out, showed its figures, but, when it is folded up, they are hidden and lost. — THEMISTOCLES.

Conviction.

Convictions will come to you in an active career, as the muscles develop in a gymnasium. — OUIDA.

Convincing.

Convincing as the multiplication table. — ANON.

Convivial.

Conwivial as a live trout in a lime-basket. — DICKENS.

Coo.

Coo,
Like voices of the gods from Bolotoo.
— BYRON.

Cool.

Cool as a snow bank. — LOUISA M. ALCOTT.

Cool as a November twilight. — ANON.

Head as cool as an usurer's. — IBID.

Cool as a dog's nose in a wire muzzle. — JOSH BILLINGS.

Cool as a deep river
In shadow.
— RUPERT BROOKE.

Cool down like a dish of tea. — COLLEY CIBBER.

Cooled, like lust in the chill of the grave. — EMERSON.

Cool as a cucumber. — JOHN GAY.

Cool as the silent shades of sleep. — ROBERT HERRICK.

Cool as a moonbeam on a frozen brook. — O. W. HOLMES.

Cool as the pool that the breeze has skimmed. — HOOD.

Cool as the call of a wind on the still of the sea — RICHARD HOVEY.

Cool as aspen leaves. — KEATS.

Cool . . . like a cutlass blade. — AMY LOWELL.

Coöperation.

We are made for coöperation, like feet, like hands, like eyelids, like the rows of the upper and lower teeth. — MARCUS AURELIUS.

Copious.

Copious as rivers. — E. B. BROWNING.

Coquette.

The heart of a coquette is like a rose, of which the lovers pluck the leaves, leaving only the thorns for the husband. — ANON.

A coquette is to a man what a toy is to a child : as long as it pleases him, he keeps on ; when it ceases to please him he discards it. — IBID.

A coquette is like a recruiting sergeant, always on the lookout for fresh victims. — DOUGLAS JERROLD.

A coquette may be compared to tinder, which lays itself out to catch sparks, but does not always succeed in lighting up a match. — HORACE SMITH.

Corneille.

Corneille is to Shakespeare as a clipped hedge is to a forest. — DR. JOHNSON.

Corpulent.

Corpulency of the body is like the corpulency of some of our institutions ; the larger they grow the more corrupt they become. — JOHN LIVINGSTON.

Correct.

Correct as a machine. — PIERRE DE COULEVAIN.

Corrupt.

Zeal corrupts like standing water. — SAMUEL BUTLER.

Corrupt — *continued.*

Corruption is like a ball of snow, when once set a rolling, it must increase. It gives momentum to the activity of the knave, but it chills the honest man, and makes him almost weary of his calling: and all that corruption attracts, it also retains; for it is easier not to fall, than only to fall once, and not to yield a single inch, then having yielded, to regain it. — C. C. COLTON.

Corrupted as the grave. — JAMES MONTGOMERY.

There is something in corruption which, like a jaundiced eye, transfers the color of itself to the object it looks upon, and sees everything stained and impure. — THOMAS PAINE.

Costly.

Costly as an election. — PIERRE DE COULEVAIN.

Cosy.

As cosy as down among country lanes. — ROBERT BUCHANAN.

Cosy as the nest of the bird. — PHŒBE CARY.

Cosy as a dormouse. — RICHARD HOVEY.

Cosy as a nest of wood-pigeons. — MISS MULOCK.

Couch.

Couch'd like a lion watching for his prey. — JAMES MONTGOMERY.

He stooped down, he couched as a lion, and as an old lion. — OLD TESTAMENT.

Coughed.

Coughed like a cow who finds feathers mixed with hay. — BALZAC.

Counsel.

Counsel to him is as good as a shoulder of mutton to a sick horse. — BEN JONSON.

Counsel in the heart of man is like deep water; but a man of understanding will draw it out. — OLD TESTAMENT.

Count.

Counted as sheep for the slaughter. — OLD TESTAMENT.

Countenance.

Her countenance looked like the gentle buds
Unfolding their beauty in early Spring.
— ANON.

Countenance as clear as friendship wears at feasts. — SHAKESPEARE.

His countenance is as Lebanon, excellent as the cedars. — OLD TESTAMENT.

His countenance was like lightning. — IBID.

Countless.

Countless, as the drops that glide
In the ocean's billowy tide.
— ANON.

Countless as locusts. — IBID.

Countless as the stars that roof our night. — AUBREY DE VERE.

Countless as the wraiths of slumber. — JULIA C. R. DORR.

Countless as the golden motes
That dance upon the sun's earth-kissing beams.
— FRANCES ANNE KEMBLE.

Countless as motes in the sunbeams. — SIR WALTER SCOTT.

Countless . . . as leaves on autumn's tempest shed. — SHELLEY.

Countless as the desert sands. — BAYARD TAYLOR.

Country.

He told me that he thought one's country like one's wife: you were born in the first, and married to the second, and had to learn all about them afterwards, — ay, and make the best of them. — GEORGE MEREDITH.

Couple.

In couples, like the clean and unclean beasts in Noah's ark. — ANON.

Fall into couples, like the birds on Valentine's day. — IBID.

Wheresoe'er we went, like Juno's
swans,
Still we went coupled, and inseparable.
— SHAKESPEARE.

Courage.

Courage is like the diamond — very brilliant; not changed by fire, capable of high polish, but except for the purpose of cutting hard bodies, useless. — C. C. COLTON.

If charg'd with Courage Man should
be,
(Like Powder in Artillery
Proportion'd to the Barrel)
Can'st thou, a Blunderbuss so large,
With scarce a Pocket-Pistol's Charge,
Presume to bounce, or quarrel?
— "FOUNDLING HOSPITAL FOR WIT," 1743.

Courage, like cowardice, is undoubtedly contagious, but some persons are not liable to catch it. — GEORGE D. PRENTICE.

Courageous.

Courageous as the cocks of Tanagra. — ANON.

Courageous and choleric as a hive. — HUGO.

Courageous as a tinker. — IBID.

Court.

Court favors lie above the common road by modesty and humble virtue trod; like trees on precipices, they display fair fruit, which none can reach but birds of prey. — WALTER HARTE.

The court is like a marble statue, I mean, it may be finely polished but it is very hard. — M. DE LA BRUYÈRE.

Courtesy.

How sweet and gracious, even in com-
mon speech,
Is that fine sense which men call
Courtesy!
Wholesome as air and genial as the
light,
Welcome in every clime as breath of
flowers. — JAMES T. FIELDS.

Courthouse.

The courthouse looks imposing; it is like a sea whose waters are the advocates deep in sagacious thought, whose waves are messengers in constant movement hurrying to and fro, whose fish and screaming birds are vile informers, whose serpents are attorney's clerks, whose banks are worn by constant course of legal action. — SUDRAKA.

Courtiers.

Courtiers are, with regard to court rumours, like old soldiers who distinguish through blasts of wind and moaning of leaves the sound of distant steps of an armed troop. — DUMAS, PÈRE.

Courting.

Courting iz like strawberries and cream, wants tew be did slow, then you get the flavor. — JOSH BILLINGS.

Courting iz like 2 little springs ov soft water that steal out from under a rock at the fut ov a mountain and run down the hill side by side singing and dansing and spattering each uther, eddying and frothing and kaskading, now hiding under bank, now full ov sun and now full ov shadder, till bimeby tha jine and then tha go slow. — IBID.

See this 'ere slipper with the paste buckle on to make it look pretty? Courting is like that, lass — all glitter and of no use to nobody. — HAROLD BRIGHOUSE.

Courtly.

Courtly as the French. — JOHN FORD.

Cover.

Covers the country as the dew. — ANON.

They covered mountain and valley like grasshoppers for their number. — PENTAUR.

Covers it, like a stone covered in grass. — D. G. ROSSETTI.

Covered as thick as a pastry-cook's shop on a Christmas-eve. — SWIFT.

Covert.

Covert as the birth of thought. — JAMES MONTGOMERY.

Stole out as covertly as starlight from the edging of a cloud. — N. P. WILLIS.

Covetous.

Covetousness, like a candle ill made, smothers the splendor of a happy fortune in its own grease. — ANON.

Covetous persons are like sponges which greedily drink in water, but return very little until they are squeezed. — G. S. BOWLES.

Covetousness, like jealousy, when it has once taken root, never leaves a man but with his life. — TOM BROWN.

A covetous man is like a dog in a wheel, that roasteth meat for others. — JOHN RAY'S "HANDBOOK OF PROVERBS," 1670.

Coward.

Base and crafty cowards are like the arrow that flieth in the dark. — BACON.

A coward in the field, is like the wise man's fool ; his heart is at his mouth, and he doth not know what he doth profess : but a coward in his faith, is like a fool in his wisdom ; his mouth is in his heart, and he dares not profess what he does know. — ARTHUR WARWICK.

Cowardly.

Cowardly as a mob. — ANON.

Cowardly as a wild duck. — SHAKESPEARE.

Cower.

Cower and shrink as Pariah before Brahma. — BULWER-LYTTON.

Cower and crouch like an English housemaid when knees are calloused with scrubbing. — HUGO.

Coxcomb.

Coxcombs keep each other company, like two knives, to whet each other. — VANBROUGH.

Coy.

Coy as a Croker's mare. — ANON.

As coy and stille as doth a mayde
Were newe spoused. — CHAUCER.

Coy as ys a mayde. — IBID.

Crabbed.

Crabbed as a cuckoo. — ANON.

Her temper is as crabbed as a thorn. — T. BUCHANAN READ.

Crack.

Every hard head has a crack in it somewhere, like a safety valve, as it were, for the steam. — BALZAC.

Crack'd your skull through like a bottle. — BEAUMONT AND FLETCHER.

Cracks like a tortured chord of harmony. — HAVARD.

Making the floor crack as if an image of stone were walking over it. — HUGO.

Crackit like a gun. — ALEXANDER LAING.

Cracked as a cocoa-nut bowled by a monkey. — GEORGE MEREDITH.

Crack and bounce like parched peas. — CHARLES READE.

Crackle.

Crackling as artillery. — R. D. BLACKMORE.

Crackling, like de bay-leaf i' de fire. — BEN JONSON.

Crackle — *continued.*

Crackled like charcoal at the flirt of a fan. — SIR RICHARD STEELE.

Crafty.

Crafty as a fox. — ANON.

Crafty as any Jesuit. — JOSEPH JOUBERT.

Crafty as a snake. — KEATS.

Cram.

Crammed in, like salted fish, in their barrel. — CARLYLE.

Cranky.

Cranky as a holy friar fed with hailstones. — BEAUMONT AND FLETCHER.

Crash.

Crashing . . . like thunder nigh, whose burst of ruin strikes the shatter'd ear with horror. — RICHARD GLOVER.

Crashing . . . like the ice of polar sea. — W. H. LECKY.

Crash as if rock were hurled upon rock. — OUIDA.

Crash, as when the whirlwind rends the ash. — SIR WALTER SCOTT.

Crashed, like a hurricane. — TENNYSON.

Crave.

Craves to see thy face as the moonblowing moon-flower's swelling heart pines for the moon. — EDWIN ARNOLD.

Craved the trumpets eager note,
As the bridled earth the spring.
— GEORGE MEREDITH.

Crawl.

Crawl like a snail. — ANON.

Crawl like shadows forth in Spring. — MATTHEW ARNOLD.

Crawl,
Like caterpillars on a wall.
— JAMES MONTGOMERY.

Crawled like a weed-clogged wave. — OSCAR WILDE.

Crazy.

Crazy as a loon. — ANON.

Crazy as a woman's watch. — IBID.

Crazy as a bedbug. — J. R. BARTLETT'S "DICTIONARY OF AMERICANISMS."

Crazy as a June bug. — WILLIAM ALLEN BUTLER.

Creak.

Wailing creak,
Like an almost human shriek.
— JOHN T. TROWBRIDGE.

Creaked like the implacable cicala's cry. — ROBERT BROWNING.

Creak like the chariot wheels of Satan. — BEN JONSON.

Cream.

Cream and mantle, like a standing pond. — SHAKESPEARE.

Creamy.

Creamy as the opening rose. — LEWIS MORRIS.

Crease.

Creased like dog's ears in a folio. — THOMAS GRAY.

Creation.

Creation, says one, lies before us, like a glorious Rainbow; but the Sun that made it lies behind us, hidden from us. — CARLYLE.

Credit.

Credit lost is like a Venice glass broken. — ANON.

Credit is like chastity; they can both stand temptation better than suspicion. — JOSH BILLINGS.

Credulous.

Credulous as a child. — GEORGE W. SMALLEY.

Like simple noble natures, credulous. — TENNYSON.

Creed.

Creeds are as thistle-down wind-tost and blown, but deeds abide throughout eternity. — GEORGE BARLOW.

Creep.

Creeping into her innocent heart like a maggot into a rose. — ANON.

Crept . . . like a chill. — E. B. BROWNING.

Creep
Like the grey mists upon the mountain side. — GERHART HAUPTMANN.

Creep like torpid Hottentots. — A. F. F. VON KOTZEBUE.

O'er our silence creep
Like whispers of the household gods that keep
A gentle empire o'er fraternal souls.
— KEATS.

Creep like shadows. — SHAKESPEARE.

Creeping like snail
Unwillingly to school. — IBID.

Creeping close as snakes in hidden weeds. — SPENSER.

Creep
Like the downy wing of sleep.
— ARTHUR SYMONS.

Softly creeping, like a breath of air,
Such as is sometimes seen, and hardly seen,
To brush the still breast of a crystal lake. — WORDSWORTH.

Crestfallen.

Crest-fallen as a dried pear. — SHAKESPEARE.

Crimson.

As crimson as August heather. — ALFRED AUSTIN.

Crimson as a comic opera climax. — J. CHEEVER GOODWIN.

Crimson, as if blood were mingled in it. — LONGFELLOW.

Crimson, like a sea of blood
Untroubled by a wave.
— WHITTIER.

Cringe.

Cringes like a toad under a harrow. — ANON.

Crinkly.

Crinkly as a coon's hair.— ANON.

Crinkly like curled maple. — LOWELL.

Crisp.

Crisp as a head of young lettuce. — ANON.

Crisp as the unshorn desert hay. — GEORGE DARLEY.

Crisp as new bank notes. — DICKENS.

Crisp as wintergreen berries. —AMY LESLIE.

Critic.

Critics are like a kind of flies, that breed,
In wild fig-trees, and when they are grown up feed
Upon the raw fruit of the nobler kind,
And by their nibbling in the outward rind
Open the pores, and make way for the sun
To ripen it sooner, than he would have done. — SAMUEL BUTLER.

Criticism is like champagne, nothing more execrable if bad, nothing more excellent if good; if meagre, muddy, vapid, and sour, both are fit only to engender colic and wind; but if rich, generous, and sparkling, they communicate a genial glow to the spirits, improve the taste, and expand the heart. — C. C. COLTON.

Critics avaunt! for you are fish of prey, and feed, like sharks, upon an infant play.
Beat every monster of the deep away; let's a fair trial have, and a clear sea. — CONGREVE.

Critic — *continued.*

A critic is like an idler amusing himself with a spy-glass; he looks at the defects of a work through the end that magnifies, then inverts the instrument to discover the virtues. — E. P. DAY.

The theatre is like a Turkish seraglio: The critics are the eunuchs. — FARQUHAR.

The critics . . . like Cerberus, are posted at all the avenues of literature, and who settle the merits of every performance. — GOLDSMITH.

A critic should be a pair of snuffers. He is oftener an extinguisher; and not seldom a thief. — JULIUS C. HARE.

Critics are a kind of freebooters in the republic of letters, who, like deer, goats, and divers other graminivorous animals, gain their subsistance by gorging upon buds and leaves of the young shrubs of the forest, thereby robbing them of verdure, and retarding their progress to maturity. — WASHINGTON IRVING.

But some will say, Criticks are a kind of Tinkers, that make more faults than they mend ordinarily. — BEN JONSON.

The eyes of critics, whether in commending or carping, are both on one side, like a turbot's. — WALTER S. LANDOR.

Critics, like surgeons, blest with curious art,
Should mark each passage to the human heart;
But not, unskillful, yet with lordly air,
Read surgeon's lectures while they scalp and tear.
— ROBERT LLOYD.

Some critics are like chimney-sweepers; they put out the fire below, and frighten the swallows from the nests above; they scrape a long time in the chimney, cover themselves with soot, and bring nothing away but a bag of cinders, and then sing out from the top of the house, as if they had built it. — LONGFELLOW.

A young critic is like a boy with a gun; he often fires at every living thing he sees; he thinks only of his own skill, not of the pain he is giving. — IBID.

Critics are the eunuchs of art; they talk about what they cannot do. — VLADIMIR DE PACHMANN.

A critic is a legless man who teaches running. — CHANNING POLLOCK.

Critics, like weather-cocks, are not infallible. — LEWIS ROSENTHAL.

The eye of the critic is often, like a microscope, made so very fine and nice that it discovers the atoms, grains, and minutest particles, without ever comprehending the whole, comparing the parts, or seeing at once the harmony. — POPE.

A true critic, in the perusal of a book, is like a dog at a feast, whose thoughts and stomach are wholly set upon what the guests fling away, and consequently is apt to snarl most when there are the fewest bones. — SWIFT.

Critics are like brushers of noblemen's clothes. — SIR HENRY WOTTON.

Croak.

Croak like raven and rook. — WILLIAM DUNBAR.

Crooked.

Crooked as a snake with the colic. — SAMUEL HOPKINS ADAMS.

Crooked as a dog's hind leg. — ANON.

Crooked as a gimlet. — IBID.

Crooked as a ram's horn. — IBID.

Crooked as Crawley brook. — IBID.

Crooked as Robin Hood's bow. — IBID.

So crooked he could hide behind a corkscrew. — IBID.

Crooked — *continued.*

So crooked he could sleep in a roundhouse. — ANON.

Crooked as the streets of Boston. — ARLO BATES.

Crooked runs
Like a Turk verse along a scimitar.
— ROBERT BROWNING.

Crooked as the letter Z. — FRANCIS GROSE'S "CLASSICAL DICTIONARY OF THE VULGAR TONGUE."

As crooked as a cammocke. — LYLY.

Crooked as an auger. — OTHEMAN STEVENS.

Cross.

Cross as a child denied a sugar plum. — ANON.

Cross as an old bear with a sore head. — IBID.

As cross as nine highways. — IBID.

Cross as the tongs. — IBID.

As cross as a red donkey. — BALZAC.

Hang you up cross-legg'd, like a hare at a poulterer. — BEAUMONT AND FLETCHER.

Cross as two sticks. — DICKENS.

Crossed.

Ankles crossed as holy statues sit. — EDWIN ARNOLD.

Like two doomed ships that pass in
storm
We had crossed each other's way.
— OSCAR WILDE.

Intricately crossed,
Like leafless underboughs, 'mid some
thick grove. — WORDSWORTH.

Crouch.

Crouching as for refuge. — ÆSCHYLUS.

Crouch'd like a slave. — AKENSIDE.

Crouched like two bulls locked horn in horn in fight. — ROBERT BROWNING.

He crouched as the panther crouches for its deadly spring. — BULWER-LYTTON.

Crouchest like the faunying whelpe. — THOMAS CHURCHYARD.

Crouching about like a cat a-mousing. — FARQUHAR.

Crouched . . . like a wild beast in his lair. — LONGFELLOW.

Crow.

Crow like chanticleer. — SHAKESPEARE.

Crowd.

He crouds to the Bar like a Pig through a Hedge. — SAMUEL BUTLER.

Crowding like the waves of ocean, one on the other. — BYRON.

Crowding one another like a flock of black goats scurrying down the hills. — FLAUBERT.

Crowded like chickens in a cluster. — JOHN H. FRERE.

Crowd, like flocking linnets. — HOOD.

Crown.

Crowned, as day crowned the dawn-enkindled wave. — SWINBURNE.

Cruel.

Cruel as a rich coxcomb in a ballroom. — ANON.

Cruel as winter. — IBID.

As cruel as Medea. — ROBERT BURTON.

Cruel as the Tartar foe,
To death inured, and nurst in scenes
of woe. — WILLIAM COLLINS.

Cruel as Medusa's sculptured face. — LORD DE TABLEY.

Cruel as Herod when he surpris'd the sleeping Children of Bethlehem. — SIR WILLIAM DAVENANT.

Cruel as the sun. — MAURICE HEWLETT.

Cruel — *continued.*

Cruel as the pinch of a painless dentist. — SYDNEY MUNDEN.

Cruel as love or life. — SWINBURNE.

Cruel as a schoolboy ere he grows
To pity. — TENNYSON.

Jealousy is as cruel as the grave. — OLD TESTAMENT.

Cruel, like the ostriches in the wilderness. — IBID.

Cruel as death. — JAMES THOMSON.

Cruelty.

Cruelty, like every other vice, requires no motive outside of itself; it only requires opportunity. — GEORGE ELIOT.

Crumble.

Crumble it like the chaff of summer threshing-floors. — MILTON.

Crumbled like a house of sand. — OUIDA.

Crumble like a ruined tower. — CHARLES G. D. ROBERTS.

Crumble as a crown,
Till Cæsar driven to lair and hounded Pope
Reel breathless and drop heartless out of hope. — SWINBURNE.

Crumple.

Crumpled like a leaf. — ANON.

Crumpled . . . like a creditor's unwelcome bill. — BULWER-LYTTON.

Crumpled like a snowball in his fist. — HOOD.

Crush.

Crushed him as a tumbrel cart crushes an egg. — BALZAC.

Crushed like an egg-shell. — IBID.

Crushing . . . like a blind Jove feels his way with thunder. — E. B. BROWNING.

Crushed as vermin. — HUGO.

Crushed as in a vise. — JACQUES JASMIN.

Crushes . . . as a child crushes grapes. — EDGAR LEE MASTERS.

Cry (Noun).

Cry of anguish that, like a pebble thrown over a precipice, revealed the depths of his despair. — BALZAC.

A cry as wild as any coming of madness. — GEORGE MEREDITH.

Cry (Verb).

My heart is crying like a tired child for one fond look, one gentle, loving word. — ANON.

Cry like babe in swathing band. — ALLAN CUNNINGHAM.

Crying like Niobe or Niagara. — O. HENRY.

Cry as an eagle freed. — HUGO.

Crying, like a wretched Shangodaya. — LONGFELLOW.

Cry of anguish, like the last dying wail of some dumb, hunted creature. — ADELAIDE A. PROCTER.

Cry like famine. — C. G. ROSSETTI.

Cries like the blood of Abel from the dust. — SHELLEY.

I cry like a travailing woman. — OLD TESTAMENT.

Cunning.

Cunning as a fox. — ANON.

Cunning as the counterfeit of wisdom. — IBID.

Cunning as the serpent of old Nile. — IBID.

Cunning as two Genoese. — BALZAC.

Cunning as a witch. — CHARLOTTE BRONTË.

Cunning as Satan. — PHILIP FRENEAU.

As cunning as Becky Sharp. — JAMES HUNEKER.

Cunning differs from wisdom as twilight from open day. — DR. JOHNSON.

Cunning — *continued.*

Cunning, like a miner, safely and unseen. — EDWARD MOORE.

Cunning as a weasel. — KANURI PROVERB.

Cunning as Captn. Drake. — JOHN RAY'S "HANDBOOK OF PROVERBS," 1670.

Cupids.

Cupids are like cooks of the camp, they can roast or boil a woman. — APHRA BEHN.

Curd.

Curd, like eager droppings into milk. — SHAKESPEARE.

Cure.

Cures are like causes in law, which may be lengthened or shortened at the discretion of the lawyer. — CHAPMAN.

Curious.

Curious as a fish. — GOETHE.

Curious as a magpie. — BETTINA VON HUTTEN.

Curiosity is like a locksmith, who departs when the door is opened. — SYDNEY MUNDEN.

Curl.

The maiden whose lip like a rose leaf is curled. — P. J. BAILEY.

Curl'd like a lamb's back. — WILLIAM BLAKE.

Curled up like some crumpled,
lonely flower-petal.
— RUPERT BROOKE.

Curled up like incense from a Mage-King's tomb. — ROBERT BROWNING.

Curled up like a blue racer in a partridge nest. — IRVIN S. COBB.

Curling, like a wreath of smoke. — COLERIDGE.

Curled and writhed like a snake stepped upon. — STEPHEN CRANE.

Curled like a pastoral crook. — DICKENS.

Curled up like hot paper. — IBID.

Curled up in his heart, like a little squirrel in its nest. — W. S. GILBERT.

Curled like the coat of a poodle. — G. B. SHAW.

Curling like tendrils of the parasite
Around a marble column.
— SHELLEY.

Curl as if a frost had stung them. — BAYARD TAYLOR.

Curling like a kinked up ostrich feather. — ELLA WHEELER WILCOX.

Curled, as when the Sirian star
Withers the ripening corn.
— OSCAR WILDE.

Curls, like ivy. — WORDSWORTH.

Curse.

Curse away!
And let me tell thee, Beauseant, a wise
proverb
The Arabs have, — "Curses are like
young chickens,
And still come home to roost."
— BULWER-LYTTON.

A curse is like a cloud — it passes. — BYRON.

An orphan's curse would drag to Hell
A spirit from on high;
But oh! more horrible than that
Is a curse in a dead man's eye!
— COLERIDGE.

Foul and cursed as if some holy temple had been robbed. — JOHN FORD.

Curses are like processions; they return to the place from which they came. — GIOVANNI RUFFINI.

Curst and shrewd as Socrates' Xantippe. — SHAKESPEARE.

Cursing like a very drab. — IBID.

Curve.

Curved like the Spring-months' russet moon. — ROBERT BROWNING.

Curved like a vault.
— D'ANNUNZIO.

His heroic stature became curved like a maple tree in autumn, bereft of its leaves. — JAN KALINČÁK.

Curved like a stallion's crop. — KIPLING.

Curved over like the edge of a waterfall. — IBID.

Curved like the crescent moon. — SOUTHEY.

Down-curving like the falling wave. — IBID.

Custom.

A bad custom is like a good cake, better broken than kept. — JOHN RAY'S "HANDBOOK OF PROVERBS," 1670.

Old customs are as the blossoms on the tree of a nation's life ; and, when they wither and fall off, death and carnage are at the roots. — ANON.

Cut.

Cuts like hail. — ANON.

Cuts like ingratitude. — IBID.

Cuts like unkindness. — IBID.

Cuts like a cold-chisel. — ALFRED HENRY LEWIS.

Cut down like the grass. — OLD TESTAMENT.

Cuts like a two-edged sword. — IBID.

Cynic.

Cynical as Mephisto. — ANON.

Cynical as Sylla. — IBID.

Cynic, like that fellow Diogenes. — ROBERT GRANT.

D

Daily.

Calls daily like a dun. — HOOD.

Dainty.

Dainty and fair as a folded rose. — ANON.

Dainty as a blushing violet. — IBID.

Dainty as Dresden china. — IBID.

Dainty as thistle-down. — IBID.

A dainty mouth like any crimson rose. — HEINRICH HEINE.

Dainty as a quail. — ZOLA.

Damnatory.

Damnatory as the spot of blood on Blue Beard's keys. — ROBERT REECE.

Damp.

Damp as a church. — ANON.

Damp like a tomb. — IBID.

The air is damp, and hush'd, and close as a sick man's room when he taketh repose an hour before death. — TENNYSON.

Dance.

Dancing like a solar mote around the atmosphere of her lips. — ANON.

Dance . . . like atoms in the sunshine. — IBID.

Dance like corks upon the waves. — IBID.

Dancing like popcorn over a hot fire. — IBID.

Dance like a town top. — BEAUMONT AND FLETCHER.

Dance like flame. — ROBERT BROWNING.

Dance — *continued.*

Dance like a lubber in a net. — WILLIAM BULLEIN.

Dancing like dervishes, who turn as on a pivot. — BYRON.

Dance like a shoal of dolphins. — JOHN DYER.

Dance up and down, like a bear asking for supper. — MAURICE HEWLETT.

Your dancing, like true wit, is best express'd
By nature only to advantage dress'd;
'Tis not a nimble bound, or a caper high,
That can pretend to please a curious eye.
Good judges no such tumblers' tricks regard;
Or think them beautiful, because they're hard.
— SOAME JENYNS.

Danced in his eyes, as the sunbeams dance on the waves of the sea. — LONGFELLOW.

Dancing like naked fauns too glad for shame. — LOWELL.

Dance like witches in their maniac mirth. — WALTER MALONE.

Danced, like wan ghosts about a funeral pyre. — THOMAS MOORE.

Dancing like a Bacchante. — OUIDA.

Dance, Like wingèd stars. — SHELLEY.

Dance like white plumes upon a hearse. — IBID.

Dance like a wither'd leaf. — TENNYSON

Dancing like a bright and buoyant flame. — CELIA THAXTER.

Dance,
Like the sun wading through the misty sky. — JAMES THOMSON.

Danced like the fairies. — VOLTAIRE.

Dance like a wave of the sea. — WILLIAM B. YEATS.

Dangerous.

Dangerous as men milliners. — ANON.

Dangerous as a machine gun. — O. HENRY.

Dangerous as the foamy race of ocean surges. — HUGO.

Dangerous as hammering dynamite. — JAMES HUNEKER.

Dangerous as to check a brute. — KINGSLEY.

More dangerous, than baits to fish. — SHAKESPEARE.

Dangle.

Dangle like a broken bough. — STEPHEN CRANE.

Dapper.

Dapper as a cock-wren. — ANON.

Dark.

Dark as the yawning grave. — AKENSIDE.

Dark as a cellar. — ANON.

Dark as a dungeon. — IBID.

Dark as a funeral scarf. — IBID.

Dark as a thief's pocket. — IBID.

Dark as futurity. — IBID.

Dark as midnight. — IBID.

Dark as the shades of night. — IBID.

Dark like a dead person in a coffin. — IBID.

Dark as Death's Eye. — P. J. BAILEY.

Dark as a wood. — R. D. BLACKMORE.

Dark as was chaos, ere the infant Sun
Was rolled together, or had tried his beams
Athwart the gloom profound.
— ROBERT BLAIR.

Dark — *continued.*

Dark as a Spaniard. — CHARLOTTE BRONTË.

Darkened, as the lighthouse will that turns upon the sea. — E. B. BROWNING.

As dark as if all the negroes of Africa had been stewed down into air. — BULWER-LYTTON.

Dark as mire. — BUNYAN.

Dark as pitch. — IBID.

Dark as misery's woeful night. — BURNS.

Dark as a sullen cloud before the sun. — BYRON.

Dark as winter. — CAMPBELL.

Darkly, as through the foliage of some wavering thicket. — CARLYLE.

Dark as death. — ALICE CARY.

Darked, as it is wonte to darke by smoked images. — CHAUCER.

Dark as a murderer's mask of crape. — ELIZA COOK.

Dark as the grave. — COWLEY.

Dark and cold, like a benighted hemisphere. — AUBREY DE VERE.

Dark as a fiend. — IBID.

Ever darker and darker, like the shadow of advancing death. — DICKENS.

Darkened, like the earth on a splendid day when a cloud flits across the sun. — DUMAS, PÈRE.

Dark as pines that autumn never sears. — GEORGE ELIOT.

Dark as Pluto's palace. — RICHARD GLOVER.

Dark as a cloud that journeys overhead. — HOOD.

Dark as the grave. — IBID.

Dark as shadows be. — IBID.

Dark as the language of the Delphic fane. — HORACE.

Dark as the back of a stag-beetle. — IRISH EPIC TALES.

Dark as the parentage of chaos. — KEATS.

Dark as the pillars of some Hindoo shrine. — KINGSLEY.

Dark as Saint Bartholomew. — W. S. LANDOR.

Darkness like the day of doom. — LONGFELLOW.

Dark as a coal-hole. — LOVER.

Dark as the swelling wave of ocean before the rising winds, when it bends its head near the coast. — JAMES MACPHERSON.

Dark as it were dipped in the death-shadow. — GERALD MASSEY.

Dark as a dead man in the ground. — SYDNEY MUNDEN.

Dark as a demon's dread thought. — MRS. OSGOOD.

Dark as the hush'd silence of the grave. — OTWAY.

Dark as night's protecting wing. — JOHN PIERPONT.

Dark as the caves wherein earth's thunders groan. — POE.

See him darkly as in a mirror. — SAINT AUGUSTINE.

As dark as a Yule midnight. — SCOTTISH PROVERB.

Dark as the bottom of a well. — W. C. RUSSELL.

Dark as care. — SCHILLER.

Dark as Egypt. — SHAKESPEARE.

Dark as Erebus. — IBID.

Dark as hell. — IBID.

Dark as ignorance. — IBID.

Dark as a cloud that the moon turns bright. — SWINBURNE.

Dark as fate. — IBID.

Dark as fear. — IBID.

Dark — *continued.*

Dark in her sight
As her measureless measure of shadow-
less pleasure was bright.
— SWINBURNE.

Dark as the heart of time. — IBID.

Galleons dark as the helmsman's bark of old that ferried to hell the dead. — IBID.

Dark as the sire that begat her, Despair. — IBID.

More dark than the dead world's tomb. — IBID.

Darkened as one that wastes by sorcerous art and knows not whence it withers. — IBID.

Dark as a land's decline. — IBID.

Silent dark as shame. — IBID.

Dark as the inside of a whale. — F. W. THOMAS.

Dark as the brooding thundercloud. — WHITTIER.

Dark as the shroudings of a bier,
As if the blessed atmosphere,
Like his own soul, was dim.
— IBID.

Dark as the waiting tomb. — MCLANDBURGH WILSON.

Dart.

Darted like an eagle. — ANEURIN.

Darted . . . like an arrow aflame. — JOSEPH CONRAD.

Darted like a skimming bird. — IBID.

Darted away like a bird that has been fluttering around its nest before it takes a distant flight. — J. FENIMORE COOPER.

Darting skyward like a rocket. — DICKENS.

Darted like a serpent. — DUMAS, PÈRE.

Darting like glittering elves at play. — MARY M. FENOLLOSA.

Darting like a flashing flame. — FIRDAUSI.

The ravenous shark, darting, like a spectre, through the blue waters. — WASHINGTON IRVING.

Dart like a rifle-bullet. — KIPLING.

Darts on like a greyhound whelp after a leveret. — W. S. LANDOR.

Dart like swallows. — LONGFELLOW.

Darted like a flight of hawks. — OUIDA.

Dart o'er stock and stone like hunted hart. — SIR WALTER SCOTT.

Their influence darts
Like subtle poison through the blood-
less veins
Of desolate society. — SHELLEY.

Dart around, as light from the meridian sun. — IBID.

Darts, like a javelin, to his destin'd goal. — CHRISTOPHER SMART.

Darts, like lichtnin' flashin'. — JAMES SMITH.

Darted away like a telegram. — MARK TWAIN.

Dash.

Dashed like a Mameluke cavalry upon a charge. — ANON.

Dashed on like a spurr'd blood-horse in a race. — BYRON.

Dashes, like a fire-flood. — CARLYLE.

Dash along, like molten diamonds glancing. — ELIZA COOK.

He dashed down among them as a sparrow-hawk dashes down. — PENTAUR.

The waves . . . dashed like a torrent of pearls. — FRANCIS S. SALTUS.

Dash them in pieces like a potter's vessel. — OLD TESTAMENT.

Daunt.

Daunt like a king that draws his troops to fight. — GEORGE SANDYS.

Dauntless.

Dauntless as deities exempt from fate. — ANON.

Dauntless as an ibis. — OUIDA.

Dauntless as death. — MATTHEW PRIOR.

Dawn.

A sudden truth dawns on me, like a light through the remainder tatters of a dream. — HOOD.

Dazzle.

Dazzles like Kama's sceptre. — JAYADEVA.

It came to passe, that a gentleman . . . chanced to glance his eyes on her, and there were they dazzled on her beautie, as lookes that are caught in the sunne with the glittering of a glasse. — LYLY.

Dazzled like the lightning in the sky. — RACINE.

Dazzle like a new-discovered star. — T. BUCHANAN READ.

Her dazzle like the sun in his Meridian. — THOMAS SHADWELL.

Dead.

Dead as Chelsea. — ANON.

Dead as a man after two doctors have visited him. — IBID.

Dead as leaves on a painted canvas. — IBID.

Dead as mackerel. — IBID.

Dead as the nail in a coffin. — IBID.

Dead as the Roman Empire. — IBID.

Dead as the wholesale district on Sunday. — IBID.

Dead as Aristophanes. — WILLIAM ARCHER.

My sweetest child,
Which like a flow'r crush'd with a blast, is dead. — SIR JOHN BEAUMONT.

Dead as a buried vestal whose whole strength
Goes when the grate above shuts heavily. — ROBERT BROWNING.

As dead to the life I once lived as if the Styx rolled between it and me. — BULWER-LYTTON.

As dead to you as the dust of your fathers. — IBID.

Dead as a herring. — SAMUEL BUTLER.

Dede as stoon. — CHAUCER.

Dead as Scrooge's partner. — HENRY A. CLAPP.

Dead as Julius Cæsar. — JOSEPH CONRAD.

Dead as Pharaoh. — DICKENS.

Dead as a salmon in a fishmonger's basket. — GEORGE FARQUHAR.

Dead as charity. — NATHANIEL FIELD.

Dead as a perished delight. — J. G. HOLLAND.

Dead as the bulrushes round little Moses,
On the old banks of the Nile.
— O. W. HOLMES.

Dead to sounds, as a ship out of soundings. — HOOD.

Dead as bricks. — IBID.

More dead than Morpheus' imaginings. — KEATS.

Ded as a dore-nayle. — LANGLAND.

Ded as dore-tree. — IBID.

Lies dead,
As a corse on the sea-shore, whose spirit has fled. — LONGFELLOW.

Dead as last year's clothes in a fashionable fine lady's wardrobe. — GEORGE MEREDITH.

The Dead are like the stars by day;
Withdrawn from mortal eye,
But not extinct, they hold their way
In glory through the sky.
— JAMES MONTGOMERY.

Dead — *continued.*

Dead as wood. — Lewis Morris.

Dead as desire in the dead. — Sydney Munden.

Dead as mutton. — Charles Reade.

Dead as a dog that lieth in a ditch. — Samuel Rowlands.

Dead as earth. — Shakespeare.

Death lies on her, like an untimely frost
Upon the sweetest flower of all the field. — Ibid.

Dead as night when stars wax dim. — Swinburne.

Dead as dreams of days that were
Before the new-born world lay bare
In heaven's wide eye. — Ibid.

Dead as the carver's figured throng. — Ibid.

Dead as the dawn's grey dew
At high midnoon of the mounting day that mocks the might of the dawn it slew. — Ibid.

Dead as yesterday. — Ibid.

As dead and sapless as last month's leaves. — Sir Henry Taylor.

Dead as dreams. — William Watson.

Dead as smelts. — Daniel Webster.

Dead as the ropes of roses on St. James street. — Israel Zangwill.

Deadly.

Deadly as nightshade. — T. B. Aldrich.

Deadly as the viper of Sumatra. — Bulwer-Lytton.

Deadly as the sting of satire. — James Cawthorn.

Deadly as the canker-worm. — Froude.

Deadly as a night frost. — Maurice Hewlett.

The venom clamours of a jealous woman poison more deadly than a dog's tooth. — Shakespeare.

Deaf.

Deaf as a post. — Anon.

As deaf as a beetle. — Ibid.

As deaf as a white cat. — Ibid.

Deaf as a door. — Nicholas Breton.

Deaf as any tradesman's dummy. — Hood.

Deaf as a nail — that you cannot hammer a meaning into. — Ibid.

She was deaf as a nut — for nuts, no doubt,
Are deaf to the grub that's hollowing out. — Ibid.

Deaf as a stone — say one of the stones
Demosthenes sucked to improve his tones;
And surely deafness no further could reach
Than to be in his mouth without hearing his speech. — Ibid.

Deaf as bricks. — Ibid.

Deaf as God and Magog. — Ibid.

Deaf as Pharaoh's mother's mother's mummy. — Ibid.

As deaf, alas! as the dead and forgotten —
(Gray has noticed the waste of breath,
In addressing the "dull, cold ear of death"). — Ibid.

Deaf as the still-born figures of Madame Tussaud,
With their eyes of glass, and their hair of flax,
That only stare whatever you "ax,"
For their ears, you know, are nothing but wax. — Ibid.

Deafe as an adder. — Ben Jonson.

Deaf — *continued.*

Deaf as winds when seamen pray. — LEE.

Deaf as the billows. — OVID.

As deaf as Ailsa Craig. — SCOTTISH PROVERB.

Deaf as the sea. — SHAKESPEARE.

Deaf as a shad. — SAM SLICK.

Deaf as fire. — SWINBURNE.

More deaf than trees. — WALLER.

Deafening.

Cries as deafening, as the shout that breaks from the bribed audience, when Fæsidius speaks. — JUVENAL.

Dear.

Dear as the land to shipwrecked mariner. — ÆSCHYLUS.

Dear as her mother holds her infant's grave. — BOGART.

Dear as the nurtured thrill of joy. — BURNS.

Dear — as his native song to Exile's ears. — BYRON.

Dear as fairy fable. — MADISON CAWEIN.

Dear as liberty. — CICERO.

Dear as the soul o'er thy memory sobbing. — JAMES G. CLARK.

Dear as freedom is. — COWPER.

Dear as a child's curling fingers. — OLIVE TILFORD DARGAN.

As dear as to the lover the smile of a gentle maid. — BARTHOLOMEW DOWLING.

Dear as the apple to thine eye. — TIMOTHY DWIGHT.

As dear to me as my own right hand. — W. S. GILBERT.

Dear, as the light that visits these sad eyes ;
Dear, as the ruddy drops that warm my heart. — GRAY.

Dear as his eyeball. — THOMAS HEYWOOD.

Dear as these mine eyes. — MARLOWE.

Dear as light. — HANNAH MORE.

Dear as the vital stream that feeds my heart. — IBID.

Dear as the vital warmth that feeds my life. — OTWAY.

Dear as my finger. — SHAKESPEARE.

As dear to me as are the ruddy drops
That visit my sad heart. — IBID.

As dear to me as life itself. — IBID.

Dearer than eye-sight, space, and liberty. — IBID.

Dear
As human heart to human heart may be. — SHELLEY.

Dear as remember'd kisses after death. — TENNYSON.

Dear as the visions of the promised bride lighted by love. — C. P. WILSON.

Death.

Death is like sleep ; and sleep shuts down our lids. — BYRON.

Deathless.

Deathless as love. — SWINBURNE.

Debase.

Debas'd by gross alloy :
As gold in mines lies mix'd with dirt and clay. — DAVID MALLET.

Debauch.

Debauches are like figs growing on a precipice : the fruit cannot be gathered by men, but only by crows and vultures. — DIOGENES.

Debt.

Debt is like a millstone about a man's neck. — ANON.

Debt— *continued.*

Debt is like any other trap, easy enough to get into, but hard enough to get out of. — JOSH BILLINGS.

Debts are now-a-days like children, begot with pleasure, but brought forth with pain. — MOLIERE.

Decay.

Decay like the rainbow's hue. — ANON.

We decay like grass of the hill ; our strength returns no more. — JAMES MACPHERSON.

All decay, like the glories of the Spring. — MISS MULOCK.

As soon decay'd and done
As is the morning's silver-melting dew.
— SHAKESPEARE.

Decay
Like corpses in a charnel.
— SHELLEY.

Deceitful.

Deceitful, like crows. — ÆSCHYLUS.

Deceitful like the devil. — WILLIAM BYRD.

Deceive.

The world
Deceived itself as maidens do with dolls. — JOHN DAVIDSON.

Deceiver.

A base deceiver, like a deep well whose mouth is covered with smiling plants. — KALIDASA.

Decency.

Decency is like gold, the same in all countries. — LI HUNG CHANG.

Deceptive.

Deceptive as the mirage of the desert. — ANON.

Deceptive as the costume of a *bal masque*. — G. K. CHESTERTON.

Decisive.

Decisive, like a flash of lightning. — LUDOVIC HALÉVY.

Decline.

Declining to change themselves, even as sulphuric acid declines to be sweet milk, though you vote so until the end of the world. — CARLYLE.

Declined, like a flower surcharged with dew. — MILTON.

Declined — like shadow in the dying of the day. — POE.

Deeds.

His deeds inimitable, like the sea
That shuts still as it opes, and leaves no tracts
Nor prints of precedent for poor men's facts. — CHAPMAN.

Deep.

Deep as the fountains of sleep. — ANON.

Deep as the void above. — IBID.

Deep as evening red. — IBID.

Deep as despair. — IBID.

Deep as ever plummet sounded. — IBID.

Deep as grief. — IBID.

Deep as the North Star. — IBID.

Deep as though the globe were split to let the waters through. — W. E. AYTOUN.

Deep as Heaven's own luminous blue. — P. J. BAILEY.

Deep as death. — IBID.

Deep in the heart as meteor stones in earth, dropped from some higher sphere. — IBID.

Deep as midnight's starry treasure. — T. L. BEDDOES.

France kept her old affection as deeply as the sepulchre the corse. — E. B. BROWNING.

Deep as hell from high heaven. — CARLYLE.

Deep as Tophet, high as heaven. — IBID.

Deep — *continued.*

Silence as deep as eternity. — IBID.

Deep as life and death. — IBID.

Deep as the murmurs of the falling floods. — JAMES CAWTHORN.

Deep and yet soft, like notes from some long chord responsive to thrilled air. — GEORGE ELIOT.

Deep as annihilation. — THOMAS HARDY.

Sighs as deep as destiny. — JEAN INGELOW.

Deep as devils grope. — SIDNEY LANIER.

Joy as deep as heaven's blue. — T. T. LYNCH.

Deep as that grave in Hell where Cæsar lies. — EDWARD MARKHAM.

As deep as Pedwell. — SCOTTISH PROVERB.

Deep and tender as the blue of a baby's eye. — JAMES WHITCOMB RILEY.

Deep as the unfathomed endless sea. — C. G. ROSSETTI.

Chasms as deep and as drear as the tomb. — JOHN RUSKIN.

Deep as hell. — SHAKESPEARE.

Deep as the sea. — IBID.

Deep as night and Heaven. — SHELLEY.

Deep as deep in water sinks a stone. — SWINBURNE.

Deep as music's heart. — IBID.

Deep as the clear unsounded sea. — IBID.

Deep as the deep dim soul of a star. — IBID.

Deep as the depths unsought
Whence faith's own hope may redeem
us nought. — IBID.

Deep as the pit of hell. — IBID.

Deeper than men's dreams of hell are deep. — IBID.

Deeper than the green sea's grass. — IBID.

Deep as hate. — IBID.

Deep as the grave. — IBID.

Deeper than time or space. — IBID.

A grief as deep as life or thought. — TENNYSON.

Deep as the shadow of Rome. — JOHN R. THOMPSON.

Deep as the bottomless pit. — G. S. VIERECK.

A tone as low and deep as love's first whisper. — N. P. WILLIS.

Deeper than the vanities of power, or in vain pomp of glory. — IBID.

Deepen.

Deepening like the dawn. — T. B. ALDRICH.

Defect.

The wise man's defects are like the eclipses of the sun; they come to every one's knowledge. — CONFUCIUS.

Defiant.

Defiant as a rosebud slipped from its parent stalk. — ANON.

Defiant as the storied Greek amid his brave Three Hundred. — MARGARET J. PRESTON.

Deformed.

Deformed as guilt. — ANON.

Deformed, like the mute dwarfs
Which wait upon a naked Indian queen.
— ROBERT BROWNING.

Degraded.

Degraded, like a hedge-born swain
That doth presume to boast of gentle
blood. — SHAKESPEARE.

Deify.

Deify me, as if some blithe wine
Or bright elixir peerless I had drunk,
And so become immortal.
— KEATS.

Dejected.

As dejected as a wet hen. — SCOTTISH PROVERB.

Deliberate.

Deliberate as a lawyer's brief. — FITZ-JAMES O'BRIEN.

Deliberately.

Deliberately as Nature. — THOREAU.

Delicate.

She was delicate and fair as moonlight. — HANS CHRISTIAN ANDERSEN.

Delicate as a lily. — ANON.

Delicate as flowers. — IBID.

Delicate as the sunset on the snow-covered summits of Mount Sfiorito. — IBID.

Delicate as invisible needle-points. — CARLYLE.

Delicate and evanescent as the colored pencilings on a frosty night from the Northern Lights. — DE QUINCEY.

Delicate as a white violet. — JOYCE KILMER.

Delicate as rose leaves. — AGNES REPPLIER.

Delicate as the tension of a lyre. — EDITH M. THOMAS.

Delicately.

Delicately, as fingers play sad music. — R. D. BLACKMORE.

Delicately, like the tap of a finger-nail on a vase. — GEORGE MEREDITH.

Delicious.

Delicious as forbidden fruit. — ANON.

Delicious as trickles of wine poured at mass-time. — ROBERT BROWNING.

Delicious as a dream. — MISS LANDON.

Delight (Noun).

These violent delights have violent ends,
And in their triumph die, like fire and powder,
Which, as they kiss, consume.
— SHAKESPEARE.

Hold delight as grape-flowers hold their wine. — SWINBURNE.

Delight as the wind's in the billow.
— IBID.

Delight (Verb).

Delight as a wave in the wind. — SWINBURNE.

Delight as in freedom won. — IBID.

Delightful.

Delightful as the song of Philomel. — ANON.

Delightful as the all-enlivening sun. — WALTER HARTE.

Delusion.

Delusions, errors, and lies are like huge, gaudy vessels, the rafters of which are rotten and worm-eaten, and those who embark in them are fated to be shipwrecked. — BUDDHA.

Delusions, like dreams, are dispelled by our awakening to the stern realities of life. — A. R. C. DALLAS.

Dear delusions, fairy charms,
As fancy dreams in virtue's arms.
— EDWARD LOVIBOND.

Delusion — like the butterfly to soar. — IMRE MADÁCH.

Delusive.

Delusive as a midnight dream. — JAMES CAWTHORN.

Democracy.

Democratic as a saint. — ANON.

The Democratic party is like a man riding backwards in a carriage: It never sees a thing until it has gone by. — BENJAMIN F. BUTLER.

Democracy — *continued.*

Democracy, like an army, has a way of persuading aristocrats to lead it. — RICHARD LE GALLIENNE.

Demur.

Demur like a posed lawyer, as if delay could remove some impediments. — THOMAS ADAMS.

Demure.

Demure as a cat. — ANON.

Demure as a nun. — IBID.

Demure as a Quaker. — IBID.

Demurely as a judge that pronounceth sentence of death. — JOHN FORD.

As demure as if butter would not melt in his mouth. — JOHN RAY'S "HANDBOOK OF PROVERBS."

Denied.

Denied,
Like spurned beggars at a palace gate.
— ANNE C. L. BOTTA.

Dense.

Dense as the fumes of ascending hell. — SWINBURNE.

Dense as the walls that fence the secret darkness of unknown time. — IBID.

Dense as darkness. — IBID.

Depart.

Departed, like Ichabod's glory. — ANON.

His fame is departed like mist, when it flies, before the rustling wind, along the brightening vale. — JAMES MACPHERSON.

Departed as a shadow. — POE.

Departed like a gleam, that for a moment in the heavy sky
Is opened when the storm is hurrying by. — SOUTHEY.

Departed as a scroll when it is rolled together. — NEW TESTAMENT.

Depart
Like blighted buds; or clouds that mimicked land
Before the sailor's eye.
— WORDSWORTH.

Descend.

Descended like a wolf on the fold. — ANON.

Descends like the foot of a crow. — ARABIC.

Dryden, descending to such game, was like an eagle stooping to catch flies. — GOLDSMITH.

Would no more descend from his calm than a bronze statue from its pedestal. — FRANCISQUE SARCEY.

Descending . . .
Like the spring whose breath is blending
All blasts of fragrance into one.
— SHELLEY.

The light of speech descends like a tongue of the Pentecost. — BAYARD TAYLOR.

Complaints of times when merit wants reward
Descend like similes from bard to bard.
—WILLIAM WHITEHEAD.

Desire (Noun).

The passions and desires, like the two twists of rope, mutually mix one with the other, and twine inextricably round the heart; producing good, if moderately indulged; but certain destruction, if suffered to become inordinate. — ROBERT BURTON.

Desire (Verb).

As flowers desire the kisses of the rain,
She his, and many a year desired in vain. — WILLIAM WATSON.

Desirous.

Desirous as the nights of youth. — D. G. ROSSETTI.

Desolate.

Desolate as a mausoleum. — ANON.

Desolate — *continued.*

Desolate as a cave
Abandoned even of the breaking wave.
— LAURENCE BINYON.

Desolate as a tomb. — HEINRICH HEINE.

Desolate as death. — FRANCIS S. SALTUS.

Despair.

Despair is like froward children, who, when you take away one of their playthings, throw the rest into the fire for madness. — P. DE CHARRON.

Despicable.

Despicable . . . as the old age of a passionate man. — ANON.

I kant consieve a more despikable objek than a proud and arrogant man; he makes me think ov an old Tom Turkey Trieing tew git mad at a red flannel pettycoat on a clothes line. — JOSH BILLINGS.

Despise.

Despised as a thing passing into oblivion. — THOMAS MORTON.

Despised, like the descending pearls of a misty morning. — JEREMY TAYLOR.

Destitute.

Destitute of sense as the gesture of the tree and the sound of the wind.
— HUGO.

Destitute . . . like a beast naked without refute, upon a plain to abide all summer showers. — JOHN LYDGATE.

Destitute as a stock-fish. — JOHN HOWARD PAYNE.

Destroy.

Destroyeth like the flash of lightning. — MAX MÜLLER.

Destroyeth the body as ivy doth the old tree, or a worm that engendereth in the kernel of the nut. — SIR WALTER RALEIGH.

Destructive.

Destructive as the bite of the rattlesnake. — ANON.

About as destructive as a blank cartridge. — IBID.

Destructive as a centre-rush in a football team. — IBID.

Destructive as hail in summer. — IBID.

Deteriorate.

Deteriorate like a fish in the sun. — AMBROSE BIERCE.

Determined.

Determined aspect like the iron jawed lady in a circus. — IRVIN S. COBB.

Detestable.

Detestable as exalted wickedness. — ROBERT BURTON.

Detested.

Detested as the gates of hell. — SCHILLER.

Detraction.

Detraction, like a crab, runneth backwards. — ANON.

Devoid.

Devoid of feeling as a eunuch is of manly joys. — ANON.

Devoid of imagination as a brick. — T. W. H. CROSLAND.

Devoted.

Devoted as a faithful dog. — GEORGE SAND.

Devotion.

Devotion is like the candle which Michael Angelo used to take in his pasteboard cap, so as not to throw his shadow upon the work on which he was engaged. — PHILLIPS BROOKS.

Devotion, like fire in froste weather, burns hottest in affliction. — SIR THOMAS OVERBURY.

Devotion — *continued.*

Devotion, like fire, goeth upward. — ZOROASTER.

Devour.

Devour me as an adversary. — BUNYAN.

Devoured it like a ravenous wolf that had been starving a fortnight in the snow. — DANIEL DEFOE.

As scorching heat the mountain snow
devours,
As thirsty earth drinks up the falling
show'rs,
Ev'n so the grave's insatiable jaws
Those rebels swallow who infringe
His laws. — GEORGE SANDYS.

Devoutly.

Devoutly as the Dervish. — HOOD.

Dewy.

Dewy as a spring morning. — AMY LESLIE.

Dewy as Aphrodite fresh risen from the foam. — OWEN SEAMAN.

Die.

Die like a dog in a ditch. — ANON.

The fresh roses on your cheeks shall
die,
Like flowers that wither in the shade.
— APHRA BEHN.

Parting day
Dies like the dolphin, whom each pang
imbues
With a new colour as it gasps away,
The last still loveliest, till — 'tis gone,
and all is gray. — BYRON.

Dies like cookery with the day that brought it forth. — CARLYLE.

Die like a rat in hole. — RANGER GULL.

A remnant of beauty was dying out upon this face of sixteen, like the pale sun which is extinguished by frightful clouds at the dawn of a winter's day. — HUGO.

It died away
Like the pale sunbeam of a weeping
day. — JACQUES JASMIN.

All my glories die,
Like flowers transplanted to a colder
sky. — LORD LYTTELTON.

She died — as die the roses
On the ruddy clouds of dawn,
When the envious sun discloses
His flame, and morning's gone.
— EVAN MACCOLL.

Dies away,
Like relics of some faded strain, loved
voices, lost for many a day.
— THOMAS MOORE.

Die as April's cowslips die. — JOHN PAYNE.

Dies away like a peal of cathedral bells. — SAINT-PIERRE.

Dies as dreams that die with the sleep they feed. — SWINBURNE.

As a star feels the sun and falters,
Touched to death by diviner eyes —
As on the old gods' untended altars
The old fire of withered worship dies.
— IBID.

Die as a leaf that dies in a day. — IBID.

Died like odor rapt in the winged wind,
Borne into alien lands and far away.
— TENNYSON.

Died away like a sigh in the shadow of the infinite vault. — GIOVANNI VERGA.

Differ.

Differ as a clipped hedge and forest. — ANON.

Differ as an Indian and a Greek. — IBID.

Differ as a Roman stylus and Mr. Waterman's fountain pen. —IBID.

Differ as a satyr to Hyperion; as a rushlight to the sun. — IBID.

Differ as a Vatican fresco and a political transparency. — IBID.

Differ — *continued.*

Differ as a whale and a tadpole. — Anon.

Differ as a Whistler nocturne and the design on a chocolate box. — Ibid.

Differ as a zephyr and a cyclone. — Ibid.

Differ as flint and chalk. — Ibid.

Differ as grass and hay. — Ibid.

Differ as Hamlet and Hercules. — Ibid.

Differ as harp and harrow. — Ibid.

Differ as locks. — Ibid.

Differ as a mangled monkey and a well made man. — Ibid.

Differ as noses. — Ibid.

Differ as pigments and a picture. — Ibid.

Differ as shine and substance. — Ibid.

Differ as simpleton and sage. — Ibid.

Differ as smoke and flame. — Ibid.

Differs as stage money from government bonds. — Ibid.

Differ as sword and tooth-pick. — Ibid.

Differ as the Central Park Menagerie and the depths of the jungle. — Ibid.

Differ as the glow-worm and the eagle. — Ibid.

Differs as the jimson weed from the violet. — Ibid.

Differ as the mid-day sun and a convalescent white bean. — Ibid.

Differ as the Parthenon of Athens and an American court house. — Ibid.

Differ as the song of the lark to the voice of the crow. — Ibid.

Differs as the tail of a comet and the tail of a pig. — Ibid.

Differ as winter and summer. — Ibid.

Differ most, as salt and sugar. — Bacon.

Differ as a nettle and a pink. — E. B. Browning.

Differ as an octave flute and a tavern gong. — William Cullen Bryant.

The true beautiful . . . differs from the false as Heaven does from Vauxhall. — Carlyle.

Differ as a breastplate and a pie-crust. — Dumas, père.

Differ as a hound of blood and a mongrel. — Charles Macklin.

Differ as a laughing brook and a cup of water. — C. M. S. McLellan.

Differ like human faces. — Nicholas Rowe.

Differ as much as chalcke and chese. — Richard Shacklock.

Difference.

Difference between a bent copper farthing and a nugget of gold. — Anon.

Difference between a Greek temple and a bird-cage, the solemn sea and a street puddle. — Ibid.

The difference between having a woman at your side and on your side. — Ibid.

Difference between tweedle dum and tweedle dee. — Ibid.

The difference of savour 'twixt vinegar and wine. — Arabian Nights.

Difference between . . . the ideal priest who is everlastingly by some one's bed and the real priest who is as glad as any one else to get to his own. — G. K. Chesterton.

Difference between the race-horse and the Shetland pony, the bantam and the Shanghai fowl, the greyhound and the poodle dog. — John W. Draper.

Difference — *continued.*

As much difference as between an organ and a bagpipe. — W. S. LANDOR.

As much difference between them as between a horse chestnut and a chestnut horse. — LEAN'S "COLLECTANEA."

As much difference as there is between beautie and vertue, bodies and shadowes, colors and life — so great odds is there between love and friendship. — LYLY.

Difference between a sonata of Beethoven and the Battle Cry of Freedom, between a gravestone-cutter's cherub and the masterpieces of Raphael. — WILLIAM MATHEWS.

The difference between a Sunday newspaper supplement on the monkeys in the Bronx Zoo and the Darwinian Theory. — GEORGE JEAN NATHAN.

The difference is as great as that between an elephant and a mosquito. — TAMIL PROVERB.

Difference . . . between jet and ivory. — SHAKESPEARE.

Different.

As different as an equinoctial is from an evangel. — ANON.

Different as dog-days and those at Christmas. — IBID.

Different as gold and platina. — IBID.

Different as swan is from goose. — IBID.

As different as paths of storm. — AMBROSE BIERCE.

As different as our faces. — C. C. COLTON.

Different an aim as a child's first journey across a floor. — HAWTHORNE.

As different . . . as a sigh from the southwest is from the northeastern breeze. — O. W. HOLMES.

Different as the two hemispheres in the time of Columbus. — GEORGE MEREDITH.

Different as dark eyes from golden hair. — SWINBURNE.

Difficult.

Difficult as a Greek puzzle. — ANON.

Difficult as to forgive the virtues of our enemies. — IBID.

Difficult as to grasp a shadow. — IBID.

Difficult as to hiss and yawn at the same time. — IBID.

Difficult as to pin a medal on a shadow. — IBID.

Difficult as to sail the sea in an egg shell. — IBID.

Difficult as to remember a rhyme made in a dream. — IBID.

Difficult as to walk a mile on stilts upon a line of feather-beds. — IBID.

Difficult as a beginning. — BYRON.

Difficult . . . as for a rattlesnake to stir without making a noise. — C. C. COLTON.

Difficult as it would be to hum an air from an opera bouffe while listening to the overture of Tannhäuser. — ARTHUR JEROME EDDY.

Difficult to grasp as the small end of a hard boiled egg. — ROBERT EDGREN.

As difficult . . . as to preserve your purse at a gaming-table or your health at a bawdy house. — FIELDING.

As difficult as for a slave girl to please a slave-dealer. — OSMANLI PROVERB.

Difficult as to distinguish colors in the darkness. — SIR RICHARD STEELE.

Difficulty.

Difficulty adds to result, as the ramming of powder sends the bullet the further. — GEORGE MACDONALD.

Difficulty — *continued.*

Difficulties, like thieves, often disappear at a glance. — ROCHEFAUCAULD.

Diffuse.

Diffused . . . like scatt'red chaffe, the which the wind away doth fan. — SPENSER.

Dignified.

Dignified as Chapels-of-Ease. — THOMAS HARDY.

Dignified, like a boy with a stiff neck. — JOSEPH C. LINCOLN.

Dilapidated.

She was a little dilapidated, like a house, with having been so long to let. — DICKENS.

Dilated.

Dilated, like a saint in ecstasy. — E. B. BROWNING.

Diligent.

Doubly diligent, like the devil's apothecary. — FRANCIS GROSE.

Diligent, like Jacob was unto his master Laban. — HUGH LATIMER.

Dim.

Dim as the land of shadows. — ANON.

As dim as dim might be. — ROBERT BUCHANAN.

Dim . . . as in a dream. — BULWER-LYTTON.

Burn dim, like lamps in noisome air. — COLERIDGE.

Dim as a ghost. — MRS. E. M. H. CORTISSOZ.

Ghastly dim and pale, as if driven by a beating storm at sea. — RICHARD HENRY DANA.

Dim as the borrow'd beams of moon or stars. — DRYDEN.

Dim as the wandering stars that burst in the blue of the Summer heaven. — FITZ-GREENE HALLECK.

Dim and sweet as moonlight in a solitary street. — LONGFELLOW.

Dim wrapt in a haze like a shrouded ghost. — SIR A. LYALL.

Dim as the dream of an idle dreamer. — ERNEST MCCAFFEY.

Dim as the shades in the angry shower. — GEORGE MEREDITH.

Dim . . . like the far golden lustre of a dark god-like town. — WILLIAM MORRIS.

Dim as the dream of a dream that was dreamed. — SYDNEY MUNDEN.

Dim as the dusk of day. — JAMES WHITCOMB RILEY.

Dimensionless.

Dimensionless as God's infinity. — EBENEZER ELLIOTT.

Diminish.

Beauties diminish, like those of a fine prospective viewed too near. — M. DE LA BRUYÈRE.

Dimly.

Dimly traced
Like moss-grown letters on a mouldering stone. — ARABIAN.

Dimly like a half-remembered dream. — GEORGE ELIOT.

Dimmed.

Dimm'd . . . like a vague remnant of some by-past scene. — CHARLOTTE BRONTË.

Dimmed and flattened, like an etching that has gone too often to the press. — JOHN CORBIN.

Dimmed and torn, like the remainder tatters of a dream. — HOOD.

Dimm'd, like to the morning mist. — THOMAS SACKVILLE.

Dimpled.

Dimpled as a baby. — O. W. Holmes.

Dimpling.

Dimpling like a brook. — Anon.

Dimpling like a maiden's cheek. — Irvin S. Cobb.

Din.

The inward din,
Like a hundred braziers working in
A caldron with their hammers.
— Southey.

Dingy.

Dingy, like a grubby lot
Of sooty sweeps, or colliers.
— Hood.

Dipping.

Dipping here and there, like diggers in California "prospecting for a placer" that will pay. — Emerson.

Dire.

Dire as the face disfeatured of a dream. — Swinburne.

Dire as when friends are rankled into foes. — James Thomson.

Direct.

Direct as a railroad. — Hood.

Direct as antique tragedy. — James Huneker.

Direct as light. — Robert G. Ingersoll.

Direct as the arrow of logic. — George Meredith.

Dirge.

Sad dirges,
Like the wind through a ruined cell,
Or the mournful surges
That ring the dead seaman's knell.
— Shelley.

Dirt.

Dirt is like wickedness; it is only when it shows so much as to be apparent to everybody that we are ashamed of it. — Mary A. Beauchamp.

Dirty.

Dirty as a hog. — John Byrom.

Dirty as earth. — Fielding.

Disagree.

Disagree like clocks. — Lyly.

Disagreeing as fire and water. — Ibid.

Disappear.

Disappear like phantoms. — Anon.

Disappearing at day break like foul night-birds of an unclean dream. — W. C. Brann.

Disappears like dew on a June morning. — Edward G. Buffum.

Slowly disappearing, like a day dream. — C. S. Calverley.

Disappeared like a shadow. — Adelbert von Chamisso.

Disappeared . . . like a man overtaken by an avalanche. — Joseph Conrad.

Disappeared, like the shadow thrown by a passing cloud. — Dickens.

Disappeared, like a cloud driven by the wind. — Dumas, père.

Disappeared, like a passing gleam. — George Eliot.

Disappear like a tale that is told. — Simeon Ford.

Disappeared like a shape in a vision — Thomas Hardy.

Disappeared, as a shadow melting into air. — Hugo.

Disappeared like buttered crumpets. — Leigh Hunt.

Disappeared like a shot. — Miss Mulock.

Disappeared like print held too close to the eye. — Arthur Ransome.

Disappear,
Like dew late strewn through the
trembling grass.
— Hayden Sands.

Disappear — *continued.*

Appeared and disappeared like a succession of lightning flashes. — José Selgas.

Disappeared as if he had vanished in the air. — Ibid.

Disappear, as if it all had vanished through the sky. — Shelley.

Disappointing.

Disappointing as wet gun-powder. — Anon.

Discipline.

Discipline, like the bridle in the hand of a good rider, should exercise its influence without appearing to do so, should be ever active, both as a support and as a restraint, yet seem to lie easily in hand. It must always be ready to check or pull up, as occasion may require ; and only when the horse is a runaway should the action of the curb be perceptible. — Julius C. Hare.

Disconnected.

Disconnected as a dream. — Max Nordau.

Discontentment.

As for discontentments, they are in the politic body like to humors in the natural, which are apt to gather a preternatural heat and to inflame ; and let no prince measure the danger of them by this, whether they be just or unjust. — Bacon.

Discordant.

Discordant as the cries of a gull. — Daudet.

Discordant as croaking frogs. —Bonnell Thornton.

Discourse.

Themistocles said that a man's discourse was like to a rich Persian carpet, the beautiful figures and patterns of which can be shown only by spreading and extending it out ; when it is contracted and folded up, they are obscured and lost. — Plutarch.

Discover.

Men of great genius as easily discover one another as freemasons can. — Fielding.

Disease.

The disease and its medicine are like two factions in a besieged town; they tear one another to pieces, but both unite against their common enemy, nature. — Richard Jefferies.

Disguise.

Weakness ineffectually seeks to disguise itself, — like a drunken man trying to show how sober he is. — C. N. Bovée.

Disgust.

Disgust, as . . . she had touched a snake. — E. B. Browning.

Disgusting, like moving cheese. — Emerson.

With disgust . . . like one who draws out a hair from fresh butter. — Osmanli Proverb.

Dishevel.

As disheveled as any naturalist's wig. — Balzac.

Dishevell'd hair,
Like eagle's plumage ruffled by the air.
— James Montgomery.

Dishonest.

Dishonest as a gas meter. — Anon.

Dishonest as local elections. — Amy Leslie.

Dishonor.

Dishonor is like the Aaron's Beard in the hedgerows ; it can only poison if it is plucked. — Ouida.

Dismal.

Dismal as a hearse. — Nicolas Boileau.

Dismal as death. — Cleanthes.

Dismal — *continued.*

Dismal as a wet Derby day. — A. E. Housman.

Dismal as a mute at a funeral. — Thackeray.

Dismal as the month in which Christmas is celebrated. — Bonnell Thornton.

Dismissed.

Dismiss'd . . . as Jove fans off the clouds. — Keats.

Disordered.

His speech was like a tangled chain ; nothing impaired, but all disordered. — Shakespeare.

Disorderly.

Disorderly,
Like to a rancke of piles that pitched
are awry. — Spenser.

Dispel.

Dispelled, as the sun did the fog. — Anon.

Disperse.

Disperse
Like cloud-obstruction when a bolt
escapes. — Robert Browning.

Dispersed like smoke wreaths. — Hugo.

Dispersed, as by a tempest. — Johann L. Uhland.

Display.

Display is like shallow water, where you can see the muddy bottom. — Alphonse Karr.

Disposition.

The disposition is moulded in a happy manner by instruction, as the shapeless material assumes a beautiful form in the hands of a skilful artist. — Demophilus.

Disputant.

True disputants are like true sportsmen, their whole delight is in the pursuit ; and a disputant no more cares for the truth than the sportsman for the hare. — Pope.

Disrobed.

Disrobed, like a pure image in a secret shrine. — Charles L. Moore.

Dissembling.

Dissembling as the sea, that now wears brows as smooth as virgins' be, tempting the merchant to invade his face, and in an hour calls his billows up, and shoots 'em at the sun, destroying all he carries on him. — Beaumont and Fletcher.

Dissension.

Dissensions like small streams, at first
begun,
Scarce seen they rise, but gather as
they run. — Samuel Garth.

Dissimilar.

As dissimilar as the pure, white, gleaming lily of the hothouse is unlike the wind-tossed, sand-sustained, yellow leaf downtrodden in the mud. — Ouida.

Dissimilar as a trading town and a watering-place. — R. S. Surtees.

Dissipated.

Dissipated like fleecy clouds across summer skies. — Anon.

Dissolve.

Dissolved like a mimic castle of morning frost when the sun exerts himself. — Anon.

Dissolved like an unsubstantial pageant. — George Eliot.

Dissolved, like a fragment of ice that melts in the summer sea. — Henry Van Dyke.

Dissolve like smoke. — Verlaine.

Distant.

Distant as America from Atlantis. — Anon.

Distant — *continued.*

Keep their distances, as if they were Montagues and Capulets. — DRYDEN.

At a safe distance, like mother ducks watching their brood. — KIPLING.

Distant as the horizon sail. — GEORGE MEREDITH.

Distant as a dream's flight. — JOHN G. NEIHARDT.

Distant as the dead. — SCHILLER.

Distinct.

Distinct as a new map. — ANON.

Distinct as thunder-peals. — P. J. BAILEY.

Distinct as vice from virtue. — CHARLOTTE BRONTË.

Distinct . . . like a gong at midnight. — E. B. BROWNING.

Distinct and individual as a pebble. — DR. JOHNSON.

Distinct as the billows, yet one as the sea. — JAMES MONTGOMERY.

Distinguished.

The piece by Voltaire . . . distinguished itself from the surrounding pieces like a slab of compact polished stone in a floor rammed together out of ruinous old bricks, and broken bottles, and mortar dust. — CARLYLE.

Distort.

Distort one's features like a paralytic stroke. — BULWER-LYTTON.

Distress (Noun).

Distress is forever going about like soot in the air. — DICKENS.

Distress (Verb).

Distressing us like some bad banquet. — CARLYLE.

Distresses . . . like old men's thoughts of love's first kiss. — JOHN DAVIDSON.

Distrest
Like a poor bird — her plundered nest
Hovering around with dolorous moan.
— WORDSWORTH.

Distribute.

Napoleon . . . distributed himself about like the five loaves in the Gospel, commanded on the battlefield all day, and drew up his plans at night. — BALZAC.

Disturbed.

Disturbed like a wind-shaken anemone. — JAMES LANE ALLEN.

Disturbing.

Disturbing . . . like a tasteless ornament. — ANON.

Disturbing as an unopened telegram. — SYDNEY MUNDEN.

Dive.

Dive, like wild-fowl for salvation. — SAMUEL BUTLER.

Dive, like ducks. — THOMAS SHADWELL.

Dive, like buckets, in concealed wells. — SHAKESPEARE.

Diverge.

But with puberty divergence begins ; and, like the radii of a circle, we go further and further apart. — SCHOPENHAUER.

Diverse.

Diverse as are the soul and the body. — BUNYAN.

Divide.

Dividing like a splitting stick. — THOMAS HARDY.

Divide me like a bribe-buck, each a haunch. — SHAKESPEARE.

And flesh from bone divides without a
pang
As dew from flower-bell drips.
— SWINBURNE.

Divine.

Divine as dreams lit by fire of appeased desire which sounds the secret of all that seems. — SWINBURNE.

Divine as evening's death. — LORD DE TABLEY.

Dizzy.

Dizzy as a goose. — ANON.

Dizzy like one in an ill dream. — IBID.

Dizzy as a moth that flutters round the flame. — BOYESEN.

Dizzy, like a man in a dream falling from a height and enduring the anguish of falling. — EDMOND AND JULES DE GONCOURT.

Docile.

Docile as a lamb. — BALZAC.

Docile as a pet spaniel. — HAWTHORNE.

Docile as a managed horse. — WORDSWORTH.

Dodge.

Dodge like the Artful Dodger. — ANON.

Dodged and scrambled around like a woman who has lost her mind on account of the arrival of a bat. — MARK TWAIN.

Doleful.

Doleful as a bull-frog crossed in love. — ANON.

Doleful as a cavern-well. — COLERIDGE.

Dolorous.

Dolorous, like some starved shape that cowers in charnel crypt. — AUBREY DE VERE.

Domestic.

Domestic as the night. — ALFRED AUSTIN.

Domesticated as marmalade. — RICHARD LE GALLIENNE.

Domineering.

Domineering as Beelzebub. — JOHN W. DE FOREST.

Dote.

Dote more on it than a fool on his bauble. — ANON.

This sluggard dotes, it seems, on slumber, like an ass on oats. — HUGO.

Double (Adjective).

Double like Janus' face. — ANON.

Double (Verb).

Double up like a jack knife. — ANON.

Double up like a foot rule. — IBID.

Doubled like a hare. — SIR SAMUEL WHITE BAKER.

Doubt.

To my doubt I was,
As glass is to the color that invests it.
— DANTE (LONGFELLOW).

Doubtful.

Doubtful antecedent is as fatal to a pronoun as to sausage. — ARLO BATES.

Doubtful it stood ;
As two spent swimmers, that do cling together
And choke their art.
— SHAKESPEARE.

Down.

Gone down like grass before the scythe. — ANON.

His foot came down like the foot of Pantagruel. — IBID.

Went down like Mercury in a chilled thermometer. — IBID.

The ship went down like lead. — COLERIDGE.

From heaven down-cast
Like red leaves he swept away.
— LONGFELLOW.

Down, like a plummet. — SOUTHEY.

Down, like the hungry hawk. — M. E. STEBBINS.

Down — *continued.*

He shall come down like rain upon the mown grass: as showers that water the earth. — OLD TESTAMENT.

Downcast.

Downcast as a woman fearing blame. — WORDSWORTH.

Downfall.

Most people's downfalls are not dangerous; they are like children who have not far to fall, and can not injure themselves. — HUGO.

Down-Trodden.

Down-trodden, as the untimely fruit
Shook from the fig-tree by a sudden storm. — COLERIDGE.

Downward.

Grew downward like old women and cow's tail. — HOOD.

Downward like a powerless corse. — JOHN LEYDEN.

Wafted downward, like the painted leaves of Autumn. — LONGFELLOW.

Drag.

Drag along like a stage procession. — ANON.

Dragged out like a languishing concertina. — WILLIAM ARCHER.

Drag like lead. — DICKENS.

Dragged . . . like a lamb to a slaughter-house. — THOMAS HOLCROFT.

Dragged like a dove into the vulture's bed. — LYCOPHRON.

Like a wounded snake drags its slow length along. — POPE.

Drama.

(*See also* Theatre *and* Play.)

The chief difference between drugs and the drama, as habits, is the ease with which one breaks away from the latter. — CHANNING POLLOCK.

The drama, like the symphony, does not teach or prove anything. — JOHN M. SYNGE.

Drape.

Draped round her pallid brow like seaweed on a clam. — SWINBURNE.

Draws.

Draws as the moon draws the sea. — ANON.

Draws tears like an onion. — IBID.

As a torch doth oil, draws. — ROBERT BURTON.

Draws like enthusiasm. — RUTH PUTNAM.

Draws . . . like a loving kiss. — W. B. RANDS.

Dread.

Dread as doom. — ANON.

Dread like the Day of Doom's tick. — ROBERT BROWNING.

Dread as vague imaginings. — TUPPER.

Dreadful.

Dreadful as the parting hour. — ANNE BRONTË.

Dreadful as the storm. — CAMPBELL.

As dreadful as the Manichean god. — COWPER.

Dreadful as a gathering storm. — JOHN HAY.

Dreadful as the God of war. — HOMER.

The King is dreadful as the grim lion in the valley. — PENTAUR.

Dreadful, as hermit's dreams in haunted shades. — POPE.

Dreadful as battle arrayed. — FRANCIS THOMPSON.

Dreadfully.

Dreadfully, as if from realms of mystical despairs. — P. H. HAYNE.

Dream (Noun).

Dreams are like portraits; and we find they please because they are confessed resemblances. — GEORGE CRABBE.

Dream (Verb).

Dreaming, like one in mood of hope by
fancy spun,
Awaiting to be wooed, and willing to
be won. — H. S. SUTTON.

Dreamy.

Dreamy like the far-off chimes of angels' bells from out the highest heaven. — KINGSLEY.

Dreamy as music. — FRANCIS S. SALTUS.

Dreamy like dim skies. — SWINBURNE.

Dreary.

Dreary as an Asian steppe. — BALZAC.

Dreary, dull, and sad as Death. — ELIZA COOK.

Dreary as an empty house. — FLAUBERT.

Thou goest like a dromedary, dreary and drowsy. — JOHN HEYWOOD.

Dress.

As the index tells the contents of the book, and directs to the particular chapter, even so do the outward habit and garments, in man or woman, give us a taste of the spirit, and point to the eternal quality of the soul; and there cannot be a more evident and gross manifestation of poor, degenerate, dunghill blood and breeding, than a rude, unpolished, disordered, and slovenly outside. — MASSINGER.

Drift.

Drifting like flakes of snow. — ANON.

Drift . . . lightly as a leaf. — P. J. BAILEY.

Drifted, light-hearted and free, and proud, like the Bedouin. — STEEN S. BLICHER.

Weary drifting, driving like a helmless bark at sea. — ALICE CARY.

Drifts on the blast, like a wind-wafted
leaf,
O'er the gulfs of the desolate sea.
— O. W. HOLMES.

Drifting like a flake of fire
Rent by a whirlwind from a blazing
spire. — IBID.

Drifted like a scarlet feather
Torn from the folded wings of clouds.
— JEAN INGELOW.

Drifts like April snow. — AMY LESLIE.

The snows are driven and drifted,
Like Tithonus' beard
Streaming dishevelled and white.
— LONGFELLOW.

Drift as wrecks on the tide. — IBID.

Drifted as an unsteered log. — WILLIAM MORRIS.

Drifting,
As the sands on sea-shore shifting.
— ELLEN B. PECK.

Drifted
Like foam or sand
Past swamp and sallow.
— SWINBURNE.

Drift like satin moons. — OSCAR WILDE.

Drink (Noun).

Strong drinks are like wars, making cripples of some men, and sending others to the grave. — W. S. DOWNEY.

Drink (Verb).

Drink like a funnel. — ANON.

Drinks like a sieve. — IBID.

Drank like a Merman. — R. H. BARHAM.

Drink — *continued.*

Drink like a fish. — Beaumont and Fletcher.

As the drop feeds its fated flower,
As finds its Alp the snowy shower,
Child of the omnific Need,
Hurled into life to do a deed,
Man drinks the water, drinks the light.
— Emerson.

Drink . . . as wells drink in November, when it rains. — Longfellow.

I drank as earth imbibes the shower,
Or as the rainbow drinks the dew ;
As ocean quaffs the rivers up
Or flushing sun inhales the sea.
— Thomas Moore.

Drink like a templar knight. — Rabelais.

Drip.

Dripping like a laborer in a foundry. — Stephen Crane.

Dripping like a mermaid. — Hugo.

Dripping as if drowned. — Ramayana.

Drive.

Driving like a bedlamite. — Cumberland.

Drives him, like a lightning. — Homer (Pope).

Drive her foes from their savage job
As a mad black Bullock would scatter
a mob. — Hood.

Drives like rain to the roots. — George Meredith.

Drive like chaff before the blust'ring wind. — George Sandys.

Drive
Like mists before the blasts of dawn.
— Swinburne.

Drives out opposition, as the sun drives out the night. — S. G. Tallentyre.

Drove like a cataract. — Tennyson.

As smoke is driven away, so drive them away. — Old Testament.

The driving is like the driving of Jehu, the son of Nimshi ; for he driveth furiously. — Ibid.

Driven.

Driven as leaves in Autumn's blast. — Edward Octavus Flagg.

Driven, like flower-seeds by the four winds sown. — Fitz-Greene Halleck.

Driven forth like a sky-rocket. — Munchausen.

Headlong driven like clouds before the blast of heaven. — Ruskin.

Driven like chaff before the wind of heaven. — Sir Walter Scott.

Driven, like the alternations of an ever-changing wind over an Æolean lyre, which move it by their motion to ever-changing melody. — Shelley.

Driven . . . like leaves before the autumnal wind. — Southey.

Driven
As foam before the wind that wakes
With the all-awakening sun, and breaks
Strong ships that rue the mirth it makes
When grace to slay is given.
— Swinburne.

Driven like starlets down the wind. — James C. Woods.

Droll.

Droll as Eliezer who wrote three hundred volumes on sowing cucumbers. — Anon.

Drone.

Droned in sweetness like a fattened bee. — C. G. Rossetti.

Droningly.

Droningly . . . like the sigh of the bleak south wind through the forest, like the crash of the troubled sea as its waves retire from the beach, like the roar of the surging blaze in the closed furnace. — Virgil.

Droop.

Droops like a broken lily. — ANON.

Droop, like to bees belated in the rain. — ALFRED AUSTIN.

Shee droopeth in her minde,
As, nipt by an ungracious winde,
Dothe some faire lillye flowre.
— ENGLISH BALLAD.

Drooping like a falling blossom. — BALZAC.

She drooped like a lily bedewed in the valley. — PATRICK BRONTË.

Droop like wreaths of snow. — E. B. BROWNING.

Droop'd as the willow when no winds can breathe. — BYRON.

Droops like some unpitied flower that the rain-fall washes down. — ALICE CARY.

She drooped like a blossom bent by the wind. — EDMONDO DE AMICIS.

Droops, like a rose, surcharged with morning dew. — DRYDEN.

Drooping like plumes. — DUMAS, PÈRE.

The maidens droop, like meadow-grass when mown. — GOETHE.

Drooping like Hyacinthus beneath the blow of the quoit. — KINGSLEY.

Drooped like a lily tired
That lolls upon the stalk.
— KIPLING.

Drooping like a rose rain-laden. — MISS LANDON.

Drooped like a yacht with idle sails struck by a sudden blast, that dips them in the salt. — GEORGE MEREDITH.

Drooping like crystals in the gulf of time. — IBID.

Droops like a flower. — BARRY PAIN.

Droop like the trees in October. — JAMES PUCKLE.

Droop, like unfolded wings half spread for flight. — T. BUCHANAN READ.

Droop like a shower-beaten flower. — D. G. ROSSETTI.

Droops . . . like over-ripen'd corn
Hanging the head of Ceres' plenteous load. — SHAKESPEARE.

Drooping like honny dew. — SPENSER.

As a vine droops, when by divorce remov'd from the embraces of the elm she lov'd. — GEORGE STEPNEY.

Drooped
Like a flower in the frost.
— CELIA THAXTER.

Drooping like a dew-laden lily. — TUPPER.

Adroop like a rained-on fowl. — WHITTIER.

Drop.

Dropped, like Icarus, in mid-sky. — T. B. ALDRICH.

Drop him like a hot potato. — ANON.

Drops like a wounded lily. — IBID.

Drops like mercury on a cold day. — IBID.

Dropped off like a repleted leech. — IBID.

Drops like a plummet. — MATTHEW ARNOLD.

Dropt like a rose o'er-blown. — APHRA BEHN.

Dropped like a lily broke down by the hail. — LADY BARNARD.

Drop off like leaves in autumn. — ROBERT BLAIR.

Fluttering to the ground, dropped like a wounded bird. — MATHILDE BLIND.

Dropped . . . like a spent horse. — GEORGE H. BOKER.

Drop — *continued.*

Dropped heavily
As century follows century
Into the deep eternity.
— E. B. Browning.

Drop like shot. — Robert Browning.

Dropped as dead. — Aubrey De Vere.

Dropped like flakes, they dropped like stars, like petals from a rose. — Emily Dickinson.

Dropped like a flower cut down by the sickle. — Dumas, père.

The blood dropped out of her cheeks as the mercury drops from a broken barometer-tube, and she melted away from her seat as an image of snow. — O. W. Holmes.

Music drops like balm into the drowsy ear. — Mrs. E. C. Judson.

Drop like hours into eternity. — Keats.

The slow mists of the evening dropped,
Dropped as a cloth upon a dead man's face. — Kipling.

He dropped like a bullock. — Ibid.

Men dropped like partridges. — Ibid.

Drop, like mellow fruit . . . into the grave. — Charles Lamb.

Dropt from the zenith like a falling star. — Milton.

Dropped like a stone down through the deep sea. — Miss Mulock.

Dropped, as by a thunder-stroke. — Shakespeare.

Drop tears as fast as the Arabian trees
Their medicinal gum. — Ibid.

Droppeth as the gentle rain from heaven. — Ibid.

Drop as a leaf drops dead. — Swinburne.

Dropping like flies, devoured
By winter as if by fire, starved, frozen, blind,
Maimed, mad with torment, dying in hell. — Ibid.

Drought.

The drouth
Is like sand spread within my mouth.
— D. G. Rossetti.

Drowned.

Drowned like pigs when they attempt to swim. — Hood.

Drowned, as by the flood of Egypt. — Old Testament.

Drowsy.

Drowsy as the hum of a bag-pipe. — Anon.

Drowsy as the clicking of a clock. — Cowper.

Drowsy as . . . Andalusian Seville. — Henry T. Finck.

Drowsy voice, like murmur of a leafy sycamore. — Alexander Smith.

Drudge.

Drudge . . . like some blind tread-mill-horse. — Imre Madách.

Drum.

The steady drummer
Drumming like a noise in dreams.
— A. E. Houseman.

Drunk.

As drunk as a beggar. — Anon.

Drunk as a boiled owl. — Ibid.

Drunk as a bunghole. — Ibid.

Drunk as a piper. — Ibid.

Drunk as a tinker. — Ibid.

Drunk as a top. — Ibid.

Drunk as David's saw. — Ibid.

Drunk as blazes. — Ibid.

As drunk as three in a bed. — Ibid.

Drunk — *continued.*

Dronken . . . as a rat. — BORDE'S "BOKE OF KNOWLEDGE," 1542.

Drunk as a lord. — GEORGE COLMAN, THE YOUNGER.

Drunk as a porter. — NATHANIEL FIELD.

Drougen [drunk] as an ape. — JOHN GRANGE.

Drunk as fish. — BEN JONSON.

Drunk as Davy's sow on a frosty night. — KIPLING.

Drunk like Lot. — ANDREW MARVELL.

Drunk as a fiddler. — THE PURITAN.

Drunk as a wheel-barrow. — SAMUEL WESLEY.

Drunk as a beast. — WHITTIER.

Drunk as a drum. — "WOMEN'S PETITION AGAINST COFFEE."

Dry.

Dry as a London newspaper. — GEORGE ADE.

Dry as a bone. — ANON.

Dry as a prohibition fight in Vermont. — IBID.

Dry as a sponge. — IBID.

Dry as nuts. — IBID.

Dry as peanut shells. — IBID.

Dry as pith. —IBID.

Dry as tinder. — IBID.

Dry as soon as tears. — IBID.

Drye as clot of clay. — OLD ENGLISH BALLAD.

Dry as desert dust. — STOPFORD A. BROOKE.

Dry as a cinder. — JOSEPH CONRAD.

Dry as a chip. — DICKENS.

Dry as a lime-basket. — IBID.

Dry as the desert. — IBID.

Dry as granite. — DR. JOHN DORAN.

Dry as ashes. — GEORGE ELIOT.

Dry as an espalier vine in winter. — ANATOLE FRANCE.

Dry as the shell on the sand. — O. W. HOLMES.

Dried like a raisin. — CHARLES LAMB.

Dry as the leaves in winter. — W. S. LANDOR.

Dry as sand. — CHARLES G. LELAND.

Dry as a pond in the Summer. — LOVER.

Dry as the tomb. — ROBERT MACKAY.

Dry as flame. — OUIDA.

Dry as dust. — SHAKESPEARE.

Dry as the remainder biscuit after a voyage. — IBID.

Dry as tinder. — SMOLLETT.

Drying up like a brook when the woods have been cleared around. — BAYARD TAYLOR.

Dry as fossil truths. — THOREAU.

Dry and yellow as parchment. — HENRY VAN DYKE.

Drizzle.

Drizling like deawy rayne. — SPENSER.

Duck.

Duck as low as any barefoot friar. — MARLOWE.

Dug.

He now dug into the poor clergyman's heart, like a miner searching for gold ; or, rather, like a sexton delving into a grave, possibly in quest of a jewel that had been buried on the dead man's bosom, but likely to find nothing save mortality and corruption. — HAWTHORNE.

Dull.

Dull as a beetle. — ANON.

Dull as a convent. — IBID.

Dull as a Dutchman. — IBID.

As dull as a hoe. — IBID.

Dull as a post. — IBID.

Dull as a Quaker meeting. — IBID.

Dull as cloudy skies. — IBID.

Dull as mutes at a funeral. — IBID.

Dull as ditch water. — IBID.

As dull as the debates of Dutch burgomasters on cheese parings and candle ends. — IBID.

Dull as Lethe. — IBID.

Dull as a dormouse. — BEAUMONT AND FLETCHER.

Dull as the earth. — IBID.

Dull as sin. — S. LAMAN BLANCHARD.

Dull as lead. — ANNE BRONTË.

Dull as any London afternoon. — E. B. BROWNING.

Dull as an archdeacon. — G. K. CHESTERTON.

Dull as laudanum. — DICKENS.

Dull as an ox. — FIELDING.

With eyes as dull as smoky glass. — NORMAN GALE.

Dull as a post. — JOHN GAY.

Dull as a bachelor beaver. — SAM SLICK.

Dull as a boiled codfish. — IBID.

Dull as a whetstone. — ROBERT HEATH.

Dull as a pig of lead. — "HELP TO DISCOURSE."

Dull as a mud-flat. — MAURICE HEWLETT.

Dull as an alderman at church, or a fat lap-dog after dinner. — THOMAS HOLCROFT.

Dull as a donkey. — HOOD.

Dull as lead. — ANDREW LANG.

Dull as a tract. — GEORGE MEREDITH.

Dull as night. — SHAKESPEARE.

Duller than a great thaw. — IBID.

Dull as catalogues. — R. B. SHERIDAN.

Dull as a sheep. — ROBERT LOUIS STEVENSON.

Sound as dull as unstrung drum. — JAMES SULLY.

Dull as the dead fume of a fallen fire. — SWINBURNE.

Dark and dull like the mould upon a skull. — FRANK WATERS.

Dull as a platonic lover. — "WOMAN TURNED BULLY."

Dull as a country squire. — WILLIAM WYCHERLEY.

Dumb.

Dumb as Philomel. — ANACREON.

Dumb as an oyster. — ANON.

Dombe as any stoon. — CHAUCER.

Doumb as a tree. — IBID.

Dumb as a senator. — COWPER.

Dumb as death. — SYDNEY DOBELL.

Dumb as a fish. — BEN JONSON.

Dumb as the grave. — KEATS.

Dumb as pillar-posts. — GEORGE MEREDITH.

Dumb as a mouse. — ENGLISH PROVERB.

As dumb as a dead cuddy. — SCOTTISH PROVERB.

Dumb as a dream. — SWINBURNE.

Dumb and mighty, as a tree grows on a fruitful soil. — IVAN TURGENEV.

Dumps.

Her dismal dumps, like doleful Dido. — NICHOLAS ROWE.

Duped.

Duped, like a monkey cheated out of an empty nutshell. — DUMAS, PÈRE.

Durable.

Durable as the black of the negro. — ANON.

More durable than steel. — IBID.

Durable as yonder spheres. — COWPER.

Durable as eternity. — HAWTHORNE.

Durable as bronze. — HENRY JAMES.

Durable as manhood. — LAMARTINE.

Durable as the firmament. — WILLIAM MATHEWS.

Dusk.

Dusk as dying stars. — BAYARD TAYLOR.

Dwarfed.

Dwarfed . . . like starved plants under Greenland skies. — GEORGE MEREDITH.

Dwell.

Love's secret may dwell,
Like Zephyr asleep in
Some rosy sea-shell.
— THOMAS MOORE.

Dwindle.

Dwindling away like echoes down a valley of rocks. — THOMAS HARDY.

She dwindled, as the fair full moon
doth turn
To swift decay and burn
Her fire away. — C. G. ROSSETTI.

E

Eager.

Eager as a bridegroom. — ANON.

Eager . . . like a mettlesome hound,
Into the fray with a plunge and a
bound. — JOHN S. BLACKIE.

Eager as men, when haply they have
heard
Of some new songster, some gay-
feathered bird,
That hath o'er blue seas strayed in
hope to find
In our thin foliage here a summer
home,
Fain would they catch the bright
things in their mind,
And cage them into sonnets as they
come. — F. W. FABER.

Eager as a cry for life. — GEORGE MEREDITH.

Eager for it as a hound. — IBID.

Eager as greyhound on his game. — SIR WALTER SCOTT.

Eager as hunters in pursuing their prey. — IBID.

Eager as a ghoul for blood. — THACKERAY.

Eager as a fine-nosed Hound. — WORDSWORTH.

Ear.

The public ear is like a common ; there is not much to be got off it, but that little is for the most part grazed down by geese and donkeys. — SAMUEL BUTLER (1835–1902).

Her little ears were like rosy shells, — they had a pearl dangling from each of them. — WILKIE COLLINS.

Flapping ears like water-flags. — SWINBURNE.

Earnest.

Earnest . . . as sober Lanesbro' dancing with the gout. — ANON.

Earnest as a seer who invokes the dead. — BULWER-LYTTON.

Earnest — *continued.*

Earnest as bees. — LEIGH HUNT.

In earnest as a mouse in a trap. — GEORGE MEREDITH.

Earnest as life and hope. — DONALD G. MITCHELL.

As a guardian Muse thou art earnest. — BAYARD TAYLOR.

Earrings.

Earrings like chandeliers. — THACKERAY.

Earth.

The earth, like a fallen woman sitting in her dark chamber and trying to forget the past, seemed tormented with remembrances of the spring and summer, and waited in apathy the inexorable winter. — ANTON TCHEKHOV.

Ease.

Like a coy maiden, Ease, when courted most,
Furtherest retires — an idol, at whose shrine
Who oft'nest sacrifice are favour'd least. — COWPER.

He taught them love of toyle; toyle which does keep obstructions from the minde, and quench the blood; ease does belong to us like sleep, like opium in our medicine, not our food. — SIR WILLIAM DAVENANT.

As much at ease as a farmer on his own acres. — THEODORE ROOSEVELT.

At ease
As a flower of the springtime of corn.
— SWINBURNE.

Easy.

Easy as for a blackbird to whistle. — ANON.

Easy as a conjurer swallowing a poker. — IBID.

Easy as breathing. — IBID.

Easy as counting the blossoms on a century plant. — IBID.

As easy as finding reasons why other people should be patient. — IBID.

Easy as for a dog to lick a dish. — IBID.

Easy as getting money in a letter. — IBID.

Easy as peeling a hard boiled egg. — IBID.

Easy as pie. — IBID.

Easy as robbing a child's bank. — IBID.

Easy as to say "Jack Robinson." — IBID.

Easy as winking. — IBID.

Easy as an old shoe. — ROBERT BROWNING.

Shall be as easy as going down the river in a boat. — DANTE.

As easy as for you to take a drink. — JOHN DAVIDSON.

Easy, as blinding a chicken on the roost with a torch. — W. N. HARBEN.

Easy as forgetting oaths. — O. W. HOLMES.

Easy as swan could bear the snowy fleece. — HOMER (POPE).

As aisy as winter shakes leaves from the trees. — LOVER.

As easy as a man dyin' wi' due warnin'. — KIPLING.

Easy as for the grass to be green. — LOWELL.

Easy as kissing. — IBID.

Easy as loving. — IBID.

About as easy as to gather a bag of feathers thrown to the four winds. — SYDNEY MUNDEN.

With as much ease as the sun outshines and dims the stars with his meridian rays. — RABELAIS.

Easy as shelling peas. — CHARLES READE.

Easy — *continued.*

Easy as a down-bed. — SHAKESPEARE.

Easy as lying. — IBID.

Easy as to set dogs on sheep. — IBID.

Easy as thanks. — IBID.

For it is easier for a camel to go through a needle's eye, than for a rich man to enter into the kingdom of God. — NEW TESTAMENT.

With as much ease as whirlwinds move feathers. — IZAAK WALTON.

Easy as fitting a new harness to an old horse. — THOMAS WATSON.

Easily.

Flows as easily as California wine out of French bottles. — ANON.

As easily as an oak looseneth its golden leaves. — P. J. BAILEY.

Easily — as you'll go to bed. — BEAUMONT AND FLETCHER.

Easily as a nurse leads a docile child. — BULWER-LYTTON.

Easily as Hocus Pocus. — SAMUEL BUTLER.

Easily as eagles cleave the air. — MRS. SARAH HALE.

Pouring as easily as hour-glass sand. — KEATS.

Easily as one might wind a watch. — DONALD G. MITCHELL.

As easily as persuading a French aristocrat in the Revolution to get aboard the tumbril that was to land him at the guillotine. — LLOYD OSBOURNE.

Easily removable as a pair of spectacles from the nose. — RABELAIS.

Easily as the eagles soar. — SCHILLER.

Gluts her vengeance with his hated blood: easily as a hawk, the bird of augury, darting from a lofty rock, comes up with a dove high in the clouds, holds her in her gripe, and with crooked talons tears out her heart, while gore and plucked feathers come tumbling from the sky.— VIRGIL.

Eat.

Eat like a hog. — ANON.

Eat like a horse. — IBID.

Eats like rust. — IBID.

Eat like wolves. — IBID.

Eat like maggots into an estate. — CHARLES LAMB.

Eating, sharply as aqua-fortis into brass, into the metal of her vanity — and her pride. — OUIDA.

Eat up like fire the ashen autumn days. — SWINBURNE.

Eat as doth a canker. — NEW TESTAMENT.

Eat your flesh as it were fire. — IBID.

Eating.

As a lamp is choked with a multitude of oil, or a little fire with overmuch wood quite extinguished; so is the natural heat with immoderate eating strangled in the body. — ROBERT BURTON.

Ebb.

Ebb like the tides of a living heart. — P. H. HAYNE.

Ebb like hopes that wither. — SWINBURNE.

Eccentric.

Eccentric as comets. — DICKENS.

Moves eccentric, like a wandering star,
Whose motion's just, though 'tis not
regular. — DRYDEN.

Echo.

An echo is like a woman, always determined to have the last word. — JOSH BILLINGS.

Echoless.

Echoless, as ripe fruit on the ground unshaken. — E. B. Browning.

Ecstacy.

With ecstacy . . . like fathers that behold their infants crawl. — Hood.

Ecstatic.

Ecstatic and inviolate as the red glad mouth of morn. — Swinburne.

Education.

A human soul without education, like marble in the quarry, which shows none of its inherent beauties, till the skill of the polisher fetches out the colors. — Addison.

Education is, to its possessor, like a golden crown, in which honour is united with intrinsic worth. — Demophilus.

Eerie.

Eerie as a witch's ballad. — Amy Leslie.

Effect.

Produced as little effect as a flake falling on the glaciers of the high Alps. — Beaconsfield.

Effective.

As effective as Gibraltar under a fusillade of grapeshot. — Anon.

Effervescent.

Effervescent as a sulphur springs geyser. — Anon.

Effervescent as young wine. — Amy Leslie.

Efficient.

Efficient as a bear trap. — Warren H. Miller.

Effortless.

Effortless as stars awakening and melting out, at eve, and morning's breaking. — N. P. Willis.

Egotism.

There's nothing like egotism. It preserves a man as ice preserves meat. — Anon.

Elastic.

Elastic as a caterpillar. — Anon.

Elastic as all flesh. — Bulwer-Lytton.

Elastic as the gas of gunpowder. — Emerson.

Elasticity.

Capable of elasticity as a washed glove. — Anon.

Elate.

Elate as Heaven. — Swinburne.

Elegant.

Elegant as a Chesterfield. — Anon.

Elegant as a Tuscan. — Ibid.

Elegant as simplicity. — Cowper.

Eloquence.

Unprofitable eloquence is like the cypress ; great and tall but bears no fruit. — Anon.

Fierce bursts of eloquence like the wail of a clarion thrilling beneath the blasts of a storm. — Ibid.

False eloquence, big empty sound,
Like showers that rush upon the ground,
Little beneath the surface goes,
All streams along and muddy flows.
— Matthew Green.

Eloquence is an engine invented to manage and wield at will the fierce democracy, and, like medicine to the sick, is only employed in the paroxysms of a disordered state. — Montaigne.

Eloquent.

Eloquent as a rattlesnake's tail. — Anon.

Eloquent as Cicero. — Ibid.

Eloquent as angels. — C. C. Colton.

With her mouth she was eloquent,
As if to her ear an angel bent,
Whispering her that she might say
The word which wipes all tears away.
— D. G. Rossetti.

Elude.

Elude us like the echo of falling waters in a dream. — ANON.

Elude the grasp like an essence. — CHARLOTTE BRONTË.

Elusive.

As elusive as the pestilence that walketh in darkness. — ANON.

Elusive as quicksilver. — IBID.

Elusive as sheet lightning playing among June clouds. — JAMES HUNEKER.

Elusive as the sea-line far, and all the secret of the wind. — GEORGE STERLING.

Embrace.

In close embrace,
Like friends that, having liv'd far apart,
Meet and relieve in tears the joy-o'erburdened heart.
— WILLIAM TENNANT.

Emotion.

All loving emotions, like plants, shoot up most rapidly in the tempestuous atmosphere of life. — RICHTER.

Emphatic.

Emphatic as an oath. — GEORGE MOORE.

Empire.

A great empire, like a great cake, is most easily diminished at the edges. — FRANKLIN.

Emptier.

Emptier than a reed. — BOCCACCIO.

Empty.

Empty as a bird's nest in December. — ANON.

Empty as a politician's address to the people. — IBID.

Empty as a quill. — IBID.

Empty of expression as a squeezed sponge of water. — IBID.

Empty as Vanity Fair. — IBID.

Empty . . . like a shell dishabited. — T. E. BROWN.

Empty of religion, as the white of an egg is of savor. — BUNYAN.

Empty as shade. — C. C. COLTON.

Empty as a church on a week-day. — DAUDET.

Empty as a cobbler's curse. — THOMAS DERMODY.

As empty of ideas as an opera. — FIELDING.

Empty as an idiot's mind. — GEORGE CABOT LODGE.

Empty as space. — GUY DE MAUPASSANT.

Empty as air-pumps drain'd of air. — WILLIAM SHENSTONE.

Empty as a skull. — TENNYSON.

Empty as wind. — MRS. TROLLOPE.

Enchanting.

Enchanting as beauty weeping in her weeds. — WILLIAM WILKIE.

Enchased.

Walls enchased like chalices. — ROBERT NOEL.

Encircled.

Encircled him as a belt. — ANON.

Encumber.

Encumbering . . . like a circumambient Bedlam. — CARLYLE.

Encumbrance.

The encumbrances of his fortune were shaken from his mind, as dew drops from a lion's mane. — DR. JOHNSON.

Ends.

I was of late as petty to his ends,
As is the morn-dew on the myrtle leaf
To his grand sea. — SHAKESPEARE.

Enduring.

Enduring as marble. — ANON.

Enduring — *continued.*

Enduring as the stars. — ANON.

Enduring as eternity. — JOSEPH CONRAD.

As enduring as a camel. — KEATS.

Energy.

Energy, even like the biblical grain of mustard-seed, will remove mountains. — HOSEA BALLOU.

In energy . . . like unto the Sun. — MAHABHARATA.

Enfold.

Enfolds . . . like mist. — JOHN KEBLE.

Enlisting.

Enlisting in the United States navy to see the world is like going to the workhouse to learn broom-making. — ABE MARTIN.

Enlivening.

Enlivening as a sneeze. — HENRY BROOKE.

Enraged.

Enraged as the wild winds to reason deaf. — R. H. HORNE.

Enshrined.

Enshrined, as in a holy altar, under guard of consecrated keepers. — RICHARD CUMBERLAND.

Enslaved.

Enslaved as a spell. — PETRARCH.

Entangled.

Entangled like vines. — ANON.

Entangled in words as a bird in lime-twigs. The more he struggles the more belimed. — THOMAS HOBBES.

In her faire lookes were his thoughts intangled, like birds of canarie, that have fallen into a silken net. — LYLY.

Entangled . . . like a mouse catched in a trap. — RABELAIS.

Enthrall.

A nameless charm enthralling, like the ghost of music melting on a rainbow spray of sound. — P. H. HAYNE.

Enthusiasm.

Enthusiasm, like a bottle rid of the cork. — GEORGE MEREDITH.

Enthusiast.

The enthusiast has been compared to a man walking in a fog ; every thing immediately round him, or in contact with him, appears sufficiently clear and luminous ; but beyond the little circle, of which he himself is the centre, all is mist, error, and confusion. — C. C. COLTON.

Enticing.

Enticing as a riddle. — P. W. SHEDD.

Entrance.

Entrancing as the gardens in a fairy romance. — ANON.

Entrances like a siren. — IBID.

Entrance as young conquerors fresh from spoil. — P. J. BAILEY.

Enveloped.

Enveloped, like a martyr's robe of flames. — PRESCOTT.

Envious.

Envious people are disarmed by their own dispositions, as iron by rust. — ANTISTHENES.

Envious as a pretty woman is of another woman, as a banker is of another banker, as a political adversary is of a rival. — HAWTHORNE.

Envious as an old maid verging on the desperation of six and thirty. — R. B. SHERIDAN.

Envy.

As rust corrupts iron, so envy corrupts man. — ANTISTHENES.

Envy, like merit, doth its shade pursue. — IBID.

Envy — *continued.*

Envy lurks at the bottom of the human heart, like a viper in its hole. — BALZAC.

Envy, like the worm, never runs but to the fairest fruit; like a cunning bloodhound, it singles out the fattest deer in the flock. — FRANCIS BEAUMONT.

A rustinesse consumeth iron: So envie consumeth the envious man. — ANTHONIE FLETCHER'S "CERTAIN VERY PROPER AND PROFITABLE SIMILIES," 1595.

As a moth gnaws a garment, so doth envy consume a man. — SAINT CHRYSOSTOM.

Envy, like a cold prison, benumbs and stupefies; and, conscious of its own impatience, folds its arms in despair. — JEREMY COLLIER.

Pity and envy, like oil and vinegar, assimilate not. — C. C. COLTON.

Envy excels in exciting jealousy, as a rat draws the crocodile from its hole. — HUGO.

Envy, like a flame soars upward. — LYVY.

Envy, like flame, blackens that which is above it, and which it cannot reach. — J. PETIT-SENN.

Ephemeral.

Ephemeral as dew. — BLISS CARMAN.

Ephemeral, like Michael Angelo's snow statue. — RUSKIN.

Epigram.

Like a bee or an epigram, all his sting is in his tail. — THOMAS ADAMS.

Equal.

Equal as flowers in the field. — EDWIN MARKHAM.

Erect.

Erect as an Indian. — ANON.

Erect as a sunbeam, upspringeth the palm. — EMERSON.

Erect as a live hydra. — HUGO.

Erect as alders. — OVID.

Grow erect as the great pine grows. — E. R. SILL.

Erect, like pillars of the temple. — SOUTHEY.

Erratic.

Erratic as electrical phenomena. — BALZAC.

Erratic
As the strong star smiles that lets no
mourner mourn.
— SWINBURNE.

Error.

Errors, like straws, upon the surface
flow;
He who would search for pearls must
dive below. — DRYDEN.

Escape.

'Scape as did Arion on the Dolphin's back. — THOMAS HEYWOOD.

My soul escaped as a bird out of the snare of the fowlers: the snare is broken, and we are escaped. — OLD TESTAMENT.

Essential.

Essential as the dew. — EDNA P. C. HAYES.

As essential to the river as a fish. — HENRY D. THOREAU.

Established.

Established for ever as the moon. — OLD TESTAMENT.

Esteemed.

Esteemed as a minstrel at a feast. — GEORGE SANDYS.

Eternal.

Eternal as life. — ANON.

Eternal as the eternal God. — J. C. GUTHRIE.

Eternal — *continued.*

Eternal as is Sion. — HUGO.

Eternal as the peace of God. — HUGH McCULLOCH.

Ethereal.

Ethereal as the air. — CHARLES SANGSTER.

Ethereal, like a lovely ghost
Soft looming in the hazy distance
dreaming. — CELIA THAXTER.

Ethereal as the sensuous pallor of waxen candles. — G. VERE TYLER.

Evanescent.

More evanescent than the rainbow. — WILLIAM ARCHER.

So evanescent that it was like a shape made in water. — DICKENS.

Evanescent as the crimson flush that tints the daybreak. — MISS LANDON.

Events.

Events, like the pendulum of a clock, have swung forward and backward, but after all, man, like the hands, has gone steadily on. — R. G. INGERSOLL.

Everlasting.

Everlasting as the sun. — WILLIAM KING.

Everlasting as the voiceless hills. — CONDÉ B. PALLEN.

Evident.

Evident as Euclid's axioms. — ANON.

Evident,
As is the universal light of day.
— JOHN BANIM.

Evident as the sun at noon. — CARLYLE.

Evident as light in dark. — GEORGE MEREDITH.

Evil (Adjective).

Evil report, like the Italian stiletto, is an assassin's weapon, worthy only of the bravo. — MADAME DE MAINTENON.

Evil as treason. — SIR THOMAS MORE.

As the fishes that are taken in an evil net, and as the birds that are caught in the snare; so are the sons of men snared in an evil time, when it falleth suddenly upon them. — OLD TESTAMENT.

Evil (Noun).

Evils, like poisons, have their uses, and there are diseases which no other remedy can reach. — THOMAS PAINE.

Exact.

Exact as clock-work. — CARLYLE.

Exacting.

Exacting as a senior clerk. — BALZAC.

Exasperated.

Exasperated . . . like the huntsman's first distant halloo to a stag. — BALZAC.

Exceed.

As far exceed . . . as doth the flower the weed. — JOHN HEYWOOD.

Excel.

As the fair lawn excels the rushy mead,
As firs the thorn, and flow'rs the pois'-
nous weed. — RICHARD JAGO.

Then I saw that wisdom excelleth folly, as far as light excelleth darkness. — OLD TESTAMENT.

Excelling, as much as orient gold surmounteth brass. — WILLIAM THOMSON.

Exchequer.

The king's exchequer was like the spleen; for when that did swell, the whole body did pine. — TRAJAN.

Excite.

Exciting as a Quaker Meeting. — GEORGE ADE.

Excite him, as the donkeys on the green did Betsy Trotwood. — DICKENS.

Excrescence.

A little rounded excrescence like a steel wart. — IRVIN S. COBB.

Exhaustless.

Exhaustless as the ocean. — OUIDA.

Exhaustless as the choral founts of night. — T. BUCHANAN READ.

Expand.

Expanded like a flower under the sun. — ANON.

Expanding like the dawn. — JOHN DAVIDSON.

Expand, as tides that ebb, or tides that flow. — LORD DE TABLEY.

Expanded like the face of the sun when it mounts above the eastern hill. — JEREMY TAYLOR.

Expect.

Expectation, like a fiery steed, anticipates the course, and pants to hear the sprightly signal start him for the goal. — ROBERT JEPHSON.

Expensive.

Expensive as glory. — SYDNEY SMITH.

Experience.

It is costly wisdom that is bought by experience. We know by experience itself, that it is a marvelous pain, to find out but a short way by long wandering. And surely, he that would prove wise by experience, he may be witty indeed, but even like a swift runner, that runneth fast out of his way, and upon the night, he knoweth not whither. — ROGER ASCHAM.

Experience, like a pale musician, holds
A dulcimer of patience in his hand,
Whence harmonies, we cannot understand,
Of God's will in his worlds, the strain unfolds
In sad, perplexed minors : deadly colds
Fall on us while we hear, and countermand
Our sanguine heart back from the fancy-land
With nightingales in visionary words.
— E. B. BROWNING.

Human experience, like the stern lights of a ship at sea, too often illuminates only the path we have passed over. — COLERIDGE.

Expire.

Expired like the sound of a melancholy echo. — ANON.

Expired like hardy plants which lose their color and perfume when transplanted to a hot-house. — IBID.

Expiring like the deserted camp-fires of a retiring army. — GEORGE W. CURTIS.

Expire like an exhausted taper. — GOLDSMITH.

Doomed to expire like blossoms that ne'er see a second sun. — RACINE.

Exploded.

As exploded as the mysteries of Eleusis. — RICHARD LE GALLIENNE.

Expression.

True expression, like the unchanging sun,
Clears and improves whate'er it shines upon. — POPE.

Expressionless.

Expressionless as a cheese. — ANON.

Expressionless as a gravestone. — IBID.

Expressionless as a Sphinx's face. — IBID.

Expressive.

Expressive as the ridge of a cat's back. — ANON.

Exquisite.

Exquisite, like the heart of a wild rose. — ANON.

Exquisite in their mechanism as the motion of the planets. — JAMES HUNEKER.

Exquisite
Like fiery chrysoprase in deep basalt.
— D. G. ROSSETTI.

Exquisite — *continued.*

Exquisite as the coming of spring and quite as natural. — OSCAR WILDE.

Extended.

Extended, like home-bound cranes. — ANON.

Extended as the heavens. — VANBRUGH.

Extinct.

Extinct as the dodo. — ANON.

Extinck as th' bison. — FINLEY PETER DUNNE.

Extinguish.

Extinguished as stars by the rising sun. — ANON.

Extinguished like a taper's flame. — AMBROSE BIERCE.

Extinguished, like a flame that sinks down hopelessly among the late decaying embers. — HAWTHORNE.

Extinguish'd, like the vital spark in death. — HOOD.

Extortion.

Extortion is like a whirlpool, that swalloweth whatever it catches. — ANON.

Extravagance.

Extravagance is like a violent fire, that is no sooner stopped in one place than it breaks out in another. — VANBRUGH.

Exult.

Exulting like a conqueror. — JOSEPH CONRAD.

Exulted as the sunrise in its might. — SWINBURNE.

Eye.

My eyes like the wheels of a chariot roll around.—ÆSCHYLUS (E. B. BROWNING).

Her eyes were like a butterfly's gorgeous wings. — JAMES LANE ALLEN.

Eyes like mountain water that's flowing on a rock. — WILLIAM ALLINGHAM.

Dovelike eyes, depths as of heaven when charged with gloom. — ANON.

Eyes like burnt holes in a blanket. — IBID.

Eyes like saucers. — IBID.

Eyes transparent as a cloudless sky. — IBID.

Eyes, brilliant and humid like the reflection of stars in a well. — EDMONDO DE AMICIS.

Languishing eyes like those of a roe looking tenderly at her young. — AMRILKAIS.

Eyes like a hind's in love-time. — EDWIN ARNOLD.

Her sparkling eyes, like Orient pearles,
Did cast a heavenlye light.
— ENGLISH BALLAD.

His eyes, like those of a pitiless judge, seemed to go to the very bottom of all questions, to read all natures, all feelings and thoughts. — BALZAC.

Burning eyes that blaze through a lace veil, like flame through cannon smoke. — IBID.

These lovely lamps, these windows of the soul. — DU BARTAS.

Eyes like flames of sulphur. — BEAUMONT AND FLETCHER.

Eyes, like torches, fling their beams around. — IBID.

Blue violet, like Pandora's eye. — THOMAS L. BEDDOES.

Eyes glazed over like harebells wet with dew. — CAROLINE BOWLES.

Her eyes are bright as stars
In the blue.
— ROBERT BRIDGES (American).

Her sunken grey eyes, like reflections from the aspect of an angel. — CHARLOTTE BRONTË.

Eye — *continued.*

Her eyes are dark and humid,
Like the depth on depth of lustre hid
i' the harebell.
— Robert Browning.

With eyes, like fresh-blown thrush-eggs on a thread,
Faint-blue and loosely floating in his head. — Ibid.

Doubting eyes,
Like a child that never knew but love
Whom words of wrath surprise.
— E. B. Browning.

Shining eyes, like antique jewels set in Parian statue-stone. — Ibid.

Eyes like the summer's light blue sky. — Bulwer-Lytton.

Beautiful eyes in the face of a handsome woman are like eloquence to speech. — Ibid.

His eyes are like a balance, apt to propend each way, and to be weighed down with every wench's looks. — Robert Burton.

Eyes like the dawn of day. — F. A. Butler.

Brilliant eyes, swift-darting as the stars. — Carlyle.

Twin violets by a shady brook were like her eyes. — Alice Cary.

Eyes, shining like thin skins full of blood. — Ibid.

What a curious workmanship is that of the eye, which is in the body, as the sun in the world; set in the head as in a watch-tower, having the softest nerves for receiving the greater multitude of spirits necessary for the act of vision. — Stephen Charnock.

Those dry eyes of his shining more like poisoned stones than living tissue. — Joseph Conrad.

Expectant yellow eyes, like a cat watching the preparation of a saucer of milk. — Ibid.

Her eyes are sapphires set in snow. — Constable.

An eye like the polar star. — Eliza Cook.

O my love has an eye,
Like a star in the sky.
— Barry Cornwall.

Honest eyes . . . Blue like the tropic skies. — D'Annunzio.

Eyes, gleaming and sparkling like lizards' eyes in the crevices of old walls.— Daudet.

Her eyes grew bright and large,
Like springs rain-fed that dilate their marge. — Aubrey De Vere.

Her eyes, like stars in midnight waters glossed. — Ibid.

Her eyes are bright as beryl stones that in the tankard wink. — Austin Dobson.

Eyes like the morning. — Ibid.

Eyes like live coals. — Dumas, père.

Her eyes like shadows in the light of torches on the Mount of Doom. — Maurice Francis Egan.

Old men's eyes are like old men's memories, they are strongest for things a long way off. — George Eliot.

When a man speaks the truth in the spirit of truth, his eye is as clear as the heavens. When he has base ends, and speaks falsely, the eye is muddy, and sometimes asquint. — Emerson.

An eye can threaten like a loaded and levelled gun, or can insult like hissing or kicking; or, in its altered mood, by beams of kindness, it can make the heart dance with joy. — Ibid.

But oh, to see his solar eyes
Like meteors which chose their way
And rived the dark like a new day.
— Ibid.

Her eyes like the radiance the sunbeams bring. — Ancient Erse.

Eyes like the summer skies when twin stars beam above. — F. A. Fahy.

Eye — *continued.*

Eyes as azure as the wave. — VIOLET FANE.

Eyes like dark blue pansies. — NORMAN GALE.

Eyes as greye as glasse. — GEORGE GASCOIGNE.

A burning eye, yellow and phosphoric like the eye of a crocodile or a lion. — GAUTIER.

The most dazzling stars are pebbles without lustre beside the diamonds of her eyes. — JOSEPH A. DE GOBINEAU.

His eyes were like the eyes of doves when washed by the dews of the morning. — GOLDSMITH.

Mary with her cheerful eyes,
Like heartsease where a dew drop lies.
— EDMUND GOSSE.

Azure eyes, like stars upon the river's brink. — IBID.

Her eyes, fair eyes, like to the purest lights,
That animate the sun, or cheer the day ;
In whom the shining sunbeams brightly play,
Whiles fancy doth on them divine delights. — ROBERT GREENE.

Her eyes two twinkling stars in winter nights. — IBID.

Her eyes like glassy streams. — IBID.

The dame had eyes like lightning, or the flash
That runs before the hot report of thunder. — IBID.

Two eyes,
Like heaven's bright lamps in matchless beauty shining. — IBID.

His eyes were grey,
Like Titan in a Summer day.
— IBID.

Eyes like violets steep'd in dew. — J. C. GUTHRIE.

Her eyes, like moonbeams glowing. — HAFIZ.

Eyes that mock the diamond's blaze. — JOHN HARRINGTON.

Eyes like twin blue stars. — HEINRICH HEINE.

Ambiguous . . . blue eyes like the china dog on the mantel piece. — O. HENRY.

Eyes frosty blue, like a winter sea that is made bright, not warm, by the sun. — MAURICE HEWLETT.

Eyes like a hare's, that look sideways for danger. — IBID.

Eyes like stars, robed in dull red. — IBID.

Shrewd old party . . . eyes like gimlets. — HEADON HILL.

The lack-lustre eye, rayless as a Beacon street door-plate in August. — O. W. HOLMES.

An eye as clear and steady as the evening star. — IBID.

Eyes . . . mild as a gazelle's. — HOOD.

Brilliant eyes,
As deeply dark as desert skies.
— LAURENCE HOPE.

Dreaming, wistful eyes,
Dark and deep as mysterious skies,
Seen from a vessel at sea. — IBID.

Wistful eyes,
As luminous and tender as Kotri's twilight spies. — IBID.

His eyes . . . deep sunk beneath his lowering brows,
Like caverns by a moonlit sea.
— R. M. MILNES.

Eyes . . . overflow like two cups filled above the brim. — HUGO.

Sweet eyes . . . tender as the deeps in yonder skies. — JEAN INGELOW.

The sophist's eye,
Like a sharp spear, went through her utterly,
Keen, cruel, perceant, stinging.
— KEATS.

Eye — *continued.*

Eyes like two streams of liquid light. — Frances Anne Kemble.

Eyes like the dawn of day. — Ibid.

Her eye
Flames like a fresh caught hind's.
— Kingsley.

Eyes that droop like summer flowers. — Miss Landon.

Eyes like the flower that was Rousseau's delight. — Andrew Lang.

O lovely eyes of azure,
Clear as the waters of a brook that run
Limpid and laughing in the summer sun! — Longfellow.

I dislike an eye that twinkles like a star. Those only are beautiful which, like the planets, have a steady, lambent light — are luminous, but not sparkling. — Ibid.

Eyes dilated, as if the spirit-world were open before him, and some beauteous vision were standing there. — Ibid.

Like the stars that nightly shine,
Thy sweet eyes shed light divine.
— Lover.

Flaw-seeing eyes, like needle points. — Lowell.

Eyes pe[a]rcing like the Sun beames. — Lyly.

Blue eyes, like Delft saucers. — Maarten Maartens.

His eyes like meteors of night. — James Macpherson.

Bright eyes
Which were like lotus-blossoms.
— Mahabharata.

Eyes . . . like restless stars in the pit of night. — Edwin Markham.

Vacant eyes, blue as the flowers of the flax plant. — Guy de Maupassant.

Unfathomable eyes, which hid their secrets under the undisturbed serenity of majestic repose, like a mountain lake, whose waters seem black on account of their depth. — Ibid.

Her eye beams as kindly and bright,
As the sun in the azure-tinged sky.
— Catulle Mendès.

Blessed eyes, like a pair of suns,
Shine in the sphere of smiling.
— Thomas Middleton.

And the bright dew-bead on the bramble lies, like liquid upon beauty's eyes. — James Montgomery.

Eyes like setting planets, weak and dim. — Charles L. Moore.

Each bright eye,
Like violets after morning's shower,
The brighter for the tears gone by.
— Thomas Moore.

Eyes, whose sleepy lid like snow on violets lies. — Ibid.

Eyes as soft as doves. — Miss Mulock.

Eyes, like reflected moonbeams on a distant lake. — Ossian.

Eyes flashed like the sun playing on water. — Ouida.

Eyes like blue heavens in a night of frost. — Ibid.

Eyes shining like the planets. — Ibid.

Her eyes were of a deep brown hue, like the velvety brown of a stag's throat. — Ibid.

Her eyes are like free-booters, living upon the spoile of stragglers. — Sir Thomas Overbury.

Eyes like an orange-grove
In whose enchanted bowers the magic fire-flies rove. — Ibid.

What eyes! [Daniel Webster's] like charcoal fire in the bottom of a deep, dark well. — Theodore Parker.

Eyes blazed like a bale-fire. — John Payne.

Eye — *continued.*

Her black eyes sparkled like sunbeams on a river : a clear, deep, liquid radiance, the reflection of ethereal fire. — Thomas L. Peacock.

Eyes . . . stared like windows at the peep of day. — Stephen Phillips.

The eye, like a shattered mirror, multiplies the images of its sorrow. — Poe.

Luminous eyes,
Brightly expressive as the twins of
Leda. — Ibid.

The eye is the window of the soul; the mouth, the door ; the intellect, the will, are seen in the eye. — Hiram Powers.

The eyes are the pioneers that first announce the soft tale of love. — Propertius.

Eyes glittering like basilisks. — Charles Reade.

Her eye worked like an ice gimlet in her daughter's face. — Ibid.

Her eyes are blue and dewy as the glimmering Summer-dawn. — James Whitcomb Riley.

Eyes as fresh and clear as morning skies. — Ibid.

With a pair o' eyes like two fried eggs. — Ibid.

Her eyes are like the open heaven
Holy and pure from sin.
— C. G. Rossetti.

Dim dried eyes like an exhausted well. — Ibid.

Eyes
As of the sky and sea on a gray day.
— D. G. Rossetti.

Her eyes were deeper than the depth
Of waters stilled at even. — Ibid.

Her dazzling eye ;
As liquid in its brilliancy as the deep
blue of midnight ocean,
When underneath, with trembling
motion,
The phosphor light floats by.
— Ruskin.

Her eyes were like a heaven, where sunlight always glows. — A. J. Ryan.

His eyes like those that Houris wear. — Sadi.

Thine eyes
Mirage of sultry prisons, flashing in —
And out, like fulg'rous lightning
through dark skies.
— Francis S. Saltus.

As a moonbeam white,
As a starbeam white,
Was her eye of iris ray.
— Ibid.

An eye like Mars, to threaten and command. — Shakespeare.

Her eyes, as murder'd with the view,
Like stars ashamed of day, themselves
withdrew. — Ibid.

Thy eyes' windows fall,
Like death, when he shuts up the
day of life. — Ibid.

His eye
Red as 'twould burn Rome. — Ibid.

His eyes, like glow-worms, shine when he doth fret. — Ibid.

Her eyes, like marigolds, had sheath'd
their light,
And canopied in darkness sweetly lay,
Till they might open to adorn the day
— Ibid.

Eyes as fair
As star-beams among twilight trees.
— Shelley.

His faint eyes,
Like dew upon a sleeping flower.
— Ibid.

Thine eyes are like the deep, blue boundless heaven. — Ibid.

Eyes like kindling flame. — Lydia H. Sigourney.

Eye — *continued.*

In her hazel eyes her thoughts lay clear
As pebbles in a brook.
— ALEXANDER SMITH.

Her goodly eyes like sapphires shining bright. — SPENSER.

An eye is, for all the world, exactly like a cannon, in this respect, That it is not so much the eye or the cannon, in themselves, as it is the carriage of the eye, and the carriage of the cannon; by which both the one and the other are enabled to do so much execution. — STERNE.

An old light smolders in her eye.
There! she looks up. They grow and glow
Like mad laughs or a rhapsody
That flickers out in woe.
— TRUMBULL STICKNEY.

Eyes as glad as summer. — SWINBURNE.

Gold-eyed as the shore-flower shelterless
Whereon the sharp-breathed sea blows bitterness,
A storm-star that the seafarers of love
Strain their wind-wearied eyes for glimpses of. — IBID.

Your grave majestic eyes
Like a bird's warbled words
Speak, and sorrow dies.
— IBID.

Eyes,
Pale as the skies.
— ARTHUR SYMONS.

His threatening eyes
Like flaming torches burned.
— TASSO.

Eyes . . . clear as the unshadowed Grecian heaven. — BAYARD TAYLOR.

Like a blue spot in the sky
Was her clear and loving eye.
— SIR HENRY TAYLOR.

Eyes like heaven's own blue. — ESAIAS TEGNER.

His eyes are like the eyelids of the morning. — OLD TESTAMENT.

Thine eyes are like the fish-pools in Heshbon, by the gate of Bathrabbim. — IBID.

Eyes like unto a flame of fire. — IBID.

But woe's me, and woe's me,
For the secrets of her eyes!
In my visions fearfully
They are ever shown to be
As fringèd pools, whereof each lies
Pallid — dark beneath the skies
Of a night that is
But one blear necropolis.
And her eyes a little tremble, in the wind of her own sighs.
— FRANCIS THOMPSON.

Like pansies dark i' the June o' the year, grow my Love's glad eyes. — JAMES THOMSON.

Her eyes are like the statues, — mild, grave, and wide. — PAUL VERLAINE.

Eyes, dark and mysterious as Night's; but, like Night's own eyes, ready, I thought, to call up the throbbing fires of a million stars. — THEODORE WATTS-DUNTON.

Eyes flashing like sapphires. — IBID.

Eyes like English skies, where seemed to play
Deep azure dreams behind the tender grey. — IBID.

O deep eyes,
Darker and softer than the bluest dusk
Of August violets, darker and deeper
Like crystal fathomless lakes in summer moons. — AUGUSTA WEBSTER.

How brilliant and mirthful the light of her eye,
Like a star glancing out from the blue of the sky. — WHITTIER.

Eyes like a bright blue-bell. — ELLA WHEELER WILCOX.

Your eyes are like fantastic moons that shiver in some stagnant lake. — OSCAR WILDE.

Eye — *continued.*

Eyes half veiled . . .
Like bluest waters seen, through mists of rain. — OSCAR WILDE.

Blue eyes shimmer with angel glances
Like spring violets over the lea.
— CONSTANCE F. WOOLSON.

Her eyes as stars of twilight fair. — WORDSWORTH.

Eyes
Like the harebells bathed in dew.
— IBID.

Eyes like sunbeams. — JOHANN ZSCHOKKE.

Eyebrow.

Eyebrows like curved snow-drifts. — MAURICE HEWLETT.

Her eyebrows like a bent bow. — "VIKRAM AND THE VAMPIRE."

Eyeless.

Eyeless as old Destiny. — SHELLEY.

Eyelid.

Eyelids close
Calmly, as to a night's repose,
Like flowers at set of sun.
— FITZ-GREENE HALLECK.

F

Fabulous.

As fabulous as Aladdin's ring. — O W. HOLMES.

As fabulous as the immortality of the giants of mythology. — THOMAS PAINE.

Fabulous as Bucephalus or Black Bess. — THACKERAY.

Face.

His face is like a street before they lay the pavement. — ANON.

Thy face, like dawn when it lights the dawn. — ARABIAN NIGHTS.

Sweet youthful face, fair as the moon at full. — EDWIN ARNOLD.

His face looks like a warrant. — BEAUMONT AND FLETCHER.

A face that cannot smile is like a bud that cannot blossom which dries up in the stalk. — HENRY WARD BEECHER.

His face is fair as heaven. — WILLIAM BLAKE.

His face is like the pippin, grown red ripe in frosty suns that shone. — ARTHUR C. BENSON.

A sharp face, like a knife in a cleft stick. — E. B. BROWNING.

He had a face like a benediction. — CERVANTES.

That face of yours looks like the title-page of a whole volume of roguery. — COLLEY CIBBER.

His face looked like a face that had refused to jell and was about to run down on his clothes. — IRVIN S. COBB.

Face,
Long as a courtier's out of place.
— COLMAN.

Face like an ancient lemon.
— JOSEPH CONRAD.

A face like a smoked herring.
— ANATOLE FRANCE.

A face like the setting sun on a summer's day, when promise of a hot day to-morrow is read in its ruddy hue.
— F. C. GRIFFITH.

Face— *continued.*

Her little face is like a walnut shell
With wrinkling lines.
— W. E. Henley.

Face like a flame. — Maurice Hewlett.

Her face like roses blown,
And in the radiance and the hush,
Her thought was shown.
— Jean Ingelow.

A face that was like an open letter in a foreign tongue. — Henry James.

His face is like a squeezed orange. — Ben Jonson.

Her face was like the earthen pitcher of Gideon : it concealed the light. — George MacDonald.

His face was like the April morn
Clad in a wintry cloud.
— David Mallet.

A face, like nestling luxury of flowers. — Gerald Massey.

Her fair face half hid, like a ripe peeping rose. — Owen Meredith.

Her face is as white
As her pillow by night.
— Ibid.

She is hid away all but her face, and that's hung about with toys and devices, like the signe of a taverne, to draw strangers. — Sir Thomas Overbury.

Faces did glister like the key-hole of a powdering-tub. — Rabelais.

A face open as day.— Rogers.

Thy face is like the full moon of heaven, allied to light, but far from my hopes. — "Romance of Antar."

Her own face was like a flower
Of the prime,
Half in sunshine, half in shower,
In the year's most tender time.
— C. G. Rossetti.

Her face was like an opening rose,
So bright to look upon :
But now it is like fallen snows,
As cold, as dead, as wan.
— Ibid.

Faces are as legible as books, with this difference in their favor, that they may be perused in much less time than printed pages, and are less liable to be misunderstood. — Frederic Saunders.

'Tis not that she paints so ill but, when she has finished her face, she joins so badly to her neck, that she looks like a mended statue, in which the connoisseur may see at once that the head is modern, though the trunk's antique.
— R. B. Sheridan.

Her face was like a lily hidden in holy dusks. — George Sterling.

Her face was like the Milky Way i' the sky,
A meeting of gentle lights without a name. — Sir John Suckling.

Thy face
Was as a water's wearied with wind.
— Swinburne.

His face was as the must that lies upon a vat of new-made wine. — Oscar Wilde.

Factions.

These factions amongst great men, they are like
Foxes, when their heads are divided,
They carry fire in their tails, and all the country,
About them goes to wreck for't.
— John Webster.

Fade.

Fade as a passing breath. — Gilbert Abbott À Beckett.

Faded as the iris after rain in April's tearful weather. — Anon.

Fades as the splendor fades from the sky, when the sun sinks to sleep. — Ibid.

Fade — *continued.*

He faded away like a pound of soap in a hard day's wash. — ANON.

Fade away like some fabled city of mythology. — IBID.

Fade like autumn leaves, and fade and die
With no kind hand to raise the head and gently close the dying eye.
— IBID.

Fade . . . like ghosts prohibited the day. — IBID.

Faded like snow. — IBID.

Faded like the morn. — ARABIAN NIGHTS.

Fades like an unfixed photograph. — WILLIAM ARCHER.

Fade like grass. — MATTHEW ARNOLD.

Fades awa' like morning dew. — SCOTTISH BALLAD.

Fade away like morning beauty from her mortal day. — WILLIAM BLAKE.

As flowers kept too long in the shade . . . fade. — E. B. BROWNING.

Fading like moonlight softly into darkness. — ROBERT BUCHANAN.

Beauty fades as a tree in winter. — ROBERT BURTON.

Fade like stars before the sun. — CAMPBELL.

Fade away like a Vesture. — CARLYLE.

Faded . . . like the mist of a breath on a mirror. — JOSEPH CONRAD.

Fade like morning's blush. — ELIZA COOK.

Fades like the rainbow's brilliant arch. — IBID.

Fades
Like the fair flow'r dishevell'd in the wind. — COWPER.

A beauty fading like the April show'rs. — WILLIAM DRUMMOND.

Fade away like a cloud and vanish. — FROUDE.

Fading, like a morning dream. — GERALD GRIFFIN.

Fades as a kiss on lips of light. — FRANK W. GUNSAULUS.

Fading away, like a pale English flower, in the shadow of the forest. — HAWTHORNE.

Faded like a dream of youth. — O. W. HOLMES.

Faded . . . like dew upon the sea. — IBID.

Fade like the roseate flush, the golden glow,
When the bright curtain of the day is rolled. — IBID.

Fade unspoken,
Like daffodils that die with sheaths unbroken. — IBID.

Fades like an old faith grown gray. — BRIAN HOOKER.

Fade away like the pale sister of the night,
When she resigns her delighted light,
Lost in the blaze of day.
— JOHN HUGHES.

Faded from me like a dream. — HUGO.

Fade like an August marigold. — JEAN INGELOW.

Fade,
As shadows passing into deeper shade.
— LONGFELLOW.

Faded slowly from the sight as blushes from the cheek. — IBID.

Fade away like a thin vapory cloud. LORD LYTTELTON.

Faded like some rich raiment worn of old. — ROSAMUND MARRIOTT WATSON.

Is all faded, like fragrance,
From the languishing late flowers.
— OWEN MEREDITH.

Fade — *continued.*

Fading . . . like a lingering star
That pales at sunrise in the waters of
light. — LLOYD MIFFLIN.

Fades like a funeral lay. — THOMAS MOORE.

Fades like a once-heard tale. — LEWIS MORRIS.

Fades like sunset flame. — CONSTANCE C. W. NADEN.

Fading like a ghost
At gray cock-crow.
— JOHN G. NEIHARDT.

How fading are the joys we dote upon!
Like apparitions seen and gone.
— JOHN NORRIS.

Faded away like a woodcock leaves a weasel. — EDWARD PEPLE.

Faded like a wreath of mist at eve. — GEORGE D. PRENTICE.

Fade . . . like a nightmare's ghastly presence, in the truthful dawn of day. — ADELAIDE A. PROCTER.

Fade as a flower in May. — R. PYNSON.

Fade like the gowans in May. — ALLAN RAMSAY.

Fade . . .
Like stars half quenched in mists of
silver dew. — SHELLEY.

Fade like vapor. — IBID.

Fade, like the hopes of youth. — SOUTHEY.

Fade like to a flowre that feeles no heate of sunne. — SPENSER.

Faded, as fields that withering winds leave dry. — SWINBURNE.

Fade like flame. — IBID.

Fade as leaves when the woods wax hoary. — IBID.

We all do fade as a leaf. — OLD TESTAMENT.

Fading as hearts forget, as shadows flee. — F. O. TICKNOR.

Fade

As placidly as when an infant dies.
— THOMAS WARD.

Fade, like waves breaking on a dreary shore. — JOHN WILSON.

Fades like the lustre of an evening cloud. — WORDSWORTH.

Fail.

Failed

Like a brief dream of unremaining
glory. — SHELLEY.

Failing like an unreplenished stream. — IBID.

Fail like the trances of the summer air. — IBID.

Fain.

Fain of the wild glad weather
As famine is fain of feast.
— SWINBURNE.

Faint.

Faint as the hum of distant bees. — ANON.

Fainter than scent of soever long-kept lavender. — MAX BEERBOHM.

Faint . . . like a lost star. — ROBERT BROWNING.

Faint as a waft from years
Long past.
— HELEN G. CONE.

As faint and helpless as a new-born babe. — LORD DE TABLEY.

Faint as the music that in dreams we hear. — MARY A. DE VERE.

I hear their cry afar
Faint like the death-song of a fallen
star. — ARTURO GRAF.

Faint as the dim ghost of a dream-sea. — RICHARD HOVEY.

Faint as the light of stars and wan. — JEAN INGELOW.

Faint as a glimmering taper's wasted light. — SIR WILLIAM JONES.

Faint as the visions in a dream. — KIPLING.

Faint — *continued.*

Faint as the Spring. — OWEN MEREDITH.

Faint . . . like chimings from some far-off tower. — AGNES C. MITCHELL.

A faint strain,
As if some echo, that among
Those minstrel halls had slumber'd long,
Were murm'ring into life again.
— THOMAS MOORE.

Faint and forlorn . . . like the breath of a spirit sighing. — MRS. NORTON.

Faint as the voice of the telephone. — MORGAN ROBERTSON.

Faint as shed flowers. — D. G. ROSSETTI.

Faint . . . as the wavering flame of spirits of wine. — W. CLARK RUSSELL.

Faint, like distant clarion feebly blown. — SIR WALTER SCOTT.

Faint as the far-off clouds of evening. — SOUTHEY.

Faint as the moonlight that rests upon your sleep, or the first glow of dawn that wakes you to new endeavor. — SUDERMANN.

Faint as the moon if the sundawn gleam. — SWINBURNE.

Faint as the shadows of ages
That sunder their season and ours.
— IBID.

Faints like a dazzled morning moon. — TENNYSON.

Faint as half-forgotten dreams. — FRANK WATERS.

Fainter than a young lamb's bleat. — WILLIAM B. YEATS.

Faintly.

Glimmering faintly like the rack of the moon in her own light cast back. — E. B. BROWNING.

Like a pale moon in vapor, faintly bright. — JOHN DYER.

Faintly as tolls the evening chime. — THOMAS MOORE.

Faintly, like falling dew. — FREDERICK TENNYSON.

Fair.

Fair as virtuous friendship : as the candid blush of him who strives with fortune to be just. — AKENSIDE.

Fair as Esther. — ANON.

Fair as a friar that is invited to dinner. — IBID.

Fair as a saint. — IBID.

Fairer than fancy ever feigned. — IBID.

Fair as Lady Dove. — IBID.

Fair as stars that shine in summer skies. — IBID.

Fair as the garden of Shiraz. — IBID.

Fair as the glorified isles of the blest. — IBID.

Mary is fair as the morning dew. — IBID.

Fair as the virgin's vows. — IBID.

Fair as the wild rose. — IBID.

Fair as winter lilies. — IBID.

Fair as youths by brides caress'd. — IBID.

As fair as summer roses. — THOMAS ASHE.

Fair as lotus when the morn kisses its opening petals red. — ANCIENT BALLAD OF HINDUSTAN.

Fair as the cup of a lily held in a maiden's hand. — EUGENE BARRY.

Fair as the floweret opening on the morn. — BEATTIE.

Fair as the bud unblasted. — BEAUMONT AND FLETCHER.

Fair — *continued.*

Fair as the morn. — MICHAEL BRUCE.

Fair as the hills of Paradise. — WILLIAM CULLEN BRYANT.

Fair as pearls. — GOTTFRIED A. BÜRGER.

As fair a thing as e'er was form'd of clay. — BYRON.

Fair as the crowning rose of the whole wreath. — IBID.

Fair, as the first that fell of womankind. — IBID.

Fair as the forest. — ALICE CARY.

Fair as Ambition's dream, or Beauty's face. — THOMAS CHATTERTON.

Faire as is the bryghte morwe [morning]. — CHAUCER.

Faire as is the rose in May. — IBID.

Fair as Eden's bowers. — COLERIDGE.

Fair, as the bosom of the swan. — IBID.

Fair withal, as spirits are. — IBID.

Fair as any goddess who sweeps through the Ivory Gate. — MORTIMER COLLINS.

As fair as truth. — BARRY CORNWALL.

Fair as cygnet's down. — NATHANIEL COTTON.

Fair as light in heaven, or flowers in spring. — ALLAN CUNNINGHAM.

Fair as Spenser's dream. — SYDNEY DOBELL.

Fair as those old fields we knew. — IBID.

Fair as a sculptor's marble dream. — JULIA C. R. DORR.

Fair as the morning's snow. — ANCIENT ERSE.

As honor fair. — FALCONER.

As Cynthia fair. — FRANCIS FAWKES.

Fair . . . as all the flowers of May. — IBID.

Fair as the flowers themselves. — JOHN FLETCHER.

Fair as Aurora. — ALICE A. FOLGER.

A face as fair as summer skies,
Where many a blush in ambush lies.
— H. B. FREEMAN.

Fair as a young maid asleep beneath new fallen snow. — GAUTIER.

Fair as the dawn in the spring time. — GIACOSA AND ILLICA.

Fair as Paphos' brooks. — ROBERT GREENE.

Fair as Helen, Sparta's pride. — ARTHUR GUITERMAN.

Fair as the Spring. — WALTER HARTE.

Fair as the summer's evening skies. — IBID.

Fair she is as foam-born Venus. — HEINRICH HEINE.

Fair, Lady Mary, as the lily in the sun. — HENRY ALFORD.

Fair as Eve in Paradise. — ROBERT HERRICK.

Fair as a god. — HOMER (POPE).

Fair as the new-born star that gilds the morn. — IBID.

Fair is she as the dreams young poets weave. — HOOD.

Fair as the wave-bleached lily of the stream. — IBID.

Fair . . . as the spotless moon upon the midnight sea. — HORACE.

She as fair as any shepherdess
That ever was in mask or Christmas
scene. — W. D. HOWELLS.

Fair as a woodland flower. — MARY JOHNSTON.

Fair — *continued.*

Fair as some wonder out of fairy land. — KEATS.

Fairer than Phœbe's sapphire-region'd star. — IBID.

As fair,
As Sion in her height of pride.
— JOHN KEBLE.

Fair as a flower, and faded just as soon. — OMAR KHAYYAM.

Fair as the sun. — KINGSLEY.

Fair as bar of gold. — KIPLING.

Fair as Aphrodite rising from the deep-blue Grecian sea. — SIGMUND KRASINSKI.

Fair as the moonlight. — MISS LANDON.

Fair as original light first from the chaos shot. — RICHARD LOVELACE.

You're fair and fresh as a morning in May. — LOVER.

Fair as the garden of God. — LORD LYTTELTON.

Fair as bride to altar lead. — EVAN MACCOLL.

Fair as a Seraph. — GEORGE MAC-HENRY.

Fair as the whitest snow on Scythian hills. — MARLOWE.

O, thou art fairer than the evening air,
Clad in the beauty of a thousand stars.
— IBID.

Fair as the spirit of the evening star. — GERALD MASSEY.

Fair as dreams. — OWEN MEREDITH.

She is fair as the spirit of light,
That floats in the ether on high.
— ADAM MICKIEWICZ.

Fair as flame. — R. M. MILNES.

Fair as the noon sky. — MILTON.

Fair as Orion. — JAMES MONTGOMERY.

Fair as the rainbow shines through darkening showers. — IBID.

Fair as the Moon's unclouded light. — EDWARD MOORE.

Your face is as fair and bright
As the foam on the wave in the morning light. — LEWIS MORRIS.

Fair as the lightning thwart the sky,
As sun-dyed snow upon the high
Untrodden heaps of threatening stone
The eagle looks upon alone.
— WILLIAM MORRIS.

Fair as an angel from the unknown land. — MISS MULOCK.

She is as fair as a peach. — MILES O'REILLY.

Fair he was, like the rainbow of heaven. — OSSIAN.

Fair as the summer-beauty of the fields. — OTWAY.

Fairer than snow on the raven's back. — IBID.

Fair as youth and love. — J. N. PATON.

Fair as a musk-willow forest. — PERSIAN.

Fair like the rose, 'midst paling flowers the queen. — PETRARCH.

As the opening blossom fair. — MATTHEW PRIOR.

Fair, like goddesses. — RABELAIS.

A face as fair as the summer dawn. — JAMES WHITCOMB RILEY.

Fine and fair as your school-boy sweetheart's hair. — IBID.

Fair as a bridal chamber. — C. G. ROSSETTI.

Fair thou art as moonrise after rain. — IBID.

Fair as the flowers that maidens pluck for an hour's delight. — D. G. ROSSETTI.

Maiden fair as a silvery dream. — FRANCIS S. SALTUS.

Fair — *continued.*

Fair as the summer. — HAYDEN SANDS.

Fair as the earliest beam of eastern light. — SIR WALTER SCOTT.

Fair as any mother's child. — SHAKESPEARE.

Fair as day. — IBID.

Fair as text B in a copy-book. — IBID.

Her face as fair as tho' she had look'd on Paradise, and caught its early beauty. — ANON.

Fair as breathing marble.— SHELLEY.

Eyes as fair as star-beams among twilight trees. — IBID.

Fair as the fabulous asphodels. — IBID.

Fairer than any wakened eyes behold. — IBID.

Fair, like stars when the moon is awakened. — IBID.

Like great god Saturne faire. — SIR PHILIP SIDNEY.

As fair as the first beams of the morning. — ROUMANIAN SONG.

Faire as Phœbus sunne. — SPENSER.

Fair as a fairy. — SWINBURNE.

Fair as a field in flower. — IBID.

Fair as all that the world may call most fair, save only the sea's own face. — IBID.

Fair as any poison-flower
Whose blossom blights the withering
bower
Whereon its blasting breath has power.
— IBID.

Fair as a star-shaped flower. — IBID.

Fair as dawn. — IBID.

Fair as dreams that die and know not what they were. — IBID.

Fair as even the wakening skies. — IBID.

Fair as flame. — IBID.

Fair as fled foam. — IBID.

Fair as heaven in spring. — IBID.

Fair as hope divines. — IBID.

Fair as life. — IBID.

Fair as peace. — IBID.

Clean and fair
As sunlight and the flowerful air.
— IBID.

Fair as the ambient gold of wallflowers. — IBID.

Fair as the eyes are fair. — IBID.

Fair as the face of the star-clothed night. — IBID.

Fair as the frondage each fleet year sees fade. — IBID.

Fair as the morning. — IBID.

Fair as the sunbright air. — IBID.

Fair as the sundawn's flame
Seen when May on her first-born day
bids earth exult in her radiant
name. — IBID.

Fair as the world's old faith of flowers. — IBID.

Fair as thine eye's beam
Hidden and shown in heaven.
— IBID.

Fair as thought could dream. — IBID.

Fair as youth. — IBID.

Fair as some Arcadian dell. — BAYARD TAYLOR.

Fair as the last star that leaves the morning air. — IBID.

Fair as the loveliest landscape of pastoral England. — IBID.

Fairer than Rachel by the palmy well,
Fairer than Ruth among the fields of
corn. — TENNYSON.

Fair as the moon. — OLD TESTAMENT.

Fair — *continued.*

Fair as the daughters of Job. — Old Testament.

Fair as lily leaves. — J. T. Trowbridge.

Fair as the day that bodes as fair a morrow. — August Von Platen.

Fair as a statue of marble. — Michael Vörösmarty.

Fair as a gorgeous fabric of the East. — Ibid.

Fair as the primrose mead, or blushing rose. — Thomas Warton.

Fair as in Mirza's Bagdad dream. — Whittier.

Fair
As Pison was to Eden's pair.
— Ibid.

Fairer than the day, or the flowery meads in May. — George Withers.

Fair as a star, when only one
Is shining in the sky.
— Wordsworth.

Fair as beams of light. — Thomas Yalden.

Faith.

Faith without works is like a bird without wings; though she may hop with her companions on earth, yet she will never fly with them to heaven; but when both are joined together, then doth the soul mount up to her eternal rest. — Francis Beaumont.

Faith, like the phœnix, soars and sings. — Richard Le Gallienne.

Faith, like light, should ever be simple and unbending. — Martin Luther.

Faith, like the itch, is catching. — Luigi Pulci.

Faith is like a lily lifted high and white. — C. G. Rossetti.

Faith, amid the disorders of a sinful life, is like the lamp burning in an ancient tomb. — Madame Swetchine.

Faithful.

Faithful as dog, the lonely shepherd's pride. — Æschylus.

Faithful as a good book. — Anon.

Faithful as the planets. — Ibid.

Faithful as wax to one settled impression. — Bulwer-Lytton.

Faithful as the sun in the heavens. — James R. Gilmore.

Faithful as the knee-joint to its socket. — Arthur Guiterman.

Faithful as the eagle to the sun, as is the steel unto the magnet. — Hugo.

Faithful as the hands of a clock to the springs. — George Meredith.

Faithful as the star is to the night. — T. Buchanan Read.

Faithful, from day to day,
As Hesperus, that leads the sun his way.
— Tasso.

Faithful as the sun. — Henry Vaughan.

Faithless.

Faithless as fair weather. — Anon.

Faithless . . . as the winds. — Aphra Behn.

Fall.

(*See also* fell.)

Sweet-falling as the evening dew. — Anon.

Fall like a thousand of brick.— Ibid.

Falling like Sierra's April flood that pours in ponderous cadence from the cliff. — Ibid.

Falls like the leaves in October. — Ibid.

Falling like the tower Siloam. —Ibid.

Fall like small birds beaten by the storm against a dead wall, dead. — P. J. Bailey.

Falling . . . softly as a snowflake. — Ibid.

Fall — *continued.*

Falling like a bolt out of the blue. — CARLYLE.

Falls and risings, like a swan upon waving water. — COLLEY CIBBER.

Fall, like the autumn-kissed leaf. — PAUL LAURENCE DUNBAR.

Fall on me like a silent dew,
Or like those maiden showers,
Which by the peep of day, do strew
A baptism o'er the flowers.
— HERRICK.

Like a leaf that quits the bough,
The mortal vesture falls.
— O. W. HOLMES.

Like a city without walls, the grandeur of the mortal falls who glories in his strength and makes not God his trust. — MACAULAY.

They fall away, like the flower on which the sun hath looked in his strength. — JAMES MACPHERSON.

He falls like an oak on the plain ; like a rock from the shaggy hill. — IBID.

Falls like some baffled thing. — ARTHUR W. E. O'SHAUGHNESSY.

Falling soft as snow on snow. — F. T. PALGRAVE.

Falling as gently as an answer to a prayer. — ADELAIDE A. PROCTER.

Falls like Lucifer,
Never to hope again.
— SHAKESPEARE.

Fall as a slaughtered beast headless. — SWINBURNE.

Fallen as leaves by the storms in their season thinned. — IBID.

Softer falls
Than petals from blown roses on the grass. — TENNYSON.

They fall like grass before the mower. — THACKERAY.

Fall off, like leaves from a withered tree. — VOLTAIRE.

False.

False as a man with a black head and a red beard. — ANON.

False as Dick's hatband. — IBID.

False friendship, like the ivy, decays and ruins the walls it embraces ; but true friendship gives new life and animation to the object it supports. — ROBERT BURTON.

False as suborn'd perjurers. — SAMUEL BUTLER.

False as the father of lies. — G. K. CHESTERTON.

False and fair-foliaged as the manchineel. — COLERIDGE.

False as a bulletin. — NAPOLEON.

False as the adulterate promises of favorites in power when poor men court them. — OTWAY.

False as the wind, the waters, and the weather. — IBID.

False as God is true.
— THOMAS PAINE.

False eloquence, like the prismatic glass,
Its gaudy colors spread on ev'ry place.
— POPE.

As false as Waghorn, and he was nineteen times falser than the deil. — SCOTTISH PROVERB.

False as an obituary. — EDGAR SALTUS.

False as dice. — SHAKESPEARE.

False as dicers' oaths. — IBID.

False as hell. — IBID.

False
As stairs of sand.
— IBID.

False as water. — IBID.

False . . . as wolf to heifer's calf. — IBID.

False as the fowler's artful snare. — SMOLLETT.

False and foul as fear. — SWINBURNE.

Falsehood.

Falsehood, like a nettle, stings those who meddle with it. — ANON.

A mixture of falsehood is like alloy in coin of gold and silver, which may make the metal work the better, but it embaseth it. — BACON.

Falsehood, like a drawing in perspective, will not bear to be examined in every point of view, because it is a good imitation of truth, as a perspective is of the reality, only in one. — C. C. COLTON.

Falsehoods, like weeds, flourish without care. Weeds care nothing for soil or rain. They not only ask no help, but they almost defy destruction. — R. G. INGERSOLL.

To tell a falsehood is like the cut of a sabre: for though the wound may heal, the scar of it will remain. — SADI.

Falsehood, like the dry-rot, flourishes the more in proportion as air and light are excluded. — WHATELY.

Falsetto.

Falsetto, like the notes of a split reed. — WASHINGTON IRVING.

Falter.

Faltering like the skylark's young. — JAMES MONTGOMERY.

Fame.

Fame is like a river, that beareth up things light and swollen, and drowns things weighty and solid; but if persons of quality and judgement concur, then it filleth all round about, and will not easily away; for the odors of ointments are more durable than those of flowers. — BACON.

Fame is like a crop of kanada thissels, very eazy tew sow, but hard tew reap. — JOSH BILLINGS.

Fame is like a whimsical mistress; she flies from those who pursue her most, and follows such as show the least regard to her. — SAMUEL CROXALL.

Fame, as a river, is narrowest where it is bred, and broadest far off. — SIR WILLIAM DAVENANT.

Fame, like a new mistress of the town, is gained with ease, but then she's lost as soon. — DRYDEN.

To some characters, fame is like an intoxicating cup placed to the lips, — they do well to turn away from it who fear it will turn their heads. But to others fame is "Love disguised", the love that answers to love in its widest, most exalted sense. — MRS. JAMESON.

Fame, like money, should neither be despised nor idolized. — L. C. JUDSON.

Fame, like a wayward Girl, will still
be coy
To those who woo her with too
slavish knees,
But makes surrender to some thoughtless Boy,
And dotes the more upon a heart at
ease. — KEATS.

Good fame is like fire: when you have kindled it, you may easily preserve it; but if you once extinguish it, you will not easily kindle it again. — PLUTARCH.

The way to fame, like the way to heaven, is through much tribulation. — STERNE.

Fragrant his fame as flowers that close not. — SWINBURNE.

Familiar.

Familiar as a popular song. — ANON.

Familiar as the sights on our streets. — IBID.

Familiar as my sleep, or want of money. — BEAUMONT AND FLETCHER.

Familiar — *continued.*

Familiar as the simple lore
That two policemen and two thieves make four.
— AMBROSE BIERCE.

Familiar as a cradle-song. — R. J. BURDETTE.

Familiar as a voice of home. — JOHN CRAWFORD.

Familiar as an oath. — LORD DE TABLEY.

Familiar, like the amulet worn on the heart. — GEORGE ELIOT.

As familiar as a fiddler. — JOHN FLETCHER.

Familiar to me as my own face in the glass; as the speech of my own tongue. — HUGO.

Familiar as eating. — MASSINGER.

Familiar as his garter. — SHAKESPEARE.

Familiar in his mouth as household words. — IBID.

Familiar as the sun and moon. — HENRY D. THOREAU.

Familiar as our childhood's stream
Or pleasant memory of a dream.
— WHITTIER.

Familiar as a book. — N. P. WILLIS.

Familiarly.

Talks as familiarly of roaring lions
As maids of thirteen do of puppy-dogs.
— SHAKESPEARE.

Family.

His family is like potatoes; all that is good of them are underground. — ANON.

The family is like a book — the children are the leaves,
The parents are the covers that protective beauty gives.
At first the pages of the book are blank and purely fair,
But time soon writeth memories and painteth pictures there.
Love is the little golden clasp that bindeth up the trust,
Oh, break it not, lest all the leaves shall scatter and be lost.
— ANON.

Fan.

It fanned his cheek
Like a meadow-gale of Spring.
— COLERIDGE.

Fanciful.

Fanciful as furnitures. — ANON.

Fancy.

Fancy, like a spright,
Prefers the silent scenes of night.
— NATHANIEL COTTON.

Fancy, like the finger of a clock,
Runs the great circuit, and is still at home. — COWPER.

Fangless.

Fangless as the fat worms of the grave. — JAMES WHITCOMB RILEY.

Fantastic.

Fantastical, like a sick man's dreams. — ANON.

Fantastic . . . as the sports of a Naiad. — BULWER-LYTTON.

Fantastic as a war-dance. — G. K. CHESTERTON.

Fantastic as a Chinese weapon. — MAURICE MAETERLINCK.

Fantastic as a woman's mood. — SIR WALTER SCOTT.

A fantastic splendor as of Aladdin and Arabian nights. — ISRAEL ZANGWILL.

Far.

Far as good is above evil. — ANON

As far from the heart as from the eyes. — IBID.

As far as finite is from infinite. — P. J. BAILEY.

Far — *continued.*

Far as mortal eye can compass sight. — BYRON.

Atom from atom yawns as far
As moon from earth, or star from star.
— EMERSON.

Far as poles asunder. — J. S. KNOWLES.

Afar as angels or the sainted dead. — GEORGE MACDONALD.

Far as imagination's eye can roll. — MONTGOMERY.

Far as human man is from the brute. — LEWIS MORRIS.

As far as sleep from waking. — JOHN G. NEIHARDT.

And no star
Is from thy mortal path so far
As streets where childhood knew the way. — D. G. ROSSETTI.

As far from help as limbo is from bliss. — SHAKESPEARE.

So far from sounding and discovery,
As is the bud bit with an envious worm,
Ere he can spread his sweet leaves to the air,
Or dedicate his beauty to the sun.
— IBID.

Far as the remotest line
That bounds imagination's flight.
— SHELLEY.

Burning far, like the light of an unmeasured star. — IBID.

Far as heaven's red labouring eye could glance. — SWINBURNE.

Far as hope from joy or sleep from truth. — IBID.

Far from earth as heaven. — IBID.

Far and wide, like the falcon that hunts through the sky. — ESAIAS TEGNER.

Fascinate.

Fascinate — as a snake would a bird. — JOSEPH CONRAD.

Fascinating.

Fascinating as a loose tooth. — ANON.

Fashion.

An Englishman of fashion is like one of those souvenirs, bound in gold vellum, enriched with delicate engravings, on thick hot-pressed paper, fit for the hands of ladies and princes, but with nothing in it worth reading or remembering. — EMERSON.

A man of fashion is like a certain blue flower, growing spontaneously in ploughed grounds, which chokes the corn, spoils the crop, and takes up the room of something better. — M. DE LA BRUYÈRE.

For fashion's sake, as bawds go to church. — JOHN WEBSTER.

Fast.

Fast as a jack rabbit in front of a prairie fire. — ANON.

Fast as a dog will lick a dish. — IBID.

As fast as the foam-flakes drift on the river. — IBID.

As fast as a fisher could let out line. — J. M. BARRIE.

Fast as Time's swift pinions can convey. — SAMUEL BOYSE.

Fast as the streaming rain. — CHATTERTON.

Gulp it down as fast as a Neapolitan beggar does a plateful of free scalding-hot macaroni. — HENRY T. FINCK.

Served as fast as you throw the five baseballs at the colored gentleman's head. — O. HENRY.

Our days run
As fast away as does the sun ;
And as a vapour, or a drop of rain
Once lost, can ne'er be found again.
— ROBERT HERRICK.

Fast as the rolling seasons bring
The hour of fate to those we love.
— O. W. HOLMES.

Fast — *continued.*

Fast as light. — HUGO.

Fast as a horse can trot. — BEN JONSON.

Spend vows as fast as vapors, which go off
Even with the fumes.
— CHARLES LAMB.

Fast as windy flames devour. — GEORGE MEREDITH.

Fading fast as rainbows. — THOMAS MOORE.

Held her fast, mercilessly, as a snake holds a little bird. — MISS MULOCK.

Fast as a dog can trot. — RABELAIS.

Fast as the magnet flies. — EDMOND ROSTAND.

As fast as the simoon's desert wind.
— FRIEDRICH RÜCKERT.

Fast as an eagle through the air. — SCHILLER.

Fast
As lagging fowls before the northern blast. — SHAKESPEARE.

Drop tears as fast as the Arabian trees
Their medicinal gum. — IBID.

Entrap the hearts of men, faster than gnats in cobwebs. — IBID.

Faster than thought or time. — IBID.

Fast as autumn days toward winter. — SWINBURNE.

Fast as fire on earth devours. — IBID.

Fast as the gin's grip of a wayfarer. — IBID.

Fast as warriors grip their brands when battle's bolt is hurled. — IBID.

Made fast as with anchors to land. — IBID.

Fast in bondage as herded beasts. — IBID.

Fast as storm could speed. — IBID.

Faster than dolphins do o'ershoot the tide, cours'd by the yawning shark. — C. J. WELLS.

Fast as a musician scatters sound
Out of an instrument.
— WORDSWORTH.

Fasten.

Like one drowning fastens upon anything that is next at hand. — JOHN EARLE.

Fastened like nails in a cartwheel. — SIR WALTER RALEIGH.

Fasten him as a nail in a sure place. — OLD TESTAMENT.

Fat.

Fat as a bacon-pig at Martlemas. — ANON.

Fat as brawn. — IBID.

Fat as a sheep's tail. — IBID.

A red bag, fat with your unpaid bills, like a landing net. — DION BOUCICAULT.

Fat as Mother Nab. — SAMUEL BUTLER.

Fat as a whale. — CHAUCER.

Fat as a barn-door fowl. — CONGREVE.

Fat as seals. — CHARLES HALLOCK.

Fatte as a foole. — LYLY.

As fat as a distillery pig. — SCOTTISH PROVERB.

As fat as a Miller's horse. — IBID.

Fat as butter. — SHAKESPEARE.

Fat as tame things. — IBID.

Fat and fulsome to mine ear
As howling after music. — IBID.

Fat as grease. — OLD TESTAMENT.

Grow fat as the heifer at grass. — IBID.

Fatal.

Fatal as Herod's worms. — ANON.

Fatal — *continued.*

Fatal as the eye of the basilisk. — ANON.

Fatal as the tongue of the serpent. — IBID.

Fatal as the shade of Death's dark valley. — P. J. BAILEY.

Fatal as the scythe of death. — COWPER.

Anger and power are as fatal as lightning. — GEORGE ELIOT.

Fatal as the Egyptian night,
When the eldest-born were slain.
— JAMES MONTGOMERY.

Fate.

My fate is like that of an eagle, who, being shot with an arrow, observes his own feathers on the arrow that kills him. — CHESTERFIELD.

Faultless.

Faultless as blown roses in June days. — EDWARD DOWDEN.

Faultless as a flower. — SWINBURNE.

Favors.

I do confess thou'rt sweet, yet find
Thee such an unthrift of thy sweets,
Thy favours are but like the wind
That kisses everything it meets.
And since thou canst with more than one,
Thou'rt worthy to be kiss'd by none.
— SIR ROBERT AYTON.

Fawn.

Fawn like spaniels. — MARLOWE.

Fawned like hounds. — SHAKESPEARE.

Fawning like a courtier parasite. — VOLTAIRE.

Fear.

Fear, like spare diet, starves the fevers of lust and quenches the flames of hell. — O. W. HOLMES.

Fear on fear, like light reflected from the dancing wave, visits all places, but can rest in none. — ROBERT JEPHSON.

As corn o'ergrown by weeds, so heedful fear
Is almost chok'd by unresisted lust.
— SHAKESPEARE.

Trembling fear, as fowl hear falcon's bells. — IBID.

Fear is like a cloak which old men huddle
About their love, as if to keep it warm.
— WORDSWORTH.

Fearful.

Fearful as a locust bane. — C. F. ALEXANDER.

Fearful, like a dog an old master drives away, and which fears the new one. — OUIDA.

Fearful as a siege. — SHAKESPEARE.

Fearless.

Fearless as the strong-winged eagle. — JAMES MACPHERSON.

Fearless as a drunkard. — THOMAS MIDDLETON.

Bred him fearless, like a sea-mew reared
In rocks of man's foot feared,
Where nought of wingless life may sing or shine. — SWINBURNE.

Fearlessly.

Fearlessly, like a happy child, too innocent to fear. — SOUTHEY.

Feast.

Feast like Dives. — ANON.

Feast like Lucullus. — IBID.

Feasting like fiends upon the infidel dead. — SHELLEY.

Feeble.

Feeble as a lamb's bleat. — ANON.

Feeble as the wing of a chicken in the pip. — CHARLOTTE BRONTË.

Feed.

Feed like an oxen at a stall. — SHAKESPEARE.

Feed on us, as worms devour our body. — SHELLEY.

Feel.

Nature meant that a fat man should have an appetite and that he should gratify it at regular intervals — meant that he should feel like the Grand Canyon before dinner and the Royal Gorge afterward. — IRVIN S. COBB.

Feelings.

It is with feelings as with waters: the shallow murmur, but the deep are dumb. — SIR WALTER RALEIGH.

The feelings, like flowers and butterflies, last longer the later they are delayed. — RICHTER.

Feet.

Her pretty feet like snails, did creep
A little out, and then,
As if they played at bo-peep,
Did soon draw in again.
— ROBERT HERRICK.

To make the tale of her charms complete,
They [her hands] were matched by the shape of her exquisite feet,
Feet so light no maid might show,
So perfectly fashioned from heel to toe,
If on the eye of a lover she stepped,
Her foot would float on the tear he wept. — JAMI.

Her feet beneath her petticoat,
Like little mice, stole in and out,
As if they feared the light.
— SIR JOHN SUCKLING.

A baby's feet, like sea-shells pink,
Might tempt, should heaven see meet,
An angel's lips to kiss, we think,
A baby's feet.
Like rose-hued sea-flowers toward the heat
They stretch and spread and wink
Their ten soft buds that part and meet.
— SWINBURNE.

Felicity.

Domestic felicity, which, like the small-pox or the plague, a man can have only once in his life. — GEORGE WASHINGTON.

Fell.

(*See also* Fall.)

Fell like piled-up cards. — ROBERT BROWNING.

Fell as thick as harvests beneath hail. — BYRON.

The charioteer fell like a fluttered leaf;
Or as feather shaken from the wing
Of some high-soaring eagle, when the hail
Falls in a whirlwind and the woods cry back. — LORD DE TABLEY.

Jussaic fell like a mass of dead flesh. — DUMAS, PÈRE.

Fell like a ninepin. — JOSÉ ECHEGARAY.

The stars of heaven fell calmly away,
Like flakes of snow in a winter day.
— JAMES HOGG.

She fell like a column of water. — W. D. HOWELLS.

He fell as one struck dead. — J. S. KNOWLES.

His face fell like a cookbook cake. — JOSEPH C. LINCOLN.

Fell, like a flail on the garnered grain. — LONGFELLOW.

Like corn before the sickle the stout Lavinians fell. — MACAULAY.

He fell, like the bank of a mountain-stream. — JAMES MACPHERSON.

She . . . fell from her full height as a stone drops from a rock into the gulf below. — OUIDA.

Like the watch-tower of a town
Which an earthquake shatters down,
Like a lightning-stricken mast,
Like a wind-uprooted tree
Spun about,
Like a foam-topped waterspout
Cast down headlong in the sea,
She fell at last. — C. G. ROSSETTI.

Fell, like ocean's feathery spray
Dashed from the boiling surge
Before the vessel's prow.
— SHELLEY.

Fell — *continued.*

Fell, like the unseen blight of a smiling day. — SHELLEY.

Fell fast, as the seared leaves that from the trembling tree the autumn whirlwind shakes. — SOUTHEY.

Fell like ripe grass before the mower's scythe. — IBID.

Fell like a thousand of brick. — SIMON SUGGS.

Fell as falls an ember from forth a flameless pile. — SWINBURNE.

Fell a spirit, as sinks the star of day beneath its watery bed of western waves. — JOSEPH TURNLEY.

But I fell ;
Fell, like the snow-flakes, from heaven
— to hell.
JOHN W. WATSON.

Fell upon his ears like fire-bell at night. — THOMAS WATSON.

Ferments.

Ferments like boiling yeast. — GEORGE MAC-HENRY.

Ferocious.

Ferocious as a catamount searching for its dinner. — ANON.

Ferocious as a bogus archangel full of cocaine. — HENRY L. MENCKEN.

Ferocious as wolves. — VOLTAIRE.

Fervent.

Fervent as the solar rays. — FRANKLIN P. ADAMS.

Fervent as fire. — ANON.

Fervent as a saint. — ELIZA COOK.

Fervent as Hesper in the brow of Eve. — GERALD MASSEY.

Fervent as fiery moon. — SWINBURNE.

Fervent as glorious noon. — ISAAC WATTS.

Festered.

Festered like buried thorns in the flesh. — IRVIN S. COBB.

Fetid.

Atmosphere as fetid as the stymphalian lake, over which no bird could fly. — ANON.

Fickle.

Fickle as friends. — ANON.

Fickle as the lightning. — IBID.

Fickle as the weather. — IBID.

Fickle as love. — BALZAC.

Fickle as the flying air. — BEAUMONT AND FLETCHER.

Fickle . . . as the winds. — APHRA BEHN.

Fickle as a feather. — ALEXANDER BROME.

Fickle as the sea. — WILLIAM CULLEN BRYANT.

Fickle and bright as a fairy throng. — ELIZA COOK.

Fickle as the sky. — JAMES GRAHAME.

Fickle as a female in hysterics. — O. W. HOLMES.

Fickle as the flood. — WILLIAM KING.

Fickle as the breezes blow. — JOSEPH B. LADD.

Fickle as a changeful dream. — WALTER SCOTT.

Fidget.

In a fit of fidgets, when she behaved like a puppy chewing a string, a clumsy woman in a side-saddle, a hen with her head cut off, or a cow stung by a hornet. — KIPLING.

Fidgety.

Fidgety as an old maid. — BALZAC.

Fierce.

Fierce as the flight of Jove's destroying flame. — AKENSIDE.

Fierce as a Japanese mask. — ANON.

Fierce as Jove. — IBID.

Fierce as lecherous desire. — IBID.

Fierce as a lion of Cotswold. — IBID.

Fierce as a mother bird. — IBID.

Fierce as a ramcat. — J. R. BARTLETT'S "DICTIONARY OF AMERICANISMS."

Fierce as those flames which shall consume, at close of all. — BHAGAVAD-GITA.

Fierce as twenty bloodhounds. — E. B. BROWNING.

Fierce as the shout of victory. — WILLIAM CULLEN BRYANT.

Fierce as the blast that tears the northern sky. — CHATTERTON.

Fierce as the fallynge thunderbolte. — IBID.

Fiers as leoun. — CHAUCER.

Fierce as sin. — P. H. HAYNE.

Fierce as a whirlwind. — HOMER.

Fierce as a tigress plundered of her young. — JUVENAL.

Fierce as the hydra. — WILLIAM KING.

Fierce as Achilles was. — MARLOWE.

Fierce as a female Leviathan. — OWEN MEREDITH.

Fierce as mounts the flame in air. — WILLIAM J. MICKLE.

Fierce as a comet. — MILTON.

Fierce as ten furies. — IBID.

Fierce as a turkey-cock. — JAMES MONTGOMERY.

As fierce as the Pentland Firth. — SCOTTISH PROVERB.

Fierce . . . as whetted scythe. — JOHN RUSKIN.

As ferce and as cruell as the feende of hel. — JOHN SKELTON.

Fierce as a famished wolf. — SOUTHEY.

Fierce as hauke in flight. — SPENSER.

Fierce as a blast of hate from hell. — SWINBURNE.

Fierce as the fervid eyes of lions. — IBID.

Fierce as flaming fire. — TASSO.

Fierce as aqua fortis. — JOHN TATHAM.

Fierce, as powers at bay. — BAYARD TAYLOR.

Fierce as wolves. — TOLSTOY.

Fiery.

Fiery as the encircling neighborhood of a forge. — D'ANNUNZIO.

Fiery as powder. — JOHN W. DE FOREST.

Fiery as a stag at bay. — THEODORE TILTON.

Fight.

Fight as fiercely in defence of his mistress as Blandimar and Paridel, of romantic fame, are said to have fought for the lovely Florimel. — ANON.

Fight like a bulldog. — IBID.

Fight like Kilkenny cats. — IBID.

Fight like sin. — IBID.

Fight like thunder. — IBID.

Fight like a dragon. — ROBERT BURTON.

Fight like mad or drunk. — SAMUEL BUTLER.

Fight like a cock. — CONGREVE.

Fight like hell-roosters. — STEPHEN CRANE.

Put up a fight like a welter-weight cinnamon bear. — O. HENRY.

Fight like a bull in a tether. — KINGSLEY.

Figure.

She had a figure like a pillow. — Anon.

Her figure is like a willow bough. — Joseph A. de Gobineau.

File.

In files they lay,
Like the mower's grass at the close of day. — Byron.

Fill.

Fill like a rush of wind and shaft of sunshine. — William Archer.

My heart feels filling like a sinking boat. — P. J. Bailey.

Filled as cloud with fire. — Swinburne.

Fill like the shadow of a cloud. — Whittier.

Filthy.

Filthy as the mouth of a fired gun. — Anon.

Final.

Final as going to Heaven. — Joseph Conrad.

Finance.

His finance is like the Indian philosophy; his earth is poised on the horns of a bull, his bull stands upon an elephant, his elephant is supported by a tortoise; and so on forever. — Edmund Burke.

Fine.

Fine as a Maypole on May-day. — Anon.

Fine as a mist of lace. — Ibid.

Fine as five-pence. — Ibid.

Fine as gossamer. — Ibid.

Fine as point lace. — Ibid.

Fine as a skein of the casuist Escobar's worked on the bone of a lie. — Robert Browning.

Fyn as ducket in Venice. — Chaucer.

Fine as an ape in purple. — Clarke's "Proverbs."

Fine as a silver dollar saloon. — Elbert Hubbard.

A sound so fine, there's nothing lies 'twixt it and silence. — J. S. Knowles.

Fine as bronze floss. — Amy Leslie.

Fine as light. — Shelley.

Fine as silkworm's thread. — Southey.

Fine as the gleamy gossamer that spreads its filmy web-work o'er the tangled mead. — Ibid.

More fine than moonbeams. — Swinburne.

Fine as ice-ferns on January panes. — Tennyson.

Fine as a hedge in May. — Samuel Wesley.

Finger.

Like reeds were those taper fingers of hers to write on each heart love's characters. — Jami.

Fire.

Fire the heart devout, like cantharidian plasters. — Burns.

Fired like a planet on its peculiar spot,
To draw nutrition, propagate, and rot.
— Pope.

Fired, as by a spell. — Shelley.

Firm.

Firm as the shaft that props the towering dome. — Æschylus.

Firm as the solid base of this great world. — Akenside.

Firm as adamant. — Anon.

Firm as a mountain. — Ibid.

Firm as the granite base of Mount Washington. — Ibid.

Firm as the iron hills. — Ibid.

Firm as the budding fruit. — Ariosto.

Firm — *continued.*

Firm as well-cured olives. — ARISTOPHANES.

Stand firm like a rock. — MARCUS AURELIUS.

Firm as butchers. — BACON.

Firm as the heart of a mountain. — AMBROSE BIERCE.

Firm in his sinew as the hind leg of a stag. — BULWER-LYTTON.

Firmer than heaven and earth. — BUNYAN.

Firm as a fortress. — BYRON.

Held firm, like a wall of rock. — CARLYLE.

Firm-founded, like the bamboo's clamping roots. — CHINESE.

Firm as Sparta's king. — SIR FRANCIS DOYLE.

Rock firm as facts. — THOMAS HARDY.

Firm as the band that clasps the antlered spoil. — O. W. HOLMES.

Firm as the rooted mountain rock. — IBID.

Firm as Atlas. — ROBERT JEPHSON.

Firm as steel. — VIRGINIA W. JOHNSON.

Firm as the tread of lions. — RICHARD LE GALLIENNE.

Firm as the oak on rocky heights. — EDWARD LOVIBOND.

Firm as Nature's self. — LOWELL.

Firm as a pillar. — GEORGE MEREDITH.

Hands firm as driven stakes. — IBID.

Firm as the poles, or earth, which never move. — GEORGE SANDYS.

Firm as faith. — SHAKESPEARE.

Firm as rocky mountains. — IBID.

Firm as the world's centre. — SHELLEY.

Firm as dust and fixed as shadows. — SWINBURNE.

Firm as a stone. — OLD TESTAMENT.

As virtue, firm. — WILLIAM THOMSON.

Firm as the fabled throne of Grecian Jove. — IBID.

Firm as the castle's feudal roof. — THOMAS WARTON.

As firm as rock in ocean. — WILLIAM WHITEHEAD.

Firm as the chain of rocks which guard the strand. — WILLIAM WILKIE.

Firm and unflinching, as the lighthouse reared
On the Island-rock.
— WORDSWORTH.

Firm as solid crystal. — IBID.

Fist

(*See also* HAND.)

Fists like shoulders of mutton. — BALZAC.

Fit (Adverb).

Fit as a rope for a thief. — ANON.

Fit as a shoulder of mutton for a sick horse. — IBID.

Fit as a fiddle. — WILLIAM HAUGHTON.

Fit as a saddle for a sow. — LEAN'S "COLLECTANEA."

As fit as a pudding for a dogges mouth. — LYLY.

Fit as a fritter for a friar's mouth. — ENGLISH PROVERB.

As fit as ten groats is for the hand of an attorney, as your French crown for your taffeta punk, as Tib's rush for Tom's forefinger, as a pancake for Shrove-Tuesday, a morris for May-day, as the nail to his hole, the cuckold to his horn, as a scolding quean to a wrangling knave, as the nun's lip to the friar's mouth ; nay, as the pudding to his skin. — SHAKESPEARE.

Fit (Adverb) — *continued.*

A word fitly spoken is like apples of gold in pictures of silver. — OLD TESTAMENT.

Fit (Verb).

Fit as a banana skin on a banana. — ANON.

Fit in like dog's teeth. — IBID.

Fits like the bark on a tree. — IBID.

Fits like feathers on a duck. — IBID.

Fit like the paper on the wall. — IBID.

Fit into his niche like a peg into a hole. — BALZAC.

Fits like a bathing suit coming out of the water. — GEORGE BROADHURST.

Fits in its place, like a marble stone accurately hewn and polished. — CARLYLE.

Fits as a shell fits a crab. — SIR A. CONAN DOYLE.

Fit as a thump with a stone in an apothecary's eye. — THOMAS FULLER, M. D.

Fitted into it like a brilliant into the setting of a ring. — HAZLITT.

Fits you like a flannel washed in hot suds. — O. HENRY.

Fit like Sunday shoes. — O. W. HOLMES.

Fitted as does a key in a well-oiled lock. — BETTINA VON HUTTEN.

Fit . . . like the leg and trouser, the hair and the comb. — HENRIK IBSEN.

Fits the present purpose like a ring to your finger. — W. S. LANDOR.

Fit her as a helmet might a hero. — AMY LESLIE.

Fitted into each other like the artfully covered pieces of wood which composed the picture puzzles of our childhood. — ALEXANDER KIELLAND.

Fit, like wheel to nave, or joint to spit. — WILLIAM KING.

Fits like a kid glove. — GEORGE MEREDITH.

Fits you like a finger stuck in the mud. — H. W. PHILLIPS.

Fitful.

Fitful and faint, like the shifting mirage of the desert. — EUGENE BARRY.

Fitful like the talking of trees. — D. G. ROSSETTI.

Fitful as the sea. — SWINBURNE.

Fitfully.

Comes fitfully like broken music. — TENNYSON.

Fits.

By fits and girds (starts), as an ague takes a goose. — JOHN RAY'S "HANDBOOK OF PROVERBS."

Fixed.

Fixed as fate. — ANON.

Fixed as the laws of the Medes and the Persians. — IBID.

Fixed as the laws of the planetary system. — IBID.

Fixed as your name on a note. — IBID.

Fixed like ony stane. — JOANNA BAILLIE.

Fixt — like conscious guilt. — APHRA BEHN.

Fix'd as the rock that braves the main. — THOMAS BLACKLOCK.

Fixed as the orb of the burning sun. — EMILY BRONTË.

Fixed as the polar star. — WILLIAM ALLEN BUTLER.

Fixed, as in death. — JOHN VANCE CHENEY.

Fixt as an island 'gainst the waves and wind. — ABRAHAM COWLEY.

Fixed — *continued.*

Eyes immovably fixed . . . like a miser torn away from his coffers, or like a mother separated from her child about to be led away to death. — DUMAS, PÈRE.

Fixed like a statue on his marble throne. — F. W. FABER.

Sullen, fix'd like some old oak's deep-rooted, knotted trunk, which hath endur'd the tempest-breathing months of thrice a hundred winters, yet remains unshaken. — RICHARD GLOVER.

Fixed as a sculptured figure. — GOETHE.

Fixedly as rocky marge. — KEATS.

Gaze fix'd . . . as one who deep in heaven some airy pageant sees. — JOHN KEBLE.

Fixed as Lochlin's thousand rocks. — JAMES MACPHERSON.

Fixed like a rock. — MAHABHARATA.

Fixed as a monument. — W. M. PRAED.

Fixt as the monument on Fish street Hill. — W. B. RHODES.

As fixed as the law of light. — CHARLES SANGSTER.

As fixed as Cheviot. — SIR WALTER SCOTT.

Fixed and indispensable as the majestic laws that rule yon rolling orbs. — SHELLEY.

Fix'd as a mountain ash. — WILLIAM SOMERVILLE.

Like the stone eyeballs of the statue fixed. — SOUTHEY.

Fixed like a sea-rock. — SWINBURNE.

Fixt
As are the roots of earth and base of
all. — TENNYSON.

Fixed as the earth. — THEOGNIS.

Fixed . . . like churchyard graves. — THEODORE TILTON.

Fix'd as oaks. — PAUL WHITEHEAD.

Fixed as a star. — WORDSWORTH.

Fixed as a sentinel. — EDWARD YOUNG.

Fizz.

Fizzes like wildfire. — ROBERT BROWNING.

Fizz . . . like the last sputtering of a firework. — BOOTH TARKINGTON.

Fizzle.

Fizzle out like a damp squib. — ANON.

Fizzled like freshly opened soda water. — KIPLING.

Fizzling like an impatient soda fountain. — HARRY LEON WILSON.

Flabby.

Flabby as a Norfolk dumpling. — ANON.

As flabby as a sponge. — GUY DE MAUPASSANT.

Flags.

There is affection in every employment, and it gives the spirit energy, and keeps the mind intent upon its work or study. This if it be not relaxed, becomes dull, and its earnestness flags, — as salt that has lost its savor, so that it has no pungency or relish ; or as bended bow, which unless it be unbent, loses the power that it derives from its elasticity. — EMANUEL SWEDENBORG.

Flame.

Flamed like a sheet of molten gold. — WILLIAM H. AINSWORTH.

Flame like torch-flames in the passionate air. — SIDNEY LANIER.

Flame, like a meteor, to the troubled air. — ROBERT LLOYD.

Flaming like a carbuncle. — RABELAIS.

Flaming, like the jaws of hell. — IBID.

Flames like morn. — SWINBURNE.

Flap.

Flapping down behind him like the back-fin of a water-serpent. — ROBERT BROWNING.

Flap as a flag as the winds go by. — JAMES WHITCOMB RILEY.

Flare.

Flare
Like a spent lamp about to die. — JOHN DAVIDSON.

Flare like torches. — LONGFELLOW.

Flared like molten brass. — JAMES MONTGOMERY.

Flared, like Titan torches flinging flakes of flame and embers, springing from the dale. — JAMES WHITCOMB RILEY.

Flares like an angered and storm-redding morn. — SWINBURNE.

Flash (Noun).

A mere flash ; as chaff and straw soon fired, burn vehemently for a while, yet out in a moment. — ROBERT BURTON.

A flash like a snow avalanche. — THOMAS WESTWOOD.

Flash (Verb).

Flashes like cut glass. — ANON.

Flash like stars. — IBID.

Eyes flashing, like shooting thunderbolts. — P. J. BAILEY.

Flashing, like a newly-awakened flame. — R. D. BLACKMORE.

Flashed like the spray of a fountain. — IBID.

Flashing like a steel blade. — GEORG M. BRANDES.

Flash'd like a jewel. — ROBERT BRIDGES (English).

Flash like a rocket. — C. S. CALVERLEY.

Flashing . . . like scimitar from its sheath. — PAUL LAURENCE DUNBAR.

Flashes . . . like a revelation. — PAUL HAMILTON HAYNE.

Flashed like dazzling arrow tipped
With amorous heat. — IBID.

Flashes like the shining soul of a jest. — W. E. HENLEY.

Flash like a heliograph. — KIPLING.

Flashing like a scythe. — RICHARD LE GALLIENNE.

Flashed like a falchion from its sheath. — LONGFELLOW.

Flashed, like a sabre in the sun. — THOMAS MOORE.

Flash like golden fire-flakes from the sky. — WILHELM MÜLLER.

Flashing like thought. — MISS MULOCK.

Flashed . . .
Like a red-hot eye from a grave.
— C. G. ROSSETTI.

Flashing like fire-flies. — IBID.

Flash like a steel blade tipped with fire. — FRANCIS S. SALTUS.

Flashing like a fiery stream. — SCHILLER.

Flashed like a strong inspiration. — SHELLEY.

Like a mirror sparkling to the sun with dazzling splendor, flashed. — SOUTHEY.

Her Eies did flash out fiery light,
Like coles that through a silver censer sparkle bright. — SPENSER.

Flash and toss
Like plumes in battle's blithest charge.
— SWINBURNE.

Flat.

Fell flat as a damp squib. — ANON.

Flat as a pricked bladder. — IBID.

Flat as your hand. — IBID.

Flat as the beaten coin. — ANTAR.

Flat as a flounder. — BEAUMONT AND FLETCHER.

Flat — *continued.*

Flat as an anvil's face. — ROBERT BROWNING.

Flat as a gravestone. — E. B. BROWNING.

Flat and bare as Hebrew verse of Bishop Hare. — JOHN BYROM.

Flat as a fillet of sole. — IRVIN S. COBB.

Flat as a juryman. — DICKENS.

Flat as a flail. — BRET HARTE.

As flat as a pancake. — LUDVIG HOLBERG (1684–1754).

Flat as a rose that has long been pressed. — O. W. HOLMES.

As flat as Æschylus in Bohn's translation. — HUGO.

Flat as a willow-pattern plate. — IBID.

Flat as an excuse. — SYDNEY MUNDEN.

Flat as the fens of Holland. — SIR WALTER SCOTT.

Flat
As dead sands be at utmost ebb that drink
The drainèd salt o' the sea.
— SWINBURNE.

Flatter.

A woman who won't flatter is like a piano that won't play. — ELLEN THORNEYCROFT FOWLER.

Flatterers.

Flatterers are cats that lick before and scratch behind. —ANON.

For as a wolf resembles a dog, so doth a flatterer a friend. A flatterer is compared to an ape, who, because she can not defend the house like a dog, labour as an ox, or bear burdens as a horse, doth therefore yet play tricks, and provoke laughter. — SIR WALTER RALEIGH.

Flattery.

Flattery is like false money : it impoverishes those that receive it. — ANON.

Flattery is like Kolone water, tew be smelt of, not swallowed. — JOSH BILLINGS.

Your flattery, like a rich jewel, has a value not only from its superior lustre, but from its extraordinary scarceness. — RICHARD CUMBERLAND.

Flattery resembles the picture of a suit of armour in this respect, that it is calculated to yield delight, not to render any actual service. — DEMOPHILUS.

Flattery is the destruction of all good fellowship ; it is like a qualmish liqueur in the midst of a bottle of wine. — DISRAELI.

Flattery is like a painted armor ; only to show. — SOCRATES.

Though flattery blossoms like friendship, yet there is a vast difference in the fruit. — IBID.

Flaunt.

Beauty . . . flaunts like the coral of summer flower. — ROBERT BRIDGES (English).

Flecked.

Flecked as a turkey egg. — ANON.

Fled.

(*See also* Fly.)

The tyrant from our shore, like a forbidden demon, fled. — AKENSIDE.

Fled, like the raven from the bird of Jove. — IBID.

Fled like leaves on the gale. — ANON.

Fled, like rats from a sinking ship. — IBID.

Sorrow fled on fleeting pinions, like the icy breath of winter that spring zephyrs waft away. — IBID.

Fly around like a bat in the twilight. — BJÖRNSTJERNE BJÖRNSON.

Fled — *continued.*

Fled from his thoughts like a sickly dream. — BULWER-LYTTON.

Like a passing thought, she fled. — BURNS.

Fled like frighted doos. — IBID.

Fled like crows when they smell powder. — SAMUEL BUTLER.

Fled like a dream. — COWPER.

Each quiet day has fled like the same moth, returning with slow wing, and pausing in the sunshine. — GEORGE ELIOT.

Like murder, chas'd by conscience, fled. — EBENEZER ELLIOTT.

Fled like the flood's foam. — EMERSON.

Fled as soon as fleet the violets. — HAROMA.

Fled like a felon. — O. W. HOLMES.

Fled like a Parthian. — HUGO.

Fled like a dusky cloud. — KIPLING.

Fled like the mist of Cona. — JAMES MACPHERSON.

Fled, as the dawn clouds flee before the sun. — JOHN PAYNE.

Fled like shadows. — PETRARCH.

Fled, as fogs disperse before the god of day. — CHARLES READE.

Fled like a mist before the radiant day. — ROSCOMMON.

Fled at will, as in a wingèd chariot. — SHELLEY.

Fled
Like insect tribes before the northern
gale. — IBID.

Fled,
Like the brief glory which dark Heaven
inherits
From the false dawn, which fades
ere it is spread,
Upon the night's devouring darkness
shed. — IBID.

Fled
Like vultures frightened from Imus
Before an earthquake's tread.
— IBID.

Fledde like a beest. — JOHN SKELTON.

Like spectres from the sight of morning, fled. — SOUTHEY.

Fled like a glittering rivulet to the tarn. — TENNYSON.

As flies the shadow of a bird, she fled. — IBID.

My best years have fled away, like dreams, or like a minstrel's lay. — WALTER VON DER VOGELWEIDE.

Fled away like a dream. — JOHN WESLEY.

Fled like a flash of light. — ELLA WHEELER WILCOX.

Fled, as time will in a dream. — N. P. WILLIS.

Fled as fast as doth the haunted fawn. — WORDSWORTH.

Fled
Like vapour, like a towering cloud,
dissolved. — IBID.

Flee.

(*See also* Fly.)

Flee like desires. — BEAUMONT AND FLETCHER.

Flee like a shamed child. — R. M. MILNES.

Flee like a dream's dim imagery. — SHELLEY.

Flee, like mist from the tempest's might. — IBID.

Flee
As clouds and winds and rays across
the sea. — SWINBURNE.

Flee as a bird to your mountain. — OLD TESTAMENT.

Flee, as fleeing from a sword. — IBID.

Fleeth also as a shadow. — IBID.

Flee — *continued.*

Flee as the air. — WHITTIER.

Fleeing like the rose of an Arctic night. — GEORGE E. WOODBERRY.

Fleet.

Fleet as a falling star. — ANON.

Fleet as a greyhound. — IBID.

Fleet as Diana. — IBID.

Fleet as kindled fire. — IBID.

Fleeter than hawk that ever flew. — EDWIN ARNOLD.

Fleet is his foot as the wild roebuck's. — C. S. CALVERLEY.

Fleet as the whirlwind. — CAMPBELL.

Flete as fleaynge cloudes that swymme before the syghte. — THOMAS CHATTERTON.

Fleet as leash-slipped greyhounds. — DANTE.

Fleet as deer the Normans ran
Through Curlieu's Pass and Ardrahan.
— T. O. DAVIS.

Fleet as fancy. — CHARLES DIBDEN, JR.

Fleet as the swallow cuts the drift. — JOSEPH R. DRAKE.

Fleets as a dream. — ELIJAH FENTON.

Fleet as the arrow from the bowstring flies,
Fleet as the eagle darting through the skies. — FIRDAUSI.

As fleet
As had they wings upon their feet.
— JACQUES JASMIN.

Fleet,
As silver-sandalled Artemis.
— FRANCES ANNE KEMBLE.

Fleet as wind. — MAHABHARATA.

Fleet as the dew. — PHILIP B. MARSTON.

Fleet as zephyr's pinion. — THOMAS MOORE.

Fleeter than the roe. — SHAKESPEARE.

Fleeter than lightning's flash. — SOPHOCLES.

Fleet as light. — SWINBURNE.

Fleet as the lightning's laugh. — IBID.

Fleet
As words of men or snowflakes on the wind. — IBID.

Fleet and slim as Atalanta. — THOMAS WESTWOOD.

Fleet as shooting star. — IBID.

Fleet as the shadows. — WORDSWORTH.

Fleet as days and months and years. — IBID.

Fleeting.

Light and fleeting as a dream of night lost in garish day. — ÆSCHYLUS.

Fleeting as a shade. — ANON.

Fleeting as joy of youth. — EDWIN ARNOLD.

Fleeting like feathers in the winde alofte. — GEORGE GASCOIGNE.

As fleeting as April sunshine. — GERHART HAUPTMANN.

Fleeting
As bubbles that swim on the beaker's brim
And break on the lips while meeting.
— CHARLES FENNO HOFFMAN.

Fleeting as a passing sigh. — SIGMUND KRASINSKI.

Fleeting as air. — SWIFT.

Fleeting like a beam of light. — TENNYSON.

Fleeting as the bow in the clouds. — TUPPER.

A thing as fleeting as the thin sea-foam. — G. S. VIERECK.

Fleeting — *continued.*

Fleeting as the wings of sleep. — VIRGIL.

Fleeting as health or beauty. — WORDSWORTH.

Flesh.

All flesh is as grass, and all the glory of man as the flower of grass. The grass withereth, and the flower thereof falleth away. — NEW TESTAMENT.

Fleshless.

Fleshless as a joint of cane. — IRVIN S. COBB.

Fleshless as bars of steel. — DUMAS, PÈRE.

Fleshless as the talons of a hawk. — EDWIN MARKHAM.

Fleshless as a skeleton. — SAINT-PIERRE.

Flexible.

Flexible as a riding whip. — ANON.

As finely flexible as linen. — GEORGE W. CURTIS.

Flexible as figures in the hands of the statistician. — ISRAEL ZANGWILL.

Flickering (Adjective).

Flickering light like the jewels of a broken necklace. — KIPLING.

Flicker (Verb).

Flickering like a flame in the wind. — ANON.

Flicker like a lamp. — SIGMUND KRASINSKI.

Flickering like dying lamps in sepulchres. — SCHILLER.

Flickers like a blown-out flame. — SWINBURNE.

Flickering like a wind-bewildered leaf. — IBID.

Flicker like fire. — IBID.

Flickering like a casement 'gainst the sun. — CHARLES T. TURNER.

Flickering like a flame, half choked by wind and dust. — G. S. VIERECK.

Flimsy.

Flimsy as gauze. — ANON.

Flimsy as gossamer. — IBID.

Flinch.

Flinch . . . like a plant in too burning a sun. — THOMAS HARDY.

Fling.

Fling . . . as a bird flings o'er his shivering plumes the fountain's spray. — WILLIAM CULLEN BRYANT.

Flung up like a fortress lifted by powder. — GEORGE MEREDITH.

Flung like vile carrion to the hound. — SIR WALTER SCOTT.

Flung as foam from a ship's swiftness. — SHELLEY.

Flip.

Flips away like whalebone from the finger. — R. D. BLACKMORE.

Flippantly.

Flippantly, as a boy not yet grown bashful. — XENOPHON.

Flirt (Noun).

A flirt is like a dipper attached to a hydrant; every one is at liberty to drink from it, but no one desires to carry it away. — N. P. WILLIS.

Flirt (Verb).

She had flirted as far and wide as the butterfly flirts with the blossoms, as it flutters on through the range of a Summer day. — OUIDA.

Flirtation.

Flirtation is like the slime on water-plants, making them hard to handle, and when caught, only to be cherished in slimy waters. — DONALD G. MITCHELL.

Flirtation — *continued.*

Flirtations are like motor cars; they either exceed the speed limit and end in a smashup, or they are so slow that a girl nearly dies of nervous prostration waiting for them to get somewhere. — HELEN ROWLAND.

Flirtation is like a circulating library, in which we seldom ask twice for the same volume. — N. P. WILLIS.

Flit.

Flitted away like a bird on a wintry night. — ANON.

Flit like a summer cloud. — IBID.

Flitting like motes in the sunbeam. — JOHN BROUGHAM.

Seasons flit before the mind as flit the snow-flakes in a winter storm, seen rather than distinguished. — WILLIAM CULLEN BRYANT.

Flittering here and there, like sunshine in the uneasy ocean-waves. — IBID.

Flitted . . . fitfully as an April sunbeam. — BULWER-LYTTON.

Flitted like a spark. — HOOD.

Flit like a ghost away. — KEATS.

Fancies flit, and wheel like butterflies on banks of thyme. — ANDREW LANG.

Flit like blown feathers. — DON MARQUIS.

Flitting like a shadow of love. — DONALD G. MITCHELL.

Flits, like a living flake of fire. — SAMUEL MINTURN PECK.

Flit over the brain like the ghosts of the dead. — THOMAS PRINGLE.

He flits like a bee. — OSMANLI PROVERB.

Flit like a swallow that stoops to lave its burnished bosom in the wave. — T. BUCHANAN READ.

Flit,
Like spendor-winged moths about a
taper. — SHELLEY.

Flit, like life's enjoyments, on rapid, rapid wing. — CAROLINE SOUTHEY.

Flitted awäy like a kite wi' a brokken string. — TENNYSON.

Flits like a sudden drift of snow against the dull grey sky. — OSCAR WILDE.

Float.

Float away like the deluding mist of a mirage. — ANON.

Floating like the Hesperian garden of old. — IBID.

Floats like the lotus in the lake, unmoved. — IBID.

Floating downward in airy play,
Like spangles dropped from the glistening crowd
That whiten by night the milky way.
— WILLIAM CULLEN BRYANT.

Floating like the Cyannean Isles in the Euxine Sea. — ROBERT BURTON.

Floats over the troubles of life as the froth above the idle wave. — WILLIAM HAZLITT.

Floats like an atmosphere. — LONGFELLOW.

Floats like an Ark safely through all the deluge of the dark. — GERALD MASSEY.

Floats like soft-melting murmurs of grief. — JAMES MONTGOMERY.

Floating in the air like so many spiders upon their cobwebs. — MUNCHAUSEN.

Floats like oil upon brown seas. — NIETZSCHE.

Floating like foam upon the wave. — SIR WALTER SCOTT.

Floating like the streamers in the wind. — SOUTHEY.

Float — *continued.*

Gently floating . . . like a faery chime of blue harebells, heard in dreams, beneath the forest trees. — A. J. Symington.

They float in its rythmic measure like leaves on a summer stream. — Ella Wheeler Wilcox.

Flock.

Flocking into the country like pigeons in the Spring. — J. Fenimore Cooper.

Flocked to his call
Like sprites that necromancy
Of a Prospero holds in thrall.
— Don Marquis.

Flood.

It flooded the crimson twilight like the close of an Angel's Psalm. — Adelaide A. Procter.

Florid.

Florid as a milk-maid. — Anon.

Florid as the Spring. — Alfred Austin.

Flounce.

Flounce like a Fish. — Robert Wolseley.

Flounder.

Floundered, like a silly creature chasing a marsh-lamp. — George Meredith.

Flounder on, like wounded whales
Tossed on the bosom of a stormy sea.
— Wordsworth.

Flourish.

Flourishes like a green bay tree. — Anon.

Flourished . . . like scripture-trees called bay. — Robert Browning.

Flourishing as a Banyan-grove. — Carlyle.

As cedars beaten with continual storms, so great men flourish. — Chapman.

Flourishes like the mountain oak. — Agnes Repplier.

Flourish as a branch. — Old Testament.

Flourish like an herb. — Ibid.

Flourish like grass of the earth. — Ibid.

Flourish like the palm tree. — Ibid.

As a flower of the field so he flourisheth. — Ibid.

Flourishing as the flowers in May. — Lewis Wager.

Flow.

Flow like a free and flowing river. — Anon.

Eloquence flows like droppings of sweet poppy syrup. — Macaulay.

Flow, like the dews of the love-breathing night, from the warmth of the sun that has set. — Thomas Moore.

Bubble, bubble, flows the stream
Like an old tune through a dream.
— Maurice Thompson.

Flow as hugely as the sea. — Shakespeare.

Flowed like light amid the shadows of the sea cast from one cloudless star. — Shelley.

Flowed by like the streaming images of sleep. — Edith Wharton.

Flow,
Like smoke, along the level of the blast,
In mighty currents.
— Wordsworth.

Fluctuant.

Fluctuant, as the ark of Noah. — Bacon.

Fluctuate.

Fluctuated like a stormy sea, urged by the secret Furies. — Thomas Ashe.

Fluctuate — *continued.*

Fluctuated as flowers in rain
That bends them and they tremble
and rise again
And heave and straighten and quiver
all through with bliss
And turn afresh their mouths up for a
kiss,
Amorous, athirst of that sweet influent
love. — SWINBURNE.

Fluctuates like a sleepy wave. — BAYARD TAYLOR.

Fluent.

Fluent as the skylark sings
When first the morn allures its wings.
— AKENSIDE.

As fluent as a parrot is,
And far more Polly-glottish.
— HOOD.

Fluent as the sea. — SHAKESPEARE.

Fluid.

Fluid as a cloud or the air. — EMERSON.

Flurried.

Helpless and flurried as a fish landed on a grassy bank with a barbed hook through his gills. — OUIDA.

Flush.

Flushed to radiance where they
stood,
Like statues by the open tomb
Of shining saints half risen.
— E. B. BROWNING.

Flushed . . . like a rose. — AUBREY DE VERE.

Rosy flushes, like warm dreams of love. — FRANCES ANNE KEMBLE.

Flushes, like some young Hebe's lip. — THOMAS MOORE.

Have ne'er by shame been taught to
blush.
Like vernal roses in the sun flush.
— IBID.

Flushed as one afire with wine. — SWINBURNE.

Flutter.

Fluttered like a dead leaf in a blast. — P. J. BAILEY.

Fluttered like a winged asp. — IBID.

Fluttering like a raven wounded. — R. D. BLACKMORE.

Its meaning flutters in me like a flame under my own breath. — E. B. BROWNING.

Fluttering, like dumb creatures before storms. — IBID.

Fluttered like a tame bird, in among its forest brothers far too strong for it. — IBID.

Flutter . . . like sparrows round an owl. — BULWER-LYTTON.

Flutters up and down like a butterfly in a garden. — SAMUEL BUTLER.

Flutters as wing'd with joy. — BYRON.

Flutters as an unreal shadow. — CARLYLE.

Flutterings as in a slumbering aviary. — DAUDET.

Fluttered like a bird with broken wings. — DICKENS.

Flutter like snowflakes. — HAMLIN GARLAND.

Fluttering like a piece of gold leaf. — HAZLITT.

Fluttered noiseless as a flame. — J. G. HOLLAND.

Fluttering like new-mown hay. — O. W. HOLMES.

Flutter like a flickering, dying lamp. — SIGMUND KRASINSKI.

Fluttered like a lark. — GERALD MASSEY.

Flutters like a bird fresh caught. — MISS MITFORD.

Flutter — *continued.*

Fluttering like a prisoned bird. — Lewis Morris.

Flutters like a flower
Along the glory of the hills.
— John Payne.

Made my own heart flutter as a bird that beats for freedom at the bars that prison it. — James Whitcomb Riley.

Gauzy wings fluttered by
Like the ghost of a daisy dropped out of the sky. — Ibid.

Fluttering like pigeons. — C. G. Rossetti.

I flutter like a child after her mother. — Sappho.

Fluttered, like a vision. — Schiller.

Like snow-coloured petals
Of blossoms that flee
From storm that unsettles
The flower as the tree
They flutter.
— Swinburne.

Fluttering like spent fire. — Ibid.

Fluttered like a callow lark,
With dim fore-feeling of the azure free,
Sustaining wing and strength of songful glee. — Bayard Taylor.

Like an angel's pinion, fluttereth. — J. T. Trowbridge.

Fly.

(*See also* Fled *and* Flee.)

Each mysterious form,
Flew like the pictures of a morning dream. — Akenside.

Flew along like a bird in a tempest. — Anon.

Flies like antic shapes in dreams. — Ibid.

His arms flew like a windmill. — Ibid.

Flying, like blown flame. — Ibid.

Flies like chaff wide scattered by the wind. — Ibid.

Flew like feathered Mercury. — Ibid.

Flew like granado. — Ibid.

Words flew out of his mouth as shot out of a gatling gun. — Ibid.

Flew like a cloth-yard shaft from a bended yew. — R. H. Barham.

Fly, like a yelping Cur with a Bottle at his Tail. — Colley Cibber.

Fly as the leaves before the autumn tempest. — Ibid.

Fly as a bird on the wings of Night. — Arabian Nights.

Fly like . . . the northern wind. — Francis Beaumont.

Fly, like a full sail. — Beaumont and Fletcher.

Fly like chaff before the wind. — James Boswell.

Flying . . . like scatterings of dead leaves in autumn-gusts. — E. B. Browning.

Flew, as if he knew
A frenzied wretch was on his back.
— Eliza Cook.

Fly as from the plague. — John Davies.

Flies like a feather in the blast. — Joseph R. Drake.

Away like a glance of thought he flew. — Ibid.

Flies like the nimble journeys of the light. — Dryden.

Fly like doves that the exalted eagle spies. — Richard Duke.

Friends have flown, like leaves whirled away by the blast. — Mrs. E. Forrester.

A headlong crowd is flying
Like a billow that has broken and is shivered into spray.
— O. W. Holmes.

Fly — *continued.*

Fly
Like the cannons that burst on the Fourth of July. — IBID.

Flew as in a dream. — HUGO.

Sparks that fly
Like chaff from a threshing-floor.
— LONGFELLOW.

Flies like a bird unfettered from her cage. — MARIA LOWELL.

Flew like sparks in burnt up paper. — LOWELL.

Fly as fast as Iris or Jove's Mercury. — MARLOWE.

Fly as fast as the hare from the horn. — BRIAN MELBANCKE.

Flown
Like a smoke melted thinner than air,
That the vacancy doth disown.
— GEORGE MEREDITH.

Flew around like the spray on a storm-driven deck.—JOAQUIN MILLER.

Flown, like morning clouds, a thousand ways. — JAMES MONTGOMERY.

All flew like the down of a thistle. — CLEMENT C. MOORE.

Swiftly flew as glancing flame. — THOMAS MOORE.

Flown are those days with their winged delights, as the odor is gone from the summer rose. — LOUISE CHANDLER MOULTON.

Flew like the swift and dazzling flight of gold-winged orioles. — OUIDA.

As before the pike will fly
Dace and roach and such small fry;
As the leaf before the gale,
As the chaff beneath the flail,
As before the wolf the flocks,
As before the hounds the fox;
As before the cat the mouse,
As the rat from falling house;
As the fiend before the spell
Of holy water, book, and bell;
As the ghost from dawning day.
— THOMAS L. PEACOCK.

Some fly, like pendulums, from good to evil,
And in that point are madder than the devil. — CHRISTOPHER PITT.

He flies like a dog that has burnt his paw. — OSMANLI PROVERB.

Flew as the spirit flies from the dead. — D. G. ROSSETTI.

Fly like eagles which pursue their prey. — GEORGE SANDYS.

Flew at him, like the young hero Siegfried when he attacked the wild, long-bearded dwarf Alberich. — JOSEPH V. VON SCHEFFEL.

Flown like the light clouds of a Summer's day. — JOHN SCOTT.

Fly, like mist before the zephyr's sigh. — SIR WALTER SCOTT.

Fly like chidden Mercury from Jove. — SHAKESPEARE.

Like falcon to the lure, away she flies. — IBID.

Fly like thought. — IBID.

Like soldiers, when their captain once doth yield,
They basely fly. — IBID.

Like a flock of rooks at a farmer's gun
Night's dreams and terrors, every one,
Fled from the brains which are their prey. — SHELLEY.

Flew like the wind. — JOHN SKELTON.

Flew at him like an hellish fiend. — SPENSER.

Flew like a wyld gote. — IBID.

Fly, like scattered sheepe. — IBID.

Flew away as lightly as the wind. — IBID.

Flying fast as roebucke through the fen. — IBID.

Flie, as leapes the deere fled from the hunter's face. — EARL OF STIRLING.

Fly as if the devil drove. — SWIFT.

Fly — *continued.*

Fly away as a dream. — IBID.

Flown as flies the blown foam's feather. — SWINBURNE.

Fly as the eagle that hasteth to eat. — OLD TESTAMENT.

Flew like a blossom blown about. — WALTER THORNBURY.

Flown,
Like birds from the nest when their wings have grown.
— JOHN T. TROWBRIDGE.

Fly,
Like doves before the gathering storm.
— G. S. VIERECK.

Flown,
Like the morning-glory's cup.
— AMELIA B. WELBY.

Fly like flower-seeds on the breeze. — N. P. WILLIS.

Foam.

Foamed like a wounded thing. — SHELLEY.

Foamed like a flagon. — M. E. STEBBINS.

Foaming at the mouth like Champagne bottles. — ISRAEL ZANGWILL.

Fold.

The soft palms fold like kissing shells. — ANON.

Folds up like a crush hat or a concertina. — IRVIN S. COBB.

Folded like a wave. — O. W. HOLMES.

Shall fold their tents like the Arabs and as silently steal away. — LONGFELLOW.

The flowers fold their cups like praying hands. — GERALD MASSEY.

Folded like thoughts in a dream. — SHELLEY.

Eyelids folded like a white-rose leaf. — SWINBURNE.

Folded up as folds a primrose when the gates of day are shut. — EUGENE FITCH WARE.

Follow.

Follow the track of blood . . .
Like to some hound that hunts a wounded fawn. — ÆSCHYLUS.

Follow like a flock of sheep. — ANON.

Follow . . . like geese on a common. — IBID.

Follow one like Anthony's pig. — IBID.

Followed fate as an Irishman a wheelbarrow. — IBID.

Follows like a shadow. — IBID.

Followed faithfully
As if 'twere his shadow.
— EDWIN ARNOLD.

Follow'd her desire, as sunlight tracks the shadow of a cloud. — THOMAS ASHE.

I be bounde to followe it,
As the carpenter his ruler.
— ENGLISH BALLAD.

Follow one another like ducks in a gutter. — BEAUMONT AND FLETCHER.

The jackals of the desert follow their prey in families, like the place-hunters of Europe. — JOHN BRIGHT.

Followed like a comet-tail. — CARLYLE.

Followed like a child after the Pied Piper. — O. HENRY.

Follow each other, like surge upon surge. — WILLIAM KNOX.

Misfortune follows him like a faithful hound. — STEPHEN PHILLIPS.

Follow, as the night the day. — SHAKESPEARE.

Followed . . . like one drawn by a charm. - E. R. SILL.

Follow — *continued.*

Youth follows life, as bees the honeybell. — BAYARD TAYLOR.

Will follow thee,
As the ripple follows the bark at sea.
— WHITTIER.

Like geese each other follow.
— GEORGE WITHERS.

Folly.

Folly is like the growth of weeds, always luxurious and spontaneous; wisdom, like flowers, requires cultivation. — HOSEA BALLOU.

Folly is like a sore on a surfeited horse, cure it in one place and it breaks out in another. — DRYDEN.

Dead flies cause the ointment of the apothecary to send forth a stinking savour: so doth a little folly him that is in reputation for wisdom and honour. — OLD TESTAMENT.

Fond.

Fond as cat is of milk. — ANON.

Fond as the miser is of his gold. — IBID.

Fond and sad as Juliet. — ROBERT BRIDGES (American).

Fond as a bride. — JOHN GAY.

Fond as hounds are of running after foxes. — HOOD.

Fonder than ignorance. — SHAKESPEARE.

Fond of an old sweetheart as a brisk widow of her third husband. — JOHN WILSON.

Fool.

Fools are as like husbands as pilchards are to herrings. — SHAKESPEARE.

A fool, like a bottle, which would make you merry in company, will make you dull alone. — VANBROUGH.

Fools, like apes, are mimics from their birth. — WILLIAM WHITEHEAD.

Foolery.

Foolery, sir, does walk about the orb like the sun: it shines every where. — SHAKESPEARE.

Foolish.

Foolish as a calf. — ANON.

Foolish as an endeavor to make a lobster climb a tree and give a report of the atmospheric conditions. — IBID.

Foolish as a peacock. — IBID.

Foolish as to scratch one's head with a firebrand. — IBID.

Foolish as the tailor who sews sleeves to the pocket holes. — IBID.

Foolish as to flash a roll of bills before a lawyer. — IBID.

Foolish as to talk of color to a blind man. — IBID.

Foolish as to try to pull hair from a bald man's head. — IBID.

Thare iz just this difference between a fule and a hen, the fule cackels before, the hen not till after the egg iz lade. — JOSH BILLINGS.

More foolish than the prodigal who
eats
The husks of sense.
— LEWIS MORRIS.

Foolish, as to look for a rainbow in the night. — SYDNEY MUNDEN.

Foolish as to have confidence to promise himself three years. — RABELAIS.

Foolish as the disturbing phantoms of the night. — WALTER TRUMBULL.

Foolish as a search would be for new sunlight to illuminate the marbles of Michael Angelo. — WILLIAM WINTER.

Forbidding.

Forbidding as a mourning card. — COMPTON MACKENZIE.

Force.

Creative force, like a musical composer, goes on unwearyingly repeating a simple air or theme, now high, now low, in solo, in chorus, ten thousand times reverberated, till it fills earth and heaven with the chant.
— EMERSON.

Forcible.

Forcible as custom. — BACON.

Forehead.

Her forehead's like the show'ry bow,
When shining sunbeams intervene,
And gild the distant mountain's brow. — BURNS.

A forehead more pure than the Parian stone. — WHITTIER.

Foremost.

Foremost in his mind,
Like the keen prow of some on-forging ship.
— PAUL LAURENCE DUNBAR.

Forged.

Forged like steel and tempered thought. — SWINBURNE.

Forgiving.

Forgiving like unto the Earth herself. — MAHABHARATA.

Forgotten.

Forgotten like waves on the sea. — ANON.

Thrown aside and forgotten as are the hoofs and horns of a buffalo. — J. FENIMORE COOPER.

By all forgot, like a flower whose stem is broken. — BARRY CORNWALL.

Forgotten, as the foliage of thy youth. — COWPER.

Forgotten like the forms of last year's clouds. — FRANKLIN.

Poor and forgotten like a clod upon the field. — HUGO.

Forgotten like an almanac out of date. — M. DE LA BRUYÈRE.

Forgotten like an antique tale
Of Hero and Leander.
— CHARLES LAMB.

Forgotten as a fallen star. — HARRY B. SMITH.

Forgotten as changes of dreams. — SWINBURNE.

Forgotten like spilt wine. — IBID.

Forgotten as a dead man out of mind. — OLD TESTAMENT.

Forgotten like a dream. — WORDSWORTH.

Forked.

Forked like the loveliest lightnings. — SWINBURNE.

Forlorn.

As forlorn as the faded coquette. — WILLIAM ALLEN BUTLER.

Forlorn
As midnight, and despairing of a morn.
— COWPER.

Forlorn,
As the night-owl's sob of fear,
As Memnon moaning at morn.
— JEAN INGELOW.

Formal.

Formal and precise, like rooms which we enter and leave, not those in which we settle and dwell. — BULWER-LYTTON.

Formal . . . as the veil of a nun. — HENRY JAMES.

Formal as a Quaker. — GEORGE P. MORRIS.

Formless.

Formless as air. — P. J. BAILEY.

Formless as midnight. — HUGO.

Forsaken.

Forsaken like some old house one moves out of and locks up when one has gotten a new one. — BJÖRNSTJERNE BJÖRNSON.

Forsaken, as ships go to old Davy. — HOOD.

Forsaken — *continued.*

Forsake us soon, like morning-stars. — JOHN POMFRET.

Forsaken, like the shadows that fly from the dawn. — WILLIAM WINTER.

Fortune.

Fortune, like other females, delights rather on favoring the young than the old. — ADDISON.

Fortune is like women, loves youth and is fickle. — ANON.

Fortune is like the market, where, many times, if you can stay a little, the price will fall; and again, it is sometimes like Sibylla's offer, which at first offereth the commodity at full, then consumeth part and part, and still holdeth up the price. — BACON.

The way of Fortune is like the milky way in the sky; which is a meeting, or knot, of a number of small stars, not seen asunder, but giving light together; so are there a number of little and scarce discerned virtues, or rather faculties and customs, that make men fortunate. — IBID.

Fortune resembles an unjust distributor of the Olympic prizes, in so much as she most frequently bestows her favours on the undeserving. — DEMOPHILUS.

False Fortune, like a fawning strumpet,
About to leave the bankrupt prodigal,
With a dissembled smile would kiss at
parting,
And flatter to the last. — DRYDEN.

Good fortune, like ripe fruit, ought to be enjoyed while it is present. — EPICTETUS.

Many fortunes, like rivers, have a pure source, but grow muddy as they grow large. — J. PETIT-SENN.

Fortune is like a widow won,
And truckles to the bold alone.
— WILLIAM SOMERVILLE.

Fortune, like other drabs, values a man gradually less for every year he lives. — SWIFT.

Fortune is like glass — the brighter the glitter, the more easily it is broken. — PUBLIUS SYRUS.

Fortune as well as women must be taken in the humor. — WYCHERLEY.

Forward.

Forward like a fierce hound straining on a leash. — SIR A. CONAN DOYLE.

Forward like a wind-blown flame. — FRANCIS THOMPSON.

Foul.

Foul as Zebedee's hen that laid three rotten eggs to a good one. — J. R. BARTLETT'S "DICTIONARY OF AMERICANISMS."

Foul, like a birding place. — THOMAS DEKKER.

Foul as a sty.
— EDGAR LEE MASTERS.

Foul as slander. — SHAKESPEARE.

Foul as Vulcan's stithy. — IBID.

Foul as bloated pestilence. — RICHARD SHEIL.

Foul as plague-polluted gloom. — SWINBURNE.

Foundling.

The devoted benches of public justice were filled by some of those foundlings of fortune, who, overwhelmed in the torrent of corruption at an early period, lay at the bottom, like drowned bodies, while soundness or sanity remained in them; but, at length, becoming buoyant by putrefaction, they rose as they rotted, and floated to the surface of the polluted stream, where they were drifted along, the objects of terror, and contagion, and abomination. — J. P. CURRAN.

Fragile.

Fragile as a lily. — ANON.

Fragile as rainbows. — IBID.

Fragile as a shade. — BALZAC.

Fragile as a dream. — WALTER MALONE.

Fragile as a leaf. — DONALD G. MITCHELL.

As fragile as a strand of rain. — JAMES WHITCOMB RILEY.

Fragile as some dream which Hope with hollow hand hath guided. — MARY A. TOWNSEND.

Fragrance.

The fragrance of her rich and delightful character still lingered about the place where she had lived, as a dried rosebud scents the drawer where it has withered and perished. — HAWTHORNE.

Fragrant.

As fragrant as clover's sod. — ANON.

Fragrant as musk. — IBID.

Fragrant as field-flowers. — BALZAC.

Fragrant . . . as May. — LORD DE TABLEY.

Fragrant as a violet on a summer's night. — EMERSON.

Fragrant as the breath of angels. — O. W. HOLMES.

Fragrant as thyme upon the mountains. — DR. JOHNSON.

Apples, as fragrant, and as bright a hue, as those which in Alcinous' gardens grew, mellowed by constant sunshine; or as those, which graced the Hesperides, in burnished rows. — JUVENAL.

Fragrant as the morning rose. — MARLOWE.

Fragrant as the frosted blossom of a May night. — GEORGE MEREDITH.

Fragrant as the dewfall. — SWINBURNE.

Fragrant as lilacs. — THACKERAY.

Fragrant as the breath of flow'rs. — WILLIAM THOMSON.

Frail.

Frail as a lily. — ANON.

Frail as flesh is. — LAMAN BLANCHARD.

Frail as the leaf in Autumn's yellow bower. — CAMPBELL.

Frail as the clouds. — DE QUINCEY.

Frail as a sigh. — SYDNEY DOBELL.

Frail as the web that misty night has spun. — O. W. HOLMES.

Frail as dishes. — HOOD.

Frail as frost-landscapes on a window-pane. — LOWELL.

Frail as the clouds of sunset. — JAMES MONTGOMERY.

Frail as glass. — PETRARCH.

Frail as a flake of snow. — A. J. RYAN.

Frail
As May's first lily in a Northern vale.
— BAYARD TAYLOR.

Frail
As perfume of the cuckoo-flower.
— TENNYSON.

Frank.

Frank as growths of spring. — GEORGE ELIOT.

Frank as a soldier. — JAMES GRAHAME.

Frank as the call of April birds.
— W. E. HENLEY.

Frank as the day. — CHARLES READE.

Frantic.

Frantic as a war dance. — ANON.

Frantic like a madman's dream. — GEORGE GRANVILLE.

Frayed.

Frayed like fretted foam. — ALFRED AUSTIN.

Freckled.

Freckled like a pard. — KEATS.

Free.

Free,
As Thames and Seine, St. Lawrence, Nile, and Ganges,
Mingled in one illimitable sea.
— GRANT ALLEN.

Free as a fly. — ANON.

Free as a gift. — IBID.

Free as a wood sawer. — IBID.

Free as egg-nog on Christmas Eve. — IBID.

Free as the diamond is free from alloy. — IBID.

Free as the sybil's leaves of yore. — IBID.

Free as thought. — IBID.

Free as a hurricane. — IBID.

Free as a mountain goat. — IBID.

As free from artifice as is the dimple in childhood's cheek. — ALFRED AUSTIN.

Free as Phœbus. — BEAUMONT AND FLETCHER.

Free as wanton winds. — APHRA BEHN.

Free, as a young calf, from sorrow. — IBID.

Free as whispering air. — IBID.

Free as bird on branch, just as ready to fly east as west. — E. B. BROWNING.

Free as light. — IBID.

Free as a babe from cheating. — ROBERT BROWNING.

Free as cloud and sunbeam are. — IBID.

Free and winding as a poet's thought through his verse. — BULWER-LYTTON.

Free and graceful . . . like Dian when the bounding hart she tracks through the morning dew. — CHÆREMON.

Free as the wind. — CHATTERTON.

Free as the light and air. — CHURCHILL.

Free as water. — WILL LEVINGTON COMFORT.

Free as the sunbeams on the chainless air. — ROBERT T. CONRAD.

Free-handed as a harlot. — JOHN DAVIDSON.

Free as a liberated ghost. — SYDNEY DOBELL.

Free and noble as clear poesy. — MICHAEL DRAYTON.

Free as nature first made man. — DRYDEN.

Free as an Arab. — EMERSON.

Free as a mountain bird. — W. S. GILBERT.

Free as a tethered ass. — IBID.

Free as the hawk. — GOETHE.

Smiling free, as rose to summer air. — DORA GREENWELL.

Free as the soul. — EDWARD HAKE.

Free, like one who trails the plough. — SAMUEL HOFFENSTEIN.

Good and free
As when poor Eve was innocent.
— JEAN INGELOW.

Free as an eagle. — KEATS.

Free as the sky-searching lark.
— IBID.

Free as the breeze. — FRANCIS SCOTT KEY.

More divinely free
Than Pacific's boundless sea.
— FREDERIC L. KNOWLES.

Free — *continued.*

Free as ambient air. — SIR ROGER L'ESTRANGE.

Free as the waters of life. — ALFRED HENRY LEWIS.

Free as a king. — THOMAS LODGE.

Free as warmth in summer's weather. — CHARLES MACKAY.

Free as breezes be on Nature's velvet flooring. — ERIC MACKAY.

Free as the thought that ye canna confine. — D. M. MOIR.

Free as Severn's waves, that spring to bless
Their parent hills.
— JAMES MONTGOMERY.

Free as the fetterless wind. — THOMAS MOORE.

Free as first innocence. — OTWAY.

Free as mountain winds. — SHAKESPEARE.

Freer than a jailer. — IBID.

Free in spirit as the mountain. — SHELLEY.

Free from flaw or stain as diamond from the mine. — D. B. W. SLADEN.

Free,
As the stars' mountain-tops be,
As the pearl, in the depths of the sea,
From the portionless king that wears it. — E. C. STEDMAN.

Free
As birds that breast and brave the sea.
— SWINBURNE.

Free as the circling sea. — IBID.

Free as heaven. — IBID.

Free-born as winds and stars and waves are free. — IBID.

Freer than birds or dreams are free. — IBID.

Free as song. — BAYARD TAYLOR.

As free as the eagle's wing. — HENRY D. THOREAU.

Free as fishing is. — IZAAK WALTON.

Free as Emperors. — WILLIAM WARD.

Free as our rivers are
Ocean-ward going.
— WHITTIER.

Free to rise
As leaves on Autumn's whirlwind borne. — IBID.

Free as India's leopard. — N. P. WILLIS.

Free as the soul of the fragrant wine. — WILLIAM WINTER.

Free as the Sun. — WORDSWORTH.

Free as our desires. — IBID.

Freely

Freely as the streams of Eden flowed. — IBID.

Freely, as the firmament embraces the world. — SCHILLER.

As freely as a conduit spout. — C. TOURNEUR.

Frequent

Frequent as the "begats" in the Bible. — ANON.

Frequent as figs at Kaunos. — ROBERT BROWNING.

Frequent as telegraph poles on a railway journey. — SYDNEY MUNDEN.

Fresh.

Fresh as an apple-tree bloom. — WILLIAM ALLINGHAM.

Fresh as May-flowers. — ANACREON.

Fresh as a buttercup. — ANON.

Fresh as a cherub. — IBID.

Fresh as a flower just blown. — IBID.

Fresh as an egg from the farm. — IBID.

Fresh as a November chrysanthemum. — IBID.

Fresh as a sea breeze. — IBID.

Fresh — *continued.*

Fresh and charming as Hebe. — IBID.

Fresh as if she had been born with the morning. — IBID.

Fresh as a young head of lettuce. — IBID.

Fresh as summer's grass. — IBID.

Fresh as the dawn. — IBID.

Fresh as the dewy field. — IBID.

Fresh as the firstlings o' the year. — IBID.

Fresh as Fiumicino's foam. — ALFRED AUSTIN.

Fresh and fragrant as a rose. — P. J. BAILEY.

Fresh as a sprouting spring upon the hills. — IBID.

As fresh as any flower. — ENGLISH BALLAD.

Her face is as fresh as a frosty morning in Autumn. — BALZAC.

Fresh as a white rosebud. — IBID.

Fresh as dew. — IBID.

Fresh as butter just from the churn. — J. R. BARTLETT'S "DICTIONARY OF AMERICANISMS."

Fresh, as the floweret opening on the morn. — BEATTIE.

Fresher than the day-star. — R. D. BLACKMORE.

Fresh as from Paradise. — ROBERT BROWNING.

Lips to lips
Fresh as the wilding hedge-rose-cup there slips
The dewdrop out of. — IBID.

Fresh as the flow'r amid the sunny showr's of May. — MICHAEL BRUCE.

Fresher than the morning dawn
When rising Phœbus first is seen.
— BURNS.

Fresh as a nursing mother. — BYRON.

Fressh as a rose. — CHAUCER.

As fressh as faucon comen out of mewe. — IBID.

As fressh as is the brighte someres day. — IBID.

Fressh as is the monthe of May. — IBID.

Fresh as sea-born Cythera. — HARTLEY COLERIDGE.

Fresh as the foamy surf. — ELIZA COOK.

Fresh and as gay
As the fairest and sweetest, that blow
On the beautiful bosom of May.
— COWPER.

All show'd as fresh, and faire, and innocent, as virgins to their lovers' first survey. — SIR WILLIAM DAVENANT.

Fresh as a clover bud. — LORD DE TABLEY.

Fresh as a lark. — DICKENS.

Fresh as butter. — IBID.

Fresh as a fresh young pear-tree blossoming. — AUSTIN DOBSON.

Fresh as primrose buds. — EDWARD DOWDEN.

As fresh as flovis that in May up spredis. — WILLIAM DUNBAR.

As fresh as rain drops. — GEORGE ELIOT.

Fresh as the trickling rainbow in July. — EMERSON.

Fresh as the wells that stand in natural rock in summer woods or violet-scented grove. — F. W. FABER.

Fresh as early day. — FRANCIS FAWKES.

Fresh, like the larks, from a dew bath in the daisies. — S. GERTRUDE FORD.

Fresh as a peach. — GOETHE.

Fresh — *continued.*

Fresh as the May-blown rose. — Richard Glover.

Fresh as a blossom bathed by April rain. — P. H. Hayne.

Fresh as the breeze blowing over the heather. — O. W. Holmes.

Fresh as the dews of our prime. — Ibid.

Fresh as April when the breezes blow. — R. M. Milnes.

Fresh and fine as a spring in winter. — Richard Hovey.

Fresh as April's heaven. — Hugo.

Fresh as a young girl. — Ibid.

Fresh as milk and roses. — Jean Ingelow.

As fresh as the fruit on the tree. — Henry James.

Fresh as the morning. — Ben Jonson.

Fresher than berries of a mountain-tree. — Keats.

Fresh as Aurora's blushing morn. — William King.

Freshening as the morning air. — C. M. S. McLellan.

Fresh as a pippin. — Theophilus Marzials.

Fresh as the drop of dew cradled at morn. — Gerald Massey.

Fresh as the orchard apple. — George Meredith.

Fresh as light from a star just discovered. — Thomas Moore.

Fresh as Spring. — Coventry Patmore.

Fresh as paint. — Sir Arthur T. Quiller-Couch.

Fresh as the welling waters. — Samuel Rogers.

Fresh as dew. — C. G. Rossetti.

Fresh as the sun. — Ibid.

Fresh as the tropic rose. — Charles Sangster.

As fresh as a May gowan. — Sir Walter Scott.

Fresh as an old oak. — Ibid.

Fresh as a bridegroom. — Shakespeare.

Fresh as Dian's visage. — Ibid.

Fresh as morning's dew distill'd on flowers. — Ibid.

Fresh as flower of May. — Spenser.

Fresh as flowers in medow greene doe grow. — Ibid.

Fresh as morning rose. — Ibid.

Fresh as a four-year-old. — R. S Surtees.

Fresh as farthing from the mint. — Swift.

Fresh as the spirit of sunrise. — Swinburne.

Fresh as a sea-flower. — Ibid.

Fresh as a man's recollections of boyhood. — Thackeray.

Fresh as the first beam glittering on a sail. — Tennyson.

Fresh as the foam, new-bathed in Paphian wells. — Ibid.

Fresh and ruddy as a parson's daughter. — Bonnell Thornton.

Fresh as a daisy. — Tolstoy.

Fresh as Eden. — Henry Vaughan.

Fresh as Spring's earliest violet. — Whittier.

Fresh as the moon. — Ibid.

Fresh as the lovely form of youthful May, when nymphs and graces in the dance unite. — Wieland.

Fresh as banner bright, unfurl'd to music suddenly. — Wordsworth.

Fresh as a lark mounting at break of day. — Ibid.

Fret.

Frets like gumm'd taffety. — ANON.

Fretting as fire frets, an inch from dry wood. — ROBERT BROWNING.

Fret as in a cage. — FREDERICK W. FABER.

Fret,
Like a pupil of Walton and Cotton,
Who remains by the brink of the water, agape,
While the jack, trout, or barbel effects its escape
Thro' the gut or silk line being rotten. — HOOD.

Fretting like a wild horse struggling to escape. — HUGO.

Frets like a gummed velvet. — SHAKESPEARE.

Friend.

A false friend is like a shadow on a dial; it appears in clear weather, but vanishes as soon as a cloud approaches. — ANON.

A true friend is like sound health; the value of it is seldom known until it is lost. — IBID.

A real friend is somewhat like a ghost or apparition; much talked of, but rarely seen. — CHARLES N. BUCK.

The malyce of a friend, is like the sting of an Aspe, which nothing can remedie, for being pearced in the hande it must be cut off, and a friend thrust to the heart it must be pulled out. — LYLY.

But as all floures that are in one Nosegay, are not of one nature, nor all Rings that are worne vppon one hande, are not of one fashion: so all friendes that associate at bedde and at boord, are not one of disposition. — IBID.

Friends are like melons: to find one good, you must a hundred try. — CLAUDE MERMET.

A friend both wise and true amid all shocks resplendent shines, like fire upon a rock's high top, which dissipates the darkness round and fills the travellers by with joy profound. — ORIENTAL.

A friend should be like money, tried before being required, not found faulty in our need. — PLUTARCH.

A profitless friend is like a fleece without hair. — OSMANLI PROVERB.

An untried friend is like an uncracked nut. — RUSSIAN PROVERB.

A new friend is as new wine; when it is old thou shalt drink it with pleasure. — SIRACH.

Old friends, like old swords, still are trusted best. — JOHN WEBSTER.

Friends, like mistresses, are avoided for obligations past. — WYCHERLEY.

Friendless.

Friendless as an alarm clock. — ANON.

Friendly.

Friendly as a spotted leopard that's been stirred up with an elephant hook. — SEWELL FORD.

Friendly as a puppy. — BETTINA VON HUTTEN.

Friendship.

The friendship of a great man is like the shadow of a bush, soon gone. — ANON.

The friendship of the ever-genial man is too often like a grate-fire, exceedingly bright to look at, but not reliable in so far as the dispensation of warmth on a really cold day is concerned. — IBID.

False friendship, like the ivy, decays and ruins the walls it embraces; but true friendship gives new life and animation to the object it supports — ROBERT BURTON.

Friendship — *continued.*

As the Sun is in the Firmament, so is friendship in the world, a most divine and heavenly band.—ROBERT BURTON.

The firmest friendships have been formed in mutual adversity, as iron is most strongly united by the fiercest flame. — C. C. COLTON.

Friendship is less apparent when
too nigh,
Like objects when they touch the
eye. — COWLEY.

As the harbour is the refuge of the ship from the tempest, so is friendship the refuge of man in adversity. — DEMOPHILUS.

Friendship, like love, is but a name,
Unless to one you stint the flame. —
The child whom many fathers share,
Hath seldom known a father's care.
'Tis thus in friendship; who depend
On many, rarely find a friend.
— JOHN GAY.

Friendship is like a debt of honor; the moment it is talked of it loses its real name, and assumes the more ungrateful form of obligation. — GOLDSMITH.

The feeling of friendship is like that of being comfortably filled with roast beef. — DR. JOHNSON.

Friendship, like love, is destroyed by long absence, though it may be increased by short intermissions. — IBID.

Friendshippe should be like the wine which Homer much commending, calleth Maroneum, whereof one pient [pint] being mingled with fiue quartes of water, yet it keepeth his old strength and vertue, not to be qualified by any discurtesie. Where salt doth grow nothing els can breede, where friendship is built, no offence can harbour. — LYLY.

Houses are like friendship; there is hardly one in a thousand worth a long lease. — OUIDA.

Friendship is like those ancient altars where the unhappy, and even the guilty, found a sure asylum. — MADAME SWETCHINE.

Friendship is like rivers, and the strand of seas, and the air, common to all the world; but tyrants, and evil customs, wars, and want of love, have made them proper and peculiar.
— JEREMY TAYLOR.

New friends, like one's best coat and patent-leather boots, are only intended for holiday wear. At other times they are neither serviceable nor comfortable; they do not answer the required purposes, are ill adapted to give us the ease we seek. A new coat, however, has this advantage, that in time it will become old and comfortable; so much can by no means be predicted with certainty of a new friend. — ANTHONY TROLLOPE.

Friendship — our friendship — is like the beautiful shadows of evening, spreading and growing till life and its light pass away. — MIHALY VITKOVICS.

The friendship of the world is like the leaves falling from the trees in autumn; while the sap of maintenance lasts, friends swarm in abundance; but in the winter of our need they leave us naked. — WARWICK.

Frightened.

As frightened as Macbeth before the ghost of Banquo. — LOUIS VEUILLOT.

Frigid.

Frigid as an iceberg. — ANON.

Frilled.

Frilled like a French chop. — ANON.

Frisk.

Frisk away,
Like school-boys, at th' expected warning,
To joy and play. — BURNS.

Frisk about like a wanton she-goat. — HORACE.

Frisky.

Frisky as colts. — DANIEL WEBSTER.

Frizzle.

Frizzled like a lawyer's wig. — R. D. BLACKMORE.

Frolic.

Frolic as the snow. — RICHARD HOVEY.

Frolicsome.

Frolicsome as a boy. — ANON.

Front.

Always in front, like a cow-catcher on a locomotive. — ANON.

Like a camel's guide, he always keeps in front. — OSMANLI PROVERB.

Frown.

Frowned like a fury. — WILLIAM BLAKE.

Frowning, as if in his unconscious arm
He held the thunder. — COWPER.

My frown is like a winter house,
Laid eastward in a bitter land.
— LORD DE TABLEY.

Frowns, like winter storms. — JAMES SHIRLEY.

Frowned like a thunder-cloud. — STEPHEN SMITH.

Frowned like Good Friday. — SPENSER.

Frugal.

Frugality, like a short and pleasant journey, is attended with much enjoyment and little toil. — DEMOPHILUS.

Frugal, like a beggar's child. — EMERSON.

Fruitful.

Fruitful as Ceres. — ANON.

As fruitful as Egypt. — ROBERT BURTON.

Fruitful as seeded earth. — GEORGE ELIOT.

Fruitful as the full-grown year. — AARON HILL.

Fruitful as the free elements. — SHAKESPEARE.

Fruitful as the land that feeds us. — IBID.

Fruitful as a sheltering palm. — SWINBURNE.

Fruitless.

Fruitless as the celebrated bee who wanted to swarm alone. — G. K. CHESTERTON.

Fruitless as it would be to explain the most difficult problems of Sir Isaac Newton to one ignorant of vulgar arithmetic. — FIELDING.

Fruitless as the lamentations of a prophet crying in the wilderness. — FRANK HORRIDGE.

Full.

Full as a goat. — ANON.

As full as a toad is of poison. — IBID.

Full of airs as a music box. — IBID.

Full of angles as the book of Euclid. — IBID.

As full of blunders as a successful career. — IBID.

Full of events as a dime novel. — IBID.

Full of poetry as a lily is of dew. — IBID.

Full of royalty as a pack of cards. — IBID.

Full of terror as a tragedy of Sophocles. — IBID.

Full of maggots as a pastoral poet's flock. — SAMUEL BUTLER.

Full as the hyve is of honey. — CHAUCER.

Full of company as a jail. — THOMAS DEKKER.

Full — *continued.*

Full as a bee with thyme. — ROBERT HERRICK.

Full of life as a multitude. — HUGO.

Chock full of noble sentiments as a bladder is of wind. — J. K. JEROME.

Full as a piper's bag. — BEN JONSON.

Full of noise as a mill. — LEAN'S "COLLECTANEA."

Full of life and light and sweetness
As a summer day's completeness.
— LOWELL.

Full of fragrant love as May's musk-roses are of morning's wine. — GERALD MASSEY.

Full of folds as a sleeping boa-constrictor. — WILLIAM MATHEWS.

Full of passion as a tiger. — BRANDER MATTHEWS.

Full as a tick. — JOHN RAY'S "HANDBOOK OF PROVERBS."

As fu' as a biled wulk. — SCOTTISH PROVERB.

As fu' as a piper. — IBID.

As fu' as the Baltic. — IBID.

Full as a plenteous river. — C. G. ROSSETTI.

As full of labour as a wise man's art. — SHAKESPEARE.

Full of quarrels as an egg is full of meat. — IBID.

Full of spirit as the month of May. — IBID.

As full of sorrows as the seas of sands. — IBID.

Full as a cup with the vine's burning dew. — SHELLEY.

As full of wisdom as a cheese of mites. — SPENSER.

Full as a feaster's hand
Fills full with bloom of bland
Bright wine his cup.
— SWINBURNE.

Full of the knowledge of the Lord, as the waters cover the sea. — OLD TESTAMENT.

Full as the summer rose. — JAMES THOMSON.

Fulsome.

As fat and fulsome to mine ear
As howling after music.
— SHAKESPEARE.

Fumbling.

Fumbling . . . like a ricketty cricket, saying its beads. — DANIEL HENRY HOLMES.

Fumbling about her like a drowning person. — HUGO.

Fume.

Fumed, like champagne that is fizzy. — BLISS CARMAN.

Fume like a stew-pot. — EDWARD SHARPHAM.

Fun.

Fun has no limits; it is like the human race and face; there is a family resemblance among all the species, but they all differ. — SAM SLICK.

Funny.

Funny as a wooden leg. — GEORGE ADE.

Funny as a barrel of monkeys. — ANON.

Funny as a clown. — IBID.

Funny as a crutch. — IBID.

As funny as a funeral in a snow storm. — IBID.

Funny as to throw an egg into an electric fan. — IBID.

Funny as an open switch. — AMY LESLIE.

Furious.

Furious as a favored child
Balked of its wish. — BYRON.

As breme [furiously] as blase of straw yset on fyre. — CHAUCER.

Furious — *continued.*

Furious . . . like a wounded bull in an arena. — DUMAS, PÈRE.

Furious as the wind. — OTWAY.

Furious . . . as a bitch is when she has lost her puppies. — VANBRUGH.

Furtively.

Embraced her tenderly but furtively like a feather curling round a lovely head, caressing yet scarce touching. — CHARLES READE.

Eyes furtively, like a guilty person. — IBID.

Fuss.

As much fuss as a bushel of salt thrown into a furnace. — ANON.

Futile.

Futile as to turn back the hands of a clock. — ANON.

Futile as a tenor in a boiler shop. — HENRY IRVING DODGE.

Future.

The Past is like a funeral gone by. The Future comes like an unwelcome guest. — EDMUND GOSSE.

G

Gabble.

Gabbled like a goose. — PHILIP FRENEAU.

Gabble like tinkers.—SHAKESPEARE.

Gabbles,
Like the laborers of Babel. — SWIFT.

Gad.

Like frisking heifer, loose in flowery meads,
She gads where'er her roving fancy leads. — AMBROSE PHILIPS.

Gaiety.

Gaiety is to good-humor as animal perfumes to vegetable fragrance. — DR. JOHNSON.

Gallant.

Gallant as the Abencerrages of Grenada. — ANTHONY HAMILTON.

Gallantly.

Gallantly as a good ship meets a heavy sea. — MISS MULOCK.

Gallantly, like an old fencer. — RABELAIS.

Gallop.

Galloping like a fury. — ANON.

Galloping, as with dispatches from the Pit,
Between his hell-born hounds.
— W. E. HENLEY.

I had seen the Arab galloping like the wind. — GUY DE MAUPASSANT.

Gambol.

Gambol like a fawn. — ANON.

Gambol like a lambkin. — IBID.

Gambol like a young cat and her first kitten. — IBID.

Gambol like a dancing skiff. — WORDSWORTH.

Game.

Game as a badger. — ANON.

Game as a fighting cock. — IBID.

Game as a lion. — IBID.

Game as a pebble. — IBID.

Game as hornets. — ALFRED HENRY LEWIS.

Gape.

Gaping mouth wide open like a dying codfish. — ANON.

Gape as it were dogs for a bone. — ALEXANDER BARCLAY.

Gape — *continued.*

Mouths that gap'd like bung-holes. — BEAUMONT AND FLETCHER.

Gape like an oyster. — IBID.

Gaping like an indolent lion. — J. FENIMORE COOPER.

Gapes like a sheriff for execution. — JOHN DAY.

Gape wider than an oyster-wife. — THOMAS DEKKER.

Like dead heaps of fishes, stranded by the storm-spray, gaping, staring. — ALFRED DOMETT.

Gaped, like the griesly mouth of hell. — SPENSER.

Gaping like a stuck pig. — SWIFT.

Garlanded.

Ribanded and garlanded like a thyrsus. — EDMUND GOSSE.

Garrulous.

Garrulous as an old maid. — ANON.

Garrulous as a magpie. — MASON L. WEEMS.

Gasp.

Gasping like a fish newly taken from the water. — EDWARD EGGLESTON.

Gasping . . . like a trout after water on a kitchen table. — FLAUBERT.

Gasping like frogs in drought. — KINGSLEY.

Gather.

Gathered like ants. — ANON.

Gather like a locust's crew. — BYRON.

Gather like night-dew. — IBID.

Like a morning mist it gathered. — O. W. HOLMES.

Gathers like a tide. — CHRISTOPHER PITT.

Gather,
Like flocks of clouds in spring's delightful weather. — SHELLEY.

Gathering . . . As broken breakers rally and roar
The loud wind down that drives off shore. — SWINBURNE.

Gather . . . like flies in the sun. — IBID.

Gathered thy children together, even as a hen gathereth her chickens under her wings. — NEW TESTAMENT.

Gathered as water spilt on the ground, which cannot be gathered up again. — OLD TESTAMENT.

Gaudy.

Gaudy as a butterfly. — WILLIAM HAZLITT.

Gaudy as the summer. — JAMES SHIRLEY.

Gaudy, like a harlequin's jacket. — THACKERAY.

Gaunt.

Gaunt as a wolf. — AUSTIN DOBSON.

Gaunt as a gibbet. — LORD DE TABLEY.

Gaunt as bitterns in the pools. — EMERSON.

Gaunt,
Like the drear soul of poverty — T. GORDON HAKE.

Gaunt as a greyhound. — JOHN RAY'S "HANDBOOK OF PROVERBS."

Gaunt as a grave. — SHAKESPEARE.

Gaunt as it were the skeleton of himself. — TENNYSON.

Gay.

Gay as a blackbird. — ANON.

Gay as a bullfinch. — IBID.

Gay as a negro funeral. — IBID.

Gay as the tropic bird's sheen is youth's fresh frolic freeness. — A H. BEESLY.

Gay and gladsome as the air. — MARY E. BLAKE.

Gay — *continued.*

Gay as Colinette. — ROBERT BRIDGES (American).

Gay as a woman's wish. — HENRY BROOKE.

Gay . . . like a Swiss guard off duty.
— ROBERT BROWNING.

Gay as a guinea. — ROBERT BUCHANAN.

Gay as the gilded summer sky. — BURNS.

Gaie as all nature at the mornyng's smile. — CHATTERTON.

Gay as gold. — "CHESTER PLAYS."

Gay as the dahlia's bloom. — ELIZA COOK.

Gay,
As the fairest and sweetest, that blow
On the beautiful bosom of May.
— COWPER.

Gay as a butterfly. — DICKENS.

Gay as a thrush. — AUSTIN DOBSON.

Gay as a chaffinch. — DUMAS, PÈRE.

Gay as larks. — LA FONTAINE.

Gay as Apollo's locks. — JOHN FORD.

Gay as the joy of a maiden's look. — SAM WALTER FOSS.

Gay,
Like to a light and brilliant butterfly,
Around a dusky flower. — GOETHE.

Gay as a mote. — WILLIAM HAZLITT.

Gay as the thistledown over the lea. — T. W. HIGGINSON.

Gay and fleeting
As bubbles that swim on the beaker's brim, and break on the lips while meeting.
— C. F. HOFFMAN.

Gay as bridal bowers with vows of many-petalled maids.—O. W. HOLMES.

Gay as the morning. — WILLIAM LIVINGSTON.

Gay as the hawthorn in May. — EVAN MACCOLL.

Gay as a rising sun. — MAHABHARATA.

Gay as lover to the altar. — GERALD MASSEY.

Colors as gay as those on angels' wings. — THOMAS MOORE.

Gay as the starling shoots thro' the skies. — F. W. H. MYERS.

Gay as if his life were young. — OTWAY.

Gay as mischief. — OUIDA.

Gay as the primrose-dell in May. — AMBROSE PHILIPS.

As the feathered warblers gay. — WILLIAM SHENSTONE.

Gay as April ere he dreams of May. — SWINBURNE.

Your voice was gay
As the voice of a bird in the dawn of a day
On a sunshiny tree.
— ARTHUR SYMONS.

Gay as the garments of gem-sprinkled gold. — BAYARD TAYLOR.

Too gay . . . like a pink ribbon on the bonnet of a Puritan woman. — HENRY D. THOREAU.

As gay as a bridegroom. — VANBRUGH.

Gay as the dancing wind. — SARAH C. WOOLSEY.

Gaily, as one who hath no care or pain. — WILLIAM WATSON.

Gay as the spring. — THOMAS YALDEN.

Gaze (Noun).

I gazed a gaze, az tho i wuz triing tu thread the rong end ov a kambrik needle. — JOSH BILLINGS.

Steady gaze, like little dogs face to face with one of their own kind. — GEORGE ELIOT.

Gaze — *continued.*

Lingering gaze, like a peacock whose eyes are inclined to his tail. — HOOD.

Gaze for gaze
As baby looks on baby.
— FRANCIS THOMPSON.

Gaze (Verb).

Gazed like one who fronts a foe. — EBENEZER ELLIOTT.

Gazed, like lion roused. — SIR WALTER SCOTT.

Gazed like the startled deer. — IBID.

General.

Broad and general as the casing air. — SHAKESPEARE.

Generosity.

Generosity is like the sea, and yet the sea hath its bounds. — ANON.

Generous.

Generous as a dream. — ANON.

Generous as the sun in spring. — P. J. BAILEY.

Generous as a lord. — J. FENIMORE COOPER.

Generous as daylight. — LEIGH HUNT.

Genial.

Genial as sunshine. — ANON.

Genial as a pawnbroker's kiss. — J. H. BLACKWOOD.

Genius.

Genius, like Shakespeare's toad, may be out at the elbows and down at the heels, yet still wears a precious jewel in its head. — HILARY BELL.

Men ov genius are like eagles, tha live on what tha kill, while men ov talents are like crows, tha live on what haz bin killed for them. — JOSH BILLINGS.

Early genius, like early cabbage, does not head well. — IBID.

Genius, like humanity, rusts for want of use. — WILLIAM HAZLITT.

The advent of genius is like what the florists style the breaking of a seedling tulip into what we may call high-caste colors. . . . It is a surprise — there is nothing to account for it. — O. W. HOLMES.

The richest genius, like the most fertile soil, when uncultivated, shoots up into the rankest weeds; and instead of vines and olives for the pleasure and use of man, produces to its slothful owner the most abundant crop of poisons. — DAVID HUME.

The mind contemplates genius through the shades of age, as the eye surveys through artificial capacity. — DR. JOHNSON.

Genius, like a torch, shines less in the broad daylight of the present than in the night of the past. — J. PETIT-SENN.

Genius is the alarm-clock of sleeping centuries. — RICHTER.

Genius, like fire, is a good servant, but a terrible master. — MRS. SIGOURNEY.

Genius as with fashion; all those are displeased at it, who are not able to follow it. — THOMAS WARTON.

Gentle.

Gentle as a fawn. — IRISH BALLAD.

Gentle as a love-sick maid. — APHRA BEHN.

Gentle as a turtle-dove. — R. D. BLACKMORE.

As gentle as the lover's sighs. — CLAUDIAN.

Gentle as the moon. — RICHARD HENRY DANA (1787–1879).

Gentle and placid as Socrates.
— DAUDET.

Gentle as sleep. — LORD DE TABLEY.

Gentle — *continued.*

Gentle as a feather-stroke.—GEORGE ELIOT.

Gentle as the falling dew. — HESIOD (COOKE).

Voice gentle as the breeze that plays in the evening among the spices of Sabara. — DR. JOHNSON.

More gentle than the wind in summer. — KEATS.

As gentle an' soft as the sweet summer air. — J. S. LE FANU.

Gentle as truth. — W. J. LINTON.

Gentle as chaines that honor binde. — RICHARD LOVELACE.

Gentle as a sigh love-fraught. — EVAN MACCOLL.

Gentle, loving, kind
Like Mary singing to her mangered child. — GEORGE MACDONALD.

Gentle as infancy. — W. T. PRICE.

Gentle as the cradle babe. — SHAKESPEARE.

They are as gentle
As zephyrs blowing below the violet.
— IBID.

Gentyll as faucoun
Or hauke of the towre. — SKELTON.

Gentle as eve. — JOHN TAYLOR.

Music that gentler on the spirit lies,
Than tir'd eyelids upon tir'd eyes.
— TENNYSON.

The queen as soft and gentle, like a moonbeam white and fair. — LUDWIG UHLAND.

Gentle as an infant child. — WORDSWORTH.

Gentle as the morning light. — IBID.

Gentle as a jay on tree. — "WORLDE AND THE CHYLDE."

Gently.

Gently as to make no more noise than a spider attaching its thread. — BALZAC.

Gently as a rabbit goes. — R. D. BLACKMORE.

Gently, like the morning's light,
Shedding, unmark'd, an influence soft and bright,
Till all the landscape gather in the sight. — E. B. BROWNING.

Gently as a lamb. — ALICE CARY.

Gently as an angel's hand. — DICKENS.

Gentle as falls a mother's tender speech. — JULIA C. R. DORR.

Breathe as gently, as a perfumed pair of sucking bellows, in some sweet lady's chamber. — JOHN FORD.

Gently like thoughts that come and go, the snowflakes fall, each one a gem. — W. H. GIBSON.

Falling as gently as an answer to a prayer. — ADELAIDE A. PROCTER.

Gently as the dew mingles with the darkening maze. — JAMES WHITCOMB RILEY.

Gently as any sucking dove. — SHAKESPEARE.

Gently as the twilight takes the parting day. — THOMAS WARD.

Gently, as morning-dews distil. — ISAAC WATTS.

Ghastly.

Ghastly as broad-eyed slumber. — ANON.

Ghastly as smiles on some fair maniac's face
Smiling unconscious o'er her bridegroom's corse. — GEORGE ELIOT.

Ghastly as a laugh in hell. — THOMAS HARDY.

Ghastly as a tyrant's dream. — SHELLEY.

Face ghastly . . . like a dead man's by the sepulchral lamp. — SOUTHEY.

Ghost.

Ghosts, like the ladies, never speak till they are spoke to. — R. M. MILNES.

Ghostly as remembered mirth. — WILLIAM WATSON.

Gibber.

Gibbers like a dead man's ghost that clamours for the licht it's lost. — J. B. SELKIRK.

Giddy.

Giddy as a dancing dervish. — LAURENCE HOUSMAN.

As giddy as an hour-old ghost that stares into eternity. — JAMES WHITCOMB RILEY.

Gift.

Gifts are like fish-hooks; for who is not aware that the greedy char is deceived by the fly which he swallows. — MARTIAL.

A gift is as a precious stone in the eyes of him that hath it: whithersoever it turneth, it prospereth. — OLD TESTAMENT.

Gilded.

Gilded as a glittering toy. — DICKENS.

Girl.

A girl is like a flower fresh gathered; but a guilty woman is a flower trodden under foot. — BALZAC.

The presence of a young girl is like the presence of a flower, the one gives its perfume to all that approach it, the other her grace to all that surround her. — LOUIS DESNOYERS.

Glad.

Glad as one would give me a crown. — ANON.

Glad as a fly. — ARABIAN NIGHTS.

Every heart was glad,
As if the taxes were abolished.
— T. L. BEDDOES.

Glad as singing-birds. — E. B. BROWNING.

As glad as April skies. — ELIZA COOK.

Glad as children come from school. — GEORGE GASCOIGNE.

As glad as fish that were but lately caught
And straight again were cast into the pool. — IBID.

Glad as the clay-red
Blaring of battle-horns.
— RICHARD HOVEY.

Glad as the bird up the summer vault singing. — E. M. KELLY.

Glad as the skylark's earliest song. — MISS LANDON.

His face as glad as dawn. — FIONA MACLEOD.

Glad, like the young spring's earliest rose. — J. C. MANGAN.

Glad as a blossoming tree. — EDWIN MARKHAM.

Glad of life as leaves in spring. — JOSEPHINE P. PEABODY.

Glad as a fowl of a fair day. — ENGLISH PROVERB.

Glad as brief delay. — SIR WALTER SCOTT.

Glad as a bird whose flight is impelled and sustained by love. — SWINBURNE.

Glad as the golden spring to greet
Its first live leaflet's play. — IBID.

Glad as a soul in pain, who hears from heaven
The angels singing of his sins forgiven.
— WHITTIER.

His voice as glad as April bird's. — IBID.

Glad as fruition. — C. P. WILSON.

Glad as gardens. — JOHN WILSON.

Gladden.

Gladdening to our eyes as the flowers in May. — R. D. BLACKMORE.

Gladden — *continued.*

Gladdens like a beam in spring . . . making blithe each daisie one by one. — ALEXANDER SMITH.

Gladsome.

Gladsome as the first-born of the spring. — COLERIDGE.

Gladsome as summer. — ROBERT TANNEHILL.

Glance (Noun).

Glances that shoot and illuminate like the sudden gleams that glow through autumn clouds. — ANON.

The glance of the eyes like the fawn's soft gaze. — ARABIAN NIGHTS.

Gave a glance as from the depths of a tomb. — STEPHEN CRANE.

Glance like lightning. — DUMAS, PÈRE.

A glance as bright as a gnome's in his mine of gold. — P. H. HAYNE.

The first glance of a soul which does not yet know itself is like the dawn in the sky. — HUGO.

The glances of women are like certain apparently peaceful but really formidable machines. You pass them every day quietly, with impunity and without suspicion of danger. There comes a moment when you forget even that they are there. You come and go, you muse, and talk, and laugh. Suddenly you feel that you are seized! It is done. The wheels have caught you, the glance has captured you. It has taken you, no matter how or where, by any portion whatever of your thought which was trailing, through any absence of mind. You are lost. You will be drawn in entirely. A train of mysterious forces has gained possession of you. You struggle in vain. No human succor is possible. You will be drawn down from wheel to wheel, from anguish to anguish, from torture to torture. You, your mind, your fortune, your soul; and you will not escape from the terrible machine, until, according as you are in the power of a malevolent nature, or a noble heart, you will be disfigured by shame or transfigured by love. — IBID.

A glance . . . such as Voltaire would have thrown upon a provincial academician who had proposed a rhyme to him. — IBID.

His glance was like a gimlet, cold and piercing. — IBID.

Fair lady, a glance of your eye is like the returning sun in the spring — it melts away the frost of age, and gives a new warmth of vigor to all nature. — ARTHUR MURPHY.

A glance like water brimming with the sky or hyacinth-light where forest-shadows fall. — D. G. ROSSETTI.

A glance like the sunshine that flashes on steel. — WHITTIER.

Glance (Verb).

Glances like one who expects a blow. — ANON.

Javelins glanced like leven-light on white mail-shirt. — ARABIAN NIGHTS.

Glancing white, like streams in sunny valleys. — THOMAS MILLER.

Glancing like a sabre's gleam. — OUIDA.

Glanc'd like rays of glory. — ALLAN RAMSAY.

Glance . . . as the glints of a thousand gems. — JAMES WHITCOMB RILEY.

Glanced by like a star in a storm. — G. H. SASS.

Glance and gleam like the green heights of sunset heaven. — SWINBURNE.

Glancing like a dragon-fly. — TENNYSON.

Glare.

Eye . . . glared like a full moon, or a broad burnished shield. — ADDISON.

Glares like the maniac's moon, whose light is madness. — ANON.

Glaring like mad. — ARISTOPHANES.

Glaring at each other like two gaunt wolves with a famished brood. — MATHILDE BLIND.

Glare like gates of hell.
— ROBERT BROWNING.

Glare like the eye of an enemy.
— JOSEPH CONRAD.

Glaring like a lion in a trap. — O. HENRY.

Glare,
Like to a dreadful comet in the air.
— ROBERT HERRICK.

Glares like a tiger. — HUGO.

Glares like an excited cat. — KIPLING.

Glared like hot iron. — IBID.

Glaring like red insanity. — MISS LANDON.

Broad and glaring as the eye of the Cyclops. — W. S. LANDOR.

As glares the famished eagle from the
Digentian rock
On a choice lamb that bounds alone
before Bandusia's flock,
Herminus glared on Sextus.
— MACAULAY.

Glared like a torch amidst creation's tomb. — JAMES MONTGOMERY.

Glare,
Like fiery serpents hissing through
the air. — IBID.

Glare, as when a torch is hurled before a sleeper's eyes. — BAYARD TAYLOR.

Glares, like a troubled Spirit. — WORDSWORTH.

Gleam.

Gleams like a naked sword. — ANON.

Gleamed like fireflies. — IBID.

Gleamed like gold from the evening rays. — IBID.

Gleam like sunny heavens. — IBID.

Gleaming like the chamomile. — ARABIAN NIGHTS.

Gleamed as the lightning glitters against the murky night. — EDWIN ARNOLD.

Gleamed like a praying-carpet at the foot of those divinest altars. — IBID.

Gleam like glass. — P. J. BAILEY.

Gleaming like the white moonlight. — IBID.

Gleaming like a flash of lightning. — BALZAC.

Gleamed upon the water like a bride at her looking-glass. — R. D. BLACKMORE.

Gleamed like star-motes in the milky-way. — MATHILDE BLIND.

Gleameth like a seraph sword. — E. B. BROWNING.

Glare
Like gates of hell.
— ROBERT BROWNING.

Gleamed like Saint Sophia's dome when all the faithful troop to morning prayer. — IBID.

Gleam . . . like the phosphor of the foam upon the shore. — ROBERT BUCHANAN.

Gleams, like a seraph from the sky descending. — BYRON.

Gleams like flint. — MADISON CAWEIN.

Gleam
Like the bright rainbow on an evening
stream. — COLERIDGE.

Golden gleams,
Like the bright miracles we see in
dreams. — JULIA C. R. DORR.

Gleaming like shot silk in the sunshine. — SIR A. CONAN DOYLE.

Gleam — *continued.*

Gleamed like the flocks of cloudlets bright in sunny air at morn. — F. W. FABER.

Gleamed . . . like sapphires in the mid-day hours. — PAUL FERROLL.

Gleamed as funeral lamps in a sepulchral chamber. — FLAUBERT.

The sand . . . gleamed like mica dust. — GAUTIER.

Gleamed . . . like a star beam, one star beam of some high predominant star. — ARTHUR HENRY HALLAM.

Gleamed and shone, like a splinter of daylight downward thrown. — WALLACE HARNEY.

Gleams, like to the angel's sword. — CHARLES HARPUR.

Gleams like an angel-market. — W. E. HENLEY.

Gleams like a diamond on a dancing girl. — O. W. HOLMES.

Gleam like gold. — PHILANDER CHASE JOHNSON.

Gleaming like rose-hued pearls below the wave. — FRANCES ANNE KEMBLE.

Gleam like pale wells of precious malachite. — IBID.

Gleams like a dream in his face. — H. C. KENDALL.

Gleam like the golden flash of a moon-lit stream. — MISS LANDON.

Gleams like the taper in the blaze of day. — ROBERT LLOYD.

Like a river, frozen and star-lit, gleamed his coat of mail. — LONGFELLOW.

Gleamed like a grate of brass. — IBID.

Gleamed on the hillside like a patch of snow. — IBID.

Gleam, like midnight's boreal dances. — LOWELL.

Gleamed like moonshine on wet sands. — GEORGE MACDONALD.

Gleam, like drifted gold in summer's cloudless beam. — JAMES MONTGOMERY.

Gleam'd, like the meteors of a northern sky. — IBID.

Gleam like the pearls that sprinkle
A virgin's golden hair. — NANAKKASH.

Gleamed like the young moon's crescent. — PILPAY.

Gleam, like glow-worm in the night. — T. BUCHANAN READ.

Gleams like a rising harvest moon. — IBID.

Gleams like the galleon rare of an Argonaut's dreams. — JAMES WHITCOMB RILEY.

Gleams like a beacon from afar. — C. G. ROSSETTI.

Gleam
Like islands on a dark blue sea.
— SHELLEY.

Gleam like the white effigies on tombs in dim cathedrals. — ALEXANDER SMITH.

Lurid gleam, like the reflection of a sulphur fire. — SOUTHEY.

Gleams as a ghost's glory in dreams. — SWINBURNE.

Gleam broad as the brows of the billows that brighten the storm with their crests. — IBID.

Gleam like a cloud the westering sun stains red
Till all the blood of day's blithe heart be bled
And all night's heart requickened.
— IBID.

Gleams like spring's green bloom on boughs all gaunt and gnarry. — IBID.

Gleam
Like the green heights of sunset heaven.
— IBID.

Gleam — *continued.*

Gleam like a brooklet, whose bed is all unshaded. — CARMEN SYLVA.

Gleam like sea-mists o'er the plain. — BAYARD TAYLOR.

Gleamed like fancy made of golden air. — TENNYSON.

Gleam like the rosy east. — WILLIAM THOMSON.

Gleamed like a satin ribbon in the sun, or like the pearly inside of a shell. — HENRY D. THOREAU.

Gleaming like a sea. — VIRGIL.

Gleams like an angry lion's eye. — OSCAR WILDE.

Gleeful.

Gleeful as the Evil One a-counting of his imps. — CHARLES READE.

Gleeful as a brook or bird. — MAURICE THOMPSON.

Glib.

Glib as glass. — ROBERT BROWNING.

Glib as wolves. — ALFRED HENRY LEWIS.

Glib as clockwork. — JAMES WHITCOMB RILEY.

Glibly.

As glibly as a top kept in vivacious movement by the perpetual application of the lash. — BULWER-LYTTON.

Glide

Glide like a gentle stream. — ANON.

Glided like a flame of wind-blown fire. — THOMAS ASHE.

Glide like a fallen leaf. — E. B. BROWNING.

Glide away
Like a ghost at break of day.
— ROBERT BROWNING.

Glide like happiness away.—BYRON.

Glided . . . like naked demons flitting among the clouds. — J. FENIMORE COOPER.

Glide
On smoothly, as a river floweth by,
Or as on stately pinion, through the gray
Evening, the culver cuts his liquid way. — DAVID GRAY.

Glide like the flitting arrow. — THOMAS HASTINGS.

Glide
As thought through spirits sanctified.
— PAUL HAMILTON HAYNE.

Like phantoms painted on the magic slide,
Forth from the darkness of the past we glide,
As living shadows for a moment seen
In airy pageant on the eternal screen.
— O. W. HOLMES.

Let my soft minutes glide securely on, like subterraneous streams, unheard, unknown. — BISHOP NORRIS.

Glide over her mind as water over a glass. — HARRIET PARR.

Glide to and fro like ghosts of buried centuries. — POE.

Like shuttles through the loom, so swiftly glide
My feather'd hours.
— GEORGE SANDYS.

Gliding like a vision o'er the ground. — SOUTHEY.

Glided like a dream. — CELIA THAXTER.

Gliding like morning mist
Enkindled by the sun.
— WORDSWORTH.

Glimmer.

Glimmering faintly like the rack
O' the moon in her own light cast back.
— E. B. BROWNING.

Glimmer like a star in autumn's hazy night. — WILLIAM CULLEN BRYANT.

Glimmers . . . like starry twinklers that momently break
Through the rifts of the gathering tempest's rack.
— JOSEPH R. DRAKE.

Glimmer — *continued.*

Glimmering, like the balance-pan
That weighs its guinea as he weighs
his man. — O. W. HOLMES.

Glimmer, like the last flicker of a night-light. — HUGO.

Glimmer like a coral grove. — WALTER MALONE.

Glimmer like a butterfly. — DON MARQUIS.

The firelight glimmers upon the walls of your cherished home, like the Vestal fire of red upon the figures of adoring angels, or like the flame of Hebrew sacrifice, whose incense bore hearts to Heaven. — DONALD G. MITCHELL.

Tresses glimmering and gleaming like glad waters running over shelving shallows, rimmed with clover. — JAMES WHITCOMB RILEY.

Glimmers like a meteor. — SAMUEL ROGERS.

Glimmered like fire. — FRANCIS S. SALTUS.

He glimmered apart
In solemn gloom
Like a dying lamp in a haunted tomb.
— R. H. STODDARD.

Glimmered through the misty sphere like moonlit marble. — BAYARD TAYLOR.

Glimmered like a faint, vanishing tinge of blood on snow. — HENRY VAN DYKE.

Glimmered like a pine tree dimly
viewed
Through Alpine vapors.
— WORDSWORTH.

Glint.

Glints like polished jet. — ANON.

Glints like sunshine. — IBID.

Glints . . like a lance that flees. — D G. ROSSETTI.

Glint, like thousands of suns from the dew-drops. — SCHILLER.

Glisten.

Glistens like the forehead of morning. — ANON.

Glistened as still
As when on moonlit eves no zephyr
spills the glistening dew.
— EDWIN ARNOLD.

Glistening, like a maid at her own ideas. — R. D. BLACKMORE.

Glistened like dormer-windows piled with snow. — IBID.

Glistened like a plate of beaten silver. — J. FENIMORE COOPER.

Glistened like the path of diamonds in the sun. — DICKENS.

Glistening . . . like the track of moonlight on the sea. — THOMAS HARDY.

Glistens like a star. — EMMA LAZARUS.

Glistened as the tears in a widow's eyes. — CAMILLE LEMONNIER.

Glistened like the dews of morn. — LONGFELLOW.

Glistened like the sun in water. — IBID.

Glistened like the glow of precious stones. — GEORGE MAC-HENRY.

His eyes dilated and glistened like the last flame that shoots up from an expiring fire. — GUY DE MAUPASSANT.

Glistens like a clump of stars. — COSMO MONKHOUSE.

Glistening like gossamer. — JAMES MONTGOMERY.

Glisten like the glistening eyes of nightingales in vernal leaves. — ROBERT NOEL.

Glistening like satin. — OUIDA.

Glistened, like a globe of burnished gold. — POE.

Glisten — *continued.*

Glistened like an emerald,
Beneath the glow-worm's sheen.
— FRANCIS S. SALTUS.

Glistring lyke glasse. — SKELTON.

Eye glistened like that of a rattlesnake. — SMOLLETT.

Glistened like a tin roof in the noonday sun. — HENRY M. STANLEY.

Glistening like the eyes of love. — JOSEPH TURNLEY.

Glitter (Noun).

Has a cold cheerless glitter, like the new furniture in a warehouse. — ALEXANDER SMITH.

Glitter (Verb).

Glittering like an Eastern Caliph. — ANON.

Glittered like spun glass. — IBID.

Robes glitter like young sedge grass. — IBID.

Glittered in the gloom
Like a gilt epitaph within a tomb.
— AMBROSE BIERCE.

Glittering, like a splendid wave that rises out of shapeless gloom. — LAURENCE BINYON.

Cold glitter as of ice. — CARLYLE.

Glittered as if strewn with powdered pumice. — D'ANNUNZIO.

Glittering as snow in the sunshine. — DAUDET.

Glittered like dragon-flies. — DR. JOHN DORAN.

Glittered like fish from the sweep-net. — DUMAS, PÈRE.

Glitters like a star. — GOETHE.

Glitter like heaven new-born.—IBID.

Glittered like dew. — RANGER GULL.

Glittering like a lost jewel, which some ill-fated wanderer might pick up, and thenceforth be haunted by strange phantoms of guilt, sinkings of the heart, and unaccountable misfortune. — HAWTHORNE.

Glittered and sparkled as if diamonds had been flung against it by the double handful. — IBID.

Glitter like an angel's ladder. — A. E. HOUSMAN.

Glittering as a parterre. — HUGO.

Glitters like a sea of light. — SIGMUND KRASINSKI.

Glittered like a winter sun. — OWEN MEREDITH.

Glittering as steel. — OUIDA.

Eye glittered like rattlesnake's. — CHARLES READE.

Genius glittered like the gloriola of a saint. — IBID.

Glittered like a sickle of tin. — EDGAR SALTUS.

Glittering like the spangled dew-drop. — SIR WALTER SCOTT.

His armor glytteryde as dyd a glede. — RICHARD SHEIL.

Glittering as the wine-bright jacinth-stone. — SWINBURNE.

Glittering as wine. — IBID.

Glittered like a bed of flowers. — TENNYSON.

Glitter like a swarm of fire-flies tangled in a silver braid. — IBID.

Glittered . . . like sleet-bound trees in wintry skies. — JOHN TRUMBULL.

Glitter . . . like the bayonets of a regiment on parade. —JOHN C. VAN DYKE.

Glitter . . . like the glass pendants of a chandelier. — IBID.

They glitter in my fancy like the distant multihedral
Steeples, domes and sunlit turrets of some beautiful cathedral.
— EUGENE FITCH WARE.

Glittering like an argent shield. — OSCAR WILDE.

Globular.

Globular like a hazel-nut. — BARON MUNCHAUSEN.

Glossy.

Glossy as a mole. — ANON.

Gloomy.

Gloomy as a graveyard on a wet Sunday. — ANON.

Gloomy as a hobgoblin. — DICKENS.

Gloomy outside, like a rusty chest. — DRYDEN.

Gloomy as night.— HOMER (POPE).

Begloomed like seas empurpled under cloud. — ROBERT NOEL.

Gloomy and dogged like a dangerous maniac in his cell. — CHARLES READE.

Gloomy, like a gathered tempest. — ISAAC WATTS.

Glorified.

Glorified . . . like the angel St. John saw in the sun. — THOMAS HARDY.

Glorified like the illuminated figures in the painted chronicles. — OUIDA.

Glorious.

Glorious as a victory for the victor. — ANON.

Glorious as when Pericles ruled over Athens. — IBID.

Glorious as the sun. — BEAUMONT AND FLETCHER.

Glorious . . . as spreads before us the sky's unspeakable blue. — MARY GEOGHEGAN.

Glorious as the morning star of heaven. — ROBERT GREENE.

As glorious as the portal of the sun. — IBID.

Glorious as a heavenly promise. — G. T. HILL.

Glorious as the rainbow's birth. — GERALD MASSEY.

Glorious as the Spring. — MASSINGER.

Glorious as a midnight star. — C. G. ROSSETTI.

Glorious as purple twilight. — IBID.

Thou art
As glorious to this night, being o'er my head,
As is a winged messenger of heaven
Unto the white-upturned wondering eyes
Of mortals. — SHAKESPEARE.

Sweet and glorious as compassion. — SWINBURNE.

Glorious as the sea. — IBID.

Rose glorious as with gleam of gold unpriced. — IBID.

Glorious as if a glimpse were given
Within the western gates of heaven.
— CELIA THAXTER.

Glorious as unclouded May. — JOHN TOBIN.

Glorious as the new-built town. — WALLER.

Glorious, like the seer-seen angel
Standing in the sun. — WHITTIER.

Glory.

Glory is like a circle in the water,
Which never ceaseth to enlarge itself,
Till by broad spreading it disperse to naught. — SHAKESPEARE.

As the vine is the glory of the trees it clasps, as the grapes of the vine, as the bull of the herd, as the standing corn of the fruitful field, thou and thou alone art the glory of those who love thee. — VIRGIL.

Glories, like glow-worms, afar off shine bright,
But look'd too near have neither heat nor light. — JOHN WEBSTER.

Glossy.

Glossy as a shark's tooth. — ARLO BATES.

Glossy — *continued.*

As glossy and black as a scarab. — ROBERT BROWNING.

Glossy like laurel. — HELEN H. JACKSON.

Glossy as a heron's wing. — THOMAS MOORE.

Glossy as the finest silk.—ORIENTAL.

Glow (Noun).

Healthy glow, as a fine frosty morning. — GEORGE GISSING.

Glow (Verb).

Her eye balls . . . glowed like flaming carbuncles. — W. H. AINSWORTH.

Glow like a blacksmith's forge. — ANON.

Glowing like molten iron. — IBID.

Glow like the gates of the New Jerusalem. — IBID.

Glow like the golden fleece. — IBID.

Glow like the vernal grass. — IBID.

Glow and glimmer soft as ocean blush of Indian shells. — MATHILDE BLIND.

Cheeks glow red as tomatoes. — ROBERT BROWNING.

Glowing in the green, like flakes of fire. — WILLIAM CULLEN BRYANT.

Glow,
As if her veins ran lightning.
— BYRON.

Aglow, like fruit when it colors. — WILLIAM CANTON.

Glow . . . like a pool of flaming blood. — JOSEPH CONRAD.

Glowing like sunset-clouds upon the borders of the Tappan-Zee. — F. S. COZZENS.

Glows like a painter's palette. — T. W. H. CROSLAND.

Glows as some rain-burnished rose. — LORD DE TABLEY.

Glowed like June. — C. G. DUFFY.

Glow like adoration. — EBENEZER ELLIOTT.

Blush and glow like angel's wings. — IBID.

Glow like webs of golden tissue in the sun. — F. W. FABER.

Glow like twin roses in the verdant bush. — FRANCIS FAWKES.

Glowin' like a circus poster. — SEWELL FORD.

Glowing like a bride robed to meet the bridal hour. — S. GERTRUDE FORD.

Glow . . . like Laura's cheek when blushes rise. — JOHN GAY.

I glow as with new wine. — GOETHE.

Glowed like a household fire. — HAWTHORNE.

Glows like a red flame in the dark. — IBID.

Glowed like sunshine. — IBID.

Glowed like a coal,
In the throat of the furnace.
— W. E. HENLEY.

Glows like a kiln. — IBID.

Soft and glowing as a summer's eve. — HENRIK HERTZ.

Glow like a queen's missal. — O. W. HOLMES.

Glowed like the morn beneath Aurora's wings. — IBID.

Glows like the old prophets. — J. G. HOLLAND.

Glow like fiery meteors. — HOMER (POPE).

Golden glow,
Like Iris just bedabbled in her bow.
— HOOD.

Glow like a self-enkindled star. — LEMUEL HOPKINS.

Glows, like a peak at dawn. — HUGO.

Glow like flashing seas of green. — HELEN H. JACKSON.

Glow — *continued.*

Glow
Like the northern lights on snow.
— KEATS.

Glows like the diamond in the presence of radium. — ANDREW LANG.

Glowed like angels in the sun. — GERALD MASSEY.

Glowed like a watch fire in the Wilderness. — IBID.

Glowing imperial as the sun-toucht rose. — IBID.

Glowing like anthracite coal. — DONALD G. MITCHELL.

Glowed like a torch amid creation's tomb. — JAMES MONTGOMERY.

In youthful beauty glows,
Like Phœbus, when he bends to cast
His beams upon a rose.
— THOMAS MOORE.

Glowed like the arbutus or beech of the Umbrian hills. — J. H. NEWMAN.

Glow like paint on death's shrunk cheek. — MILES O'REILLY.

Jewels . . . glowing like sunbeams. — OUIDA.

The Court, it glows, and shines like rotten wood. — SIR WALTER RALEIGH.

Glows like a golden group of buttercups. — T. BUCHANAN READ.

Glowed, like great archangels moving slow
On some celestial road. — IBID.

Her white forehead glowed like a rose. — CHARLES READE.

Glow like a flower. — C. G. ROSSETTI.

Glowed like the first splendors of the morn. — JOSÉ SELGAS.

Glowed like plated Mars.— SHAKESPEARE.

Glows like solid amethyst. — SHELLEY.

Glowing like the vital morn. — IBID.

Glow
As a heart burns with some divine thing done. — SWINBURNE.

Glow . . . like the sunset's flush on a field of snow. — BAYARD TAYLOR.

Glows, like baker's oven. — WILLIAM TENNANT.

Glowed as a cloud worn thin. — WALTER THORNBURY.

Glow like a great pearl. — JOHN C. VAN DYKE.

With beauty glows like that of Venus, where she rose naked in blushing charms from Ocean's hoary wave. — JOSEPH WARTON.

Glum.

Glum as an oyster. — ANON.

Glum as mud. — IBID.

As glum as a man who has found a penny and lost a sixpence. — SCOTTISH PROVERB.

Glum as an undertaker. — THACKERAY.

Gluttonous.

Gluttonous as curiosity. — LEWIS CARROLL.

Gnarled.

Gnarled like olive branches. — GUY DE MAUPASSANT.

Gnaw.

Gnaw me, like a burning worm. — BUNYAN.

Gnawed as with a file. — D. G. ROSSETTI.

Gnaw like fire. — SWINBURNE.

Pain gnaws at my heart like a rat that gnaws at a bean
In the dusty dark of a ghost-frequented house. — ARTHUR SYMONS.

Go.

(*See also* Gone.)

Go along like sixty. — Anon.

Go like a house afire. — Ibid.

Going as if he had trod upon eggs. — Robert Burton.

Go along like blazes. — De Quincey.

The multitude goes, like the flower
and the weed,
That wither away to let others succeed.
— William Knox.

Goeth . . . as an ox goeth to the slaughter. — Old Testament.

Out of his nostrils goeth smoke, as out of a seething pot or caldron. — Ibid.

God.

For God is like a skilful Geometrician, who, when more easily and with one stroke of his Compass he might describe or divide a right line, had yet rather do this in a circle or longer way, according to the constituted and forelaid principle of his art. — Sir Thomas Browne.

Gold.

Gold in the house is like sun in the world. — Arabian Nights.

Gold, like the sun, which melts wax and hardens clay, expands great souls and contracts bad hearts. — Rivarol.

Golden.

Golden as the fruits of autumn. — Anon.

Golden as the sun. — P. J. Bailey.

Golden as the sunlight. — Flaubert.

Golden as honey in the sun. — Lowell.

Golden as the glow of morning sunlight. — Clinton Scollard.

Gold as golden as the gold of hives. — Swinburne.

Golden as water kindled with presage of dawn or night. — Ibid.

Golden as a star. — Thomas Wade.

Golden as the façade of St. Mark's with dancing reflections. — Israel Zangwill.

Gone.

Gone as a gone goose. — Anon.

Gone as a shadow goes. — R. D. Blackmore.

Gone as evanescent cloudlands. — Mathilde Blind.

Gone, like traces on the deep,
Like a spectre grasp'd in sleep,
Dews inhal'd from morning glades,
Melting snows, and gliding shades.
— Henry Brooke.

Quite gone . . . like a lost star. — Robert Browning.

Gone . . . like ice on a June day. — Carlyle.

Gone into their snares like a thread into a needle. — Fedor Dostoevsky.

Gone, like a vapor which the potent morn kills, and in killing glorifies. — David Gray.

Gone like the bubble that bursts in the
sun;
Gone like the grain when the reaper is
done;
Gone like the dew on the fresh morn-
ing grass;
Gone without parting farewell; and
alas!
Gone with a flavor of hydrogen gas!
— Bret Harte.

Gone like the locust band, when whirlwinds bear
Their flimsy legions through the waste
of air. — Reginald Heber.

Gone, like smoke dissolved in air. — Aaron Hill.

Gone, like the tenants that quit with-
out warning,
Down the back entry of time.
— O. W. Holmes.

Gone, like the spray. — Kingsley.

Gone — *continued.*

Thou art gone from my gaze like a beautiful dream. — GEORGE LINLEY.

Gone was every trace of sorrow,
As the fog from off the river,
As the mist from off the meadow.
— LONGFELLOW.

Gane, like the flowers o' spring awa', or like a vision perished. — ALEXANDER McLAUGHLAN.

Seen no more,
Gone, like the wind that raised the wave,
The spent wave on the shore.
— GEORGE MEREDITH.

Gone like a meteor. — THOMAS MOORE.

Gone, like the thoughts that once were ours. — IBID.

Gone like all things else that men set life upon. — F. W. H. MYERS.

To-day we are here, to-morrow gone, like the shadow that vanisheth, like the grass that withereth, or like the flower that fadeth; or indeed like anything, or rather like nothing. — OTWAY.

Gone, as an angel's wing through an opening cloud is seen, and then withdrawn. — JOHN PIERPONT.

Gone as soon as a grain of corn thrown to an ant. — PLAUTUS.

Gone as an unreturning river. — C. G. ROSSETTI.

Like the dew on the mountain,
Like the foam on the river,
Like the bubble on the fountain,
Thou art gone, and forever.
— SIR WALTER SCOTT.

Gone like the bloom upon the heather. — J. B. SELKIRK.

Gone, as they never had been. — BAYARD TAYLOR.

Gone like shadow when it declineth. — OLD TESTAMENT.

Your early splendor's gone
Like stars into a cloud withdrawn —
Like music laid asleep
In dried up fountains.
— WILLIAM WALLACE.

Gone, like the summer lightning's gleam. — FRANK WATERS.

Gone
As the fox-hunter follows the sound of the horn. — WHITTIER.

The red man has gone like the mist on the air. — IBID.

Gone as a cloud faded into the sky — W. B. YEATS.

Good.

Good as a feast. — ANON.

Good as an addled egg. — IBID.

Good as an idle bird. — IBID.

Good as ever went upon the ground. — IBID.

Good as new. — IBID.

Beauty is as good as ready money — IBID.

Good as truth. — IBID.

Good as dew to flowers. — IBID.

Good as gold. — BALZAC.

Good as white bread and just as insipid. — IBID.

Good as wheat. — J. R. BARTLETT'S "DICTIONARY OF AMERICANISMS."

As good as a show. — BULWER-LYTTON.

Good as a play. — CHARLES II.

As good music as when pigs play on the organ. — CLARKE'S "PROVERBS."

Good as ever water wet. — HAZLITT'S "PROVERBS."

Good as ever trod upon shoe leather. — "LONDON CHANTICLEERS."

Good as bread. — LONGFELLOW.

Good — *continued.*

Good as puppet show. — NORTHALL'S "FOLK PHRASES."

Good as ever flew in the air. — JOHN RAY'S "HANDBOOK OF PROVERBS."

Good as a sermon. — SOUTHEY.

Good as a comedy. — JOHN TAYLOR.

To do good to the base is like sowing the sea. — THEOGNIS.

Good-nature.

Good-nature, like a bee, collects honey from every herb. Ill-nature, like a spider, sucks poison from the sweetest flower. — ANON.

Goodness.

True goodness is like the glow-worm in this, that it shines most when no eyes, except those of heaven, are upon it. — A. J. C. HARE.

As a horse when he has run, a bee when he has made honey, so man when he has done a good act does not call out for others to come and see, but he goes on to another act, as the vine goes on to produce again the grapes in season. — MARCUS AURELIUS.

Goodness, like the Sun, enlightens all. — SAMUEL BOYSE.

Goodnesse is like the art prospective: one point center, begetting infinite rayes. — SIR THOMAS OVERBURY.

Your goodness is as a morning cloud, and as the early dew it goeth away. — OLD TESTAMENT.

Good-will.

Good-will, like a good name, is got by many actions, and lost by one. — FRANCIS JEFFREY.

Gore.

Gore like the tusks of a boar. — ANON.

Gorgeous.

Gorgeous as a sultana. — ANON.

Gorgeous as are a rivulet's banks in June. — WILLIAM CULLEN BRYANT.

Gorgeous as the heavens. — DE QUINCEY.

Gorgeous as the sun at midsummer. — SHAKESPEARE.

Gossip.

A gossip in a village is like a viper in a bed. — ANON.

Gossip, like ennui, is born of idleness. — NINON DE LENCLOS.

Gossipin' about like a cracked bell-clapper. — GEORGE MEREDITH.

Gossip must often have been likened to the winged insects bearing pollen to the flowers; it fertilizes many a vacuous reverie. — IBID.

Govern.

Govern the lips as they were palace doors, the King within. — EDWIN ARNOLD.

Government.

A government tumbling and drifting on the whirlpool and mud-deluges, floating atop in a conspicuous manner, no whither, like the carcass of a drowned ass. — CARLYLE.

But when a government is grown in strength,
Like some old oak, rough with its armed bark,
It yields not to the tug, but only nods,
And turns to sullen state.
— DRYDEN.

Government, like dress, is the badge of lost innocence. — THOMAS PAINE.

Graceful.

Graceful as an Alpine sapling. — ANON.

Graceful as a bird on the wing. — IBID.

Graceful as a fawn. — IBID.

Graceful as the arch of a rainbow. — IBID.

Graceful — *continued.*

Graceful as a fairy-tale. — WILLIAM ARCHER.

Graceful as a black frigate with snow white sails. — BALZAC.

Graceful as a springborn fairy. — PAUL HAMILTON HAYNE.

Graceful as Mars. — HOMER (POPE).

Graceful as a snake of the paradise of Asia. — DAVID DE LA GAMME.

Graceful as the willow-bough o'er the streamlet weeping. — LOVER.

As warm and graceful as May. — EDWARD LOVIBOND.

She is graceful as the greenly waving boughs in summer wind. — GERALD MASSEY.

Graceful as a Naiad. — GEORGE MOORE.

Graceful as a faun. — SAMUEL ROGERS.

Graceful as an ivy bough born to cling and lean. — C. G. ROSSETTI.

Graceful as a bow just bent. — RUSKIN.

Graceful and free
As honeysuckles and the lilies be.
— D. B. W. SLADEN.

Graceful as a couchant goddess. — ANTHONY TROLLOPE.

Graceful as the sapphirine tide. — JOSEPH TURNLEY.

Graceful as the shawl-designs
Of Delhi or Umritsir.
— WHITTIER.

Gracefully.

Flit about as gracefully as a pickax in a sack. — IBID.

Gracious.

All gracious and good as when God made the living creatures, and none was afraid. — BLISS CARMAN.

Gracious as a mediæval queen. — THOMAS HEYWOOD.

As gracious as the morn. — HUGO.

Gracious as the golden maiden morn
When darkness craves her blessing.
— SWINBURNE.

Gracious as a duchess. — THACKERAY.

Grand.

Grand like Barbarossa's beard. — ANON.

Grand as a victory. — IBID.

Grand as thought. — BALZAC.

Grand as a Greek statue. — ROBERT BROWNING.

As grand as the world. — JOSEPH A. DE GOBINEAU.

Grand as floor-walkers. — O. HENRY.

Grand as the frigate on the wind. — JEAN INGELOW.

Grand as the passion felt but never spoken. — TRACY ROBINSON.

Grand,
As though a distant singing sea broke on a tuneful strand.
— C. G. ROSSETTI.

Grand
As any stone that decks a monarch's hand.
— D. B. W. SLADEN.

Grand as doomsday and as grave. — TENNYSON.

Grasp.

Grasps, like death. — EBENEZER ELLIOTT.

Grasp as firm
As his whose arm is nerved by glory's zeal. — GERALD GRIFFIN.

Grasp like a scourge. — T. BUCHANAN READ.

Grasps as in water, the more she grasped the less she held. — SIR PHILIP SIDNEY.

Grate.

Grate like a sawblade under the file. — HENRIK IBSEN.

Grating like arsenic. — JOHN WOLCOTT.

Grateful.

Thou touchest me gratefully, like Nature's wholesome breath. — NICCOLO TOMMASEO (D. G. ROSSETTI).

Gratis.

Gratis, as yesternight. — CARLYLE.

Gratitude.

Gratitude is like the good faith of traders, it maintains commerce; and we often pay, not because it is just to discharge our debts, but that we may more readily find people to trust us. — ROCHEFOUCAULD.

Grave.

Grave as an old gate-post. — ANON.

Grave as Pascal. — IBID.

Grave, as the manner of noble men is. — E. B. BROWNING.

Grave as an organ. — DICKENS.

Grave and thoughtful as rich mourners. — DIOGENES.

Grave as actors do in Lent. — PIERCE EGAN.

Grave as a mourning hearse. — IBID.

Grave as Libanius, slumbering o'er the laws. — ELIJAH FENTON.

Grave as saints. — J. J. JUSSERAND.

As grave as Porcius Cato when he met with a repulse which he had never expected nor dreamt of. — MARCELLINUS.

Grave as an eye dwelling on blood. — GEORGE MEREDITH.

Grave as a judge. — "POOR ROBIN'S ALMANACK."

Grave
As the unwilling herald of the king.
— ARTHUR SYMONS.

Grave as from a funeral. — TENNYSON.

Gravity.

Gravity in a woman is like to a gray beard upon a breaching boise chinne, which a good scholemaister would cause to be clipt, and the wise husband to be avoyded. — LYLY.

Gray.

Gray as grannun's cat. — ANON.

Gray as the inside of a pewter dish. — IBID.

Gray hairs are like the light of a soft moon, silvering over the evening of life. — IBID.

Grey as a badger. — R. H. BARHAM.

Gray as shallow sea. — CUCHULAIN.

Grey as a hoary monolith. — G. K. CHESTERTON.

Misty gray, like a cow's breath on a frosty morning. — IRVIN S. COBB.

Grey as time. — GEORGE DARLEY.

Gray, like a shield embossed in silver. — LONGFELLOW.

Grey, like the soft creeping twilight. — WILLIAM MORRIS.

Gray as smoke. — JOHN G. NEIHARDT.

Gray as glass. — SHAKESPEARE.

Grey, like a storm-extinguished day. — SHELLEY.

Grey as a flower ruined. — SWINBURNE.

Grey as the morn. — J. A. SYMONDS.

Her eyes are grey like morning dew. — W. B. YEATS.

Great.

Great as a lord. — FRANCES FAWKES.

It is with great men as with high mountains. They oppress us with awe when we stand under them: they disappoint our insatiable imaginations when we are nigh, but not quite close to them: and then, the further we recede from them, the more astonishing they appear; until . . . they at one moment seem miraculously lifted above earth, and the next strike our fancies as let down from heaven.
— J. C. HARE.

I think myself as great
As Cæsar riding in the Roman street,
With captive kings at his triumphant car. — MARLOWE.

Greed.

Greedy as a hog. — ANON.

Greed was like a slip-knot drawn more and more tightly about his heart, till reason at length was stifled. — BALZAC.

As greedy as ten cocks scraping in a dunghill for ae barley pickle. — SCOTTISH PROVERB.

Greedy as a cormorant. — JOHN SKELTON.

Greedy as hell's mouth. — LEONARD WRIGHT.

Green.

Green as May. — JAMES LANE ALLEN.

Green as a gooseberry. — ANON.

Green as a gourd. — IBID.

Green as a lizard. — IBID.

Green as bottled glass. — IBID.

Green as emeralds. — IBID.

Green as grass. — IBID.

Green as the deep waters. — IBID.

Green as the sea. — IBID.

Green as a leaf. — THOMAS ASHE.

As green as any privet-hedge a bird might choose to build in. — E. B. BROWNING.

Green as blissful Eden. — R. C. DUTT.

Green as the mantled pool. — HOOD

Green as hope before it grieves. — MISS LANDON.

Green as a meadow by Chaucer. — RICHARD LE GALLIENNE.

As green as the leaves of the fir tree. — "MABINOGION."

Green as jealousy. —GEORGE MEREDITH.

Green as an arum leaf. — OUIDA.

Green as the grave of a loved one. — C. G. ROSSETTI.

Green as leeks. — SHAKESPEARE.

Green as the forest's night. — SHELLEY.

Green as summer. — SWINBURNE.

Green as the salt-sea billows. — WORDSWORTH.

Greetings.

Christmas greetings are like pots of ore;
The hollower they are they sing the more. — AMBROSE BIERCE.

Grew.

Grew like the summer grass. — SHAKESPEARE.

Grew,
Like a pale flower by some sad maiden cherished. — SHELLEY.

Grey.

(*See* Gray.)

Grief.

Woman's grief is like a summer storm, short as it is violent. — JOANNA BAILLIE.

Genuine grief is like penitence, not clamorous, but subdued. — JOSH BILLINGS.

Grief — *continued.*

Grief and passion are like floods raised in little brooks by a sudden rain. — DRYDEN.

Grief, like wine, the tongue will render free. — J. M. LEGARE.

Grief, like night, is salutary. It cools down the soul by the putting out its fevered fires; and if it oppresses her, it also compresses her energies. The load once gone, she will go forth with greater buoyancy to new pleasures. — JOHN PULSFORD.

Grief
Was as a last year's leaf
Blown dead far down the wind's way.
— SWINBURNE.

Grieve.

Grieve like the stranger-tended child,
Which seeks its mother's arms, and sees and feels them not.
— CELIA THAXTER.

Grim.

Grim as a judge. — ANON.

Grim as Cerberus. — IBID.

Grim as death. — IBID.

Grim as a voice from the grave. — A. H. BEESLY.

Grim as a Swiss guard. — ROBERT BROWNING.

Grim as a grizzly fighting for her cub. — JOHN G. NEIHARDT.

Grim as a crow. — JOSEPH SKIPSEY.

Grim as dreams that quicken from dead men's graves. — SWINBURNE.

Grim as hell. — IBID.

Grin.

Grin like a Cheshire cat, from ear to ear. — ANON.

Grinning like one bringing rare news. — J. M. BARRIE.

Grinning like enchanted apes. — THOMAS CARLYLE.

Grin like a basket of chips. — FRANCIS GROSE.

Grins like some fantastic nightly spectre. — A. G. OEHLENSCHLAGER.

Grin like lions
Upon the pikes o' the hunters.
— SHAKESPEARE.

Grip.

Grips like a vise. — ANON.

Grips like hoops of steel. — IBID.

Grip like some kind of sinning. — ROBERT W. SERVICE.

Gripe.

Gripe as hard Cassibelan. — SHAKESPEARE.

Gripe like a convulsion. — COLERIDGE.

Groan.

Groaned
Like some sad prophet, that foresaw the doom
Of those whom best he loved, and could not save.
— DRYDEN.

Groans like a cannon-ball. — RICHARD LOVELACE.

Groaneth, like a door on rusty hinges. — TUPPER.

Groaning like a dying horse. — WILLIAM WARD.

Grog.

Grog, like grief, is fatal stuff for any man to sup;
For when it fails to pull him down, it's sure to blow him up.
— JOHN G. SAXE.

Grooved.

Grooved like the sunken spaces between the fingers. — JOHN BURROUGHS.

Grope.

Groping blindly as in a dream. — HUGO.

Groped like a blind man finding his way. — GUY DE MAUPASSANT.

Gross.

Grosse as a hog. — MIDDLETON.

Gross as a mountain. — SHAKESPEARE.

Gross as ignorance made drunk. — IBID.

Ground.

Ground,
Like a thousand vanquish'd men in
bloody flight. — SHAKESPEARE.

Groundless.

Groundless as the dreams of philosophy. — LAURENCE STERNE.

Group.

As the moths around a taper,
As the bees around a rose,
As the gnats around a vapour,
So the spirits group and close
Round about a holy childhood as if
drinking its repose.
— E. B. BROWNING.

Grovel.

Grovel like swine. — ANON.

Grow.

Grow like a cow's tail, downwards. — ANON.

Grows like Jimson weed in a pile of compost. — IBID.

We do not make our thoughts; they grow in us like grain in a wood. — P. J. BAILEY.

Growing like smoke. — FRANCES HODGSON BURNETT.

Grow like grass in May. — GEORGE ELIOT.

Like some fair plant beneath my careful hand
He grew, he flourish'd and he grac'd
the land. — HOMER (POPE).

That grows with gazing on, like lover's beauty. — GERALD MASSEY.

Grew like the summer grass. — SHAKESPEARE.

Grow like weeds on a neglected tomb. — SHELLEY.

Grows great as the moon through the month. — SWINBURNE.

Growl.

Growled within himself like a little double-bass. — DICKENS.

Growls, roars and breaks itself, like our eternal and powerless despair. — DUMAS, PÈRE.

Growl, like a rescendo in the double bass. — LOVER.

He growls like a bear that has burnt his paw. — OSMANLI PROVERB.

Grunt.

Grunt like a bear when he is a-moaning. — ULPIAN FULWELL.

Grunting like some pounded animal — MAURICE HEWLETT.

Grunted like a pig under a tub. — LYLY.

Grunts like a hog. — MARLOWE.

Guarded.

As well guarded as a prince in his castle. — JAMES OTIS.

Guest.

A guest, like a fish, has an unpleasant odor after three days. — GUIDO CAVALCANTI.

Guileless.

Guileless and simple as a six-year-old child that has never left its mother. — BALZAC.

Guileless as a candidate. — RICHARD LE GALLIENNE.

Guileless as infancy. — T. N. TALFOURD.

Gulp.

Gulped as . . . swallowing sobs. — JOSEPH CONRAD.

Gulped it down fast as a Neapolitan beggar a plateful of pure scalding-hot macaroni. — H. T. FINCK.

Gulp — *continued.*

Gulped down pleasures as a dog does his dinner. — IBID.

Gurgled.

Gurgled like the cry of a drowning man. — W. C. RUSSELL.

Gush.

Gush like a fountain at its source. — DONALD G. MITCHELL.

Gushes like nectar from Hebe's Olympian bottle. — W. H. VENABLES.

His heart
Gush'd like a river-fountain of the hills,
Ceaseless and lavish, at a kindly smile,
A word of welcome, or a tone of love.
— WHITTIER.

Gusts.

His speech came in gusts, like linnets in the pauses of the wind. — WILLIAM DE MORGAN.

H

Habit.

Habit may be likened to a cable; every day we weave a thread, and soon we cannot break it. — ANON.

Habits are like the wrinkles on a man's brow; if you will smooth out the one, I will smooth out the other. — JOSH BILLINGS.

Bad habits are as infectious by example as the plague itself by contact. — FIELDING.

Hack.

Hacked like a hand-saw. — SHAKESPEARE.

Hacked like dull wood of every day. — FRANCIS THOMPSON.

Haggard.

Haggard and wan as slain men. — EDWIN ARNOLD.

Haggard as spectres. — SCHILLER.

Haggard as crime. — SWINBURNE.

Haggard as fear. — IBID.

Haggard as hell. — IBID.

Haggard as the face of night. — IBID.

Hair.

Her hair was like the threads of gold. — SCOTTISH BALLAD.

Her hair is like the curling mist
That shades the mountain-side at e'en. — BURNS.

Her dusky hair, like silver night elbowing the gloom of twilight. — DARREL FIGGIS.

Hair like weed. — MAURICE HEWLETT.

His blond hair like gold from the furnace. — CHARLES NODIER.

Hair like the mist of the hill, soft and curling in the day of the sun. — OSSIAN.

Her hair is like the golden corn
A low wind breathes upon:
Or like the golden harvest-moon
When all the mists are gone:
Or like a stream with golden sands
On which the sun has shone
Day after day in summertime
Ere autumn leaves are wan.
— C. G. ROSSETTI.

Her hair, like golden threads, play'd with her breath. — SHAKESPEARE.

Hairless.

Hairless as an egg. — ROBERT HERRICK.

Hairy.

Hairy as a mastodon. — JOSEPH CONRAD.

Hand.

He had a hand like a bunch of bananas. — R. F. OUTCAULT.

Hands like rugged bark. — HOOD.

A baby's hands, like rosebuds furled. — SWINBURNE.

Handily.

Handily as a Tacoma Indian picks hops. — AMY LESLIE.

Handsome.

Handsome as houris. — ANON.

Handsome as paint. — IBID.

Handsome as a new stake-rope on a thirty-dollar pony. — O. HENRY.

Handsome as a Detaille chevalier. — AMY LESLIE.

Handsome as one full on drugs. — ALFRED HENRY LEWIS.

Handsome as a hackman's hat. — SYDNEY MUNDEN.

Handy.

Handy as a hen. — ANON.

Handy as a poker in Hell. — IBID.

Handy as a robin after a rain. — IBID.

Handy as a pocket in a shirt. — J. R. BARTLETT'S "DICTIONARY OF AMERICANISMS."

Handy as a pig with a musket. — NORTHALL'S "FOLK PHRASES."

As handy as a corkscrew in Kentucky. — J. P. WILSON.

Hang.

Hang as high as Haman. — ANON.

Hanging like Mahomet's coffin, between earth and heaven. — IBID.

Hang together like bees. — IBID.

Hang together like birds. — IBID.

Hang together like burrs. — IBID.

Hangs together like a rope of sand. — IBID.

Like Mahomet's coffin, the shocking word hung half-way 'twixt the root and the tip of the tongue. —R. H. BARHAM.

One snowy cloud hangs, like an avalanche of frozen light upon the peak of night's cerulean Alp. — T. L. BEDDOES.

Hung, like words of transport trembling on the tongue, too strong for utterance. — ROBERT BLOOMFIELD.

Hang like Mahomet in the air. — SAMUEL BUTLER.

You dosed me with a drug that hangs about my tongue like a pound-weight on a humming-bird's wing. — J. FENIMORE COOPER.

Hangs his head . . . like bending lilies over-charg'd with rain. — RICHARD DUKE.

Hung like heaven around. — GERALD MASSEY.

Hang like a tail. — GEORGE MEREDITH.

Hangs on the heart like a nightmare. — OWEN MEREDITH.

Hung like mists o'er sleeping streams
In uninhabitable lands.
— T. BUCHANAN READ.

Hung like a vapor in the cloudless sky. — SAMUEL ROGERS.

Hung like an icicle on a Dutchman's beard. — SHAKESPEARE.

His listless hand
Hung like dead bone within its withered
skin. — IBID.

Hangs like flax on a distaff. — IBID.

Hang me in a bottle like a cat, and shoot at me. — IBID.

Hang upon him like a disease. — IBID.

Hang upon my tongue like a new-married wife about her husband's neck. — IBID.

She hangs upon the cheek of night
Like a rich jewel in an Ethiope's ear.
— IBID.

Hang — *continued.*

Hang on her lips like a padlock on a pedlar's budget. — EDWARD SHARPHAM.

Hung like bees on mountain-flowers. — SHELLEY.

Hang like night on heaven above me. — IBID.

Hangs heavy as the dewiest poppy. — ARTHUR UPSON.

Hang like sackcloth on a wanton nun. — THOMAS WADE.

Hanker.

Hanker as strongly as do pianists in the presence of an open keyboard. — JAMES HUNEKER.

Happiness.

Happiness is like sunshine; it is made up of very little beams. — ANON.

Happiness, like the blue of the sky, cannot be lasting, for the earth, to yield its fruits, requires the rain, and man to estimate at their true value this life and the next, has need of tears. — FERNAN CABALLERO.

Happiness, like a refreshing stream, flows from heart to heart in endless circulation. — HENRY GROVE.

Happiness is reflective, like the light of heaven; and every countenance, bright with smiles, and glowing with innocent enjoyment, is a mirror transmitting to others the ways of a supreme and evershining benevolence. — WASHINGTON IRVING.

Happiness, like a snail, is never found from home, nor without a home. — L. C. JUDSON.

Happiness is like game, if you aim at it from too long a distance, you must miss it. — ALPHONSE KARR.

False happiness is like false money; it passes for a time as well as the true, and serves some ordinary purposes; but when it is brought to the touch we find the lightness and alloy and feel the loss. — POPE.

Happiness is like a sunbeam, which the least shadow intercepts, while adversity is often as the rain of spring. — CHINESE PROVERB.

Happy.

Happy as a big sunflower. — ANON.

Happy as a boy at a baseball game. — IBID.

Happy as a June bug. — IBID.

Happy as a prince. — IBID.

Happy as a pussy that sees cream. — IBID.

Happy as a queen. — IBID.

Happy as a turtle dove. — IBID.

Happy as a wave that dances on the sea. — IBID.

Happy as the sunlight. — THOMAS ASHE.

Happy as Heaven. — P. J. BAILEY.

Happy as a reprieved thief. — BALZAC.

Happy as a clam at high water. — J. R. BARTLETT'S "DICTIONARY OF AMERICANISMS."

Happy az a dinner-bell. — JOSH BILLINGS.

Happy as a May-pole. — R. D. BLACKMORE.

Happy as birds in the spring. — WILLIAM BLAKE.

Happy as a lark. — ANNE BRONTË.

Happy as the kine in the fields. — BULWER-LYTTON.

Happy as birds that sing on a tree — SIR JAMES CARNEGIE.

Happy as a fish in water. — VICTOR CHERBULIEZ.

Happy as Spirits cleansed. — AUBREY DE VERE.

Happy — *continued.*

Happy as ol' maids an' died onmarried. — FINLEY PETER DUNNE.

Happy as a king. — JOHN GAY.

Happy as the blest above. — GEORGE GRANVILLE.

Happy as a Sunday in Paris, full of song, and dance, and laughter. — FITZ-GREENE HALLECK.

Happy as the Day. — J. G. HOLLAND.

Happy as a lord. — HUGO.

Happy as the Bird whose nest
Is heaven'd in the heart of purple
Hills. — GERALD MASSEY.

Happy as a miner when he has discovered a vein of precious metal. — GUY DE MAUPASSANT.

Happy as a schoolgirl going home for the holidays. — IBID.

Happy as a priest at a wedding. — GEORGE MOORE.

Happy as an enfranchised bird. — THOMAS MOORE.

Happy as a poor man with a bag of gold. — MISS MULOCK.

Happy as a pig in muck. — NORTHALL'S "FOLK PHRASES."

Happy as a young lamb. — OUIDA.

Happy as heroes after battles won. — MATTHEW PRIOR.

As happy as the day is lang. — SCOTTISH PROVERB.

Happy as the fairest of all. — SHAKESPEARE.

As happy as a serf who leaves the king ennobled. — ALEXANDER SMITH.

Happy as a rose-tree in sunshine. — THACKERAY.

Happy as a child. — WORDSWORTH.

Happy as a Lover. — IBID.

As happy as birds in their bowers. — IBID.

Happy as a wave. — IBID.

Hard (Adjective).

Hard as a brick. — ANON.

Hard as a cobble-stone. — IBID.

Hard as a cricket-ball. — IBID.

Hard as granite. — IBID.

Hard as hail stones. — IBID.

As hard as horn. — IBID.

Hard as marble. — IBID.

As hard as the rocks of Dundee. — IBID.

Hard as flint. — ROBERT BURTON.

Hard as adamant. — CAWDRAY'S "TREASURIE OR STORE-HOUSE OF SMILIES."

Hard as a 1907 prune. — HELEN GREEN.

Hard as a barren stepmother's slap. — LADY GREGORY.

Hard as wire. — JOHN HEYWOOD.

As hard as the heart of a religious foe-curser. — O. W. HOLMES.

Hard as an egg at Easter. — LEAN'S "COLLECTANEA."

Hard as nails. — IBID.

Hard as iron. — THOMAS LODGE.

Hardeneth like the Adama[n]t. — LYLY.

Fingers, hard as a lobster's claws. — GUY DE MAUPASSANT.

Hard as the devil's nagnails. — NORTHALL'S "FOLK PHRASES."

Hard as a sheet of brass. — OUIDA.

Hard as a pine-knot. — JAMES K. PAULDING.

Hard as steel. — SHAKESPEARE.

Hard as the palm of ploughman. — IBID.

Hard — *continued.*

Hard as the push of death. — SWINBURNE.

Hard as a piece of the nether millstone. — OLD TESTAMENT.

Hard as Severn salmon dried in Wales. — NED WARD.

Hard as a flint stone. — LEONARD WRIGHT'S "A DISPLAY OF DUTIE."

Hard (Adverb).

Hard as being good. — ANON.

As hard as to shave an egg. — IBID.

As hard to answer as why cats love fish. — IBID.

Hard to climb as Parnassus. — IBID.

As hard to hold as an eel by the tail. — IBID.

As hard as for an empty sack to stand upright. — BENJAMIN FRANKLIN.

Hard as death. — HAWTHORNE.

Hard to enter my belief as Dives into heaven. — THOMAS HEYWOOD.

Hardy.

Hardy as a mountain pine. — ANON.

Hardy as Highland heather. — W. DUDGEON.

Hardy as a forest pig. —NORTHALL'S "FOLK PHRASES."

Hardy as the Nemean lion's nerve. — SHAKESPEARE.

Harmless.

Harmless as a strawberry festival. — ANON.

Harmless as Sancho's ass. — IBID.

Harmless as the turtle-dove. — PATRICK BRONTË.

Harmless and pleasant as the murmur of brook and wind. — ROBERT BUCHANAN.

Harmless as an infant's play. — COWPER.

Harmlesse as the bee that doeth but taste the flower and flee away. — WILLIAM DRUMMOND.

Harmless as reptiles kept in spirits. — SYDNEY MUNDEN.

Harmless as the turtle of the woods. — OTWAY.

Harmless as a paper tiger. — CHINESE PROVERB.

Harmless as my life's first day. — SWINBURNE.

Harmless as the lightning life of song. — IBID.

Harmless . . . as petals of a flower. — BAYARD TAYLOR.

Harmless as doves. — NEW TESTAMENT.

Harmless as a babe. — WORDSWORTH.

Harsh.

Harsh as blame on ear unused to aught save Angels' tongues. — ROBERT BROWNING.

Harsh as . . . a grating wheel. — JOHN DAVIES.

Harsh as truth. — WILLIAM LLOYD GARRISON.

Harsh as the bitterness of death. — SWINBURNE.

Like a jagged shell's lips, harsh. — IBID.

Of harsher import than the curfew-knell
That spoke the Norman Conqueror's
stern behest. — WORDSWORTH.

Haste.

Hastened like homing pigeons, which do not look behind. — HAMLIN GARLAND.

Haste . . . like flaming tapers brightening as they wasted. — JAMES WHITCOMB RILEY.

Like as the waves make towards the
pebbled shore,
So do our minutes hasten to their end.
— SHAKESPEARE.

Haste — *continued.*

Hastes . . . like as war horse to the fray. — WULFFER.

Hasty.

As hasty as Hopkins, that came to jail over night and was hanged the next morning. — ENGLISH PROVERB.

Hasty as fire. — SHAKESPEARE.

Hasty, like a Scotch jig. — IBID.

Hate (Noun).

Hate is like fire; it makes even light rubbish deadly. — GEORGE ELIOT.

Hate without an object is like a shooting-match without a target. — HUGO.

Hate (Verb).

Hate like poison. — ANON.

Hates as Heaven hates falsehood. — BEAUMONT AND FLETCHER.

Hate like cat and dog. — CARLYLE.

Whose breath I hate
As reek o' the rotten fens.
— HUGO.

I do hate him as I do hell pains. — SHAKESPEARE.

Hate is as an unfilled can. — IBID.

Hateful.

Hateful as death. — CARLYLE.

Hateful to me as the gate of Hades is that man who hides one thing in his heart and speaks another. — HOMER.

Hateful as hell. — JOHN PHILIPS.

Hateful as Cocytus' misty mouth. — SHAKESPEARE.

Hateful to me as the reek of a lime-kiln. — IBID.

Hateful as the grave. — SWINBURNE.

Hatred.

Hatred without a desire for vengeance is like a seed falling on stony ground. — BALZAC.

Haughty.

Haughty as the devil. — POPE.

Haunt.

Haunts like a knell. — WILLIAM AYTOUN.

Haunt us as eagles haunt the mountain air. — P. J. BAILEY.

Your beauty haunts me like a fevered dream. — LADY DUFFERIN.

Haunts . . . like some sweet cadenced strain. — G. H. ELLWANGER.

Haunts the memory, like the wild imagings of a fevered nightmare. — R. W. FRASER.

Haunted as a robber-path through wilderness of wood. — HUGO.

Haunted . . . like a regret. — LAMARTINE.

Haunts like a wild melody.
— THOMAS MOORE.

Haunt . . . like an avenging fiend.
— MISS MULOCK.

Vex and haunt me like a tale of my own future destiny. — SCHILLER.

Haunt thee like a wicked conscience. — SHAKESPEARE.

Haunt one like a ghost. — EDWARD SHARPHAM.

Haunting like spectres. — T. N. TALFOURD.

Haunted me like a passion.
— WORDSWORTH.

Hazy.

Hazy of thought, as a calf looks at a butcher. — ANON.

Hazy, like an oil-lamp full of fungus. — R. D. BLACKMORE.

Head.

Head as hairy as Faunus. — E. B. BROWNING.

Many heads t' obstruct intrigues,
As slowest Insects have most Legs.
— SAMUEL BUTLER.

Head — *continued.*

The head of a woman is like a weather cock on the top of a house, which turns with the slightest wind. — Molière.

The head, like the stomach, is most easily infected with poison when it is empty. — Richter.

His head is like a stomach and intestines which let the food pass through them undigested. — Schopenhauer.

I hang the head
As flowers with frost, or grasses beat
down with storms.—Shakespeare.

Headstrong.

Headstrong as an allegory on the banks of the Nile. — R. B. Sheridan.

Headway.

Making headway like birds aflying. — Anon.

Makes such head as a fire does in a raging wind. — Dickens.

Heal.

Healing as a Sabbath psalm. — Alice W. Brotherton.

Health.

A man too busy to take care of his health is like a mechanic too busy to look after his tools. — Anon.

Health is like munny, we never hav a true idea ov its value until we lose it. — Josh Billings.

Health and good humor are to the human body like sunshine to vegetation. — Massillon.

Healthy.

Healthy as a May morning. — Anon.

Healthy as pity for all the conquered. — Ibid.

Healthy as a May hedge in bloom. — Sir A. Conan Doyle.

Healthful as poignant brine. — William Watson.

Heap (Noun).

All in a heap, like a slaughtered lamb. — Shakespeare.

Heap (Verb).

Heaped like Pelion on Ossa. — Anon.

Heaped like a host in battle overthrown. — William Cullen Bryant.

Heart.

A heart is like a fan, and why? —
'Twill flutter when a beau is nigh:
Oft times with gentle words he'll take it;
Play with it for a while, then break it.
— Anon.

The heart of a man is like a delicate weed,
That requires to be trampled on boldly indeed. — Ibid.

A flinty heart within a snowy breast
Is like base mold lock'd in a golden chest. — Francis Beaumont.

The human heart is like Indian rubber: a little swells it, but a great deal will not burst it. If "little more than nothing will disturb it, little less than all things will suffice" to break it. — Anne Brontë.

The heart is like the sky, a part of heaven;
But changes, night and day, too, like the sky;
Now o'er it clouds and thunder must be driven,
And darkness and destruction as on high;
But when it hath been scorch'd and pierc'd and riven,
Its storms expire in water-drops; the eye
Pours forth, at last, the heart's blood turn'd to tears. — Byron.

A maiden's heart is as champagne, ever struggling upward. — C. S. Calverley.

The heart is like the tree that gives balm for the wounds of man, only when the iron has wounded it. — Chateaubriand.

Heart — *continued.*

My heart is like the fair sea-shell,
There's music ever in it.
— ELIZA COOK.

A woman's heart is as intricate as a ravelled skein of silk. — DUMAS, PÈRE.

Some hearts are like a melting peach, but with a larger, coarser, harder stone. — J. C. HARE.

Hearts, like apples, are hard and sour,
Till crushed by Pain's resistless power.
— J. C. HOLLAND.

The heart of a man has been compared to flowers; but unlike them, it does not wait for the blowing of the wind to be scattered abroad. It is so fleeting and changeful. — YOHIDA KENKŌ.

His heart was like a bookful of girls' song. — FRANCIS LEDWIDGE.

Her heart, like the lake, was as pure
and as calm,
Till love o'er it came, like a breeze
o'er the sea,
And made the heart heave of sweet
Mary machree. — LOVER.

The human heart is like a millstone in a mill; when you put wheat under it, it turns and grinds, and bruises the wheat into flour; if you put no wheat in it, it still grinds on; but then it is itself it grinds, and slowly wears away. — MARTIN LUTHER.

My heart is like a hearth where Cupid is making a fire . . . methinks Venus and Nature stand with each of them a pair of bellowes, the one cooling my low birth, the other kindling my lofty affections. — LYLY.

The heart is like an instrument whose strings steal nobler music from life's many frets. — GERALD MASSEY.

A wise man's heart is like a broad hearth that keeps the coales [his passions] from burning the house. — SIR THOMAS OVERBURY.

A heart is like a new house — the ones that dry the plastering are not the true tenants. — ÉDUARD PAILLERON.

His heart is like a mountain of iron. — PENTAUR.

The hearts of pretty women, like New Year's bonbons, are wrapped in enigmas. — J. PETIT-SENN.

A woman's heart, like the moon, is always changing, but there is always a man in it. — PUNCH.

Heavy hearts, like heavy clouds in the sky, are best relieved by the letting of water. — RIVAROL.

My heart is like a singing bird
Whose nest is in a watered shoot;
My heart is like an apple-tree
Whose boughs are bent with thickset
fruit;
My heart is like a rainbow shell
That paddles in a halcyon sea;
My heart is gladder than all these
Because my love is come to me.
— C. G. ROSSETTI.

Her heart is like an ordered house
Good fairies harbour in. — IBID.

A noble heart, like the sun, showeth its greatest countenance in its lowest estate. — SIR PHILIP SIDNEY.

Burning lips and a wicked heart are like a potsherd covered with silver dross. — OLD TESTAMENT.

A woman's heart is just like a lithographer's stone, — what is once written upon it cannot be rubbed out. — THACKERAY.

My heart is like fire in a close vessel: I am ready to burst for want of vent. — JOHN WESLEY.

Her heart is like an outbound ship
That at its anchor swings.
— WHITTIER.

Heart as calm as lakes that sleep,
In frosty moonlight glistening.
— WORDSWORTH

Hearty.

Hearty as a buck. — Anon.

Hearty as an O.K. — Ibid.

Hearty as an oak. — Samuel Foote.

Hearty . . . like a trombone thoroughly impregnated with cheerful views of life. — Charles Reade.

Heat.

Heats like the hammered anvil.— O. W. Holmes.

Heave.

Heaved and sighed like the dying gasp of a syphon bottle. — Anon.

Heaves . . .
Like a mighty ship in pain,
Facing the tempest with struggle and strain. — E. B. Browning.

Heaves like a water-weed that opens to the wave. — Ibid.

Heaves like a long-swept wave about to break. — Byron.

Heaved like the surface of the sea. — Dumas, père.

Heaved as in his breast the waves of life kept heaving to and fro. — Hood.

Heaving . . . like the sea in the background of a marine piece at the theatre. — George Meredith.

Heaved like ridgy waves. — Ossian.

Heart heaved as a man's death-smitten with a dart
That smites him sleeping, warm and full of life. — Swinburne.

Heaven.

Heaven is like unto treasure hid in a field; the which when a man hath found, he hideth, and for joy thereof goeth and selleth all that he hath, and buyeth that field. — New Testament.

Heavily.

Laboring heavily — like a tramp freighter in a heavy sea. —E. D. Price.

Heavily, as sorrow-laden. — Hawthorne.

Heavy.

Heavy as a boarding-house dumpling. — Anon.

Heavy as death. — Matthew Arnold

Heavy as a panegyric. — Congreve.

Heavy as the hand of death. — Dickens.

Head as heavy as alderman's. — Fielding.

Hung heavy as an opiate. — Thomas Hardy.

Heavy and lumpish . . . like a defunct nightmare, which had perished in the midst of its wickedness, and left its flabby corpse on the breast of the tormented one, to be gotten rid of as it might. — Hawthorne.

Heavy, like a spade that digs in clay. — R. H. Horne.

Heavy as remembered sin
That will not suffer sleep or thought to ease. — Kipling.

Lies heavy . . . like murder on a guilty soul. — Schiller.

Heavy as lead. — Skelton.

Heavier than the sands of the sea. — Old Testament.

Heavy as a Dutchman. — Mrs. Henry Wood.

Heavy as frost. — Wordsworth.

Heeds.

Heeds
As the seven Seas should a pebble cast. — Edward Fitzgerald.

Held.

Held on like a summer cold. — George Ade.

Held back like a hearse horse. — Anon.

Held on like grim death. — Ibid.

Held — *continued.*

Held on to him like a life-belt. — Lloyd Osbourne.

Held you . . .
As flesh holds flesh, and the soul the soul. — Swinburne.

Help.

As far from help as limbo is from bliss. — Shakespeare.

Helpless.

Helpless as a babe. — Anon.

Helpless, as a cat in a trap. — Ibid.

Helpless as a corpse. — Ibid.

Helpless as Balaam. — Ibid.

Helpless as a king of England. — Emerson.

Helpless as an infant caterpillar in a nest of hungry ants. — James Montgomery Flagg.

Helpless as the dead. — W. S. Gilbert.

Helpless as a turtle on its back. — O. Henry.

Helpless as a lame beggar. — Ouida.

Helpless and flurried as a fish landed on a grassy bank with a barbed hook through its gills. — Ibid.

Helpless as a ship in stays. — Robert Louis Stevenson.

Helpless, like doves driven headlong down by a murky tempest. — Virgil.

Helpless as a sailor cast on desert rock. — Wordsworth.

Helpless . . . as the blind. — Ibid.

Helter-Skelter.

Helter-skelter . . . like a crowd of frightened porpoises a shoal of sharks pursue. — Robert Browning.

Heresy.

Heresies perish not with their authors, but, like the river Arethusa, though they lose their currents in one place, they rise up again in another. — Sir Thomas Browne.

Hero.

Like the young lion wounded by the dart,
Whose fury kindled at the galling smart;
The hero rouses with redoubled rage,
Flies on the foe, and foams upon the stage. — Paul Whitehead.

Heroic.

Heroic as martyrdom. — Ouida.

Heroism.

Heroism, like Plotinus, is almost ashamed of its body. — Emerson.

Hesitate.

Hesitating like stag at bay. — John Clare.

Hesitating, fluttering, like the bird with young wing, weak and dubious. — George Eliot.

Hesitating like a bather about to make his plunge. — Thomas Hardy.

Hesitate, like the submissive voice of an inferior. — Sir Walter Scott.

Hew.

Hew'd away, like doctors of theology
When they dispute with sceptics.
— Byron.

Hewn as if with stroke of swords in tempest steeled. — Swinburne.

Hide.

Hid, like a thought of God, unuttered. — P. J. Bailey.

Closely hid as Rameses in the pyramid. — Julia C. R. Dorr.

Hide ourself as Adam at the voice of the Lord God in the garden. — Emerson.

Hidden . . . like the works of a watch beneath the hands. — H. A. Jones.

Hide — *continued.*

Hide like gentle nuns from human eyes. — SIDNEY LANIER.

Hid like incense in a flower's heart. — GERALD MASSEY.

Hid like a buried star. — JAMES MONTGOMERY.

Hid, as in a grave. — ROWE.

Hid
Safe from the glare of the day like an
eye under its lid.
— FRANK D. SHERMAN.

Hidden . . . like a dark well, whose unseen brink is overgrown with waving grass. — VALMIKI.

Hideous.

Hideous as midnight. — ANON.

Hideous as evil. — HUGO.

Hideous as the witch of Endor. — HENRY MACKENZIE.

Hideous like a savage at his altar. — NIETZSCHE.

Hideous as a skeleton. — ANTON TCHEKHOV.

High.

High as a kite. — ANON.

High as summer-surge swells. — IBID.

Higher than Gilroy's kite. — IBID.

High as the herald-star. — EDWIN ARNOLD.

High as man's desires. — BEACONSFIELD.

High . . . as the stars were above the clouds. — A. C. BENSON.

Higher than the price ov gold. — JOSH BILLINGS.

High as the stars. — CARLYLE.

High as the head of Fame. — CONGREVE.

High as the spheres. — IBID.

Piled high as the skies. — FREDERICK THE GREAT.

High as the berries of a wild ash tree. — KEATS.

High as Jove's roof. — SIR ROGER L'ESTRANGE.

High as that peak in Heaven where Milton kneels. — EDWIN MARKHAM.

High as most fantastic woman's wits could reach. — OTWAY.

As high as Gilderoy. — SCOTTISH PROVERB.

High as heaven itself. — SHAKESPEARE.

High as the sunniest heights of kindliest thought. — SWINBURNE.

As high as heaven. — OLD TESTAMENT.

High as manhood's noon. — WORDSWORTH.

Hilarious.

Hilarious as a sailor ashore. — ANON.

Hinders.

Hinders . . . like water, that by force of its own pressing violence and abundance cannot find a ready issue through the neck of a bottle, or of a narrow sluice. — MONTAIGNE.

Hiss.

Hiss like a steam kettle. — ANON.

Hiss . . . like shot from guns. — E. B. BROWNING.

The sea hissed like twenty thousand kettles! — JOSEPH CONRAD.

Hissed like a forked serpent. — AUBREY DE VERE.

Hiss, like a goose with a flock of goslings. — SAM SLICK.

Hissing like a snake. — HUGO.

Hiss like vipers. — SIGMUND KRASINSKI.

Hissed like a rocket. — CAMILLE LEMONNIER.

Hisses like red-hot iron. — W. C. RUSSELL.

Hiss — *continued.*

Hisses and roars, as when fire is with water commixed and contending. — SCHILLER.

Hiss as of a rushing wind. — SHELLEY.

Hisses as with mouths of snakes and wolves at bay. — SWINBURNE.

Hiss like bottle(d) ale. — JOHN TAYLOR.

History.

History is like sacred music, because truth is essential to it. — CERVANTES.

History, like religion, unites all learning and power. — RICHTER.

Hoarse.

Hoarse as the rustling of autumnal breeze. — HENRY BROOKE.

Hoarse as a raven. — CHARLES READE.

Hoarse as warning prophets in an evil age. — BAYARD TAYLOR.

Hoarse
As when a hawker hawks his wares.
— TENNYSON.

Hoary.

Hoary as the glacier's head
Faced to the moon.
— GEORGE MEREDITH.

Hoary as ashes that show not a gleam. — SWINBURNE.

Hoar as the hawthorn blossom in spring. — IBID.

Hoary as weeds cast up from the hoary sea. — IBID.

Hobble.

Hobbles as a goose.—JOHN SKELTON.

Hold.

Hold on like grim death. — ANON.

Hold him, like an eagle that has seized an eaglet in his talons. — BALZAC.

Hold together like burrs. — WILLIAM CAMDEN'S "REMAINS CONCERNING BRITAIN."

Holds as tight as a horse-leech. — DICKENS.

Holds him fast
As a night-flag round the mast.
— GEORGE MEREDITH.

Her arms the master hold,
As on wounds the scarf winds tight.
— IBID.

Hold like colors of a shell.— TENNYSON.

Taken hold upon me, as the pangs of a woman that travaileth. — OLD TESTAMENT.

Holds . . . together as the shell does the egg. — JOHN C. VAN DYKE.

Holler.

Holler like a loon. — ANON.

Holler . . . like a calf for its mammy. — BOOTH TARKINGTON.

Hollow.

Hollow as a gun. — ANON.

Hollow as the soul of an echo. — IBID.

Hollow as the murmur of the midnight sea after the tempest nursed itself to rest. — IBID.

As hollow as an egg shell. — P. J. BAILEY.

Hollow and wasteful as a whirlwind. — IBID.

Hollow as is the armour of a ghost. — T. L. BEDDOES.

Hollow as an actor's laugh. — GELETT BURGESS.

Hollow like a niche in a column. — FEDOR DOSTOEVSKY.

Hollow and dead as the empty shell of last year's nut. — VIOLET FANE.

As hollow as any trumpet in Europe. — FIELDING.

Hollow — *continued.*

Hollower than an echo fallen
Across some clear abyss.
— JEAN INGELOW.

Hollow as the unbowell'd winds. — H. H. MILMAN.

Hollow, as a sepulchre. — M. D. POST.

Hollow as a drum. — CHARLES READE.

Hollow like a breathing shell. — D. G. ROSSETTI.

Hollow as a ghost. — SHAKESPEARE.

Hollow as the hopes and fears of men. — TENNYSON.

Holy.

As holy, as the symbol that we lay on the still bosom of our white-robed dead. — O. W. HOLMES.

Holy as heaven a mother's tender love. — MRS. NORTON.

Holy as the watch of an invisible spirit. — POE.

Holy as bowers where angels have flown. — A. J. RYAN.

Holy as a choir of nuns. — R. D. WILLIAMS.

Holy as a spire rear'd o'er the house of God. — JOHN WILSON.

Holy as one from an angel clime. — WILLIAM WINTER.

Home.

As much at home . . . as a fish in water. — BALZAC.

Homeless.

Homeless as the dogs in the Constantinople streets. — PIERRE DE COULEVAIN.

Homely.

Homely as a hedge-fence. — ANON.

Homely as the queen of spades. — IBID.

Homely as a stump fence. — ARTEMUS WARD.

Homer.

In the Odyssey, Homer may be likened to the setting sun, whose grandeur still remains, though his beams have lost their meridian heat. — LONGINUS.

Honest.

Honest a man as ever brake bread. — ANON.

Honest a man as ever trod on shoe leather. — IBID.

Honest as a cat when the meat is out of reach. — IBID.

Honest as a mirror. — IBID.

Honest as the day is long. — IBID.

Honest as the sun. — IBID.

Honest as the skin between his brows. — "GAMMER GURTON'S NEEDLE."

Honest as a tar. — JAMES GRAHAME.

Honest a man as ever lived by bread. — THOMAS HEYWOOD.

Bluffly honest as a northwest wind. — LOWELL.

Honest a man as any in the cards, when all the Kings are out. — BRIAN MELBANCKE.

Honest as the skin between his brows. — SHAKESPEARE.

Honest as the nature of man first made, ere fraud and vice were fashions. — OTWAY.

Honesty.

Honesty iz like a 7 per cent. interest ; it will beat all kind of speckerlashuns in the long run. — JOSH BILLINGS.

Honesty
Is like a stock of money laid to sleep,
Which, ne'er so little broke, does
never keep.
— CYRIL TOURNEUR.

Honeyed.

Honeyed as the damask rose. — NORA HOPPER.

Honor.

Honor that is gained and broken upon another hath the quickest reflection, like diamonds cut with facets; and therefore let a man contend to excel any competitors of his in honor, in outshooting them, if he can, in their own bow. — BACON.

Honour is like the eye, which cannot suffer the least injury without damage; it is a precious stone, the price of which is lessened by the least flaw. — BOSSUET.

Honor is like a widow, won
With brisk attempt and putting on;
With entering manfully, and urging,
Not slow approaches, like a virgin.
— SAMUEL BUTLER.

Honour is like that glossy bubble
That finds philosophers such trouble,
Whose least part crack'd, the whole does fly
And wits are crack'd to find out why.
— IBID.

Woman's honour is nice as ermine; 'twill not bear a soil. — DRYDEN.

Honour doth appeare to statesmen like a vision in the night,
And jugler-like workes o' th' deluded sight.
— WILLIAM HARBINGTON.

Honor and he agree as well together as a satin suit and woolen stockings. — JOHN MARSTON.

Honor . . . like power, disdains being questioned. — NICHOLAS ROWE.

Honor, like life, when once lost, never returns. — PUBLIUS SYRUS.

As snow in summer, and as rain in harvest, so honour is not seemly for a fool. — OLD TESTAMENT.

Hooded.

Hooded like a hawk. — CONGREVE.

Hoot.

Hooted at like an old tale. — SHAKESPEARE.

Hop.

Hop as light as bird from brier. — SHAKESPEARE.

Hope.

Our hopes, like towering falcons, aim at objects in an airy height:
The little pleasure of the game is afar off to view the flight. — ANON.

It is equally precarious to moor a ship by an insufficient anchor, and to ground hope on a capricious temper. — DEMOPHILUS.

A woman's hopes are woven as sunbeams; a shadow annihilates them. — GEORGE ELIOT.

Hope, like the glimmering taper's light
Adorns and cheers the way;
And still, as darker grows the night,
Emits a brighter ray.
— GOLDSMITH.

Our hopes, like withered leaves, fall fast. — LONGFELLOW.

As froth on the face of the deep,
As foam on the crest of the sea,
As dreams at the waking of sleep,
As gourd of a day and a night,
As harvest that no man shall reap,
As vintage that never shall be,
Is hope if it cling not aright,
O my God unto Thee.
— C. G. ROSSETTI.

Hope is like a harebell trembling from its birth. — IBID.

Who builds his hope in air of your fair looks,
Lives like a drunken sailor on a mast;
Ready, with every nod, to tumble down
Into the fatal bowels of the deep.
— SHAKESPEARE.

Hope is like the sun, which, as we journey towards it, casts the shadow of our burden behind us. — SAMUEL SMILES.

Hope — *continued.*

Hope has left you like a painted dream. — Joseph Stansbury.

As some adventurous flower, on savage craig-side grown,
Seems nourished hour by hour from its wild self alone,
So lives inveterate Hope, on her own hardihood.
— William Watson.

Hopeful.

Hopeful as the break of day. — T. B. Aldrich.

Hopeful as Prometheus. — George MacDonald.

Hopeless.

Hopeless and as full of fear
As are the blasted banks of Erebus.
— Marlowe.

Hopeless as telling Belshazzar his dream. — T. N. Page.

As hopeless as for the musician to pour his notes into the ear of a deaf man. — J. McNeill Whistler.

Horned.

Horned like the crescent moon. — Shelley.

Horny.

Horny as a camel's knee. — Anatole France.

Horny as a briar rose. — Hugo.

Horrible.

Horrible as viper-bitten bodies. — George Meredith.

Horrible, like the shrieks of witches. — Munchausen.

Horrid.

Horrid as a murderer's dream. — Dr. Johnson.

Horrid as the witches in Macbeth. — Bonnell Thornton.

Horse.

A white horse and a beautiful woman are akin, and two troublesome things to manage : the first is difficult to be kept clean ; and the second, honest. — Samuel Foote.

Hospitable.

Hospitable as an old Siracusan. — Dumas, père.

Hostile.

By nature as hostile to mystery as the sunshine to a dark corner. — Hawthorne.

Hostility.

Hostility between two people is like fire, and the evil-fated backbiter supplies fuel. Afterwards, when they are reconciled together, the backbiter is hated and despised by both parties. — Anon.

Hot.

Hot as a black pudding. — Anon.

Hot as a coal. — Ibid.

Hot as a pone cake. — Ibid.

As hot as hot might be. — Ibid.

Hot as Jove. — Ibid.

Hot as love's flaming climate. — Ibid.

Hot as pepper. — Ibid.

Hot as ten thousand suns in one. — Ibid.

Hot as the hinges of hell. — Ibid.

Hot as Tophet. — Ibid.

Hot as a volcano. — Ibid.

Hot as the devil's kitchen. — J. R. Bartlett's "Dictionary of Americanisms."

Hot as the fire of the Lord out of heaven could make it. — Bunyan.

Hot as a basted turkey. — Will Carleton.

Hot as hell-fire. — Dryden.

Hot — *continued.*

Agonies as hot as flames of sulphur. — JOHN FORD.

Hot as hate. — HAMLIN GARLAND.

Love is as hot as pepper'd brandy. — WILLIAM KING.

Hot as a toast. — LYLY.

Hot as hay harvest. — BRIAN MELBANCKE.

Hot as flame. — OUIDA.

Hot as coals of glowing fire. — SHAKESPEARE.

Hot as gunpowder. — IBID.

Hot as molten lead. — IBID.

Hot as monkeys. — IBID.

Hot as Perseus. — IBID.

Hot as hell. — SWINBURNE.

Hot like Mars. — IBID.

Hot and close as fire. — IBID.

Hot as an oven. — OLD TESTAMENT.

Hot as a swinked gypsy. — FRANCIS THOMPSON.

Hot as Indian curry. — ISRAEL ZANGWILL.

House.

A house without woman or firelight is like a body without soul or spirit. — FRANKLIN.

Houses are like friendship ; there is hardly one in a thousand worth a long lease. — OUIDA.

Hover.

Hover as a hawk. — ANON.

Hover like a moth around a flame. — IBID.

Hovered round the work like rainbow round a fountain. — P. J. BAILEY.

Hovering like the summer sky. — M. A. BROWNE.

Hover — like a moth intoxicated with light. — JOHN GALSWORTHY.

Hovering near,
Like some base vulture in the battle's rear. — REGINALD HEBER.

Hovered, like a spectre, in the background of all her imaginations. — KINGSLEY.

Strives and hovers
As a bird above the brood her bosom covers. — SWINBURNE.

Hovers as birds that impend on the sea. — IBID.

Howl.

Howl like a dervish. — ANON.

Howl like a vagabond for bread. — IBID.

Howled like a just-lugged bear. — ROBERT BROWNING.

Howling, like a wolf, flies the famished northern blast. — WILLIAM CULLEN BRYANT.

Howl'd for help as wolves do for a meal. — BYRON.

Howl like a wolf. — DICKENS.

Howls like a thousand demons. — GEORGE ELIOT.

Howling like a pig in a gate. — KINGSLEY.

Howl like a wild beast. — KIPLING.

Howled like a pack of famished dogs. — LAMARTINE.

Howlings, like a herd of ravenous wolves disappointed of their prey. — WILLIAM H. PRESCOTT.

Howling like savage creatures grazed by death. — CHARLES READE.

Howling, like a slaughtered town. — SHELLEY.

Huddle.

Huddle together at random . . . like the forms of dreams. — ÆSCHYLUS.

Huddled in rows, like wrinkles in some old gown. — ROBERT BRIDGES (AMERICAN).

Huddle — *continued.*

Huddled like beasts beneath the drovers' whips. — JOHN MASEFIELD.

Hueless.

Hueless as a ghost. — COLERIDGE.

Cheeks hueless as a brandy-peach. — O. W. HOLMES.

Hueless as young ivory. — GEORGE CABOT LODGE.

Hug.

Hug me as a devil hugs a witch. — ANON.

Hug like a bear. — IBID.

Hug like a boa-constrictor. — IBID.

To be hugged by a bony man is about as luxurious as sitting on a picket fence. — IBID.

Huge.

Huge as a planet. — KEATS.

As huge as Ossa piled on Pelion. — OWEN MEREDITH.

Huge as high Olympus. — SHAKESPEARE.

Hum.

Hum like a cobbler. — ANON.

Hum,
Like listless topers singing o'er their cups. — ARABIC.

Hum and murmur like a hive. — E. B. BROWNING.

Hummed . . . as the sea in shells. — IBID.

Humming, like bees that are swarming. — HEINRICH HEINE.

Humming like a hornet. — LONGFELLOW.

Humming . . . like a hive of bees. — JOAQUIN MILLER.

Human.

Human as a kiss. — VANCE THOMPSON.

Humble.

Humble as a grateful almsman. — ANON.

Humble as a worm. — IBID.

Humble as Uriah Heep. — IBID.

Humble as is a lamb. — ALEXANDER BARCLAY.

Humble as a Jesuit to his superior. — SAMUEL BUTLER.

As humble as the grass. — BLISS CARMAN.

As humble as the child of one that sweats, to eat the dear-earn'd bread of honest thrift. — JOHN FORD.

Humbly, like a praying nun. — O. W. HOLMES.

Humble as a stone. — HOOD.

Humble as a worm. — IBID.

Humbly as they used to creep
To holy altars.
— SHAKESPEARE.

Humility.

Humility like darkness reveals the heavenly lights.—HENRY D. THOREAU.

Humor.

A sense of humor is to a lonely citizen of the world what is to a shipwrecked sailor on a desert the knife with which he hews the logs to make his hut, and cuts the fruit by which he lives. — BETTINA VON HUTTEN.

Humorous.

Humorous as April. — ANON.

Humorous as wind. — JOHN DRYDEN.

Humorous as winter. — SHAKESPEARE.

Hunger.

Hungering hard as frost that feeds on flowers. — SWINBURNE.

Hungry.

Hungry as a bear. — ANON.

Hungry as a church mouse. — IBID.

Hungry — *continued.*

Hungry as a diamond without a karat. — ANON.

Hungry as a graven image. — J. R. BARTLETT'S "DICTIONARY OF AMERICANISMS."

Hungry as a tired hound. — "THE CHRISTMAS PRINCE."

Hungry as a horse. — CLARKE'S "PHRASEOLOGIA PUERILIS."

Hungry as devouring flame. — EBENEZER ELLIOTT.

Hungry as the chap that said a turkey was too much for one, not enough for two. — O. W. HOLMES.

Hungry as the jaws of a gaol. — "JACKE DRUM'S ENTERTAINMENTS."

Hungry as if it were the last day of Lent. — HENRI MURGER.

Hungry as a hunter. — NORTHALL'S "FOLK PHRASES."

Hungry as a wolf. — JOHN PALGRAVE.

Hungry as a kite. — SIR WALTER SCOTT.

Hungry as the sea,
And can digest as much.
— SHAKESPEARE.

Hungry as a hawk. — JOHN TAYLOR.

Hungry as the winter. — ANTON TCHEKOV.

Hungry as the grave. — JAMES THOMSON.

Hunted.

Hunted like a stag. — ANON.

A man [Voltaire] hunted by the little devils that dwell unchained within him ; like Pentheus by the Mænads, like Actæon by his own Dogs. — CARLYLE.

Hurled.

Hurled as a stone from out of a catapult. — TENNYSON.

Hurry.

Hurried, like one distraught. — T. B. ALDRICH.

Hurried like a torrent through a strait. — JOHN DAVIDSON.

Hurried like moon-ray flashes through the drifting snow. — MILES O'REILLY.

Hurry . . . like the leaf in a roaring whirlwind. — TENNYSON.

Hurt.

Hurts one like the day
Let suddenly on sick eyes.
— E. B. BROWNING.

Husband.

Husbands are like apples, they shouldn't be picked till they are ripe. — ANON.

Husbands, like spectacles, to fit every age, from fifteen to fourscore. — GOLDSMITH.

Hushed.

Hushed, as in waiting for a bird to sing. — RICHARD HOVEY.

Lies hushed, like a seer in a vision. W. D. HOWELLS.

Hushed like an infant on its mother's breast. — GERALD MASSEY.

Hushed, as if nature were retired. — OTWAY.

Hush as death. — SHAKESPEARE.

Hushed as midnight. — IBID.

Hushed soft as the leaves and the grasses
Are hushed if the storm's foot draws near. — SWINBURNE.

Hush'd . . . as a sick man's room when he taketh repose. — TENNYSON.

Hushed as the warm Numidian heaven. — WHITTIER.

Hushed as night. — WORDSWORTH.

Hushed
As the unbreathing air, when not a leaf
Stirs in the mighty woods. — IBID.

Hustle.

Hustle like fiery-eyed dragons. — Henrik Ibsen.

Hustle about me like pent-up air. — D. G. Rossetti.

How close-packed the mob is, they hustle like a herd of swine. — Theocritus.

Hypocrite.

An hypocrite is like unto an apple, that is very faire and beautiful without, but within is corrupted and rotten. — Anthonie Fletcher's "Certain Very Proper and Profitable Similes," 1595.

Hypocrites! for ye are like unto whited sepulchres, which indeed appear beautiful outward, but are within full of dead men's bones, and of all uncleanness. — New Testament.

Hysterical.

Hysterical as a tree full of chickens. — Irvin S. Cobb.

I

Ideas.

Our ideas, like orange-plants, spread out in proportion to the size of the box which imprisons the roots. — Bulwer-Lytton.

Ideas are for the most part like bad sixpences and we spend our lives in trying to pass them off on one another. — Samuel Butler (1835–1902).

Ideas are like shadows — substantial enough until we try to grasp them. — Ibid.

An idea, like a ghost (according to the common notion of ghosts), must be spoken to a little before it will explain itself. — Dickens.

A fixed idea is like a gimlet; every year gives it another turn. To pull it out the first year is like plucking out the hair by the roots; in the second year, like tearing the skin; in the third, like breaking the bones; and in the fourth, like removing the very brain itself. — Hugo.

An idea is like a meteor; at the critical moment, the confused meditations which have preceded it open a way, and a spark flashes forth. . . . These flashes are generated in the conscience in its states of cloud and darkness. — Ibid.

Our ideas, like pictures, are made up of lights and shadows. — Joubert.

A fixed idea is like the iron rod which sculptors put in their statues. It impales and sustains. — Taine.

Ideas are like beards; men do not have them until they grow up. — Voltaire.

Idle.

Idle as digging in the bottom of the river for the stars we see reflected on the surface. — Anon.

Idle as railing at a deaf man. — Ibid.

Idle as to aim at inscrutable things beyond the moon. — Ibid.

Idle as a lazzarone. — J. Ashby-Sterry.

As idle as a dial when the sun
Sulks in the clouds.
— Alfred Austin.

Idle as the stroke of a cane on the hide of rhinoceros. — Bulwer-Lytton.

Idle as air. — Alice Cary.

As idle as a painted ship upon a painted ocean. — Coleridge.

Idle — *continued.*

Idle, as the dreams of maids. — WALTER HARTE.

Idle as a summer noon. — OMAR KHAYYAM.

Looks idle, perhaps, and foolish, like a hat on its block in the store. — JOYCE KILMER.

Idle, and mean as a collier's whelp. — KIPLING.

Idleness.

Idleness feeds on the empty day
As a chameleon on the air.
— RICHARD HOVEY.

Idly.

As idly as a babe that sees the painted pictures of a book. — BAYARD TAYLOR.

Ignorance.

He makes his ignorance pass for reserve, and, like a hunting-nag, leaps over what he cannot get through. — SAMUEL BUTLER.

Ignorant.

Ignorant as a pig is of the side pocket of a pool table. — ANON.

Ignorant as a bookseller. — COLERIDGE.

As invincibly ignorant as a town-fop judging of a new play. — DRYDEN.

Ignorant as a Tripoline ambassador, or an envoy from Mujac. — GOLDSMITH.

Ignorant as a raw kitchen wench. — GEORGE MEREDITH.

The ignorant person is like a cock out of season, which crows at midnight. — OSMANLI PROVERB.

Ignorant as dirt. — SHAKESPEARE.

Ignorant as a child. — THOREAU.

Illimitable.

Illimitable as the boundless sea. — ANON.

Illiterate.

Illiterate as the lowliest hedger and ditcher. — EUGENE FIELD.

Ill-Natured.

Ill-natured as an old maid. — CONGREVE.

Illuminated.

Illuminated him as the burning taper lights up consecrated plate. — GEORGE MEREDITH.

Illusion.

Illusion like the tints of pearl,
Or changing colors of the sky,
Or ribbons of a dancing girl
That mend her beauty to the eye.
— EMERSON.

Illusive.

Illusive, like a dream. — JULIA C. R. DORR.

Immaculate.

Immaculate as an angel. — ANON.

Immaculate as Tanit. — FLAUBERT.

Immaculate as a sheet of white paper. — SAMUEL FOOTE.

Hearts immaculate as light. — J. G. HOLLAND.

Immaculate as fresh snow. — T. N. PAGE.

Immaterial.

Immaterial as a ghost. — JOSEPH CONRAD.

Immaterial as a moonbeam. — EDGAR SALTUS.

Immediately.

Immediately, like a repeating clock of which the spring has been touched. — G. B. SHAW.

Immense.

Immense as the sea. — SWINBURNE.

Immobile.

As immobile as an unruffled lake on a perfect summer's day. — D. R. ANDERSON.

Immobile — *continued.*

Immobile as a Sphinx's face. — ANON.

Immobility.

Immobility lay on his limbs like a leaden garment. — JOSEPH CONRAD.

Immortal.

Immortal as the stars. — MATHILDE BLIND.

Immortal as air or as fire is. — SWINBURNE.

Immortal as art and as love. — IBID.

Immortal as the sun. — ARTHUR SYMONS.

Poetry is the first and last of all knowledge: it is immortal as the heart of man. — WORDSWORTH.

Immovable.

Immovable as the figure of Mercury. — ANON.

Grenadiers . . . stood their ground immovable, like rocks, steadily spouting fire-torrents. — CARLYLE.

Immovable as a pump or a lamppost. — DICKENS.

Immovable as a leopard crouching in the jungle. — FLAUBERT.

Immovable as a picture. — IBID.

Immovable, as if it were painted on the wall. — HAWTHORNE.

Immovable as a setter at the scent of quail. — O. HENRY.

Immovable, like the owner's names, cut in brass, and nailed to their doors. — THOMAS HOLCROFT.

Immovable in the flow of the rout as rocks in running water. — HUGO.

Immovable as a man of iron. — KINGSLEY.

Immovable as the sun. — THEOGNIS.

Immovably.

As immovably as the pillars that prop the universe. — FISHER AMES.

Immutable.

Immutable as the laws of the Medes and Persians. — ANON.

Impalpable.

Impalpable as stars-beams in deep seas. — PAUL HAMILTON HAYNE.

Impalpable as a rainbow on the clouds. — MISS MITFORD.

Impartial.

Impartial as bullets in a battle. — ANON.

Impartially.

Impartially as the grave. — KIPLING.

Impassable.

Impassable as marble. — ANON.

Impassable, as the veil of the Image of Sais. — BULWER-LYTTON.

Impassive.

Impassive as a figure of carved ivory. — ANON.

Impassive as an Indian idol. — IBID.

Impassive as the copper head on a penny. — KIPLING.

Impassive as an angel. — SIR RICHARD STEELE.

Impatient.

Impatient as a lover. — ANON.

Impatient as a boy. — SIGMUND KRASINSKI.

Impatient as a hungry infant. — SYDNEY MUNDEN.

Impend.

Impends, like a crag over the brow of a lofty precipice. — O. W. HOLMES.

Impenetrable.

Impenetrable as a hedgehog. — ANON.

Impenetrable to the view as the deep blue of a glacier. — D'ANNUNZIO.

Impenetrable as granite. — OUIDA.

Impenetrable as rhinoceri. — IBID.

Impenitent.

Impenitent as a stone. — ANON.

Imperceptible.

Imperceptible as the spots on the sun or the shadows on a sunlit seat. — SWINBURNE.

Imperceptibly.

Imperceptibly as old age comes on. — W. S. GILBERT.

Imperfect.

Imperfect as discourses in a dream. — GEORGE GRANVILLE.

Imperfection.

Our inborn human imperfection is part of the order of things, like the constant deformation of the petal in the plant. — TAINE.

Imperishable.

Imperishable as eternity. — P. J. BAILEY.

Impersonal.

Impersonal as Shakespeare. — CHARLOTTE BRONTË.

Impersonal as the justice of God. — HUGO.

Impertinent.

Impertinent as puns. — G. K. CHESTERTON.

Imperturbable.

Imperturbable as diplomatists. — BALZAC.

Impervious.

Impervious as a statue to all sight and sound. — OUIDA.

Impetuous.

As eager flames, with opposition pent,
Break out impetuous when they find a rent. — GEORGE GRANVILLE.

Impetuous as a poet. — JOUBERT.

Impetuous as a wild boar. — SIR WALTER SCOTT.

Implacable.

Implacable as the voice of Doom. — CARLYLE.

Implacable an adversary as a wife suing for alimony. — VANBRUGH.

Implacable as the wind. — VIRGIL.

Important.

Important as a militia officer on a training day. — J. R. BARTLETT'S "DICTIONARY OF AMERICANISMS."

Important as life eternal and death eternal. — CARLYLE.

Important as the linch-pin. — O. W. HOLMES.

Imposing.

Imposing as a set of solid gold teeth. — REX BEACH.

Impossible.

Impossible as an echo without a voice to start it. — ANON.

Impossible as for a blind man to describe color. — IBID.

Impossible as for a lawyer to feel compassion gratis. — IBID.

Impossible as for one buried alive to lift his gravestone. — IBID.

Impossible as for the full-grown bird to live imprisoned in the eggshell. — IBID.

Impossible as for the man in the moon to come down. — IBID.

Impossible as for the poles to come together till the earth is crushed. — IBID.

Impossible as for widows to feed on
dreams and wishes;
Like hags on visionary dishes.
— IBID.

Impossible as to count the waves. — IBID.

Impossible as to hiss and yawn at the same time. — IBID.

Impossible as to hold the wind with a net. — IBID.

Impossible — *continued.*

Impossible as to join in a procession and look out the window. — ANON.

Impossible as to jump away from your shadow. — IBID.

Impossible as to mend a bell. — IBID.

Impossible as to paint a sound. — IBID.

Impossible as to recall the days that are past. — IBID.

Impossible as to reconcile cats and rats, or hounds and hares. — IBID.

Impossible as to replace a hatched chicken in its shell. — IBID.

Impossible as to stem the eternal flood of time. — IBID.

Impossible as to wash a black man white. — IBID.

Impossible as to wet the sea. — IBID.

As impossible for him to take flight of fancy as it would be for a watchmaker to put together a chronometer with nothing except a two-pound hammer and a whip-saw in the way of tools. — JOSEPH CONRAD.

Impossible as it would be for a full balloon not to go up. — DICKENS.

A little girl without a doll is almost as unfortunate and quite as impossible as a woman without children. — HUGO.

Impossible as for a blind man to copy Raphael. — LONDON TELEGRAPH.

Truth is as impossible to be soiled by any outward touch as the sunbeam. — MILTON.

As impossible as that a man should walk in procession at his own funeral. — THOMAS PAINE.

Impossible as to cut fire into steaks, or draw water with a fish-net. — RABELAIS.

Impossible as a centaur or a griffin. — JOHN SKELTON.

Impossible as to get the whole music of the spheres into a sonata. — ROBERT LOUIS STEVENSON.

Impotent.

Impotent as "the strengthless tribes of the dead." — ANDREW LANG.

Impractical.

Impractical as to attempt to satisfy a tiger's hunger with *pâté de foie gras.* — ANON.

Impressionable.

Impressionable as an Æolian harp to the rise or fall of a passing wind. — BULWER-LYTTON.

Impudent.

Impudent as a young barrister after getting a verdict by mistake. — ANON.

Inaccessible.

Inaccessible as the best defended fortress. — FIELDING.

Inaccessible, like some tall cliff. — SCHILLER.

Inanimate.

Inanimate as a statue. — ANON.

Inanimate as mutton. — IBID.

Inanimate as the picture on a postal card. — IBID.

Inaudible.

Inaudible like spirits. — E. B. BROWNING.

Inaudible as dreams. — COLERIDGE.

Inaudible . . . like a damp Æolian harp. — GEORGE DU MAURIER.

Inborn.

Inborn, as fragrance in the heart of flowers. — OUIDA.

Incalculable.

Carlyle's course through the world of books is as incalculable as a bee's in a clover-field. — ARCHIBALD MACMECHAN.

Incapable.

Incapable as quicksilver of lying still. — FIELDING.

Incarnate.

Incarnate, as all summer in flower. — SWINBURNE.

Incessant.

Incessant streams supplies
Like the red star that fires th' autumnal skies. — HOMER (POPE).

Incessant . . . as the sound of the sea. — MARY JOHNSTON.

Like a broker's mouth, he speaks incessantly. — OSMANLI PROVERB.

Incessant as the squeaking cry of a monkey. — IVAN TURGENEV.

Incomes.

Our incomes, like our shoes, if too small, will gall and pinch us, but if too large, will cause us to stumble and to trip. — C. C. COLTON.

Incomprehensible.

Incomprehensible as a man starting a long journey without a good book. — LAMARTINE.

Incongruous.

As incongruous as a blacksmith with a white silk apron. — ANON.

Incongruous as a joke on a gravestone or a ledger. — IBID.

Incongruous as Matthew Arnold jumping rope. — IBID.

Incongruous as a merry dirge, or sacramental bacchanal. — P. J. BAILEY.

Incongruous as a wedding-dress at a funeral. — J. M. BARRIE.

Inconsistent.

Inconsistent as the seas or as the wind. — FIELDING.

Inconsistent as the sharpest antithesis. — RUFUS W. GRISWOLD.

Inconstant.

Inconstant as the wind. — ANON.

Inconstant as the shadows we survey. — SAMUEL BOYSE.

Inconstant as the moon. — SAMUEL BUTLER.

Inconstant . . . like the veriest flower
'neath whose dream folds fair
Some poisonous germ lies brooding.
— MICHAEL DELEVANTE.

Inconstant as a ship with a broken helm. — EGYPTIAN.

More inconstant than the wind. — SHAKESPEARE.

Inconstant as waves. — SMOLLETT.

Inconstant as the waving sea. — EARL OF STIRLING.

Incorruptible.

Incorruptible, unending, free,
Like the moon's golden road upon the sea. — F. W. H. MYERS.

Increase.

Increase like wind and oil on a fatal fire. — ANON.

Increased, like a spreading sore. — ANDREW LANG.

Increased as fast as the calendar of saints. — THOMAS PAINE.

Increased my fury, as the beating of a drum stimulates the soldier in courage. — POE.

Increased as the chant of the dawn that the choir of the noon outsings. — SWINBURNE.

Incredible.

Incredible as the fulfilment of an amazing and startling dream in which he could take the world in his arms — all the suffering world. — JOSEPH CONRAD.

Indecorum.

A great indecorum, to use men like old shoes or broken glasses, which are flung to the dunghill. — ROBERT BURTON.

Indefinite.

Indefinite, like the quality of the best manners. — S. WEIR MITCHELL.

Indelible.

Indelible as Domesday Book. — EMERSON.

Indented.

Indented like a saw. — ROBERT BURTON.

Independent.

Independent as a bird. — ANON.

Independence, like honor, is a rocky island without a beach. — NAPOLEON.

Independent as if he had paid twopence for a park chair. — HARRY LEON WILSON.

Indestructible.

Indestructible as are the stars. — SCHILLER.

Indifferent.

Indifferent as my right hand and my left. — ANON.

Indifferent as rain. — G. K. CHESTERTON.

Indifferent as the moon. — CHARLES READE.

Indifferently.

Indifferently as the herring's backbone doth lie in the midst of the fish. — ANON.

As indifferently as a boy plucks down a cranberry bough. — OUIDA.

Indigestible.

Indigestible as cold plum pudding. — BETTINA VON HUTTEN.

Indispensable.

Indispensable as your skin. — ANON.

Indispensable as clean linen. — EMERSON.

Indispensable
As the majestic laws
That rule yon rolling orbs.
— SHELLEY.

Indistinct.

Indistinct, like a vapor exhaled by the earth. — JOSEPH CONRAD.

Indistinct, like language uttered in a dream. — COWPER.

Indistinct like the echo of a symphony dying away. — FLAUBERT.

Indistinct as the premonition of calamity. — HAWTHORNE.

Indistinct as water is in water.
— SHAKESPEARE.

Indistinct as a camel's track between Mourzouk and Darfour. — HENRY D. THOREAU.

Indistinctly visible as through a white gauze veil. — MRS. TROLLOPE.

Indistinguishable.

Indistinguishable . . . like a celebrity in a crowd. — J. M. BARRIE.

Individuals.

Individuals, like nations, must have suitable broad and natural boundaries, even a considerable neutral ground, between them. — HENRY D. THOREAU.

Indolent.

Indolent as an old bachelor. — GOETHE.

Indolent, like the face of a happy lotus-eater. — ROBERT HICHENS.

Indolent as a lazy breeze of midsummer. — JAMES WHITCOMB RILEY.

Indolent as a warm rain. — TRUMBULL STICKNEY.

Industrious.

Industrious as an ant. — HENRYK SIENKIEWICZ.

Ineffective.

Ineffective as a safety razor at a negro ball. — ANON.

Ineffectual.

Ineffectual as plaint from a tomb. — ANON.

Ineffectual, like geese babbling at a vulture. — IBID.

Inefficient.

Inefficient as Nester Roqueplan's diatribe against the sun. — ANON.

Ineradicable.

Ineradicable as sin. — HAWTHORNE.

Ineradicable, like some persistent vegetable growth, because its seed is an element of the very soil out of which it springs. — WALTER PATER.

Inert.

Inert as stone. — ANON.

Inert as a dead body. — HUGO.

Inevitable.

Inevitable as death. — ANON.

Inevitable as the unfolding of the lily bud to the sun. — IBID.

Inevitable as the brute mother shields her young from attacks of the hereditary enemy. — GEORGE ELIOT.

Influences . . . inevitable as those musical vibrations which take possession of us with a rhythmic empire that no sooner ceases than we desire it to begin again. — IBID.

Inexcusable.

Inexcusable as Peter's denial of our Lord. — JOHN A. BINGHAM.

Inexhaustible.

Inexhaustible as the Hoard of King Nibelung, which twelve wagons in twelve days, at the rate of three journeys a day, could not carry off. — CARLYLE.

Inexhaustible as the deep sea. — OUIDA.

Inexorable.

Inexorable as that of Destiny and Doom. — CARLYLE.

Inexorable as the grave. — DE QUINCEY.

Inexorably.

A premonition embraces inexorably, like the closing of a folding umbrella. — ANON.

Infamous.

Infamous as Hell. — EARL OF ROCHESTER.

Infatuating.

Infatuating as a houri. — ANON.

Infectious.

More infectious than the poison of the spider. — ANON.

Inference.

Inferences are like shadows on the wall — they are thrown from an object, and are monstrous distortions of it. — GEORGE MEREDITH.

Infidelity.

Infidelity, like death, admits of no degrees. — MADAME DE GIRARDIN.

Infinite.

Infinite as the dividing of the foam and the sifting of the sea-sand. — ANON.

Infinite as the soul. — ARTHUR SYMONS.

Inflamed.

Inflamed as spirits damned in hell may feel. — BOIARDO.

Gloriously inflamed . . . like an aerial mist across the sky. — F. W. FABER.

Inflamed like the crimson rose. — PERSIAN.

Inflexible.

Inflexible as a granite block. — ANON.

Inflexible as an oak. — GOLDSMITH.

Influence.

Of as little influence as the letter "p" in pneumonia. — ANON.

Infrequent.

Infrequent as a porterhouse steak in a ten-dollar-a-week boarding-house. — SIMEON FORD.

Inherent.

Inherent as the sheen of a bird's plumage, as the texture of a flower's petal. — JOHN BURROUGHS.

Inherent, like the laws of gravity. — FROUDE.

Injurious.

Injurious as the tainted breath of fame. — THOMAS YALDEN.

Ink.

A small drop of ink,
Falling like dew, upon a thought, produces that which makes thousands,
perhaps millions, think.
— BYRON.

Innocence.

Innocence is like an umbrella: when once we've lost it we must never hope to see it back again. — PUNCH.

Innocence is like a polished armor; it adorns and it defends. — SOUTH.

Innocent.

Innocent as a cloistered nun. — ANON.

Innocent as a dove. — IBID.

Innocent as a lamb. — IBID.

Innocent as flowers. — IBID.

Innocent as angels. — BALZAC.

Innocent as a new-born babe. — IBID.

Innocent as 2 merino lambs. — JOSH BILLINGS.

Innocent as an infant. — R. D. BLACKMORE.

Innocent as a babe. — ROBERT BROWNING.

As innocent as a new-laid egg. — WILLIAM S. GILBERT.

Innocent as a child. — GOLDSMITH.

Innocent as the wayside fly. — CYRIL HARCOURT.

Innocent as sleep. — AARON HILL.

Innocent as an almanac. — JAMES HUNEKER.

Innocent
As youth before its charm is spent.
— G. E. MONTGOMERY.

As innocent as a devil of two years old. — ENGLISH PROVERB.

Innocent as grace itself. — SHAKESPEARE.

Innocent as milk. — SPENSER.

Innocent as the age of gold. — ROBERT LOUIS STEVENSON.

Innocent as a child unborn. — SAMUEL WESLEY.

Innumerable.

Innumerable as the gay motes that people the sunbeams. — ANON.

Innumerable as the stars of night. — MILTON.

Innumerable as maggots. — ROBERT LOUIS STEVENSON.

As the sand which is by the sea shore innumerable. — NEW TESTAMENT.

Inoffensive.

Inoffensive as the stone with which, at play, a boy makes ducks and drakes. — DUMAS, PÈRE.

Inoffensive as a glass of water. — HUGO.

Insatiate.

Insatiate as a Puritan. — "THE HONEST LAWYER," 1616.

Inscrutable.

Inscrutable as a sphinx. — ANON.

Inseparable.

Inseparable, as a shadow to a body. — ROBERT BURTON.

Inseparable as Athos, Porthos and Aramis. — FEDOR DOSTOEVSKY.

Inseparable as finger and thumb. — FARQUHAR.

Inseparable — *continued.*

Inseparable as peanuts and the Bowery. — KATE FIELD.

Inseparable as beauty and love. — MRS. JAMESON.

Wheresoe'er we went, like Juno's swans,
Still we went coupled, and inseparable.
— SHAKESPEARE.

Insidious.

Insidious as the odor of poppy leaves. — ANON.

Insinuating.

Insinuating as a corkscrew boring into a tender cork. — ANON.

Insinuating as ink. — IBID.

Insipid.

Insipid company as a looking-glass. — BEACONSFIELD.

Insipid as an old acquaintance. — COLLEY CIBBER.

Insipid things — like sandwiches of veal. — HOOD.

Insipid as a garden much watered. — HORACE.

Insipid, and dull as a drone,
Though near to each other
As sister and brother,
They both take their airing alone.
— ROBERT LLOYD.

Insistent.

Insistent as remorse. — HUGO.

Insoluble.

An enigma, dark and insoluble as that of the Sphinx. — DE QUINCEY.

Inspire.

Kindred thoughts inspire,
As summer clouds flash forth electric fire. — SAMUEL ROGERS.

Instant.

Instantly, like a bullet from the barrel. — ANON.

Emotion extinguished instantly, like a lighted match in a water-butt. — HERMANN SUDERMANN.

Instant as a thought. — N. P. WILLIS.

Instinctive.

Instinctive in her as its song to a bird, as its swiftness to a chamois. — OUIDA.

Intangible.

Intangible as a shadow. — BALZAC.

Intangible and indescribable as the tints of morning or evening. — HENRY D. THOREAU.

Intellect.

The intellect of the wise is like glass: it admits the light of heaven, and reflects it. — J. C. HARE.

The highest intellects, like the tops of mountains, are the first to catch and reflect the dawn. — MACAULAY.

Intense.

Intense as a trumpet sounding in the knights to tilt. — ROBERT BROWNING.

Intense as the cling of the sun to the lips of the earth. — RICHARD HOVEY.

Intense as life. — THEODORE WINTHROP.

Intercede.

Intercede like an angel of mercy. — DUMAS, PÈRE.

Interlocked.

Interlocked like a couple of preposterous gladiators. — DICKENS.

Interminable.

Interminable as a Lapland day. — ANON.

Intermingled.

Intermingled like the tares among the wheat. — BACON.

Intermittently.

Intermittently, like the click of a blind man's cane. — IRVIN S. COBB.

Intimate.

Intimate, fluctant, free, like the clasp and the cling of waters. — BLISS CARMAN.

Intolerable.

Intolerable as a fortunate fool. — SYDNEY MUNDEN.

Intoxicated.

Intoxicated as a colt that has been turned into a meadow. — GUY DE MAUPASSANT.

Intoxicating.

Intoxicating, like all joys that are soon lost. — JULES SANDEAU.

Wildly intoxicating as a mad gallop. — W. H. AINSWORTH.

Intricate.

Intricate as the hardest proposition in Euclid. — ANON.

Intricate as a thicket. — HUGO.

Intrigue.

Intrigues of state, like games of whist, require a partner, and in both, success is the joint effect of chance and skill ; but the former differ from the latter in one particular — the knaves rule the kings. — C. C. COLTON.

Intrude.

Intrude like comets on the heavenly solitude. — MATTHEW ARNOLD.

Invade.

Invades like the ocean. — ANON.

Invaluable.

Invaluable as the virtue of conformity in the army and navy. — HENRY D. THOREAU.

Invariable.

Invariable as the laws of gravitation. — ANON.

Invariable as the waxen image of a little old lady under a glass case. — GEORGE ELIOT.

Inventive.

Inventive as an excuse. — ANON.

Invigorating.

As invigorating as a bath of salt water when the skin is peeled off. — JAMES HUNEKER.

Inviolable.

Inviolable as recorded oaths. — ROBERT JEPHSON.

Invisible.

Invisible like the gods. — ANON.

Invisible as thought. — GEORGE ELIOT.

Invisible as air. — JUVENAL.

Invisible,
As a nose on a man's face, or a weathercock on a steeple.
— SHAKESPEARE.

Involuntarily.

Work involuntarily, like the heart. — SCHOPENHAUER.

Involved.

Involved like a cart involved in mud and muddle. — STEPHEN CRANE.

Inwoven.

Inwoven,
Like sunlight through acacia woods at even.
— SHELLEY.

Irksome.

It is irksome to them so to live, as to a bird in a cage, or a dog in a kennel. — ROBERT BURTON.

Irrecoverable.

As irrecoverable as a lump of butter in a greyhound's mouth. — ANON.

Irregular.

Irregular as a toper's walk. — RICHARD LE GALLIENNE.

Irreparable.

Irreparable as taking away life. — SIR RICHARD STEELE.

Irresistible.

Irresistible as the force of gravity. — ANON.

Irresistible, like a man with eight trumps in his hand at a whist table. — IBID.

Irresistible as when from some tall
peak into the plain
Thunder and smoke and crash the
rolling rocks.
— EDWIN ARNOLD.

Irresistible as the needle to the pole. — BULWER-LYTTON.

Irresolute.

Irresolute as Adriadne when she was urged to fly. — W. S. LANDOR.

Irrevocable.

Irrevocable as death. — CHARLOTTE BRONTË.

Irritating.

Irritating as a hundred needles forgotten in an armchair. — DAUDET.

Issue.

Issuing, as from a fountain. — ANON.

J

Jabber.

Jabbering like rooks. — ANON.

Jabbering . . . like two intriguing ducks. — RICHARD CUMBERLAND.

Jangled.

Like sweet bells jangled, out of tune, and harsh. — SHAKESPEARE.

Jar.

Jarred on the ear like a squeaking lead-pencil. — WILLIAM ARCHER.

Jarred horrid, like the rusted hinge upon a door of hell, like the shrill scream outbursting from a frightened charger's throat, like the rasp of a tang of brass against an iron gate. — HUGO.

Jars like a butting ram. — WILLIAM J. LAMPTON.

Jarring.

Jarring sound, like a cracked bell. — MICHAEL DRAYTON.

Jargon.

Jargoning like a foreigner at his food. — LONGFELLOW.

Jaunty.

Jaunty as the nimble flit of a cabaret dancer in midnight season form. — GRANTLAND RICE.

Jaw.

A jaw like a nutcracker. — ANON.

A jaw like a vise. — IBID.

An old lady with a jaw like a flat-iron. — MAURICE HEWLETT.

Jealous.

Jealous as a barren wife. — CONGREVE.

Jealous as a pet greyhound. — HUGO.

Jealous as a Spaniard. — IBID.

Jealous as a Spanish miser. — CHARLES MACKLIN.

As jealous as a nine-day's lover. — H. C. MERIVALE.

Jealous as a Barbary cock pigeon over his hen. — SHAKESPEARE.

Jealous as a cat. — TORRIANO'S "ITALIAN PROVERBS."

Jealous as a couple of hairdressers. — R. C. TRENCH.

Jealous as a Venetian. — VOLTAIRE.

Jealousy.

Jealousy is like
A polished glass held to the lips when life's in doubt;
If there be breath, 'twill catch the damp, and show it.
— DRYDEN.

Jerk.

Jerky as a ride on a buckboard. — ANON.

Jerking . . . like the lid of a boiling pot. — BLISS CARMAN.

Jerked his head like a bird. — DICKENS.

Jerky as a cinematograph. — J. K. JEROME.

Jerky like a clockwork snake. — H. G. WELLS.

Jest.

Good jests bite like lambs, not like dogs. — ANON.

Jests, like sweetmeats, have often a sour sauce. — IBID.

Jingle.

Jingle . . . like rattling handcuffs. — IRVIN S. COBB.

Jingled like a carriage horse. — KIPLING.

Jingle like a crate of broken crockery. — W. J. LOCKE.

Jocund.

Jocund as June. — WALTER MALONE.

Joined.

Joyned as burre to burre. — ALEXANDER BARCLAY.

Joined like a five-fold twisted cord. — JOHN DAVIES.

Joints.

Like a fishing rod, all joints. — ANON.

Joker.

Practical jokers, like physicians, seldom take their prescriptions with pleasure. — JOSEPH JEFFERSON.

Jolly.

Jolly as a shoe-brush. — EDWIN BOOTH.

Jolly as a country host. — ANDREW MARVELL.

Jolly as a sandboy. — NORTHALL'S "FOLK PHRASES."

As jolly as a play. — JAMES WHITCOMB RILEY.

Jolt.

Jolted like a solitary penny in an iron bank. — ANON.

Jostle.

Jostled like a crowd of people rushing to catch a train. — ANON.

Came jostling together like heads and sticks on the last day of Donnybrook. — W. BAYLE BERNARD.

Joy (Noun).

Joy is like a fitful gleam,
Discerned through shadowy mists of dream. — GRANT ALLEN.

For joys that are gone, when remembered again,
Like flowers bereft of their sweets by the frost,
Are poor withered things that do but retain
The thorns of the rose, when its fragrance is lost.
— E. F. ANDREWS.

Joy like the joy of a leaf that unfolds in the sun;
Joy like the joy of a child in the borders of sleep. — RICHARD HOVEY.

For joys are like sunbeams, — more fleeting than they,
And sorrows cast shadows between;
And friends that in moments of brightness are won,
Like gossamer, only are seen — in the sun. — LOVER.

Joy — *continued.*

Joy is like restless day; but peace divine
Like quiet night;
Lead me, O Lord, — till perfect Day shall shine
Through Peace to Light.
— ADELAIDE ANNE PROCTER.

Joy is like the ague; one good day between two bad ones. — DANISH PROVERB.

Joy in this world is like a rainbow, which in the morning only appears in the west, or towards the evening sky; but in the latter hours of day casts its triumphal arch over the east, or morning sky. — RICHTER.

As bitter wormwood never doth delicious honey yield,
Nor can the cheerful grape be reap'd from thistles in the field;
So who, in this uncertain life, deceitful joys pursue,
They fruits do seek upon such trees on which it never grew.
— FLORENCE WILSON.

Joy (Verb).

Joy'd as the spring, when March his sighs has spent,
And April's sweet rash tears are decoy'd by May. — DAVENANT.

Joyful.

Joyful as flowers when they are filled to the brim with dew. — ANON.

Joyful as a nest. — IBID.

Joyful as a fly. — ARABIAN NIGHTS.

Joyful as the back of a gravestone. — NORTHALL'S "FOLK PHRASES."

Joyfully as the shepherd bears a strayed lamb to the fold. — CHARLES READE.

Joyful as the light. — C. G. ROSSETTI.

Joyful as the sea. — SWINBURNE.

Joyless.

Joyless as the winter days which bound the earth under bands of iron and let no living thing or creeping herb rejoice or procreate. — OUIDA.

Joyless as the blind. — WORDSWORTH.

Joyous.

Joyous as a child. — ANON.

Joyous as the trill of a skylark. — IBID.

Joyous as the song of the wren. — J. FENIMORE COOPER.

Joyous, like a rising star. — JOHN HAY.

Joyous as a bobolink. — KEATS.

Joyous as the morning ray. — SHELLEY.

Joyous as the cadence of the sea. — BAYARD TAYLOR.

Joyous as the laughter of a child. — CELIA THAXTER.

Jubilant.

Jubilant as old sleigh bells. — JAMES WHITCOMB RILEY.

Jubilant as earth. — SWINBURNE.

Judgment.

The judgment of the wise is, like gold, distinguished for its superior weight. — DEMOPHILUS.

'Tis with our judgments as our watches, — none
Go just alike, yet each believes his own.
— POPE.

Jump.

Jumping about like a toad in a thunderstorm. — ANON.

Jumped at it like a trout at a May-fly. — IBID.

Jumped like a bird for a berry. — IBID.

Jump like Harlequin. — EMERSON.

Jump — *continued.*

Jumps, like a sole from the pan. — Hood.

Jumpy as a cat. — Kipling.

Justice.

Justice is like the north star, which is fixed, and all the rest revolve about it. — Confucius.

Justice is like the Kingdom of God: It is not without us as a fact; it is within us as a great yearning. — George Eliot.

As honor, just. — David Mallet.

Human justice, like Luther's drunken peasant, when saved from falling on one side, topples over on the other. — Mazzini.

Justice, like lightning, ever should appear;
To few men ruin, but to all men fear.
— Thomas Randolph.

K

Keen.

Wit as keen as archer's dart. — A. A. Adee.

Keen as a bride. — Anon.

Keen as the sight of an eagle. — Ibid.

Keen as the sun. — Ibid.

Keen, like the horn of the cuspèd moon. — Arabian Nights.

As keen for profit as a Polish Jew. — Balzac.

Keen as the torture of impending bankruptcy. — Ibid.

As keen as a miser after his pay. — Jules Q. de Beaurepaire.

Keen as Jove's lightning wing'd athwart the sky. — William Broome.

As keen as anguish. — James Cawthorn.

Keen as a poniard-thrust. — Eliza Cook.

Keen as arrows. — Flaubert.

Keen as a razor. — John Gay.

Keen as a hawk. — Hood.

Keen as a sword. — Kipling.

Keen like a spear. — Sidney Lanier.

Keen as a wolf. — James Montgomery.

Keen of glance as a falcon. — Ouida.

Keen as steel. — Ibid.

Keen as a blinded man . . .
Smells in the dark the cold odour of the earth. — Stephen Phillips.

Keen as undrawn sword. — Frank Richardson.

Keen as is razor's edge invisible. — Shakespeare.

Keen as the engine
Which tortures and which kills.
— Shelley

Keen as a sword's edge. — Swinburne.

Keen as burns the passion of the rose. — Ibid.

Keen as death to smite. — Ibid.

Keen as flame. — Ibid.

Keen as hate. — Ibid.

Keen as iron in the flesh. — Ibid.

Keen as lightning's life. — Ibid.

Eyes as keen as pain. — Ibid.

Keen as sleep and strife. — Ibid.

Keen as the fire's own fang. — Ibid.

Keen — *continued.*

Keen as the heart of Mars. — SWINBURNE.

Keen as hunger. — IBID.

Keen as the heart's desire. — IBID.

Keen as the manslayer's knife. — IBID.

Keen as the sea's thrill towards a kindling star. — IBID.

Keen as desertion. — SIR HENRY TAYLOR.

Keen as a sabre from its sheath. — WHITTIER.

Keen and eager as a fine-nosed hound. — WORDSWORTH.

His face was keen as is the wind
That cuts along the hawthorn fence.
— IBID.

Kill.

Kills the illusion as surely as would the introduction of a Queen Anne cottage in the scenery of a Roman play. — ARTHUR ACHESON.

Kill like lightning flashes. — ANON.

Kill one another by the look, like cockatrices. — SHAKESPEARE.

Killing.

Killing as a plague. — MASSINGER.

Looks . . . as killing as the basilisk's. — IBID.

As killing as the canker to the rose. — MILTON.

Kind.

Kind as a kite. — ANON.

Kind as a turtle. — ANON.

As kind as the month of maying. — H. C. BEECHING.

Kind as cream. — BULWER-LYTTON.

Kind as a glove. — CARR'S "DIALECT OF CRAVEN."

As kynde as any wyf from Denmark unto Ynde. — CHAUCER.

Kind as is the life of love. — "JACKE DRUM'S ENTERTAINMENT," 1601.

Kind as kings upon their coronation day. — DRYDEN.

Kind as Cleopatra. — GEORGE GASCOIGNE.

She's as kind as new faln April showers. — RICHARD LOVELACE.

Kinde as Alceste. — JOHN LYDGATE.

Kind as consent. — SYDNEY MUNDEN.

Kind as hovering dove. — C. G. ROSSETTI.

Like the sunlight kind. — SWINBURNE.

Kind as harvest in autumn. — IBID.

Kind as the fostering air. — IBID.

Kind as the sun in heaven. — IBID.

She meeker, kinder than the turtle-dove or pelican. — GEORGE WITHER.

Kindly.

Kindly as night dew. — P. J. BAILEY.

Kindly as the spirit of society. — WORDSWORTH.

Kindle.

Kindling like a Christmas feaster
When some wild chorus shakes the
vinous air. — O. W. HOLMES.

Kindled like as heaven in June. — SWINBURNE.

Heart kindling as the heart of heaven. — IBID.

Kindling, as dawn a frost-bound precipice. — IBID.

Kindling as a rose at breath of sunrise. — IBID.

Kindles and burns,
Like a fiery star in the upper air.
— WHITTIER.

Kindness.

Little acts of kindness are stowed away in the heart, like bags of lavender in a drawer, to sweeten every object around them. — ANON.

Kindness — *continued.*

To do a kindness to a bad man is like sowing your seed in the sea. — PHOCYLIDES.

Kindness, like grain, increases by sowing. — ENGLISH PROVERB.

King.

Kings are like stars, — they rise and set, they have
The worship of the world, but no repose. — SHELLEY.

Kingly.

Kingly as Charlemagne on his throne in the West. — AGNES REPPLIER.

Kiss.

Her kisses were like tire explosions. — ANON.

Kissing . . . is as a prologue to a play. — FIELDING.

The kisses of thy deathless lips,
Like strange star-pulses, throbbed through space. — PAUL HAMILTON HAYNE.

Kiss as close as a scallop. — BEN JONSON.

Came kissing like rich airs from secret shores
To those who sail into the eternal dawn. — GERALD MASSEY.

Kisses as unctuous as oil. — FRANCIS S. SALTUS.

Kisses like sweet, sad, subtle scents of myrrh. — IBID.

Kisses are like grains of gold or silver found upon the ground, of no value themselves, but precious as showing that a mine is near. — GEORGE VILLIERS.

Kneel.

Knelt like a child marble-sculptured and white
That seems kneeling to pray on the tomb of a knight.
— E. B. BROWNING.

Kneeling . . . like a painted lady on an altar tomb. — MAURICE HEWLETT.

Knotted.

Knotted like water-snakes. — SHELLEY.

Know.

I know him as well as if I had gone through him with a lantern. — ANON.

I know him like a book. — IBID.

Knowing it as the moon her traditional influence upon the tides. — GEORGE MEREDITH.

To know as well as a beggar knows his dish. — JAMES PILKINGTON.

Knowing.

Knowing as the stars. — CONGREVE.

Knowledge.

He picked up knowledge to wear it on his head like the plumes of horses in a parade. — ANON.

The distributions and partitions of knowledge are . . . like the branches of a tree, that meet in a stem, which hath a dimension and quantity of entireness and continuance, before it come to discontinue and break itself into arms and boughs. — BACON.

Knowledge is like money, — the more a man gets, the more he craves. — JOSH BILLINGS.

Knowledge is like capital : the more there is in a country, the greater the disparities in wealth between one man and another. — BULWER-LYTTON.

Knowledge . . . like a great rough diamond ; it may do very well in a closet by way of curiosity, and also for its intrinsic value ; but it will never be worn or shine, if it is not polished. — CHESTERFIELD.

Knowledge, like our blood, must circulate. — DENHAM.

Knowledge — *continued.*

A little knowledge in some people is like little boys throwing stones into mysterious lakes. They make a great clatter but the silence was more wonderful. — RICHARD LE GALLIENNE.

Knowledge of books is like that sort of lantern which hides him who carries it, and serves only to pass through secret and gloomy paths of its own; but in the possession of a man of business, it is as a torch in the hand of one who is willing and able to show those who are bewildered, the way which leads to their prosperity and welfare. — SIR RICHARD STEELE.

L

Labor.

Laboring like galley slaves. — ANON.

Labour like a thresher. — BEAUMONT AND FLETCHER.

Labored heavily like a tramp freighter in a heavy sea. — E. D. PRICE.

Labours like the drops of rain on the sandy ground. — SIR WALTER RALEIGH.

Labyrinth.

Labyrinth you there, like a hid scent in an unbudded rose. — KEATS.

Laced.

Laced,
Like an hour-glass, exceedingly small
in the waist.
— THOMAS MOORE.

Lady.

Ladies, like barristers, must wait to be chosen. — ANON.

A fine lady is a squirrel-headed thing, with small airs and small notions; about as applicable to the business of life as a pair of tweezers to the clearing of a forest. — GEORGE ELIOT.

Ladies, like variegated tulips, show
'T is to their changes half their charms
we owe. — POPE.

Great ladies, like great merchants, set but the higher prizes upon what they have, because they are not in necessity of taking the first offer. — WYCHERLEY.

Lag.

Lagged behind,
Like boat against the tide and wind.
— SAMUEL BUTLER.

Lament.

Lament like a virgin girded with sackcloth for the husband of her youth. — OLD TESTAMENT.

Lamentation.

A lamentation.
Like some old prophet wailing.
— LONGFELLOW.

Lamentation is the only musician that always, like a screech-owl, alights and sits on the roof of an angry man. — PLUTARCH.

Language.

Languages, like our bodies, are in a perpetual flux, and stand in the need of recruits to supply those words that are continually falling, through disuse. — FELTON.

Written language is like a mirror which it is necessary to have in order that man know himself and be sure that he exists. — LAMARTINE.

Language rises like a spring among the mountains; it increases into a rivulet; then it becomes a river (the water is still unpolluted), but when

Language — *continued.*

the river has passed through a town the water must be filtered. And Milton was mentioned as the first filter, the first stylist. — GEORGE MOORE.

Language is like amber in its efficacy to circulate the electric spirit of truth; it is also like amber in embalming and preserving the relics of ancient wisdom, although one is not seldom puzzled to decipher its contents. — G. A. SALA.

Languid.

Languid as one from slumber newly come. — LORD DE TABLEY.

As languid as a lilied pond. — NORMAN GALE.

A mind languid as a drooping wing. — JAYADEVA.

Languid, like a lovesick maid. — SWIFT.

Languidly.

Languidly, as voluptuously, as a water-lily at rest on the water's breast. — OUIDA.

Languidly as a lost desire
Upon a sumach's fading fire.
— ELIZABETH S. P. WARD.

Languish.

Languish like a withering flower. — OTWAY.

Languisheth
As lily drooping to death,
As a drought-worn bird with failing breath,
As a lovely vine without a stay,
As a tree whereof the owner saith,
"Hew it down to-day."
— C. G. ROSSETTI.

Even as poor birds, deceived with painted grapes,
Do surfeit by the eye and pine the maw,
Even so she languisheth in her mishaps,
As those poor birds that helpless berries saw. — SHAKESPEARE.

Languish as the leafe faln from the tree. — SPENSER.

Lank.

Lank as an unthrift's purse. — DONNE.

Lank as a greyhound. — SMOLLETT.

Lank as a ghost. — WORDSWORTH.

Lap.

Lapped her like a vapor. — HOOD.

Lapse.

Days, weeks and months lapsed like soft measures, rhyming each with each. — J. G. HOLLAND.

Large.

Large as life and twice as natural. — NORTHALL'S "FOLK PHRASES."

Lash.

Lashing her face like the wing of a raven driven by the storm. — LAMARTINE.

Last.

Lasts about as long as a keg of cider at a barn raising. — ALFRED HENRY LEWIS.

Didn't last him as long as a ten-dollar bill would a Democrat the night before election. — "BRICK" POMEROY.

Lasting.

Lasting as the pyramids. — AGNES REPPLIER.

As lasting . . . as the vestal fire. — CHRISTOPHER SMART.

Lasting, as the lilac crocus of autumn. — TUPPER.

Late.

Comes too late;
'Tis like a pardon after execution.
— SHAKESPEARE.

Laugh (Noun).

Her laugh is like rare wine. — ROBERT BRIDGES (American).

Laugh — *continued*

Her laff is like a singin' brook that bubbles as it passes. — SAM WALTER FOSS.

Gave a short laugh like the closing of a padlock. — O. HENRY.

A laugh like a suffocating wheeze. — LEVER.

Her laugh is like a roundelay — so ringing sweet and clear. — JAMES WHITCOMB RILEY.

Her laugh is like sunshine. — FRANCIS S. SALTUS.

Laugh (Verb).

Laugh like a loon. — ANON.

Laughing like a stentor. — IBID.

Laughed like a bell. — R. D. BLACKMORE.

Laughed as if he had drowned a dog. — E. B. BROWNING.

Laugh on one side, like the masks of the ancients. — DUMAS, PÈRE.

To laugh like Robin Goodfellow — a long, loud, hearty horse laugh. — ROBERT FORBY'S "VOCABULARY OF EAST ANGLIA."

Laughed like the sun. — RICHARD LE GALLIENNE.

Laughed as incessantly as a bird sings. — GUY DE MAUPASSANT.

Laughed like a bowlful of jelly. — CLEMENT C. MOORE.

Laugh like a swarm of flies. — RABELAIS.

He laughed like the screech of a rusty hinge. — JAMES WHITCOMB RILEY.

Laugh, like parrots, at a bag-piper. — SHAKESPEARE.

Laughed, like a happy fountain in a cave brightening the gloomy rocks. — ALEXANDER SMITH.

Laughs like beech-leaves ringing in the light. — TRUMBULL STICKNEY.

Laughter.

Laughter rich as woodland thunder. — EMERSON.

Laughter and tears are meant to turn the same machinery of sensibility; one is wind-power, and the other water-power: that is all. — O. W. HOLMES.

Laughter like a chime of bells. — CHARLES READE.

Soft laughter as of light that stirs the sea
With darkling sense of dawn ere dawn may be. — SWINBURNE.

Laughter soft as tears. — IBID.

For as the crackling of thorns under a pot, so is the laughter of the fool. — OLD TESTAMENT.

Sweet laughter in mirthfulness artlessly flowing
Like zephyrs at play through a fairy flute blowing.
— R. D. WILLIAMS.

Lavish.

Lavish as the moon. — NORA HOPPER.

Lavish, as all the dew were turn'd to gems. — GERALD MASSEY.

Law.

Laws are like cobwebs; the small flies are caught, the great break through. — ANACHARSIS.

So he that goes to law, as the proverb is, holds a wolf by the ears, or, as a sheep in a storm runs for shelter to a briar, if he prosecute his cause he is consumed, if he surcease his suit he loseth all; what difference? — ROBERT BURTON.

The knowledge of the law is like a deep well, out of which each man draweth according to the strength of his understanding. — COKE.

Law — *continued.*

Strict laws are like a steel bodice, good for growing limbs; but when the joints are knit, they are not helps but burdens. — SIR F. FANE.

Solon used to say that speech was the image of actions; . . . that laws were like cobwebs, — for that if any trifling or powerless thing fell into them, they held it fast; while if it were something weightier, it broke through them and was off. — DIOGENES LAERTIUS.

Law is like a sieve; it is very easy to see through it, but a man must be considerably reduced before he can get through it. — S. G. MORTON.

The law is like the axle of a carriage — you can turn it wherever you please. — RUSSIAN PROVERB.

Laws are not made like lime-twigs or nets, to catch everything that toucheth them, but rather like sea-marks, to avoid the shipwreck of ignorant passengers. — SIR PHILIP SIDNEY.

Lawful.

Lawful as eating. — SHAKESPEARE.

Lawless.

Lawless as a town bull. — ANON.

Lawless as the sea or wind. — WALLER.

Lawless, like the stormy wind. — WILLIAM WILKIE.

Lawsuit.

A lawsuit is like an ill-managed dispute, in which the first object is soon out of sight, and the parties end upon a matter wholly foreign to that on which they began. — EDMUND BURKE.

Lax.

Lax like cut string. — H. G. WELLS.

Lay.

Lay like a bank of stage snow. — O. HENRY.

Lay, like a smile upon the lips of sleep. — RUSKIN.

Lay, like winds that die in water. — SHELLEY.

In silver slumber lay,
Like the evening starre adorn'd with dewy ray. — SPENSER.

But he lay like a warrior taking his rest,
With his martial cloak around him. — CHARLES WOLFE.

Laziness.

Laziness is a good deal like money — the more a man has of it, the more he seems to want. — JOSH BILLINGS.

Lazy.

Lazy as a toad at the bottom of a well. — ANON.

Lazy as Joe the Marine, who laid down his musket to sneeze. — IBID.

Lazy as a lobster. — BALZAC.

Lazy as Ludham's dog that leaned his head against the wall to bark. — THOMAS FULLER.

Lazy as a ship in the doldrums. — WILLIAM D. O'CONNOR.

Lead.

Leads the passions, like the orb that guides,
From pole to pole, the palpitating tides. — O. W. HOLMES.

Leads them like a thing
Made by some other deity than nature. — SHAKESPEARE.

Lead thee, as a staff directs the blind. — SWIFT.

Lead as a mother. — SWINBURNE.

Led lovingly like hound in huntsman's leash
Or child by finger. — IBID.

Leak.

Leaks like a sieve. — ANON.

Leaking like a lobster-pot. — KIPLING.

Lean (Adjective).

Lean as a dog in Lent. — ANON.

Lean as Sancho's ass. — IBID.

Leene was his hors as is a rake. — CHAUCER.

Lean as a lath. — THOMAS HEYWOOD.

Lean as a backgammon board. — W. S. LANDOR.

Lean as a lantern. — LANGLAND.

Lean like bull-beef. — RICHARD MATHER.

Lean as a skeleton. — THOMAS SHADWELL.

Leaner than fleshless misery. — SHELLEY.

As lean as a lizard. — JAMES SMITH.

Lean as death. — TENNYSON.

Lean (Verb).

They leaned towards each other like young saplings weakened at the root. — GRACE MACGOWAN COOKE.

Leap.

Leap like a cock at a blackberry. — ANON.

Leaps, like happy hearts by holiday made light. — BERNARD BARTON.

Leaped in the air like a shot rabbit. — R. D. BLACKMORE.

Leaps like a young horse
Who bites against the new bit in his teeth,
And tugs and struggles against the new-tried rein. — E. B. BROWNING.

Leap such leap
As lands the feet in Heaven.
— ROBERT BROWNING.

Leapt like a tongue of fire that cleaves the smoke. — IBID.

Leaps like a bared sword. — KIPLING.

Leap like trout in May. — IBID.

Leaped as if stung by an electric shock. — GEORGE B. MCCUTCHEON.

Leapt like a leaping sword. — JOAQUIN MILLER.

Leap away lyke froges. — JOHN SKELTON.

Leaped like a roebuck from the plain. — H. AND J. SMITH.

Leaping like wanton kids in pleasant spring. — SPENSER.

He leaped like a man shot. — ROBERT LOUIS STEVENSON.

Leap, like moody madness to the changing moon. — JOHN STRUTHERS.

Leaps clear as a flame from the pyres of the dead. — SWINBURNE.

Leaps like fire. — IBID.

Leap up
As red wine mantling in a royal cup.
— IBID.

Leaps up as the foe's heart leaps. — IBID.

Leapt like a passing thought. — TENNYSON.

Leap, like the noise of a flame of fire that devoureth the stubble, as a strong people set in battle array. — OLD TESTAMENT.

Leapt as lightly as weanling fawns that leap around the doe. — THEOCRITUS.

Leap like a caressing angel. — N. P. WILLIS.

Learning.

Learning is like a lark, that can mount, and sing, and please herself, and nothing else; but may know that she holdeth as well as the hawk, that can soar aloft, and can also descend and strike upon the prey. — BACON.

Wear your learning like your watch, in a private pocket, and do not pull it out and strike it merely to show that you have one. — CHESTERFIELD.

Learning is like mercury, one of the most powerful and excellent things in the world in skillful hands; in unskillful, the most mischievous. — POPE.

Learning — *continued.*

Learning, like money, may be of so base a coin as to be utterly void of use. — SHENSTONE.

Learning, like the lunar beam, affords light. — YOUNG.

Leave.

Leaves . . . as silent lightning leaves the starless night. — SHELLEY.

Lecherous.

Lecherous as a he-goat. — ANON.

As lecherous as a she-ferret. — BEAUMONT AND FLETCHER.

Lecherous as a monkey. — SHAKESPEARE.

Lecture.

A new lecture is like any new tool. We use it for a while with pleasure. Then it blisters our hands and we hate to touch it. By-and-by our hands get callous, and then we no longer have any sensitiveness about it. But if we give it up the callouses disappear; and if we meddle with it again, we miss the novelty and get the blisters. — O. W. HOLMES.

Leer.

Leers like Æsop's fox upon a crane whose neck he craves for his chirurgian. — JOSEPH HALL.

Leers at me with eyes askance like a seducer. — NIETZSCHE.

Leered at her like a satyr. — THACKERAY.

Legendary.

Legendary as the Flying Dutchman. — ANON.

Leisure.

At leisure, as a laird dies. — ANON.

At leisure, as flax groweth. — WILLIAM CAMDEN'S "REMAINS."

Lenient.

Lenient as soft opiates to the mind. — COWPER.

Leprous.

He was leprous as snow. — OLD TESTAMENT.

Level.

Level as a pond. — ANON.

Level as a sea. — LORD DE TABLEY.

Level as the cannon to his blank. — SHAKESPEARE.

Lewd.

Lewd as drunkards that fall out. — SAMUEL BUTLER.

Liar.

Liars act like the salt miners, they undermine the truth, but leave just so much standing as is necessary to support the edifice. — RICHTER.

Liberal.

A hand as lib'ral as the light of day. — COWPER.

Liberal as the air. — SHAKESPEARE.

Libertine.

Libertines are like hideous spiders, that often catch pretty butterflies. — DIDEROT.

Liberty.

Liberty has its roots in the hearts of the people, as the tree in the hearts of the earth; like the tree it raises and spreads its branches to heaven; like the tree it is ceaseless in its growth, and it covers generations with its shade. — HUGO.

Lie (Noun).

A great lie is like a great fish on dry land; it may fret and fling, and make a frightful bother, but it cannot hurt you; you have only to keep still and it will die of itself. — GEORGE CRABBE.

A lie is like a snow-ball; the longer it is rolled, the larger it is. — LUTHER.

A lie is like a vizard, that may cover the face, indeed, but can never become it. — ROBERT SOUTH.

Lie (Verb).

Lie as fast as dog can lick a plate. — ANON.

Lies like an auctioneer. — IBID.

Lies like a tooth-drawer. — IBID.

Lies like print. — IBID.

Lie like a charlatan. — BALZAC.

Lie like a political program. — IBID.

Lie like a gas meter. — HAROLD BRIGHOUSE.

Swere and lye as a womman kan. — CHAUCER.

He lies like a hedgehog rolled up the wrong way, tormenting himself with prickles. — HOOD.

Lies like a feller with a family horse t' sell. — ABE MARTIN.

Lies like a smile of sunshine among lilies. — GERALD MASSEY.

Lie like a book of anecdotes. — HANNAH MORE.

Lies like truth. — SHAKESPEARE.

Life.

Life is like a tale ended ere 'tis told. — T. B. ALDRICH.

In life, as in chess, one's own pawns block one's way. A man's very wealth, ease, leisure, children, books, which should help him to win, more often checkmate him. — CHARLES BUXTON.

Life, as a windmill, grinds the bread of Life. — LORD DE TABLEY.

This Life, which seems so fair, is like a bubble blown up in the air by sportive children's breath. — WILLIAM DRUMMOND.

Life is like a game of whist. I don't enjoy the game much; but I like to play my cards well, and see what will be the end of it. — GEORGE ELIOT.

Life is a train of moods like a string of beads, and as we pass through them, they prove to be many-colored lenses which paint the world their own hue, and each shows only what lies in its focus. — EMERSON.

Man's life is like unto a winter's day,
Some break their fast and so depart away,
Others stay dinner then depart full fed;
The longest age but sups and goes to bed.
Oh, reader, then behold and see,
As we are now so must you be.
— BISHOP HENSHAW.

Life is like yon fisher's boat
Gay she quits the friendly shore.
— W. H. LEATHAM.

Life is, after all, like baccarat or billiards. . . . It is no use winning unless there be a gallery to look on and applaud. — OUIDA.

Like a morning dream, life becomes more and more bright the longer we live, and the reason of everything appears more clear. — J. P. RICHTER.

Life, like the water of the seas, freshens only when it ascends upwards. — IBID.

After all, life is like soda-water. Childhood, effervescence corked down and wired; manhood, some sparkle, more vapidity; old age, empty bottle, cart it away with the rubbish. — T. W. ROBERTSON.

Life is like a beautiful and winding lane, on either side bright flowers, and beautiful butterflies, and tempting fruits, which we scarcely pause to admire and to taste, so eager are we to hasten to an opening which we imagine will be more beautiful still. By degrees as we advance, the trees grow bleak; the flowers and butterflies fail, the fruits disappear, and we find we have arrived — to reach a desert waste. — G. A. SALA.

Our life is like a journey on which, as we advance, the landscape takes a different view from that which it pre-

Life — *continued.*

sented at first, and changes again, as we come nearer. — SCHOPENHAUER.

A wise man is never disappointed. Man's life is like a game at tables; if at any time the cast you most shall need does not come up, let that which comes instead of it be mended by your play. — THOMAS SHADWELL.

Life, like a dome of many-colored glass,
Stains the white radiance of eternity.
— SHELLEY.

The vanity of human life is like a river, constantly passing away, and yet constantly coming on. — SWIFT.

Life is like wine; who would drink it pure, must not draw it to the dregs. — SIR WILLIAM TEMPLE.

When all is done, Human Life is, at the greatest and the best, but like a forward Child, that must be Play'd with and Humor'd a little to keep it quiet till it falls asleep, and then the Care is over. — IBID.

My life is like a stroll upon the beach,
As near the ocean's edge as I can go.
— HENRY D. THOREAU.

My life is like the summer rose
That opens in the morning sky,
But, ere the shades of evening close,
Is scattered on the ground — to die.
— R. H. WILDE.

Lifeless.

Lifeless as the grave. — ANON.

Lifeless as a string of dead fish. — G. K. CHESTERTON.

Lifeless and lumpish as the bagpipe's drowsy drone. — ROBERT LLOYD.

Lifeless as a mouse in an exhausted receiver. — WILLIAM MATHEWS.

Lifeless as the icy moon. — LEWIS MORRIS.

Lift.

Lifts the head like conscious innocence. — ANON.

Lifting my heart to her, as the spring wind lifts the clouds. — R. D. BLACKMORE.

Lifting his feet like a knife grinder. — DAUDET.

Her favour lifts him up, as the sun moisture. — SIR THOMAS OVERBURY.

Light (Adjective).

Light as the leaf that summer's breeze
Has wafted o'er the glassy seas.
—ANACREON.

Light as flake of foam. — HANS CHRISTIAN ANDERSEN.

Light and clean as the foaming surf that the wind severs from the broken wave. — ANON.

Light and speedy as a steam-roller. — IBID.

Light as a fly. — IBID.

Light as a sack of feathers. — IBID.

Light as down. — IBID.

Passed as light as October leaves blown over the forest floor. — IBID.

Light as the leaf of the aspen. — IBID.

Light as the bow with its gay blossoms springing. — IBID.

Light as the spider's silken lair. — IBID.

Light as thistledown. — IBID.

Light as vain praise. — IBID.

Light as whipped cream. — IBID.

Oaths as light as wind. — IBID.

Light enough to float in the sweat of an ice pitcher. — IBID.

Light-hearted as a robin. — IBID.

As light as leafe on tree. — OLD ENGLISH BALLAD.

Light as hope. — BAUDELAIRE.

Light as a wind-blown leaf. — CHARLOTTE BECKER.

Light — *continued.*

Light as cobwebs. — R. D. BLACKMORE.

Light-footed as a hare. — H. H. BOYESEN.

Light as the fabric which swells in the ambient air. — SAMUEL BOYSE.

Light as a feather whisk. — ROBERT BROWNING.

Light as the whispers of a dream. — WILLIAM CULLEN BRYANT.

Light as a faint wreath of snow
That tremblest to fall in the wind.
— ROBERT BUCHANAN.

Light as day. — BUNYAN.

Light as any lambie. — BURNS.

Light as a Nereid in her ocean sledge. — BYRON.

Light as dreams. — GIOSUÈ CARDUCCI.

Light as gossamer. — CARLYLE.

Light as winds that stir the willow. — ALICE CARY.

Light as leef on lynde. — CHAUCER.

Light as the busy clouds. — COLERIDGE.

Light as the sea-fowl rocking in the storm. — J. FENIMORE COOPER.

Light as froth. — JOHN DAVIES.

Light as a snowflake. — AUSTIN DOBSON.

Light as an empty dream at break of day. — DRYDEN.

Light as the vapours of a morning dream. — IBID.

Light as the light. — FARQUHAR.

Light as air. — FIELDING.

Light as the feather on the head of beaux. — JOHN GAY.

Light as vapor. — RICHARD HOVEY.

Light like a sunbeam shattered into mist. — IBID.

Light-hearted as a boy. — IBID.

Light as a rustling foot on last year's leaves. — JEAN INGELOW.

Light . . . as cork. — HENRY JAMES.

Light as love's angel. — MISS LANDON.

Light as fairy footsteps. — EVAN MACCOLL.

As light as a leaf unbound
From the grasp of its parent tree.
— ERNEST MCGAFFEY.

Light as the flying seed-ball. — GEORGE MEREDITH.

Light as a bubble that flies from the tub,
Whisked by the laundry-wife out of her suds. — IBID.

Steps . . . light as though a winged angel trod,
Over earth's flowers, and feared to brush away,
Their delicate hues.
— H. H. MILMAN.

Light as the angel shapes that bless
An infant's dream.
— THOMAS MOORE.

Light as the bridegrooms bound to their young loves. — IBID.

Light and feathery as squirrel-tails. — JOHN MUIR.

Light as the breeze that brushed the orient dew. — SAMUEL ROGERS.

Light as the tinkling leaves, that wander wide
When Vallombrosa mourns her pride.
— JOHN RUSKIN.

Light as a happy wave. — SCHILLER.

Light as the dancing skiff borne on the silvery tide. — IBID.

Light as the rainbow's leap into space. — IBID.

Light as a beam of Dian. — OWEN SEAMAN.

Light — *continued.*

Trifles light as air. — SHAKESPEARE.

Light as the mote that danceth in the beam. — H. AND J. SMITH.

Light as a feather. — SOPHOCLES.

Light as a lady's plumes.—SOUTHEY.

Light as a robe of peace. — IBID.

Light as a warrior's summer-garb in peace. — IBID.

Light as a laugh of glee. — SWINBURNE.

Heart is as light as a leaf on a tree. — IBID.

Light as a spring south-wind. —IBID.

Light as foam. — IBID.

Light as laugh of flame. — IBID.

Light as riotous insolence. — IBID.

A hand at the door taps light as the hand of my heart's delight. — IBID.

Light as the spray that disperses. — IBID.

Light as floating leaf of orchard snow, loosed by the pulse of Spring. — BAYARD TAYLOR.

Gallop . . . light as any antelope upon the hills of the Gavilòn. — IBID.

Light as the singing bird that wings the air. — TENNYSON.

Light as a dry leaf in the winter woods. — CELIA THAXTER.

A step as light as the summer air. — WHITTIER.

Light as a buoyant bark from wave to wave. — WORDSWORTH.

Light as a sunbeam glides along the hills. — IBID.

Light (Noun).

Tender light, like the first moonrise of midnight. — BYRON.

Lights as of dawn beyond the tomb. — HUGO.

Happy light, like those dream-smiles which are the speech of sleep. — GERALD MASSEY.

A redder light shone through the dell,
As if the very gates of hell
Swung suddenly ajar. — WHITTIER.

Lighter.

Lighter than vanity. — BUNYAN.

Lighter than any linnet's feather. — RICHARD REALF.

Lighter than air. — SAMUEL ROGERS.

Lighter than dandelion down. — PHILIP H. SAVAGE.

Lightly.

Lightly as the skimming of swallows. — ANON.

Lightly and softly,
As a queen's languid and imperial arm
Which scatters crowns among her lovers. — ROBERT BROWNING.

Set as lightly as a mouse-trap. — MAURICE HEWLETT.

Lightly as swimming shadows dusk the lake. — GERALD MASSEY.

Lightly as a kite rushes through the gloom of the dawn. — OUIDA.

Lightly as bird on wing. — SAMUEL WARD.

Like.

About as like as an apple to an oyster. — ANON.

As like as the two halves of an apple. — IBID.

As like as two pins. — IBID.

As like each other as a sword and scythe. — P. J. BAILEY.

As like him as flakes ov snow. — JOSH BILLINGS.

As like as hand to another hand — ROBERT BROWNING.

Like as twins. — IBID.

Like — *continued.*

Is na mare like . . . than the nyght oule resemblis the papingay. — GAWAIN DOUGLAS.

Like as chalk and coles. — JAMES HURDIS.

As lyke as one pease is to another. — LYLY.

As like him as an eagle to an eagle. — OUIDA.

Like a leaf on a withering limb,
The fluttering life still clung to him.
— T. BUCHANAN READ.

No more like than chalk and cheese. — SAMUEL ROWLAND.

No more like my father
Than I to Hercules.
— SHAKESPEARE.

Alike as my fingers is to my fingers. — IBID.

As like, as rain to water, or devil to his dam. — IBID.

Like as eggs. — IBID.

As like this as a crab is like an apple. — IBID.

As like you,
As cherry is to cherry.
— IBID.

Day like to day, face like to face, as waves in some calm sea. — WILLIAM WATSON.

Likely.

Likely as to see a pig fly. — ANON.

As lykely to obtain thy wish, as the Wolfe is to catch [eat] the Moone. — LYLY.

Limber.

Limber as a watch chain. — ANON.

Limber az a lover. — JOSH BILLINGS.

His back as limber as a canker worm's. — O. W. HOLMES.

Limber as a frog. — KIPLING.

Limber as eelskins. — MIDDLETON.

Limber as a washed paper collar. — STEPHEN SMITH.

Limp.

Limp as a rag. — ANON.

Limp as a glove. — IBID.

Limp like cut vine-twig. — ROBERT BROWNING.

Limp as bags of oats. — ELBERT HUBBARD.

Limp as your grandma's Mother Hubbard gown. — WALLACE IRWIN.

Limp as a chewed rag. — KIPLING.

Limp (Verb).

Limping like a sore-footed soldier striding to the band. — ISRAEL ZANGWILL.

Limpid.

Limpid as a cold blue lake on a mountain. — ANON.

Limpid as a diamond. — D'ANNUNZIO.

Limpid as the eye of a heron. — OSMANLI PROVERB.

Limpid as the mountain stream. — JOHN SKELTON.

Line.

Lines as vivid and as durable as the exergues of the Carthaginian medals. — POE.

Lined.

Lined like the rind of a cantaloupe. — O. HENRY.

Linger.

Linger in the memory like the silvery embellishments of a great singer. — ANON.

Lingers like an old faith. — IBID.

Lingered . . . like innocent birds loath to be gone from the spot where their nest has been. — J. M. BARRIE.

The soft memory of her virtues . . . lingers like twilight hues. — WILLIAM CULLEN BRYANT.

Linger — *continued*.

Linger there,
Like hopeless love without despair.
— RUFUS DAWES.

Lingering about like a bailiff. — DICKENS.

I am lingering yet, as sometimes in the blaze of day
A milk-and-watery moon
Stains with its dim and fading ray
The lustrous blue of noon.
— O. W. HOLMES.

Ling'ring now,
Like the last of the leaves left on Autumn's sere and faded bough.
— THOMAS MOORE.

Lingered in the air like dying rolls of abrupt thunder. — SAINTE-BEUVE.

She lingers my desires,
Like to a step-dame, or a dowager,
Long withering out a young man's revenue. — SHAKESPEARE.

Lingering like an unloved guest. — SHELLEY.

Lingering a minute, like outcast spirits, who wait, and see, through the heaven's gate, angels within it. — THACKERAY.

Link.

Linked, like rose-buds in a wreath. — ANON.

Linked like a river by ripples following ripples. — EDWIN ARNOLD.

His vulture nature had already linked itself to this poor little soul as a spider binds a fluttering insect in its web, which the little thing tries vainly to break. — PAUL BOURGET.

Linked each to each by labor, like a bee. — HOOD.

Link in sympathy like the keys
Of an organ. — WHITTIER.

Lip.

A lip like Persuasion's, calling on us to kiss it. — ANACREON.

Lips just tinted like pink shells. — ANON.

Lips that flamed like scarlet wine. — IBID.

Lips like coralline. — ARABIAN NIGHTS.

Dainty lips like double carnelian. — IBID.

Lips, as smooth and tender . . . as rose-leaves in a coppice wild. — THOMAS ASHE.

Curving lips like wave half-furled. — ALFRED AUSTIN.

Lips like rosebuds peeping out of snow. — P. J. BAILEY.

Music lives within thy lips like a nightingale in roses. — IBID.

Her lippes, erst like the corall redde,
Did waxe both wan and pale.
— ENGLISH BALLAD.

Lippes like roses dropping dew. — IBID.

Her lips were like pomegranate blossoms. — ARLO BATES.

A lip like ripest cherries. — BEAUMONT AND FLETCHER.

The Circassian damsel's . . . lips are like taverns of wine. — IBID.

Lips
Curved like an archer's bow to send the bitter arrows out.
— E. B. BROWNING.

Lips shook
Like a rose leaning o'er a brook,
Which vibrates though it is not struck.
— IBID.

Lips with such sweetness in their honeyed deeps
As fills the rose in which a fairy sleeps. — BULWER-LYTTON.

Lips like the red of Christmas holly. — FRANCES HODGSON BURNETT.

Her lips are like the cherries ripe
That sunny walls from Boreas screen.

Lip — *continued.*

They tempt the taste and charm the sight. — BURNS.

Her lips like dewy rosebuds are. — WILFRED CAMPBELL.

Lippes rede as rose. — CHAUCER.

Her lips are like two budded roses whom ranks of lilies neighbor nigh. — H. CONSTABLE.

Lips gay like the rose. — LADY FLORENCE DIXIE.

Her lips are like the muscatel. — AUSTIN DOBSON.

Like rubies are created their two lips. — FAZIL-BEY.

Lips as rounded as a cherry. — EDMUND GOSSE.

Lips like warm carnations. — IBID.

Her lips are roses over-washed with dew,
Or like the purple of Narciss' flower.
— ROBERT GREENE.

With lips, like hanging fruit, whose hue
Is ruby 'neath a bloom of blue.
— T. GORDON HAKE.

Lips that spoil the ruby's praise. — JOHN HARRINGTON.

Red lips like a living, laughing rose. — LAURENCE HOPE.

A quiet smile played around his lips,
As the eddies and dimples of the tide play round the bows of ships.
— LONGFELLOW.

Lips,
That open like the morn, breathing perfumes,
On such as dare approach them.
— PHILIP MASSINGER.

Lips . . . like a ripe raspberry. — CATULLE MENDÈS.

Lips like the carmine's ruddy glow. — FRANCIS S. SALTUS.

Lips, like roses dropping myrrh. — GEORGE SANDYS.

Lips . . . like roses ere they blow. — JOHN G. SAXE.

Ruby lips . . . like rosebuds in spring. — STEPHEN SMITH.

Her lips lyke cherries charming men to byte. — SPENSER.

Lips like rose-petals blown apart. — F. L. STANTON.

Lips like blood spilt on it. — JOHN M. SYNGE.

Lips like the honeyed lips of Hylas. — BAYARD TAYLOR.

Lips, parting like a loose bow, that just has launched its arrow. — IBID.

My lips are like a thread of scarlet. — OLD TESTAMENT.

His lips like lilies, dropping sweet-smelling myrrh. — IBID.

The red colour of her lips like that of a gourd. — "VIKRAM AND THE VAMPIRE."

From lips as the lips of Hylas sweet,
And moved like twin roses which zephyrs meet. — WHITTIER.

Through the open lips shone visibly a delicate line of pearl,
Like a white vein within a rosy shell.
— N. P. WILLIS.

Lipp'd like a lily, and as white as it. — IBID.

Like sunset were her lips. — W. B. YEATS.

Liquid.

Liquid as an Illinois road in April. — GEORGE FITCH.

Liquidation.

A liquidation is something like a chemical process, from which the clever insolvent merchant endeavors to emerge as a saturated solution. — BALZAC.

Listen.

Listened . . . like a stag whose mysterious faculties had detected the footsteps of the distant hounds in the gale. — J. FENIMORE COOPER.

Listen — *continued.*

Listened like one in whom a train of novel ideas had been excited by the reasoning of the other. — IBID.

It is like eating vanilla cream in Paradise listening to beautiful music. — CAMILLE LEMONNIER.

Holding his breath and listening . . . like a burglar who is going to break into a house. — GUY DE MAUPASSANT.

Listened like a cushat dove that listens to its mate alone. — C. G. ROSSETTI.

Listless.

Listless as the summer-stricken air. — SWINBURNE.

Literature.

Literature, like virtue, is its own reward. — CHESTERFIELD.

Literature, like nobility, runs in the blood. — HAZLITT.

Literature, like a gypsy, to be picturesque, should be a little ragged. — DOUGLAS JERROLD.

Lithe.

Lithe as a panther. — T. B. ALDRICH.

Lithe as a snake. — ANON.

Lithe as a tiger. — IBID.

Lithe as leech. — ROBERT BROWNING.

Lithe as a feather duster. — GELETT BURGESS.

Lithe as a rat. — FRANK DANBY.

Lyth as lasse of Kent. — MICHAEL DRAYTON.

Lithe as willow. — RICHARD HOVEY.

Lithe as lips
That curl in touching you.
— SWINBURNE.

Lithe as the dark-eyed Syrian gazelle. — BAYARD TAYLOR.

Little.

Little as Tom Thumb. — NED WARD'S "NUPTIAL DIALOGUES AND DEBATES," 1710.

Live.

Live like a king. — ANON.

Live like a lord. — IBID.

Live like a prince. — IBID.

Live like fighting cocks. — IBID.

Will live together like two wanton vines. — BEAUMONT AND FLETCHER.

He would live like a lamp, to the last wink,
And crawl upon the utmost verge of life.
— DRYDEN.

I live in the town like a lion in his desert, or an eagle in his rock, too great for friendship or society, and condemned to solitude by unhappy elevation and dreaded ascendency. — DR. JOHNSON.

Lively.

Lively and changeable, like a flame in the wind. — ANON.

Lively as a cricket. — IBID.

Lively as fire. — ROBERT BRIDGES (English).

As lively as tints of young Iris' bow. — J. G. COOPER.

Lively as a chaffinch. — DUMAS, PÈRE.

Lively as the smiling day. — AARON HILL.

Lively as a squirrel. — O. W. HOLMES.

Lively as grasshoppers. — LOVER.

Livid.

As pale and livid as any skull unearthed from a graveyard. — BALZAC.

Lips as livid as the opening lilac-leaves. — O. W. HOLMES.

Livid as Lazarus lately from death. — SIDNEY LANIER.

Loathe.

Loathe worse than a leper's mouth.
— SWINBURNE.

Loathsome.

Loathsome as the briny sea to him who languishes with thirst. — AKENSIDE.

Loathsome as death. — JAMES MONTGOMERY.

Loathsome as a toad. — SHAKESPEARE.

Lock.

Locked in, like a fly in amber. — ANON.

Lock'd up like veins of metal. — KEATS.

Locked as in a wrestle together. — SWINBURNE.

Loll.

Lolling, like one indifferent, fabricates a heaven of gold. — CHARLES LAMB.

Loll about . . . like gorged snakes. — HAROLD FREDERIC.

London.

London is like a shelled corn-cob on the Derby day. — O. W. HOLMES.

Lone.

As lone as a churchyard. — BULWER-LYTTON.

Lone as the corse within its shroud,
Lone — as a solitary cloud,
A single cloud on a sunny day,
While all the rest of heaven is clear.
— BYRON.

Lone like an eagle's nest. — MISS LANDON.

Lone as incarnate death.— SHELLEY.

Lonely.

Lonely as a deserted ship. — ANON.

Lonely as a ghost. — IBID.

Lonely as a trance. — HARTLEY COLERIDGE.

Lonely as a crow in a strange country. — JOSEPH CONRAD.

There is nothing so lonely in the world as the girl who has got to look after herself. — IBID.

As lonely as the sun. — SIR FRANCIS H. DOYLE.

Lonely as the Arctic Sea. — HAMLIN GARLAND.

Lonely in her gloom as a pale Angel of the Grove. — THOMAS MOORE.

Lonely as the home of kings
When the slow hours on leaden wings
Oppress the friendless great.
— LEWIS MORRIS.

Lonely, as sovereigns are. — OUIDA.

Lonely as a catamount. — SAM SLICK.

Lonely as in a garden-close
Slumbers the solitary rose.
— ARTHUR SYMONS.

Lonely . . . as a crow on the sands. — WORDSWORTH.

I wandered lonely as a cloud
That floats on high o'er vales and hills.
— IBID.

Lonesome.

Lonesome as a bell-buoy at sea. — ANON.

Lonesome as a walnut rolling in a barrel. — EDNA FERBER.

Long.

Long as a day without bread. — ANON.

Long as a Devonshire lane, — which has no turning. — IBID.

Long as an obituary. — IBID.

Long as the moral law. — IBID.

Long as a Thanksgiving sermon. — J. R. BARTLETT'S "DICTIONARY OF AMERICANISMS."

Long as death. — E. B. BROWNING.

Long as an epic. — BULWER-LYTTON

Long — *continued.*

Face as long as an undertaker's. — IBID.

Longer than a lawsuit. — THOMAS DEKKER.

Long and slender, like a cat's elbow. — THOMAS FULLER.

Long as the spear of Aaron. — CHARLES B. LOOMIS.

Her sorrow as long
As the passage of numberless ages in slumberless song. — SWINBURNE.

Long-winded.

Long-winded as a tornado. — J. R. BARTLETT'S "DICTIONARY OF AMERICANISMS."

Look (Noun).

His look was like a sad embrace. — MATTHEW ARNOLD.

With a look . . . that would split a pitcher, as the Irish say. — CARLYLE.

A look like a noose. — HUGO.

Look like Let-me-be. — LEAN'S "COLLECTANEA."

Gave her a look like red lightning. — CHARLES READE.

Look (Verb).

Looks as if butter would not melt in his mouth. — ANON.

Looked as if he would jump down your throat. — IBID.

Looked as if he had eaten his bed-straw. — IBID.

He looked like a composite picture of five thousand orphans too late to catch a picnic steamboat. — O. HENRY.

Look like the far end o' a French fiddle. — ALEXANDER HISLOP'S "PROVERBS OF SCOTLAND."

To look as if he were hanged already. — SIR JOHN TAYLOR.

She looks like an old coach new painted, affecting an unseemly smugness, whilst she is ready to drop to pieces. — VANBRUGH.

Loom.

Looms in the distant landscape of the Past,
Like a burnt tower upon a blackened heath. — LONGFELLOW.

Loose.

Loose as . . . negligence. — JAMES CAWTHORN.

Loose as the stubble in the field. — GEORGE CROLY.

Loose as a vine-branch blowing in the morn. — AUSTIN DOBSON.

Loose as the wrapper of a two-for-fiver. — O. HENRY.

Loose as Cossack pantaloons. — O. W. HOLMES.

Loose as eggs in a nest. — W. S. LANDOR.

Hang loose about him, like a giant's robe
Upon a dwarfish thief.
— SHAKESPEARE.

Loose as the flame that flutters on the grate. — ALEXANDER SMITH.

Loose, like a Comet's refluent tresses, hung her heavenly hair dispersed. — SOUTHEY.

Loose as the petals of roses discrowned. — SWINBURNE.

Loose as the breeze that plays along the downs. — JAMES THOMSON.

The reins loose as flying ribbons. — LEWIS WALLACE.

Loose as a cloud-wreath on the sky. — WHITTIER.

Loosely.

Loosely like embroidered robes thrown o'er some funeral bier.— JOHN BRENT.

Loquacious.

As loquacious as Polonius. — James Huneker.

Loquacity.

Whose loquacity, like an over-full bottle, could never pour forth a small dose. — Charles Eliot.

Lording.

Lording it like a Bashaw. — Anon.

Lorn.

Lorn,
As needs must Samson when his hair
is shorn.
— Robert Browning.

Lorn as the hung-up lute, that ne'er
hath spoken
Since the sad day its master-cord was
broken! — Thomas Moore.

Lost.

Lost as Eden. — Anon.

Lost, like a river running into an unknown sea. — Ibid.

Lost like a predestined soul. — Ibid.

Lost, like autumnal leaves, when North winds rage. — Congreve.

Lost himself in thought as though he had fallen out of the world. — Joseph Conrad.

Lost, like a star in day. — Henry Ellison.

Lost like the day of Job's awful curse, in the third chapter, third and fourth verse. — Bret Harte.

Lost, like the lightning in
The sullen cloud.
— O. W. Holmes.

As lost, as any needle in a stack of hay. — Hood.

Lost in the gulf of chance to fall, as oblivion swallows thought. — Alfred de Musset.

Lost like stars beyond dark trees. — D. G. Rossetti.

Lost, like the light flickering of a cottage's fire. — Sir Walter Scott.

Lost as in a trance. — Esaias Tegner.

Loud.

Loud as a horn. — Anon.

Loud as the blows of a hammer. — Ibid.

Loud as the voice of an auctioneer. — Ibid.

Loud as Tom of Lincoln. — Ibid.

Crying your name as loud and hastily as men i' th' streets do fire. — Beaumont and Fletcher.

Loud as a culverin. — R. D. Blackmore.

Louder than harvest thunderstorm. — Ibid.

Loud as Sinai's trumpet-sound. — William Blake.

Helpless, naked, piping loud,
Like a fiend hid in a cloud.
— Ibid.

As lowde as bloweth wynde in helle. — Chaucer.

Loud as a king's defiance. — Coleridge.

Tumultuous and very loud . . like the roll of an immense and remote drum beating the charge of the gale. — Joseph Conrad.

Loud as thunder. — Sydney Dobell.

Loud as the sea. — Richard Duke.

Loud as Jupiter's thunder. — Pierce Egan.

As loud as Heav'n's quick-darted flame. — William Hamilton.

Loud as the trumpet rolls its sound. — Ibid.

Loud as when blust'ring Boreas issues
forth,
To bring the sweeping whirlwind from
the north. — Walter Harte.

Loud — *continued.*

Loud as the storm-wind that tumbles the main. — O. W. Holmes.

Loud, as the shout encount'ring armies yield. — Homer (Pope).

Loud as the surges when the tempest blows. — Ibid.

Loud as cavalry to the charge. — George Meredith.

Loud as from numbers without number. — Milton.

Dreadful sounds,
Loud as tides that burst their bounds.
— John Scott.

Speak as loud as Mars. — Shakespeare.

Loud as the clank of an ironmonger. — Shelley.

Loud as the voice of nature. — Ibid.

Loud as the summer forest in the storm, as the river that roars among rocks. — Southey.

Loud, as when the tempest-tossed forest roars to the roaring wind. — Ibid.

Loud as when the wintry whirlwinds blow. — Ibid.

Lowd as larke in ayre. — Spenser.

Loud as the winds when stormy spring
Makes all the woodland rage and ring.
— Swinburne.

Loud as when the storm at ebb-tide rends the beach. — Ibid.

Loud as the trumpet of surviving Fame. — Waller.

Loud as the ocean when a tempest blows. — William Wilkie.

Loud as the silver trumpet's martial noise. — Ibid.

Loud as any mill. — Wordsworth.

Lounge.

Lounged like a boy of the South. — Robert Browning.

Love (Noun).

Love is like the rose: so sweet, that one always tries to gather it in spite of the thorns. — Anon.

Love is like the sunbeam that gleams through the shower
And kisses off gently the dews from the flower;
That cheers up the blossoms and bids them be gay,
And lends the fragrance that perfumes the day. — Ibid.

Love, like a cough, can't be hidden. — Ibid.

Love, like fire, cannot subsist without continual movement; as soon as it ceases to hope and fear, it ceases to exist. — Ibid.

Like threads of silver seen through crystal beads let love through good deeds show. — Edwin Arnold.

Love is like the rose,
And a month it may not see,
Ere it withers where it grows.
— P. J. Bailey.

In love, a woman is like a lyre that surrenders its secrets only to the hand that knows how to touch its strings. — Balzac.

The wrongs of love, like the notes of a solvent debtor, bear interest. — Ibid.

Love is like youth, he thirsts,
He scorns to be his mother's page;
But when the proceeding times assuage
The former heate, he will complaine,
And wish those pleasant houres againe.
— Francis Beaumont.

Luv is like the measles, one kant alwus tell when one ketched it and ain't ap tew hav it severe but onst, and then it ain't kounted much unless it strikes inly. — Josh Billings.

Love — *continued.*

Love is like the wild rose-briar ;
Friendship like the holly-tree.
The holly is dark when the rose-briar
blooms,
But which will bloom most constantly?
The wild rose-briar is sweet in spring,
Its summer blossoms scent the air ;
Yet wait till winter comes again,
And who will call the wild-briar fair?
Then, scorn the silly rose-wreath now,
And deck thee with the holly's sheen,
That, when December blights thy brow
He still may leave thy garland green.
— Emily Brontë.

Women's love, like lichens on a rock, will still grow where even charity can find no soil to nurture itself. — C. N. Bovée.

Love, like death, levels all ranks and lays the shepherd's crook beside the sceptre. — Bulwer-Lytton.

Love's very much like bathing. At first we go souse to the bottom, if we're not drowned, then we gather pluck, grow calm, strike out gently, and make a deal pleasanter thing of it afore we're done. — Ibid.

Oh, my luve is like a red, red rose
That's newly sprung in June ;
Oh, my luve is like the melodie
That's sweetly play'd in tune.
— Burns.

Love is increased by injuries, as the Sunbeams are more gracious after a cloud. — Robert Burton.

As the Sun is in the Firmament, so is Love in the world. — Ibid.

Love is a fire that burns and sparkles
In men as naturally as in charcoals.
— Samuel Butler.

All love at first, like generous wine,
Ferments and frets, until 'tis fine ;
But when 'tis settled on the lye,
And from the impurer matter free,
Becomes the richer still, the older,
And proves the pleasanter, the colder.
— Ibid.

Love-passions are like parables, by which men still mean something else.
— Samuel Butler.

Love in your heart as idly burns
As fire in antique Roman urns.
— Ibid.

Love, like the cold bath, is never negative, it seldom leaves us where it finds us ; if once we plunge into it, it will either heighten our virtues or inflame our vices. — C. C. Colton.

Love, like death, a universal leveller of mankind. — Congreve.

Love, like a greedy hawk, if we give way,
Does over-gorge himself with his own
prey. — Abraham Cowley.

Love, like a scene, at distance should
appear,
But marriage views the gross daubed
landscape near. — Dryden.

Love, like fire, when once kindled, is soon blown into a flame. — Fielding.

Look as it is with some true April day,
Whose various weather stores the world
with flowers ;
The sun his glorious beams doth fair
display,
Then rains and shines again, and
straight it lowers,
And twenty changes in one hour doth
prove ;
So, and more changing is a woman's
love. — Phineas Fletcher.

Love is most like an owl that cannot fly, though wings he has, and lurks in every hole. Beware of him ; the villain, old in sin, shuns the front door, and by the back comes in. — Folengo.

Love like a little bird is made, that
hops about from bough to bough :
Into my bosom it has strayed and at
my heart is pecking now.
— Goldoni.

Love is like a landscape which doth
stand,
Smooth at a distance, rough at hand.
— Robert Hegge.

Love — *continued.*

Love, like the opening of heaven to the saints, shows for a moment, even to the dullest man, the possibilities of the human race. — ARTHUR HELPS.

Love rushed through him as a river in flood. — MAURICE HEWLETT.

O, love, love, love!
Love is like a dizziness;
It winna let a poor body
Gang about his bizziness.
— HOGG.

Love is like a well profound,
From which two souls have right to draw,
And in whose waters will be drowned,
The one who takes the other's law.
— J. G. HOLLAND.

Love is like spring: it laughs through the cold and the snow; it perfumes the night and flourishes under graves. — ARSÈNE HOUSSAYE.

Love is like epidemic diseases, the more one is afraid of it, the more is one exposed to it. — IBID.

Love's like the measles — all the worse when it comes late in life. — DOUGLAS JERROLD.

Love is like medical science — the art of assisting Nature. — LALLEMAND.

Love, like beauty, strong to lure;
Love, like joy, makes man her thrall,
Strong to please and conquer all.
— ERNST LANGE.

Love, like the flower that courts the sun's kind ray,
Will flourish only in the smiles of day.
— JOHN LANGHORNE.

True love, like the eye, can bear no flaw. — LAVATER.

Love, like the lark, while soaring sings;
Wouldst have him spread again his wings?
What careth he for higher skies
Who on the heart of harvest lies,
And finds both sun and firmament
Closed in the round of his content?
— W. J. LINTON.

Loue is likened to the Emerald which cracketh rather then consenteth to any disloyaltie, and can there be any greater villany then being secreat not to be constant, or being constant not to be secret. — LYLY.

Love gotten with witchcraft, is as unpleasant as fish taken with medicines unwholesome. — IBID.

Love is like a charming romance which is read with avidity, and often with such impatience that many pages are skipped to reach the dénouement sooner. — THOMAS MARÉCHAL.

Love, like arm'd Death, is strong. — EDWARD MOORE.

'Tis love, like the sun, that gives light to the year,
The sweetest of blessings that life can give;
Our pleasures it brightens, drives sorrow away,
Gives joy to the night, and enlivens the day.
— IBID.

Ah! love is like a tender flower
Hid in the opening leaves of life,
Which, when the springtide calls, has power,
To scorn the elemental strife.
— LEWIS MORRIS.

Love, like the creeping vine, withers if it has nothing to embrace. — NISUMI.

Love before marriage is like a too short preface before a book without end. — J. PETIT-SENN.

Love, like death, makes all distinction void. — MATTHEW PRIOR.

Love, like men, dies oftener of excess than hunger. — RICHTER.

Love's as cunnin' a little thing as a hummin'-bird upon the wing. — JAMES WHITCOMB RILEY.

Love — *continued.*

Love is like a red-currant wine — it first tastes sweet, but afterward shuddery. — T. W. Robertson.

True love is like ghosts, which everybody talks about and few have seen. — Rochefoucauld.

Love, like other little boys,
Cries for hearts, as they for toys.
— Earl of Rochester.

Love, like flowers, endureth but a spring. — Ronsard.

Love is like a lovely rose the world's delight. — C. G. Rossetti.

Love is like the moon: when it does not increase, it decreases. — Sèqur.

Love is like a child,
That longs for everything that he can come by. — Shakespeare.

Love like a shadow flies, when substance love pursues;
Pursuing that that flies, and flying what pursues. — Ibid.

Love, that comes too late,
Like a remorseful pardon slowly carried,
To a great sender turns a sour offence,
Crying, that's good that's gone.
— Ibid.

Love is like understanding, that grows bright
Gazing on many truths; 'tis like thy light, Imagination. — Shelley.

Love like air is widely given;
Power nor chance can these restrain;
Truest, noblest gifts of heaven!
Only purest in the plain.
— William Shenstone.

Love is an April's doubting day:
Awhile we see the tempest lower;
Anon the radiant heaven survey,
And quite forget the flitting shower.
— Ibid.

Love is like a tune that's played, and life a tale that's told. — W. W. Story.

True love, like the lightning that flashes, must kindle from eye to eye and strike into the heart. — Franz von Suppé.

Love is awful as immortal death. — Ibid.

Better is a dinner of herbs where love is, than a stalled ox and hatred therewith. — Old Testament.

The love of a woman is like a mushroom, — it grows in one night and will serve somewhat pleasantly next morning for breakfast, but afterwards waxes fulsome and unwholesome. — Cyril Tourneur.

Emotional effusions are like licorice-root. When you take your first suck at it, it doesn't seem so bad, but it leaves a very bad taste in your mouth afterward. — Turgenev.

In love as in war, a fortress that parleys is half taken. — Marguerite de Valois.

Love . . . like a pirate, takes you by spreading false colors. — Vanbrugh.

Love, like virtue, is its own reward. — Ibid.

Love, like fortune, turns upon a heel, and is very much given to rising and falling. — Ibid.

Love, my sweet Lidi! resembles the fugitive shadows of morning; shorter and shorter they grow and at length disappear. — Mihaly Vitkovics.

Love's like a torch which, if secur'd from blasts,
Will fainter burn, but then it longer lasts:
Expos'd to storms of jealousy and doubt,
The blaze grows greater, but 'tis sooner out. — William Walsh.

Love, like a bird, hath perch'd upon a spray
For thee and me to hearken what he sings.
— William Watson.

Love — *continued.*

Love . . . as pure as Angel-worship, when the just
And beautiful of Heaven are bow'd in prayer! — WHITTIER.

Love as strong as that which binds the peopled Universe. — IBID.

Love is a lamp unseen, burning to waste, or, if its light is found, nursed for our idle hour, then idly broken. — N. P. WILLIS.

Love, like ambition, dies as 'tis enjoyed. — THOMAS YALDEN.

Love (Verb).

Love as a cat loves mustard. — ANON.

Loved as a guardian angel. — IBID.

As reeds and willows love the water side,
So love loves with the idle to abide.
— FRANCIS BEAUMONT.

Loved as patriots. — E. B. BROWNING.

Love . . . dearly, like pig and pie. — ROBERT BURTON.

Love as a Welshman does toasted cheese. — JOHN DAY.

Love as the dog does a whip. — JOHN RAY'S "HANDBOOK OF PROVERBS."

Love as the devil loves holy water. — SWIFT.

Love him as Frenchmen love Napoleon. — SWINBURNE.

My spirit loved and loves him yet,
Like some poor girl whose heart is set
On one whose rank exceeds her own.
— TENNYSON.

Loveliness.

Loveliness
Stays like the light, after the sun is set.
— RICHARD SHEIL.

Loveliness,
Like a rich tint that makes a picture warm
Is lurking in the chestnut of thy tress,
Enriching it, as moonlight after storm
Mingles dark shadows into gentleness.
— N. P. WILLIS.

Lovely.

Lovely as the first green in the wood. — ANON.

Lovely as Venus. — IBID.

Lovely as sleep. — BION.

Lovely as an angel's dream. — EMILY BRONTË.

Lovely as all excellence. —WILLIAM BROWNE.

Lucid and lovely as the morning star. — MICHAEL BRUCE.

Lovely as Love. — BYRON.

Lovely as day. — GEORGE COLMAN, THE YOUNGER.

Lovely and piteous, like a frosted flower. — HELEN G. CONE.

Lovely as the morning. — BARRY CORNWALL.

Lovely as fairies. — FIRDAUSI.

Lovely as seraphs. — WASHINGTON IRVING.

Lovely as lilies ungathered. — HARRIET E. HAMILTON KING.

Lovely as May. — JOHN LOGAN.

Lovely as is the maiden moon in May. — WALTER MALONE.

Lovely as a bridegroom. — MISS MITFORD.

Lovely as an infant's dream
On the waking mother's breast.
— JAMES MONTGOMERY.

Lovely as the first beam of the sun. — OSSIAN.

Lovely as adolescence. — OUIDA.

Lovely as an obelisk in a desert. — T. N. PAGE.

Lovely as light. — MATTHEW PRIOR.

Lovely — *continued.*

Lovely as the Lord of Night. — RAMAYANA.

Lovely as a queen. — D. G. ROSSETTI.

Lovely as the smiling infant spring. — SIR WALTER SCOTT.

Lovely as a budding rose. — SOUTHEY.

Lovely as nymphs. — IBID.

Lovely as the youthful dreams of Hope. — IBID.

Lovely as a landscape in a dream. — TENNYSON.

Lovely as the violet. — TUPPER.

Lovely as a Lapland night. — WORDSWORTH.

Lovely as spring's first rose. — IBID.

Lover.

Lovers are like walking ghosts, they always haunt the spot of their misdeeds. — GEORGE H. BOKER.

Lovers like sick folks may say what they please. — JEREMY COLLIER.

A lover is like a hunter, if the game be got with too much ease he cares not for it. — ROBERT MEAD.

The quarrels of lovers are like summer showers, that leave the country more verdant and beautiful. — MADAME NECKER.

Young lovers, like game cocks, are made bolder by being kept without light. — VANBRUGH.

Loving.

Loving as a mother's voice. — CARLYLE.

Low.

Low as the grave. — ANON.

Low as horse's hoof. — SCOTCH BALLAD.

Low as zephyr, telling secrets to his rose. — T. L. BEDDOES.

Lying low, like a malignant little animal under a hedge. — JOSEPH CONRAD.

Low as a bushy bramble. — CHARLES MACKLIN.

Low as a baboon's forehead. — SYDNEY MUNDEN.

Low as Hell. — D. G. ROSSETTI.

Fall low as Persian to the sun. — CHARLES SANGSTER.

Low as to the fiends. — SHAKESPEARE.

As low as hell's from heaven. — IBID.

Low as the softest breath that passes
in summer at evening
O'er the Æolian strings, felt there when
nothing is moving,
Save the thistle-down, lighter than air,
and the leaf of the aspen.
— SOUTHEY.

Low as broken crown. — SWINBURNE.

Lower.

Lowers like a storm. — CHRISTOPHER PITT.

Lowering as a storm-flushed moon. — SWINBURNE.

Lowly.

Lowly as a flower. — MADISON CAWEIN.

Lowly as a slave. — TUPPER.

Loyal.

Loyal as a dove. — ANON.

Loyal to her plighted faith as is the sun in Heaven. — JOHN FORD.

Loyal as the Liberty on a golden ten-dollar piece. — O. W. HOLMES.

Loyal as prairie scout. — AMY LESLIE.

Lucent.

Softly lucent as a rounded moon. — LOWELL.

Lucid.

Lucid as a Japanese sphere of rock-crystal. — O. W. HOLMES.

Lucid and lovely as the morning star. — JOHN LOGAN.

Lucid as the dawn. — JOHN SKELTON.

Lucid as daylight. — S. G. TALLENTYRE.

Lucid as air. — JOHN WILSON.

Lugubrious.

Lugubrious as a tombstone. — RENNOLD WOLF.

Lull.

Lull'd like the depth of ocean when at rest. — BYRON.

Lulling as falling water's hollow noise. — JOHN GAY.

It lulled like the lull in a storm. — OUIDA.

Luminous.

Luminous as jelly. — AMBROSE BIERCE.

Luminous as a panther's skin. — SIR A. CONAN DOYLE.

As luminous as the sun's intensest beam. — CHARLES SANGSTER.

Luminous as a lit-up ballroom. — H. DE VERE STACPOOLE.

Lure.

Lured as the fowler lures the bird. — LOPE DE VEGA.

Lurid.

Lurid as a comic opera climax. — J. CHEEVER GOODWIN.

Lurid as hell. — GEORGE CABOT LODGE.

Lurid as anguish. — SWINBURNE.

Lurk.

Lurk behind, like a concealed root. — CERVANTES.

Lurked as comfortably as a shy bird in its native thicket.—JOSEPH CONRAD.

Lurk like vermin. — JOHN DAVIDSON.

Lurks like embers raked in ashes. — DRYDEN.

Lurks and clings as withering, damning blight. — GEORGE ELIOT.

Lurking . . . like a concealed enemy. — FIELDING.

Lurks like a mole underneath the visible surface of manners. — THOMAS HARDY.

Lurk, like a snake under the innocent
shade
Of a spread summer-leaf.
— THOMAS MIDDLETON.

Lurking like a savage thing
Crouching for a treacherous spring.
— MAURICE THOMPSON.

Luscious.

Luscious as locusts. — SHAKESPEARE.

Lust.

Lust, like a lawless headlong flood,
Impregnated with ooze and mud,
Descending fast on every side,
Once mingles with the sacred tide,
Farewell the soul-enliv'ning scene!
The banks that wore a smiling green,
With rank defilement overspread,
Bewail their flow'ry beauties dead.
— COWPER.

Base lust,
With all her powders, paintings, and best pride,
Is but a fair house built by a ditch side. — THOMAS MIDDLETON.

Lusts are like agues; the fit is not always on, and yet the man is not rid of the disease ; and some men's lusts, like some agues, have not such returns as others. — HERBERT SPENCER.

Our headlong lusts, like a young fiery horse,
Start and flee raging in a violent course.
— ISAAC WATTS.

Lustful.

As lustful as Messalina. — ROBERT BURTON.

Lustrous.

Lustrous as satin. — ANON.

Lustrous, thick like horsehairs. — ROBERT BROWNING.

Lustrous as agate. — GAUTIER.

Lustrous as ebony. — SHAKESPEARE.

Lustrous as laughter. — SWINBURNE.

Lustrous as the day.— JOHN TAYLOR.

Lustrous as sun-set. — THOMAS WADE.

Lusty.

Lusty as leaves in June. — GERALD MASSEY.

Lusty as Nature. — WALT WHITMAN

Luxuriant.

Luxuriant as the vine. — ANON.

Luxurious.

Luxurious as a cluster of grapes. — WILLIAM M. REEDY.

Luxury.

Luxury, like wine, both stimulates and weakens. — ALPHONSE KARR.

M

Machine.

The Ford machine is like a bathtub. Everybody wants one, but nobody wants to be seen in it. — CHAUNCEY M. DEPEW.

Mad.

Mad as a hatter. — ANON.

Mad as an adder. — IBID.

Mad as a rat in a trap. — IBID.

Mad as a wet cat. — IBID.

Mad as blazes. — IBID.

Mad as tigers. — IBID.

Mad as all wrath. — J. R. BARTLETT'S "DICTIONARY OF AMERICANISMS."

Mad as a bull among bumble bees. — IBID.

Mad as May butter. — BEAUMONT AND FLETCHER.

As Staring madde like March Hares. — ANDREW BORDE (1490–1549.)

As mad as Orlando for his Angelica, or Hercules for his Hylas. — ROBERT BURTON.

He is as mad as a March hare. — CERVANTES.

Mad . . . like the warrior in the fight. — BARRY CORNWALL.

Mad as a drunken squaw. — ALFRED HENRY LEWIS.

Mad as the delirious dream
Of one who, on an Indian stream
Floating in a Morphean bark,
Feeds on the charmèd lotus leaf.
— T. BUCHANAN READ.

Mad as Ajax. — SHAKESPEARE.

More mad
Than Telamon for his shield.
— IBID.

Mad as the vexed sea. — IBID.

Maddening.

Lived maddeningly, like a man who has a drumming in his ear. — MAURICE HEWLETT.

Magnanimous.

Magnanimous as Agamemnon. — SHAKESPEARE.

Magnificent.

Magnificent as Mrs. Siddons as Lady Macbeth. — THACKERAY.

Maid.

The spotless maid is like the blooming rose
Which on its native stem unsullied grows. — ARIOSTO.

Maidens, like moths, are ever caught by glare,
And Mammon wins his way where seraphs might despair.
— BYRON.

Maids are like contentment in this life,
Which all the world have sought, but none enjoy'd.
— SIR JOHN DAVIES.

A maiden is like a half-blown damask rose, fair as a dream and full of the sweet fragrance of the purity of dawning womanhood. — ANNIE E. LANCASTER.

Majestic.

Majestic as a statue. — ANON.

Majestic as Cæsar. — IBID.

Majestic as Juno. — IBID.

Like Jove, majestic. — GEORGE GRANVILLE.

Majestic as the sun at noon. — ORIENTAL.

Port as Majestic as Astley's horse dances. — ANTHONY PASQUIN.

Majestic in its movement as a sonnet of Milton. — ISRAEL ZANGWILL.

Majorities.

Decision by majorities is as much an expedient as lighting by gas. — GLADSTONE.

Malicious.

Malicious as a satyr. — ANON.

Malicious as Saul to David. — IBID.

Maliciously like poison. — SHAKESPEARE.

Malicious as Satan. — THACKERAY.

Man.

Man is a social creature, and we are made to be helpful to each other; we are like the wheels of a watch, that none of them can do their work alone, without the concurrence of the rest. — ANON.

Some men are like a brook, noisy but shallow. — IBID.

Man is like a razor, the sharper for being stropped. — IBID.

Some men, like wagons, rattle most when there's nothing in them. — IBID.

Tall men, like tall houses, are usually ill furnished in the upper story. — BACON.

The majority of men are like animals — they take fright and are reassured by trifles. — BALZAC.

A Man is like unto a fort in a strange land, easy to capture, but hard to hold; but a woman of virtue is like an eel in a bathtub, not easily to be acquired, but difficult to lose. — GELETT BURGESS.

Men but like visions are, Time all doth claime,
He lives, who dies to winne a lasting name. — WILLIAM DRUMMOND.

Men, like musical instruments, seem made to be played upon. —
C. N. BOVÉE.

An honest man is like a plain coat, which without welt [fold] or guard, keepeth the body from wind and weather, and being well made fits him best that wears it; and where the stuff is more regarded than the fashion, there is not much ado in the putting of it on. So, the mind of an honest man, without tricks or compliments, keeps the credit of a good conscience from the scandal of the world and the worm of Iniquity; which being wrought by the Workman of Heaven, fits him best that wears it to His service; and where Virtue is more esteemed than Vanity, it is put on and worn with that ease that shows excellency of the Workman. — NICHOLAS BRETON

Man — *continued.*

Men are like old ships, easy towed, but hard to steer. — ROBERT BRIDGES (American).

Man is like a book . . . the commonality only look to his binding. — BULWER-LYTTON.

A young man is like a fair new house, the carpenter leaves it well built, in good repair, a solid stuff ; but a bad tenant lets it rain in, and for want of reparation fall to decay, etc. Our Parents, Tutors, Friends, spare no cost to bring us up in our youth in all manner of virtuous education ; but when we are left to ourselves idleness as a tempest drives all virtuous notions out of our minds, etc., and *nihili sumus*, on a sudden, by sloth and such bad ways, we come to naught. — ROBERT BURTON.

Man is like a napkin, the more neatly the housewife doubles him, the more carefully she lays him on the shelf. — IBID.

We are like billiard balls in a game played by unskillful players, continually being nearly sent into a pocket, but hardly ever getting right into one, except by a fluke. — SAMUEL BUTLER (1835–1902).

In fact, man ain't constructed for a heavy strain of bliss.
Human beings are like boilers, and the same rules, it would seem,
Have an equal application to affection and steam. — WM. ALLEN BUTLER.

A young man of high talent, and high though still temper, like a young mettled colt, 'breaks-off his neck-halter', and bounds forth, from his peculiar manger, into the wide world ; which, alas, he finds all rigorously fenced-in. Richest clover-fields tempt his eye ; but to him they are forbidden pasture : either pining in progressive starvation, he must stand ; or, in mad exasperation, must rush to and fro, leaping against sheer stone-walls, which he cannot leap over, which only lacerate and lame him ; till at last, after thousand attempts and endurances, he, as if by miracle, clears his way : not indeed into luxuriant and luxurious clover, yet into a certain bosky wilderness where existence is still possible, and Freedom, though waited on by Scarcity, is not without sweetness. — CARLYLE.

Some men are like musical glasses, — to produce their finest tone, you must keep them wet. — COLERIDGE.

Great men, like great cities, have many crooked arts and dark alleys in their hearts, whereby he that knows them may save himself much time and trouble. — C. C. COLTON.

Great men, like comets, are eccentric in their courses, and formed to do extensive good, by modes unintelligible to vulgar minds. — IBID.

A good man, like a well trained wrestler, ought to struggle against adversity with the whole energy of his faculties. — DEMOPHILUS.

Why do you make such haste to have done loving me ? You men are like watches, wound up for striking twelve immediately ; but after you are satisfied, the very next that follows, is the solitary sound of a single one. — DRYDEN.

Men are like Geneva watches with crystal faces which expose the whole movement. — EMERSON.

Men are like wine, — not good before the lees of clownishness be settled. — FELTHAM.

Such men grew wiser as well as better, the farther they departed from home, and seemed like rivers, whose streams are not only increased, but refined, as they traveled from their source. — GOLDSMITH.

Wise men, like wine, are best when old ; pretty women, like bread, are best when young. — SAM SLICK.

Man — *continued.*

As no two pots will boil alike, so with men ; they seethe in trouble with a difference. — MAURICE HEWLETT.

A bad man is like an earthen vessel, easy to break, and hard to mend. A good man is like a golden vessel, — hard to break, and easy to mend. — HITOPADESA.

Men, like peaches and pears, grow sweet a little while before they begin to decay. — O. W. HOLMES.

As is the race of leaves, such is that of men ; some leaves the wind scatters upon the ground, and others the budding wood produces, for they come again in the season of Spring. So is the race of men, one springs up and the other dies. — HOMER.

A man whose great qualities want the ornament of superficial attractions, is like a naked mountain with mines of gold, which will be frequented only till the treasure is exhausted. — DR. JOHNSON.

Good men, like the sea, should still
maintain
Their noble tastes in midst of all fresh
humours,
That flow about them, to corrupt their
streams,
Bearing no season, much less salt of
goodness. — BEN JONSON.

Like to the falling of a star,
Or as the flights of eagles are;
Or like the fresh spring's gaudy hue,
Or silver drops of morning dew;
Or like a wind that chafes the flood,
Or bubbles which on water stood:
Ev'n such is man, whose borrow'd light
Is straight call'd in, and paid to-night.
The wind blows out, the bubble dies;
The spring entom'd in autumn lies;
The dew dries up, the star is shot;
The flight is past — and man forgot.
— HENRY KING.

Wise men are like moorlands — ride as far as you will on the sound ground, you are sure to come upon a soft place at last. — KINGSLEY.

Man is like a tree which is shaken that its fruit may drop to the ground. — LAMARTINE.

Great men stand like solitary towers! — LONGFELLOW.

Great men are like meteors : they glitter and are consumed to enlighten the world. — NAPOLEON.

Men are like money : we must take them for their value, whatever may be the effigy. — MADAME NECKER.

A man, like a watch, is to be valued for his manner of going. — WILLIAM PENN.

Man, like the generous vine, supported
lives ;
The strength he gains is from the embrace he gives. — POPE.

Men like bullets, go farthest when they are smoothest. — J. P. RICHTER.

Man is like horse-radish : the more it is grated the more it bites. — IBID.

Men are weathercocks, which are never constant or fixed, but when they are, they are worn out or rusty. — ROUSSEAU.

Most men are like plants : they possess properties which chance discovers. — SAINT-RÉAL.

At ten, Mercury is in the ascendant ; and at that age, a man, like this planet, is characterized by extreme mobility within a narrow sphere where trifles have a great effect upon him ; but under the guidance of so crafty and eloquent a god, he easily makes great progress. Venus begins her sway during his twentieth year, and then a man is wholly given up to the love of women. At thirty, Mars comes to the front, and he is now all energy and strength — daring, pugnacious, and arrogant. — SCHOPENHAUER.

Man — *continued.*

Men, like butterflies,
Shew not their mealy wings but to the summer;
And not a man, for being simply man,
Hath any honour. — SHAKESPEARE.

Man, like this sublunary world, is born the sport of two cross planets, love and scorn. — SIR EDWARD SHERBURNE.

If you were to say that man was like a time glass — that both must run out, and both render up their dust, I should listen to you with more attention, because I should feel something like surprise at the sudden relation you had struck out between two such apparently dissimilar ideas as a man and a time glass. — SYDNEY SMITH.

It is in men as in soils, where sometimes there is a vein of gold which the owner knows not of. — SWIFT.

Man, like everything else that lives, changes with the air that sustains him. — TAINE.

A man, like a book, must have an index; he is divided into chapters, sections, pages, prefaces, and appendix; in size, quarto, octavo, or duodecimo, and bound in cloth, morocco, antique, or half calf; the dress, the gait, the behavior, are an index to the contents of this strange book, and give you the number of the page. — T. DEWITT TALMAGE.

Man is like to vanity: his days are as a shadow that passeth away. — OLD TESTAMENT.

Great men are like oaks, under the branches of which men are happy in finding a refuge in the time of storm and rain; but when they have to pass a sunny day under them, they take pleasure in cutting the bark and breaking the branches. — THEMISTOCLES.

Great men are like great bells; every sound they utter strikes our ears with the noise of thunder. — J. PENFORD THOMAS.

Man, like to Cassia, is proved best being bruised. — JOHN WEBSTER.

Every man is like the apostle Peter in one respect, that his tongue betrays him. — R. G. WHITE.

Man's like the earth, his hair like grasse is grown,
His veins the rivers are, his heart the stone.
— "WITS RECREATIONS," 1640.

Man-Worship.

This thing of man-worship I am a stranger to; I don't like it; it taints every action of life; it is like a skunk getting into a house — long after he has cleared out, you smell him in every room and closet, from the cellar to the garret. — DAVID CROCKETT.

Manageable.

Manageable as chess-pieces. — GEORGE MEREDITH.

Manful.

Manful as the man of stone. — A. E. HOUSMAN.

Manfully.

Manfully, like one who speaks the honest truth. — SOUTHEY.

Manifest.

As clear and as manifest as the nose in a man's face. — ROBERT BURTON.

Manifest as day. — "WARNING FOR FAIRE WOMEN," 1599.

Manifold.

Manifold
As are the passions of uncertain man.
— SAMUEL DANIEL.

Mankind.

The world is like a vast sea; mankind like a vessel sailing on its tempestuous bosom. Our prudence is its sails, the sciences serve us for oars, good or bad fortune are the favourable or contrary winds, and judgment is the rudder: without this last, the vessel is tossed by every billow, and will find shipwreck in every breeze. — GOLDSMITH.

Manners.

Fine manners are like personal beauty, — a letter of credit everywhere. — C. A. BARTOL.

Manners . . . Like a great rough diamond, it may do very well in a closet by way of curiosity, and also for its intrinsic value. — CHESTERFIELD.

Manners, like fashions, still from courts descend,
And what the great begin, the vulgar end. — PAUL WHITEHEAD.

Mantle.

Mantle like a flame of fire. — LONGFELLOW.

Cream and mantle, like a standing pond. — SHAKESPEARE.

Many.

As many lives as a cat. — BUNYAN.

As feele (many) as of leves ben on trees in somer. — CHAUCER.

As many as the phases of the mind's emotion. — HAYDEN SANDS.

March.

March like a rough tumbling storm. — BEAUMONT AND FLETCHER.

March like an endless rhyme. — KIPLING.

Marriage.

Marriage is like to casting dice. If chance bring you a virtuous and good-tempered wife your lot is happy. If you gain instead a gadding, gossiping, and thriftless quean, no wife is yours, but everlasting plague in woman's garb; the habitable globe holds not so dire a torment anywhere. — EPICHARMUS.

Like a dog with a bottle fast tied to his tail,
Like vermin in a trap or a thief in a jail,
Like a Tory in a bog
Or an ape with a clog:
Such is the man who, when he might go free,
Does his liberty lose
For a matrimony noose,
And sells himself into captivity.
— THOMAS FLATMAN.

Marriage is not like the hill of Olympus, wholly clear, without clouds. — THOMAS FULLER.

Marriage to maids is like a war to men; the battle causes fear, but the sweet hope of winning at the last still draws them on. — NATHANIEL LEE.

It is a signe that nothing will asswage your love but marriage: for such is the tying of two in wedlocks, as is the tuning of two lutes in one key, for striking the strings of one, strawes will stirre upon the strings of the other, and in two mindes linked in love, one cannot be delighted, but the other rejoiceth. — LYLY.

You know some of our Grub Street wits compared marriage to a country dance, which scheme I extremely approved, but when I read it I thought it should have been set to the tune of "Love forever"; but they say it never did go to that tune, nor ever would. — ELIZABETH R. MONTAGU.

Marriage is like a flaming candle-light
Placed in the window on a summer's night,
Inviting all the insects of the air
To come and singe their pretty winglets there. — ENGLISH SONG.

Married.

Married people, for being so closely united, are but the apter to part: as knots, the harder they are pulled, break the sooner. — POPE.

Marry.

Every man who marries is like the Doge who weds the Adriatic sea: he knows not what he may find therein, — treasures, pearls, monsters, unknown storms. — HEINRICH HEINE.

Marrying.

Marrying . . . 'tis like going a long voyage to sea, where after a while even the calms are distasteful, and the storms dangerous: one seldom sees a new object, 'tis still a deal of sea, sea; husband, husband, every day, — till one's quite cloy'd with it. — APHRA BEHN.

Marrying a widow is an easy business, like leaping the hedge where another has gone over before. — VANBRUGH.

Marrying to increase love is like gaming to become rich. — WYCHERLEY.

Mars.

Mars like the curse on a woman's lips. — EDWARD PEPLE.

Masculine.

Masculine as a fox chase. — HENRY MACKENZIE.

Masterful.

Masterful as the blind instinct that compels the migration of schools of fish. — HENRY A. CLAPP.

Masterful as fate. — SWINBURNE.

Masterless.

Masterless as will-o'-the-wisps. — AGNES REPPLIER.

Match.

As evenly matched as two cubes of the same size. — ANON.

Mature.

Matured like flowers by the light of the sun. — ANON.

Maxim.

A maxim is like the seed of a plant, which the soul it is thrown into must expand into leaves and flowers and fruit. — MADAME DE SARTORY.

Maxims . . . have the same use with the burning-glass; to collect the diffused rays of wit and learning in authors, and make them point with warmth and quickness upon the reader's imagination. — SWIFT.

Meagre.

Meagre as death itself. — JOHN BYROM.

Mean.

Mean as a miser. — ANON.

Mean as an earth-worm. — DUMAS, PÈRE.

Mean as falsehood. — MISS MULOCK.

Mean as dust, and dead as dreams. — WILLIAM WATSON.

Meander.

Meandered . . . like a lazy brook among water-meadows. — MAURICE HEWLETT.

Meandering . . . like a silver scarf outblown
On the fluttering of the gale.
— FRANK WATERS.

Meaningless.

Meaningless as shredded hay. — FRANKLIN P. ADAMS.

Meaningless as an imprint on a wornout coin. — ANON.

Meaningless, like the head of a corpse. — JOSEPH CONRAD.

Meaningless as the boom of waves in a drowning head. — EDITH WHARTON.

Meditate.

Meditate deeply, like a warning whisper from Providence. — HUGO.

Meditative.

Meditative, like a girl trying to decide which dress to wear to the party. — O. HENRY.

Meek.

Meek as a Madonna. — ANON.

Meek as a mouse. — IBID.

Meek as mustard. — IBID.

Meek — *continued.*

Meek as a violet. — Anon.

Meek as Moses. — Ibid.

Meek as a matron in mantle gray. — Joanna Baillie.

Meek as the turtle-dove. — Robert Blair.

Meek as the man Moses. — Cowper.

Meeke as is a mayde. — Chaucer.

As meke as ever was any lamb. — Ibid.

As a lamb she sitteth meke and stille, as leef on lynde [Linden tree]. — Ibid.

Meek as any baby. — Maurice Hewlett.

As Hester meke. — John Lydgate.

Meek as a dove. — George Meredith.

Meek as gruel. — Ibid.

Meek as the gentlest of those who in life's sunny valley lie sheltered and warm. — Thomas Moore.

Meek as a saint. — Pope.

Meek as May. — Ibid.

More meek than lambs. — Theocritus.

Meek, like to a bankrupt beggar. — Shakespeare.

Shee meeker, kinder than
The turtle-dove or pelican.
— George Wither.

Leans meekly, like a flower
By the still river tempted from its stem
And on its bosom floating.
— N. P. Willis.

Meek and patient as a sheathèd sword. — Wordsworth.

Meet.

As meet as a rope for a thief. — John Heywood.

Melancholy.

Melancholy as a graveyard on a rainy day. — Anon.

Melancholy as a hearse-plume. — Ibid.

Melancholy as a mourning-coach in a snowstorm. — Ibid.

Melancholy as a squeezed lemon. — Ibid.

Melancholy as a tailor. — Ibid.

Melancholy as the moon at full. — P. J. Bailey.

Melancholy as a Quaker meeting-house by moonlight. — J. R. Bartlett's "Dictionary of Americanisms."

Melancholy . . . like a gamester that has lost his money. — Beaumont and Fletcher.

Melancholy as a cow. — George H. Boker.

Melancholy as Monks and Hermits. — Robert Burton.

Melancholy as Irish melodies. — Bliss Carman.

Melancholy as an unbraced drum. — Mrs. Centlivre.

Melancholy sound . . . like the weeping of a solitary, deserted human heart. — Guy de Maupassant.

Melancholy as a slighted damsel. — Goethe.

Melancholy, like the voice of a child that was spending its infancy without playfulness. — Hawthorne.

Melancholic as midnight. — Ben Jonson.

Melancholy as a cat. — Lyly.

A melancholy strain,
Like the low moaning of the distant sea.
— Poe.

Melancholy as a gib cat. — Shakespeare.

Melancholy as a lodge in a warren — Ibid.

Mellow.

Mellow as the far-off lute. — ANON.

Mellow, like a plum which has hung in the sun. — IBID.

Mellow as the anger of waters in caves of the sea-shore. — JOHN W. DE FOREST.

Mellow like the sunlight. — MARY JOHNSTON.

Mellow, like a peach that is ready to drop in your lap. — LOVER.

Mellow as a lamp in a lighted room. — ALICE DUER MILLER.

Melodious.

Melodious as the strain that floats on high,
To soothe the sleep of blameless infancy. — JOHN LEYDEN.

Wild wordless melodies of love like murmur of dreaming brooks in Paradise. — THEODORE WATTS-DUNTON.

Melt.

Melts like the fitful vapor. — GRANT ALLEN.

Melted away like an image of snow. — ANON.

Melts like a passing smoke, a nightly dream. — MATTHEW ARNOLD.

Melt as in a dream. — THOMAS BOYD.

Melted as a star might do,
Still smiling as she melted slow.
— E. B. BROWNING.

Melts in the furnace of desire,
Like glass, that's but the ice of fire.
— SAMUEL BUTLER.

Melt, like man, to Time. — BYRON.

Melted like a phantasm. — CALDERON.

Melt like two hungry torrents. — GEORGE CHAPMAN.

Melting, like ghosts before the rising sun. — CHARLES CHURCHILL.

Melt like straggling snow that falls on fire. — AARON HILL.

Melted like an image of snow. — O. W. HOLMES.

Melting as a lover's prayer. — JOHN HUGHES.

Melt away into the darkness like a snowflake in the water. — HUGO.

Melt like gold refined. — JEAN INGELOW.

Melts in, like the smile that sinks in the face of the dreamer. — EBENEZER JONES.

Sweet Pleasure melteth,
Like the bubbles when rain pelteth.
— KEATS.

Melted, as the rose
Blendeth its odour with the violet.
— IBID.

Melts like a pearl in pot of vinegar. — J. H. MCCARTHY.

Melting, like mist, away. — THOMAS MOORE.

Melted like vapor in the sun. — GEORGE P. MORRIS.

Fond duties melt away like April snows. — MISS MULOCK.

Like frost work in the morning ray,
The fancied fabric melts away.
— SIR WALTER SCOTT.

Melt away,
Like dissolving spray.
— SHELLEY.

Melt, like cloud to cloud. — IBID.

Melts away
Like moonlight in the heaven of spreading day. — IBID.

Melted, as in a crucible. — WILLIAM W. STORY.

He melted like a cloud in the silent summer heaven. — TENNYSON.

Melt like mist. — IBID.

Melt away as waters which run continual. — OLD TESTAMENT.

Melt — *continued.*

Melted like wax. — OLD TESTAMENT.

Melt as an iceberg in the tropics. — TUPPER.

Melt . . . like the sun from the day. — JOHN WILSON.

Memorable.

Memorable as the grave. — DE QUINCEY.

Memory.

Like to a coin, passing from hand to
hand,
Are common memories, and day by
day
The sharpness of their impress wears
away. — ARLO BATES.

Then Memory disclosed her face divine, that like the calm nocturnal lights doth shine within the soul. — GEORGE ELIOT.

Memory is like a purse, if it be overfull that it cannot shut, all will drop out of it. — THOMAS FULLER.

His memory was like a miser's pocket, from which you cannot entice a quarter of a kopek. — NIKOLAI V. GOGOL.

Sweet is the memory of departed friends. Like the mellow rays of the declining sun, it falls tenderly, yet sadly, on the heart. — WASHINGTON IRVING.

Memory is like moonlight, the reflection of brighter rays from an object no longer seen. — G. P. R. JAMES.

Our memory is like a sieve, the holes of which in time get larger and larger ; the older we get, the quicker anything intrusted to it slips from the memory, whereas what was fixed fast in it in early days is there still. — SCHOPENHAUER.

Memory like books that remain a long time shut up in the dust needs to be opened from time to time ; it is necessary, so to speak, to open the leaves, that it may be ready in time of need. — SENECA.

Menace.

Swell menacingly like the first whisper of a rising wind. — JOSEPH CONRAD.

Mend.

Mend as sour ale in summer. — HEYWOOD'S "PROVERBS."

Men.

(*See* Man.)

Mendacity.

We believe that mendacity, like marriage, is essentially a human convention and that in Heaven there is neither lying nor giving the lie. — NEW YORK SUN.

Merciless.

Merciless as a male tiger. — ANON.

Merciless as Cæsar. — IBID.

Merciless as the grave. — IBID.

Merciless . . . as that of trying to read the Universal Riddle. — LAFCADIO HEARN.

Merciless as ambition. — JOUBERT.

Merciless as Othello. — OUIDA.

Merciless as waste desire. — JOHN PAYNE.

Mercy.

As freely as the firmament embraces the world, so mercy must encircle friend and foe. — SCHILLER.

The quality of mercy is not strained.
It droppeth, as the gentle rain from
heaven
Upon the place beneath : it is twice
blessed ;
It blesseth him that gives, and him
that takes. — SHAKESPEARE.

Mercy is like a rainbow, we must never look for it after dark. — SAMUEL SQUIRE.

Merit.

True merit is like a river; the deeper it is the less noise it makes. — HALIFAX.

Merit is like musk, which although remaining concealed through the diffusion of its perfume, the nostrils are apprised thereof. — PILPAY.

True merit, like the pearl inside the oyster, is content to remain quiet until it finds an opening. — PUNCH.

True merit, like the light of a glow-worm, shines conspicuous to all except the object which emits it. — ELIZABETH RICORD.

Merit, like the show inside the circus, is of comparatively little use as drawing card; it is the bluff and buncombe, the banging drum and megaphone of the barker, which is the successful magnet. — LESLIE DE VAUX.

Merry.

Merry as a haystack sleeper. — ANON.

Merry as a two-year-old. — IBID.

Merry as cap and can. — IBID.

Merry as crickets in an oven. — IBID.

Merry as flowers in May. — IBID.

Merry as mice in malt. — IBID.

Merry as spring. — IBID.

Merry as the maids. — BUNYAN.

Merry as a kitten. — BURNS.

Merry as a marriage bell. — BYRON.

As merry as a fiddler. — "THE CHRISTMAS PRINCE."

Merry as the month of May. — BARRY CORNWALL.

Merry as popinjay. — MICHAEL DRAYTON.

Merry as birds on the bough. — FREDERICK THE GREAT.

As merry as king in his delight. — ROBERT GREENE.

Merry as an alimony bell. — O. HENRY.

As merry as a pie. — "KING'S HALFE-PENNY-WORTH OF WIT IN A PENNY-WORTH OF PAPER."

Merry as larks. — W. S. LANDOR.

Merry as spring groves full of birds. — GERALD MASSEY.

Merry as it were June. — MISS MULOCK.

Merry as singing birds. — C. E. NORTON.

Merry as three beans in a blue bladder. — "POOR ROBIN'S ALMANACK."

As merry as a grig. — ENGLISH PROVERB.

As merry as the maltman. — SCOTTISH PROVERB.

Merry as the day is long. — SHAKESPEARE.

As merry, as when our nuptial day was done,
And tapers burned to bedward.
— IBID.

Merry as crickets. — IBID.

Merry as an ape. — SWIFT.

Meshed.

The red
Is meshed in the brown,
Like a rubied sun in a Venice sail.
— FRANCIS THOMPSON.

Method.

Method is like packing things in a box; a good packer will get in half as much again as a bad one. — SIR RICHARD CECIL.

Middle.

Standing exactly in the middle of his face like the white in the centre of a target. — ANON.

Mighty.

Mighty as an ivy-suffocated tower against a field of johnny-jump-ups. — Amy Leslie.

Mild.

Mild and peaceful as Socrates. — Anon.

Mild as the ev'ning's humid ray. — Thomas Blacklock.

Mild as an English summer lingering on the brink of autumn. — Bulwer-Lytton.

Mild,
As a mother with her child.
— Coleridge.

Mild as an emulsion. — George Colman, the younger.

Mild as any lamb that ever pastured in the fields. — Dickens.

Mild as any maid. — Michael Drayton.

Mild as the gentlest season of the year. — Francis Fawkes.

Mild as the dove ey'd morn awakes the May. — Elijah Fenton.

As mild and humble in her thoughts,
As was Aspasia unto Cyprus.
— Robert Greene.

Mild as the voice of comfort to despair. — Walter Harte.

Mild as summer's mildest shower. — Reginald Heber.

Mild as sighing saints. — Aaron Hill.

Mild as moonbeams crazed with murderous hates. — O. W. Holmes.

Mild,
Like the soft snoring of a child. — Hood.

Mild as a star in water. — Keats.

Mild
As grazing ox unworried in the meads.
— Ibid.

Mild eye like the dawn. — C. J. Kickham.

Mild, as the never wrathful dove. — John Langhorne.

Mild as a saint whose errors are forgiven. — William Livingston.

Mild as the zephyr, like zephyr that throws
Its sweets on the sweet-breathing May.
— Edward Lovibond.

Mild as the call of spring to buried flowers. — George Mac-Henry.

Mild as milk. — James C. Mangan.

Mild as an evening heaven around Hesper bright. — George Meredith.

Mild as the April eve. — William J. Mickle.

Mild, as when Zephyrus or Flora breathes. — Milton.

Mild, like the hour of the setting sun. — Ossian.

Mild as the moon's light. — John Payne.

Mild as the lamb. — Ambrose Philips.

Mild as the moon. — J. R. Planché.

Mild as May. — Pope.

Mild as op'ning gleams of promised heav'n. — Ibid.

Mild as the murmurs of the Bird of Woe. — Mrs. Mary Robinson.

Mild as a dove. — Shakespeare.

Mild as the opening morn of May. — William Shenstone.

As Juno mild. — Sir Philip Sidney.

Mild as the murmuring of Hymettian bees
And honied as their harvest.
— Swinburne.

Mild as very sleep. — Ibid.

All mild and gentle as the silver moon
Sitting heaven's blue aboon.
— Esaias Tegner.

Mild as the kisses of connubial love. — Henry Kirke White.

Mild — *continued.*

Mild as the murmurs of the moonlight wave. — IBID.

Mild as the opening morn's serenest ray. — WILLIAM WHITEHEAD.

Mild as the close of summer's softest day. — IBID.

Mild as Mr. Tupper's precepts. — WILLIAM WINTER.

Mince.

Mince like a maiden bride. — NICHOLAS BRETON.

Minced like a nestling's food. — BAYARD TAYLOR.

Mind.

Old minds are like old horses; you must exercise them if you wish to keep them in working order. — JOHN ADAMS.

Little minds, like weak liquors, are soonest soured. — ANON.

The mind is like a sheet of white paper in this, that the impressions it receives the oftenest, and retains the longest, are black ones. — EDWIN ARNOLD.

The mind's action is like that of an engineer who works under water. He goes down in a diving-bell, and is hidden. The work progresses, and the structure rises, but it does not show above water at all. It is there, but it is deep-seated and concealed. — HENRY WARD BEECHER.

Successful minds work like a gimlet, to a single point. — C. N. BOVÉE.

Our minds are like certain vehicles, — when they have little to carry they make much noise about it, but when heavily loaded they run quietly. — ELIHU BURRITT.

A wise man's mind, as Seneca holds, is like the state of the world above the Moon, ever serene. — ROBERT BURTON.

The mind, that broods o'er guilty woes,
Is like the Scorpion girt by fire,
In circle narrowing as it glows,
The flames around their captive close.
. . . . . .
So writhes the mind Remorse hath riven,
Unfit for earth, undoom'd for heaven,
Darkness above, despair beneath,
Around it flame, within it death.
— BYRON.

A weak mind is like a microscope, which magnifies trifling things, but cannot receive great ones. — CHESTERFIELD.

The mind, when imbued with the lessons of wisdom, is like a charioteer; for it restrains the desires implanted in us, and brings us back to virtue. — DEMOPHILUS.

His mind was like a bottle, extended with the delectable liquor of observation. — DRYDEN.

The mind is like a trunk. If well packed, it holds almost everything; if ill packed, next to nothing. — JULIUS C. HARE.

Minds like fine pictures are by distance proved,
And objects proper, only as removed.
— WALTER HARTE.

Sick minds are like sick men that burn with fevers,
Who when they drink, please but a present taste,
And after bear a more impatient fit.
— BEN JONSON.

The mind of man is like the sea, which is neither agreeable to the beholder nor the voyager, in a calm or in a storm, but is so to both when a little agitated by gentle gales; and so the mind, when moved by soft and easy passions or affections. — CHARLES LAMB.

For as the precious stone Autharsitis beeing throwne into the fyre looketh blacke and halfe dead, but being cast into the water glistreth like the Sunne beames : so the precious minde of man once put into the flame of loue, is as it were vglye, and loseth his vertue, but sprinckled with the water of wisdome, and detestation of such fond delightes, it shineth like the golden rayes of Phœbus. — LYLY.

The mind is like the eye, for, though it may see all other objects, it cannot see itself, and therefore cannot judge of itself. — PHILO.

As land is improved by sowing it with various seeds, so is the mind by exercising it with different studies. — PLINY.

To the mind's eye things will appear,
At distance through an artful glass,
But bring the flattering objects near,
They're all a senseless gloomy mass.
— MATTHEW PRIOR.

Our minds are like our stomachs ; they are whetted by the change of their food, variety supplies both with fresh appetite. — QUINTILIAN.

Thy mind is like a mirror swung in space,
And whirling on a thread. Now it reflecteth
The heavens, and now the earth. Now doth the lightning
Write hieroglyphs upon it, and anon
Some deep-sea monster glooms it with his bulk. — AMÉLIE RIVES.

As the soil, however rich it may be, cannot be productive without culture, so the mind without cultivation can never produce good fruit. — SENECA.

For 'tis the mind that makes the body rich ;
And as the sun breaks through the darkest clouds,
So honor peereth in the meanest habit.
What, is the jay more precious than the lark,
Because his feathers are more beautiful. — SHAKESPEARE.

The chaste mind, like a polished plane, may admit foul thoughts, without receiving their tincture. — STERNE.

Mindless.

Mindless as the beasts that browse. — VIOLET FANE.

Mingle.

Mingled . . . like the fragments of a couple of broken lantern slides swept up together. — R. C. BATES.

Our two spirits mingled like scents from varying roses that remain one sweetness, nor can ever more be singled. — GEORGE ELIOT.

Mingled in these vulgar controversies like a knight of romance among caitiff brawlers. — HENRY HALLAM.

Mingle into one,
Like blended streams that make one music as they run. — HOOD.

They had mingled their hearts together as they grew up, as two saplings planted near, mingle their branches as they become trees. — HUGO.

Mingle . . . like sunshine and rain. — WILLIAM KNOX.

Mingling foes,
Like billows dash'd in conflict.
— JAMES MONTGOMERY.

My soul is commingled with thine,
As water is mingled with wine.
— ORIENTAL.

Meet and mingle like human fear and hope. — A. J. RYAN.

Mirth.

Mirth is like a flash of lightning that breaks through a gloom of clouds and glitters for a moment; cheerfulness keeps up a daylight in the mind and fills it with a steady and perpetual serenity. — ADDISON.

Mirth, like light, will all too often take its birth mid darkness and decay. — MISS LANDON.

Mirthful.

Mirthful as an undertaker's mute. — BALZAC.

Mischievous.

Mischievous as a kitten. — ANON.

Mischievous as a monkey. — BALZAC.

Mischievous as a marmoset. — OUIDA.

Miser.

The wealth of misers, like the evening sun sinking below the horizon, contributes nothing to the enjoyment of mankind. — DEMOPHILUS.

The miser swimming in gold seems to me like a thirsty fish. — J. PETIT-SENN.

Miserable.

Miserable as a frost-bitten apple. — ANON.

Miserable as the fifth act of a tragedy. — IBID.

Misfortune.

Misfortunes are like the creations of Cadmus, they destroy one another. — BULWER-LYTTON.

Mishap.

Mishaps are like knives, that either serve us or cut us, as we grasp them by the blade or the handle. — LOWELL.

Mistress.

Mistresses, like friends, are lost by letting 'em handle your money. — VANBRUGH.

Mistresses are like books. If you pore upon them too much, they doze you, and make you unfit for company; but if used discreetly you are the fitter for conversation by 'em. — WILLIAM WYCHERLEY.

Misty.

Misty as a shape in a dream. — GEORGE MEREDITH.

Mix.

Mix, like bards, the useful with the sweet. — JOEL BARLOW.

Mix as mists do. — ROBERT BROWNING.

Mixed together like jackstraws. — IRVIN S. COBB.

Are mixed as the mist of some devilish dream. — KIPLING.

Mix them up
Like self-destroying poisons in one cup. — SHELLEY.

Moan.

Moaned like a chafed spirit warring with its lot. — ANON.

Moaned like a dismal autumn wind. — T. B. ALDRICH.

Moaned like a drinker in grievous plight. — ARABIAN NIGHTS.

Moan like the doves. — ASSYRIAN.

Moans like a dying hound. — HENRY H. BROWNELL.

Moans . . . like wind through ill-shut casements. — E. B. BROWNING.

Moan like nightbirds. — CARLYLE.

Moan, like the voice of one who crieth
In the wilderness alone.
— LONGFELLOW.

Moaned like some stricken thing . . . strangled with its own despair. — DON MARQUIS.

Moaning, like the voices of spirits departing in pain. — OWEN MEREDITH.

A wild and desolate moan,
As a sea heart-broken on the hard brown stone.
— JOAQUIN MILLER.

Moans like a tender infant in its cradle,
Whose nurse had left it.
— OTWAY.

Moan, like me who hath lost the last and best. — T. BUCHANAN READ.

Moan— *continued.*

As running rivers moan
On their course alone,
So I moan
Left alone. — C. G. ROSSETTI.

Moan like the waves at set of autumn days. — ELIZA SCUDDER.

The forest moans and vibrates like a vast Æolian harp. — JOHN C. VAN DYKE.

Moaned . . . like a dirge. — FRANK WATERS.

Mob.

The mob, like the ocean, is very seldom agitated without some cause superior and exterior to itself; but . . . both are capable of doing the greatest mischief after the cause which first set them in motion has ceased to act. — C. C. COLTON.

Mobile.

Mobile as humanity. — DUMAS, FILS.

Mock.

Mocks as whom the fen-fire leads
By the creed-wrought faith of faithless souls that mock their doubts with creeds. — SWINBURNE.

Modern.

Modern as an arc light. —AMY LESLIE.

Modest.

Modest as a squash. — ANON.

Modest and shy as a nun. — WILLIAM CULLEN BRYANT.

In her modesty, like a star among earthly lights. — CARLYLE.

Modest as the violet in dewy dell. — F. A. FAHY.

Modest as a maid a-christening. — CHARLES MACKLIN.

Modest as justice. — SHAKESPEARE.

Modest as morning when she coldly eyes
The youthful Phœbus. — IBID.

Modest as the dove. — IBID.

Modest as a primrose. — ELIZABETH S. P. WARD.

Modest as a flower. — ELLA WHEELER WILCOX.

Moist.

Moist as a cold toad's skin. — ANON.

Moist as a desert with dew. — SWINBURNE.

Molten.

Molten as lead. — SWINBURNE.

Momentary.

Momentary as a sound. — SHAKESPEARE.

Monarchy.

Monarchy is like a work of nature, well composed both to grow and continue. — BACON.

A monarchy is like a man-of-war — bad shots between wind and water hurt it exceedingly; there is danger of capsizing. But democracy is a raft. You cannot easily upturn it. It is a wet place, but it is a pretty safe one. — JOSEPH COOK.

Money.

Public money is like holy water: every one helps himself to it. — ANON.

Money is like manure; of very little use unless it be spread. — BACON.

Munny is like promises, easier maid than kept. — JOSH BILLINGS.

Money is like the manna of the wilderness: sweet and wholesome if it is gathered and used by faith each day: breeding worms if hoarded by doubt. — HUGH O. PENTICOST.

Money is like whiskey: a certain quantity of it improves the condition, but too much brings about bestiality. — CHANNING POLLOCK.

A man without money is like a ship without sails. — DUTCH PROVERB.

Money — *continued.*

His money comes from him like drops of blood. — JOHN RAY'S "HANDBOOK OF PROVERBS."

A man without money is like a bird without wings; if he soars he falls to the ground and dies. — ROUMANIAN PROVERB.

Monotonous.

Monotonous as the dress of charity children. — ANON.

Monotonous as mutton. — RICHARD LE GALLIENNE.

Monotonous as the sea. — RICHARD M. MILNES.

Mood.

Moody as a poet. — THOMAS SHADWELL.

Mope.

Mope like birds that are changing feather. — LONGFELLOW.

Mopish.

I am as mopish as if I were married and lived in a provincial town. — G. H. LEWES.

Moral.

Moral as peppermint. — ANON.

Moral as the tents of Abraham. — W. H. MALLOCK.

Morals.

In morals as in metals . . . you cannot work gold without supporting it with alloy. — OUIDA.

Mortal.

Mortal as an old man's life. — SHAKESPEARE.

Mortality.

Mortality
Weighs heavily on me like unwilling sleep. — KEATS.

Motionless.

Motionless as a corpse. — ANON.

Motionless as a figure cut in stone. — IBID.

Motionless as a monument. — IBID.

Motionless, like the sun over Avalon. — WILLIAM ARCHER.

Motionless as the fixed rock. — EDWIN ARNOLD.

Motionless as a babe asleep. — ALFRED AUSTIN.

Motionless as a tombstone. — R. D BLACKMORE.

Motionless as a statue. — FERNAN CABALLERO.

Motionless, like one who sees but does not understand. — DUMAS, PÈRE.

Motionless as a king's mummy in a catacomb. — FLAUBERT.

Motionless, like a woman of wax. — MAURICE HEWLETT.

Motionless, as if thunder-stricken. — HUGO.

Standing as motionless as pillar set
To guide a wanderer in a pathless waste. — JEAN INGELOW.

Postured motionless,
Like natural sculpture in cathedral cavern. — KEATS.

Stood motionless . . . like some exquisite chrys-elephantine statue, all ivory and gold. — CHARLES KINGSLEY.

Motionless as a spectre. — GUY DE MAUPASSANT.

Motionless as the distant purple hills
On which the shadows of the white clouds rest.
— R. K. MUNKITTRICK.

As motionless as death. — THOMAS L. PEACOCK.

Motionless, like a bereaved creature. — CHARLES READE.

Motionless, as if she were seeking in her mind the explanation of some mystery or the key of some riddle. — JOSÉ SELGAS.

Motionless — *continued.*

Motionless,
As a stone above a grave.
— WILLIAM W. STORY.

Stood motionless, as if transfixed. — IVAN VAZOV.

Motionless as a pool. — VIRGIL.

Motionless as an idol. — WHITTIER.

Motionless as rocks. — IBID.

Mottled.

Mottled and dappled like an April trout. — ANON.

Mount.

Mounts as a soul from flesh escaping. — BLISS CARMAN.

Mounting like a flame. — C. G. ROSSETTI.

Mourn.

Mourned like a turtle. — ANON.

She mourns, like the sweet wind grieving in
The pines on an autumn night.
— BARRY CORNWALL.

Mournful and low, like the song of the tomb. — OSSIAN.

Mourn like a turtle-dove but late robb'd of his mate. — GEORGE SANDYS.

Mourn like a sick child. — ALEXANDER SMITH.

Mourn like a boy beaten. — SWINBURNE.

Mourn as a dove. — OLD TESTAMENT.

Mourn'd
Like a living thing distressed.
— WHITTIER.

Mournful.

Mournful as the grave. — ANON.

Mournful as the rhythm of the seas. — IBID.

A voice as mournful as the dying light in the west — for a vague reminder of Death is divinely set in the heavens, and the sun above gives the same warning that is given here on earth by the flowers and the bright insects of the day. — BALZAC.

Mournful — but mournful of another's crime,
She look'd as if she sat by Eden's door,
And grieved for those who could return no more.
— BYRON.

Mournful as . . . Memnon's harp. — KEATS.

Mournful as the dancing of dead leaves. — GERALD MASSEY.

Mournful as the dead below. — R. M. MILNES.

Mournful, like the voice of one who raves. — CELIA THAXTER.

Mouth (Noun).

He had a mouth like a whirlpool. — ANON.

Her mouth turned up voluptuously like the antique masks of Erigone. — IBID.

A mouth as it were Solomon's seal. — ARABIAN NIGHTS.

That little mouth is like in this,
The rose-bush that so fair is,
For sly envenomed serpents hiss
In dark leaves where their lair is.
— HEINRICH HEINE.

A dainty mouth like a crimson rose. — IBID.

A mouth like the whale that swallowed a whole fleet. — THOMAS LODGE.

Mouth that looked like a red gash from a sabre cut. — GUY DE MAUPASSANT.

His mouth opened like the end of a sawmill. — EDGAR W. NYE.

Mouth was like a red rose rinsed with rain. — JAMES WHITCOMB RILEY.

Mouth tremulous light as a seabird's motion oversea. — SWINBURNE.

Mouth — *continued.*

Her mouth
Was as a rose athirst that pants for
drouth. — IBID.

Red mouth like a venomous flower. — IBID.

Mouth sweeter than cherries. — IBID.

A red mouth like a wound. — ARTHUR SYMONS.

As a pomegranate, cut in twain,
White-seeded, is her crimson mouth.
— OSCAR WILDE.

Mouth (Verb).

Mouths a sentence, as curs mouth a bone. — CHURCHILL.

Mouthed, like a chawbacon. — CHARLES READE.

Move.

Moving constantly, like the spheres. — ANON.

Gently she moved in the calmness of
beauty,
Moved as the bough to the light breeze
of morning. — ARABIAN.

Moving like heaven still in the self-same moving. — PHINEAS FLETCHER.

A wizard wind did faintly move,
Like a whisper through a dream.
— OWEN MEREDITH.

When everything moves equally, nothing moves apparently : as on a ship. — PASCAL.

Moving, like a skeptic's thought,
Cut of nowhere into naught.
— JAMES WHITCOMB RILEY.

Moved one like the finest eloquence. — ALEXANDER SMITH.

Moveless.

Moveless as a worm beneath a stone
Which some one's stumbling foot has
spurned aside.
— E. B. BROWNING.

Moveless, as a long-forgotten lyre
Suspended in the solitary dome
Of some mysterious and deserted fane.
— SHELLEY.

Muddy.

Muddy as a little pigeon-toed drummer after a long march. — GEORGE COLMAN, THE YOUNGER.

Muddy as sheep-dogs. — HENRI MURGER.

Muffled.

Muffled and dumb like barefoot dervishes. — EMERSON.

Multiply.

Multiply in swarms, like vermin. — HUGO.

Their forms and features multiplied,
As the reflection of a light
Between two burnished mirrors gleams,
Or lamps upon a bridge at night
Stretch on and on before the sight,
Till the long vista endless seems.
— LONGFELLOW.

Multiply in seed like Abraham. — RABELAIS.

Multiplied like grasshoppers upon the face of the land. — IBID.

Multiply as the bud of the field. — OLD TESTAMENT.

Multiply thy seed as the stars of heaven. — IBID.

Multiply like insects in the sun. — CHARLES WAGNER.

Multitude.

Applause
Waits on success ; the fickle multitude,
Like the straw that floats along the
stream,
Glide with the current still and follow
fortune. — FRANKLIN.

Even as the sand that is upon the sea shore in multitude. — OLD TESTAMENT.

As the stars of heaven for multitude. — IBID.

Multitudinous.

Multitudinous tongues, like the whispering leaves of a wind-stirred oak. — HAWTHORNE.

Like coral insects multitudinous. — JEAN INGELOW.

Multitudinous as the desert sand
Borne on the storm. — SHELLEY.

Mum.

Mum as an oyster. — ANON.

Mumble

Mumble as if he were at his matins. — THOMAS LODGE.

Murder.

Murder, like talent, seems occasionally to run in families. — G. H. LEWES.

Murderous.

Murderous as a cannon ball. — ANON.

Murmur (Noun).

A vague and monotonous murmur, like that of the waves on a shore where the wind dies away with approaching night. — ANON.

Murmurs passed along the valleys, like the banshee's lonely croon. — IBID.

A murmur like the sough of bees
Hidden among the noon-stilled linden
trees. — LOWELL.

A deep sullen murmur . . . like the moaning noise that goes before the whirlwind on the deep. — MACAULAY.

Murmurs, like the sea's, dying uncomprehended. — T. BUCHANAN READ.

A murmur like the winds that break
Into green waves the prairie's grassy
lake. — WHITTIER.

Murmur (Verb).

Murmurs like a dreaming sea. — ANON.

Murmuring like bees at honey-time. — IBID.

Murmuring like the sound of the sea. — ROBERT HUGH BENSON.

Murmured like a shell. — R. D. BLACKMORE.

Murmur like a hive. — E. B. BROWNING.

Murmur like the moan of far-off seas. — ROBERT BUCHANAN.

They murmureden as dooth a swarm of been. — CHAUCER.

Murmured like a whispering priest. — AUBREY DE VERE.

Murmur like the gales of spring. — IBID.

Murm'ring they move, as when old ocean roars. — HOMER (POPE).

Murmured like the humming of a bee. — HOOD.

Murmur like the wind in the leaves. — MARY JOHNSTON.

Murmur as of waves upon a seashore. — LONGFELLOW.

Murmur like the rustle of dead leaves. — IBID.

Murmuring to her ears
Like to a falling stream, which, passing slow,
Is wont to nourish sleep and quietness.
— SIR WALTER RALEIGH.

Murmured like seas that are tempesting. — C. G. ROSSETTI.

Low like dirge-wail or requiem they murmured. — D. G. ROSSETTI.

Murmurs . . . like a bell that calls to prayer. — JOHN RUSKIN.

Murmured like a noontide bee. — SHELLEY.

Murmuring like the ocean roar. — IBID.

Murmured . . . like breathings of a shell. — ELIZABETH O. SMITH.

Murmur . . . as when at twilight hour the summer breeze moves o'er the elmy vale. — SOUTHEY.

Murmur — *continued.*

Murmur like a shell. — Robert Louis Stevenson.

Murmurs as who talks in dreams with death. — Swinburne.

Murmur like the wind among the trees. — S. G. Tallentyre.

The verse murmurs . . . like the moan of doves in immemorial elms. — Tennyson.

A veiled stream murmurs like thoughts of Heaven in a dream. — Thomas Wade.

Murmurous.

Murmurous as the August bees
That fill the forest deep
Around the roots of trees.
— Arthur Symons.

Muscle.

Muscles as tense as those of the tiger waiting for his leap. — Albion W. Tourgée.

Muscular.

Muscular as dogmeat. — Rex Beach.

Muse.

The muse, like mortal females, may be woo'd :
In turns she'll seem a Paphian, or a prude ;
Fierce as a bride when first she feels affright,
Mild as the same upon the second night ;
Wild as the wife of alderman or peer,
Now for his grace, and now a grenadier.
— Byron.

Music.

Music at meals is like a carbuncle set in gold, or a signet of an emerald highly burnished. — Anon.

The music of Carryl was like the memory of joys that are past, pleasant and mournful to the soul. — James Macpherson.

Rippling music like the sweet babble of brook over stones. — Harriet M. Miller.

Music as sweet as the music which seems
Breathed softly and faint in the ear of our dreams. — Whittier.

Musical.

Musical as brooks that run o'er yellow shallows in the sun. — T. B. Aldrich.

Musical as rain drops on a roof. — Anon.

Musical as a stream in Bunyan's delectable Mountains. — Ibid.

Voices musical as birds or brooks. — Aubrey De Vere.

Musically as the pine cone to the breeze. — George Gilfillan.

Musical as the holes of a flute without the flute. — O. Henry.

Bells, as musical
As those that, on the golden-shafted trees
Of Eden, shake in the eternal breeze.
— Thomas Moore.

Sweet and musical as bright Apollo's lute strung with his hair. — Shakespeare.

Mutable.

Mutable as the wind. — Richard D. Stoker.

Mutable as sand. — Swinburne.

Mute.

Mute as a funeral procession. — Anon.

Mute as a poker. — Ibid.

Mute as death. — Ibid.

Mute as fate. — Ibid.

Mute as Mumchance, who was hanged for saying nothing. — Ibid.

Mute as the Tiber. — Ibid.

Mute as fishes. — Balzac.

Mute — *continued.*

Mute as mice. — EMILY BRONTË.

Mute as snow. — E. B. BROWNING.

Mute as the dead. — CAMPBELL.

Mute, like one who pondered on strange and unaccountable events. — J. FENIMORE COOPER.

Mute as the grave. — ABRAHAM COWLEY.

Mute as the wine we drink. — BARTHOLOMEW DOWLING.

As mute as the tomb. — DUMAS, PÈRE.

As mute and motionless as statues. — GOLDSMITH.

Stood mute as silence was in Heaven. — MILTON.

Soldiers . . . as mute as on parade. — MISS MULOCK.

Mute, like a flame. — D. G. ROSSETTI.

Mute as if I tongueless were. — GEORGE SANDYS.

Mute as fox's 'mongst mangling hounds. — SIR WALTER SCOTT.

Mute as the grave. — IBID.

As mute as Pygmalion. — JAMES SMITH.

Mute as a maiden. — SWINBURNE.

Mute as the mouth which felt death's wave o'erflow it. — IBID.

As mute as Jedorough Tower. — WORDSWORTH.

Mutely.

Mutely as birds skim through air. — BULWER-LYTTON.

Mutter.

Muttering like the murmur of hurried priest dispatching a prayer. — HUGO.

Mutter like sullen bulls. — KINGSLEY.

He sits muttering in his beard. His voice
Is like a river flowing underground.
— LONGFELLOW.

Muttering like smoked bees. — SWINBURNE.

Mutters like a dim despair. — FRANK WATERS.

Myriad.

Myriad as the leaves by Autumn sent,
Up forest aisles and down.
— MARGARET E. EASTER.

Mysterious.

Mysterious as a rose leaf. — ANON.

Mysterious as a sphinx. — IBID.

Mysterious as a star. — IBID.

Mysterious as the sea. — IBID.

Misterious as an echo. — JOSH BILLINGS.

Mystery.

As great a mystery as the serpent-crest of the king's crown on the pillars of Egypt. — ANON.

Mystical.

Mystical . . . like a singing in a dream. — E. B. BROWNING.

Mystical as an astrological symbol. — RICHARD LE GALLIENNE.

Mystical as some dreamland arched with unfathomed azure. — JAMES WHITCOMB RILEY.

Myth.

As much of a myth as Lohengrin. — ANON.

Mythical as the glass of blood quaffed by Sombreuil's daughter. — THOMAS WATSON.

N

Naked.

Naked as an Indian's back. — ANON.

Naked as night. — IBID.

Naked as the graces. — IBID.

Naked as a frog. — BEAUMONT AND FLETCHER.

Naked as a flower. — MADISON CAWEIN.

As naked . . . as a corowne withe out stones. — CHAUCER.

Poor and naked as a fakir. — JOSEPH CONRAD.

Like winter-earth, naked. — COWLEY.

As naked as Norfolk dumpling. — JOHN DAY.

Naked as a worm. — DUMAS, PÈRE.

Naked as a peeled apple. — O. W. HOLMES.

Naked as a nedle. — LANGLAND.

Naked as my nail. — MASSINGER.

The country is naked as the sea. — JULES SANDEAU.

Naked as the vulgar air. — SHAKESPEARE.

As naked as their mothers bore them. — SWIFT.

Naked as apes. — VOLTAIRE.

Naked as a Tower. — WORDSWORTH.

Name.

Women's good name, O my lady, is like curded milk, the least dust fouleth it ; and like glass, which, if it be cracked, may not be mended. — ARABIAN NIGHTS.

A good name is like a precious ointment ; it filleth all around about, and will not easily away ; for the odors of ointments are more durable than those of flowers. — BACON.

Names like jewels flashing the night of time. — JOSEPH CONRAD.

A man's name is not like a mantle, which merely hangs about him, and which one perchance may safely twitch and pull, but a perfectly fitting garment, which like the skin has grown over and over him, at which one cannot rake and scrape without injuring the man himself. — GOETHE.

A great name without merit is like an epitaph on a coffin. — MADAME DE PUISIEUX.

A good name is better than precious ointment ; and the day of death than the day of one's birth. — OLD TESTAMENT.

A good name is like sweet-smelling ointment. — IBID.

Nameless.

Nameless as God. — HUGO.

Narrow.

The nations narrow and expand,
As tides that ebb, or tides that flow.
— LORD DE TABLEY.

Nasty.

Nasty as the opaque whiteness of boiled veal. — ANON.

Nation.

Nations, like individuals, are powerful in the degree that they command the sympathies of their neighbors. — C. N. BOVÉE.

I have seen some nations like overloaded asses,
Kick off their burdens, meaning the higher classes. — BYRON.

Every nation seems to me like a plant, of which the lower class is the root, the middle class the stem, and the upper class the flower. — PIERRE DE COULEVAIN.

Nations, like individuals, live and die ; but civilization cannot die. — GIUSEPPE MAZZINI.

Nation — *continued.*

A warring nation, like an orator, should know when to stop. — NEW REPUBLIC.

Like men, nations are purified and strengthened by trials. — SAMUEL SMILES.

Natural.

Natural as the breeze
That stirs amongst the forest trees.
— SARAH F. ADAMS.

Natural as for ivy to climb a tree. — ANON.

Natural as life. — IBID.

Natural as milk to a calf. — IBID.

Natural as nature. — IBID.

As natural as that a genius should wear queer clothes. — IBID.

Natural as the Marseillaise to a French riot. — IBID.

Natural as whooping to owls. — IBID.

'Tis as natural for women to pride themselves in fine clothes as 'tis for a peacock to spread his tail. — IBID.

Natural to die as to be born. — BACON.

Natural as grinning to a hyena. — J. R. BARTLETT'S "DICTIONARY OF AMERICANISMS."

Natral as the bee tow the flower. — JOSH BILLINGS.

Natural as dancing bears to a bagpiper. — TOM BROWN.

Natural as to eat, sleep, and wear a nightcap. — JOHN FORD.

Natural as the love of life in the merest dumb thing that knows nothing of ideas, of Country, realms, and policies, nothing of war. — JOHN GALSWORTHY.

Natural as bird-notes. — HAWTHORNE.

Natural as daylight. — IBID.

Natural as primping at a looking-glass. — O. W. HOLMES.

Natural as dunghill steam. — GEORGE MEREDITH.

Natural as sunlight on the sea. — OSCAR WILDE.

Natural as light. — N. P. WILLIS.

Natural as dreams to feverish sleep. — WORDSWORTH.

Naturally.

Naturally as a bird warbles in May. — ANON.

As naturally as a chestnut bursts its pod, and a chicken its shell. — IBID.

Naturally as fungus grows out of a dying tree. — IBID.

Naturally as pigs squeak. — SAMUEL BUTLER.

As naturally as the descendant from a line of suicides thinks of killing himself. — HAWTHORNE.

Naturally as the bleating of a sheep. — WILLIAM HAZLITT.

Naturally as needles turn to the loadstone. — FRANCES LITTLE.

As naturally as bees swarm and follow their queen. — HENRY D. THOREAU.

Nature.

Nature, like man, sometimes weeps for gladness. — BEACONSFIELD.

Fine natures are like fine poems, — a glance at the first two lines suffices for a guess into the beauty that waits you if you read on. — BULWER-LYTTON.

Our nature is like the sea, which gains by the flow of the tide in one place what it has lost by the ebb in another. — SIR RICHARD CECIL.

Nature, like liberty, is but restrained
By the same laws which first herself
ordained. — POPE.

Nature — *continued.*

Nature, like oil, will rise uppermost. — JAMES RALPH.

Nature, like a loving mother, is ever trying to keep land and sea, mountain and valley, each in its place, to hush the angry winds and waves, balance the extremes of heat and cold, of rain and drought, that peace, harmony, and heart may reign supreme. — ELIZABETH CADY STANTON.

The finest qualities of our nature, like the bloom on fruits, can be preserved only by the most delicate handling. — HENRY D. THOREAU.

Naughty.

Naughty as Gautick, where the devil struck for shorter hours. — ANON.

Near.

Near as two ha'pennies for a penny. — ANON.

Near as one second is to another. — IBID.

Near as the bark to [the] tree. — WILLIAM CAMDEN'S "REMAINS."

As neere is Fancie to Beautie, as the pricke to the rose, as the stalke to the rynde, as the earth to the roote. — LYLY.

More near and near,
Like doves about a dovecote, wheeling round. — TENNYSON.

Nearsighted.

Near-sighted as a mole. — ANON.

Neat.

Neat as a nail. — ANON.

Neat as a new pin. — IBID.

Neat as ninepence. — IBID.

Neat as wax. — IBID.

Neat as fresh spring herbs. — GEORGE ELIOT.

Neat as wax-work. — HENRY J. FINN.

Neat as a postman's knock. — GEORGE MEREDITH.

Necessary.

As necessary as breathing is to live. — ANON.

Necessary as for the butterfly to escape from the worm to become a butterfly. — IBID.

As necessary as skin to the apple. — IBID.

As necessary as Churches. — ROBERT BURTON.

Necessary . . . as friction in mechanics. — C. C. COLTON.

Necessary as one's digestion. — THOMAS HEYWOOD.

Necessary . . . as rakehells in an army. — JOHN WEBSTER.

Necessary . . . as the gargoyle on the spire and the high altar are necessary parts of a Gothic cathedral. — H. G. WELLS.

Neck.

Her neck is like the neck of doe. — ARABIAN NIGHTS.

A neck like an ingot of silver. — IBID.

A neck as white as whale's bone,
Compased with a lace of stone.
— ROBERT GREENE.

Her neck like a stately tower,
Where love himself imprisoned lies,
To watch for glances, every hour,
From her divine and sacred eyes.
— THOMAS LODGE.

Thy neck is like the swan, and fair as the pearl. — LOVER.

Her snowie neck lyke to a marble towre. — SPENSER.

Thy neck is as a tower of ivory. — OLD TESTAMENT.

Thy neck is like the tower of David builded for an armoury, whereon ther. hang a thousand bucklers, all shields of mighty men. — IBID.

Need.

Need . . . as pansies need the dew. — ANON.

Need a wife as much as a dog does a side-pocket. — GROSE'S "DICTIONARY OF THE VULGAR TONGUE."

Needful.

Needful as the sun. — GRANT ALLEN.

As needful to the forest-tree as sun and gentle shower. — TUPPER.

Neglected.

Neglected, as the moon by day. — SWIFT.

Negligence.

Wanton negligence is like a net,
Which for unwary feet the powers have set. — ANON.

Nervous.

Nervous as a cat that hears a mouse in the wall. — ANON.

Nervous as a witch. — IBID.

Nervous as a watch. — F. MARION CRAWFORD.

Nervous as a mouse. — G. B. SHAW.

New.

New as day. — BEN JONSON.

New as sight. — FRANCIS THOMPSON.

Newspaper.

A newspaper, like a theatre, must mainly owe its continuance in life to the fact that it pleases many persons; and in order to please many persons it will, unconsciously perhaps, respond to their several tastes, reflect their various qualities, and reproduce their views. — WILLIAM WINTER.

Nice.

Nice as Marie Antoinette playing milkmaid. — ANON.

As nice as ninepence. — IBID.

Nyse as a nonne's henne. — SIR THOMAS WILSON.

Nimble.

Nimble as a bee on a tar-barrel. — ANON.

Nimble as a cow in a cage. — IBID.

Nimble as a lizard. — IBID.

Nimble as an eel. — IBID.

As nimble as a wireless spark, that hurdles the ether, pole-vaults the oceans and circles the ends of the earth in a flash. — IBID.

Nimble as ninepence. — IBID.

Nimble as roes. — CARLYLE.

Nimble as thought. — CERVANTES.

Nimble as quicksilver. — GEORGE COLMAN, THE YOUNGER.

Nimble, like a shadow. — JOHN FLETCHER.

Nimble as a hare. — SWIFT.

Nimble-fingered as a harper. — JOHN TAYLOR.

Nimble as quarrel from a crossbow shot. — FRANCOIS VILLON.

Nimbly.

Nimbly as juggler's balls from cup to cup. — JAMES PUCKLE.

Nod.

Nodded like a plume. —DICKENS.

Nodded in bright array, like hollyhocks heavy with blossoms. — LONGFELLOW.

Nodded her head like a mandarin. — CHARLES READE.

Nodded at each other like a congregation of Anabaptists. — SMOLLETT.

Noise.

To catch a squirrel make a noise like a nut. — ANON.

As much fuss and noise as a one-legged man falling down stairs. — IBID.

Make noises like a drunken Zulu trying to sing a Swedish folk song. — IRVIN S. COBB.

Noise — *continued.*

Make a noise like an assessment. — O. HENRY.

The noise was in the beast's belly like unto the questyng of thirty couple hounds. — THOMAS MALORY.

Noiseless.

Noiseless as a shadow. — ANON.

Noiseless as a lapwing. — IBID.

Noiseless as the circulation of the blood. — IBID.

Noiseless as the gathering storm before the tempest. — IBID.

Noiseless as the sunlight. — THOMAS ASHE.

Noiseless as a bright mist rolls down a hill. — CHARLOTTE BRONTË.

As noiseless as the trail of the swift snake and pilgrim snail. — T. G. HAKE.

Noiseless as night's soft shade. — AARON HILL.

Noiseless as fear in a wide wilderness. — KEATS.

Noiseless as the passing mountain rain. — IBID.

Noiseless as a black shadow. — KIPLING.

Noiseless . . . as the falling dew — GEORGE MAC-HENRY.

Noiseless as sleep. — T. BUCHANAN READ.

Noiseless as the years descend. — IBID.

Noiseless as the owlet's wing. — IBID.

Noiseless as if velvet-shod. — WHITTIER.

Noiselessly.

Noiselessly as the daylight comes back
when night is done,
And the crimson streak on an ocean's
cheek grows into the great sun.
— MRS. C. F. ALEXANDER.

Noiselessly as the springtime her crown
of verdure weaves,
And all the trees on all the hills open
their thousand leaves. — IBID.

As noiselessly as fairies' feet that press
The dewdropt grass.
— JOHN PAYNE.

Glide noiselessly as spirits of the night. — MICHAEL SCOTT.

Noisy.

Noisy as a boiler-shop. — ANON.

Noisy as a menagerie. — IBID.

Noisy as a creditors' meeting. — IBID.

Noisy as a flock of crow-blackbirds in the migration season. — IBID.

Noisy as a cookstove falling down stairs. — IBID.

Noisy as burial-howlers at full cry. — IBID.

Noisy as a living skeleton having a fit on a hardwood floor. — IBID.

Noisy as a dozen drums. — "FOUNDLING HOSPITAL FOR WIT."

Noisy as a kettle-drum. — O. W. HOLMES.

Noisy as at a fair. — GEORGE MEREDITH.

Noisy as women bathing in a river. — OSMANLI PROVERB.

As noisy as a hen with one chicken. — CHARLES READE.

Nonsense.

Nonsense : like to the thundering tone of unspoke speeches . . . like the fiery tombstone of a cabbage. — RICHARD CORBET.

Nonsense — like swimming on a carpet. — CHARLES READE.

Low nonsense is like that in the Barrel, which is altogether flat, tasteless and insipid. High nonsense is like that in the Bottle, which has in Reality no mere Strength and Spirit than the other, but frets, and flies, and bounces, and by the help of a little Wind that is got in it, imitates the Passions of much nobler liquor. — SIR RICHARD STEELE.

Nose.

Flabby nose like a brinjall, or egg-plant. — ARABIAN NIGHTS.

Nose like a promontory. — ROBERT BURTON.

Sharp nose like a sharp autumn evening, inclined to be frosty towards the end. — DICKENS.

With angry bottle nose,
Like a red cabbage rose.
— HORACE SMITH.

Notch.

Notched him like a carbonado. — SHAKESPEARE.

Novel.

A novel, like a bundle of wood, the more fagots it contains the greater its value. — BULWER-LYTTON.

A novel is typically as far removed from a play as a bird is from a fish . . . any attempt to transform one into the other is apt to result in a sort of flying-fish, a betwixt-and-between-thing. — BLISS PERRY.

A novel is the world's truth with a beautiful woman walking through it. — DAVID SWING.

Nude.

As nude as a raw oyster. — IRVIN S. COBB.

Numb.

Growing numb from the feet up,
Like one stepping deeper and deeper
into a stream of ice.
— EDGAR LEE MASTERS.

Numberless.

Numberless as are the dead. — P. J. BAILEY.

As numberless as they that at last will throng into the valley of Jehosaphat. — SIGMUND KRASINSKI.

Numberless as the gay motes that people the sunbeams. — MILTON.

Numerous.

Numerous as grains of silver in the bowels of the Rockies. — ANON.

Numerous as hailstones. — IBID.

Numerous as insects on the banks of the Nile. — IBID.

Numerous as maggots in a Cheshire cheese. — IBID.

Numerous as the breaths a patriarch has breathed. — IBID.

Numerous as the heads of Briareus. — IBID.

Numerous as the holes in the mantle of Diogenes. — IBID.

Numerous as the leaves of the forest. — IBID.

Numerous as the mouths of the Ganges. — IBID.

Numerous as the mouths of the Nile. — IBID.

Numerous as the pearls of morning-dew, which hang on herbs and flowers. — IBID.

As numerous as the stars of heaven
Are the fond hopes to mortals given.
— RICHARD DABNEY.

Numerous as sands upon the ocean shore. — PHILIP FRENEAU.

Numerous as unsold shares in an over-capitalized mining company. — F. C. GRIFFITH.

Num'rous as birds that o'er the forest play. — WALTER HARTE.

Numerous as the fish that sail the wide sea over. — ITALIAN LOVE SONG.

Numerous as shadows haunting fairily
The brain. — KEATS.

Numerous as a night of stars. — GERALD MASSEY.

Numerous as leaves that strew the autumnal gale. — SHELLEY.

Numerous as the hairs of his head. — PAUL WIGGINS.

Numerous as the writings of Ibid. — IBID.

O

Oaths.

Lovers' oaths are like mariners' prayers, uttered in extremity; but when the tempest is o'er, and that the vessel leaves tumbling, they fall from protesting to cursing. — JOHN WEBSTER.

Lovers' oaths are like fetters made of glass, that glisten fair, but couple no restraint. — ZENO.

Obdurate.

Obdurate as the grave. — WELSH BALLAD.

Obdurate as a bailiff where his dues are concerned. — BALZAC.

Obedience.

Passive obedience, like jumping off a castle-roof at the word of a czar. — EMERSON.

Obedient.

Obedient as the needle to the pole. — ANON.

Obedient as the yew to the tender's will. — IBID.

Obedient as a puppet. — GEORGE MEREDITH.

Obedient as the scabbard. — SHAKESPEARE.

Obediently.

Obediently bent as a willow wand. — OUIDA.

Obey.

Obeyed, as the she-wolf obeys her mate, with a growl. — HUGO.

Obey,
Like children under wise paternal sway.
— SOUTHEY.

Obligation.

Like an Irishman's obligation, all on one side. — G. F. NORTHALL.

Obnoxious.

Obnoxious as an alligator. — TOM TAYLOR.

Obscure (Adjective).

Obscure as Mallarmé. — ISRAEL ZANGWILL.

Obscure (Verb).

Obscured as with a veil. — ANON.

Obscurely.

Moves obscurely like the hand of fate. — AARON HILL.

Observations.

His observations are like a sieve, that lets the finer flour pass, and retains only the bran of things. — SAMUEL BUTLER.

Obsolete.

Obsolete as a Congress shoe. — ANON.

Obsolete as the coalscuttle bonnet and the hoopskirt. — IBID.

Obsolete as the Minotaur of Crete. — ANDREW LANG.

Obstinate.

Obstinate as a discharged school-director. — ANON.

Obstinate as a mule. — IBID.

Obstinate as death. — DRYDEN.

Obstinate as a pig, will neither lead nor drive. — THOMAS FULLER.

Obstinate . . . like the corpse in the fable, threatening the driver of the hearse with vengeance dire at every gate of fatal charnel-house. — SIGMUND KRASINSKI.

Obstinate as sin. — STRINDBERG.

Obtrusive.

Obtrusive as violent colors in a sober woof. — ANON.

Obvious.

Obvious as circus parade. — ANON.

Obvious as noonday sun. — ROBERT BROWNING.

Obvious — *continued.*

Obvious as stars on a clear night. — Alfred Henry Lewis.

Obvious as the midnight stars. — William J. Mickle.

Obvious as the gloss upon a new silk hat. — H. G. Wells.

Occupation.

As the Oxe is most apt for the plough, the Horse for the carte, and the hound for hunting: So ought men to chuse that occupation, and Trade of life, wherunto by nature they are most apt. As he which hath no house of his owne, wandereth here and there: So he which followeth no certaine Trade of life, must foolishly assay many sorts and chaunces. — Robert Cawdray's "A Treasurie or Store-house of Similes," 1600.

Odd.

Odd as the gesticulations and antic motions of the Satyrs. — Bacon.

Odorous.

Odorous as an angel's fresh-culled crown. — P. J. Bailey.

Odorous as a bouquet. — Hugo.

Odorous as incense gathered in the skies. — Richard Savage.

Off.

Off like a snip. — Anon.

Off, like chimera, glinting, flitting, gay and light and free. — Ibid.

Off like the lid of a pumpkin pie. — Ibid.

Off like a shot. — R. H. Barham.

Gang off like a squib or a cracker on a rejoicing night, in a noise and a stink, and are never heard of after. — Charles Macklin.

Offensive.

Offensive as the sun to weak eyes. — Anon.

Offensive . . . as a smell of cooking in the drawing room — Edith Wharton.

Office.

High office is like a pyramid: only two kinds of animals reach the summit, — reptiles and eagles. — D'Alembert.

Ogle.

Ogle like a provincial tenor. — Dumas, fils.

Oily.

Oily as the King's constable's lamp. — Dr. Johnson.

Old.

Old as a serpent. — Anon.

Old as Charing-Cross. — Ibid.

Old as circus jokes. — Ibid.

Old as creation. — Ibid.

Old as Eve. — Ibid.

Old as grey eternity. — Ibid.

Old as Hercules. — Ibid.

Old as Jericho. — Ibid.

Old as man. — Ibid.

Old as Methuselah.— Ibid.

Old as Nestor. — Ibid.

Old as poverty. — Ibid.

Old as Solomon. — Ibid.

Old as the age of stone. — Ibid.

Old as the hills. — Ibid.

Old as the Prophet Ezekiel. — Ibid.

Old as the rebuilding of Samaria. — Ibid.

Old as Trilobites. — Ibid.

Old as Zoroaster. — Ibid.

Old as Paradise. — Bulwer-Lytton.

Old as my little finger. — John Day.

As old as Fate. — Lord De Tabley.

Old as Time. — Austin Dobson.

Old — *continued.*

Ever old and ever new as love. — George Du Maurier.

Old as thought. — Elbert Hubbard.

Old as Priam. — Longfellow.

As old as human nature. — W. H. Mallock.

As old as heartache. — Meredith Nicholson.

As old as the itch. — Spanish Proverb.

Old as Sibylla. — Shakespeare.

Old as the shepherds. — G. B. Shaw.

Old as the earth is old. — Arthur Symons.

Wax old like a garment. — New Testament.

Old as hope. — Francis Thompson.

One.

In one,
As all the stars found utterance through
the sun. — Swinburne.

Oozing.

The damp oozed up through the thick brick floor like water through the sides of a Moorish jar. — Balzac.

Oozing like a leg of mutton on the spit. — T. F. Meagher.

Opaque.

Opaque as the sky. — Anon.

Open (Adjective).

Open as a smile. — E. B. Browning.

Open as shore to the sea. — Rose T. Cooke.

Open as the mid-day. — R. Davenport.

Open as the inn gates to receive guests. — George Gascoigne.

Wide open like the church portals when the bride and bridegroom enter. — O. W. Holmes.

Open as a plate. — George Meredith.

Minds open as a well-read book. — Charles Sangster.

Open as day for melting charity. — Shakespeare.

Open (Verb).

Opened inertly like the hands of the dead. — Hugo.

To lay oneself open like an oyster. — "A Knack to Knowe a Knave."

The dreadful truth was opened like a gulf. — James S. Knowles.

Open-mouthed.

Open-mouthed, like a crow at a walnut. — Balzac.

Open-mouthed as a young child
Wondering with a mind at fault.
— George Meredith.

Opera.

Old operas are like old bonnets: they ought to be remodelled, retrimmed from time to time. — A. E. Housman.

An opera, like a pillory, may be said,
To nail our ears down and expose our
head. — Young.

Opinion.

Opinions, like showers, are generated in high places. — C. C. Colton.

Social opinion is like a sharp knife. There are foolish people who regard it only with terror, and dare not touch or meddle with it; there are more foolish people, who, in rashness or defiance, seize it by the blade, and get cut and mangled for their pains; and there are wise people, who grasp it discreetly by the handle, and use it to carve out their own purposes. — Mrs. Jameson.

Opinions! — they are like the clothes we wear, which warm us, not with their heat, but with ours. — Walter Pater.

Opinion — *continued.*

Opinion is like a pendulum and obeys the same law. If it goes past the center of gravity on one side, it must go a like distance on the other; and it is only after a certain time that it finds the true point at which it can remain at rest. — SCHOPENHAUER.

Opinions, like fashions, always descend from those of quality to the middle sort; and thence to the vulgar, where they are dropped and vanish. — SWIFT.

Opportunity.

Lost opportunities are like precious jewels locked in the casket of regret, whose key is held in the unchanging past. — ANON.

Opportunitays, like eggs, don't kum but one at a time. — JOSH BILLINGS.

Opposed.

Opposed as the two poles. — ROBERT BROWNING.

Opposite.

Opposite as black and white. — ANON.

Opposite as fire and water. — IBID.

Opposite as oil and vinegar. — IBID.

Opposite as the poles. — IBID.

Opposite as day and darkness. — THOMAS DEKKER.

Opposite as the spheres. — HUGO.

Opposite as men's thoughts and their words. — LYLY.

Opposite as heaven and hell. — WORDSWORTH.

Opposition.

Opposition to a man in love is like oil to fire. — OUIDA.

Oppress.

Oppressed like foul air. — DICKENS.

Oppresses like a crown of gold. — ALEXANDER SMITH.

Oppression.

Ideal oppression . . . something like a fly serving spiders. — HUGO.

Oratory.

Oratory, like the drama, abhors lengthiness ; like the drama, it must keep doing. — BULWER-LYTTON.

Order.

Ordered as the morning light. — TUPPER.

Orderliness.

Painful orderliness, like a city procession under the conduct of the police. — GEORGE MEREDITH.

Orderly.

Orderly, like fresh veiled nuns. — BALZAC.

Oriental.

Oriental as a rug. — ANON.

Original.

Original as original sin. — ANON.

Ornamental.

Ornamental as a band-wagon. — ANON.

Ornamental as the signs of old London. — IBID.

Orthodoxy.

Orthodoxy combined with brilliancy is like glycerine combined with vaccine — it enables a little to go a very long way. — H. D. TRAILL.

Oscillated.

The earth . . . oscillated like a thin crust beneath our feet. — CHARLES R. DARWIN.

Out.

In and out like a needle through cloth. — ANON.

Come out like beetles when the lights are out. — J. M. BARRIE.

Out like a burnt taper's flame. — R. H. DANA.

Out — *continued.*

Go out, like an untended lamp. — Schiller.

Outpoured.

Abundance is outpoured
Like worship at a shrine adored.
— Bayard Taylor.

Outrageous.

Outrageous as the sea, dark, wasteful, wild. — Milton.

Outspoken.

Outspoken as a north-wester. — Anon.

Overcast.

Overcast,
Like a snow-covered pine in the vast
Dim forests of Orkadale.
— Longfellow.

Overcome.

Overcome us like a summer's cloud. — Shakespeare.

Overflow.

Overflowing like a crock of salt-rising dough in a warm kitchen. — Irvin S. Cobb.

My being overflowed,
Wert like a golden chalice to bright wine
Which else had sunk into the thirsty dust. — Shelley.

Overtake.

Overtake . . . like sea waves. — T. Edgar Pemberton.

Overturned.

Idols are overturned like new-mown grass. — Sigmund Krasinski.

Overwhelm.

Overwhelmed, like the miner upon whom a roof has just fallen. — Dumas, père.

As when a torrent, swell'd with wintry rains,
Pours from the mountains o'er the delug'd plains,
And pines and oaks, from their foundations torn,
A country's ruins ! to the seas are borne :
Fierce Ajax thus o'erwhelms the yielding throng. — Homer (Pope).

O'erwhelming his fair sight,
Like misty vapors when they blot the sky. — Shakespeare.

P

Packed.

Packed like Norfolk biffins. — Anon.

Packed like the leaves in a closed book. — O. W. Holmes.

Pagan.

Pagan as the Muses. — Anon.

Pain (Noun).

Pain . . . like the bitterness of dissolution. — Thomas Hardy.

Pain and pleasure, like light and darkness, succeed each other. — Sterne.

They shall be in pain as a woman that travaileth. — Old Testament.

Pain (Verb).

Pains like a horrible vulgarism. — Lafcadio Hearn.

Painful.

Painful, as a visit to the dentist. — Guy de Maupassant.

Painted.

Painted like the leaves of Autumn. — Longfellow.

Painted like the sky of morning. — Ibid.

Painting.

As is painting, so is poetry : some pieces will strike you more if you stand near, and some, if you are at a greater distance : one loves the dark ; another, which is not afraid of the critic's subtle judgment, chooses to be seen in the light ; the one has pleased once, the other will give pleasure if ten times repeated. — HORACE.

Pale

Pale as an Angel of the Grave. — ANON.

Pale as Banquo's ghost. — IBID.

Pale as linen. — IBID.

Pale as parchment. -- IBID.

Pale as the gleam of a glow-worm. — IBID.

Pale as the haggard features of despair. — IBID.

Pale as the rose-leaves withered in the northern gale. — IBID.

Pale as turnips were his cheeks. — IBID.

Pale as with the sickness that promised death. — IBID.

Grew pale, like a flower that is cut off. — ASSYRIAN.

Pale as a moon that moves alone through lonely space. — ALFRED AUSTIN.

Pale as snowdrift in the frost. — C. D. BELL.

Pale as the moon before the solar ray — SAMUEL BOYSE.

Pale as a white stone. — CHARLOTTE BRONTË.

Pale as baby carved in stone. — E. B. BROWNING.

Pale . . . as one who saw an ecstasy beyond a foretold agony. — IBID.

Pale as crocus grows
Close beside a rose-tree's root.
— IBID.

Pale as the silver cross of Savoy. — IBID.

Pale as a spectre. — BULWER-LYTTON.

Pale like only lily. — BURNS.

Pale as ashes, or a clout. — SAMUEL BUTLER.

Pale as death. — IBID.

Pale . . . as any lead. — CHAUCER.

Like a dede ymage, pale and wan. — IBID.

Palle as asshen colde. — IBID.

Pale as a witch. — RICHARD CUMBERLAND.

Pale as driven by a beating storm at sea. — R. H. DANA.

Pale as a new cheese. — THOMAS DEKKER.

Pale as a wreath of Alpine snow. — LORD DE TABLEY.

Pale as a candle. — DICKENS.

Pale as a muffin. — IBID.

Pale as fires when mastered by the night. — DRYDEN.

Pale as a ghost. — DUMAS, PÈRE.

Pale as a sheet. — IBID.

Pale
Like a white, bright boat in the sky's vast seas.
— MARGARET EWING.

Pale and thin as an autumn moon. — F. W. FABER.

Pearly pale,
Like a white transparent veil.
— IBID.

Pale and meagre as a court page. — FIELDING.

Pale as a moonbeam. — FLAUBERT.

Pale as brow of one on whom the axe is falling. — GOETHE.

Pale as a petulant star. — HELEN HAY

Pale — *continued.*

Pale as the tender tints that blush upon a baby's cheek. — J. R. HAYES.

Pale as wordless grief. — F. W. HOME.

Pale as frosty snow-drops. — HOOD.

Pale, like cheeks that feel the chill of affright. — IBID.

Pale as the Champa flowers. — LAURENCE HOPE.

Pale as a lover dying of despair. — ARSÈNE HOUSSAYE.

Pale as a trappist. — IBID.

Pale as a corpse. — HUGO.

Pale she was
As lily yet unsmiled on by the sun.
— JEAN INGELOW.

Pale as the moonlight beam. — MRS. INGLIS.

Pale as smooth-sculptured stone. — KEATS.

Pale as Orithyia when she was borne away. — W. S. LANDOR.

More pale than the meadows of Anjou. — ANDREW LANG.

Pale as an unawakened Galatea. — AMY LESLIE.

Pale as pale November dawn. — IBID.

Pale as is the face of one
Who sinks exhausted in oblivion after
a night of deep debauchery.
— GEORGE CABOT LODGE.

Pale as light. — IBID.

Pale as are the dead. — MACAULAY.

Pale as ascending ghost cast back to day. — DAVID MALLET.

Pale as a lily crowned with moonlight.— GERALD MASSEY.

Pale as a pearl. — IBID.

Pale as the sister of death. — GEORGE MEREDITH.

Pale as a snowdrop in Cashmere. — OWEN MEREDITH.

Pale . . . as the icy moon. — LEWIS MORRIS.

Pale as marble. — ROBERT MORRIS.

Pale as the angel of consumption. — HENRI MURGER.

Pale as despairing woe. — ORIENTAL.

Pale as the ended night. — JOHN PAYNE.

Pale as Paris plaster. — J. R. PLANCHÉ.

Pale like those to whom dead Lazarus burst the tomb. — CHARLES READE.

Pale as a rain-washed rose. — AGNES REPPLIER.

Pale as blossoms. — JAMES WHITCOMB RILEY.

Pale
As the fair changing moon.
— C. G. ROSSETTI.

Pale as whom the Fates astound. — IBID.

Pale as Parian statues. — IBID.

Pale as transparent Psyche-wings. — D. G. ROSSETTI.

Pale as bread. — SADI.

Pale as a whitewashed wall. — SCHILLER.

Pale and wan, as watchlight by the bed of some departing man. — SIR WALTER SCOTT.

Pale as clay. — IBID.

Pale as any clout in the versal world. — SHAKESPEARE.

Pale, as if a bear was at his heels. — IBID.

Pale as milk. — IBID.

Pale lustre like the silver moon. — IBID.

Pale as his shirt. — IBID.

Pale — *continued.*

Pale as the breath of blue smoke in far woodlands. — WILLIAM SHARP.

Pale as yonder waning moon. — SHELLEY.

Pale — like the white shore
Of Albion. — IBID.

Pale and pure as a maiden secluded in secret and cherished in fear. — SWINBURNE.

Pale and sweet as a dream's delight. — IBID.

Pale as grass or later flowers. — IBID.

Pale as the duskiest lily's leaf. — IBID.

Pale as the front of oblivion. — IBID.

Pale as the glimmer of stars on moorland meres. — IBID.

Pale as the moon in star-forsaken skies. — IBID.

Pale . . . as twilight. — IBID.

Paler than young snow. — IBID.

Skies as pale, as moonlight in a shadowy sea. — ARTHUR SYMONS.

Pale as a tear. — JOHN B. TABB.

Pale as a tablecloth. — THACKERAY.

Pale as Jephtha's daughter. — TENNYSON.

Pale as the passing of a ghost. — IBID.

Pale sad faces like faint flames dying. — G. S. VIERECK.

Paled.

Paled, as a candle by the sun. — OUIDA.

Paleness.

A death-like paleness . . . like one who trembling waits his fatal doom. — ARIOSTO.

Paleness, like winter. — BEAUMONT AND FLETCHER.

A sudden pale,
Like lawn being spread upon the blushing rose. — SHAKESPEARE.

Pall.

Pall on the temper, like a twice told tale. — AKENSIDE.

Contemplation palls upon the spirit
Like the chill silence of an autumn sun.
— KINGSLEY.

Pallid.

Pallid as coffined clay. — EMILY BRONTË.

Pallid as a saint. — E. B. BROWNING.

Pallid as the snow. — EBENEZER ELLIOTT.

Pallid as a corpse. — HOOD.

Grew pallid and shrank,
As a taper in sunlight sinks faint and aghast. — T. BUCHANAN READ.

Pallid and pink as the palm of the flag-flower that flickers with fear of the flies as they float. — SWINBURNE.

Pallid as a ghost. — WORDSWORTH.

Palpitate.

Palpitating . . . like a white soul tossed out to eternity with thrills of time upon it. — E. B. BROWNING.

Palpitating at the least emotion like the nostrils of an amorous tigress. — GAUTIER.

Like the birch-leaf palpitated. — LONGFELLOW.

Palpitant as men's pulses palpitate
Between the flowing and ebbing tides of fate
That wash their lifelong waifs of weal and woe
Through night and light and twilight to and fro. — SWINBURNE.

Pamper.

Pampering of their paunches, like a monk that maketh his jubilee. — HUGH LATIMER.

Pang.

A pang
As hot as death's is chill with fierce
convulse. — KEATS.

Pant.

Panting like the hounds of summer,
When they scent the stately deer.
— W. E. AYTOUN.

Pant like a netted lioness. — E. B. BROWNING.

Pant like climbers. — IBID.

Pant as in a dream. — COLERIDGE.

Panting like a spent hound. — SIR A. CONAN DOYLE.

Panting, like a bird that has often beaten his wings in vain against his cage. — DRYDEN.

Softly panting like a bride. — ROBERT HERRICK.

Panted like a forge bellows. — HUGO.

Panting, like a run-down hare. — DOUGLAS JERROLD.

The country was panting like a wrestler lying under the knees of his successful opponent. — GUY DE MAUPASSANT.

Panting, like an engine with its steam up. — J. R. PLANCHÉ.

Panting, and swept as by the sense of death. — SWINBURNE.

Panted like a sick man's fitful breath. — IBID.

Panted hard,
Like one that feels a nightmare on
his bed. — TENNYSON.

As the hart panteth after the water brooks, so panteth my soul after thee, O God. — OLD TESTAMENT.

Parch.

Mouth parched like a shade that comes to salute friends of former days. — DUMAS, PÈRE.

Parch'd like the fallow destitute of corn. — FRANCIS FAWKES.

Parch to the peppered palate like a pea. — HOOD.

Pardon.

God pardons like a mother who kisses away the repentant tears of her child. — HENRY WARD BEECHER.

Paris.

Paris — like a pretty woman, has mysterious fits of ugliness or beauty. — BALZAC.

Parted.

Parted like a scattered flock before a lion. — SYDNEY DOBELL.

Parted like a stone from a sling. — CHARLES READE.

Parted thence,
As pearls from diamonds dropped.
— SHAKESPEARE.

Parting.

Partings are like postscripts to a letter — indiscreet utterances that do as much mischief to the speaker as to those who overhear them. — BALZAC.

Pass.

Our memory passes like a ripple in the water, or a breeze in the air. — AMIEL.

Passes like a mode. — ANON.

Passed like an uncurbed cavalry. — IBID.

Time passes like the wind. — IBID.

Pass like a rolled syllable of midnight thunder from the coming day. — P. J. BAILEY.

One solitary and foreseeing thought, passed, like a planet's transit o'er the sun. — IBID.

Passed, like the foam of the wave — JANE BARLOW.

As shadows cast by cloud and sun
flit o'er the summer grass,
So, in thy sight, Almighty One!
earth's generations pass.
— WILLIAM CULLEN BRYANT.

Pass — *continued.*

Passed away as fairies vanish at the break of day. — Hartley Coleridge.

Thy grace must pass
As unremembered things.
— Lord De Tabley.

Time passed away as a tale which is told. — Dickens.

Passed out as quickly as a sunbeam. — Ibid.

New generations pass,
Like shadows on the grass.
— Julia C. R. Dorr.

Passed like a meteor. — Dumas, père.

Pass away as in vision. — Frederic Harrison.

The generations pass, like autumn's fruits,
Garnered, consumed, and springing fresh to life.
— James A. Hillhouse.

Passed away like waves. — Hugo.

Pass away —
As flowers that bloom at morn, at eve decay. — Francis Scott Key.

Oh, why should the spirit of mortal be proud?
Like a swift-fleeting meteor, a fast flying cloud,
A flash of the lightning, a break of the wave,
Man passes from life to his rest in the grave. — William Knox.

Little troubles pass like little ripples in a sunny river. — W. S. Landor.

Passed like the mournful cry of sunward sailing cranes. — Longfellow.

When she had passed, it seemed like the ceasing of exquisite music. — Ibid.

Passed like a dream away. — Macaulay.

They pass like a shade away. — James Macpherson.

They pass
Like a breath from the face of a glass. — Don Marquis.

Pass away, like a thin cloud that melts across the moon. — James Montgomery.

Passed
Like autumn foliage withering in the blast. — Ibid.

Passed like a day-dream. — Thomas Moore.

All gently pass away,
Like mists that flee
From a summer sea. — Ibid.

All my days
Passed like an empty vision.
— Lewis Morris.

Pass'd, like swift clouds across a windy sky. — A. J. Munby.

Passed along the waves like the chariot of Neptune. — Munchausen.

Passed away, like shadows of the moon. — Adelaide A. Procter.

Passed away,
Like the remembrance of a guest that tarrieth but a day.
— C. G. Rossetti.

Pass'd by me
As misers do by beggars.
— Shakespeare.

Passed, like a cloud on the blast. — Shelley.

Must pass, as grains of sand must fall,
Beneath the infinite calm sea
Of ages and eternity.
— Harry B. Smith.

Passed away like summer clouds. — Southey.

And pass as love and sorrow pass,
As shadows flashing down a glass,
As dew-flowers blowing in flowerless grass. — Swinburne.

Passes as the grey dew from the morning mountain grasses. — Ibid.

Pass as the flight of a year. — Ibid.

Pass — *continued.*

Passed, like a sudden squall that tears
the sea,
Yet leaves a sun to smile the billows
down. — BAYARD TAYLOR.

Pass like a light. — TENNYSON.

Passeth away as a cloud. — OLD TESTAMENT.

Pass through thy hand as a river. — IBID.

Passed, like a sweet but transient dream. — FRANK WATERS.

As a cloud of the sunset, slow melting
in heaven,
As a star that is lost when the daylight
is given,
As a glad dream of slumber, which
wakens in bliss,
She hath pass'd to the world of the
holy from this. — WHITTIER.

Pass,
Like shadows through a twilight
land. — OSCAR WILDE.

Passed like a fancy that is swept away. — WORDSWORTH.

Passion.

Passions are like fire and water, good servants, but bad masters. — ANON.

The passions are like fire, useful in a thousand ways and dangerous only in one, through their excess. — C. N. BOVÉE.

A man without a passion is like a vessel waiting for wind and not budging. — ARSÈNE HOUSSAYE.

Passions are like roses, the more you cut them, the more they grow. — IBID.

Passions are cheap things, common as nuts, and just as often rotten. — GEORGE W. LOVELL.

Passions, among pure thoughts hid,
Like serpents under flowerets sleeping.
— THOMAS MOORE.

Passion, like the sun at noon,
That burns o'er all he sees,
Awhile as warm, will set as soon—
Then, call it none of these. — IBID.

Our passions are like convulsive fits, which, though they make us stronger for the time, leave us weaker ever after. — POPE.

Passions are likened best to floods and streams; the shallow murmur, but the deep are dumb. — SIR WALTER RALEIGH.

Passions are like storms which, full of the present mischief, serve to purify the atmosphere. — SIR GEORGE RAMSAY.

Our passions, like the seasons turn;
And now we laugh, and now we mourn.
— NICHOLAS ROWE.

Passionate.

Passionate as young love. — ANON.

Passionate men, like fleet hounds, are apt to overrun the scent. — IBID.

Passionate as the Hun. — J. H. NEWMAN.

A passionate man is like a weak spring, that cannot stand long locked. — WILLIAM PENN.

The passionate are like men standing on their heads; they see all things the wrong way. — PLATO.

Passionate as an April day. — WILLIAM ROWLEY.

Passive.

Passive as a monument. — ANON.

Passive as a tabby-cat. — IBID.

Passive — like dead bodies, with open, fixed eyes. — JOSEPH CONRAD.

Past.

The Past is like a funeral gone by. The Future comes like an unwelcome guest. — EDMUND GOSSE.

Pat.

Truths, as pat as paving stones in cities. — N. P. WILLIS.

Pat he comes, like the catastrophe of the old comedy. — SHAKESPEARE.

Pathetic.

Pathetic as an autumn leaf. — GEORGE MOORE.

Pathetic as the violets that bloom on a grave. — OSCAR WILDE.

Patience.

Patience under misfortunes is like opiates in a fever; tossing and tumbling only irritate the distemper. — ANON.

Patience is so like fortitude, that she seems either her sister or her daughter. — ARISTOTLE.

Grisilde-like in patience. — JOHN LYDGATE.

Patient.

Patient as rocks. — ANON.

A poor man without patience is like a lamp without oil. — ARABIAN PROVERB.

Patient, like a marble man. — E. B. BROWNING.

Patient as a stone. — CHARLES G. DUFFY.

Patient as a god. — DUMAS, PÈRE.

Patient as death. — MAURICE HEWLETT.

As patient under injury as any Christian saint of old. — J. G. HOLLAND.

Patient as destiny. — ROBERT G. INGERSOLL.

Patient as an ant. — KEATS.

Patient as a hen-bird. — IBID.

Gazing patient at the sky;
Like some marble carven nun,
With folded hands when work is done,
Who mute upon her tomb doth pray,
Till resurrection day. — KINGSLEY.

Patient as sheep. — MACAULAY.

Patient as earth. — RAMAYANA.

Patient as a gentle stream. — SHAKESPEARE.

Patient as the female dove. — IBID.

As pacient and as styll.
And as ful of good wil.
As fayre Isiphill. — SKELTON.

Patient as the hours. — SWINBURNE.

Patient as the lamb is she. — GEORGE WITHER.

Patiently.

Patiently as an old worn horse. — GEORGE MEREDITH.

Patiently as the spider weaves the broken web. — BULWER-LYTTON.

Patterings.

Patterings like an April's rain. — O. W. HOLMES.

Pause.

A felicitous pause
A pause as of a thoughtful reasoner.
— BULWER-LYTTON.

Paused.

Paused, like some slow ship with sail unfurled waiting, in seas by scarce a wavelet curled. — GEORGE ELIOT.

Peace.

Like the rainbow,
Peace rests upon the earth, but its
arch is lost in heaven.
— BULWER-LYTTON.

Peaceful.

Peaceful as sleep. — BEAUMONT AND FLETCHER.

Peaceful as the advance of summer. — M. D. CONWAY.

Peaceful as stars at twilight. — HUGO.

Peaceful as two pups in a basket. — ALFRED HENRY LEWIS.

Peaceful — *continued.*

Peaceful as two six-shooters on the same belt. — IBID.

Peaceful . . . as a virgin lake. — LOWELL.

Peaceful as summer woods. — GEORGE MACDONALD.

Peaceful as a hired hand. — JAMES WHITCOMB RILEY.

Peaceful as dew-mist from an evening sky. — BAYARD TAYLOR.

Peaceful as falls the dew. — WILLIAM WINTER.

Peaceful as the morning. — WORDSWORTH.

Peacefully.

Sleeping as peacefully as a little girl tired of playing. — GUY DE MAUPASSANT.

Ran the sweet strain peacefully like a river in its flow. — ELLA M. MOORE.

Peaked.

Peaked as a pen. — ANON.

Peal.

Peals
Like the eternal thunders of the deep.
— BYRON.

Pearls.

Pearls are like girls, they require quite as much attention. — BEACONSFIELD.

Pedantry.

Pedantry in learning is like hypocrisy in religion, — a form of knowledge without the power of it. — ADDISON.

Pedantry and taste are as inconsistent as gayety and melancholy. — J. C. LAVATER.

Peel.

Peel, like slippery elms in spring. — EUGENE FITCH WARE.

Peep.

Peep like Venus rising from her shell. — JAMES MONTGOMERY.

Countless eyes,
Peeping like stars through the blue
ev'ning skies.
— THOMAS MOORE.

Peep, like moss-grown rocks, half-seen,
Half hidden in the copse.
— SIR WALTER SCOTT.

Peeps like a star o'er ocean's western edge. — SHELLEY.

Peeping like modest virgins from secluded bowers. — FANNY FORESTER.

Peeping and peering like an excited parrot. — KINGSLEY.

Peevish.

Peevish as a sick monkey. — JAMES PUCKLE.

Pellucid.

Pellucid as a pearl. — ROBERT BROWNING.

Pendant.

Pendant like berries on the branches. — MUNCHAUSEN.

Penetrate.

Penetrating as fear. — ANON.

Penetrating as the east wind. — IBID.

Penetrates like a vapor. — HUGO.

Penetrated him like a gimlet. — GUY DE MAUPASSANT.

Pensive.

Pensive as a sailor in a coach. — BALZAC.

Pensiv as a wel fed kitten. — JOSH BILLINGS.

People.

The people in mass are like metal in the ore; and, as all the iron that ever came from a Swedish mine would never hew a block or divide a plank until it was fashioned into the shape of a hatchet or a saw, so the strength of a people can never perhaps be made capable of producing much effect in

People — *continued.*

war, till it is extracted partially and moulded into that factitious and highly polished instrument called an army. — SIR ARCHIBALD ALISON.

Impatient people, according to Bacon, are like the bees, and kill themselves in stinging others. — GEORGE ELIOT.

Peoples, like planets, possess the right to an eclipse. And all is well, provided that the light returns and that the eclipse does not degenerate into night. Dawn and resurrection are synonymous. — HUGO.

It is with narrow soul'd people as with narrow necked bottles, the less they have in them the more noise they make in pouring it out. — POPE.

Perceive.

If a fool be associated with a man all his life he will perceive the truth as little as a spoon perceives the taste of soup. — BUDDHA.

Perfect.

Perfect as an astronomical chart. — ANON.

Perfect as the dew-bead. — GEORGE ELIOT.

A poem round and perfect as a star. — ALEXANDER SMITH.

Perfect as a flame
That springs and spreads, till each glad limb became
A note of rapture in the tune of life.
— SWINBURNE.

Perfection.

Complete in perfection as a great line in poetry, as the flight of a bird, as the curve of a falling wave. — RICHARD LE GALLIENNE.

Perforate.

Perforated like a civil war battle flag. — ANON.

Perforate, like a honeycomb. — THOMAS WADE.

Perfumed.

Perfumed like a milliner. — SHAKESPEARE.

Perilous.

The crisis was perilous, but not without its charm : such as an Indian, perhaps, feels when he slips over the rapid in his canoe. — HUGO.

Perish.

Perish . . . like a microbe in hot water. — ANON.

Perish, through their over-confidence, like Icarus. — BACON.

Perish, as the quickening breath of God . . . is withdrawn. — BRYANT.

They perish as a robe outworn,
As faded leaves they float away.
— LORD DE TABLEY.

Perish like leaves. — EMERSON.

Perish as the summer fly. — H. A. JONES.

Perisheth, and is past by, like the Pearle in the Fable. — BEN JONSON.

Perished with him like a rocket which falls
And quenches its light in earth.
— EDGAR LEE MASTERS.

Perishing,
As though they were but things of dust and ashes. — MONTGOMERY.

Perished like the pageant of a dream. — T. L. PEACOCK.

Perished like some gift of earth. — SCHILLER.

Perish, as haze in sunrise on the red sea-line. — SWINBURNE.

Perish as the snow built up of sleep. — IBID.

Perish forever like his own dung. — OLD TESTAMENT.

Permanent.

Permanent as marble. — BAYARD TAYLOR.

Perpendicular.

Perpendicular like poplars. — BYRON.

Perplexing.

Perplexing as the question: "Do angels ever come back and pay their debts?" — ANON.

Persistence.

Persistence . . . like the obstinacy of a rancid odour clinging to the hair. — HUGO.

Persistent.

Persistent as a mosquito. — ANON.

Persons.

Vain and frivolous persons, like empty vessels, are easily laid hold of and borne along by the ears. — DEMOPHILUS.

Persuasive.

Persuasive as the tongue of seraphs. — THOMAS BLACKLOCK.

Pert.

Pert as a school-girl well can be. — W. S. GILBERT.

Peart as a circus pony. — JOEL CHANDLER HARRIS.

Pervade.

Pervading his frame like a raging fever. — DUMAS, PÈRE.

Perverse.

Perverse as a camel, which can neither be stopped when he is going nor moved when he is resting. — ANON.

Perverse as a hog. — SMOLLETT.

Phantasmagoric.

Phantasmagoric, like a mirage beyond the horizon. — RICHARD LE GALLIENNE.

Philosophy.

As swallows give us intimation of fair weather, so the lessons of philosophy point out to us the way to attain tranquility of mind. — DEMOPHILUS.

Physician.

One prompt physician, like a sculler plies,
And all his art, and all his skill applies;
But two physicians, like a pair of oars,
Convey you soonest to the Stygian shores. — ANON.

Physicians, like beer, are best when they are old; and lawyers, like bread, when they are young and new. — THOMAS FULLER.

Pick.

Picked out like a kernel from a nut. — R. C. BATES.

Pick as clean as a bone. — SAMUEL WESLEY.

Picturesque.

Picturesque as the "frolic architecture of the snow." — ANON.

As picturesque,
As the figures we see in an arabesque.
— R. H. BARHAM.

Pierce.

Pierced like pard by hunters' steel. — BYRON.

Pierce as the lightning flashes. — ELIZA COOK.

Pierced like lightning. — THOMAS NASH.

He pierces like a lady's needle. — OSMANLI PROVERB.

It shall as level to your judgment pierce
As day does to your eye.
— SHAKESPEARE.

Piercing.

Piercing as light. — ANON.

Piercing . . . as the air. — FRANCIS FAWKES.

Piercing as the mid-day sun. — SHAKESPEARE.

Piercing — *continued.*

Piercing, like the morn, now it has darted
Its lustre on all hidden things.
— SHELLEY.

Piled.

Piled . . . like sacks of wheat in a granary. — LONGFELLOW.

Pinch.

Pinches like a trap that shuts. — SWINBURNE.

Pine.

Pines she like to the hyacinth out on the path of the hill-top ; shepherds tread it aside, and its purples lie lost on the herbage. — SAPPHO.

Like an eagle caged I pine
On this dull unchanging shore.
— EPES SARGENT.

Pink.

Pink as the lip of the sea-shell. — ANON.

Pink as the rose in Galatea's cheek. — ALFRED AUSTIN.

Pink as the cheeks of sweet-and-twenty. — TEMPLE BAILEY.

Pink as a rose leaf is pink. — FRANK D. SHERMAN.

Pinned.

Pinned to the mire of the murky, the charnel river
Like fair fresh flowers on the filthy breast of a hag. — AGNES LEE.

Pious.

Pious as a broken-kneed post-horse. — WILLIAM B. BERNARD.

Pious as a virgin enclosed. — MAURICE HEWLETT.

Pious as a Pope. — HOOD.

Pipe.

A pipe is like a Christian in many ways ; sure it's made o' clay like a Christian, and has the spark o' life in it, and while the breath is in it the spark is alive ; but when the breath is out of it, the spark dies, and then it grows cowld like a Christian ; and isn't it a pleasant companion like a Christian? — LOVER.

Piquant.

Piquant as the waters of the Scheldt. — GEORGES EEKHOUD.

Pirouette.

Pirouetted like a bit of fantoccini. — OUIDA.

Piteous.

Piteous as a spirit wailing in a world of tears. — GERALD MASSEY.

Pitiable.

Pitiable, like every ignorant man who wins a triumph. — HUGO.

Pitiful.

Pitiful as he that's hired for death
And loves the slaying yet better than the hire. — SWINBURNE.

Pitifully.

Pitifully as a poor girl of the pavement will pretend to be a clergyman's daughter. — G. B. SHAW.

Pitiless.

Pitiless as a Maxim gun. — ANON.

Pitiless as northern night. — J. W. BARBER.

Pitiless as night. — AMBROSE BIERCE.

Pitiless as the grave. — GERALD MASSEY.

Pitiless as driving sleet. — JOHN G. NEIHARDT.

As pitiless to them as the Hyrcanian tiger to a lamb chop in the original wool. — NEW YORK SUN.

Pitiless as the strokes of an iron hammer. — OUIDA.

Pitiless as hail from heaven. — C. C. FRASER-TYTLER.

Pity.

As much pity is to be taken of a woman weeping, as of a goose going barefoot. — ROBERT BURTON.

And pity, like a naked, new-born babe,
Striding the blast, or heaven's cherubin, hors'd
Upon the sightless couriers of the air,
Shall blow the horrid deed in every eye,
That tears shall drown the wind.
— SHAKESPEARE.

Place.

Out of place as a faro layout in a Sunday school. — ALFRED HENRY LEWIS.

Placeless.

Placeless, as spirits. — COLERIDGE.

Placid.

Placid as a duck pond. — ANON.

Placid as a mill-pond. — IBID.

Placid as a scarecrow in a field of scoundrels. — IBID.

Placid as a soft-shell crab in a plate of parsley. — IBID.

Placid as Socrates. — IBID.

Placid as Paradise. — EDWIN ARNOLD.

Placid as a hearthstone. — EUGENE FIELD.

Placid as a stone. — HUGO.

Placidly . . . as waiting to be sheeted home. — JEAN INGELOW.

Placid as a swan that drifts in a dream. — LOWELL.

Plain.

Plain as A. B. C. — ANON.

Plain as a hat on a rack. — IBID.

Plain as a steeple. — IBID.

Plain as a pack-saddle. — IBID.

Plain as the shepherd nymph in russet weeds. — IBID.

Plain as two and two make four. — IBID.

Plain as your own miniken-breeches. — BEAUMONT AND FLETCHER.

As plain as noon-day. — GEORGE H. BOKER.

She dresses as plain as the lily that modestly grows in the valley. — PATRICK BRONTË.

Plain as truth. — CHAPMAN.

Plain as a demonstration in Euclid. — GEORGE COLMAN, THE YOUNGER.

Her dress was as plain as an umbrella cover. — JOSEPH CONRAD.

Plain as plainness. — JOHN DAVIES.

As plain to everybody as the sun. — DICKENS.

As plain as water's water. — GEORGE ELIOT.

Plain as a pikestaff. — SAMUEL FOOTE.

Plain as a dropped egg on a plate of hash. — SEWELL FORD.

Plain as the way to market. — FRANKLIN.

Plain as the sunlight. — FROUDE.

As plain as the moral law. — BRET HARTE.

Plain as the man with lantern. — HOOD.

Plain as whisper in the ear. — IBID.

Plain as the record on the prophet's scroll. — O. W. HOLMES.

As plain as a hole in a grindstone. — IBID.

As plain as the round shield of the sun blazing on high. — JAMES HUNEKER.

Plain as print. — LOVER.

Plaine . . . as the high way. — LYLY.

Plain — *continued.*

Plain as the sun in heaven. — MACAULAY.

Plain . . . as a rudimentary sum in arithmetic. — GEORGE MEREDITH.

Plain as the light in the sun or as the man in the moon. — OTWAY.

Plain as a nose in a man's face. — RABELAIS.

Plain as the plain bald pate of Father Time himself. — SHAKESPEARE.

Plain as way to parish church. — IBID.

Plain and smooth like a Quaker's meeting. — JAMES SMITH.

Plain as the sun at noonday. — STERNE.

Plain as the glistening planets shine when winds have cleared the skies. — ROBERT LOUIS STEVENSON.

Plain as a weed. — BAYARD TAYLOR.

Plainly.

Plainly as heaven sees earth and earth sees heaven. — SHAKESPEARE.

Plainly as shoulder-straps mark a soldier. — ANON.

Plastic.

Plastic as potter's clay. — ANON.

Play.

A bad play is like a cabbage, — all leaves. — ANON.

A play is like a cigar, it requires judicious puffing. — IBID.

Most plays are like pills ; if you swallow them whole they are sweet ; but, if they are chewed, like a pill, you will, like the critic, find them bitter. — IBID.

A play is like a cigar ; if it is a failure no amount of puffing will make it draw, but if it is a success, everybody wants a box. — HENRY J. BYRON.

Like hungry guests, a sitting audience
looks :
Plays are like suppers ; poets are the
cooks.
The founder's you : the table is this
place :
The carvers we : the prologue is the
grace.
Each act a course; each scene, a different dish,
Though we're in Lent, I doubt you're
still for flesh.
Satire's the sauce, high-seasoned, sharp,
and rough.
Kind masks and beaux, I hope you're
pepper-proof ?
Wit is the wine ; but 'tis so scarce the
true
Poets, like vintners, balderdash and
brew.
Your surly scenes, where rant and
bloodshed join,
Are butcher's meat, a battle's a sirloin.
Your scenes of love, so flowing, soft
and chaste,
Are water-gruel without salt or taste.
— FARQUHAR.

A play, like a bill, is of no value till it is accepted ; nor indeed when it is, very often. — FIELDING.

A play is like a picture : the actors are the colors, and they must blend with one another if a perfect work is to be produced. — JOSEPH JEFFERSON.

Plays are exactly like Portraits Drawn in the Garb and Fashion of the time when Painted. You see one Habit in the time of King Charles I. ; another quite different from that, both for Men and Woman, in Queen Elizabeths time ; another under Henry the Eighth different from both ; and so backward all various. — JAMES WRIGHT'S "HISTORIA HISTRIONICA."

For plays, like women, by the world
are thought,
When you speak kindly of 'em, very
naught. — WYCHERLEY.

Playful.

Playful as a frolic boy. — ANON.

Playful as a rabbit. — GEORGE P. MORRIS.

Playwright.

A wise playwright should act like the man who gives a magnificent feast: he should seek to delight the spectators, that each on departing may feel he has eaten and drunk just the things he would chiefly have chosen himself: not set but one dish for all palates, one writing for all sorts of tastes. — ASTYDAMUS, JUNIOR.

Plead.

Plead like angels, trumpet-tongued. — SHAKESPEARE.

Pleading like a frightened child. — ROBERT LOUIS STEVENSON.

Pleasant.

Pleasant as youth with all its blossoms crown'd. — COWPER.

Pleasant as a wave. — LORD DE TABLEY.

Pleasant as health. — GERALD GRIFFIN.

As pleasant about the house as a gleam of sunshine, falling on the floor through a shadow of twinkling leaves, or as a ray of firelight that dances on the wall, while evening is drawing nigh. — HAWTHORNE.

Pleasant as the shower which falls on the sunny field. — JAMES MACPHERSON.

Pleasant as the thunder of heaven, before the showers of spring. — IBID.

Pleasant as the gale of spring, that sighs on the hunter's ear. — OSSIAN.

Pleasant as budding tree. — C. G. ROSSETTI.

Pleasant as a scented mouth to kiss. — SWINBURNE.

Pleasant as roses in the thickets blown. — WORDSWORTH.

Pleased.

Pleased as Punch. — ANON.

Pleased, as infants are with sleep. — SIR WILLIAM DAVENANT.

Pleasure.

But pleasures are like poppies spread,
You seize the flower, its bloom is shed;
Or like the snow falls in the river,
A moment white — then melts for ever;
Or like the borealis race,
That flit ere you can point their place;
Or like the rainbow's lovely form,
Evanishing amid the storm.
— BURNS.

Pleasure, like an over-fed lamp, is extinguished by the excess of its own aliment. — HANNAH MORE.

Pleasures like the flow'r,
Frail and fleeting ever;
Now decks the bow'r,
Now 'tis gone for ever.
— FREDERICK REYNOLDS.

Pleasures are like liqueurs: They must be drunk but in small glasses. — ROUMAINILLE.

Plentiful.

Plentiful as bacteria in bad butter. — ANON.

Plentiful as sage brush in the desert. — IBID.

Plentiful as shingles on the shore. — IBID.

Plentiful as wells in the Old Testament. — IBID.

Plentiful as plebeians in Oxford Street. — SAMUEL WARREN.

Plentitude.

Spiritual sweets to plentitude,
As bees gorge full their cells.
— KEATS.

Plenty.

Plenty as the grass. — ANON.

As plenty as blackberries. — SHAKESPEARE.

Pliant.

Pliant as a glove. — Balzac.

Pliant as a reed. — Charlotte Brontë.

Pliant as the torrent flows. — John G. Cooper.

Pliant as a wand of willow. — Longfellow.

Pliable as wax. — James Shirley.

Pliant as the air. — Bayard Taylor.

Plod.

Plods on like a steed in a mill. — Eliza Cook.

Pluck.

Plucked like a berry from a bush. — R. C. Bates.

Plumed.

Plumed like a hearse. — Anon.

Plumed like a storm-portending cloud. — P. J. Bailey.

Plump.

Plump as an orange. — Anon.

Plump as plenty. — Ibid.

Plump as a peach. — Dickens.

Plump as ripe clusters. — Richard Duke.

Plump as a pudding. — Hawthorne.

Plump as a cherry. — Robert Herrick.

Plump as a partridge. — Lover.

Plump as a melon under a glass. — George Meredith.

Plump as mastiffs. — Plautus.

As plump as a miller's sparrow. — Scottish Proverb.

Plump, like tiny skins of wine. — James Whitcomb Riley.

As plump as plump can be. — C. G. Rossetti.

Plump as stall'd theology. — Young.

Plunge.

Plunged like a mad horse. — Anon.

He was plunged in rushing water like a diver holding on to a stake planted in the bed of a swollen river. — Joseph Conrad.

Plunging like the sea. — J. G. Holland.

Pockets.

Pockets . . . looked like a pool table's after a fifteen-ball run. — O. Henry.

Poems.

Poems, like rivers, convey to their destination what must without their appliances be unhandled: these to ports and arsenals, this to the human heart. — W. S. Landor.

Poetry.

Poetry, good sir, in my opinion, is like a tender virgin, very young and extremely beautiful, whom divers other virgins — namely, all other sciences — make it their business to enrich, polish, and adorn. — Cervantes.

There is as much difference between good poetry and fine verses, as between the smell of a flower garden, and a perfumer's shop. — Julius C. Hare.

Wisdom and poetry are like fruit for children, unwholesome if too fresh. — W. S. Landor.

Poëtry is to philosophy what the Sabbath is to the rest of the week. — W. B. Yeats.

Poets.

Poets are like birds: the least thing makes them sing. — Chateaubriand.

For party poets are like wasps, who dart
Death to themselves, and to their foes but smart. — George Crabbe.

Poets, like Lovers, should be bold and dare,
They spoil their business with an overcare. — Dryden.

Poets — *continued.*

Poets, like painters, their machinery claim,
And verse bestows the varnish and the frame. — O. W. Holmes.

Poets, like candles, are all puffers,
And critics are the candle snuffers.
— Robert Lloyd.

Poets, like angels, where they once appear,
Hallow the place. — John Norris.

Fir'd at first sight with what the Muse imparts,
In fearless youth we tempt the height of arts,
While from the bounded level of our mind
Short views we take, nor see the lengths behind;
But more advanc'd, behold, with strange surprise,
New distant scenes of endless science rise.
So pleas'd at first the tow'ring Alps we try,
Mount o'er the vales, and seem to tread the sky;
Th' eternal snows appear already past,
And the first clouds and mountains seem the last;
But these attain'd, we tremble to survey
The growing labours of the lengthen'd way:
Th' increasing prospect tires our wandering eyes;
Hills peep o'er hills, and Alps on Alps arise. — Pope.[1]

Poignant.

Poignant and silent like the terrible questioning of one's conscience. — Joseph Conrad.

Point.

Points like death's lean lifted finger. — Robert Browning.

[1] Dr. Johnson, in his "Lives of the Poets," says that this simile on poets is "perhaps the best the English language affords."

Pointed.

Pointed as a wasp's sting. — Anon.

Pointed as a poniard. — Thomas Nash.

Poise.

Poise as of humming-birds hanging in air. — F. W. H. Myers.

Poison.

Poisoned his life, as a rusted nail driven through an oak-tree in its prime corrodes and kills. — Ouida.

Polished.

Polished as the bosom of a star. — T. B. Aldrich.

Polite.

Perlite as a dancing master. — Josh Billings.

Polite as wax. — O. Henry.

Politeness.

Politeness is like an air cushion; there's nothing in it, but it eases the joints wonderfully. — W. C. Gannett.

Political.

Political men, like goats, usually thrive best among equalities. — W. S. Landor.

Politicians.

Politicians, like the earth, are flattened at the polls. — Anon.

Pollute.

Polluted as a harlot. — Anon.

Pompous.

Pompous as an undertaker. — Thackeray.

Poor.

Poor as a cab-driver in Venice. — Anon.

Poor as a rat. — Ibid.

Poor as skunk's misery. — Ibid.

As poor as winter. — Ibid.

Poor as wood. — Josh Billings.

Poor — *continued.*

Poor as an owlet. — Bunyan.

As poor as some church mouse. — Lord De Tabley.

Poorer than a retired Spanish ensign. — Fortserré.

Poor as Job's turkey. — Marston.

Poor as a sheep new shorn. — George Peele.

Poor as virtue and as friendless. — Ibid.

Poor as a pauper's pottage. — John G. Saxe.

Poor as truth. — Francis Seager.

Poor as Job. — Shakespeare.

Poor as winter. — Ibid.

Pop.

Popping about like a parched pea. — Anon.

Popular.

Popular as love. — Lamartine.

Popular as a film drama. — G. B. Shaw.

Populous.

Populous as a hive. — Anon.

Populous as an ant-hill. — Hugo.

Positions.

High positions are like the summit of high steep rocks. Eagles and reptiles alone can reach them. — Madame Necker.

Positive.

Positive as a Scotchman. — Anon.

Positive as the earth is firm. — Shakespeare.

Posture.

Posturing, for all the world just like the man on the slack rope at our fair. — Hannah More.

Posturing as proudly as a matador. — Julian Street.

Potent.

Potent as Irish whiskey. — Anon.

Potent an evil as Shakespeare's French fiddle. — W. C. Brann.

Pounce.

Pounced like a kite on a chick. — Anon.

Pounce like a vulture. — Ibid.

Pounced . . . like lightning. — Wilkie Collins.

Pounced like a falcon. — George Meredith.

Pout.

Pout like a disappointed child. — Charlotte Brontë.

Pouting.

With laughing eyes and dewy lips, pouting like the purple tip that points the rose's bud. — Catullus.

Pouting lip like the print upon a pound of butter. — Samuel Foote.

Poverty.

Poverty is like an upper story, since the poor take precedency of all. — Pilpay.

Power.

Power, like the diamond, dazzles the beholder, and also the wearer; it dignifies meanness; it magnifies littleness; to what is contemptible, it gives authority; to what is low, exaltation. — C. C. Colton.

Power, like the hasty Vine, climbes up apace to the Supporter, but if not skilfully attended and dress'd, instead of spreading and bearing fruit, grows high and naked, and then, like empty title, being soon useless to others, becomes neglected and unable to support itself. — Sir William Davenant.

Power, like a desolating pestilence,
Pollutes whate'er it touches.
— Shelley.

Powerful.

Powerful as the tyranny of fashion. — J. H. St. J. de Crèvecœur.

Powerful as the sacerdotalism of Mediæval Europe. — Froude.

Powerful as death. — Pope.

Powerless.

Powerless as an infant. — Anon.

Powerless as grubs. — Ibid.

Powerless as stubble exposed to the draught of a furnace. — Charlotte Brontë.

Powerless . . . as a stone. — E. B. Browning.

Powerless as the wind
That passeth idly by. — Shelley.

Praise.

Praise, like gold and diamonds, owes its value only to its scarcity. — Dr. Johnson.

Praise to a young wit is like rain to a tender flower. — Pope.

Praise is like ambergris; a little whiff of it, and by snatches, is very agreeable; but when a man holds a great lump of it to his nose, it is a stink and strikes down. — Swift.

As the fining pot for silver, and the furnace for gold; so is a man to his praise. — Old Testament.

Prance.

Prance like uncurbed cavalry. — Anon.

Pranced round it like a pair of cannibals about to eat a victim. — Balzac.

Prancing like a bean-fed horse. — Kipling.

Prate.

Prate like a parrot. — Anon.

Prating of the stars
Like an old soldier of his scars.
— P. J. Bailey.

Prate like one i' the stocks. — Shakespeare.

Prattle.

Prattled like a babbling brook. — C. S. Calverley.

Prattle like a magpie. — Congreve.

Prattlers, like swallows, destroy the pleasure of conversation by incessant loquacity. — Demophilus.

Prattles like a child at play. — Coventry Patmore.

Prayers.

God puts our prayers like rose-leaves between the leaves of his book of remembrance, and when the volume is opened at last, there shall be a precious fragrance springing from them. — C. H. Spurgeon.

Preach.

A woman preacher is like a dog walking on his hind legs. It is not done well; but you are surprised to find it done at all. — Dr. Johnson.

Precept.

Precepts are like seeds; they are little things which do much good. — Seneca.

Precious.

Precious as the Sibyl's leaves. — Anon.

Precious as enterprise. — Hafiz.

Precious as a Grecian vase. — Richard Le Gallienne.

Precious,
As are the conceal'd comforts of a man,
Lock'd in a woman's love.
— Thomas Lodge.

More precious
Than the rich-jewell'd coffer of Darius.
— Shakespeare.

Precious as is friend. — "Wit Restored."

Precious — *continued.*

More precious far
Than that accumulated store of gold
And orient gems, which, for a day of need,
The Sultan hides deep in ancestral tombs. — WORDSWORTH.

Prejudice.

Prejudice, like the spider, makes everywhere its home, and lives where there seems nothing to live on. — THOMAS PAINE.

Prepared.

Prepared as a bride adorned for her husband. — NEW TESTAMENT.

Preposterous.

Preposterous . . . as natural color upon a fashionable cheek. — JOHN BROUGHAM.

Preserved.

She was well preserved by a tranquil existence, like winter fruit in a closed cupboard. — GUY DE MAUPASSANT.

Press.

Pressed it to his heart as holy sinners press the scapular. — E. W. HORNUNG.

Pressed in my heart, like flowers within a book. — LONGFELLOW.

Pressed her like corn that has been crushed in the mill. — GUY DE MAUPASSANT.

Press one as men press a sponge. — "REPUBLICA: A MERYE ENTERLUDE."

Presumptuous.

Presumptuous as Haman the halt. — JOHN HEYWOOD.

Pretty.

Pretty as a Pingree potato patch. — ANON.

Pretty as a red wagon. — IBID.

Pretty as a September peach. — IBID.

Pretty as a picture. — IBID.

She was as pretty as the spring time. — BALZAC.

Pretty as a peach
Such as school boys always long for when they're hangin' out of reach.
— PHŒBE CARY.

A little girl, pretty as an angel. — HENDRIK CONSCIENCE.

Pretty as a seraph. — GAUTIER.

Pretty as a rosebud debutante. — AMY LESLIE.

Pretty as a diamond flush. — ALFRED HENRY LEWIS.

Pretty as Paint. — NORTHALL'S "FOLK PHRASES."

Pretty, like a toy cowboy with a chamois shirt and a nine-dollar sombrero. — EDGAR W. NYE.

Prey.

Prey . . . like a fox in midst of harvest-time. — MARLOWE.

Prey on itself,
Like monsters of the deep.
— SHAKESPEARE.

Prick.

Pricks like thorn. — SHAKESPEARE.

Pride.

'Tis as natural for women to pride themselves in fine clothes as 'tis for a peacock to spread his tail. — ANON.

Pride is like the beautiful acacia, that lifts its head proudly above its neighbor plants — forgetting that it too, like them, has its roots in the dirt. — C. N. BOVÉE.

Pride, like the magnet, constantly points to one object, — self, — self; but, unlike the magnet, it has no attractive pole, but at all points repels. — C. C. COLTON.

Pride, like ambition, is sometimes virtuous and sometimes vicious, according to the character in which it is found, and the object to which it is directed. — FULKE GREVILLE.

Pride — *continued.*

Pride is like vapour which ascendeth high, and presently vanishes away.— PLUTARCH.

Pride, like laudanum and other poisonous medicines, is beneficial in small, though injurious in large quantities. No man who is not pleased with himself, even in a personal sense, can please others. — FREDERICK SAUNDERS.

Earthly pride is like the passing flower, that springs to fall, and blossoms to die. — H. K. WHITE.

Pride, like anger, builds among the stars ; but pleasure, lark like, nests upon the ground. — YOUNG.

Prim.

Prim as a Quaker. — G. P. MORRIS.

Prime.

Prime as a fiddle. — ANON.

Prime as goats. — SHAKESPEARE.

Primitive.

Primitive . . . like the praam and the canoe. — HUGO.

Prince.

Princes are like to heavenly bodies, which cause good or evil times ; and which have much veneration, but no rest. — BACON.

Princes, like beauties, from their youth
Are strangers to the voice of Truth.
— JOHN GAY.

The name of a Prince is like the sweete deaw, which falleth as well vppon lowe shrubbes, as hygh trees, and resembleth a true glasse, where-in the poore maye see theyr faces with the rych, or a cleare streame where-in all maye drincke that are drye : not they onelye that are wealthy. — LYLY.

Principle.

A good principle was never found solitary in any breast. — JANE PORTER.

Principles, like troops of the line, are undisturbed, and stand fast. — RICHTER.

Print.

He that commeth in print because he woulde be knowen, is like the foole that commeth into the Market because he would be seene. — LYLY.

Privacy.

No more privacy than a goldfish. — IRVIN S. COBB.

Private.

Love should be as private a sentiment as a toothbrush. — O. HENRY.

Privilege.

Kings will lose their privilege, as stars which have completed their time lose their splendor. — DUMAS, PÈRE.

Prize.

Prized as a stray gift. — THOMAS N. TALFOURD.

Probe.

Probing with a cautious touch, like a treasure-seeker in a dark cavern. — HAWTHORNE.

Prodigal.

Prodigal as winter rain. — FRANCIS LEDWIDGE.

Prodigious.

As prodigious, as that of the Sun's swift motion of Heavens. — ROBERT BURTON.

Prodigious as the pyramid of Cheops. — EUGENE FIELD.

Productive.

Vigorously productive, as those fabulous dragon's teeth. — MILTON.

Productive as the Sun. — POPE.

Profession.

In the long run it is with a profession as with marriage — we come to feel only the annoyances. — BALZAC.

Profitless.

Cease thy counsel,
Which falls into mine ears as profitless
As water in a sieve.
— SHAKESPEARE.

Profound.

Profound as an allegory. — ANON.

Profound as an Arctic night. — IBID.

Profound as a genuflection. — IBID.

Profound as that Serbonian bog. — MILTON.

Profuse.

As profusely as a raspberry is furnished with seeds. — ANON.

Progress.

A common progress; like vessels on a common tide. — DANIEL WEBSTER.

Progressive.

Progressive as time. — ANON.

Progressive as a stream. — COWPER.

Prologue.

Prologues, like compliments, are loss of time;
'Tis penning bows and making legs in rhyme. — DAVID GARRICK.

Prologues are like a forlorn hope, sent out
Before the play, to skirmish and to scout. — P. A. MOTTEUX.

Prominent.

Prominent as a ten-cent lemon on a fruitstand. — ANON.

Promise.

Promises are like pie-crust, made to be broken. — ANON.

Promises are like Adonis' gardens,
That one day bloom'd and fruitful were the next. — SHAKESPEARE.

A large promise without performance is like a false fire to a great piece, which dischargeth a good expectation with a bad report. — ARTHUR WARWICK.

Prompt.

Prompt as powder to the linstock. — C. G. DUFFY.

Property.

Property is like snow; if it falleth level to-day, it will be blown into drifts to-morrow. — CATHERINE SINCLAIR.

Prophetic.

Prophetic as the palm of Parsifal's hand. — AMY LESLIE.

Proportion.

Proportioned like the columns of the temple. — BYRON.

Prosper.

Prosper as gardener's crops do in the rottenest ground. — MIDDLETON.

Prosperity.

Prosperity destroyeth the fool; it is like poison, like ratsbane. — THOMAS HOOKER.

Prosperous.

Prosperous as the angels are. — E. B. BROWNING.

Protruding.

Protruding, like the clue to a Lilliputian murder mystery. — O. HENRY.

Proud.

Proud as a cock. — ANON.

Proud as any prince. — IBID.

Proud as a Government mule. — IBID.

Proud as a king. — IBID.

Proud as Lucifer. — IBID.

Proud as a popinjay. — IBID.

Proud as a Spanish Grandee. — IBID.

Proud as a tiger-lily. — IBID.

Proud as Juno. — IBID.

Proud as Punch. — IBID.

Proud as Sheba's queen. — IBID.

Proud — *continued.*

Proud as the man who got rich manufacturing soldiers' shoes out of pasteboard instead of leather. — Ibid.

Proud as any queen. — George Barlow.

Proud as a mulatto in a negro congregation. — J. R. Bartlett's "Dictionary of Americanisms."

Proud as the Pope behind the peacock-fans. — Robert Browning.

Proud as a freeborn peasant. — Byron.

Proud as a peacock. — Chaucer.

Proud as Gascon. — Dumas, père.

Proud as all the Guzmans put together. — Anthony Hamilton.

Proud as a peer. — Bret Harte.

Proud as a young bull. — Richard Le Gallienne.

Proud as a hen with one chicken. — B. Lowsley.

Proud as the day is long. — Lyly.

Proud as a lion when passion-stirred. — Edwin Markham.

Proud as waves that on the beach
Lay their war-crests down and die.
— Thomas Moore.

Proud as an emperor. — Miss Mulock.

Proud as a lord's bastard. — English Proverb.

As proud as a Highlander. — Scottish Proverb.

Proud as an empress on her marriage-day. — Charles Sangster.

Proud as a boy with a brand-new top. — John G. Saxe.

Proud as an enjoyer. — Shakespeare.

Proud as a child who will what he would. — Arthur Symons.

Proud as the Bourbons. — Thackeray.

Proudly.

Proudly, like a bold swimmer. — Hugo.

Flows . . . as proudly as Tiber by Rome. — Edward Lovibond.

Proved.

Proved like steel in tempering fire. — Byron.

Proverb.

Ginowine proverbs ar like good kambrick needles — short, sharp, and shiny. — Josh Billings.

Proverbs are like arrows ; they fly not only fast but straight. — Ibid.

Proverbs, like the sacred books of each nation, are the sanctuary of the Institutions. — Emerson.

Provocative.

Provocative of tears as an onion. — Hawthorne.

Prowl.

Prowl, like stealthy cats. — Frederick S. Cozzens.

Public.

The public, like the delicate Greek Narcissus, is sleepily enamoured of itself ; and the name of its only other perfect lover is Echo. — Sir Walter Raleigh (1861–).

Puff (Noun).

Puff like a paragraph praising a pill. — O. W. Holmes.

Puff (Verb).

Puffed himself up like a ship in full sail. — Hans Christian Andersen.

Puffing out like canvas in a gale. — Anon.

Puffing like the bellows of a blacksmith. — Ibid.

Puffed like a leaky steam pipe. — O. Henry.

Puffed like a swimmer in the breakers. — George Meredith.

Puffy.

Puffy as a cheesecake. — Sir A. Conan Doyle.

Puffy as a bolster. — Thackeray.

Pull.

Pulled and hauled like a rag baby being contended for by a litter of bull pups. — Anon.

Pun.

People that make puns are like wanton boys that put coppers on the railroad tracks. They amuse themselves and other children but their little trick may upset a freight train of conversation for the sake of a battered witticism. — O. W. Holmes.

A pun is somewhat like a cherry: though there may be a slight outward indication of partition — of a duplicity of meaning — yet no gentleman need make two bites at it against his own pleasure. — Thomas Hood.

A pun is like a stumbling-block, that a man cannot always avoid without hitting his shins against it, but the sooner he clears himself from it the better. — James Quin.

Pun . . . where a word, like the tongue of a jackdaw, speaks twice as much by being split. — Swift.

Punctual.

Punctual as a bride at a wedding. — Balzac.

Punctual as Springtide. — Robert Browning.

Punctual — like morning. — James Whitcomb Riley.

Punctual as lovers to the moment sworn. — Young.

Punster.

A punster is to a humorist what a burro is to a horse. — Elbert Hubbard.

Pure.

Pure as a Madonna. — Anon.

Pure as a plaster cast mummy with cement toes. — Ibid.

Pure as a virgin's kiss. — Ibid.

Pure as crystal. — Ibid.

Pure as Heaven's snowy flake. — Ibid.

Like infant's slumbers, pure and light. — Ibid.

Pure as love's heart is. — Ibid.

Pure as Memphian skies that never knew a storm. — Ibid.

Pure as mountain dew. — Ibid.

Pure as purest crystallization. — Ibid.

Pure as the blush of maiden modesty. — Ibid.

Pure as the dream of a child just descended from the heavens. — Ibid.

Pure as the lily. — Ibid.

Pure as the saints above. — Ibid.

Pure as the pines. — Ibid.

Pure as the unsullied wing of a bird. — Ibid.

Pure and pointed as a star. — P. J. Bailey.

Pure as the dead. — Ibid.

Pure as the black of the eye. — Ibid.

As pure as the flame that burns upon an altar. — Balzac.

Pure as the breth of a white male infant. — Josh Billings.

Pure az the utterances ov angells. — Ibid.

Pure as the dawn of Heaven's unclouded day. — Thomas Blacklock.

Pure as the silver from the crucible. — Robert Blair.

As pure and glad as he whom first God in Eden placed. — Robert Bridges (English).

Pure — *continued.*

Pure as the expanse of Heaven. — HENRY BROOKE.

Pure as blossoms, which are newly blowne. — WILLIAM BROWNE.

Pure as the grapes in wine. — E. B. BROWNING.

Pure as chalk. — ROBERT BROWNING.

Pure as the Arctic fox that suits the snow. — IBID.

Pure as buds before they blow. — MICHAEL BRUCE.

Pure as the sky. — BULWER-LYTTON.

Pure as Psyche ere she grew a wife. — BYRON.

Pure as the prayer which
Childhood wafts above.
— IBID.

Pure as the first blush of day. — CALDERON.

As pure as gold yfined. — CHAUCER.

Pure as the babe. — COLERIDGE.

Pure as a Saint's adoring sigh. — GEORGE DARLEY.

Pure as fire. — THOMAS DEKKER.

Pure . . . like aureole round the forehead of a saint. — AUBREY DE VERE.

Pure as the stars in yon blue sky. — DR. JOHN DORAN.

Pure as the breath of the fragrant pine. — JULIA C. R. DORR.

Pure as the angel forms above. — J. D. DRAKE.

Pure as winter snow. — F. A. FAHY.

Pure as unwritten papers. — JOHN FORD.

Pure as consecrated water. — GAUTIER.

Pure as the summer sun of Southern heaven. — W. S. GILBERT.

Like Diana pure. — RICHARD GLOVER.

Pure like the heart of water,
You are pure like the core of earth.
— GOETHE.

Pure as smooth-carven marble. — IAN HAMILTON.

Pure as the virgin who first led Agrippa. — HAWTHORNE.

Pure as infant's brow. — PAUL HAMILTON HAYNE.

Pure as the Hindoo's votive lamp
On Ganges' sacred tide.
— MARY E. HEWITT.

Pure as the dew that filters through the rose. — O. W. HOLMES.

Pure as the quarry's whitest block. — IBID.

Pure as starlight shall their deeds of daring glow. — W. D. HOWELLS.

Pure as a burning ember. — HUGO.

Pure as spirits. — IBID.

Pure as the thoughts of infant innocence. — DR. JOHNSON.

Pure as the ice-drop that froze on the mountain. — KEATS.

As pure from sin and stain, as his when Eden held his virgin heart. — JOHN KEBLE.

Pure as the light of day. — KINGSBURY.

Pure as purest vestal virgin. — SIGMUND KRASINSKI.

Pure as buds before they blow. — JOHN LOGAN.

Pure, as the charities of the skies. — IBID.

Pure as the kiss that waked Endymion. — GEORGE MAC-HENRY.

Pure as the white stars sweeping through the sky. — MAHABHARATA.

Pure as the wild white rain. — EDWIN MARKHAM.

Pure — *continued.*

Pure as the first opening of the blooms in May. — MARSTON.

She is as pure, as good, and as beautiful as an angel. — GUY DE MAUPASSANT.

As pure as April's snowdrops are. — OWEN MEREDITH.

Pure as the snow-rob'd angel that guards the holy altar. — WILLIAM J. MICKLE.

Pure as sanctity's best shrine. — THOMAS MIDDLETON.

Pure as the white clouds,
That sail around the moon.
— MISS MITFORD.

Pure as a wreath of snow on April flowers. — JAMES MONTGOMERY.

Pure as angel thoughts. — THOMAS MOORE.

Pure as the young moon's coronet. — IBID.

Pure as bright Aurora's ray. — G. P. MORRIS.

Pure as any maid. — LEWIS MORRIS.

Pure as the pure in heart that shall see God. — MISS MULOCK.

Pure as Cato's daughter. — OTWAY.

Pure as the sunbeams gild the placid deep,
When zephyrs close their wings in listless sleep. — ANDREW PARK.

Pure as a bride's blush. — COVENTRY PATMORE.

Pure as the permeating fires
That smoulder in the opal's veins.
— IBID.

Pure as the wishes breathed in prayer. — POE.

Pure as the summer skies. — W. M. PRAED.

Pure and chaste as the falling snow. — T. BUCHANAN READ.

Pure as any gowan [daisy]. — H. RIDDELL.

As pure and clear as the cherry-blossoms blow in the land of Thus-and-So. — JAMES WHITCOMB RILEY.

Pure as a joyous prayer. — IBID.

Pure as the dove. — C. G. ROSSETTI.

Pure as virgin purity. — IBID.

As pure as a mountain spring. — RUSKIN.

Pure as thoughts that thrill a saint. — A. J. RYAN.

Pure as grace. — SHAKESPEARE.

Pure as sin with baptism. — IBID.

Pure as speechless infancy. — SHELLEY.

Pure as an infant's thoughts. — SOUTHEY.

Pure and painless as a virgin's dreams. — SWINBURNE.

Pure as at the daydawn of the world. — IBID.

Pure as faith. — IBID.

Pure as Eden's dew. — IBID.

Desire pure as babe's that nestles toward the breast. — IBID.

Pure as fire or flowers or snows. — IBID.

Pure as heaven. — IBID.

Pure as love's heart is. — IBID.

Pure as one purged of pain that passion bore. — IBID.

Pure as the dawn and the dew. — IBID.

Pure as the depth of pain. — IBID.

Pure as the wind and the sun. — IBID.

Pure as truth. — IBID.

Pure as morns of Paradise. — BAYARD TAYLOR.

Pure — *continued.*

Purer than snow. — OLD TESTAMENT.

Pure words: as silver tried in a furnace of earth, purified seven times. — IBID.

Pure as the breath of dawn. — CELIA THAXTER.

Pure,
As is the lily or the mountain snow.
— JAMES THOMSON.

Pure as the snowy leaves that fold
Over the flower's heart of gold.
— HENRY VAN DYKE.

Pure as melting dew. — GARCILASO DE LA VEGA.

Pure as the snowflake ere it falls and takes the stain of earth. — ALARIC A. WATTS.

Pure as Angel-worship. — WHITTIER.

Pure as the mountains of perpetual snow. — WILLIAM WINTER.

Pure as nature is. — WORDSWORTH.

Purge.

Purges as with fire of purgatory. — SWINBURNE.

Purified.

Purified from passion's stain,
Like the moon, in gentle splendour,
ruling o'er the peaceful main.
— BERNARD BARTON.

Purified as by fire. — FRANÇOIS COPPÉE.

Purpose.

Purposes, like eggs, unless they be hatched into action, soon run into rottenness. — SAMUEL SMILES.

Purposeless.

Purposeless as to give a goose hay. — ANON.

Purple.

Purpled as with stains of wine. — T. B. ALDRICH.

Purple as a pansy. — ANON.

Purple as the Nile. — IBID.

Purple like that of a prelate. — JOHN DENNIS.

Purple . . . like robes of a king. — ROBERT NOEL.

Purple like the unplucked plum. — ELIZABETH D. STODDARD.

Purple, like the blush of even. — WORDSWORTH.

Pursue.

Pursue like a shadow. — ANON.

Pursuing like a whirlwind. — SAMUEL BUTLER.

The howl pursued me like a vengeance. — JOSEPH CONRAD.

Pursued like a June bug by a duck. — SAM JONES.

Pursued as hawk pursues its prey. — EDNA DEAN PROCTOR.

Pursued like raging hounds. — SHELLEY.

Pursued them like the Furies. — VOLTAIRE.

Pursuit.

The pursuit was like Jacob's ladder — if it did lead to heaven it was certainly an awfully long journey, and very hard on one's legs. — LEVER.

Push.

Pushed like a fencing master. — COLLEY CIBBER.

Pushed, like a fish to its native sea. — GEORGE MEREDITH.

Push on — like ambition. — SYDNEY MUNDEN.

Puzzled.

Puzzled as a hen when her ducklings suddenly take to the water. — ANON.

A puzzled look, like a foreigner trying to catch the meaning of words in a language he does not understand. — BALZAC.

Q

Quail.

Quails like a naughty child. — G. B. Shaw.

Quake.

Quake like an aspen leaf. — Anon.

Quaking like an owl out in the sunshine. — Balzac.

Quaked like river-shaken rush. — William Morris.

Quarrel.

Thus love and quarrels (April weather)
Like vinegar and oil together
Join in an easy mingled strife,
To make the salad up of life.
— Robert Lloyd.

The quarrels of lovers are like showers that leave the country more verdant and beautiful. — Madame Necker.

Quarrelsome.

Quarrel like the two halves of a Seidlitz powder. — Anon.

Quarrelsome, like a sparrow. — Dickens.

Quarrelous as the weasel. — Shakespeare.

Queer.

As queer as Dick's hatband, made of pea-straw, that went nine times round, and would not meet at last. — Anon.

Quench.

Quench in tears like a star in the sea. — P. J. Bailey.

Quenched . . . like torch-flame choked in dust. — Robert Browning.

Quenched like a consumed torch. — Spenser.

Quenched as a flame. — Swinburne.

Querulous.

Voice was sweet indeed, but it was thin and querulous like that of a feeble slave in misery, who despairs altogether, yet cannot refrain himself from weeping and lamentation. — Coleridge.

Question.

I was to my questioning like glass unto the color which it clothes. — Dante.

Most questions are like a plank: have two sides. — Sydney Munden.

Quick.

Quick as a flash. — Anon.

Quick as an arrow. — Ibid.

Quick as a wink. — Ibid.

Quick as gunpowder. — Ibid.

Quick as the flash of a quail's wing. — Ibid.

Quick as the twinkling of a bed-post. — Ibid.

Quick as you can say Jack Robinson. — Ibid.

Quick as hell can scorch a feather. — Ibid.

Quick as a stab. — J. M. Barrie.

Quick as greased lightning. — J. R. Bartlett's "Dictionary of Americanisms."

Quick, as a darted beam of light. — R. D. Blackmore.

Quick as a fear. — E. B. Browning.

Quick as finches in a blossomed tree. — Ibid.

Quick as thought. — Thomas Carew.

Quick as an eyelid's beat. — Cavalcanti.

Quick of scent as a vulture. — Cumberland.

Quick as a dart. — Goethe.

Change quick, like eyes that brighten. — Judah HaLevi.

Quick — *continued.*

Quick as barrels popping at a bird. — GEORGE MEREDITH.

Quick as torrents run. — IBID.

Quick as wings. — IBID.

Quick as an imp. — ADA PATTERSON.

Thy wit is as quick as the greyhound's mouth. — SHAKESPEARE.

Fly as quick to Delia's arms, as yonder halcyon skims the stream. — WILLIAM SHENSTONE.

Quick as the morning ray, or ev'ning beam. — WILLIAM THOMSON.

Quick as the lightning's flash. — JUAN VALERA.

Quick as light. — HENRY VAUGHAN.

Quick as thought. — "WIT RESTORED."

Quickening.

Quickening as sunshine. — FRANK HARRIS.

Quickly.

Quickly as a cabbage bed produces snails. — ANON.

Quickly as a scalded cat goes through a back window. — IBID.

As quickly as iron in the fire passes through the various stages between warmth and white heat. — J. M. BARRIE.

Quickly as iron to the magnet. — HELEN H. JACKSON.

Quickly as a dream that dawn devours. — EUGENE LEE-HAMILTON.

Quiet.

Quiet as a graveyard. — ANON.

Quiet as a wasp in one's nose. — IBID.

Quiet as death. — IBID.

Quiet as dreaming trees. — IBID.

Quiet as murder. — IBID.

Quiet as the hush of evening. — IBID.

As quiet as the lighting of a fly on a feather-duster. — IBID.

Quiet as two kittens. — IBID.

Quiet fish are talkative in comparison. — IBID.

Quiet as a woman the first day and a half after she's married. — BEAUMONT AND FLETCHER.

Quiet as despair. — ROBERT BROWNING.

Quiet as are quiet skies. — ELLEN BURROUGHS.

Quiet as a sepulchre. — DICKENS.

Quiet as a sleeping boa. — HAMLIN GARLAND.

Quiet as a statue. — W. E. HENLEY.

Quiet as if shod with felt. — HOOD.

Quiet as a mouse. — ARSÈNE HOUSSAYE.

Quiet as a stone. — KEATS.

Quiet as a nest of monasteries. — AMY LESLIE.

Quiet as a heart that beats no more. — LONGFELLOW.

Quiet as the tranquil sky. — IBID.

Quiet, as of dreaming Trees. — GERALD MASSEY.

Quiet as if the finger of God's will had bade the human mechanism "be still." — MISS MULOCK.

Quiet as at anchor in a dead calm. — MUNCHAUSEN.

As quiet as a settin' hen. — SCOTTISH PROVERB.

Quiet as a lamb. — SHAKESPEARE.

Quiet as the sun. — SWINBURNE.

Quiet as a moonbeam. — ELIZABETH S. P. WARD.

Quiet as a Nun
Breathless with adoration.
— WORDSWORTH.

Quieted.

Quieted like love overcoming strife. — ADELAIDE A. PROCTER.

Quietly.

Began as quietly as a roaring March. — J. M. BARRIE.

Float quietly, like Angels winnowing by. — F. W. FABER.

Quietly as a cloud. — KIPLING.

As quietly as spots of sky
Among the evening clouds.
— WORDSWORTH.

Quietness.

Quietness like the serene glow of a halo. — JOSEPH CONRAD.

Better is an handful with quietness, than both the hands full with travail and vexation of spirit. — OLD TESTAMENT.

Quiver.

Quiver like a fiddle string. — ANON.

Quiver like a leaf in the wind. — IBID.

Quiver like jelly. — IBID.

Tremulous quiver, like an arrow full drawn by the strong. — EUGENE BARRY.

Quiver, like a weed in water. — R. D. BLACKMORE.

Quivering . . . like a vibrant music-string stretched from mountain peak to sky. — E. B. BROWNING.

Quiver, as if they stood upon the verge of an imminent peril. — GEORGE W. CURTIS.

Quivers like the tail of swine gladdened by a corn feast. — AUBREY DE VERE.

Quivering . . . like a cunning animal whose hiding-places are surrounded by swift-advancing flame. — GEORGE ELIOT.

Quivered like a harp of which the strings are ready to spring. — FLAUBERT.

Quivers as if it were nipped with frost. — KALIDASA.

Quivered . . . as a breakwater-pile quivers to the rush of landward-racing seas. — KIPLING.

Quivering like a man's hand when he raises it to say good-bye. — IBID.

Quivered like a willow wand. — JOAQUIN MILLER.

Quivered like forest-leaves. — D. G. ROSSETTI.

Quiver . . .
Like weeds unfolding in the ocean.
— SHELLEY.

Quivering as when life is hard on death. — SWINBURNE.

Quiver,
Like jewels in the river.
— THEODORE TILTON.

R

Race.

Races as dust and surf of the sea. — SWINBURNE.

Radiant.

Radiant . . . as moon that breaks a stormy night. — ÆSCHYLUS.

Radiant . . . like a young moon. — ARABIAN NIGHTS.

Radiant as morning. — ALFRED AUSTIN.

Radiant like a diamond. — P. J. BAILEY.

Radiant . . . like paths of the gods. — CARLYLE.

Radiant as the day. — SIR SAMUEL FERGUSON.

Radiant — *continued.*

Radiant as the queen of love. — HOMER (POPE).

Radiant as the blossomed lea. — PHILANDER CHASE JOHNSON.

Radiant as the starry night. — "LAYS OF ANCIENT INDIA."

Radiant as snow. — OWEN MEREDITH.

Radiant as summer sun in morn. — JAMES WHITCOMB RILEY.

Radiant as a lark. — OWEN SEAMAN.

Radiant as the air around a star. — SHELLEY.

Radiant, like the phantoms of the dawn. — IBID.

Radiant as the bloom of day. — WILLIAM THOMSON.

Radiant as Hope, when Hope was young. — ALARIC A. WATTS.

Radiant as sunlit clustering goldenrod. — C. P. WILSON.

Radiate.

Radiated like the stars. — JAMES MONTGOMERY.

Rage (Noun).

Heaven has no rage like love to hatred turned. — CONGREVE.

Rage (Verb).

Raged like Satan with a toothache. — ANON.

Rage like a lion. — ROBERT BURTON.

Immeasurable thirst
Raged as a flame.
— LORD DE TABLEY.

Raging like an unexpected fire. — GOETHE.

Rages . . . like a leopard caged. — MAURICE HEWLETT.

Rage like a thirst. — IBID.

Hector rages like the force of fire. — HOMER (POPE).

Like a wild thing, suddenly aware
That it is caged, which flings and bruises all
Its body at the bars, he rose, and raged. — JEAN INGELOW.

Raging as burning Hercules. — WILLIAM J. MICKLE.

Raging as Demon of Dante. — WALTER PARKE.

Rage like a fury. — J. R. PLANCHÉ.

Rage, like demons in their Stygian cage. — JOHN RUSKIN.

Rage like an angry bear, chafed with sweat. — SHAKESPEARE.

Raged within me, like a scorpion's nest
Built in my entrails. — SHELLEY.

Rage . . . like boiling liquor in a seething pot. — TASSO.

Raging like one mad in flight. — THEOCRITUS.

Rage as old Voltaire at Ferney. — N. P. WILLIS.

Ragged.

Ragged as the mouth of a Cornish cave. — G. K. CHESTERTON.

As ragged and dirty as a Leith carter's pony. — SCOTTISH PROVERB.

Ragged as Lazarus. — SHAKESPEARE.

Rail.

Rail like a rude costermonger. — BEAUMONT AND FLETCHER.

Raillery.

Raillery, like salt, should be used sparingly. — DEMOPHILUS.

Railroads.

Railroads are like the human race, they have their stopping places and their termini ; but unlike the human race they can make a return journey. — E. P. DAY.

Rally.

Rally like bees. — ANON.

Rampant.

Rampant, like the split-eagle of the Austrian Empire. — BULWER-LYTTON.

Rampant, like a lion roused to wrath. — CHARLES HARPUR.

Ran.

Tyll the bloode from ther bassonetts ranne
As the roke doth in the rayne.
— "THE BATTLE OF OTTERBOURNE."

Random.

At random, like Bullies Oaths. — ROBERT WOLSELEY.

Rang.

Rang like a God-swept lyre. — ANON.

My head rang like a guard-room gong. — KIPLING.

Rang like a musket-butt on flagstones. — IBID.

Rang out like hollow woods, at hunting-tide. — TENNYSON.

Rank.

Rank as any pole-cat.—BEN JONSON.

Rank as pumpkin-pips. — OWEN SEAMAN.

Rank as a fox. — SHAKESPEARE.

Rank as any flax-wench. — IBID.

Rankle.

Rankle like poisons in the soul. — TUPPER.

Ransack.

Ransacked like an old workbox. — WILLIAM ARCHER.

Rapacious.

As a vulture rapacious. — SMOLLETT.

Rapid.

Rapid as a charge of Arab horse. — ANON.

Rapid as lightning. — WILLIAM BARTRAM.

Rapid as the winds of Spring. — CUCHULAIN.

Rapid as the shadow of a cloud. — THOMAS HARDY.

Rapid as the ever-wheeling sun. — AARON HILL.

Rapid as the storm-wind. — HAFIZ PASHA.

Rapidly.

Rapidly as drummer-sticks. — GEORGE MEREDITH.

Rapt.

Rapt as sleep. — HAMLIN GARLAND.

Rapture.

Rapture like the rage of hate allayed
With ruin and ravin that its might hath made. — SWINBURNE.

Rare.

Rare as a blue rose. — ANON.

Rare as a snowbird in hell. — IBID.

Rare as a sunflower in the desert — IBID.

Rare as venison in a poor man's kitchen. — IBID.

Rare as a winter swallow. — BALZAC.

As rare almost as hedge-rows in the wild. — COWPER.

Rare as an Albino in Africa. — W. R. HEREFORD.

As rare to see the Sunne with-out a light, as a fayre woeman with-out a lover. — LYLY.

As rare as wings upon a cat, or flowers of air, a rabbit's horns, or ropes of tortoise-hair. — ORIENTAL.

Rare as a comet. — JAMES RALPH.

Rare as a play that does not yawn you, or a woman that does not deceive you. — CHARLES READE.

Rare — *continued.*

Rarer than a phœnix. — AGNES REPPLIER.

Rare to be found as black swans. — DANIEL ROGER'S "MATRIMONIALL HONOUR," 1642.

Rare as the stars upon a clouded night. — LOUISE MORGAN SILL.

Rare as a dodo. — ROBERT LOUIS STEVENSON.

Like snow at Midsummer, exceeding rare. — JOHN TAYLOR.

Rare as Homers and Miltons, rare as Platos and Newtons. — EDWIN P. WHIPPLE.

Rash.

Rash as fire. — SHAKESPEARE.

Rattle.

She rattles away like a woman's tongue. — W. H. AINSWORTH.

Rattled in his ear like coins dropped on a barroom floor. — ANON.

Rattled like a parchment drum. — IBID.

Rattle like peas in a bladder. — IBID.

Rattled like a pair of castanets. — DAUDET.

His bones
Rattle in his skin, like beans tossed in
a bladder.
— PHILIP MASSINGER.

Rattled like shutters in a blast. — ELLA WHEELER WILCOX.

Rave.

Raved like a bedlamite. — ANON.

Rave like a madman. — IBID.

Rave like an epileptic dervish. — ROBERT BROWNING.

Rave like beasts stupefied. — ROBERT BURTON.

Rave like a man in Bedlam. — GEORGE COLMAN, THE YOUNGER.

Raved like a fiend. — J. G. HOLLAND.

Rave like a fury. — W. S. LANDOR.

Raving like a mad creature. — JANE PORTER.

Rave like Shakespeare's jealous Moor. — CHRISTOPHER SMART.

Raving . . . like a Maenad starting up at the rattle of the sacred emblems, when the triennial orgies lash her with the cry of Bacchus, and Cithæron's yell calls her into the night. — VIRGIL.

Ravenous.

Ravenous as winter wolf. — COLERIDGE.

Ravenous as the fitful sea. — SWINBURNE.

Ravenous as a prairie's fire. — FRANK WATERS.

Ravish.

Ravish like enchanting harmony. — SHAKESPEARE.

Ravishment.

Ravishments more keen
Than Hermes' pipe. — KEATS.

Raw.

Raw as a Lyndhaven on the half-shell. — GEORGE BRONSON-HOWARD.

Rayless.

The lack-lustre eye, rayless as a Beacon-street door-plate in August. — O. W. HOLMES.

Reach.

Out of reach of him,
As the sun! As the stars — a million,
million times
Beyond the sun. — J. S. KNOWLES.

React.

React like the pendulum. — C. C. COLTON.

Reader.

Like the tiger, that seldom desists from pursuing man, after having once preyed upon human flesh, the reader, who has once gratified his appetite with calumny, makes, ever after, the most agreeable feast upon murdered reputation. — GOLDSMITH.

Readily.

Readily as the smith can labor at his forge. — ANON.

Readily as water rushes into a hollow. — IBID.

Met the gale as readily as the butterflies meet the sun. — ELIZA COOK.

As readily as a child takes sweetmeats at Mardi Gras. — OUIDA.

Readily as condemned men take reprieve. — SWINBURNE.

Reading.

Much reading is like much eating, — wholly useless without digestion. — ROBERT SOUTH.

Ready.

Ready like a porcupine for cold weather. — ANON.

Ready like the golden censer for the aloes and cassia. — IBID.

Ready as a primed cannon. — CARLYLE.

Ready as bird that sees the sprinkled corn. — GEORGE ELIOT.

Ready all,
As Echo, waiting for a call.
— THOMAS MOORE.

He stood ready for the battle like a bull that has whetted his horns. — PENTAUR.

Ready as a borrower's cap. — SHAKESPEARE.

Real.

Real as man's wonder what his soul may be. — MARTHA G. DICKINSON.

Real as the violets of April days. — IBID.

Real as the stars. — RICHARD LE GALLIENNE.

Real as a hand. — VANCE THOMPSON.

Reality.

No more to do with reality than the toy men in a child's Noah's Ark. — H. A. JONES.

Reason.

Reasons are like liquors, and there are some of such nature as none but strong heads can bear. — EDMUND BURKE.

Reason is to faith as the eye is to the telescope. — JOHN CAIRD.

Reason, like virtue, in a medium lies :
A hair-breadth more might make us mad, not wise.
— WALTER HARTE.

Human reason is like a drunken man on horseback ; set it up on one side, and it tumbles over on the other. — LUTHER.

Reasonable.

As reasonable as to expect that the tiger will spare the hart, to browse upon the herbage. — C. C. COLTON.

Rebellious.

Rebellious as the sea. — THOMAS HEYWOOD.

Recede.

Receding as the skies. — ROBERT LEIGHTON.

Recedes as a dream recedes. — SWINBURNE.

Receding as a cloud in air. — BAYARD TAYLOR.

Receded, as mists fade before a morning sun. — BARRETT WENDELL.

Reckless.

Loud-voiced and reckless as the wide tide-race
That whips our harbor-mouth!
— KIPLING.

Reclined.

Reclined like some vacuous beauty lounging in a guarded harem. — O. Henry.

Recognition.

About as much chance of recognition as would the breathings of a lute under an elevated train. — Anon.

Recoil.

Recoiled as . . . he had seen a snake in his path. — Joseph Conrad.

Recoiled as if an unclean creature touched him. — Richard H. Dana, senior.

Recoiled from its purpose, as from the verge of a crag. — Longfellow.

Recoiled, as if she had been face to face with an apparition. — Guy de Maupassant.

Like an over-charged gun, recoil. — Shakespeare.

Recoils, and climbs and closes,
As a wave of the sea turned back.
— Swinburne.

Recreation.

Recreation is intended to the mind, as whetting is to the scythe; to sharpen the edge of it, which otherwise would grow dull and blunt. He, therefore, that spends his whole time in recreation, is ever whetting, never mowing: his grass may grow, and his steed starve. As, contrarily, he, that always toils and never recreates, is ever mowing, never whetting; labouring much to little purpose: as good no scythe, as no edge. Then only doth the work go forward, when the scythe is so seasonably and moderately whetted, that it may cut; and so cuts, that it may have the help of sharpening. I would also so interchange, that I neither be dull with work, nor idle and wanton with recreation. — Joseph Hall.

Red.

Red as any rose in June. — C. F. Alexander.

Red, like a cardinal. — Leonid Andreyev.

Red as a beet. — Anon.

Red as a blister. — Ibid.

Red as a brick. — Ibid.

Red as a cherry. — Ibid.

Red as a coal. — Ibid.

Red as a danger signal. — Ibid.

Red as a hunter's face. — Ibid.

Red as a petticoat. — Ibid.

Red as a red wagon. — Ibid.

Red as Roger's nose, who was christened with pump water. — Ibid.

Red as asoka flowers. — Ibid.

Red as a turkey-cock. — Ibid.

Red as fields of heather on fire. — — Ibid.

Red as the fire of a pipe. — Ibid.

Red as the heather bell. — Ibid.

Glowed red, like the ishrik seeds, fresh fallen, unbroken, bright. — Arabic.

Red as a plum. — R. D. Blackmore.

Red as with wine out of season. — E. B. Browning.

Face of him . . . red as that of the foggiest rising Moon. — Carlyle.

Red as the highest colour'd Gallic wine. — Chatterton.

Red as a fox. — Chaucer.

Rede as blood. — Ibid.

Rede as rose. — Ibid.

Rede,
As doth where that men melte lede.
— Ibid.

Reed as the bristles of a sowes erys. — Ibid.

Red — *continued.*

Red as a tile. — DANIEL DEFOE.

Red as beetroot. — DICKENS.

Red as gore. — MICHAEL FIELD.

Red as beef. — FIELDING.

Red as the sangaree. — RICHARD GARNETT.

Red as deep as bull's blood. — GIBBON.

Red as the blood-drops from a wounded heart. — FRANK W. GUNSAULUS.

Red as coral. — ANTHONY HAMILTON.

Dry red, like old blood. — MAURICE HEWLETT.

With hue as red as the rosy bed
Which a bee would choose to dream in.
— C. F. HOFFMAN.

Red as the beacon-light. — HOGG.

Red as an angry sunset. — JEAN INGELOW.

Red as the rose is red. — OMAR KHAYYAM.

Red as slaughter. — KIPLING.

Red as the fire of a furnace. — LAMARTINE.

Red as a beacon the wind has upblown. — SIDNEY LANIER.

Red as if he were going to choke. — GEORGE MACDONALD.

Nose had got as red with passion as the protuberance of a turkey-cock when gobbling out its unutterable feelings of disdain. — IBID.

Red as murder. — GEORGE MEREDITH.

Red as the British Army. — IBID.

Red as a dawn. — HENRY MORLEY.

Red as a lobster. — THOMAS NASH.

Red as Cupid's bed of red rose-leaves shed on Mount Hymettus. — MILES O'REILLY.

Red as a mazer from an alder-tree. — RABELAIS.

Red as Mont Blanc at morning glows. — T. BUCHANAN READ.

Red . . . as the forge's mouth. — IBID.

Red as from the broken heart. — D. G. ROSSETTI.

Red, like a ruby. — RUSKIN.

Red as fire. — SHAKESPEARE.

Red as Mars. — IBID.

Red as new-enkindled fire. — IBID.

Red as Titan's face. — IBID.

Red, as it had drunk the evening beams. — SOUTHEY.

Red did show like roses in a bed of lillies shed. — SPENSER.

Red as dawn. — SWINBURNE.

Red as hate. — IBID.

Red as hot brows of shame. — IBID.

Red as love or shame. — IBID.

Lips red as morning's rise. — IBID.

Red as the rains of hell. — IBID.

Red as a poppy. — THACKERAY.

Red as mountain-ash berries. — ZACHARIAS TOPÉLIUS.

Red as the Baldinsville skool-house. — ARTEMUS WARD.

Red as the reddest ruby. — THEODORE WATTS-DUNTON.

Red as the banner which enshrouds
The warrior-dead when strife is done.
— WHITTIER.

Red as the naked hand of doom. — IBID.

Red as ruddy clover. — WORDSWORTH.

Redolent.

Redolent . . . as a clover-field of honey. — GEORGE W. CURTIS.

Reek.

Reeking as if with a cloud of incense. — Max Nordau.

Reeked as a wet red grave. — Swinburne.

Reeked as fumes from hell. — Ibid.

Reel.

Reeling as a clubbed man reels before he collapses. — Joseph Conrad.

Reel like masts on ocean's swell. — O. W. Holmes.

Reeling, to and fro, like a reed. — Hugo.

He reels like a ship that has met with waves raised by the southeast wind. — Osmanli Proverb.

Reel like a leaf that's drawn to a water-wheel. — D. G. Rossetti.

Reels as any reed under the wind. — Swinburne.

Reeled
As waves wind-thwarted on the sea
— Ibid.

Reels like a falling cedar. — Tasso.

Reels, as the golden Autumn woodland reels
Athwart the smoke of burning weeds.
— Tennyson.

Reel to and fro and stagger like a drunkard. — Old Testament.

Refines.

Refines as by fire. — Robert Browning.

Reflection.

All serious reflections are like reflections in water — a pebble will disturb them, and make a dull pond sparkle. — George Eliot.

Reform.

Reform, like charity, must begin at home. — Carlyle.

Refresh.

Refreshes like the first gush of spring, or the break of an April shower. — Donald G. Mitchell.

Refreshed, as men in barren lands in drought are soothed by hearing the glad fall of a welcome rain. — Ouida.

Refreshed as by the sight of fresh grass in midwinter or early spring. — Henry D. Thoreau.

Refreshes me like a tonic. — Israel Zangwill.

Refreshing.

Refreshing like a quaff from a crystal spring to a dying man. — Anon.

Regal.

Regal as Juno. — C. S. Calverley.

Regretted.

Regretted like the nightingale's last note. — Wordsworth.

Regular.

Regular as sunrise. — Anon.

Regular as military drums. — Dickens.

Regular as the private garden of a Grand Duke. — Arsène Houssaye.

Regular as a lath. — Lowell.

Regularly.

Regularly as light and shadow on April days. — J. Fitzgerald Molloy.

Regularly as clock-work. — Sir Walter Scott.

Rejoice.

Rejoice
As at our first love's voice.
— Lord De Tabley.

Like the mother of some victor chief rejoices. — Aubrey De Vere.

Rejoice like grasshoppers on summer days. — Homer (Pope).

Rejoicing like a cloud of morn. — Shelley.

Rejoice — *continued.*

Rejoice,
Like Kouli-Kan, in plunder of the proud. — YOUNG.

Relations.

Relations are like drugs, — useful, sometimes, and even pleasant, if taken in small quantities and seldom, — and the truly wise avoid them. — MARY A. BEAUCHAMP.

Relax.

Beneath his glance the strong-knit joints relax
As the weak knees before the headsman's axe. — O. W. HOLMES.

Relent.

Relent her
As blooming spring unbends the brow
Of surly, savage winter. — BURNS.

Relentless.

Relentless as fate. — ANON.

Relentless as a curse. — GEORGE ELIOT.

As relentless as a Greek tragedy. — JAMES HUNEKER.

Relentless as an invalid. — GEORGE MEREDITH.

Reliable.

Reliable as an old wheel-horse. — ANON.

Religion.

Religion is like the Fashion : one Man wears his Doublet slashed, another laced, another plain ; but every Man has a Doublet. So every man has his Religion. We differ about Trimming. — SELDEN.

Without a belief in personal immortality, religion is surely like an arch resting on one pillar, like a bridge ending in an abyss. — MAX MÜLLER.

Reluctantly.

Reluctantly . . . like the steps of a bride to the altar. — DONALD G. MITCHELL.

Rely.

On Thee let my spirit rely —
Like some rude dial, that, fix'd on earth,
Still looks for its light from the sky. — THOMAS MOORE.

Remain.

Remaining, like marten-holes in a sand-cliff. — THOMAS HARDY.

Remorseless.

Remorseless as an infant's bier. — KEATS.

Remorselessly.

Remorselessly as the ocean moves in upon the shore. — O. W. HOLMES.

Remote.

Remote as a dream. — ANON.

Remote, like echoed voice of one the tombs among. — AUBREY DE VERE.

Remote, as the dead lords of song,
Great masters who have made us what we are. — JEAN INGELOW.

Remote and minute as the chief scene of our infancy. — GEORGE MEREDITH.

Remote as the stars are. — CHARLES L. MOORE.

As remote in thought as . . . the Apostles or the Cæsars. — ROBERT LOUIS STEVENSON.

Removes.

Two removes are as bad as a fire. — ANON.

Rend.

Whose rage doth rend
Like interrupted waters. — SHAKESPEARE.

Renew.

Renewed, like Juno's virtue. — ANON.

As embers touch'd with sulphurs do renew,
So will her sight kindle fresh flames in you. — FRANCIS BEAUMONT.

Renew — *continued.*

Renew thy youth, as eagle from the nest. — C. G. Rossetti.

Thy youth is renewed like the eagle's. — Old Testament.

Renewable.

Renewable, as some appetites are. — Charles Lamb.

Renowned.

Renowned as the sun. — Homer (Pope).

Rent.

Is rent as carrion by the vulturous beaks
That feed on fame and soil it.
— Swinburne.

Repeating.

Repeating . . . like a drunken man with a tune in his head. — Richard Le Gallienne.

Repel.

Repel one like a cudgel. — C. N. Bovée.

Repellent.

As repellent as a boy's drum. — J. M. Barrie.

Repelling.

More repelling than an abyss. — George Meredith.

Repetition.

To tease by ceaseless repetition; like the unvaried continued action of a bore. — Samuel Richardson.

Repose (Noun).

Half-repose, like a shepherd keeping sheep. — E. B. Browning.

Repose, like that of a sphinx. — Bulwer-Lytton.

Repose (Verb).

Repose, as feebler wings do in a quiet nest. — George Eliot.

Repose, like birds who nightly nestle in the trees. — "Hymn to Time."

Reposes,
Like relics in an urn.
— Wordsworth.

Reposeful.

Reposeful as a statue. — Anon.

Reproduce.

He could have reproduced like an echo. — Joseph Conrad.

Reproof.

Reproof is a medicine like mercury or opium; if it be improperly administered, it will do harm instead of good. — Horace Mann.

Reputation.

Reputation, like beavers and cloaks, shall last some people twice the time of others. — Douglas Jerrold.

The reputation of a man is like his shadow; it sometimes follows and sometimes precedes him, sometimes longer and sometimes shorter than his natural size. — French Proverb.

Reputation, like other mistresses, is never true to a man in his absence. — Wycherley.

Repute.

Good repute is like fire: once kindled, it is easily kept alive; but when extinguished, not easily lighted again. — Plutarch.

Requisite.

Requisite . . . as steele in a weapon. — Lyly.

Resembles.

Resembles, as a pastoral resembles a symphony. — Alfred Ayres.

Resembles, as bottles bottles. — George Meredith.

Resemble . . .
As much as an apple doth an oyster.
— Shakespeare.

Resistless.

Resistless as the wind. — THOMAS BLACKLOCK.

Resistless as the spirit of the night. — CHARLOTTE BROOKE.

Resistless as a cannon ball. — JEFFERY FARNOL.

Resistless as a flash that strikes from Heaven. — ROBERT JEPHSON.

Resolute.

Resolute as a drunken Irishman. — ANON.

Resolute as thunder. — JOHN FORD.

Resolute as iron. — HAWTHORNE.

Resound.

Voice, resounding as a brass trumpet. — GAUTIER.

Resounds like Sylvan revelry. — REGINALD HEBER.

Resounding, like the blast of funeral trumpets. — LONGFELLOW.

Resounds like heaven's thunder. — SHAKESPEARE.

Resourceful.

Resourceful as D'Artagnan. — ANON.

Respectable.

Respectable as a long face. — BULWER-LYTTON.

Resplendent.

Resplendent as the noonday sun. — ANON.

Resplendent as the autumn moon. — IBID.

Resplendent as a bridegroom. — GREGORY OF NAZIANZUS.

Resplendent as the summer noon. — THOMAS MOORE.

Resplendent as a beam of the morning star. — J. T. TROWBRIDGE.

Respond.

Respond as steel answers to the magnet. — ANON.

Responds like the strings of an Æolian harp. — IBID.

Responsive.

Like the tun'd string responsive to the touch. — RICHARD JAGO.

Rest.

At rest, as the ark in the temple. — BACON.

Rested on him as lightly as freckles on his nose. — ALICE CALDWELL HEGAN.

Rest,
Like beauty nestling in a young man's
breast. — CHARLES LAMB.

Rested in strange wise,
As when some creature utterly outworn
Sinks into bed and lies.
— D. G. ROSSETTI.

Restless.

Restless as a gypsy. — ANON.

Restless as ambition. — IBID.

Restless as Hamlet. — IBID.

Restless as leaves. — IBID.

Restless as quicksilver. — IBID.

Restless as the sea. — ALFRED AUSTIN.

Restless as a riot. — REX BEACH.

Restless . . . as the winds. — APHRA BEHN.

Restless as the nest-deserted bird. — E. B. BROWNING.

Restless, like a dog whose master is absent. — DUMAS, PÈRE.

Restless as the fire that blows and spreads and leaps from high to higher where'er is aught to seize or to subdue. — GEORGE ELIOT.

Restless as the winter storm. — REGINALD HEBER.

Restless as water that winds onward through the plains. — HUGO.

Restless as butterflies. — LEIGH HUNT.

Restless — *continued.*

He was as restless as a wild beast in a cage. — GEORGE MACDONALD.

Restless as if fluttering wings bore thee on thy wanderings. — C. E. NORTON.

Restless as the desert wind. — ALBERT BIGELOW PAINE.

Restless as a brook. — HIRAM RICH.

Restless as hyenas. — EDGAR SALTUS.

Restless . . . like the touch'd needle till it find the star. — GEORGE SANDYS.

Restless as Ulysses. — THACKERAY.

Restless as Niagara. — TUPPER.

Restless as a veering wind. — WORDSWORTH.

Restoration.

A restoration is like an old oil painting, blackened by time, and re-varnished. — HUGO.

Restored.

Restored
Like a re-appearing Star.
— WORDSWORTH.

Restraint.

This restraint,
Like English mastiffs
That grow fierce with tying,
Makes her too passionately apprehend
Those pleasures she's kept from.
— JOHN WEBSTER.

Retain.

Retained their wonted vigour . . . as clocks once set in motion do yet go, the hand being absent. — WILLIAM CARTWRIGHT.

Retire.

Calmly retire, like evening light. — NATHANIEL COTTON.

Retired . . . like the moon in the west, when she foresees the shower and hides her fair head in a cloud. — JAMES MACPHERSON.

Gloomily retired ; like clouds that long having threatened rain, vanish behind the hills. — IBID.

Retire within himself, like a tortoise when attacked. — VOLTAIRE.

Retired as noontide dew. — WORDSWORTH.

Retreat.

Retreated . . . like a panther which draws back to take its spring. — DUMAS, PERE.

Return.

Return, like the postman. — ANON.

Return, like a late summer when the year grows old. — WILLIAM CULLEN BRYANT.

Return upon you like pent waters. — CARLYLE.

Return, like stars replenished at Joy's golden urn. — HOOD.

Returned, like the first messenger of Noah. — HENRY MACKENZIE.

Returning like dew that hath been to heaven, dropping in rain. — GERALD MASSEY.

An echo returned on the cold gray
morn,
Like the breath of a spirit sighing.
— MRS. NORTON.

Returned like a leaden shilling. — SIR RICHARD STEELE.

As a dog returneth to his vomit, so a fool returneth to his folly. — OLD TESTAMENT.

Returning like the Patriarch's dove,
Wing-weary from the eternal sea.
— WHITTIER.

Returning, like a ghost unlaid. — WORDSWORTH.

Revealed.

Through the driving mists revealed,
Like the lifting of the Host, by incense-
cloud almost concealed.
— LONGFELLOW.

Revel.

Revelled in my changeful dreams, like petrel on the sea. — EMILY BRONTË.

Reverend.

Reverend as Lear. — JEAN INGELOW.

Reverential.

Reverential, as though he were handling sacred vessels. — IRVIN S. COBB.

Tender and reverential . . . as a nun over her missal. — O. W. HOLMES.

Reverently.

Reverently as any pilgrim to the papal seat. — E. B. BROWNING.

Reverie.

A certain amount of reverie is good, like a narcotic in discreet doses. — HUGO.

Reverie, like a mist, leaves no trace behind. — IBID.

Revive.

Revive, like a dash of cold water in the face of the fainting. — ANON.

Revive, like Hector's body. — E. B. BROWNING.

She was like a fading plant revived by showers of rain. — CHARLES READE.

Nature revives, like a dim winking lamp,
That flashes brightly with parting light,
And straight is dark forever.
— NICHOLAS ROWE.

Sad death, revived with her sweet inspection,
And feeble spirit inly felt reflection ;
As withered weed through cruell winter's tine,
That feels the warmth of sunny beams reflection,
Liftes up his head that did before decline,
And gins to spread his leafe before the faire sunshine. — SPENSER.

Revive as the corn. — OLD TESTAMENT.

Reviving.

As reviving as a friend's visit. — CHARLOTTE BRONTË.

As reviving as an epigram. — A. E. HOUSMAN.

Revolve.

Revolving what I had heard, like a curious man over a riddle. — ANON.

Rheumatic.

Rheumatic as two dry toasts. — SHAKESPEARE.

Rhythmic.

Rhythmic as the swish of a swinging scythe. — ANON.

Rich.

Rich as flakes of virgin gold. — ANON.

Rich as Golconda. — IBID.

Rich as lords. — IBID.

Rich as mud. — IBID.

Rich as the mint. — IBID.

Rich in invisible treasures, like a bud of unborn sweets, and thick about the heart with ripe and rosy beauty. — P. J. BAILEY.

Rich as Crœsus. — ROBERT BURTON.

Rich as Stamboul's diadem. — BYRON.

Rich and as red as the mellowing blushes of maiden of eighteen. — LUIZ DE CAMOENS.

Richer than Ormuz bazaars. — CARLYLE.

Rich and ripe as Autumn's store. — HARTLEY COLERIDGE.

Rich as Pluto. — GEORGE COLMAN, THE YOUNGER.

Rich as Chaucer's speech. — SYDNEY DOBELL.

Rich — *continued.*

Rich as love. — EMERSON.

Rich as the merchant ships that crowd the strand. — FRANCIS FAWKES.

As feathers do lift up, and carry high, the foules and birds of the aire: So the riches and dignities of this world, are wont to extol and carry men, into the air and clouds of vanitie. — ANTHONIE FLETCHER'S "CERTAIN VERY PROPER AND PROFITABLE SIMILES," 1595.

Rich as a platter of gravy. — SEWELL FORD.

Rich as newshorn sheep. — JOHN HEYWOOD.

Rich as the rose's dye. — MRS. INGLIS.

Rich as a Millais in its tint and tone. — GERALD MASSEY.

Rich as a rose can be. — JOAQUIN MILLER.

A wise rich man is like the backe or stocke of the chimney, and his wealth the fire; he receives it not for his own need, but to reflect the heat to others' good. — SIR THOMAS OVERBURY.

Rich as an alum seller. — OSMANLI PROVERB.

Rich as Job. — RABELAIS.

As rich with unconscious art as the first song birds of May. — JAMES WHITCOMB RILEY.

Rich as the robes of heaven. — JOHN G. SAXE.

And I as rich in having such a jewel,
As twenty seas, if all their sand were pearl,
The water nectar, and the rocks pure gold. — SHAKESPEARE.

Rich . . .
As is the ooze and bottom of the sea,
With sunken wrack and sumless treasuries. — IBID.

Rich as Emperor-moths. — TENNYSON.

Rich as for the nuptials of a king. — IBID.

Rich as the pillars which support the sky. — WILLIAM THOMSON.

Riches.

Riches are like muck which stinks in a heap, but spread abroad, make the earth fruitful. — ANON.

Riches, like insects, while concealed they lie,
Wait but for wings, and in their season fly. — POPE.

Worldly riches are like nuts; many clothes are torn in getting them, many a tooth broken in cracking them, but never a belly filled with eating them. — RALPH VENNING.

Riddle.

Riddled like a pepper castor. — AUSTIN DOBSON.

Riddled with thrusts like a sieve. — DUMAS, PÈRE.

Riddled like a piece of lace. — ZOLA.

Ride.

Ride
Like fire on some high errand of the race. — W. E. HENLEY.

Ridiculous.

Ridiculous as a wig on the head of Apollo. — ANON.

A lord without riches is like a soldier without arms — very ridiculous. — IBID.

Ridiculous as a lover. — DEMETRIOS BIKELAS.

As ridiculous as to venture your life for another man's quarrel. — SHADWELL.

Ridiculous as to imitate the inimitable. — SIR RICHARD STEELE.

Ridgy.

Ridgy as backs of mountain-chains. — HUGO.

Rife.

Rife as flies at midsummer. — ANON.

Right.

Right as a glove. — ANON.

Right as a golden guinea. — IBID.

Right as a nail. — IBID.

Right as a pie. — IBID.

Right as a right angle. — IBID.

Right as ninepins. — IBID.

Right as rain. — IBID.

Right as the Church of England. — IBID.

Right as the day. — IBID.

Right as a conquerour. — ENGLISH BALLAD.

Right as a trivet. — R. H. BARHAM.

Right as the town clock. — BEACONSFIELD.

Right as a gun. — BEAUMONT AND FLETCHER.

Right as a line. — JOHN HEYWOOD.

Right as a fiddle. — LYDGATE.

Right as my leg. — RABELAIS.

Right as right. — "THE PURITAN."

Right as my glove. — SIR WALTER SCOTT.

As right as a ram's horn. — SKELTON.

Right as ninepence. — ROBERT LOUIS STEVENSON.

Righteous.

Righteous as redemption. — SWINBURNE.

Righteousness.

Righteousnesses are as filthy rags. — BUNYAN.

Thy righteousness is like the great mountains; thy judgments are a great deep. — OLD TESTAMENT.

Rigid.

Rigid as a rock. — ANON.

Rigid as if chiselled from stone. — IBID.

Rigid as a sheet of metal. — BALZAC.

Rigid as the will of Fate. — WILLIAM CULLEN BRYANT.

About as rigid as a concertina. — JOSEPH CONRAD.

Rigid as embodied duty. — DAUDET.

Rigid as his starched collar. — IBID.

Rigid as stone. — JAMES B. KENYON.

Rigid as a Greek masque. — BRANDER MATTHEWS.

Stood rigid, as if in a trance. — J. H. McCARTHY.

Rigid as a prison's blank stone wall. — MARGARET E. SANGSTER.

Ring.

Ringing like mad. — ANON.

Rings like a bugle in the night. — IBID.

Ring like Dodonæan brass. — E. B. BROWNING.

Ringing, as if a choir of golden-nested birds in heaven were singing. — E. C. JUDSON.

My heart rings out in music, like a lark hung in the charmed palace of the morn. — GERALD MASSEY.

Ring as trumpets blown for battle. — SWINBURNE.

Rings as the blast of martial mirth when trumpets fire men's hearts for fray. — IBID.

Rings clean as the clear wind's cry through the roar of the surge on the rocks. — IBID.

Ringed.

Ringed like curtain rods. — JOHN DAVIES.

Ripe.

Ripe as the melting cluster. — JOHN GAY.

Ripe as June. — HOOD.

As ripe and rosy . . . as a mellow little pippin that had tumbled in the weeds. — JAMES WHITCOMB RILEY.

Ripe as the wine. — R. H. STODDARD.

Ripen.

Ripened into speech,
Like the sap that turns to nectar in
the velvet of the peach.
— W. W. HARNEY.

The peril ripens like a wound o' the
flesh
That gathers poison.
— SWINBURNE.

Rippled.

Rippled like flowing waters by the wind. — BYRON.

Rippled like an over-fleeting wave. — TENNYSON.

Rise.

Rises and falls like a swan upon roaring water. — ANON.

Rise as a vapor. — IBID.

Rose like a phœnix, from the fires of time. — IBID.

Rose like sunlight from the sea. — IBID.

Rise like the white clouds on April skies. — IBID.

Rising like springs ingathered. — R. D. BLACKMORE.

Rising like water-columns from the sea. — BYRON.

Joy rises in me, like a summer's morn. — COLERIDGE.

Rose like a kite. — COWPER.

Rose like a bewildering strain of oriental music. — F. W. FABER.

Rise out of the hearth, like the garden of Hesperides. — GIBBON.

Rising like pillared fire. — ARTHUR HENRY HALLAM.

Rising in the middle of it like a lump of self-raising dough. — O. HENRY.

Rising in the air like eagle on the wing. — HOOD.

Rose like dim fancies when a dream begins. — IBID.

Rising like Aphrodite from the wave. — KINGSLEY.

Rose red as a beacon the wind had upblown. — SIDNEY LANIER.

Rising like the ruined arch of some aerial aqueduct. — LONGFELLOW.

Rose like an exhalation. — MILTON.

He (Burke) rose like a rocket, he fell like a stick. — THOMAS PAINE.

Rise from the ground like feather'd Mercury. — SHAKESPEARE.

Rises as ocean at the enchantment of the moon. — SHELLEY.

Rising as a shoreward sea. — SWINBURNE.

Rose like dust before the whirlwind's force. — BAYARD TAYLOR.

Rise up as a great lion. — OLD TESTAMENT.

True to rise as leaves on Autumn's whirlwind borne. — WHITTIER.

Rise,
Like spring-doves from the startled
wood. — IBID.

Roam.

Roam as wolves in a wolfish horde. — SWINBURNE.

Roar (Noun).

A single roar like the roar of a mortar-battery. — KIPLING.

Roar . . . like the sound of a beast in pain. — IBID.

Roar — *continued.*

The roar of battle rose,
Like the roar of a burning forest, when
a strong north wind blows.
— MACAULAY.

Roaring like thunder borne upon the breeze. — JOHN RUSKIN.

Roar as of an ocean foaming. — SHELLEY.

Roar,
Like the din of wintry breakers on a
sounding wall of shore.
— BAYARD TAYLOR.

Roar (Verb).

Roar as doth the sea. — ANON.

Roared like a burning devil. — IBID.

Roared like a burning lumber yard. — IBID.

Roars like a demon in torture. — IBID.

Roars like a lion. — IBID.

Roars like a mad bull. — IBID.

Roared like an angry sea. — IBID.

A roar deep as the murmuring of Ætna. — JOHN BANIM.

Roaring like Juno in the Tragedy. — ROBERT BURTON.

Roared and murmured like a mountain stream dashing or winding as its torrent strays. — BYRON.

Roared like breakers in the night. — AUBREY DE VERE.

Roar as by the evil one possessed. — GOETHE.

Roaring like a foundered horse. — MAURICE HEWLETT.

Roaring like a tempest. — HUGO.

Roars in the gloaming
Like an ocean of seething champagne.
— KINGSLEY.

Roared like water which rushes from a lock when the gates are open. — CAMILLE LEMONNIER.

Roaring like a lion for his food. — ROBERT LLOYD.

Roars like a flame that is fanned. — LONGFELLOW.

Roared as if smitten by some god. — LUCIAN.

Roar like a devil with a man in his belly. — ANDREW MARVELL.

Roared like a battle. — JOHN MASEFIELD.

Roar like mad waves upon the shore. — MISS MULOCK.

Roars like a bull. — MUNCHAUSEN.

Roars . . . like a swift pursuing hound. — ARTHUR O'SHAUGHNESSY.

Roar
Like ocean battling with the shore.
— T. BUCHANAN READ.

Roareth like the sea. — OLD TESTAMENT.

Roars like a bull of Bashan. — THACKERAY.

Rough repetition roars in rudest
rhyme,
As clappers clinkle in one charming
chime. — BONNELL THORNTON.

Roaring like a bear. — WILLIAM WARD.

Roar like lions for their prey. — WORDSWORTH.

Robber.

Robbers are like rane, tha fall on the just and the unjust. — JOSH BILLINGS.

Robust.

Robust as ever rural labor bred. — WORDSWORTH.

Rock.

Rocked like a leaf. — ANON.

Rocked like a ship at sea. — IBID.

The earth rocking as a ship borne over the waves. — SAMUEL BEAL.

Rock — *continued.*

The burning phrase
Rocked on like ocean's tidal swell.
— LORD DE TABLEY.

Rock'd like Yankee in his chair. — HOOD.

Rocking like the stately lilies beneath the stately sky.—C. G. ROSSETTI.

Like sea-birds in the sunny main, rock idly. — SOUTHEY.

Rocked like a mass of jelly that has been invisibly shaken. — HERMANN SUDERMANN.

Head was on her breast, rock'd like a nautilus in calm mid-ocean. — N. P. WILLIS.

Roll.

Rolls like a whale in the sea. — ANON.

Rolling like a sea. — MATTHEW ARNOLD.

I rolled myself like a hedgehog against the sharp points of my own thoughts. — JOSEPH VON EICHENDORFF.

Rolled in money like pigs in mud. — HOOD.

Rolls like a scow in the wake of a liner. — ELBERT HUBBARD.

Rolled up like a scroll. — C. G. ROSSETTI.

Rolled like the willowy and tumultuous sea. — SOUTHEY.

Rolling like a wreath of snow. — IBID.

Roll
As waves that race and find no goal.
— SWINBURNE.

Roll'd about like tumbled fruit in grass. — TENNYSON.

Romans.

The Romans were like sheep, for that a man might better drive a flock of them, than one of them ; for in a flock, if you could get some few to go right, the rest would follow. — CATO.

Romantic.

As romantic as a Bouguereau canvas. — JAMES HUNEKER.

Romantic as the Alcoran. — BONNELL THORNTON.

Root.

Rooting . . . like pigs arter ground-nuts. — BENJAMIN P. SHILLABER (MRS. PARTINGTON).

Rosy.

Rosy-cheeked as a winter apple. — ANON.

Rosy as a peony. — IBID.

Rosy as pinks. — C. S. CALVERLEY.

Rosy as the dawn. — FLAUBERT.

Rosy . . . like ripened peaches in the morning light. — R. H. HORNE.

As rosy as a bride. — HUGO.

Rosy as a victorious candidate. — GEORGE MEREDITH.

Rosy as the morn. — SHELLEY.

Rosy as rifts of dawn. — CELIA THAXTER.

Rosy as the candle-shade. — EDITH WHARTON.

Rot.

Rot as corn ungarnered.
— SWINBURNE.

Rotten.

Rotten as the poisonous heap the sea throws up for waste. — SARAH FLOWER ADAMS.

Rotten as the gills of an old mushroom. — ANON.

Rotten
As ever oak or stone was sound.
— SHAKESPEARE.

Rotten as dirt. — STERNE.

Rotting.

Rotting in my gizzard, like Sancho's suppressed witticisms. — SIR WALTER SCOTT.

Rough.

Rough like butter spread over stale bread. — ANON.

Rough as the back of a hedgehog. — J. R. BARTLETT'S "DICTIONARY OF AMERICANISMS."

Rough as hemp. — CARLYLE.

Rough as a Sea Porkypine. — DICKENS.

Rough as a storm. — DRYDEN.

Rough as bearskins. — ROBERT HEATH.

Rough as nutmeg-graters. — AARON HILL.

Rough as the winds. — OTWAY.

Were she as rough
As are the swelling Adriatic seas.
— SHAKESPEARE.

Rough as a Russian bear. — JOHN TAYLOR.

Round (Adjective).

Round as a circus ring. — ANON.

Round as a dish. — IBID.

Round as a dumpling. — IBID.

Round as a juggler's box. — IBID.

Round as a length of stovepipe. — IBID.

Round as a pearl. — IBID.

Round as a rosebud. — IBID.

Round as a turnip. — IBID.

Round as a windmill. — IBID.

Round as the full moon. — IBID.

Round as the globe. — IBID.

Rounde as a thymbyll. — MS. ASHMOL. (15th Century).

Round like wells. — BACON.

Round and sound as a mountain apple. — ROBERT BROWNING.

Round as any Jonian jug. — JOHN BYROM

Round as Giotto's O. — CARLYLE.

Rounde as appille was his face. — CHAUCER.

A round disc of fire, somewhat like a guinea. — HAVELOCK ELLIS.

Round as the globe. — JOHN GAY.

Round as Norval's shield. — HOOD.

Round as platter of delf. — IBID.

Round as a quoit. — CAMILLE LEMONNIER.

Round like pumpkins. — GUY DE MAUPASSANT.

Round as a tun. — MIDDLETON.

Round as the shield of my fathers. — OSSIAN.

Round as a dish. — RABELAIS.

Round as a hoop. — IBID.

Round and perfect as a star. — ALEXANDER SMITH.

Round as a pearl or tear. — SWINBURNE.

Round and pale as a pair of suet dumplings. — THACKERAY.

Round as a moyn. — "TOWNELEY MYSTERIES AND MIRACLE PLAYS."

Round as a kettle. — SAMUEL WESLEY.

Round as an Orbe. — J. WILKINS.

Round as a horn. — ALEXANDER WILSON.

Round (Adverb).

Round and round like a boiling potful. — J. M. BARRIE.

Round and round, like a dance of snow
In a dazzling drift. — IBID.

Round and round they flew,
As when, in spring, about a chimney-top,
A cloud of twittering swallows, just returned,
Wheel round and round, and turn and wheel again,
Unwinding their swift track.
— WILLIAM CULLEN BRYANT.

Round — *continued.*

Round and round in the same circle, like a dog in a wheel, or a horse in a mill. — ROBERT BURTON.

Go round and round like Catherine wheels. — O. HENRY.

Circles round, like the soft waving wings of noonday dreams. — SHELLEY.

Round-Shouldered.

Round-shouldered as a grindstone. — ANON.

Rouse.

Rouses me, as with a cherub's trump. — COLERIDGE.

Roused, like homeward wishes in wanderer's heart. — EDMUND GOSSE.

Rouse . . . like rattling peal of thunder. — JOHN HUGHES.

Rouse and startle, like a call to arms. — GRACE KING.

Rous'd like a huntsman to the chase. — SWINBURNE.

Rousing.

Rousing as a bugle. — OUIDA.

Routed.

Routed . . . like a lost army. — SWINBURNE.

Rows.

In rows, like figures in a sum. — DICKENS.

A row, like a Quaker gone delirious. — HOOD.

Ruddy.

Ruddy as a parson's daughter. — ANON.

Ruddy like a winter apple. — JOSEPH CONRAD.

Ruddy and fresh as the waking morn. — EUGENE FIELD.

Ruddy as if baked by heat of sun or glowing forge. — HOOD.

Ruddy as bimba fruit. — KALIDASA.

Ruddy as gold his cheek. — MATTHEW PRIOR.

Ruddy read as any chery. — "SQUIRE OF LOW DEGREE."

His lips waxed ruddy as light. — SWINBURNE.

More ruddy in body than rubies. — OLD TESTAMENT.

Rude.

As rude as rage. — ANON.

Rude as a bear. — SWIFT.

Ruffles.

Ruffles as a breeze ruffles the surface of a pond. — ANON.

Rugged.

Rugged as a Saracen. — SAMUEL BUTLER.

Rugged as the coat of a colt that has been bred upon a common. — IBID.

Rugged as burrs. — JOHN HEYWOOD.

Rugged as Ailsa crag. — J. S. KNOWLES.

Ruin.

Fell slowly into ruin, like all dwellings to which the presence of man no longer communicates life. — HUGO.

Ruinous.

Ruinous as guilt. — THACKERAY.

Rule (Noun).

Rules, like crutches, ne'er became of any use but to the lame. — ROBERT LLOYD.

He that hath no rule over his own spirit is like a city that is broken down, and without walls. — OLD TESTAMENT.

Rule (Verb).

Ruled as straight as a sheet of music-paper. — BALZAC.

Ruled, like a wandering planet. — SHAKESPEARE.

Rumbling.

Rumbling like a restless torrent lashing the mountain-side. — ÆSCHYLUS.

Ruminate.

Ruminates like an hostess that hath no arithmetic but her brain to set down her reckoning. — SHAKESPEARE.

Rumor.

Rumors fructify about it like the burgeoning of toad stools on a fat muck heap. — ANON.

Run.

Run from it as a mendicant friar from an alms. — THOMAS ADAMS.

Running like a high sea. — ANON.

Running like a lapwing. — IBID.

Ran like a madman. — IBID.

Run like a millrace. — IBID.

Runs like a spout. — IBID.

Run like fire through stubble. — IBID.

Run like the devil. — IBID.

Running like the Devil's mill. — IBID.

Run like the east wind. — IBID.

Running things into the ground, like a dog after the hare. — IBID.

Run like wildfire. — IBID.

Run like winking. — IBID.

Runs . . . as the surge of health returning to the sick. — ARABIAN NIGHTS.

Runne like a fountayne free. — ENGLISH BALLAD.

Running as if they had hot coals in their shoes. — BJÖRNSTJERNE BJÖRNSON.

Just as a wheel, that's running down a hill
Which has no bottom, must keep running still. — JOHN BYROM.

I ran like the drift on the ice low curled
When the winds of Yule are abroad on the world. — BLISS CARMAN.

Ran like hell-hounds. — HAMLIN GARLAND.

Ran . . . as a wolfe, that taketh his praye. — JOHN GOWER.

Running like a hunted deer. — HOOD.

Run like fire in summer furze. — GEORGE MEREDITH.

Runs like the prey of the forest. — IBID.

Ran, as in the terror of a dream. — JAMES MONTGOMERY.

Ran like a shiver. — MAX NORDAU.

Run like water off a duck's back. — RAY'S "COLLECTANEA."

Running like a leaping wave. — E. R. SILL.

Ran,
Like scatt'red chaffe, the which the wind away doth fan.
— SPENSER.

Run ravening as the Gadarean swine. — SWINBURNE.

Run like oil. — OLD TESTAMENT.

Run like the lightnings. — IBID.

Rush (Noun).

A rush somewhat like the opening of an Oklahoma reservation. — GEORGE ADE.

A rushing like the rushing of mighty waters. — OLD TESTAMENT.

Sullen rush upon the air,
Such as the unseen wings of spirits make. — WHITTIER.

Rush (Verb).

Rushes . . . like a tempest-troubled brook. — ANON.

As the billows fling shells on the shore,
As the sun pours light o'er the sea,
As the lark scatters song evermore,
So rushes my love to thee. — IBID.

Rush — *continued.*

Rushed as a storm. — John Armstrong.

Rush, like a rocket tearing up the sky. — P. J. Bailey.

Rush . . . open-mouthed, like a crow at a walnut. — Balzac.

The blood rushed like a burning torrent through his veins. — Ibid.

Armies rush'd like warring mighty seas. — William Blake.

Like an unruly deluge, rushed on. — William Broome.

Rush
Like clans from their hills at the voice of the battle.
— J. J. Callahan.

Two souls, like two dew-drops, rushed into one. — Carlyle.

Rush like rain. — Ferdinand Freiligrath.

Rush, like mountain torrent, swollen by the melted snow. — Goethe.

Rush like a fiery torrent. — Homer.

Rushed like fairies. — Ibid.

Rushed like a torrid hurricane. — Hood.

Rushed upon us like a lava torrent. — Sigmund Krasinski.

Rush like gudgeons to the bait. — Robert Lloyd.

Rushed like a man insane. — Longfellow.

Rushed as a wind that is keen and cold and relentless. — Ibid.

Like prisoners from the dungeon gloom,
Like birds escaping from a snare,
Like schoolboys at the hour of play,
All left at once the pent-up room,
And rushed into the open air.
— Ibid.

Rushes like a boar against the shouting chase. — Macaulay.

Rushed out upon the wayfarers like ambushed bandits. — George Meredith.

Rushed in as rush the waters through a cave
That tunnels half a sea-girt lonely rock. — William Morris.

Rushed like the hot blood in the veins of a fever-stricken child. — Sydney Munden.

As rusheth a foamy stream from the dark shady steep of Cromla when thunder is rolling above, and dark brown night rests on the hill ; so fierce, so vast, so terrible, rush forward, the sons of Erin. — Ossian.

Rushing like a flood. — E. H. Plumptre.

Rush . . . like ravenous wolves in night's dark cloud, driven abroad by the blind rage of lawless hunger. — Virgil.

Russia.

Russia, like the elephant, is rather unwieldy in attacking others, but most formidable in defending herself. She proposes this dilemma to all invaders — a dilemma that Napoleon discovered too late. The horns of it are short and simple, but strong. Come unto me with few, and I will overwhelm you; come to me with many, and you shall overwhelm yourselves. — C. C. Colton.

Rustle (Noun).

The rustling of their gowns seems like the crumpling of bank bills. — Émile Augier.

A silken rustle,
Like the meeting of guests at a festival.
— T. Buchanan Read.

Rustle (Verb).

Rustling . . . like autumn leaves that tremble and foretell the sable storm. — Hood.

Rustling like the secret darkness of the soul. — Richard Hovey.

Rustle — *continued.*

The dead laurels of the dead
Rustle for a moment only,
Like withered leaves in lonely
Churchyards at some passing tread.
— LONGFELLOW.

Rustling like a flock of sea-fowl. — JAMES MACPHERSON.

Rustling like a summer rain. — IBID.

Ruthless.

Ruthless as the sea. — MAURICE HEWLETT.

Ruthless as a baby with a worm. — TENNYSON.

Ruthlessly.

Ruthlessly as you lop a branch. — RICHARD LE GALLIENNE.

S

Sacred.

Sacred as cats to a priest in Thebes. — ANON.

Sacred as Hindoo gods. — IBID.

Sacred as a shrine. — BULWER-LYTTON.

Sacred as the crocodiles were to the ancient Egyptians. — IBID.

Sacred as churchyard turf. — ELIZA COOK.

Sacred as an unvoiced prayer. — GEORGE MEREDITH.

Sacred as the monarch's hall. — WHITTIER.

Sad.

Sad as the sunless sea. — FRANKLIN P. ADAMS.

Sad as a subpœna. — ANON.

Sad as a wail over the dead. — IBID.

Sad as doom. — IBID.

As sad as Fate. — IBID.

Sad as if steering to dim eternity. — IBID.

Sad as the eyeball of sorrow behind a shroud. — IBID.

A song as sad as the wild waves be. — IBID.

Sad as silence when a song is spent. — ALFRED AUSTIN.

Sad as death. — APHRA BEHN.

Sad as the groans of dying innocence. — IBID.

Sad as a thousand sighs, when the dark winds sob through the yews. — HENRY BROOKE.

Sad as wisdom cut off from fellowship. — E. B. BROWNING.

Sad as Melancholy. — ROBERT BURTON.

Sad as angels for the good man's sin. — CAMPBELL.

Serenely sad as eternity. — CARLYLE.

Sad as bull liver. — WILLIAM CARR'S "THE DIALECT OF CRAVEN."

Sad as twilight. — GEORGE ELIOT.

Sad as the gust that sweeps the clouded sky. — O. W. HOLMES.

Sad as eve. — HUGO.

Sad as an image of despair. — SIGMUND KRASINSKI.

Sad as raindrops on a grave. — GEORGE P. LATHROP.

My heart is as sad as a black stone under the blue sea. — LOVER.

Sad as the tears the sullen Winter weeps. — GEORGE MAC-HENRY.

Sad, like the sun in the day of mist, when his face is watery and dim. — JAMES MACPHERSON.

Sad — *continued.*

Sad as the wind that sighs
Through cypress trees under rainy
skies. — PHILIP B. MARSTON.

Sad as the shriek of the midnight blast. — GERALD MASSEY.

Sad as wailing winds. — IBID.

Sad as the last line of a brave romance. — GEORGE MEREDITH.

Sad . . . as the ghostly past. — OWEN MEREDITH.

Sad my thoughts as willows bending,
O'er the borders of the tomb.
— G. P. MORRIS.

Sad as tears to the eyes that are bright. — A. J. RYAN.

Sad
Like the echo mad
Of some plaintive spirit strain.
— FRANCIS S. SALTUS.

Sad as night. — SHAKESPEARE.

Sad as a lump of lead. — SPENSER.

Sad as twilight on the deep. — GEORGE STERLING.

Sad as a soul estranged. — SWINBURNE.

Sad as a wintry withering moon. — IBID.

Bare and sad as banishment. — IBID.

Sad as doom. — IBID.

Sadder than a banquet skeleton. — FREDERICK TENNYSON.

Sadness.

A little tinge of sadness floats upon her eye, like the haze upon a summer landscape. — DONALD G. MITCHELL.

Safe.

Safe as a tortoise under its shell. — ALEXANDER ADAM.

Safe as a blockhouse. — ANON.

Safe as a child on its mother's breast. — IBID.

Safe as a crow in a gutter. — IBID.

Safe as a mouse in a cheese. — IBID.

Safe as a mouse in a mill. — IBID.

Safe as a rat in a trap. — IBID.

Safe as a sardine. — IBID.

Safe as Solomon's birds. — IBID.

Safe as a thief in a mill. — IBID.

Safe as a wall of brass. — IBID.

Safe as caged. — IBID.

Safe as brandy. — MISS A. E. BAKER'S "NORTHAMPTONSHIRE GLOSSARY."

Saif tu take as a fotograph. — JOSH BILLINGS.

Safe from harm as sings the lark when sucked up out of sight in vortices of glory and blue air. — E. B. BROWNING.

Safe as the Bank of England. — BULWER-LYTTON.

As safe and sacred from the step of man
As an invisible world. — COLERIDGE.

Safe as my life. — R. DAVENPORT'S "NEW TRICKS TO CHEAT THE DEVIL."

Safe as a stone in a peach. — ALFRED HEAD.

Safe as a fish. — "HELP TO DISCOURSE."

Safe as a fox in a trap. — KINGSLEY.

Safe as in the bank. — RICHARD LE GALLIENNE.

Safe as in bed. — CHARLES READE.

Safe as Priam is in Ilion. — SHAKESPEARE.

Safe as thy gold in the strong box. — WILLIAM SOMERVILLE.

Safe as hunted wolf within his lair. — THEODORE WATTS-DUNTON.

Sag.

Sags like a fisherman's hat. — IRVIN S. COBB.

Sag — *continued.*

Sagging down like a Welsh wallet. — THOMAS DEKKER.

Saggy.

Saggy, like a paper bag full of sour milk. — REX BEACH.

Saggy as a sponge full of treacle. — ANGUS MCNEILL.

Sagacious.

Sagacious as the Roman. — J. H. NEWMAN.

Sage.

Sage as Cato. — ANON.

Sail.

Sailed skyward, like burnt onion-peelings. — ROBERT BROWNING.

Sallow.

Sallow as Autumn. — OWEN MEREDITH.

Salt.

Salt as a sea sponge. — OWEN MEREDITH.

Salt as the sea-wind. — WHITTIER.

Salute.

Salute as ceremoniously as lawyers when they meet after a long vacation. — MIDDLETON.

Sane.

About as sane as a lunatic's dream. — ANON.

Sanguine.

Sanguine as the morning skies. — LORD DE TABLEY.

Sanguine, like a globe of blood. — FRANCIS THOMPSON.

Sank.

Sank into the bottom as a stone. — OLD TESTAMENT.

Sap.

Sapped as weak sand by water. — SWINBURNE.

Sarcasm.

A true sarcasm is like a sword-stick; it appears, at first sight, to be much more innocent than it really is, till, all of a sudden, there leaps something out of it — sharp and deadly and incisive — which makes you tremble and recoil. — SYDNEY SMITH.

Satire.

Satire should, like a polished razor keen,
Wound with a touch that's scarcely felt or seen.
— LADY MARY WORTLEY MONTAGU.

Satire is a sort of glass wherein beholders do generally discover everybody's face but their own. — SWIFT.

For Satyre, that most needful part of our Poetry, it has of late been more abus'd, and is grown more degenerate than any other; most commonly, like a Sword in the hands of a Madman, it runs a Tilt at all manner of Persons without any sort of distinction or reason; and so ill-guided is this furious Career, that the Thrusts are most aim'd where the Enemy is best arm'd. — ROBERT WOLSELEY.

Saucy.

Saucy as the wave. — ELIZA COOK.

Sassy ez a jay-bird. — JOEL CHANDLER HARRIS.

Saucy as sin. — AMBROSE BIERCE.

Saucy,
Like a proudly waving plume.
— JOHN T. TROWBRIDGE.

Saunters.

Saunters . . . like an idle river very leasurely strolling down a flat country to the sea. — DICKENS.

Savage.

Savage as a bear with a sore head. — ANON.

Savage as an Apache. — IBID.

Savage — *continued.*

Savage at heart as a tiger chained. — EDWIN ARNOLD.

Sayings.

Great men's sayings are like silver gilt ; use wears the gilt off the silver, and all the sparkle goes out of the sayings if they are repeated. — BALZAC.

Scald.

Scald like molten lead. — SHAKESPEARE.

Scamper.

Scamper off and disappear like a flight of partridges. — FERNÁN CABALLERO.

Scampering as if the Devil drove them. — RABELAIS.

Fitfully scampered like fireflies over the waste. — "VIKRAM AND THE VAMPIRE."

Scandal.

Scandal, like dirt, will rub out when dry. — SIR T. BERNARD.

In scandal, as in robbery, the receiver is always as bad as the thief. — CHESTERFIELD.

Scandal, like a reptile crawling over bright grass, leaves a trail and a stain. — ALLAN CUNNINGHAM.

Scandals are like dandelion seeds, — they are arrow-headed and stick where they fall, and bring forth and multiply fourfold. — OUIDA.

Scandal, like the Nile, is fed by innumerable streams, but it is extremely difficult to trace it to its source. — PUNCH.

Scant.

Scant as hair in leprosy. — ROBERT BROWNING.

Scant as winter underwood. — GEORGE MEREDITH.

Scanty.

Scanty as the gleaning after harvest. — TUPPER.

Scarce.

Scarce as feathers on a fish. — ANON.

Scarce as furs in hell. — IBID.

Scarce as orange plumes on St. Patrick's Day. — IBID.

Scarce as pin-feathers on a bullfrog. — IBID.

Scarce as Scotch orators. — IBID.

Scarce as snakes in Ireland. — IBID.

Scarce as hens' teeth. — J. R. BARTLETT'S "DICTIONARY OF AMERICANISMS."

Scare.

Scaring the ladies like a crow-keeper. — SHAKESPEARE.

Scared.

Scared like a wild bird flies. — R. D. BLACKMORE.

Scared, like to a man that with a ghost was marred. — WILLIAM DUNBAR.

Scared as a jack-rabbit that has heard the howl of a wolf. — ALFRED HENRY LEWIS.

Scared look, like a bird's driven right into the fowler's nest. — MISS MULOCK.

Scarlet.

Scarlet as Major Bagstock. — DR. JOHN DORAN.

Scars.

Hath more scars of sorrow in his heart
Than foeman's marks upon his batter'd shield. — SHAKESPEARE.

Scathe.

Love doth scathe
The gentle heart, as northern blasts do roses. — KEATS.

Scatter.

Scatters them like a shot in a preserve. — ANON.

Scattered like the bones of dead bodies torn from one another by wolves after the battle. — IBID.

Scatter — *continued.*

Scattered like chaff before the wind. — ANON.

Scattered like a flock. — E. B. BROWNING.

Scattered with as little premeditation as the birds scattered their songs. — BLISS CARMAN.

The people I love most are scattered as the sands of the dry river beds fly before the fall hurricane. — J. FENIMORE COOPER.

Scattered like foam along the wave. — GEORGE CROLY.

Like the Jews, scattered. — THOMAS DEKKER.

Scattered like mown and withered grass. — GOETHE.

Scatter like smoke. — MAURICE HEWLETT.

Scattered all along, like emptied sea-shells on the sand. — O. W. HOLMES.

Scattered . . .
As leaves when wild winds blow.
— IBID.

She scatters the spray as the chaff in the stroke of the flail. — IBID.

Scattered like a mad sea. — LAMARTINE.

Scattering drops like beads of wampum. — LONGFELLOW.

Scattered were they, like flakes of snow. — IBID.

Scattered wide
Like silt and seaweed by the force and
fluctuations of the tide. — IBID.

Scattered, like treasures of the lost Hesperides. — ADELAIDE A. PROCTER.

Scatter . . . as if they had been balloons in a wind. — GEORGE MEREDITH.

Scattered . . . like loose spray before the wind. — IBID.

They scattered like a brood of partridges. — OSMANLI PROVERB.

Scattering, like hope through fear. — RICHARD SAVAGE.

Scattered like foam on the torrent. — SHELLEY.

Like a glow-worm golden
In a dell of dew,
Scattering unbeholden
Its aërial hue
Among the flowers and grass, which
screen it from the view. — IBID.

Scattered, like a cloud of summer dust. — IBID.

Like sheep from the wolf, scattering. — SOUTHEY.

Scattered them as crows. — SWINBURNE.

Scatter as wild swans parting adrift on the wan green waste. — IBID.

Scatters as leaves blown down the wind. — ARTHUR SYMONS.

Scattered abroad, as sheep having no shepherd. — NEW TESTAMENT.

Scattereth the hoarfrost like ashes. — OLD TESTAMENT.

Scatter them as the stubble that passeth away by the wind of the wilderness. — IBID.

Scattered upon the hills, as sheep that have not a shepherd. — IBID.

Scatter like quicksilver. — JOHN WEBSTER.

Scattered like dust before the storm. — LUDWIG UHLAND.

Scattered . . . like chaff before the winnower's fan. — WHITTIER.

Scattered like the chaff blown from the threshing-floor of God. — IBID.

Scattering, like birds escaped the fowler's net. — WORDSWORTH.

Scenery.

Fine scenery is like fine music — you have to fill it up with your own fine thoughts or there is no fineness in it. — ELLEN T. FOWLER.

Scented.

Sweetly scented as the incense smoking on Vesta's altars. — JOHN FORD.

Sceptics.

Sceptics, like dolphins, change when dying. — LADY BLESSINGTON.

Science.

The sciences, even the best, — mathematics and astronomy, — are like sportsmen, who seize whatever prey offers, even without being able to make any use of it. — EMERSON.

Science is, like virtue, its own exceeding great reward. — CHARLES KINGSLEY.

Scintillate.

Scintillate and snap like sparks from an electrical conductor. —EDWARD DOWDEN.

Scintillate like a human St. Catherine wheel. — RICHARD LE GALLIENNE.

Scintillating as a poet's rapture. — AMY LESLIE.

Scold (Noun).

As arrant a scold as Xanthippe. — ROBERT BURTON.

Scold (Verb).

Rail and scold like butter-women. — IBID.

Scold like a wet parrot. — STEPHEN CRANE.

Scold like an oyster-woman at Billingsgate. — HALLIWELL'S "DICTIONARY."

Scold like shrewish wives at tavern door. — HOOD.

Scold and rail
Like porters o'er a pot of ale. — SWIFT.

Scorch.

Scorched like a drop of fire from a brandished torch. — ROBERT BROWNING.

Scorches like a cave-hid dragon's breath. — GEORGE ELIOT.

Scorched like lightning. — FITZ-JAMES O'BRIEN.

Scorn.

Scorn you as old Æsop's bull the frogs. — TUPPER.

Scornful.

Scornful as spirit fallen, its own tormentor. — O. W. HOLMES.

Scornful as honor is. — W. J. LINTON.

Scowl.

Scowled like a thunder cloud. — EMILY BRONTË.

Scowling like a winter sky. — MRS. MARY ROBINSON.

Scramble.

Scrambling like a cat up a wall. — RABELAIS.

Scratching.

Scratching like a death-watch-tick. — ROBERT BROWNING.

Scream.

Screaming like a pigge half stickt. — ANON.

Scream, like a trumpet whining through a catacomb. — P. J. BAILEY.

Scribbler.

For the Scribblers are infinite, that like Mushrooms or Flys are born and dye in small circles of time ; whereas Books, like Proverbs, receive their Chief Value from the Stamp and Esteem of Ages through which they have passed. — SIR WILLIAM TEMPLE.

Scruple.

There are less worthy offerings, than the first scruple of an unscrupulous life. It is like the first pure drops that fall from a long turbid and dust-choked fountain. — OUIDA.

Scud.

Scud like a wild bird. — KEATS.

Scuttle.

Scuttle off . . . like a brace of teal ducks getting out of a walrus' way. — IRVIN S. COBB.

Sealed.

Sealed up, like the valley of Rasselas, against the intrusion of the world. — DE QUINCEY.

Sealed as the voice of a frost-bound stream. — SWINBURNE.

Seamed.

Seamed as if by a burn. — D'ANNUNZIO.

Sear.

Seared like hot iron. — ANON.

Sears like a brand. — J. H. NEWMAN.

Seasonable.

Seasonable as snow in summer. — ANON.

Seasoned.

Seasoned as twin beams of soundest oak. — BAYARD TAYLOR.

Seclude.

Secluded as an anchorite. — BERNARD BARTON.

Secluded as a chimney corner. — JOHN BURROUGHS.

Secrecy.

Dissimulation and secrecy are like the alloy mingled with pure ore: a little is necessary, and will not debase the coin below its proper standard. — CHESTERFIELD.

Secret (Adjective).

Secret as rocks under sea. — T. L. BEDDOES.

Secret as the grave. — BYRON.

Secret as the head of Nilus. — CONGREVE.

Secret as the night. — IBID.

Secret as thought. — FRANCIS FAWKES.

Secret as a confessor. — JOHN GAY.

More secret than a nest of nightingales. — KEATS.

Secreter than the isle of Delos. — IBID.

Secret as the magnet-stone. — G. P. LATHROP.

Secret as your midwife. — EDWARD SHARPHAM.

Secret as a coach-horse. — R. B. SHERIDAN.

Secret (Noun).

Secrets are like maidens: the closer they are kept locked up, the more certain they are to escape. — BALZAC.

A secret is like silence: you cannot talk about it, and keep it. It is like money; when once you know there is any concealed, it is half discovered. — PAUL CHATFIELD.

State secrets are like mortal poison: as long as that poison is in its box and the box closed, it is not injurious; out of the box, it kills. — DUMAS, PÈRE.

A secret in his mouth is like a wild bird in a cage, whose door no sooner opens, than 'tis out. — BEN JONSON.

Keep your own secrets, as the seed keeps the color of the flower. — ALICE MEYNELL.

A secret at home is like a rock under tide. — MISS MULOCK.

Secretly.

Secretly as a lion in his den. — OLD TESTAMENT.

Lieth secret, as a serpent. — TUPPER.

In secret, as a miser tells his gold. — N. P. WILLIS.

Secure.

Secure as the grave. — ANON.

Secure as in the cell of a saint. — SAMUEL FOOTE.

Secure as happy yesterdays. — LOWELL.

Secure as the firmament. — GEORGE MEREDITH.

Secure, as evening shuts behind the day. — T. BUCHANAN READ.

Secure as sleep. — SHAKESPEARE.

Secure as the orchard-turf. — BAYARD TAYLOR.

Secure as a mathematical demonstration. — THEOBALD.

Sedate.

Sedate, like Plato. — THOMAS PAINE.

Seedy.

Seedy as a raspberry. — ALICE CALDWELL HEGAN.

Seedy as a caraway umbrel late in the season. — O. W. HOLMES.

Seek.

Seeking, like a bleating lamb
Left out at night in shutting up the fold. — E. B. BROWNING.

Seeks as does an old tailor his needle's eye. — DANTE.

As rivers seek the sea,
Much more deep than they,
So my soul seeks Thee
Far away. — C. G. ROSSETTI.

Seemly.

Seemly as a cow in a cage, a dog in a doublet, or a sow with a saddle. — ANON.

Seethe.

Seething, like the waves of an angry sea. — ANON.

Selfish.

Selfish as a fox. — ANON.

Self-praise.

Self-praise is like water poured on fire to make it burn the brighter. — ANON.

Sense.

No more sense than a shoat (young pig) in pickle. — THOMAS LODGE.

Plain good sense, like a dish of solid beef or mutton, is proper only for peasants; but a ragout of folly, well dressed with a sharp sauce of wit, is fit to be served up at an Emperor's table. — LORD LYTTELTON.

Senses.

Our senses like false glasses show,
Smooth beauty where browes wrinkled are,
And make the cosen'd fancy glow.
— WILLIAM HARBINGTON.

The senses are like the sun. The sun makes the heavens invisible and the earth clear; the senses obscure heavenly things and open up earthly ones. — PHILO JUDÆUS.

Senseless.

Senseless as flint. — ANON.

Senseless as stones. — THOMAS HEYWOOD.

Sensibility.

Fine sensibilities are like woodbines, delightful luxuries of beauty to twine around a solid, upright stem of understanding; but very poor things, if, unsustained by strength, they are left to creep along the ground. — JOHN FOSTER.

Sensitive.

Sensitive as a flower. — ANON.

Sensitive as truth in Heaven. — WALTER HARTE.

Sensual.

Sensual pleasures are like soap bubbles, sparkling, evanescent. The pleasures of intellect are calm, beautiful, sublime, ever enduring and climbing upward to the borders of the unseen world. — JOHN H. AUGHEY.

Sensuous.

Sensuous as ether. — ANON.

Sentences.

Sentences are like sharp nails which force truth upon our memory. — DIDEROT.

His [Bacon's] sentences bend beneath the weight of his thought like a branch beneath the weight of its fruit. — ALEXANDER SMITH.

Sentiment.

How beautiful is noble sentiment : like gossamer gauze, beautiful and cheap, which will stand no wear and tear. — CARLYLE.

Sentiment, like religion, had its superstition and its martyrdom. — HENRY MACKENZIE.

Separate.

Separate them one from another, as a shepherd divideth his sheep from the goats. — NEW TESTAMENT.

Sere.

Sere and dead
As any leaves of summer shed
From crimson bough when autumn grieves. — W. D. HOWELLS.

Serene.

Serene and ephemeral as a little smiling sun. — ANON.

Serene as a star in a bright mist. — BALZAC.

Serene, like a deep, smooth, and still lake. — BUDDHA.

Serene as night. — BYRON.

Serene . . . like envoys from the skies. — NATHANIEL COTTON.

Serene and calm, as when the Spring
The new-created world began.
— DRYDEN.

Serene as the dawn. — HUGO.

More serene than Cordelia's countenance. — KEATS.

Serene as summer in Arcadian hills. — CHARLES L. MOORE.

Serene as a Quaker's meeting. — JAMES RALPH.

Serene as a winter sunset. — SAINT-PIERRE.

Serene, as in armour of faith. — MARGARET E. SANGSTER.

Serene and pleased a look as Patience ere put on. — JAMES THOMSON.

Serene as light. — ISAAC WATTS.

Serene as day. — WORDSWORTH.

Serenely.

Serenely as the stars gaze through the air
Straight on each other.
— E. B. BROWNING.

Serious.

Serious as a philosopher. — MILES P. ANDREWS.

Serious as an owl. — ANON.

Serious as a portmanteau. — IBID.

Serious as a doctor. — DUMAS, PÈRE.

Serious . . . as one would whisper that a lion's near. — HOOD.

Serious as the fifth act of a tragedy. — JOSEPH JEFFERSON.

Serious as taxes. — GEORGE HENRY LEWES.

Serious as a pope. — FRANCISQUE SARCEY.

Serviceable.

Serviceable as his inkstand. — GEORGE MEREDITH.

Set.

Her jaw was set like a steel latch. — IRVIN S. COBB.

Set, as a piece of sculpture. — DICKENS.

Set my face like a flint. — OLD TESTAMENT.

Settlements.

Settlements between married people are like throwing oneself out of the window a second time in order to discover how it happened the first time. — BJÖRNSTJERNE BJÖRNSON.

Sever.

Sever'd, like a flight of fowl
Scatter'd by winds and high tempestuous gusts. — SHAKESPEARE.

Severe.

Stood severe . . . like a Greek temple at mid-day in a southern clime. — BULWER-LYTTON.

Severe as vengeance. — COWPER.

Shabby.

Shabby as a sheepskin book. — AUSTIN DOBSON.

Shade.

Shaded over, like rainy clouds just ripe for showering tears. — HOOD.

Shadow.

Shadow . . . like a puddle of ink. — MARK TWAIN.

Shadowy.

Shadowy, like half-comprehended notions that float dim through children's brains. — CHARLOTTE BRONTË.

Shadowy as a dream. — EMMA LAZARUS.

Shadowless.

Shadowless as Heaven. — ROBERT COLLYER.

Shady.

With a past as shady
As the grove where Dian hides.
— BERT LESTON TAYLOR.

Shake.

(*See also* Shook.)

Shake like an aspen leaf. — ANON.

Shakes like jelly. — IBID.

Cease those aching sighs,
Which shake the tear-drops from thine eyes,
As morning wind, with wing fresh wet,
Shakes dew out of the violet.
— P. J. BAILEY.

Shake him up like a shirt in a hurricane. — J. R. BARTLETT'S "DICTIONARY OF AMERICANISMS."

Shakes like a tenant recreant. — BEAUMONT AND FLETCHER.

Shakes with passion, like a horse shaking off a fly. — JULES Q. DE BEAUREPAIRE.

Shake like withered leaves. — ALICE CARY.

Shake like a shadow. — GUIDO CAVALCANTI.

Head shaking like one of those drunken satyrs in the pictures of Rubens. — DUMAS, PÈRE.

Shaken as if an earthquake passed. — MICHAEL FIELD.

Shaken as by a shudder. — FLAUBERT.

Shaking like an ague. — WILLIAM HARBINGTON.

Shaking as with the cold fit of the Roman fever. — HAWTHORNE.

Shaking like pent up winds. — ROBERT JEPHSON.

Tremulous shake,
As in a palsied Druid's harp unstrung.
— KEATS.

Shaken like a press of spears. — D. G. ROSSETTI.

Shaked like a coward. — SHAKESPEARE.

Shake like a field of beaten corn. — IBID.

Shakes, like a thing unfirm. — IBID.

Shaking . . . like a drunkard after a debauch. — ROBERT LOUIS STEVENSON.

Shakes like flame. — SWINBURNE.

Shaken like spray from the sea. — IBID.

Shake — *continued.*

Shake,
As winds tall cedars toss on mountains hoar. TASSO.

Shaky.

Like the magnetic needle, shaky but steadfast. — CARLYLE.

Shallow.

As shallow as a pan. — BOOTH TARKINGTON.

Shame (Noun).

Shame sits, like a foul vulture on a corse. — J. S. KNOWLES.

Shame (Verb).

Would shame those stars,
As daylight doth a lamp.
— SHAKESPEARE.

Shamed as a Mayflower shames an autumn leaf. — SWINBURNE.

Shameful.

Shameful . . . as impotence in love. — POPE.

Shameful as a sin. — FRANCIS THOMPSON.

Shameless.

Shameless as a nude statue. — SYDNEY MUNDEN.

Shaped.

Shaped like an olive. — GEORGE ADE.

A female shaped like a washer. — CHARLES WAYLAND TOWNE.

Shapeless.

Shapeless as an old shoe. — ANON.

Shapeless as a shadow. — SWINBURNE.

Sharp.

As sharp as a razor. — ANON.

Sharp as a steel trap. — IBID.

Sharp as a tiger's tooth. — IBID.

As sharp as if he lived on Tewksbury mustard. — IBID.

Sharp as the bristles of a hedgehog. — IBID.

Sharp as the tooth of time. — IBID.

Sharp as vinegar. — IBID.

Sharp, like the shrill swallow's cry. — IBID.

So sharp that you could shave a sleeping mouse without waking her. — IBID.

Sharp as the little end of nothing. — J. R. BARTLETT'S "DICTIONARY OF AMERICANISMS."

Sharp, like the crack of a pistol. — R. D. BLACKMORE.

A pang as sharp as ever wrenched confession from the lips of a prisoner in the cells of the Inquisition. — BULWER-LYTTON.

Like the prick of a needle, duly sharp. — CARLYLE.

Sharpe as brere. — CHAUCER.

Sharp as the gore-soaked lashes
Of men's whips.
— ELIZA COOK.

Sharp as a winter's morning. — RICHARD CORBET.

Sharp-sighted as a hawk. — RICHARD CUMBERLAND.

Sharp like the claws of ravening beasts. — JOHN FOX.

Sharp as the bee-sting. — JAMES GRAINGER.

Sharp like a quince. — WILLIAM HAZLITT.

Sharp as a handsaw. — JOHN HEYWOOD.

Sharp as her needle. — IBID.

Sharp as a beak. — HUGO.

Sharp as truth. — IBID.

Sharp as frost. — ERIC MACKAY.

Sharp as a sickle is the edge of shade and shine. — GEORGE MEREDITH.

Sharp as the enchanter's sword. — IBID.

Sharp — *continued.*

Sharp as a ferret at a field-rat's hole. — MISS MULOCK.

Sharp as a sword drawn from a shuddering wound. — ALFRED NOYES.

Sharp as thistles are. — OVID.

Short and sharp, like a donkey's gallop. — SAMUEL PEGGE.

Sharp as javelins. — RUSKIN.

Sharp as dirk rammed down in its sheath. — DUNCAN C. SCOTT.

Sharp as my needle. — SHAKESPEARE.

More sharp than filed steel. — IBID.

How sharper than a serpent's tooth it is
To have a thankless child.
— IBID.

Nose was as sharp as a pen. — IBID.

Sharp as his spur. — IBID.

Sharp as a bayonet. — SHELLEY.

Sharp as tenterhooks. — SKELTON.

Sharp as . . . oyster strumpet. — SWIFT.

Sharp as the north sets when the snows are out. — SWINBURNE.

More sharp than is the naked side of war. — IBID.

Sharp as a terrier. — TOM TAYLOR.

Sharp as reproach. — TENNYSON.

Sharp as a two-edged sword. — OLD TESTAMENT.

Sharper than a thorn. — IBID.

Sharp as a thistle. — "TOWNELEY MYSTERIES, OR MIRACLE PLAYS."

Sharply.

Breaking as sharply as the ice blade that loosens from the eave to slice the air and splinter into scales of flying frost. — JAMES WHITCOMB RILEY.

Sharply as the blow which breaks
Prison bolts and chains.
— WHITTIER.

Shatter.

Shattered as if a shell had exploded inside. — JOSEPH CONRAD.

Shattered like stormy spray. — GEORGE MEREDITH.

Shattered, as though they had stood a siege at Rome. — T. BUCHANAN READ.

Shattered, like a stranded bark
On the wrathful woful marge of earth and sea. — SWINBURNE.

Shed.

Sheds gladness like a morn of sweet sunshine. — ANON.

Shed great thoughts as easily as an oak looseneth its golden leaves in a kindly largess to the soil it grew on. — P. J. BAILEY.

The glory of the morn is shed, like a celestial benison. — LONGFELLOW.

Shed loose as the petals of roses discrowned
On the floors of the forest.
— SWINBURNE.

Sheer.

Sheer as chaos to the irrevocable past. — D. G. ROSSETTI.

The rays run sheer as fire from the sun through the dusk of the pinewood. — SWINBURNE.

Shelter.

Shelters him
As birds within the green shade of the grove. — D. G. ROSSETTI.

Shield.

Shields me like an angel's wing. — MRS. FORRESTER.

Shift.

Shifting as a weathercock. — ANON

Shift as the sands. — IBID.

Shift — *continued.*

Shifting as the tints of the rainbow. — BULWER-LYTTON.

Shift, like fortune's favours. — BURNS.

Shifting, like the weather. — COWPER.

Shifts its scenery like a diorama. — GEORGE ELIOT.

She shifts and changes like the moon. — ROBERT HERRICK.

Shifting like the boundaries of a dream. — CHARLES L. MOORE.

Shifted like restless clouds. — SHELLEY.

Shifty.

Shifty as a huckster's opening deal
For bargain under smoothest market face. — GEORGE MEREDITH.

Shimmer.

Shimmered like silver. — ARABIAN NIGHTS.

Shimmered like the sun. — SCOTTISH BALLAD.

Shimmered . . . like meteor-fires that haunt a fairy dell. — BAYARD TAYLOR.

Shimmered like moonbeams on dancing water. — PAUL WIGGENS.

Blue eyes shimmer with angel glances,
Like spring violets over the lea.
— CONSTANCE F. WOOLSON.

Shine.

Shone like a glowworm's head. — ANON.

Shines like a nigger's heel. — IBID.

Shines like armor. — IBID.

Shines like burnished metal. — IBID.

Shines like fire in cat's eye. — IBID.

Shines like frost in the moonlight. — IBID.

Shine like immortals. — IBID.

Shone like the bristles of a blacking-brush. — IBID.

Shines like the gleam of a sword. — IBID.

Shone like the jetty down on the black hogs of Hassaqua. — IBID.

Shone like polished ebony. — IBID.

Shone like satin. — IBID.

Shines like shot silk in the sunshine. — IBID.

Shining like glowing flame. — ARISTO.

Shine at all points like a constellation. — P. J. BAILEY.

Shine like a diamond on a dead man's hand. — IBID.

Shine through them as live coals through ashes. — IBID.

Shine as Phœbus doth in a May morning. — ALEXANDER BARCLAY.

Shine like dragon's scales. — BEAUMONT AND FLETCHER.

Shines like a newly lit flame. — JOSH BILLINGS.

Shone like a cherry by candle-light. — R. D. BLACKMORE.

She shines like the birch in the sunlight's play. — HJALMAR H. BOYESEN.

Shine like jet. — CHARLOTTE BRONTË.

Shone like flames blown in the wind. — O. M. BROWN.

Shone
Like yealow flowres and grasse farre off, in one;
Or like the mixture nature doth display
Upon the quaint wings of the popinjay.
— WILLIAM BROWNE.

Shine like the sun in the firmament of heaven. — BUNYAN.

Shone as seraphs shine. — BYRON.

Shines like a phosphoric sea. — IBID.

Shine — *continued.*

Shines like snow. — Ibid.

Shining like a bed of daffodils. — Alice Cary.

Shine like red buttons set on a holiday coat. — Ibid.

Shoon as the burned gold. — Chaucer.

Shine as brighte as sunne. — Thomas Churchyard.

Shining out like the gold that 'd been purged of its dross. — Eliza Cook.

Shine like gleams which sparkle in the crowns of kings barbaric. — J. G. Cooper.

Shine, like a veil before a holy shrine. — Mrs. E. M. H. Cortissoz.

Shine with such lustre as the tear that flows down Virtue's manly cheek for other's woes. — Erasmus Darwin.

Shine out like the spine of a frosty hill in the wintry sun. — Aubrey De Vere.

Shine out like flowering meads in spring. — Ibid.

Shine like cherub's cheeks. — Dickens.

Stalks shine
Like the burnished spears of a field of gold.
— Paul Laurence Dunbar.

Shines like a beau in a new birthday suit. — Fielding.

Shining as a saint on a holy pyx. — Flaubert.

Shine in heav'n as bright
As doth the sun in his transcendent might. — Giles Fletcher.

Shine as bright as smiling day. — Ibid.

The winking buttons on the gown
Shone like the lamps of London Town.
— Norman Gale.

On prince or bride no diamond stone
Half so gracious ever shone,
As the light of enterprise
Beaming from a young man's eyes.
— Hafiz (Emerson).

The wistful stars
Shine like good memories.
— W. E. Henley.

Shone like the evening star. — O. W. Holmes.

Shone like Jove's own lightning. — Homer (Pope).

Shone like an aureole round the head of some modern saint. — A. E. Housman.

Their souls shine like living torches. — James Huneker.

Shone like the bubbling foam about a keel. — Keats.

Shone like a friendly twinkling star. — Frances Anne Kemble.

Shining as the Alps, when that the sun
Gems their pale robes with diamonds.
— Ibid.

The pile of fish . . . shone like a dump of fluid silver. — Kipling.

A smouldering fire, shining like lamps through rents in sepulchres. — Sigmund Krasinski.

Shone like an illuminated letter. — Richard Le Gallienne.

Lakes . . . shining like polished mirrors. — Lever.

Shone beneath, as the fire shines through the ashes. — George Henry Lewes.

Shone like ocean's snowy foam. — John Leyden.

Shine as immortal poems. — Longfellow.

Shining like the Sunne in earth. — Lyly.

Shone like Joshua's sun. — Gerald Massey.

Shine — *continued.*

Shone like love's eyes soft with tears. — JOAQUIN MILLER.

Shone like a meteor streaming to the wind. — MILTON.

Shine sweetly through the gloom,
Like glimpses of eternal day beyond the tomb.
— JAMES MONTGOMERY.

Shine,
Like golden ingots from a fairy mine.
— THOMAS MOORE.

Shine like Nereïd's hair. — IBID.

Shine like a goldsmith's shop in Cheapside. — THOMAS NABBES.

Shine, like woodland flowers which paint the desert glades,
And waste their sweetness in unfrequented shades.
— AMBROSE PHILIPS.

Shines like rotten wood. — SIR WALTER RALEIGH.

Gleam and shine
Like jewels in a stream of wine.
— JAMES WHITCOMB RILEY.

Shone like a keen Damascus blade. — CLINTON SCOLLARD.

Shine
As gloriously as the Venus of the sky.
— SHAKESPEARE.

Shone like mountains in the morn. — SHELLEY.

Shine like obelisks of fire. — IBID.

Shine like pyramids of fire. — IBID.

Shone like the reflex of a thousand minds. — IBID.

Shone like a sunbeam. — WILLIAM SOTHEBY.

Shone like a single star, serene in a night of darkness. — SOUTHEY.

Shone like silver in the sunshine. — IBID.

Shone like the brook that o'er its pebbled course runs glittering gayly to the noontide sun. — IBID.

Shone like the waves that glow around a midnight keel in liquid light. — IBID.

Shyne as brightest skye. — SPENSER.

Shone as heaven's light. — IBID.

Shined far away, like glauncing light of Phœbus brightest ray. — IBID.

Shone and shivered like wings of angels blown by the sun's breath. — SWINBURNE.

Shines as a cloud-constraining star. — IBID.

Shone like a burning brand. — IBID.

Shone like a drop of dew. — IBID.

Shining like all April in one day. — IBID.

Shining like a sunbeam-smitten tear. — IBID.

Shone like the star that shines down storm. — IBID.

Shine sweet like stars when darkness feels them strong. — IBID.

Shone like suns aglow. — IBID.

Shone like isles of tawny gold. — BAYARD TAYLOR.

Like a sheathless sabre . . . shines. — IBID.

Shines like fire in swamps. — TENNYSON.

Shone as a wintry sun. — FREDERICK TENNYSON.

Shine as the brightness of the firmament. — OLD TESTAMENT.

Shone like silver threads in tangles blown. — MAURICE THOMPSON.

Shone like the robe of a queen. — WALTER THORNBURY.

Shin'd like molten glass. — HENRY VAUGHAN.

Shine like fairy flags unfurled. — THEODORE WATTS-DUNTON.

Shine — *continued.*

Snines like burnished brass. — PAUL WIGGENS.

Shines as calmly as some distant star. — SARAH WILLIAMS.

Shine, eminent as a planet's light. — N. P. WILLIS.

Ship.

Ships are like flies in the spider's web of the sea. — HUGO.

Shiver.

Shiver as the swimmer when he makes his first plunge. — ANON.

Shivered like a tyrant king when he smelt gunpowder. — IBID.

Shivered as if in a deadly chill. — J. M. BARRIE.

Shivered as with an ague-fit. — ROBERT M. BIRD.

Shivered in my heart like a suffering child in a cold cradle. — CHARLOTTE BRONTË.

Shiver
Like the lotus in the river.
— E. B. BROWNING.

A shivering thing;
Like a young bird missing its mother's wing. — ELIZA COOK.

Shivers, like a signal-flame held high. — HUGO.

Shivered . . . like tautened wire. — JOHN MASEFIELD.

Made one shiver unpleasantly, as when the Espanña comes to close quarters with the infuriated brute at a bull fight. — GUY DE MAUPASSANT.

Shiver'd, like wither'd moss. — JAMES MONTGOMERY.

Shivering in the wind like the sails in the sea song. — JOHN POOLE.

Shiver'd like an egg. — SHAKESPEARE.

Shivering as if a bullet had struck him. — G. B. SHAW.

Shock.

Shock like tornado tempests. — CARLYLE.

Shocked me like a bullet. — BADGER CLARK.

Shock my spirit . . . like the vibration of a bell. — COVENTRY PATMORE.

Shook.

(*See also* Shake.)

Shook like a strong oak in a blast. — ANON.

Shook it like a terrier with a rat. — HOOD.

Shook as one that looks on death. — JEAN INGELOW.

Like bullrushes on side of brook,
Or aspen leaf, her joints all shook.
— WILLIAM KING.

Shook like windy weeds. — LONGFELLOW.

Shook like custards. — OUIDA.

Shook as the quivering plumes upon the hearse. — POE.

Shook like a spied spy. — IBID.

Shook . . . like cold jelly. — CHARLES READE.

Shook like an autumn leaf. — D. G. ROSSETTI.

Shook . . . like shingle at the ocean's mercy. — JOHN RUSKIN.

Shook, like reeds beside a frozen brook. — SIR WALTER SCOTT.

Shook, like the Aspen leaves in the wind. — IBID.

Shook like a palsied limb. — SOUTHEY.

Shook like loosened music. — FRANCIS THOMPSON.

Her waving hair shook like music. — IBID.

Shook like a poppy-field. — G. W. THORNBURY.

Shook — *continued.*

Shook, as the blackbird's throat
With its last big note.
— Oscar Wilde.

Shoot.

Shot like a bullet from a gun. — O. W. Holmes.

Shot like a rabbit in a ride. — Kipling.

Shot, like meteors changed from stars to gleams of lightning. — James Montgomery.

Shoot through the sparkling foam like an ocean-bird set free. — Epes Sargent.

Shoots like a meteor through the storm. — Sir Walter Scott.

Shoots, as a fire to smite some towering town. — Swinburne.

Shorn.

Shorn as Samson. — Tupper.

Short.

Short as the life of a wave. — Leonid Andreyev.

Short as Mahomet's dream. — Anon.

Short, thick and round, — like a suet-pudding. — Ibid.

Short as a militia drummer-boy. — J. B. Buckstone.

Short as wash-day-dinner graces. — Irwin Russell.

Short as any dream. — Shakespeare.

Short as a lawyer's beard. — John Webster.

Shout.

Universal shout, like a volcano's burst. — Edwin Atherstone.

Shout, like the hoarse peals of vultures. — Dryden.

Shouted and laughed, like a school full of boys from their benches set free. — O. W. Holmes.

Shouts like Egypt, when her priests have found,
A new Osiris, for the old one drowned.
— Juvenal.

Shout like a storm on hills of pine. — Bayard Taylor.

Shout, as they that tread the grapes. — Old Testament.

Shrew.

As a mushroom is among roses, so is a shrew in a costly establishment. — W. S. Downey.

Shrewish.

Shrewish to a jest as a woman to advice. — Bulwer-Lytton.

Curst and shrewd as Socrates' Xanthippe. — Shakespeare.

Shriek (Noun).

A shriek, as of a soul in Hades. — Anon.

Shriek . . . such as might have risen only out of hell. — Poe.

Shrieks like mandrakes' torn out of the earth. — Shakespeare.

A shriek and a yell
Like the devils of hell.
— Thackeray.

Shriek (Verb).

Like one who wakens in a grave and shrieks,
The still house seemed to shriek.
— E. B. Browning.

Shriek,
Like a frayed bird in the gray owlet's beak.
— Hood.

Shrieks like laughter in the demoned hills. — Richard Hovey.

Shriek . . . as if a frightful memory whipped thy soul for some infernal crime. — H. C. Kendall.

Shriek . . . during shipwrecks, like the cursed inhabitants of the Bay of the Dead, who await their prey in the ships lost at sea. — Lamartine.

Shriek — *continued.*

Shriek like a storm-wind. — Swinburne.

Shrieking, like a soul in pain. — Celia Thaxter.

Shrill.

Shrill
As ever started through a sea-bird's bill. — Byron.

Though thy voice be shrill, like rasping file on steel. — Emerson.

A cry more shrill than Diana surprised by Actæon. — Gautier.

Shrill . . like the tingling steel of an elfin gong. — P. H. Hayne.

Shrill as bird on topmost twig. — C. G. Rossetti.

Shrink.

Shrink as from a haunted place. — Anon.

Shrinking like an old man into his shoulders. — Ibid.

Shrinks inward like a walnut. — Ibid.

Shrinks like a Yonkers celebrity when he hits Broadway. — Ibid.

Shrunk like a withered hand. — P. J. Bailey.

Shrink, as if I had been wandering among volcanic-looking hills, and had suddenly felt the ground quiver. — Charlotte Brontë.

Shrink into a point like death. — E. B. Browning.

Shrink up like a crushed snail. — Robert Browning.

Shrunken . . . like a withered branch. — Buddha.

Shrunk up like a bean in a pod. — Alice Cary.

Shrinking back, like one that had mistook. — Coleridge.

Shrink,
As from a precipice's brink. — Eliza Cook.

Shrink as a snail. — "Coventry Mysteries."

Shrinks, like the sick moon at the wholesome morn. — William Crashaw.

Shrink like parchment in consuming flame. — John Dryden.

Shrinks as some fair tulip by a storm oppressed
Shrinks up and folds its silken arms to rest. — Ibid.

Shrank
As one who sees a loathed sight. — Maurice F. Egan.

Shrank like the snow that watchers in the vale see narrowed on the height each summer morn. — George Eliot.

Shrank like a leaf in Fall. — Eugene Field.

Shrinking like a snail withdrawing into its shell. — Herman Heijermans, Jr.

Shrunk away as a frost-bitten apple. — Washington Irving.

Shrunk away, within him, like a dried filbert in its shell. — Ibid.

Shrank as from a sudden and mortal danger. — Mary Johnston.

Shrank, like things with breath,
Whose ripeness feels the touch of death. — C. F. Keary.

Shrank as the beetle shrinks beneath the pin when village children stab him in their sport. — Kipling.

Shrank, like boys, who, unaware,
Ranging the woods to start a hare,
Come to the mouth of the dark lair where,
Growling low, a fierce old bear
Lies amidst bones and blood. — Macaulay.

Shrink — *continued.*

Shrink as though Death were passing in his shroud. — JOHN MASEFIELD.

Shrank as at prick of steel. — GEORGE MEREDITH.

Shrank — like parchment at the touch of flame. — IBID.

Shrink, as from a serpent in a knot of flowers. — H. H. MILMAN.

He shrinks, as from a viewless blow. — RICHARD M. MILNES.

Shrinking as violets do in summer ray. — THOMAS MOORE.

Shrink as though some cowardly sin were between them. — OUIDA.

Shrank,
As a taper in sunlight sinks faint and
aghast. — T. BUCHANAN READ.

Shrinks like scorched parchment from the fiery ordeal of true criticism. — R. B. SHERIDAN.

Shrinks, as might love from scorn. — SWINBURNE.

Shrank away tremulously, as fairies in the story-books, before a superior bad angel. — THACKERAY.

Shrinks like a beggar in the cold. — J. T. TROWBRIDGE.

Shrink . . . like guilty things surprised. — E. P. WHIPPLE.

Shrivel.

Shrivelled like belated daisies, before a north wind. — ANON.

Shrivels like a scroll. — O. W. HOLMES.

Shrivelled like a burning scroll. — H. H. MILMAN.

Shrivel, like leaves when summer's green recedes. — J. H. NEWMAN.

Shrivelling up his face, like an autumn leaf. — SMOLLETT.

Shriveled.

Shriveled . . . like the pictures of mummies you see in books. — MARK TWAIN.

Shrouded.

Shrouded as a corpse with storm's grey shroud. — SWINBURNE.

Imagination shrouded, like the drawing-room furniture. — EDITH WHARTON.

Shudder (Noun).

He felt the sort of shudder which a bull-dog would feel who should scent a wolf in his master's clothes. — HUGO.

A shudder like that of the deer when he sees the hounds again upon his track. — IBID.

Shudder (Verb).

Shuddered like some woman's over-fat pug when a street dog bristles up at him. — O. HENRY.

Shuddered like a man in a fever. — MAURICE HEWLETT.

Shuddered as at a swift cleaving of cold steel. — GEORGE MEREDITH.

Shuddering like a shot bird. — SWINBURNE.

Shun.

Shun wickedness as swallows shun pestilent places. — ST. AUGUSTINE.

Shun him like the plague. — ROBERT BROWNING.

Shun her like garlic. — BYRON.

Shunned like a viper. — MATHEW CAREY.

Shunned like base praise and hireling's mart. — AUBREY DE VERE.

Shunn'd him as a sailor shuns the rocks. — DRYDEN.

Shun as moles shun light. — O. HENRY.

Shun him like the pest. — EDWARD SHARPHAM.

Shun — *continued.*

Shun as sullen night-ravens do the sun. — Henry Vaughan.

Shun, like a shattered bark, the storm. — Wordsworth.

Shut.

As shut as evening flowers. — Anon.

Shut as the leaves of a white rose may
Ere the wan bud blooms out perfectly.
— James Whitcomb Riley.

Shut like a purse. — Swift.

My heart is shut
As a sealed spring of fire.
— Swinburne.

Shut from approach like sea-nymph in a shell. — N. P. Willis.

Shy.

Shy as lightning. — De Quincey.

Shy
As some stray fawn that seeks its mother. — Austin Dobson.

As shy and secret as a maid. — Lowell.

Shy as the squirrel. — George Meredith.

Shyer than the forest doe
Twinkling slim through branches green.
— Ibid.

Shy as a wren in the hedgerow. — George Moore.

Shy as the fawn. — Ambrose Philips.

Sick.

Sick as a cat with eating rats.—Anon.

Sick as a horse. — J. R. Bartlett's "Dictionary of Americanisms."

As sick as a dog. — Richard Jago.

Sick as a Dover packet-boat. — George Meredith.

Sick at heart as the mouse, that the cat lets go a little way, and then darts and replaces. — Charles Reade.

Sick as Lent. — Swinburne.

Sickly.

Sickly as faint weather. — Beaumont and Fletcher.

Side.

All on one side, like a bird with one wing. — G. F. Northall.

Sideways.

Sideways, like an amorous dove. — George Darley.

Spread sideways like a drawing net. — Swinburne.

Went sideways as a big fish flaps
And shoves with head and body.
— Ibid.

Side by Side.

Side by side,
Like tombs of pilgrims that have died
About the Holy Sepulchre.
— D. G. Rossetti.

Sift.

Sifted fine as flour. — Dickens.

Sifted, drifted, like the sun of sands in wastes Arabian. — Andrew Lang

Sifted like great snowdrifts o'er the landscape. — Longfellow.

Sift you as wheat. — New Testament.

Sigh (Noun).

A sort of sigh, like the grunt of an overburdened St. Joseph. — Balzac.

Sighed with such a sigh as drops from agony to exhaustion. — E. B. Browning.

A sigh like driven wind or foam. — Bliss Carman.

My sighs, like silent air, unheeded, never move her. — Robert Crawford.

Profound sigh, like a man unloosed from the tightest bonds. — Dumas, père.

Sigh — *continued.*

Pitiful sigh, like a gust of chill, damp wind out of a long-closed vault, the door of which has accidentally been set ajar. — HAWTHORNE.

A sigh like the long-drawn breath of a fog-horn. — EDGAR W. NYE.

A great sigh, like that of a giant who is stoned. — EDGAR QUINET.

With low, uneasy sigh ;
Like the voice of wandering spirits,
Lamenting through the sky.
— FRANCIS S. SALTUS.

A sigh like that of a saint desirous of dissolution. — SIR WALTER SCOTT.

Sigh (Verb).

Sighed like the dying gasp of a syphon bottle. — ANON.

Sighing . . . as though the sea were mourning above an ancient grief. — BLISS CARMAN.

The sails did sigh like sedge. — COLERIDGE.

Sighed like Boreas. — GERALD GRIFFIN.

Sigh like a dog that hath lost his master. — THOMAS LODGE.

He sighs like David's son for Sheba's queen. — EDWARD LOVIBOND.

Sighs as men sigh relieved from care. — LOWELL.

Sighing . . . like a tomb-searcher. — THOMAS MOORE.

Sigh,
Like some sweet plaintive melody of ages long gone by.
— WILLIAM MOTHERWELL.

Sighed as if a deadly burthen had been taken from her breast. — POE.

Sighing as April sighs for May. — T. BUCHANAN READ.

Sighing like furnace. — SHAKESPEARE.

Sigh, like a school-boy that had lost his A, B, C. — IBID.

Sigh like Tom o' Bedlam. — IBID.

Sighed like a man near fainting. — ROBERT LOUIS STEVENSON.

Sighs
As a voiceless crying of old love
That died and never spoke.
— ARTHUR SYMONS.

He sighed like a zephyr. — MARK TWAIN.

Sighs, like a spirit, deep along the cheerless waste. — H. K. WHITE.

Silence.

Silence . . . like an adoring host in ecstasy. — LAURENCE BINYON.

Silence sank
Like music on my heart.
— COLERIDGE.

A silence like that of dreams. — O. W. HOLMES.

Silence, like a poultice, comes
To heal the blows of sound.
— IBID.

We rest in silence, like two gems upcurl'd
In the recesses of a pearly shell.
— KEATS.

A deep silence, like the fearful calm
That slumbers in the storm's portentous pause. — SHELLEY.

Silence . . . like a flower closed in the night. — CHARLES WELLS.

Silenced.

Silenced with a scorn as bitter to the taste as myrrh. — CLINTON SCOLLARD.

Silent.

Silent . . . like a forgotten melody. — HAMILTON AÏDÉ.

Silent as a man being shaved. — NICCOLO ALBIZZI.

Silent as a catacomb. — ANON.

Silent — *continued.*

Silent as a father confessor. — Ibid.

Silent as death. — Ibid.

Silent as Fate. — Ibid.

Silent as Messina during a sirocco. — Ibid.

Silent as the day gives way to night. — Ibid.

Silent as the lips of Memnon.— Ibid.

Silent as the Sphinx. — Ibid.

Silent men like silent waters are deep and dangerous. — Ibid.

Silent as the foot of time. — A. L. Barbauld.

Silent as the growth of flowers. — Aphra Behn.

Silent as thought. — Béranger.

The living seemed as silent as the slain. — Ambrose Bierce.

Silent as a church. — Charlotte Brontë.

Silent as an Indian. — Ibid.

Silent as a ghost. — W. H. Burleigh.

Silent as night. — Thomas Carew.

Silent . . . like Sleeping Beauty's Castle. — Carlyle.

Silent as snow falls on the earth. — Chinese.

Silent as your shadow. — Colley Cibber.

Silent and pure as the heaven above. — D'Annunzio.

Silent as a saint. — Aubrey De Vere.

Silent as a flame that fails. — Dickens.

Silent as the elves. — George Eliot.

Silent and troubled, like a man who feels he hath done that which he shall one day rue. — F. W. Faber.

Silent as evening. — Francis Fawkes.

Silent as shut cups
And windless reeds.
— Zona Gale.

Silent as a Japanese. — Goldsmith.

Silent like a glacier bed. — Edmund Gosse.

Silent as midnight's falling meteor slides into the stillness of the far-off land. — O. W. Holmes.

Silent as a mummy. — Hood.

Silent as a stone. — Ibid.

Glide as silent as a Dryad
That disappears among the trees.
—Richard Hovey.

Silent as sleep or shadow. — Jean Ingelow.

Silent as at the gentle Lethe's tide. — William Irving.

Silent as a consecrated urn. — Keats.

Silent as a tomb. — Ibid.

Silent as a sentinel on an outpost. — Hugh Kelly.

Silent as the Trafalgar Square lions. — Amy Leslie.

Silent as the ev'nings ayre. — Richard Lovelace.

Silent as a country churchyard. — Macaulay.

Silent as a hound at fault. — Charles Macklin.

Silent as the sleeping seas. — Gerald Massey.

Silent as the evening sky. — George Meredith.

Silent as the moon. — Milton.

Silent as the depth of night. — James Montgomery.

Silent, like a sundial in the shade. — Sydney Munden.

Silent — *continued.*

Silent as a tree. — Josephine P. Peabody.

Silent as the silence where men lie slain. — C. G. Rossetti.

Silent and slight as the fall of a half-checked tear on a maiden cheek. — Ruskin.

Silent as the grave. — Schiller.

Silent as a corpse. — Shelley.

Silent as a noonday sky when larks with heat are mute. — Alexander Smith.

Silent as a steam calliope with a broken boiler. — New York Sun.

Silent as a politician. — Swift.

Silent as a mountain lawn. — Swinburne.

Silent as time. — Ibid.

Silent as a stooping cloud. — Ibid.

Silent as a cloud that sleeps in midday on a mountain peak. — Bayard Taylor.

Silent in conversation as a country lover. — Vanbrugh.

Silent as the mighty marching
Of earth and all the planets round the
sun. — Thomas Wade.

Silent . . . as the hush'd grouping of a dream. — Whittier.

Silent as despair. — Ibid.

Silent as a picture. — Wordsworth.

Silent as a standing pool. — Ibid.

Silent as the skies. — Ibid.

Silently.

Silently as a snail slips over a cabbage leaf on a dewy morning. — J. R. Bartlett's "Dictionary of Amfricanisms."

Silently as a dream. — Cowper.

Silently as a fish in a stream. — Sir A. Conan Doyle.

Fall silently like dew on roses. — Dryden.

Silently, like thoughts that come and go, the snowflakes fall, each one a gem. — W. H. Gibson.

Silently . . . as colours steal into the pear or plum. — Robert Herrick.

E'en like the passage of an angel's tear
That falls through the clear ether
silently. — Keats.

Silently as a cloud rolls out of the mouth of a valley. — Kipling.

Silently as the winds of the desert sweep upward and northward over the plains. — Ouida.

Eat his dinner as silently as a brother of La Trappe. — Thackeray.

Silently as bubbles burst. — William R. Thayer.

As the water follows the moon, silently, with fluid steps, anywhere round the globe. — Walt Whitman.

Silly.

Silly as calves. — Anon.

Silly as an old maid at a marriage. — Congreve.

You look . . . as silly as a tumbler when he's been upside down and has got on his heels again. — George Eliot.

Silly as an owlish roysterer's glazed stare at the young aurora. — George Meredith.

Silly as a booby. — Mason L. Weems.

Silvery.

Silvery as a song. — Gerald Massey.

Simile.

And similes in each dull line,
Like glow-worms in the dark should
shine. — Edward Moore.

What liuely similitudes & comparisons, as the righteous man to a baie tree, the Soule to a thirstie Hart, vnitie to oyntment and the dew of Hermon. — HENRY PEACHAM.

Similes are like songs in love ;
They much describe ; they nothing prove. — PRIOR.

Similes prove nothing, but yet greatly lighten and relieve the tedium of argument. — SOUTH.

Simmer.

Simmer like a sea pent volcano. — O. W. HOLMES.

Simper.

She simpers as a mare when she eats thistles. — ANON.

Simper like a porrage pot in the fire when it first begins to seethe. — THOMAS NASH.

Simper like a bride on her wedding day. — JOHN RAY'S "HANDBOOK OF PROVERBS."

Simple.

Simple as A. B. C. — ANON.

Simple as a Greek temple. — IBID.

Simple as a nun's prayer. — IBID.

Simple as a schoolboy's logic. — IBID.

Simple as a squash. — IBID.

Simple as rolling off a log. — IBID.

Simple as the choice of Hercules between virtue and vice. — IBID.

Simple as a child. — BALZAC.

Simple as the flowers in the field. — R. D. BLACKMORE.

Simple as milking. — IBID.

Simple as playful lamb. — ROBERT BLOOMFIELD.

Symple as byrde in bouer. — CHAUCER.

Symple as dowve of tree. — IBID.

As simple as a saint might bathe in lakes of prayer. — RICHARD HOVEY.

Simple as miracles always are after they are wrought. — F. W. H. MYERS.

Simpler than the infancy of truth. — SHAKESPEARE.

Simple as breath. — ARTHUR SYMONS.

Simple as a snow-drop. — ELIZABETH S. P. WARD.

Simply.

Simply as Augustus went on foot to the Capital. — ÉMILE BOURGEOIS.

Simply as breathing. — LOWELL.

Heart-whole, and simply as a bird that feels the onset of the spring. — F. W. H. MYERS.

Sin.

Sin is like a mountain with two aspects according to whether it is viewed before or after it has been reached : yet both aspects are real. — SAMUEL BUTLER (1835–1902).

Sins are like circles in the water when a stone is thrown into it — one produces another. — MATTHEW HENRY.

Sincere.

Sincere as sunlight. — ANON.

As truth, sincere. — DAVID MALLET.

About as sincere as the look upon the face of an undertaker conducting a nine-hundred dollar funeral. — HENRY L. MENCKEN.

Sincerity is like travelling on a plain, beaten road, which commonly brings a man sooner to his journey's end than byways, in which men often lose themselves. — JOHN TILLOTSON.

Sinew.

Sinews like a vine. — ALFRED AUSTIN.

Sinful.

Sinful as sin. — FIELDING.

Sing.

Sing like a bird called a swine. — ANON.

Sing like a cobbler. — IBID.

Singest like an angel in the clouds. — COLERIDGE.

Sing like a swan, as if thou went'st to bliss. — SIR JOHN DAVIES.

Sing like an angel. — JOHN EVELYN.

Singing as sweetly and making as heavenly a noise as doth an arbour of nightingales in a calm-winded night. — JOHN GRANGE.

Sing-song like a stiff puffet on a humdrum barrel-organ. — LEIGH HUNT.

Sings like the sighing of a tempest spent. — DR. JOHNSON.

Singing . . . like the shouting of a backstay in a gale. — KIPLING.

Sings, like an inspired young Sibyl. — THOMAS MOORE.

He sings like an empty water jar. — OSMANLI PROVERB.

She sings
As if a choir of spirits swept
From earth with throbbing wings.
— C. G. ROSSETTI.

About the caldron sing,
Like elves and fairies in a ring.
— SHAKESPEARE.

Sang like sirens. — VOLTAIRE.

Single.

Single as the sun. — SWINBURNE.

Singly.

The good things of life are not to be had singly, but come to us with a mixture, — like a schoolboy's holiday, with a task affixed to the tail of it. — CHARLES LAMB.

Sinister.

Sinister as murky midnight pools. — JAMES HUNEKER.

Sink.

Sink like a lark falling suddenly to earth. — ANON.

Sinks like a plummet. — IBID.

Sinks, like a seaweed, into whence she rose. — IBID.

Sunk
Like a blade sent home to its scabbard.
— ROBERT BROWNING.

Sink lower than the grave. — BUNYAN.

Then sinks, as beauty fades and passion cools,
The scorn of coxcombs, and the jest of fools. — JAMES CAWTHORN.

Sunk like lead into the sea. — COLERIDGE.

Sinks like a lily from the storm. — ELIZA COOK.

Sink like fall of summer eve. — REGINALD HEBER.

The erect body sank like a sword driven home into the scabbard. — KIPLING.

The nerves of Power
Sink, as a lute's in rain.
— W. S. LANDOR.

Sank
As one that kneels before a virgin shrine. — JOHN PAYNE.

Sinks eclipsed, as at the dawn a star when cover'd by the solar ray. — PETRARCH.

Sinks, like a strain of vesper-song. — FRANK SEWALL.

I sank under it like a baby fed on starch. — G. B. SHAW.

Sink down as a sunset in sea-mist. — SWINBURNE.

Sink as the pausing of music. — BAYARD TAYLOR.

They sank into the bottom as a stone. — OLD TESTAMENT.

Sank as lead in the mighty waters. — IBID.

Sinless.

Sinless as Eden. — SHELLEY.

Sinless as the spring. — SWINBURNE.

Sit.

Sits careless of wave's ebb and flow,
Like a love beacon on a desert coast,
Showing where all her hope was
wrecked and lost. — HOOD.

Sat like patience on a monument,
Smiling at grief. — SHAKESPEARE.

Sit up all night like a watching candle. — THOMAS TOMKIS.

Skeptic.

The skeptic, when he plunges into the depths of infidelity, like the miser who leaps from the shipwreck, will find that the treasures which he bears about him, will only sink him deeper in the abyss. — C. C. COLTON.

Skilless.

Skilless as unpractis'd infancy. — SHAKESPEARE.

Skim.

The little man skimmed down the hill,
Like a swallow down the wind.
— JOHN HAY.

Lightly skimming. . . .
Like winds which gently brush the plying grass. — AMBROSE PHILIPS.

Skinny.

Skinny as an anchorite. — CHARLES MACKAY.

Skip.

Skip like a young kid. — ANON.

He skips like hail on a pack-saddle. — IBID.

Skip like a calf. — OLD TESTAMENT.

Mountains skipped like rams, and the little hills like lambs. — IBID.

Skulk.

Skulk like the dishonor'd wretch, whose hireling steel, in secret lifted, reeks with human gore. — SMOLLETT.

Skulk . . . like a dog shivering. — SWINBURNE.

Slacken.

Slacken like a bow-string slipped. — EDWIN ARNOLD.

Slain.

Slain and lost,
Like a sweet flower nipp'd with untimely frost. — TASSO.

Slam.

Door slam like the smacking of an iron lip. — IRVIN S. COBB.

Slander.

Slanders are like flies, that pass all over a man's good parts to light on his sores. — ANON.

Slander, like the pestilence, which rages at noonday, sweeps all before it, levelling without distinction the good and the bad. — STERNE.

Slanderous.

Slanderous as Satan. — SHAKESPEARE.

Slash.

Slash,
Like to a censer in a barber's shop.
— SHAKESPEARE.

Slaughter.

Slaughtered like cattle in the shambles. — PRESCOTT.

Slay.

Slay like thunderbolts. — ANON.

Slay, as folk that nae defence might ma. — JOHN BARBOUR.

Slays like lightning. — GEORGE ELIOT.

Slays as plague's blind breath. — SWINBURNE.

Sleek.

Sleek and round as a German sausage. — PETER C. ASBJÖRNSEN.

Sleek as a dray horse. — GEORGE COLMAN, THE YOUNGER.

Sleek — *continued.*

A skin as sleek as a maiden's cheek. — ELIZA COOK.

Sleek as Mr. Pecksniff. — DICKENS.

Sleek as a mouse. — GAY.

Sleek as a cat. — MAURICE HEWLETT.

Sleek as silk. — HOOD.

Sleek as a horn-book. — BEN JONSON.

Sleeker than Night-swollen mushrooms. — KEATS.

Sleep (Noun).

My sleep was like a summer sky that held the music of a lark. — GEORGE STERLING.

Sleep (Verb).

Never bothered — sleeps like a hall-boy. — FRANKLIN P. ADAMS.

Sleep like a bud. — ANON.

Sleep like a dead man. — IBID.

Slept like a log. — IBID.

Sealed sleep as water-lilies know. — EDWIN ARNOLD.

Sleep like a top. — BEAUMONT AND FLETCHER.

Sleep as soundly as a constable. — RICHARD BRATHWAITE.

Dante sleeps afar,
Like Scipio, buried by the upbraiding
shore. —BYRON.

Sleep like a jewel on the breast of faith. — J. H. HOLLAND.

Time
Slept, as he sleeps upon the silent face
Of a dark dial in a sunless place.
— HOOD.

Sleep, like wrecks in the unfathom'd main. — MISS LANDON.

Like a lull'd babe she slept, and knew no fear. — OTWAY.

Sleeps like a dream in a grave. — A. J. RYAN.

Sleep she as sound as careless infancy. — SHAKESPEARE.

She slept, as sleeps the blossom, hushed amid the silent air. — E. O. SMITH.

Sleep as a slain man sleeps. — SWINBURNE.

As a pearl within its shell, the happy spirit sleeps in me. — BAYARD TAYLOR.

Sleep . . . like sinless flowers that heed not the world and its maddening din. — E. W. WATSON.

Sleeping, like the darkness at noontide. — LADY WILDE.

Sleeps, like a caterpillar sheathed in ice. — WORDSWORTH.

Sleepless.

Sleepless as owls. — ANON.

Sleepless of soul as wind or wave or fire. — SWINBURNE.

Slender.

Slender as a cat's elbow. — ANON.

Slender as a lath. — IBID.

Slender as a reed. — IBID.

Fair and slender as the pine tree. — SERVIAN BALLAD.

Slender as a young poplar. — BALZAC.

How slender a tract, as scant as Alcibiades his land in a Map. — ROBERT BURTON.

As slender in the middle as a Cow in the waist. — IBID.

Like the hazel-twig
Is straight and slender.
— SHAKESPEARE.

A girl tall and slender as a palm. — HEINRICH ZSCHOKKE.

Slick.

Slick as a ribbon. — ANON.

Slick as greased lightning. — J. R. BARTLETT'S "DICTIONARY OF AMERICANISMS."

Slick — *continued.*

Slick as sin. — Ibid.

Slick as a whistle. — Ibid.

Slick as grease. — Ibid.

Slick as a butterfly's wing. — Thomas Davies.

Slick as soap grease. — O. Henry.

Slide.

Slid like water. — John G. Holland.

Slide off them like July rain off a duck's back feathers. — Thomas Hughes.

Slid like an evil dream. — Kipling.

Slid like a corpse afloat. — D. G. Rossetti.

Around him slid like a wave. — Bayard Taylor.

Slideth back as a backsliding heifer. — Old Testament.

Slight.

Slight . . . as a dew-drop. — Dickens.

Slight as a crescent moon at night. — Theodosia Garrison.

Slight as a vagrant plume
Shed from some passing wing.
— Laura R. Searing.

Slight as indeed a dew-drop. — Swinburne.

Slight as the sea's sight of the sea-mew,
Slight as the sun's sight of the star.
— Ibid.

Slighted.

Slighted and betrayed ;
And like a rose, just gathered from the stalk,
But only smelt, and cheaply thrown aside,
To wither on the ground.
— Dryden.

Slighted like a rivalled toy. — Robert U. Johnson.

Slink.

Slinking . . . like a sad and humiliated man. — Hugo.

The stars slink off like thieves, in company with Night. — Friedrich Rückert.

Slink like spectres. — John C. Van Dyke.

Slip.

Slip away like shadows into shade. — P. J. Bailey.

Slips on like the lapse of water. — Bulwer-Lytton.

Slip frae me like a knotless thread. — Burns.

Slipped from his fingers, like drops of quicksilver. — F. Marion Crawford.

Time slipping by you, as if it was an animal at rustic sports with his tail soaped. — Dickens.

Slippes as a dew-drop slips from some flower-cup o'erweighted. — Edward Dowden.

Slip like bending rushes from your hand. — Dryden.

Slipped like a shadow. — Bret Harte.

Slips like water through a sieve. — Hood.

Slipp'd me like his greyhound,
Which runs himself and catches for his master.
— Shakespeare.

All earthly things are doomed to fall away and slip back into Chaos, like a boatman who just manages to make head against the stream, if the tension of his arms happens to relax, and the current whirls away the boat headlong down the river's bed. — Virgil.

Slippery.

Slippery and smooth as a serpent. — Arne Garbog.

Slippery — *continued.*

Slippery as an eel's tail. — JOHN HEYWOOD.

As slippery as the Gordian knot was hard. — SHAKESPEARE.

Slippery as ice. — THEODORE WATTS-DUNTON.

Slope.

Sloped, as if leaning on the air. — CHARLOTTE BRONTË.

Sloping like a roof. — JOSEPH CONRAD.

Sloped,
As slopes a wild brook o'er a little
stone. — TENNYSON.

Sloth.

Sloth, like rust, consumes faster than labor wears, while the key often used is always bright. — FRANKLIN.

As the door turneth upon his hinges, so doth the slothful upon his bed. — OLD TESTAMENT.

Slow.

Slow as a plumber going for his tools. — ANON.

Slow as cold molasses. — IBID.

Slow as molasses in January. — IBID.

Slow as the hand on clock's face. — ROBERT BUCHANAN.

Slow as the white cloud in the sky. — IBID.

Slow, like water-lilies floating down a rill. — BYRON.

A voice as soft and slow
As might proceed from angel's tongue
If angel's heart were sorrow-wrung,
And wish'd to speak its woe.
— ROBERT CHAMBERS.

Slow as minor friars on sacred errands go. — DANTE.

Slow-swelling like God's thunder underground. — EURIPIDES.

Slow as at Oxford, on some gaudy day,
Fat beadles, in magnificent array,
With big bellies bear the ponderous
treat
And heavily lag on, with the vast loady
meat. — FRANCIS FAWKES.

Slow as old Saturn through prodigious space. — IBID.

Slow as an oak
To woodman's stroke.
— RICHARD GARNETT.

Slow, like the tired heaving of a grief-worn breast. — O. W. HOLMES.

Slow, as the strokes of a pump. — HOOD.

Slow, like a bell. — HUGO.

Slow as a worm. — KIPLING.

Exact and slow,
Like wooden monarchs at a puppet
show. — ROBERT LLOYD.

Slow,
Like a sexton ringing the village bell,
When the evening sun is low.
— LONGFELLOW.

It goes slow, comes slow, like a big
mill-wheel
On some broad stream, with long green
weeds a-sway,
And soft and slow it rises and it falls,
Still going onward.
— WILLIAM MORRIS.

Slow as lawyers mount to heaven. — CHARLES READE.

Slow as the snail. — SAMUEL ROGERS.

Hobbled slow as a broken-winded mare. — SIR WALTER SCOTT.

Seldome and slowe, like the scantye droppes of a fountaine neare a drye. — CAROLINE SOUTHEY.

Slowlier than life into breath . . . it moves. — SWINBURNE.

Slowly.

Slowly, as a man in doubt. — E. B. BROWNING.

Slowly — *continued.*

Slowly like one impelled by an unseen force. — Agnes and Egerton Castle.

It came on slowly, like a cloud when there is no wind. — Dickens.

Slowly as shadows creep at set of sun. — Julia C. R. Dorr.

Works as slowly as old Doctor Time in curing folly. — George Eliot.

Her heart beat more and more slowly, more gently and uncertainly, like a spring which is growing exhausted, like an echo which is sinking away. — Flaubert.

Slowly, as falls a tear that slowly starts
From some great agony.
— Norman Gale.

Slowly filling with life as a moon with silver. — Richard Le Gallienne.

Slowly, as when walking-beam first feels the gathering bead of steam. — O. W. Holmes.

Sail, slowly as an icy isle
Upon a calm sea drifting.
— Keats.

He slowly moves, like a cloud of thunder, when the sultry plain of summer is silent and dark. — Ossian.

As slowly, as sadly, as a hare that the greyhounds have coursed drags itself through the grasses and ferns. — Ouida.

Slowly like the heave and roll of a glassy sea. — John C. Van Dyke.

Sluggish.

Sluggish as "the dull weed that rots by Lethe's wharf." — Anon.

Sluggish . . . like a greasy bog. — Joseph Conrad.

Sluggish as liquid pitch. — W. C. Russell.

Slumber.

Slumbers as in a grave. — Robert Browning.

Slumbered like Goldsmith's Madam Blaize, bedizened and brocaded. — Austin Dobson.

Slumbers like a beam of moonlight. — Henry Ellison.

Slumber like a stone. — Emerson.

Slumber like the leaves of a lily at nightfall. — O. W. Holmes.

Slumbering quietly,
Like forms which sculptors carve.
— Shelley.

Slumberest here like a caged bird that never knew its pinions. — N. P. Willis.

Sly.

Sly as a fox. — Anon.

Sly as old boots. — Ibid.

Sly as submarine. — Ibid.

Sly as a ring-dove. — Miss Mitford.

Slyly.

Slyly as a wild deer. — Hawthorne.

Smack.

Smack like a tight cork from a bottle. — O. W. Holmes.

Small.

Small as tiny stars lighting some ruined world. — Anon.

Smaller than the point of a fine needle. — Ibid.

Small as atoms. — Massinger.

Small as minced meat. — Rabelais.

Small as the dust before the wind. — Old Testament.

Beat them as small as the dust of the earth. — Ibid.

As small as the hoar frost on the ground. — Ibid.

Smart (Adjective)

Smart as a whip. — Anon.

Smart as a sixpence. — Dickens.

Smart (Verb).

Smart as lizards' stings. — SHAKESPEARE.

Smashed.

Smashed like a cocoa-nut by a sledge-hammer. — ANON.

Smashed, as glass when it encounters adamant. — IBID.

Smell.

Smells like a fertilizer factory on a sunny afternoon. — ANON.

Smellynge as the rose ay fresh and redolent. — ALEXANDER BARCLAY.

Smells as sweet as any posy. — THOMAS KILLIGREW.

Smells worse than a tallow-chandler's shop in the dog-days. — CHARLES MACKLIN

He smells like a fish ; a very ancient and fish-like smell. — SHAKESPEARE.

Smells of gunpowder like a soldier's pouch. — R. B. SHERIDAN.

Smile (Noun).

The smiles of his dark-blue eyes sparkle like the sea when first lighted up by the rays of the sun. — ALCIPHRON.

Smiles and tears, like sunshine and rain, are necessary for the development of life. — ANON.

Smiled, as mountains smile to see the spring. — ANCIENT BALLAD OF HINDUSTAN.

Her smiles were like the glowing sunshine. — SERVIAN BALLAD.

Her smile was like a summer morn. — BURNS.

Smile as gay as th' sun o' th' May. — ALICE CARY.

Charming smiles thy beauteous face
adorn,
As May's white blossoms gaily deck the
thorn. — CHATTERTON.

Smiles . . . sweet as the flow'rs in bloom of spring array'd. — IBID.

A smile as fine as wine. — FREDERICK S. COZZENS.

'Twould force a misanthrope to hang a smile upon his lip, as dewdrop on a thorn. — MICHAEL FIELD.

Smile like the bloom of the morning. — EDWARD OCTAVUS FLAGG.

Smiles, like meteors of the night,
Just give one flash of momentary light.
— WALTER HARTE.

Smiles as thick on rosy lips as ripples on the sea. — O. W. HOLMES.

A grim smile, like lion that has found a way of exit. — HUGO.

Smile like morning gold. — IBID.

Her smile was such as a sultan might, in a blissful and fond moment, bestow on a slave his gold gems had enriched. — IBID.

Her smile grateful as the dissolution of the ice. — DR. JOHNSON.

Wan smiles flickered, like the northern dawn, across her worn cheeks' ice-field. — KINGSLEY.

He strove to clothe his agony in smiles,
Which he would force up in his poor
pale cheeks,
Like ill-timed guests that had no proper
dwelling there.
— CHARLES LAMB.

The smiles which play on my cheek in public are to my heart as moonbeams falling on some rock of ice ; they shine, but warm not. — M. G. LEWIS.

Capacious . . . smile, like the exaggerated reflection of a concave mirror. — LOVER.

A half smile, like the moonlight of laughter, dawned on her face. — GEORGE MACDONALD.

Her smile as sunshine on a ripening land. — GERALD MASSEY.

Smile — *continued.*

Its smile is as a thankful hymn. — IBID.

Her smile — it was like the golden wine
Poured in the spirit, as in a cup.
— OWEN MEREDITH.

Thy smiles, like sunflowers in the golden light they love. — H. H. MILMAN.

Childhood . . . smiles, like glimpses of heaven. — DONALD G. MITCHELL.

Smile like sunlight in a rippling sea. — LEWIS MORRIS.

Her smile is like the noon-splendor of a day of June. — JAMES WHITCOMB RILEY.

As a meteor bright,
As a comet bright,
Was her smile of pearl and spray.
— FRANCIS S. SALTUS.

How like the dewdrops on a drooping flower are smiles from gentle eyes.— JOHN G. SAXE.

Smiles, which spread like radiance from the cloud-surrounded moon. — SHELLEY.

A half smile hovering round her happy lips like a bright butterfly around a flower. — ALEXANDER SMITH.

Smile . . . like sunshine opening through a shower in vernal skies. — SOUTHEY.

A smile
Sweet as good Angels wear when they present
Their mortal charge before the throne of Heaven. — IBID.

Smile, it was like sunshine in a shady place. — ROBERT LOUIS STEVENSON.

Crimson smile,
Like seas hid by a meadow-land.
— TRUMBULL STICKNEY.

Smiles more sweet than flowers. — SWINBURNE.

A smile that was like sunrise on a sea strewn with wreckage. — EDITH WHARTON.

Her smile is as a listening child's
Who hears its mother's call.
— WHITTIER.

A smile which cheered — like the breaking day. — IBID.

A smile as joyous, frank, and innocent
As that with which a babe awakes from sleep.
— SARAH WILLIAMS.

Around the lips a smile played like the shadow of a silver cloud upon a sunlit stream. — J. C. WILSON.

A smile . . . as sleeps a sunbeam on a stone. — WILLIAM WINTER.

An innocent smile, like a sunbeam kissing a velvet rose. — IBID.

Smile (Verb).

She smiled as though somebody were talking to her inside. — MARGUERITE AUDOUX.

Like the wine and roses, smiles. — ANACREON.

Smiling like a star on the darkest night. — ANON.

Smiles like a sweet June rose. — IBID.

Smiling triumphantly the while like one who had discovered a cure for duty. — J. M. BARRIE.

Smiling as a basket of chips. — J. R. BARTLETT'S "DICTIONARY OF AMERICANISMS."

Smile like a cherub. — WILLIAM BLAKE.

Smiled like a siren. — IBID.

Smiled like the flowers of Eden. — PATRICK BRONTË.

Smiled like Italy. — E. B. BROWNING.

Smiling like a fiend who has deceived God. — ROBERT BROWNING.

Smile — *continued.*

Smile, as infants at a sudden light. — COLERIDGE.

Smiling, like a sickly moralist. — IBID.

Smiling like a child in the grass, dreaming deep of the flowers, and their golden beguiling. — ISA CRAIG.

Smiles like clockwork. — DICKENS.

The singer smiled, as doubtless Orpheus smiled, to see the animals both great and small, the mountainous elephant and the scampering mouse, held by the ears in decent audience. — GEORGE ELIOT.

Smiling free as a rose in summer air. — DORA GREENWALL.

Smiling like a cherry. — THOMAS HEYWOOD.

Smiling like a new-blown flower. — R. H. HORNE.

Faint-smiling like a star
Through autumn mists.
— KEATS.

Smiled like a paradise. — GERALD MASSEY.

Smiled with superior love, as Jupiter
On Juno smiles, when he impregns the clouds
That shed May flowers. — MILTON.

Smiling like heaven. — WILLIAM MORRIS.

Smile, like the sun in his glory on the bud. — W. M. PRAED.

Smiles like a May morning. — ALLAN RAMSAY.

Smile like summer after snow. — C. G. ROSSETTI.

Smiled, as all the world were his. — THOMAS SACKVILLE.

Smiling, as some fly had tickled slumber,
Not as death's dart, being laughed at.
— SHAKESPEARE.

Smiling as smiles the fowler when flutters the bird to the gin. — ROBERT LOUIS STEVENSON.

Smile like an Oil Trust. — NEW YORK SUN.

Smiled as dawn on the spirit of man. — SWINBURNE.

Smiled as one living even on craft and hate. — IBID.

Smiling dim
As the smile on a lip still fearful.
— IBID.

Smiled,
As though the spirit and sense unreconciled
Sank laughing back, and would not ere its hour
Let life put forth the irrevocable flower. — IBID.

Smiled . . . like song's triumphant breath. — IBID.

Smiling, like a star in the blackest night. — IBID.

Smiling as a master at one
That is not of his school, nor any school
But that where blind and naked Ignorance
Delivers brawling judgments, unashamed. — TENNYSON.

Smiling . . . like beauty waking from a happy dream. — JOHN WILSON.

Smirk.

Smirk . . . like a dog scratching his ear. — AMÉLIE RIVES.

Smite.

Smiting like a cry. — MATHILDE BLIND.

Smites it as acid smites the red rust. — SAMUEL HOFFENSTEIN.

Smote him like a judgment from above. — JAMES MONTGOMERY.

Smiteth as a staff. — TUPPER.

Smote on my ears like a tocsin. — THOMAS WESTWOOD.

Smoke.

Smoked like a herring. — ROBERT BROWNING.

Smoking like a crater. — DAUDET.

Smoked like a gammon of bacon. — ANTHONY HAMILTON.

Smoked like a chimney. — R. H. BARHAM.

Smoking like a boiler at the heat. — J. S. KNOWLES.

Smoking like an iron works. — TOM TAYLOR.

Smoky.

Smoky as an Irish hut. — JAMES HOWELL.

Smooth.

Smooth as the surface of a pebble. — ADDISON.

Smooth like a china cup. — WILLIAM ALLINGHAM.

Smooth as the stem of a young palm. — AMRIOLKAIS.

Smooth as a bowling green. — ANON.

Smooth as a bulrush. — IBID.

Smooth as a carpet. — IBID.

Smooth as a die. — IBID.

Smooth as a door knob. — IBID.

Smooth as an oil'd thunderbolt. — IBID.

Smooth as a perfect peach. — IBID.

Smooth as a poker table. — IBID.

Smooth as a rose leaf. — IBID.

Smooth as the mirrors in the Palace of Peace. — IBID.

Smooth as the palm of one's hand. — IBID.

Smooth as wax. — IBID.

Smooth as a snow cloud. — IBID.

Smooth as a spirit's wing. — BULWER-LYTTON.

Smothe it was as it were late shave. — CHAUCER.

Smooth as smoothest beaver hat. — JOHN DAVIES.

Smooth as a new laid egg. — DICKENS.

Smooth as sheet of polished brass. — JOSEPH R. DRAKE.

Smooth as the back of a razor. — GEORGE DU MAURIER.

Smooth as the dusky down on the elk. — ANCIENT ERSE.

Smooth as fungus, daughter of the rain. — FRANCIS FAWKES.

Smooth as the surface of well polish'd brass. — IBID.

Smooth and shining, as a sword out of a sheath. — FLAUBERT.

A skin as smoth as silke. — GEORGE GASCOIGNE.

Smooth as glass. — JOHN GAY.

Smooth as a billiard-table. — ANTHONY HAMILTON.

Smooth as ice. — THOMAS HEYWOOD.

Smooth as the pond can be. — O. W. HOLMES.

Smooth as a file. — LEIGH HUNT.

Smooth as a road in Venice. — MARY JOHNSTON.

Smooth as a billiard ball. — BEN JONSON.

Skin as smooth as any rush. — IBID.

Smooth as a silver shield. — GEORGE CABOT LODGE.

Smooth as jet. — LYLY.

Smooth as the gliding stream.— JAMES MACPHERSON.

Smooth as velvet. — CHARLES READE.

Smoother than the fur of cats. — JAMES WHITCOMB RILEY.

Smooth — *continued.*

Tones as smooth as honey. — C. G. Rossetti.

Smooth as a mirror. — Saint-Pierre.

Smooth as oil. — Shakespeare.

Smooth as monumental alabaster. — Ibid.

Smooth as the elephant's new polished tooth. — Sir Edward Sherburne.

Smooth as Pan. — Sir Philip Sidney.

Smooth as a billow. — Alexander Smith.

As Parian marble smooth. — William Somerville.

Smooth as the level lake, when not a
breeze
Dies o'er the sleeping surface.
— Southey.

Smooth as the liquid passage of a bird. — Trumbull Stickney.

Smoother than butter. — Old Testament.

Smooth as the flight of a dream. — Edith M. Thomas.

Smooth as a floor. — Mary A. Tincker.

Smooth as a mole. — John Withals' "Dictionary in English and Latin."

Smooth as marble or a waveless sea. — Wordsworth.

Smoothly.

When things went smoothly as a baby drugged. — E. B. Browning.

Smoothly glide
As ships drop down a river with the
tide. — Jean Ingelow.

Smoothly . . . like the noiseless flow of a river of oil. — Plato.

Smothered.

Smothered like a whisper in a storm. — Herman George Scheffauer.

Smudged.

Smudged, like a shopkeeper's account-book. — Osmanli Proverb.

Smug.

Smug as April. — Beaumont and Fletcher.

Snap.

Snapped like a fiddle string. — Anon.

Snap like a pipe stem. — Ibid.

Snap like the lash of a whip. — Ibid.

Snapping like too high-stretched treble strings. — Donne.

Snapping like a mad dog. — George Eliot.

Snapped up — like a steel gin. — Maurice Hewlett.

Snapped like the threads of a lyre. — Adelaide A. Procter.

Snappy.

Snappy as a fresh string bean. — Anon.

Snarl.

Snarl at pleasure, like a stoic. — Chesterfield.

Snarl like a monster at meat. — Hamlin Garland.

Snarled like an old dog. — Maurice Hewlett.

Snarling like the hound a wolf has checked. — Hugo.

Snarled like Malemutes over a mildewed bone. — Robert W. Service.

Snarl like Guthrie for the public weal. — Smollett.

Sniff.

Looked at it and sniffed at it daintily — like a reluctant patient going under the ether. — Irvin S. Cobb.

Sniffing like a dog after game. — Guy de Maupassant.

Snigger.

Snigger, like a yokel's smile. — GEORGE MEREDITH.

Snobbishness.

Snobbishness is like death in a quotation from Horace, which I hope you never have heard, "beating with equal foot at poor men's doors, and kicking at the gates of Emperors." — THACKERAY.

Snore.

Snoring like a pig. — ANON.

Snored like an organ. — AMBROSE BIERCE.

A groaning intermitting sound like Gog and Magog snoring. — HOOD.

Snore like a porc-pisce (porpoise). — BEN JONSON.

Snore like over-gorged humans. — KIPLING.

Snores like sawin' planks. — ALFRED HENRY LEWIS.

Snoring like old boots. — MOLIÈRE.

Snores like the base-pipe of an Organ. — SHADWELL.

Snort.

Snorting like an under-sea volcano. — SAMUEL FERGUSON.

Snorting like a horse. — SHAKESPEARE.

Snug.

As snug as a pig in pea-straw. — RICHARD DAVENPORT.

Snug as a parson. — FLAUBERT.

Snug
As a bug
In a rug. — FRANKLIN.

I'm as snugly shut
As a glad little worm in the heart of a nut. — JAMES WHITCOMB RILEY.

As snug as a snag in a bog. — EUGENE FITCH WARE.

Fitted as snugly as bits in a puzzle. — EDITH WHARTON.

Snug as a child that hides itself in sport
'Mid a green hay-cock in a sunny field. — WORDSWORTH.

Soar.

Soars like a bird on the wing. — ANON.

Soars like a cloud. — IBID.

Soars like smoke. — EURIPIDES.

Soaring like pride. — JULIA WARD HOWE.

The burthened heart should soar in mirth like Morn's young prophet-lark. — GERALD MASSEY.

Soars like a seraph. — OWEN MEREDITH.

Up, like a kite made of foolscap, it shall soar, with a long tail of rubbish behind, to the skies. — THOMAS MOORE.

Soar like white-winged sea-birds into the Infinite Deep. — MISS MULOCK.

Soars, like a wild bird from a cypress bough, into the poets' heaven. — MRS. NORTON.

Soared like incense to the skies. — C. G. ROSSETTI.

My fancy soars like a kite and faints in the blue infinite. — ROBERT LOUIS STEVENSON.

Sob.

Sobs like an Æolian. — ANON.

Sobs like a child in a dream. — JAMES BALLANTINE.

Sobbing, as if the body and soul were torn. — BULWER-LYTTON.

Sobbing like a lover by his false one left in sorrow and in pain. — J. S. GUTHRIE.

Sob, like ocean's tremor when it turns to ebb. — CHARLES L. MOORE.

Sobbed like tears at the heart of May. — D. G. ROSSETTI.

Sober.

As sober as an ice-cream soda on New Year's Eve. — Anon.

Sober as if he had supped with Diogenes. — Bulwer-Lytton.

Sober as a judge. — Fielding.

Sober as a hymn. — W. E. Henley.

Sober as is the tender voice of home. — Lewis Morris.

Sober as a vicar. — John G. Saxe.

Sociable.

Sociable ez a basket er kittens. — Joel Chandler Harris.

Society.

Society is like air ; very high up, it is sublimated — too low down, a perfect choke-damp. — Anon.

Society, like the Roman youth at the circus, never shows mercy to the fallen gladiator. — Balzac.

Man in society is like a flow'r,
Blown in its native bed ; 'tis there alone
His facilities expanded in full bloom
Shine out, there only reach their proper use. — Cowper.

Society as cold as the glacier of an unsunned cavern. — O. W. Holmes.

Society is like a lawn, where every roughness is smoothed, every bramble eradicated, and where the eye is delighted by the smiling verdure of a velvet surface. — Washington Irving.

Society is like a large piece of frozen water ; and skating well is the great art of social life. — Miss Landon.

Society, like a woman, requires a special painter to delineate it in accordance with its own taste. — Sainte-Beuve.

Society is like the air — necessary to breathe but insufficient to live on. — George Santayana.

Society is in this respect like a fire — the wise man warming himself at a proper distance from it ; not coming too close like a fool, who, on getting scorched, runs away and shivers in solitude, loud in his complaint that the fire burns. — Schopenhauer.

Society is like the echoing hills. It gives back to the speaker his words ; groan for groan, song for song. — David Thomas.

Soft.

Soft as the satin fringe that shades the eyelids of thy fragrant maids. — T. B. Aldrich.

Soft as the broken solar beam,
That trembles in the solar stream.
— Anacreon.

Soft as misted star. — Mary Louisa Anderson.

Soft and creamy as a charlotte russe. — Anon.

Soft and supple as lady's glove. — Ibid.

Soft as a Dartmoor bog. — Ibid.

Soft as a flute. — Ibid.

Soft as a government job. — Ibid.

Soft as a jelly fish. — Ibid.

Soft as a shadow. — Ibid.

Soft as foot can fall. — Ibid.

Soft as marshmallows. — Ibid.

Soft as mush. — Ibid.

Soft as pudding. — Ibid.

Soft as sad music. — Ibid.

Soft as showers that fall on April meads. — Ibid.

Soft as soap. — Ibid.

Soft as the evening wind murmuring among willows. — Ibid.

Soft as the hands of indolence. — Ibid.

Soft as the murmurs of a virgin's sigh. — Ibid.

Soft — *continued.*

Delicately soft as the sand that has been trod on by dainty seraphs. — ANON.

Soft as the snow on the sea. — IBID.

Soft as zephyr of a summer sky. — IBID.

Softly as a milk tooth leaving a baby's gum. — IBID.

Softly as on ice that will scarcely bear. — IBID.

Softly . . . like the footfalls of departed spirits. — IBID.

Soft as silk in her touch. — ARABIAN NIGHTS.

Soft as threaded pearls. — IBID.

Softer than zephyr's wing. — IBID.

Soft as the breath of even. — HARRIET AUBER.

Thy sweet words drop upon the ear as soft as rose leaves on a wall. — P. J. BAILEY.

Softly sublime like lightnings in repose. — IBID.

Soft as the sunlight. — W. C. BENNETT.

Softly like a stream of oil. — WILLIAM BROWNE.

Soft voice as a laughing dream. — R. D. BLACKMORE.

Soft as the breeze flitting over the flowers. — IBID.

Soft as the dew on flowers of spring,
Sweet as the hidden drops that swell
their honey-throated chalicing.
— ROBERT BRIDGES (English).

Soft as Muses' string. — E. B. BROWNING.

Soft as a mother's kiss. — IBID.

Soft as a silent hush. — IBID.

Softly, as the last repenting drops
Of a thunder-shower. — IBID.

Soft as a sofa. — BULWER-LYTTON.

Soft as wool. — ROBERT BURTON.

Soft as the murmurs of a virgin's sigh. — WILLIAM BYRD.

Soft as the callow cygnet in its nest. — BYRON.

Soft as the gentler breathing of the lute. — IBID.

Soft as harp that houri strings his long entrancing note. — IBID.

Soft as the melody of youthful days. — IBID.

Soft as the memory of buried love. — IBID.

Soft as the unfledged birdling when at rest. — IBID.

Soft as the eyes of a girl. — WILFRED CAMPBELL.

Soft as a bed of roses blown. — THOMAS CAREW.

Soft as duffel. — CARLYLE.

Soft as sunset. — IBID.

Soft as snow that falls on snow. — ALICE CARY.

Soft as a bank of moss. — CAWDRAY'S "TREASURIE OR STOREHOUSE OF SIMILIES," 1600.

Soft as love. — JAMES CAWTHORN.

Soft as silence. — W. E. CHANNING.

Soft as the breath of morn in bloom of spring. — CHATTERTON.

Soft as the cooing of the turtle dove. — IBID.

Soft as the moss where hissing adders dwell. — IBID.

Softe as the sommer flowrets. — IBID.

As soft as honey-dew. — COLERIDGE.

Soft as the passing wind. — COWPER.

Soft as the breath of a sleeper. — ISA CRAIG.

Soft — *continued.*

Soft, his accents fill, like voices of departed friends heard in our dreams, or music in the air, when night-spirits warble their magic minstrelsy. — RICHARD CUMBERLAND.

Soft as pity. — GEORGE DARLEY.

Soft as the murmurs of a weeping spring. — SIR WILLIAM DAVENANT.

As soft and sleek as girlish cheek. — AUSTIN DOBSON.

Soft as a baby's breath. — JULIA C. R. DORR.

Soft as spirit's sigh. — IBID.

Soft as summer. — ERNEST DOWSON.

Soft as prayer. — IBID.

Skin as soft as Naples silk. — MICHAEL DRAYTON.

Soft as Lempster wool. — IBID.

Soft and caressing as a melody. — DUMAS, PÈRE.

Soft as a whisper. — GEORGE DU MAURIER.

Soft . . . like a whispered dream of sleeping music. — GEORGE ELIOT.

Soft as pattering drops that fall from off the eaves in fancy dance when clouds are breaking. — IBID.

Soft and fluid as a cloud on the air. — EMERSON.

Soft as the songs of some shy hidden bird
From the low fields of woodlands nightly heard.
— F. W. FABER.

Soft as the voice of summer's evening gale. — WILLIAM FALCONER.

Soft as love. — IBID.

Soft as the breath of distant flutes at hours
When silent evening closes up the flowers. — JOHN GAY.

Soft as when Venus stroked the beard of Jove. — IBID.

Soft as the stringed harp's moan. — GERALD GRIFFIN.

Soft as is the falling thistle downe. — JOSEPH HALL.

Cheeks, soft as September's rose
Blushing but faintly on its faltering stem.
— P. H. HAYNE.

Soft as silkworms. — STEPHEN HAWES.

Soft as the whisper shut within a shell. — W. E. HENLEY.

Soft as jelly. — THOMAS HEYWOOD.

Soft as sleep. — HESIOD.

Soft as pity, and as blest. — AARON HILL.

Soft as upper air. — IBID.

Soft as rain. — O. W. HOLMES.

As soft as swan's down. — IBID.

Soft as the moonbeams when they sought Endymion's fragrant bower. — IBID.

Soft as a flute. — HOOD.

Soft as flowers. — IBID.

Sounds upon the air most soothing soft,
Like humming bees busy about the brooms. — IBID.

Soft as a dream of beauty. — RICHARD HOVEY.

Soft as the division in the wool of a sheep. — HUGO.

Soft as love's first word. — JEAN INGELOW.

Soft . . . as cob-webs. — BEN JONSON.

Soft as cream. — IBID.

Soft as Memnon's harp at morning. — JOHN KEBLE.

Soft as imprison'd martyr's deathbed calm. — IBID.

Soft as the face of maid. — FREDERIC L. KNOWLES.

Soft — *continued.*

Soft as a dying violet-breath. — SIDNEY LANIER.

Soft and still, like birds half hidden in a nest. — LONGFELLOW.

Soft as velvet. — JOHN LYDGATE.

Soft as silke. — LYLY.

Soft as the swan-down where Summer sleeps. — GEORGE MAC-HENRY.

Soft as the sighings of the gale, that wakes the flowery year. — DAVID MALLET.

Soft as dew-drops when they settle
In a fair flower's open petal.
— PHILIP B. MARSTON.

Soft as light-fall on unfolding flowers. — GERALD MASSEY.

Soft and thick as a feather bed. — GUY DE MAUPASSANT.

Soft as a kiss. — JOAQUIN MILLER.

Soft as moonlight. — MISS MITFORD.

Soft as evening o'er the ocean,
When she charms the waves to rest.
— JAMES MONTGOMERY.

Soft as in moments of bliss long ago. — THOMAS MOORE.

Soft as lightning in May. — IBID.

Soft as the back of a swan. — THOMAS NASH.

Soft as angels. — OTWAY.

Soft as a baby's cheek. — T. N. PAGE.

Soft as twin-violets moist with early dew. — ANDREW PARK.

Her voice . . . soft as Zephyr sighs on morning's lily cheek. — ROBERT POLLOK.

Soft as yielding air. — MATTHEW PRIOR.

Soft as a pillow. — W. B. RANDS.

Soft as angels' wings. — JAMES WHITCOMB RILEY.

Soft as a sunny shadow
When day is almost done.
— C. G. ROSSETTI.

Soft as music's measure. — IBID.

Soft as spring. — D. G. ROSSETTI.

Soft as the gleam after sunset
That hangs like a halo of grace
Where the daylight had died in the valley.
— A. J. RYAN.

Soft as air. — SHAKESPEARE.

Soft as sinews of the new-born babe. — IBID.

Soft as dove's down. — IBID.

Soft as the parasite's silk. — IBID.

Soft as young down. — IBID.

Soft as an Incarnation of the Sun. — SHELLEY.

Soft as sleep. — IBID.

Soft as thoughts of budding love. — IBID.

Softer than the West wind's sigh. — IBID.

Soft as the wild duck's tender young, that floats on Avon's tide. — SHENSTONE.

Soft as a spirit prayer. — SEBA SMITH.

Soft as a man with a dead child speaks. — CARL SANBURG.

Whispering soft, like the last low accents of an expiring saint. — STERNE.

Soft like the waxe, each image shall receive. — EARL OF STIRLING.

Soft as pap. — SWIFT.

Softer than the dawn. — IBID.

Soft and listless as the slumber-stricken air. — SWINBURNE.

Soft as a low long sigh. — IBID.

Soft as lip is soft to lip. — IBID.

Soft as at noon the slow sea's rise and fall. — IBID.

Soft — *continued.*

Soft . . . as desire that prevails and fades. — SWINBURNE.

Soft as fire in dew. — IBID.

Soft as hate speaks within itself apart. — IBID.

Soft as heaven the stream that girdles hell. — IBID.

Soft as lips that laugh. — IBID.

Soft as o'er her babe the smile of Mary. — IBID.

Soft as a weak wind blows. — IBID.

Soft as sleep sings in a tired man's ear. — IBID.

Soft as snow lights on her snow-soft flesh. — IBID.

Soft as swan's plumes are. — IBID.

Borne soft as the babe from the bearing-bed. — IBID.

Soft . . .
As the clouds and beams of night.
— IBID.

Soft as the least wave's lapse in a still small reach. — IBID.

Soft as the loosening of wound arms in sleep. — IBID.

Soft
As thoughts of beauty sleeping.
— ARTHUR SYMONS.

Soft, as Heaven's angelic messenger might touch the lips of prayer, and make them blest. — BAYARD TAYLOR.

Soft as lonely maiden's thoughts on him she loves. — ESAIAS TEGNER.

There is sweet music here that softer falls
Than petals from blown roses on the grass. — TENNYSON.

Softer than oil. — OLD TESTAMENT.

Soft as satin. — THACKERAY.

Soft as a sleeping cat. — THEOCRITUS.

Soft as the nightingale's harmonious woe,
In dewy even-tide, when cowslips drop
Their sleepy heads, and languish in the breeze.
— WILLIAM THOMPSON.

Soft as the blowbell. — THOMAS TICKELL.

Soft, like summer night. — MARK TWAIN.

Soft as a peacock steps. — FAZIO DEGLI UBERTI.

The air as soft as lovers' jest. — EMANUEL VON GIEBEL.

Soft as summer breeze. — SAMUEL WARD.

Soft as the wind of spring-tide in the trees. — ROSAMUND MARRIOTT WATSON.

Soft as fall of thistle-down. — WHITTIER.

Soft as the flow of an infant's breath. — IBID.

Soft as the landscape of a dream. — IBID.

Soft as a lady's hand. — ELLA WHEELER WILCOX.

Soft as a cloud. — WORDSWORTH.

Softly.

Tread softly, — softly, like the foot
Of winter, shod with fleecy snow.
— BARRY CORNWALL.

Softly as if over a pavement of down. — DAUDET.

Walked as softly as the ghost in Hamlet. — DICKENS.

Softly as moonlight steals upon the skies. — JULIA C. R. DORR.

Softly . . . as music that floats through a dream. — MINNIE GILMORE.

Softly as a burglar goes. — O. HENRY.

Stepping softly like a scout. — IBID.

Softly — *continued.*

More softly than the east could blow
Arion's magic to the Atlantic isles.
— KEATS.

Softly among the pines as a young witch gathering simples. — RICHARD LE GALLIENNE.

Softly as full-blown flower
Unfolds its heart to welcome in the dawn. — HENRY VAN DYKE.

Softly . . . like low aërial music when some angel hovers near. — LADY WILDE.

Softness.

A softness like the atmosphere of dreams. — MRS. NORTON.

Soil.

Soil'd, like the soil'd tissue of white violets left, freshly gather'd, on their native bank, by children whom their nurses call with haste indoors from the sun's eye. — MATTHEW ARNOLD.

Soilless.

Soilless as pearls. — OUIDA.

Soldier.

Though a soldier in time of peace is like a chimney in summer, yet what wise man would pluck down his chimney because his almanac told him it was the middle of June. — TOM BROWN.

A good soldier, like a good horse, cannot be of a bad color. — O. W. HOLMES.

Soldiers are like cloaks, — one thinks of us only when it rains. — MARSHAL SAXE.

Solemn.

Solemn as a judge. — ANON.

Solemn as a slate gravestone. — IBID.

Solemn as a thunderbolt. — IBID.

As solemn as any catafalque. — IBID.

Solemn as organ music. — IBID.

Solemn as a king on a five-franc piece. — BALZAC.

Solemn, as a thought of God. — E. B. BROWNING.

Solemn as despair. — BULWER-LYTTON.

Solemn, like the cloudy groan of dying thunder on the distant wind. — BYRON.

Solemn as the long stops upon an organ. — DRYDEN.

Solemn as an owl. — GOETHE.

Solemn as a dying nun. — MAURICE HEWLETT.

Solemn as putty. — KIPLING.

Solemn as a parson's clerk. — GEORGE MEREDITH.

Solemn as a monkey after committing a mischief. — RABELAIS.

Solemnly.

Moved as solemnly as a dowager when she condescends to complete a quadrille at the close of a ball. — BALZAC.

Solemnly as Gargellis (gargoyles) on a wall gryn and stare. — "RUIN OF A REALM."

Solid.

Solid as old times. — ANON.

Solid as the eternal rocks. — IBID.

Solid like a principle. — JOSEPH CONRAD.

Solid as glass. — HOOD.

Solid as a sod house. — A. H. LEWIS.

Solid as the Pyramids. — BRANDER MATTHEWS.

Solid as a haystack. — RUSKIN.

Solid, like a cactus stem. — IBID.

Solid as bricks. — G. B. SHAW.

As solid as a landed estate. — ROBERT LOUIS STEVENSON.

Solid — *continued.*

Solid as a wall. — Tupper.

Solid as a globe of mud. — Mark Twain.

Solitary.

Solitary . . . like some colossal Pillar of the Cyclops. — Carlyle.

Solitary . . . like a lighthouse keeper above the sea. — Joseph Conrad.

Solitary . . . like a swallow left behind at the migrating season of his tribe. — Ibid.

Solitary as a tomb. — Hugo.

Solitude.

Solitude, like some unsounded bell. — Mary A. Townsend.

Sombre.

Sombre as sorrow. — Anon.

Sombre as the night. — Dante.

Sombre as Othello. — Ignatius Donnelly.

Sombre like a cathedral. — Hugo.

Song.

Songs are like painted window-panes!
In darkness wrapped the church remains,
If from the market-place we view it;
But let us now inside repair,
And greet the holy chapel there!
At once the whole seems clear and bright,
Each ornament is bathed in light,
And fraught with meaning to the sight.
— Goethe.

Sonorous.

Sonorous as a fountain's notes. — Anon.

Sonorous as the inside of a violin. — Octave Mirbeau.

Soothe.

Soothes the ear like the echo of distant music. — Edmondo de Amicis.

Soothed like the music of a tomtom. — O. Henry.

Soothes like a caress of angels. — Donald G. Mitchell.

Soothing.

Soothing as the gospel. — Anon.

Soothing as the breath of spring. — F. W. Faber.

More soothing than the pretty hummer
That stays one moment in an open flower
And buzzes cheerily from bower to bower.
— Keats.

Soothing as the wash of the sea. — Kipling.

Soothing as the gale of eve. — H. H. Milman.

Soothingly.

Soothingly as childhood pressed to bosom. — Whittier.

Sophistry.

Sophistry is like a window curtain — it pleases as an ornament, but its true use is to keep out the light. — Anon.

As creeping ivy clings to wood or stone,
And hides the ruin that it feeds upon,
So sophistry cleaves close to and protects
Sin's rotten trunk, concealing its defects.
— Cowper.

Sophistry, like poison, is at once detected and nauseated when presented to us in a concentrated form; but a falsity which, when stated barely in a few sentences, would not deceive a child, may deceive half the world if diluted in a quarto volume. — Whately.

Sore.

Sore as a mashed thumb. — Irvin S. Cobb.

Sorrow.

Youth's sorrows, like April showers, are transitory. — Anon.

Sorrow — *continued.*

Sorrow for a husband is like pain in the elbow, sharp and short. — IBID.

Sorrowful as death. — OUIDA.

Sorrow concealed, like an oven stopp'd,
Doth burn the heart to cinders.
— SHAKESPEARE.

Sorrow, like a heavy-hanging bell,
Once set on ringing, with his own weight goes;
Then little strength rings out the doleful knell. — IBID.

Sorrow, like cloud that flies,
Like a cloud in clearing skies,
Passed away. — SWINBURNE.

Soubrette.

A soubrette is like a bottle of vinegar, — mother is always there. — EDITH M. HUDNALL.

Soul.

The humble soul is like the violet, which grows low, hangs the head downward, and hides itself with its own leaves. — FREDERIKA BREMER.

Souls fly forth, like sparks of light
From clear white fires by whirlwinds fanned. — WILLIAM J. DAWSON.

My soul is like those sieves in which gold-washers of Mexico gather bits of the pure metal in the torrents of the Cordilleras. The sand falls through them, the gold remains. — LAMARTINE.

My soul is like the oar that momently
Dies in a desperate stress beneath the wave,
Then glitters out again and sweeps the sea:
Each second I'm new-born from some new grave. — SIDNEY LANIER.

As the waifs cast up by the sea change with the changing season, so the tides of the soul throw up their changing drift on the sand, but the sea beyond is one for ever. — D. G. ROSSETTI.

An evil soul, producing holy witness,
Is like a villain with a smiling cheek;
A good apple rotten at the heart.
O, what a goodly outside falsehood hath.
— SHAKESPEARE.

Body and Soul like peevish man and wife, united jar, and yet are loath to part. — EDWARD YOUNG.

Soulless.

Soulless as the fragments of a broken statue. — ANON.

Soulless as is the brute. — LEWIS MORRIS.

Sound (Adjective).

Sound as an acorn. — ANON.

Sound as a trout. — IBID.

Sound as a watch. — IBID.

Heart as sound as an oak. — BEAUMONT AND FLETCHER.

Sound as old wine. — IBID.

Sound as a rock. — BULWER-LYTTON.

Sound-hearted to the core, like some perfect fruit ripened in a sunny nook of an English garden. — HENRY A. CLAPP.

Sound as a biscuit. — CONGREVE.

Sound as a nut. — EMERSON.

Sound as a roach. — JOHN GAY.

Sound as a fish. — MARTIN LUTHER.

Sound as iron. — CHARLES READE.

Sound as an honest man's conscience when he's dying. — WILLIAM ROWLEY.

He hath a heart as sound as a bell, and his tongue is the clapper. — SHAKESPEARE.

Sound as a top. — THACKERAY.

Sound (Verb).

No one was at the organ, yet it went on sounding — sounding like the songs of the archangels in their bursts of mystic ecstasy. — GUSTAVO A. BECQUÉR.

Sound — *continued.*

The voice sounds as a prophet's word. — Fitz-Greene Halleck.

Sounded like a felon's heart in skeleton ribs. — George Meredith.

Soundless.

Soundless as a tomb. — Thomas Hardy.

Soundless as light. — Miss Mulock.

Sour.

Sour as Melancholy. — Robert Burton.

Sour as verjuice. — Thomas Dekker.

As sour as though he had swallowed
A sloe-bush. — Maria Lowell.

Sour as a rotten orange. — J. H. McCarthy.

Sour as lees in wine. — Brian Melbancke.

Sour as sorrel. — Thomas Sackville.

Sovereign.

As sovereign as the blood of hearts. — Shakespeare.

Spacious.

Spacious as the element. — John Davidson.

Spangle.

Spangled . . . like leaves that laden are with trembling dew. — Robert Herrick.

Sparkling spangles . . . like morning sunshine tinselling the dew. — Ibid.

Sparkle.

Sparkles like a fresh glass of champagne.— Anon.

Sparkle like a ruby. — Ibid.

Sparkle like a seething caldron. — Ibid.

Sparkled as a sword-blade in the sunshine. — Ibid.

Sparkled as a bubbling spring. — Welsh Ballad.

Sparkling like the dancing of new stars. — R. D. Blackmore.

Sparkling like an ocean flower. — Horatius Bonar.

Sparkle like brooks in the morning sun. — William Cullen Bryant.

Sparkling like snow-wreaths in the early sun. — Ibid.

Sparkled like a garnet in the light. — Fernan Caballero.

Sparkling like a star. — Ibid.

The sea sparkled as if it smiled. — Bliss Carman.

Sparkling . . . like creatures in whose
sunny veins
The blood is running bright.
— Barry Cornwall.

Sparkle . . . like iron that comes molten from the fire. — Dante.

Sparkling all over, like a harlequin. — Dickens.

Sparkle like half-seen fairy eyes. — S. H. Dickson.

Sparkling as Mercutio. — Dr. John Doran.

All sparkling, like a goddess. — Dryden.

Sparkles . . . like the glimmer of a lance. — Francis M. Finch.

Sparkles like a lusty wine new broached. — John Ford.

Sparkles like the sea, whose wave at Algiers breaks upon the shore. — Ferdinand Freiligrath.

Sparkling, as if a Naiad's silvery feet
In quiet and coy retreat,
Glanced through the star-gleams on
calm summer nights.
— P. H. Hayne.

Sparkles like Ariadne's crown. — Robert Herrick.

Sparkle — *continued.*

Sparkle like the celestial mountains in the visions of the saints. — ROBERT HICHENS.

Sparkling and roseate as the dewy fingers of Aurora. — O. W. HOLMES.

Sparkle like fairy boon. — HOOD.

Sparkling like diamond rocks in the sun's rays. — FRANCES ANNE KEMBLE.

Eye sparkled, like the wine-cup's brim. — MISS LANDON.

Sparkling as dewdrops. — C. G. LELAND.

Sparkled like white bait in the meshes of a net. — CAMILLE LEMONIER.

Sparkle like the sea round the boat at night. — JAMES MACPHERSON.

Sparkling like lightning on a dusky sky. — MAHABHARATA.

Sparkling . . . like a man's thought transfigured into fire. — JOHN MASEFIELD.

Sparkling . . . like a coquette in a vaudeville. — OUIDA.

Sparkled like a jewel in the light. — IBID.

Sparkling like a son of morning. — SCHILLER.

Sparkle like the beaten flint. — SHAKESPEARE.

Sparkled like falling tears. — BAYARD TAYLOR.

Sparkles like a grain of salt. — TENNYSON.

Sparkled like the colour of burnished brass. — OLD TESTAMENT.

Sparkling like young wine which has ceased to ferment. — TURGENEV.

Sparkling like all the stars of heaven had fallen down. — MARK TWAIN.

Sparkle as a gold mine. — HENRY WATTERSON.

Spasm.

No spasms are like the spasms of expiring liberty, and no wailing such as her convulsions extort. — LYMAN BEECHER.

Spasms are like waves, they cannot go down the very moment the wind of trouble is lulled. — CHARLES READE.

Spattering.

Spattering off in a steady stream, like a buck-shot spilling from a canister. — IRVIN S. COBB.

Lightning spattered the sky as a thrown egg spatters a barn door. — KIPLING.

Speak.

Parliamentary speaking, like playing on the fiddle, requires practice. — BEACONSFIELD.

Speak as if he would jump down your throat. — JOHN SKELTON.

Spake
As who bids dead men wake.
— SWINBURNE.

Speak like a capon that had the cough. — NICHOLAS UDALL.

Speck.

Many a speck,
Like the water-snake's belly and the toad's back. — SHELLEY.

Speckled.

Speckled like a toad. — SHELLEY.

Speech.

Long and curious speeches are as fit for dispatch as a robe, or mantle, with a long train, is for a race. — BACON.

Considered as the last finish of education, or of human culture, worth and acquirement, the art of speech is noble, and even divine ; it is like the kindling of a Heaven's light to show us what a glorious world exists, and has perfected itself, in a man. — CARLYLE.

Speech — *continued.*

As a vessel is known by the sound, whether it be cracked or not, so men are proved by their speeches whether they be wise or foolish. — DEMOSTHENES.

Her artless speech, like chrystal, shows the thing it would hide, but only covers. — J. S. KNOWLES.

Solon used to say that speech was the image of actions ; . . . that laws were like cobwebs, — for that if any trifling or powerless thing fell into them, they held it fast ; while if it were something weightier, it broke through them and was off. — DIOGENES LAERTIUS.

A printed speech is like a dried flower : the substance, indeed, is there, but the color is faded and the perfume gone. — PROSPER LORAIN.

Speech is like the cloth of Arras, opened and put abroad, whereby the imagery doth appear in figure, while in thoughts they lie but in packs. — PLUTARCH.

His speech was like a tangled chain ; nothing impaired, but all disordered. — SHAKESPEARE.

Swift with speech like fire in fiery lands
To melt the steel's edge in the headsman's hands. — SWINBURNE.

Speech was like to tapestry ; and like it, when it was spread it showed its figures, but when it was folded up, hid and spoiled them. — THEMISTOCLES.

Speechless.

Speechless as a stone. — E. B. BROWNING.

Speechless as a mummy. — HOOD.

Like some sad statue, speechless. — POPE.

Speed.

Sped, like a phantom. — P. D. GRAY.

Sped like meteors through the sky. — BYRON.

Like a shaft dismissed I sped away. — RICHARD GARNETT.

Speeding . . . like an arrow. — THOMAS HARDY.

Sped like plagues and pestilences. — ROBERT JEPHSON.

Speeds from the earth like a bird on the wing. — WILLIAM KNOX.

He sped as speeds the wind. — LEWIS MORRIS.

Speed, like yellow leaves before the gale,
When Autumn winds are strongest.
— T. L. PEACOCK.

Speeds like the horseman who travels in haste. — THOMAS PRINGLE.

As a swallow chases the summer, we sped. — T. BUCHANAN READ.

Sped, like some swift cloud that wings the wide air's wilderness. — SHELLEY.

Speedy.

About as speedy as a steam-roller. — GEORGE ADE.

Spellbound.

Spellbound as in a vice. — ANON.

Stood spellbound, like a child to whom his nurse is telling some wonderful story. — BALZAC.

Spent.

Past and spent,
Like stars extinguished in the firmament. — HOOD.

Spicy.

Spicy as a cinnamon bear. — ANON.

Spin.

Spin like a dervish. — ANON.

Spins like a top. — IBID.

Spin round like a withered leaf blown from the tree. — IBID.

Spin — *continued.*

Spinning like a plummet down
Into the spacious gulf of deep blue air.
— LORD DE TABLEY.

Spinning like water flung from a top. — LORD DUNSANY.

Spinning like bubbles in a river. — EMERSON.

Spins like a fretful midge. — D. G. ROSSETTI.

Spinning like mill wheels. — JULIAN STREET.

Spineless.

Spineless as a chocolate eclair. — ANON.

Spineless as a jelly-fish. — IBID.

Spirit.

Spirit is like the thread whereon are strung the beads or worlds of life. — P. J. BAILEY.

A healthy spirit like a healthy frame craves aliment in plenty. — ROBERT BROWNING.

Spiritual.

Spiritual as a bunch of roses. — C. M. S. McLELLAN.

Spirituality.

Spirituality . . . as refined and spotless as the Jungfrau's silvery peak. — MARK TWAIN.

Spit.

Spit like fire. — ANON.

Spitted them like larks. — GILBERT ABBOTT À. BECKETT.

Spit like hump-back'd cats. — HOOD.

Spiteful.

Spiteful as an old maid. — ANON.

Spiteful as a monkey. — BALZAC.

Spiteful as the light. — ABRAHAM COWLEY.

Splashed.

Splashed like a sweet star-spray. — D. G. ROSSETTI.

Splendid.

Splendid as the sun. — FLAUBERT.

Splendid as a general's plume at the gallop. — GEORGE MEREDITH.

Splendid as trembling gems. — EDGAR SALTUS.

Splendid as the limbs of that supreme
incarnate beauty through men's visions gleam,
Whereof all fairest things are even
but shadow or dream.
— SWINBURNE.

Cold and splendid as death if dawn be bright. — IBID.

Splendid and strange as the sea that upbears as an ark. — IBID.

Splendor.

Splendor like an angel's love. — LORD DE TABLEY.

In fearful splendor, like the Northern Lights' red glare. — LUDWIG UHLAND.

Splinter.

Splinter'd like an icicle. — TENNYSON.

Split.

Split like a fired shell. — DICKENS.

Split,
Like fields of ice rent by the polar
wind. — WORDSWORTH.

Splotched.

Splotched like a brandy drunkard's face with red stains. — IRVIN S. COBB.

Spontaneous.

Spontaneous as a crystal fountain. — ANON.

Spontaneous as . . . a tree resigning its leaves to the wind. — SIR WALTER SCOTT.

Sported.

Sported like gilded insects on the wing. — JAMES MONTGOMERY.

Spotted.

Spotted like a pack of cards. — ANON.

Spotted — *continued.*

Spotted, as thickly as the leopard's dappled skin. — HOOD.

Spotted, like the field-bean's flower. — R. H. HORNE.

Spotless.

Spotless as snow. — ROBERT BLOOMFIELD.

Spotless as the flow'ring thorn. — BURNS.

Heart as spotless as the doves. — J. G. COOPER.

Spotless as an angel. — THOMAS HEYWOOD.

Spotless as the noon. — IBID.

Spotless as a Glastonbury nun. — RICHARD HOVEY.

Spotless as Saint Dorothy. — IBID.

Spotless as lilies. — LONGFELLOW.

Spotless and sincere, as the chaste vows of the holy vestals are. — OTWAY.

Spotless as a lily's leaf. — A. J. RYAN.

Spouting.

Spouting like a sperm-whale. — IRVIN S. COBB.

Sprawl.

Sprawl like a toad. — ANON

Sprawling . . . like a cowherd taking a siesta. — FLAUBERT.

Spread.

Spread out like a circus parade. — ANON.

Spreads like an inflammation. — IBID.

Spreads like ivy. — IBID.

Spreads like gossip. — IBID.

Spreads like honeysuckle in Virginia. — IBID.

Spreads like a lie. — IBID.

Spread like a rushing torrent. — IBID.

Spreads like measles in a country school. — IBID.

Spread like a drop of oil on a pool. — IBID.

Spread like a cinder shower from Vesuvius. — IBID.

Spreads . . . like the great voice of the sea. — BALZAC.

Spread like fingers. — R. D. BLACKMORE.

Spreads like fire. — BULWER-LYTTON.

Spreading his hands and all of his fingers, like the threads of a spider's web. — IBID.

Spread like wild-geese. — CHAPMAN.

The conflagration spread like a flaming garland. — CHATEAUBRIAND.

Spread like fire among stubble. — SANFORD COX.

Spreads like a memory. — GIOSUÈ CARDUCCI.

Spread like fog. — DRYDEN.

An innumerable crowd spread like a black robe over the shore. — HAMLIN GARLAND.

Roots . . . spreading like huge creeping snakes over the surface of the evil. — ERNST H. HAECKEL.

Spread, like distant morning in the skies. — JOHN HUGHES.

Calumny spreads like an oil-spot: we endeavor to cleanse it, but the mark remains. — MADAME DE LESPINASSE.

The fancy of this exclusion spread immediately, like a gangrene, over the whole body of the monarchy. — SIR ROGER L'ESTRANGE.

Spreads like a snow-ball. — WILLIAM J. LOCKE.

Spread like an ocean. — EDWARD LOVIBOND.

Spread — *continued.*

Spreading like a mighty flock of sheep. — WALTER MALONE.

Spread out, wide as the width of mind. — LEWIS MORRIS.

Spreads like a surface. — JOHN POMFRET.

Spread like wildfire. — RAY'S "COLLECTANEA."

Spread like a contagion. — MRS. MARY ROBERTS RINEHART.

As the delicate rose
To the sun's sweet strength
Doth herself unclose,
Breadth and length ;
So spreads my heart to thee.
— C. G. ROSSETTI.

Silence spread . . . like water that a pebble stirs. — D. G. ROSSETTI.

Spreads like scandal after a sewing bee. — WILLIAM SAGE.

Spread like evil ulcers. — SENECA.

Spread like a quenchless fire. — SHELLEY.

Spread
Like radiance from the cloud-surrounded morn. — IBID.

Spreads, like the round ocean, girdled with the sky. — SOUTHEY.

Her rich locks spread like sunbeams on the wind. — TASSO.

Spread . . . abroad as the four winds of heaven. — OLD TESTAMENT.

As the valleys are they spread forth. — IBID.

Spreading himself like a green bay tree. — IBID.

Spread like a halo round a misty moon. — WORDSWORTH.

Spread like a sea. — IBID.

Spread like plagues. — IBID.

Spread like day. — IBID.

The slaughter spread like flame. — IBID.

Sprightly.

As sprightly as a jumping-jack in the hands of a man with St. Vitus dance. — ANON.

Sprightly, as a hayfield. — R. D. BLACKMORE.

Sprightly as unyok'd heifers. — RICHARD DUKE.

Sprightly as light. — WILLIAM PATTISON.

Spring (Verb).

Springs like a hunted deer. — ANON.

Sprang to his feet like one recalled to life. — IBID.

Spring up like mushrooms. — IBID.

Spring up as weeds in neglected soil. — IBID.

Springing up like dandelions after a spring shower. — IBID.

Sprang to his feet like a startled roebuck. — BALZAC.

Sprang, like an uncaged beast. — ROBERT BROWNING.

Sprang like sparks from an anvil. — BULWER-LYTTON.

Sprang as from a sudden trumpet's clang. — BYRON.

Sprang forward like a courser for the goal. — J. FENIMORE COOPER.

Sprang, like the twin fountains of Benasji, from a divided source. — DR. JOHN DORAN.

Spring like a stag. — A. L. GORDON.

Springeth up as doth a welle. — JOHN GOWER.

Sprang like a wave
In the wind.
— W. E. HENLEY.

Spring
Like an arrow released from the strain
of the string.
— T. W. HIGGINSON.

Spring — *continued.*

Spring up like mushrooms in a September night. — G. B. Hill.

Springeth like Neptune. — Homer.

Oh never despair, for our hopes oftentime
Spring swiftly as flow'rs in some tropical clime,
Where the spot that was barren and scentless at night
Is blooming and fragrant at morning's first light. — Lover.

Sprang like a lily from the dirt of poverty. — Gerald Massey.

Sprang, as smitten with a mortal wound. — James Montgomery.

Spring as at the shout of war. — Samuel Rogers.

Springest like a cloud of fire. — Shelley.

Springs like a mettled steed when the spur stingeth. — M. E. Stebbins.

They shall spring up as among the grass, as willows by the water courses. — Old Testament.

Spring as the grass. — Ibid.

Spring forth like spectres starting from the storm-swept earth. — Whittier.

Sprang like an arrow shot straight from the bow. — Ella Wheeler Wilcox.

Spring (Noun).

The coming of spring is like the creation of Cosmos out of Chaos and the realization of the Golden Age. — Henry D. Thoreau.

Sprinkled.

Sprinkled with stars, like Ariadne's tiar. — Keats.

Sprout.

Sprout like saplings on French soil. — Balzac.

Sprout like rose-buds. — Dryden.

Spruce.

Spruce and shining like a new sabre. — Edmond About.

Spruce as an onion. — Anon.

Spry.

Spry as a Sparrow. — George Ade.

Spry as a cat. — Anon.

Spry as the chaff in the stroke of the flail. — O. W. Holmes.

Spry as a life-long Dimmycrat. — Abe Martin.

Spry as a cricket. — Sylvester Judd.

Spunky.

As spunky as a growin' flea. — George Outram.

Spurn.

Spurned like any reptile. — Dickens.

I spurn thee like a cur out of my way. — Shakespeare.

Sputter.

The words came sputtering out of his mouth like the beer from a barrel without a bung. — Friedrich Rückert.

Squabble.

To pass life in squabbling thus is to bear on the collar without relaxing, like the luckless remount horses at the rivers, who do not rest even when they stop, and who always draw though they cease to march. — Beaumarchais.

Squabble like brother and sister. Sir Richard Steele.

Squalid.

Squalid, like the traveler when he emerges from his bath of dust. — Virgil.

Squat (Adjective).

Squat as the figure of bronze upon a Chinese drawing. — Campbell.

Squat — *continued.*

Squatting things like toads. — HOOD.

Squat as a flounder. — RABELAIS.

Squat (Verb).

Squat like a toad. — MILTON.

Squat like a hermit on a tree stump lonely. — NIETZSCHE.

Squat into the ground like moles. — RABELAIS.

The soul squats down in the flesh, like a tinker drunk in a ditch. — SWINBURNE.

Squeak.

Squeaks like a rusty hinge. — ANON.

Squeaked like guinea-pigs. — IBID.

As Pokers do, whose tails are
Squeaked. — AUSTIN DOBSON.

Squeak like a Bart'lemew fiddle. — CHARLES LAMB.

Squeaking like a metal banner on a tower. — HENRYK SIENKIEWICZ.

He squeaks out like a hurt chicken. — ALEXANDER WILSON.

Squirm.

Squirming like a scorched moth. — G. VERE TYLER.

Squirm like a speared Eel. — ARTEMUS WARD.

Stable.

Stable as earth. — THOMAS BLACKLOCK.

Stage (*see* Theatre).

Stagger.

Staggered away as a defeated man staggers away from the field of battle. — JOSEPH CONRAD.

Staggered . . . like a child that is just allowed to go alone. — HUGO.

Staggers, like a sinking mast. — IBID.

Staggering like a quivering aspen leaf. — MARLOWE.

Staggers like a starveling cripple. — DONALD G. MITCHELL.

Like an old oke, whose pith and sap is
seare,
At puffe of every storm doth stagger.
— SPENSER.

Stagger like a drunken man. — OLD TESTAMENT.

Staggering . . . like tiplers answering Father Mathew's call. — WHITTIER.

Stain.

Stains, like sunshine falling through heraldic panes that rise between the altar and the sky. — BAYARD TAYLOR.

Stained.

Stained like pale honey oozed from
topmost rocks
Sun-bleached the lifelong summer.
— ROBERT BROWNING.

Stained, like meerschaum, through and through. — O. W. HOLMES.

Stain'd, as meadows yet not dry,
With miry slime left on them by a
flood. — SHAKESPEARE.

Stainless.

Stainless as a star. — ANON.

Stainless as driven snow. — IBID.

Springing stainless, like some mountain stream. — CONSTANCE C. W. NADEN.

Stainless as the air of Heaven. — RUSKIN.

Stainless white,
Like ivory bathed in still moonlight.
— WHITTIER.

Stale.

Stale as the hot rolls dug out of Pompeii. — ANON.

Stale as old beer. — IBID.

Stale as a black velvet cloak. — BEAUMONT AND FLETCHER.

Stale — *continued.*

Unspeakably stale
Like vats in desuetude shrunk.
— JOHN DAVIDSON.

Stale as custom. — "SIR THOMAS MORE" (Pseudo-Shakespearean).

Stale as sea-beef. — THOMAS NASH.

Stalk.

Stalk like an imperial peacock. — ANON.

Their words, like stage processions, stalk along. — ROBERT LLOYD.

Stamp.

Stamping her feet like an Italian actor representing anger. — EDMONDO DE AMICIS.

Stamp themselves upon his consciousness as the signet on soft wax. — O. W. HOLMES.

Stand.

Stands as firm as Gibraltar. — ANON.

Stands forth like morning from the shades of night. — IBID.

Stands like Mumphazard, who was hanged for saying nothing. — IBID.

Stands where he did, like Scotland. — IBID.

Stood like some erring angel that had lost his radiance. — BALZAC.

See! There is Jackson standing like a stone wall. — BERNARD E. BEE.

Stands at gaze
As might a wolf just fasten'd on his prey.
— CALDERON.

Grenadiers . . . stand there, like a fixed stone-dam in that wild whirlpool of ruin. — CARLYLE.

Stood like the Law and Gospel, one with the sanction of earth and one with the blessing of heaven. — LONGFELLOW.

Stood like a sentinel under inspection. — GEORGE MEREDITH.

Stand like statues cut in stone. — GEORGE SANDYS.

Stood, like veteran, worn, but unsubdued. — SIR WALTER SCOTT.

Stand at your door like a sheriff's post. — SHAKESPEARE.

Stand
Like wonder-wounded hearers.
— IBID.

Stood like a man at a mark with a whole army shooting at me. — IBID.

Stand on end,
Like quills upon the fretful porcupine.
— IBID.

Stand like flame transformed to marble. — SHELLEY.

Starch.

Starched as a formal City Matron. — JAMES RALPH.

Stare (Noun).

The stare, like that of a child who begins to see for the first time. — BALZAC.

Stare (Verb).

Stare like a glass eye. — ANON.

Stare like a mad bull. — IBID.

Staring like an idiot. — IBID.

Staring like a sick face. — IBID.

Stared in my face like a flash of light. — BALZAC.

Mortals stare aghast
As though heaven's bounteous windows were slammed fast
Incontinent.
— ROBERT BROWNING.

Stared like a pig poisoned. — BENJAMIN FRANKLIN.

Stared . . . like a detected thief. — HAWTHORNE.

Staring like Pythoness possessed. — HOOD.

Staring at her as if she had been an angel out of Heaven. — KINGSLEY.

Stare — *continued.*

Stare, like wild things of the wood about a fire. — LOWELL.

Stares as he had seen Medusa's head. — MASSINGER.

Stared, as one who would command
Sight of what has filled his ear.
— GEORGE MEREDITH.

Stared listlessly,
Like those who walk in sleep.
— WILLIAM MORRIS.

Eyes staring like a dead pig's. — RABELAIS.

Like dumb statues, or breathing stones,
Stared each on other.
— SHAKESPEARE.

Stared . . . as professional critics do at a new poet. — JOSEPH V. VON SCHEFFEL.

Stared like the Gorgon's head. — SMOLLETT.

Staring like a stuck pig. — SWIFT.

Stared aghast at her a minute, as Macbeth might on beholding Banquo's sudden appearance at his ball-supper. — THACKERAY.

Stared like a dead body. — H. G. WELLS.

Stark.

Stark, as the soul of sin. — FRANKLIN R. ADAMS.

Stark as a statue. — T. B. ALDRICH.

Stark as a gust of the sea. — BLISS CARMAN.

Stark,
Like the sea-rejected thing
Sea-sucked white.
— GEORGE MEREDITH.

Stark as the winter snow. — D. G. ROSSETTI.

Start.

Start like sparkles from a fire. — GEORGE CHAPMAN.

Start as from some dreadful dream. — DRYDEN.

Starting as at the sight of an enemy. — DUMAS, PERE.

Start, like a frightened roe. — W. S. GILBERT.

I started as one startles from a dream. — J. G. HOLLAND.

Starts like a ghost. — HOOD.

Start like lightning greased. — IBID.

Start as flames from ashes. — LONGFELLOW.

Start and quiver, as when some ignorant hand touches the barb hid in a long healed wound. — MISS MULOCK.

Started, like a greyhound from the slips when the sportsman cries halloo. — SIR WALTER SCOTT.

Starts, like one that spies an adder. — SHAKESPEARE.

Start like a shying horse. — STRINDBERG.

Started like a guilty thing. — MRS. TROLLOPE.

She starts like a sleeper who wakes from dreaming. — ELLA WHEELER WILCOX.

Startle.

Startles . . . like a blasphemy. — ADDISON.

Startled like shying steeds. — ARABIAN NIGHTS.

Startle like a wound in the flesh. — CONFUCIUS.

Startled like a moon-caught ghost. — JOHN DAVIDSON.

Startle, like a call to arms. — GRACE KING.

Startles like a pistol shot at a wedding. — SYDNEY MUNDEN.

Startled, as if some new-created thing
Enriched the earth, or Faery of the woods
Bounded before him.
— WORDSWORTH.

State.

States, as great engines, move slowly. — Bacon.

A great modern state is like a gigantic vessel built without any watertight compartments, which, if it be unskilfully steered, may perish when it strikes a single rock. — Viscount Bryce.

It is with states as with clocks, which must have some dead weight hanging at them to help and regulate the motion of the finer and more useful parts. — Pope.

Stately.

Stately as a column. — Æschylus.

Stately as a Roman legion. — Anon.

Stately as an oak. — Ibid.

Stately as a steeple. — Ibid.

Tall and stately as a pine. — Ibid.

Stately as a forest monarch. — Ibid.

Stately and pure as the swan on the lake. — Sir Samuel Ferguson.

Stately as a deer with antlers. — Longfellow.

Stately as a palm-tree standing before the moon. — George Meredith.

Stately as a ship under full sail. — Owen Meredith.

Stately like the stars. — C. G. Rossetti.

Stately as a queen. — Thackeray.

Stately as a King. — Walter Thornbury.

Statesman.

A statesman, we are told, should follow public opinion. Doubtless . . . as a coachman follows his horses; having firm hold on the reins, and guiding them. — J. C. Hare.

I look upon an able statesman out of office like a huge whale, that will endeavor to overturn the ship unless he has an empty cask to play with. — Sir Richard Steele.

An honest statesman to a prince,
Is like a cedar planted by a spring.
The spring bathes the tree's roots, the grateful tree,
Rewards it with its shadow.
— John Webster.

Stationary.

I am somewhat like the weathercocks, which only become stationary when they are rusty. — Voltaire.

Staunch.

Staunch as a bloodhound. — Anon.

Staunch as steel. — Ibid.

Stay (Noun).

Stand at a stay; like a stale at chess, where it is no mate, but yet the game can not stir. — Bacon.

Stay (Verb).

Stay, like fairies, till the cock crow them away. — Donne.

Stay . . . about as long as a tenderfoot would stick on an untamed bronco. — O. Henry.

Steadfast.

Steadfast as the steered-by star. — Alfred Austin.

Steadfast as the light of a diamond. — Bulwer-Lytton.

Steadfast as the sun. — Carlyle.

Steadfast as the eternal throne. — Alice Cary.

Steadfast as a wall. — Chaucer.

Stands steadfast, like tower which blast of wind can never shake. — Dante.

Steadfast, as the throne of God. — Aubrey De Vere.

Steadfast as a principle. — Keats.

Steadfast — *continued.*

Steadfast as the pole-star. — HANNAH MORE.

Steadfast as a fixed star. — C. G. ROSSETTI.

Steadfast as the everlasting rocks. — SOUTHEY.

Steadfast as a sea-mew's wing. — SWINBURNE.

Steadfast as clouds or hours in flight. — IBID.

Steadfastly.

Steadfastly as look the twin stars down into unfathomable wells. — N. P. WILLIS.

Steady.

Steady as a church. — ANON.

Steady as a clock. — IBID.

Steady as a rock. — IBID.

Steady as Old Time. — IBID.

Braced and steady, like a game man facing a firing squad. — IRVIN S. COBB.

Steady,
Like eyes suffused with rapture.
— COLERIDGE.

Steady
As if our footsteps had begun
To print the golden streets already!
— O. W. HOLMES.

Steady as a church. — ALFRED HENRY LEWIS.

Steady as clock-work. — MISS MULOCK.

Steady as the ocean waves.— CHARLES SANGSTER.

Steady as tramp of marching feet. — CELIA THAXTER.

Steady as a mill. — MARK TWAIN.

Steady as a hay wagon. — JUAN VALERA.

Steady as the pole. — ISAAC WATTS.

Steadily.

Like the drip from a loose faucet . . . steadily. — MARGARET DELAND.

Burned steadily, like a candle set in a window. — MARY JOHNSTON.

Steadiness.

I looked with steadiness, as sailors look
On the north star, or watch-tower's distant lamp. — WORDSWORTH.

Steal.

Steal o'er my soul in sweetness
As the moonlight steals over the sea.
— ANON.

Steals lingering like a river smooth along its grassy borders. — CAMPBELL.

Steal along like an Argus. — CHARLES HALLOCK.

Stealthily.

Stealthily, as if on shoes of felt, as if on paws of velvet. — CARLYLE.

Stealthily like rocks that tear a ship's life out under the smooth sea. — JOSEPH CONRAD.

Stealthy.

Stealthy as a cat. — BALZAC.

Steep.

Steep, like the ladder of a hay-mow. — R. D. BLACKMORE.

Steep as a house-side. — DANIEL DEFOE.

Steep as a sheet of glass. — EMILY LAWLESS.

Steaming.

Steaming like a brewer's vat. — HOOD.

Stern.

Stern as a stone bust of Augustus Cæsar. — ANON.

Stern as block of bogwood oak. — R D. BLACKMORE.

Stern as Vengeance. — BULWER-LYTTON.

Stern — *continued.*

An iron Queen,
Stern as her flinty judgment seat of
doom.
— LORD DE TABLEY.

Stern as Richard in Bosworth Field. — PIERCE EGAN.

Stern as Pluto's sceptre. — KEATS.

Stern as a mailed knight that had been grappling death. — GERALD MASSEY.

Stern as the noon of night. — IBID.

As stern as e'er was knitted in the folds of rancorous discontent. — RICHARD SHEIL.

Stern and still
As hours and years that change and
anguish fill. — SWINBURNE.

Stern as Medea in her dragon car. — IBID.

Stick.

Sticking as close together as two dried figs. — ANON.

Sticks like a cockle burr to a sheep's coat. — IBID.

Stick like a leech. — IBID.

Sticks like a porous plaster. — IBID.

Sticks like fly paper. — IBID.

Stick like wax. — IBID.

Stick like a Comanche on a mustang. The worse it jumps, the tighter he sticks. — J. R. BARTLETT'S "DICTIONARY OF AMERICANISMS."

Stick to it, like a clenched nail. — R. D. BLACKMORE.

Stick to her point like a fox to his own tail. — DION BOUCICAULT.

Stick like burrs. — BUNYAN.

Sticks as close . . . as a shadow to a body. — ROBERT BURTON.

Stick like pitch. — CONGREVE.

Sticks like a weasel. — GOLDSMITH.

Stuck together like a sheet of buns. — O. W. HOLMES.

Sticks to me like a bobolink on a sapling, in a wood. — SYLVESTER JUDD.

Stick as close as my shirt does to my back on a sultry, sweating day. — "LONDON CHANTICLEERS."

Like fruit unripe, sticks on the tree. — SHAKESPEARE.

Stick like rust. — CYRIL TOURNEUR.

Stick . . . as a country postmaster to his offiss. — ARTEMUS WARD.

Stiff.

Stiff as a board. — ANON.

Stiff as a fakir in a box left too long buried. — IBID.

Stiff as a frozen shadow. — IBID.

Stiff as a plaster mask. — IBID.

Stiff as a poker. — IBID.

Stiff as a post. — IBID.

Stiff as hedge-stakes. — IBID.

Stiff as steel. — IBID.

Stiff like a state coachman. — DICKENS.

Sitting stiffly by, like a functionary presiding over an interview, previous to an execution. — IBID.

Stiff as a dead body. — JONATHAN DICKINSON.

Stiff as the corpse of a hanged man. — DUMAS, PÈRE.

Stiff like a side of coarse leather. — J. T. FIELDS.

He stood . . . stiff as a marble statue. — GOETHE.

Stiff as a pointer's tail. — MAURICE HEWLETT.

Stiff as a rubbing brush. — THOMAS HEYWOOD.

Stiffly, and like one slain and cold. — EBENEZER JONES.

Stiff — *continued.*

Stiff as coat of mail. — W. S. LANDOR.

Stiff as a ramrod. — LEVER.

Stiff as a turnpike. — CHARLES MACKLIN.

Stiff as iron bars. — GUY DE MAUPASSANT.

Stiff as oak-leaves after frost. — GEORGE MEREDITH.

Stiff as logwood. — IBID.

Stiff like a soldier on parade. — CHARLES READE.

Stiff as a stone. — JOHN RUSKIN.

As stiff as a brick-built-wall. — J. K. STEPHEN.

Stiff as a viper frozen. — TENNYSON.

Stiff as Lot's wife. — IBID.

Stiff as a dry Quaker. — THOMAS WADE.

Still (Adjective).

Still as a church mouse. — ANON.

Still as a sheltered place when winds blow loud. — IBID.

Still as a tomb. — IBID.

Still as the stump of a tree. — IBID.

Still as a cat in a gutter. — "APPIUS AND VIRGINIA."

Great thoughts are still as stars. — P. J. BAILEY.

Still as one in sleep. — ALEXANDER BARCLAY.

Still as a crow's nest, in the ded ov winter. — JOSH BILLINGS.

Still as a log. — R. D. BLACKMORE.

Still as a mouse. — CHARLOTTE BRONTË.

Still as a prostrate column. — IBID.

Still as a vision. — E. B. BROWNING.

Still as when a silent mouth in frost
Breathes. — IBID.

Still as if spell-bound. — BULWER-LYTTON.

Still as the moonbeam. — IBID.

Still as a statue. — BYRON.

Still as a summer noon. — BLISS CARMAN.

Stille as any stoone. — CHAUCER.

Sat stille, as if he were in a traunce. — IBID.

As stille as the dede were. — IBID.

Still as a slave before his lord. — COLERIDGE.

Still like leaves forged of heavy metal. — JOSEPH CONRAD.

Still as old Chaos, before Motion's birth. — COWLEY.

Still as if struck with death. — JULIA C. R. DORR.

Still like a clock worn out with eating time,
The wheels of weary life at last stood still. — DRYDEN.

Still as a graveyard. — O. HENRY.

Still as tombstone. — HOMER.

Still as salt. — W. D. HOWELLS.

Still as a pool. — HUGO.

Still as a rock set in the watery deep. — JEAN INGELOW.

Dead-still as a marble man. — KEATS.

Still as children's thoughts. — THOMAS KILLIGREW.

Still as a chimney. — KINGSLEY.

Still as beggars at the gate of greatness. — KIPLING.

Silence stiller than the shore
Swept by Charon's stealthy car.
— F. L. KNOWLES.

Still as the moonlight. — GEORGE MACDONALD.

Fall still as oak-leaves after frost. — GEORGE MEREDITH.

Still — *continued.*

Still as an island stood our ship. — RICHARD M. MILNES.

Still as the Spring-tide comes. — LEWIS MORRIS.

As still
As snowflakes fall upon the sod.
— JOHN PIERPONT.

Still as a sow in beans. — PEDRO PINEDA'S "SPANISH DICTIONARY."

Still as the hour of death. — T. BUCHANAN READ.

Still, as one who broods or grieves. — D. G. ROSSETTI.

Still as the gleam of a star through the dark. — A. J. RYAN.

Still as a shadow. — DUNCAN C. SCOTT.

Still as the grave. — SHAKESPEARE.

Still as a wavelet in a pool. — WILLIAM SHARP.

Still as some far tropic sea where no winds murmur, nor waves be. — IBID.

Still as a brooding dove. — SHELLEY.

Still as clapper in a mill. — SKELTON.

Still as the gentle calm, when the hush'd wave no longer foams before the rapid storm. — SMOLLETT.

Still as any stake. — SPENSER.

Still as a ghostly lake. — HOWARD V. SUTHERLAND.

Still as fair shapes fixed on some wondrous wall
Of minster-aisle or cloister-close or hall
To take even time's eye prisoner with delight. — SWINBURNE.

Still as a stone. — OLD TESTAMENT.

Still, like Sunday. — MARK TWAIN.

Still as an image of a boy in stone. — THEODORE WATTS-DUNTON.

Still as the dawn. — ELLA WHEELER WILCOX.

Still as a picture. — WHITTIER.

Still as Eden ere the birth of man. — N. P. WILLIS.

Still as starlight. — IBID.

Still
As the mute swan that floats adown the stream. — WORDSWORTH.

Still (Verb).

Stilling her spirit like the waving of a wand of peace. — JAMES LANE ALLEN.

Stimulating.

About as stimulating as a mouthful of sawdust and water. — ANON.

Stimulating as ginger cordial. — G. B. SHAW.

Sting.

Sting like a hornet. — ANON.

Stung like a nettle. — IBID.

Stung like bees unhived. — ROBERT BROWNING.

Sting like a serpent. — ROBERT BURTON.

Care stings like pois'nous asps to fury wrought. — NATHANIEL COTTON.

Stung . . . like amber asp. — MATTHEW GREEN.

Stinging, like the wind when frosts are keen. — HENRIK HERTZ.

Stings like fire. — LUCRETIUS.

Stung like a bee in the warm core of a rose. — OUIDA.

He stings like a scorpion. — OSMANLI PROVERB.

Stung like fire. — SWINBURNE.

Stingeth like an adder. — OLD TESTAMENT.

Stink.

Stink like a polecat. — ANON.

Stink like carrion. — IBID.

Stinks like a poison'd cat behind a hanging. — BEAUMONT AND FLETCHER.

Stink — *continued.*

His memory stinks like the snuff of a candle when it is put out. — ROBERT BURTON.

Stank as the pitte of helle. — CHAUCER.

Stynken as a goot. — IBID.

Stinks and shines, and shines and stinks, like a dead mackerel in the moonlight. — JOHN RANDOLPH.

Stunk like wash-polluted pigs. — WILLIAM TENNANT.

Stir.

Stirs the blood like trumpet-blast. — WILLIAM ARCHER.

Stirr'd, like a clarion-blast. — MATTHEW ARNOLD.

Stirred her soul like organ music. — BALZAC.

Stirring like the sight of glorious triumph. — JOSEPH CONRAD.

Stir as with hope and bliss. — MRS. E. M. H. CORTISSOZ.

Stir like tide-worn sea-weed. — FANNIE STEARNS DAVIS.

That dream is in my heart, stirring, like spring within the unconscious earth setting the unborn summer in array. — F. W. FABER.

Stirs one like a martial tune. — RICHARD LE GALLIENNE.

Stirring as music. — J. H. GARDINER.

Stirred like drifted snows. — THOMAS G. HAKE.

Stirred . . . as the dive of a kingfisher stirs a quiet pool. — THOMAS HARDY.

Divinely stirred,
As if the vanished soul of Keats,
Had found its new birth in a bird.
— P. H. HAYNE.

Stirred as tempest stirs the forest branches. — HOOD.

Stirred, like insects settled on a dancing leaf. — IBID.

Stir like the hail of musketry in fight. — SIGMUND KRASINSKI.

Love's sweet mystery stirring at their hearts, like first spring motions in the veins o' the flowers. — GERALD MASSEY.

My heart is stirred,
Like childhood's when it hears the carol of a bird.
— ROBERT NICOLL.

Stirred him up like the tap of a drum. — JAMES WHITCOMB RILEY.

Stirred like springtide waters. — SWINBURNE.

And with such song the hollow ways were stirred
As of a god's heart hidden in a bird,
Or as the whole soul of the sun in spring
Should find full utterance in one flower-soft word. — IBID.

Stirs my spirits like a raging sea. — CHARLES WELLS.

Stirs, like the trumpet's call to strife. — WHITTIER.

Stirr'd like the ocean when a tempest blows. — WILLIAM WILKIE.

Stolid.

Stolid as a Dutchman. — ANON.

Stolid as an ox. — IBID.

Stoop.

Stoop
Like timid silence shrinking from the breeze. — R. H. BELL.

Stoops like a bow. — BULWER-LYTTON.

Stooped like sprinters before a signal. — STEPHEN CRANE.

Stooped, like a bird with a broken wing. — DUMAS, PÈRE.

Stop.

Stop progress, like a block in the pit entrance to a theater. — GEORGE MEREDITH.

Storm.

Storm like a caged lion. — ANON.

Storm like a mad thing. — OUIDA.

Stormed like a perfect hurricane.— SMOLLETT.

Stormy.

Stormy as a multitude. — HUGO.

Story.

A good story is like a bitter pill with the sugar coating inside of it. — O. HENRY.

Stout.

Stout of fibre as hemp. — CARLYLE.

Stout as bergs of Arctic ice. — GEORGE MEREDITH.

Stout as death. — OTWAY.

Straight.

Straight as a candle. — HANS CHRISTIAN ANDERSEN.

Straight as an angel's flight. — ANON.

Straight as an Indian's hair. — IBID.

Straight as a lance. — IBID.

Straight as a pine. — IBID.

Straight as a ramrod. — IBID.

Straight as a rush. — IBID.

Straight as a string. — IBID.

Straight as columns of fire. — IBID.

Straight, as if he had swallowed a stick. — IBID.

Straight as the backbone of a herring. — IBID.

Straight as a cane. — ARABIAN NIGHTS.

Straight as a temple-shaft. — EDWIN ARNOLD.

Straight as a shooting star. — WILLIAM AUSTIN.

Straight as a die. — ALEXANDER BARCLAY.

Straight as a loon's leg. — J. R. BARTLETT'S "DICTIONARY OF AMERICANISMS."

Straight as a shingle. — IBID.

Straight as truth. — BEAUMONT AND FLETCHER.

Straight as poplars. — CHARLOTTE BRONTË.

Straight . . . like graves dug side by side at measured lengths. — E. B. BROWNING.

Straight to its aim as the aim of the rifle-ball of a Tyrolese. — BULWER-LYTTON.

Straight as a rule. — BUNYAN.

Straight as a beadle's wand. — C. S. CALVERLEY.

Straight as a bull's back against the white sky. — BLISS CARMAN.

Straight as line. — CHAUCER.

Straight as a lily on its stem. — WILKIE COLLINS.

Straight as a tower. — T. O. DAVIS.

Straight as any plummet line. — DICKENS.

Straight as a crow flies. — IBID.

As straight as a beggar can spit. — KIPLING.

Go as straight as a schoolboy at Christmas. — LEAN'S "COLLECTANEA."

Straight as a spear. — NATHANIEL LEE.

Straight like a sala-tree. — MAHABHARATA.

Straight as Circe's wand. — MARLOWE.

Gleams straight like the glow which a
ploughing keel doth break
From the grim sea around, with light
on her bow and light in her raging
wake. — WESTLAND MARSTON.

Straight like vine poles. — GUY DE MAUPASSANT.

Straight — *continued.*

Fly straight as the emissary eagle back to Jove. — GEORGE MEREDITH.

Straight as the flight of the dove. — IBID.

Straight, — like a webfoot to water. — IBID.

Straight as a dart. — PILPAY.

Straight as the palm tree. — PRIOR.

Straight as a Seer's thought into the blue of the immaculate heavens. — RICHARD REALF.

Straight as thought could span. — SWINBURNE.

Straight as bolt from crossbow sped. — MARK TWAIN.

Straight as a wall. — IVAN VAZOV.

Straight as a Sioux chief. — BOOKER T. WASHINGTON.

Straighten.

Straightened himself up like a liberty-pole. — MARK TWAIN.

Straightforward.

As straightforward as a tile falling on your head. — JOSEPH CONRAD.

Strain.

A faint strain,
As if some echo, that among
Those minstrel halls had slumber'd long,
Were murm'ring into life again.
— THOMAS MOORE.

One great strain of joy as the sea breaking. — SWINBURNE.

Strange.

As strange as a wedding without a bridegroom. — ANON.

Strange
As Hindostanee to an Ind-born man
Accustomed many years to English speech. — E. B. BROWNING.

Strange as death. — IBID.

Strange to me as dreams of distant spheres. — IBID.

Strange as the stars. — G. K. CHESTERTON.

Strange as a vision. — AGNES M. F. DARMESTETER.

Strange as a dream. — LEWIS MORRIS.

Strange as a dreamer's mad imagings. — SHELLEY.

I feel as new and strange as a free spirit which had shaken off the wrappings of this life. — ALEXANDER SMITH.

Strange as the curlew's song. — R. H. STODDARD.

Strange . . . like a fine lady swapping her moles for the mange. — SWIFT.

Strange as are night and morning, stars and sun. — SWINBURNE.

Strange as chance or doom. — IBID.

Strange as hope's green blossom touched with time's harsh rust. — IBID.

Strange as life. — IBID.

Strange as light
That cleaves in twain the shadow of night
Before the wide-winged world takes flight
That thunder speaks to depth and height
And quells the quiet hour with sound.
— IBID.

Strange as sleep. — IBID.

Strange as heaven. — IBID.

Strange as fate. — IBID.

Strange as the sea. — IBID.

Strange as a wild flower. — THOREAU.

Strangely.

Strangely there, as would a bower of roses in Siberia. — MRS. TROLLOPE.

Stream.

Streaming like feathers of a shuttlecock. — AMBROSE BIERCE.

Stream — *continued.*

Branches stream like the dishevelled hair
Of women in the sadness of despair.
— WILLIAM CULLEN BRYANT.

Streamed o'er his memory like a forest's flame. — O. W. HOLMES.

Streaming like a flag of battle. — GEORGE MEREDITH.

Streamed like curtain-rents
Fluttered by a wind. — IBID.

Her locks streamed like the torch
Borne by a racer at full speed,
Or like the mane of horses in their flight
Or like an angel when she stems the light
Straight towards the sun,
Or like a caged thing freed,
Or like a flying flag when armies run.
— C. G. ROSSETTI.

Stream like a comet's flashing hair — SHELLEY.

Stream, like a sunset. — FREDERICK TENNYSON.

Strengthening.

As strengthening to the mind as drinking sweetened wind out of a toy balloon. — W. C. BRANN.

Strengthless.

Strengthless as a noon-belated moon,
Or as the glazing eyes of watery heaven,
When the sick night sinks into deadly swoon. — FRANCIS THOMPSON.

Strenuously.

Strenuously as ever Cavalier strove for the White Rose. — OUIDA.

Stretch.

Stretch away, like the perspective of a dream. — PAUL BOURGET.

Stretch . . . like a bow-string by the forceful arm of some bold archer strained. — LUCIAN.

Stretched as far as doth the mind of man. — MARLOWE.

Stretching out his hand like the wings of a bird. — RABELAIS.

Laura stretched her gleaming neck
Like a rush-imbedded swan,
Like a lily from the beck,
Like a moonlit poplar branch,
Like a vessel at the launch
When its last restraint is gone.
— C. G. ROSSETTI.

Stretched along, like a wounded knight. — SHAKESPEARE.

Stretch like imploring arms. — BAYARD TAYLOR.

Stretched out the heavens as a curtain. — OLD TESTAMENT.

Strew.

Strewn round as like a dead world's shroud in ghastly fragments torn. — E. B. BROWNING.

Strewed like the leaves that vanish in the soil. — O. W. HOLMES.

Strewn . . . like bridal chamber floors. — SHELLEY.

Stricken.

Stricken down as a broken pillar. — RUTH PUTNAM.

Stride.

Fortune striding, like a vast Colossus. — DRYDEN.

The strides of the lame are like the glances of the one-eyed ; they do not speedily reach their aim. — HUGO.

Strife.

Dark with strife,
Like heaven's own sun that storming clouds bedim. — SWINBURNE.

Strike.

Strike like a battering ram. — ANON.

Strike like a trip-hammer. — IBID.

Strikes like lightning. — ROBERT BURTON.

Strike — *continued.*

The ocean strikes like a lion with its heavy paw, seizing and dismembering at the same moment. — HUGO.

Striped.

Striped like a viper's loins. — R. D. BLACKMORE.

Striped like a zebra. — KEATS.

Strive.

Strive not as doth a crocke (pitcher) with a wall. — CHAUCER.

Strove
As toward the sundawn strives the lark. — SWINBURNE.

Strove as in toils. — IBID.

Strove . . . like song's triumphant breath. — IBID.

Strong.

Strong as the mainstay of the laboring bark. — ÆSCHYLUS.

Strong as Zeus. — ÆSCHYLUS (E. B. BROWNING).

Strong as an eagle. — ANON.

Strong as a Flander's mare. — IBID.

Strong as hate. — IBID.

Strong as Hercules. — IBID.

Strong as mustard. — IBID.

Strong as an ox. — IBID.

Strong as the voice of Fate. — BULWER-LYTTON.

Strong as the spirit of the storm. — W. WILFRED CAMPBELL.

Strong as beechwood in the blast. — CAMPBELL.

Strong as bulls. — CARLYLE.

Strong as the Harz-rock, rooted in the depths of the world. — IBID.

Strong as an host of armed Deities. — COLERIDGE.

Strong as brandy. — FARQUHAR.

As the lion strong. — FRANCIS FAWKES.

Strong in silence as mysteries locked up in Jove's own bosom. — JOHN FORD.

Strong as earth's first kings.— FITZ-GREENE HALLECK.

As strong as instinct. — HAWTHORNE.

Strong as the enginery that works the world. — J. A. HILLHOUSE.

Stronger than thunder's winged force. — HORACE.

Strong as the wind. — MARY JOHNSTON.

Strong as fire. — KINGSLEY.

Strong as a jail. — LEVER.

Strong as iron bands. — LONGFELLOW.

Strong as a storm. — JAMES MACPHERSON.

Strong as a sea-swell. — GERALD MASSEY.

Strong as God. — NIETZSCHE.

Strong as a young goat. — OUIDA.

Strong, like an iron chain. — PILPAY.

Strong as the devil himself. — RABELAIS.

Strong as Sampson. — IBID.

Strong . . . as young Desire. — T. BUCHANAN READ.

Strong as strong Ajax's red right hand. — C. G. ROSSETTI.

Strong as necessity. — RICHARD SAVAGE.

Confirmations strong
As proofs of holy writ.
— SHAKESPEARE.

Strong as Pluto's gates. — IBID.

Strong as the axletree. — IBID.

Strong as . . . rash gunpowder. — IBID.

Strong — *continued.*

Strong as a wild swan's pinions. — SWINBURNE.

Strong as grows the yearning of the blossom toward the fruit. — IBID.

Strong as love. — IBID.

Strong as the seas. — IBID.

Strong as the worldwide sun. — IBID.

Strong as sheer truth. — IBID.

Strong as time. — IBID.

Strong like fate. — IBID.

Strong, and bold, and free as the milk-white foal of the Nedjidee.— BAYARD TAYLOR.

Strong as death. — OLD TESTAMENT.

Strong as iron. — IBID.

Strong as an oaken staff. — HENRY VAN DYKE.

As the deluge strong. — ISAAC WATTS.

Strong as a Monarch's signet. — N. P. WILLIS.

Strong as guilty fear. — WORDSWORTH.

Struggle.

Struggling like a flower towards Heaven. — ANON.

Struggling like a man led towards death and crucifixion. — CARLYLE.

Struggled, like an old lawyer between two fees. — CONGREVE.

Struggled instinctively like an animal under a net. — JOSEPH CONRAD.

Struggles, like a living creature making its way from under a great snowdrift. — GEORGE ELIOT.

Struggling like a captive dove which wishes to resume its flight. — FLAUBERT.

Struggled, like a dragon-doubt glooming a lonely spirit. — CHARLES HARPUR.

She struggled against silence like soda-water against the cork. — ANTHONY HOPE.

Struggle, like a wild, frantic bird that is rending its plumage in its desperation. — HUGO.

Struggling like black spirits in hell. — IBID.

Struggled together like foes in a burning city. — LONGFELLOW.

Struggle, like a stricken hare
When swoops the monarch bird of air.
— T. BUCHANAN READ.

Struggling like an animal in an air pump. — SIR RICHARD STEELE.

Struggling . . . like a wild beast tangled in a net. — RABINDRANATH TAGORE.

Struggled like a bird chained and restive. — WALTER THORNBURY.

Strut.

Strut like a new church warden. — THOMAS ADAMS.

Struts like a cock o' the walk. — ANON.

Strut like a peacock. — IBID.

Struts like a Thespian. — IBID.

Strutted through hell, and pushed
the devils by,
Like a magnifico of Venice.
— GEORGE H. BOKER.

Strutting like a turkey cock. — FIELDING.

Struts like a juggler. — JOHN FORD.

Struts like a crow. — SMOLLETT.

Stubborn.

Stubborn as a mule. — ANON.

As stubborn as the will of kings. — AMBROSE BIERCE.

As stubborn as Muirkirk iron. — HOGG.

Stubborn as a stone. — HUGO.

Stubborn — *continued.*

Stubborn people are like reproaches, and we have a right to laugh at them. — IBID.

Stubborn as the Rocky Mountains. — RICHARD LE GALLIENNE.

Stubborn as an elephant's leg, no bending in her. — WILLIAM ROWLEY.

More stubborn-hard than hammer'd iron. — SHAKESPEARE.

Stuck.

Stuck on like burrs. — BEAUMONT AND FLETCHER.

Stuck to me like cobbler's wax. — R. D. BLACKMORE.

Stuck like leeches. — IBID.

Stuck there like a curious seal. — MICHAEL DRAYTON.

Stuck as close ter ole Marster's heel as de shadder sticks to de tree. — T. N. PAGE.

Studded.

Studded with I's as a boiled ham is stuck full of cloves. — LYMAN F. GEORGE.

Study.

Study is like the heaven's glorious sun,
That will not be deep-search'd with
saucy looks. — SHAKESPEARE.

Stuff.

Stuff up his lust, as minutes fill up hours. — SHAKESPEARE.

Stumble.

Stumbling, like a cat shod with walnuts. — ANON.

Stumbled like fat sheep. — STEPHEN CRANE.

Stunning.

Stunning as a shock of electricity. — JOHN BROUGHAM.

Stupid.

Stupid as an excuse. — ANON.

Stupid as a sloth. — IBID.

Stupid as a fact. — BALZAC.

Stupid as a stone. — ROBERT BROWNING.

Loftily stupid, like dumb idols. — CARLYLE.

Stupid as a coot. — COWAN'S "DICTIONARY OF SEA PROVERBS."

Stupid as a little downy owl. — GEORGE DU MAURIER.

Stupid . . . like Falstaff in his old age. — THOMAS H. HUXLEY.

Stupid as a log. — ISAAC JACKMAN.

Stupid as hounds chasing an iron deer. — SYDNEY MUNDEN.

Stupid as a post. — CLEMENT ROBINSON.

Stupid as the swine. — HANS SACHS.

Stupid as a hog. — TOLSTOY.

Sturdy.

Sturdy as a wild ass colt. — COWPER.

Style.

Our style should be like a skeine of silke, to be carried and found by the right thred, not ravel'd and perplex'd ; then all is a knot, a heape. — BEN JONSON.

Gibbon's style is too uniform ; he writes in the same flowing and pompous style on every subject. He is like Christie, the auctioneer, who says as much of a ribbon as of a Raphael. — RICHARD PORSON.

Subdued.

Subdued . . . like some strong stream made placid in the fullness of the lake. — ANON.

Subdued like Argus by the might of sound. — HOOD.

Subdued and grave,
Like schoolboys when the master's in
a passion. — IBID.

Sublime.

Sublime as Niagara. — Anon.

Sublime as the cliffs and the clouds. — Ibid.

Sublime as the sky overhead. — Balzac.

Sublime as a fact. — George Canning.

Sublime, like a gilt crockery Idol. — Carlyle.

Sublime as Milton's immemorial theme. — Sydney Dobell.

Sublime . . . as the combats of Homer. — Hugo.

Sublime, as tropic storm. — H. C. Merivale.

Sublime . . . like the sun's fir'd flame. — John Scott.

As faith sublime. — Swinburne.

Sublime and triumphant as fire or as lightning. — Ibid.

Sublime,
As God were man, to spare or to forget.
— Ibid.

Sublime as storm or sorrow. — Ibid.

Sublime as truth. — Ibid.

As Liberty, sublime. — William Thomson.

Sublime as heaven. — Ibid.

Submissive.

Submissive as a neophyte. — Anon.

Submissive as clay. — Ibid.

Submissive as putty. — Ibid.

Submissive as earth. — Hamlin Garland.

Subside.

Subside like a lanced boil. — Anon.

Subside, like a swollen bubble on the ocean tide. — George Darley.

Substance.

Substance is like a river in a continual flow, and the activities of things are in constant change, and the causes work in infinite varieties. — Marcus Aurelius.

Substantial.

Substantial as the shadow of a shade. — Calderon.

Subtle.

Subtle as a serpent. — Anon.

About as subtle as a sidewalk-worker for a second-hand clothing store. — Ibid.

Subtle as the tone of the voice or the glance of the eye. — John Burroughs.

Subtle as a snake. — Lord Lyttelton.

A point as subtle
As Ariachne's broken woof.
— Shakespeare.

Subtle as the fox for prey. — Ibid.

Subtle as thin water. — Swinburne.

Subtle as a serpent. — Bayard Taylor.

Subtle as light. — Celia Thaxter.

Subtle as a dead pig. — T. Wright.

Subtly.

Subtly as a failing of the sight. — C. L. Hildreth.

Success.

Success is like the sunshine, — it brings the rattlesnakes out. — Paul Morton.

Succeed.

Succeed each other, like monster devouring monster in a dream. — Carlyle.

Successive.

Successive, as the seasons to the sun. — P. J. Bailey.

Sudden.

Sudden, like a Fate. — T. B. ALDRICH.

Sudden as an April shower. — ANON.

Sudden as a meteor's flight. — IBID.

Sudden and swift as a raging cyclone. -- IBID.

Sudden as a sunbeam's ray. — IBID.

Sudden as a tidal wave on a summer sea. — IBID.

Sudden as the babbling brook or robin's whistle. — IBID.

Sudden as the call of spring to buried flowers. — IBID.

A sudden brightness, as when meteor swift opens the darkness. — IBID.

Sudden, as creation burst from naught. — CAMPBELL.

Sudden as conscience. — G. K. CHESTERTON.

Sudden as the crack of rifle. — EMERSON.

Sudden as kindling flames arise. — WALTER HARTE.

Sudden as a snap. — HOOD.

Sudden as lightning. — BEN JONSON.

Sudden sound as of a bowstring snapped in air. — LONGFELLOW.

Sudden as a stab. — LOWELL.

Sudden as Aphrodite from the sea. — GEORGE MACDONALD.

Sudden as the slapping of a wave. — SPENCER MOORE.

A sudden flash, as from a sunlit jewel. — LEWIS MORRIS.

Sudden like a pool that once gave back
Your image, but now drowns it and is
clear
Again. — D. G. ROSSETTI.

Sudden like a hamadryad before a dull fawn. — HENRYK SIENKIEWICZ.

Sudden as a flame. — SWINBURNE.

Suddenly.

As suddenly as sudden death. — ANON.

Rise up suddenly like the dry corpse which stood upright in the glory of life when touched by the bones of the prophet. — IBID.

Suddenly, like a thunder-bolt. — R. D. BLACKMORE.

Flashed suddenly . . . as love of youth at first sight. — BULWER-LYTTON.

Suddenly as a rain sound can pass from your ear. — JOHN FORD.

More suddenly than doth a moment go. — KEATS.

Suddenly . . . like a ghost from the tomb. — RUTH PUTNAM.

Broke as suddenly as a widow's saving bank. — WALTER TRUMBULL.

Sue.

Beggars sue as king with king
Before the Throne of Grace on high.
— C. G. ROSSETTI.

Suffer.

Suffers like a snipe shut up in a snuff-box. — HENRY P. LELAND.

Suicide.

Every suicide is like an awful poem of sorrow. — BALZAC.

Sulk.

Sulking like Achilles in his tent. — ANON.

Sulky.

Sulky as a ghost. — E. B. BROWNING.

Sulky as a bear. — THACKERAY.

Sullen.

Sullen, like lamps in sepulchres. — ROBERT BLAIR.

Sullen as an Algerine colt. — OSMANLI PROVERB.

Sullen — *continued.*

Sullen as a storm. — NICHOLAS ROWE.

Sullenly.

He looks as sullenly as a routed general. — APHRA BEHN.

Sultry.

Sultry . . . as if the air had fainted, and the pulse of Nature had run down, and ceased to beat. — N. P. WILLIS.

Sunburnt.

Sunburnt as the leaves of autumn. — ANON.

Sunday.

A world without a Sabbath would be like a man without a smile, like a summer without flowers, and like a homestead without a garden. — H. W. BEECHER.

Sunday is like a stile between the fields and toil, where we can kneel and pray, or sit and meditate. — LONGFELLOW.

Sunken.

Sunken as Atlantis. — G. K. CHESTERTON.

Hopes deep sunken like anchors under
the ice. — J. T. TROWBRIDGE.

Sunlight.

Sunlight is like the breath of life to the pomp of autumn. — HAWTHORNE.

Superfluous.

Superfluous as a fifth wheel. — ANON.

Superfluous as bells on idle horses. — RICHARD C. TRENCH.

Supernatural.

Supernatural as the Dante of Florence. — LAMARTINE.

Superior.

As superior . . . as a peak of the Alps to a highland of the Hudson. — WASHINGTON IRVING.

Superstitious.

Superstitious as sailors. — ANON.

Supper.

Your supper is like the Hidalgo's dinner; very little meat and a great deal of tablecloth. — LONGFELLOW.

Supple.

Supple as a young panther. — ANON.

Supple as the neck of a swan. — IBID.

Supple as tobacco pouches. — BALZAC.

Supple . . . as a young cat. — WILKIE COLLINS.

Supple as water. — HUGO.

Supple as a snake. — GUY DE MAUPASSANT.

Supple as if they were on springs. — IBID.

Supple as the Scythian's bow. — GEORGE MEREDITH.

Supple as a *peau de Suède* glove. — OCTAVE MIRBEAU.

Supple as Damascus steel. — OUIDA.

Suppliant.

Suppliant . . . like a white-spotted heifer on the lofty rocks, where trusting for aid she lows, telling to the herdsman her troubles. — ÆSCHYLUS.

Support.

Support themselves as swarming bees do, hang on by each other. — RUSKIN.

Supreme.

Supreme as a pope. — MILTON.

Sure.

Sure as monument of brass,
Their fame to future time shall pass.
— ARTHUR ACHESON.

Sure as a club. — ANON.

Sure as a stone drops from the hand which lets it go. — IBID.

Sure — *continued.*

Sure as birth and death. — ANON.

Sure as day and night succeed each other. — IBID.

Sure as eggs in April. — IBID.

Sure as gravity. — IBID.

As sure as Heaven. — IBID.

Sure as God's in heaven — IBID.

Sure as I'm standing here. — IBID.

Sure as March in Lent. — IBID.

Sure as needles point to the north. — IBID.

Sure as Silas Wegg is to drop into poetry. — IBID.

Sure as tares. — IBID.

As sure as that bubbles are in the form of a hemisphere. — IBID.

As sure as that wild goose never laid a tame egg. — IBID.

As sure as that the world is turned upside down every twenty-four hours. — IBID.

Sure as the coat's on your back. — IBID.

Sure as the foot of a mule. — IBID.

Sure as the opportune arrival of the detective on the final curtain of a melodrama. — IBID.

Sure as the sun shines. — IBID.

Sure as the steeple bears the bell.— IBID.

Sure as two and two make four. — IBID.

Sure as water is water. — IBID.

Sure as you're alive. — IBID.

Sure as shootin'. — IBID.

As sure as eggs and bacon. — IBID.

Sure as an obligation sealed in the butter. — JOHN BARET.

Sure as a gun. — J. R. BARTLETT'S "DICTIONARY OF AMERICANISMS."

Sure as wedlock. — BEAUMONT AND FLETCHER.

Sure as stars of hope. — R. D. BLACKMORE.

Sure as sunrise. — IBID.

Sure as you are there. — BUNYAN.

Sure as death. — CALDERON.

Sure as the wold gulls make seaward. — BLISS CARMAN.

Sure . . . as the witch-hazel towards treasure. — GEORGE W. CURTIS.

Sure as a rock. — JOHN DAVIES.

Sure as sun-up. — DICKENS.

Sure as the gospel. — DUMAS, PÈRE.

Sure as roundness in the dewdrop. — GEORGE ELIOT.

Sure as the devil's in London. — FIELDING.

Sure as the fishes swim and birds do fly. — GERHART HAUPTMANN.

Sure as a juggler's box. — W. C. HAZLITT'S "ENGLISH PROVERBS AND PROVERBIAL PHRASES."

Sure as Dover stands at Dover. — HOOD.

Sure as a horse when he knows his rider. — RICHARD HOVEY.

Sure as Time. — KIPLING.

Sure as the shaft that leaves the Parthian bow. — LUCAN.

As sure as Heaven rained manna for the Jews. — MARLOWE.

Sure as the date on a bill. —GEORGE MEREDITH.

Sure as earth lives under snows, and Love lives under pain. — MISS MULOCK.

Sure as fate. — NORTHALL'S "FOLK PHRASES."

Sure — *continued.*

Sure as God made little apples. — NORTHALL'S "FOLK PHRASES."

Sure as I'm alive. — IBID.

Sure as you are born. — IBID.

As sure as Christmas comes. — GEORGE OUTRAM.

Sure as is the march of doom. — SANDOR PETŐFI.

Sure as death and taxes are. — "POOR ROBIN'S ALMANACK."

As sure as cold engenders hail. — POPE.

Sure as key of lock. — MATTHEW PRIOR.

As sure as a gun is iron. — OPIE READ.

Sure as the sun rolls up the morn,
Or twilight from eve is born.
— CHARLES SANGSTER.

Sure as bark on a tree. — SHAKESPEARE.

Sure as day. — IBID.

Sure as I live. — IBID.

Sure as I have thought or soul. — IBID.

Sure as God made Moses. — SAM SLICK.

Sure as eggs is eggs. — IBID.

As sure as any gun. — HORACE SMITH.

As sure as wax-candles have wicks. — IBID.

Sure as I hobble on ten toes. — JAMES SMITH.

Sure as night is known from day. — SWINBURNE.

Sure as present pain is. — IBID.

Sure as truth. — IBID.

Sure as sense of beast or bird. — IBID.

Sure as comes the postman and the sun. — THACKERAY.

Sure as creed. — IZAAK WALTON.

Sure as the most certain sure. — WALT WHITMAN.

Sure as brook to run to river. — A. C. WILKE.

As sure as there's a moon in Heaven. — WORDSWORTH.

Sure-footed.

Sure-footed as a goat. — OUIDA.

Surely.

Surely as night is the shadow of the earth. — ANON.

Surely as oxygen eats iron. — IBID.

Surely as that if two men ride a horse, one must ride behind. — IBID.

Surely as the earth is moving in the spheres. — IBID.

Surely as the sea-gull loves the sea, and the sunflower loves the sun. — IBID.

Surely as a fallen stone must fall to its mother earth. — IBID.

Surely as we wish the joys of Heaven. — IBID.

Surely as fame belongs to earth. — R. D. BLACKMORE.

As surely as the internal motions of the watch are indicated on its face. — MARIE G. BROOKS.

Surely as the starry multitude
Is numbered by the sailors.
— ROBERT BROWNING.

Surely as a blind man is pulled by his dog into the butcher's shop. — MAURICE HEWLETT.

Surely as the same sunshine of heaven is on the mountain tops of east and west. — LEIGH HUNT.

Surely as musical ears are pained by a discord. — GEORGE MEREDITH.

Surely as the heavens are mirrored in the quiet seas. — IBID.

Surely as there is hope in man. — DONALD G. MITCHELL.

Surely — *continued.*

Surely as cometh the Winter, I know
There are Spring violets under the snow. — R. H. NEWELL.

Surely as Winter taketh all. — T. BUCHANAN READ.

Surely as the hours came round. — SAMUEL ROGERS.

Surely as the day-star loves the sun. — SWINBURNE.

Surely and as certainly as the hawthorn must blossom in spring and the corn burn to gold at harvest time, and the moon in her ordered wanderings change from shield to sickle, and from sickle to shield. — OSCAR WILDE.

Surge.

Surge, like hope upon a deathbed. — BYRON.

Surging as a sea. — TUPPER.

Surly.

Surly as a butcher's dog. — ANON.

Surpass.

Surpasses, as a teal does a gander; as a coach does a wheelbarrow, or a game-cock a sparrow. — ANON.

Suspense.

Suspense . . . like the irresolution of the sea at turn of tide. — P. J. BAILEY.

Suspicion.

Suspicions amongst thoughts are like bats amongst birds, they ever fly by twilight. — BACON.

Suspicion, like the fabled upas, blights
All healthy life.
— GEORGE W. LOVELL.

Suspicious.

Suspicious as a cat. — BALZAC.

Swallow.

Can . . swallow down sin like water. — BUNYAN.

Swallowed her steps like a pursuing grave. — HOOD.

Swallow . . . as easily as a great pit a small pebble. — LYLY.

Swallowed Persia, as the sand does foam. — SHELLEY.

Swarm.

Swarmed like an ant-hill. — ANON.

Swarmed like bees. — IBID.

Swarming after, as a tail follows a comet. — IBID.

As wasps, provok'd by children in their play,
Pour from their mansions by the broad high-way,
In swarms the guiltless traveller engage,
Whet all their stings, and call forth all their rage:
All rise in arms, and with a gen'ral cry
Assert their waxen domes, and buzzing progeny.
Thus from the tents the fervent legion swarms,
So loud their clamours, and so keen their arms. — HOMER (POPE).

Place swarmed like a fair. — SCHILLER.

Swart.

Swart as the night. — LONGFELLOW.

Swart as the smoke from raging furnace. — SIR WALTER SCOTT.

Swart, like my shoe. — SHAKESPEARE.

Sway.

Swayed like a column in an earthquake. — ANON.

Swaying like a lily. — IBID.

Like a branch she sways with supple ply. — ARABIAN NIGHTS.

Swayed like a flower stalk in a gale. — JOHN D. BARRY.

Swayed like a bird on a twig. — ARNOLD BENNETT.

Sway — *continued.*

Swayed and bent as gracefully as doth a lily-bell, when by the summer zephyr gently kissed. — CARTWRIGHT.

Sway, like a water-plant in a wave. — ALICE CARY.

Swayed at the top like a tree. — JOSEPH CONRAD.

Swayed rhythmically in one direction like a wheatfield in a squall. — SIR A. CONAN DOYLE.

Sway, like a trim galley, at her anchorage between two seas. — F. W. FABER.

Swayed like a river weed. — THOMAS HARDY.

Swayed like a pole in the tideway. — MAURICE HEWLETT.

Swayed . . . as the sling swings its projectile. — HUGO.

Swaying like a reed. — IBID.

Swayed, like grain-fields when the wind breathes over them. — SIGMUND KRASINSKI.

Swaying like wind-swung bell. — GEORGE MACDONALD.

Swaying about like a fat goose with enormous legs and yielding knees. — GUY DE MAUPASSANT.

Sway, as the calm joy of flowers, and living leaves before the wind. — SHELLEY.

Sway'd
Like those long mosses in the stream.
— TENNYSON.

Swayed as the reeds sway in the blast. — WHITTIER.

Swear.

Swear like a freighter. — ANON.

Swear like a costermonger. — IBID.

Swore like a Tartar. — BALZAC.

Swear like a tinker. — THOMAS CORYATE.

Swear like a drunken tapster. — DR. JOHN DORAN.

Swear like a lord. — SIR T. ELYOT.

Swears like an imp. — HUGO.

Swore like a porter. — MACAULAY.

Swore like a preacher's son. — HENRY L. MENCKEN.

Swears like a printing-office foreman and yearns for close quarters with a knife. — IBID.

Swear like a comfit-maker's wife. — SHAKESPEARE.

Swore like any trooper. — SOUTHEY.

Sweat.

Sweat like Cits in May-day Coaches. — APHRA BEHN.

Sweating like a porous pitcher. — MAURICE HEWLETT.

Sweating like a pitcher with ice-water in it. — WILLIAM T. PORTER'S "TALES OF THE SOUTHWEST."

Sweep.

Sweep like a simoon. — ANON.

Sweeps . . . along, like the broad volume of the insurgent Nile. — MATTHEW ARNOLD.

Sweep around . . . like angered eagles cheated of their prey. — P. J. BAILEY.

Swept . . . like sullying cloud from pure blue sky. — CHARLOTTE BRONTË.

Sweep like wolves on a lambkin. — T. D. BROWN.

Swept in like tides of Fundy. — F. T. BROWNE.

Sweep like a sea, barred out from land. — ROBERT BROWNING.

Swept like surge, i' the simile
Of Homer. — IBID.

Sweep, like currents journeying through the windless deep. — WILLIAM CULLEN BRYANT.

Sweep — *continued.*

Swept . . . like leaves before the autumn gale. — Ibid.

Swept . . . like ocean-tides uprising at the call of tyrant winds. — Ibid.

Sweeping along like the Huns. — Stephen Crane.

They swept him out of the street, as a fire-hose flushes the gutter. — Richard Harding Davis.

Like chain-shot, sweeps all things in its way. — Dryden.

Sweeps like spectral shade. — Goethe.

Swept like a tempestuous sea. — Hawthorne.

Sweeping like rivers that seek the main. — Hood.

Sweeping the country like locust-swarm. — Ouida.

Sweep like a wing'd will. — Emily Pfeiffer.

Sweep like bitter Nor'land gales. — T. Buchanan Read.

Sweep as the tempest o'er the deep. — Schiller.

Swept the lists like an Egypt's plague of locusts. — Owen Seaman.

Sweep it away like a leaf before a hurricane. — G. B. Shaw.

Swept
Like waves before the tempest.
— Shelley.

Swept
As storm across his soul that kept
Wild watch, and watched not well.
— Swinburne.

Swept like a torrent. — Tennyson.

Swept like a conquering army through my blood. — Louis Untermeyer.

Swept
As by a plague. — Wordsworth.

Sweet.

Sweet as odorous white lilies are. — Oscar Fay Adams.

Sweet as new-blown rose. — Thomas Adams.

Sweet as fresh fount to thirsty wanderer. — Æschylus.

Sweet as a girl graduate. — Anon.

Sweet as a nut. — Ibid.

Sweet as the infant spring. — Ibid.

Sweet as a rose. — Ibid.

Sweet and wholesome as a sprig of mignonette. — Ibid.

Sweet as a sugar plum. — Ibid.

Sweet as a vial of rose oil. — Ibid.

Kiss as sweet,
As cool fresh stream to bruised and
weary feet. — Ibid.

Sweet as honey bee. — Ibid.

Sweet as honeysuckle. — Ibid.

Sweet as lilies in May. — Ibid.

As sweet as spring's first song heard in the grove's retreat. — Ibid.

Sweet as sugar. — Ibid.

Sweet as the cup of Circe. — Ibid.

Sweet as the harmonies of Spring. — Ibid.

Sweet as the liquid notes of a plover. — Ibid.

Sweet as the notes of a fountain. — Ibid.

Sweet as the perfume of roses. — Ibid.

Faintly sweet as the reapers hear a lark afar in the sky. — Ibid.

Sweet as the solemn sounds of cherubs, when they strike their golden harps. — Ibid.

Sweet as unblown hawthorn buds. — Ibid.

Sweet as maidens deckt and dight. — Arabian Nights.

Sweet — *continued.*

Sweet as that which is forbidden. — Arabic.

Sweet as the last smile of sunset. — Edwin Arnold.

Sweeter than the comb its sweetness. — Ibid.

Sweet as the honeyed dews that drip from the budding lotus-flower. — George Arnold.

Sweet and calm as is a sister's kiss. — P. J. Bailey.

Sweete as the infant spring. — Scottish Ballad.

Sweet as the joy which sorrow hushes. — Balzac.

Sweet as new wine. — John Baret.

Sweet
As where smooth Zephyrus plays on the fleet
Face of the curled streams.
— Francis Beaumont.

Sweet as applause to the actor. — Beaumont and Fletcher.

As sweet as April. — Ibid.

Sweet as the Spring. — Ibid.

Sweet as the moonlight sleeping on the hills. — Sir William S. Bennett.

Sweet as the light of the stars. — Robert Hugh Benson.

Sweet as the look of a lover saluting the eyes of a maid. — Ambrose Bierce.

Sweet as odour of the upland thyme. — Mathilde Blind.

As sweet as perfumed shroud which the gay Roman maidens sewed for English Keats. — E. B. Browning.

As sweet as window-eglantine. — Ibid.

Sweet, as when winter storms have ceased to chide. — Bryant.

Sweeter than all perfumes. — Bunyan.

Sweet as the dewy milk-white thorn. — Burns.

Sweet as yon hawthorn's blossom. — Ibid.

Sweet as matrimony. — Robert Burton.

Sounds sweet as if a sister's voice reproved. — Byron.

Sweet as May. — Thomas Carew.

Sweet as the sundown. — Bliss Carman.

Sweet as the song of the wind in the rippling wheat. — Madison Cawein.

Sweet as the warbles of the vocal woods. — James Cawthorn.

Sweet as the voice of thraslarks [Thrushes] in the spring. — Chatterton.

Sweete as is the brembul-flour
That bereth the rede hepe [Fruit of the dog rose]. — Chaucer.

Sweet as pity. — Hartley Coleridge.

Sweet as the whispered breeze of evening. — Coleridge.

As sweet as Western wind breathes from the violets' fragrant beds. — J. G. Cooper.

Sweet as the hopes on which starv'd lovers feed. — Sir William Davenant.

Sweet as aerial chimes
Of flower-bells.
— John Davidson.

Sweet as sails in summer sky. — Lord De Tabley.

Sweet as some immeasurable rose, expanding leaf on leaf. — Aubrey De Vere.

Sweet as Anadyomene rising from the sea. — Dr. John Doran.

Sweet — *continued.*

Sweet as are the orchards, when the fruit is hanging ripe. — PAUL LAURENCE DUNBAR.

Sweet as the murmur of the brook and the rustle of the corn. — EMERSON.

Serenely sweet as vernal air. — FALCONER.

As sweet as a violet. — JOHN FORD.

Sweet . . . as the new-mown hay. — W. S. GILBERT.

Sweet as the vernal flow'r in early prime. — RICHARD GLOVER.

Sweet as the rosy morn in May. — GEORGE GRANVILLE.

Sweet as a youthful poet's dream. — CHARLES GRAY.

Sweet as the harps that hung by Babel's stream. — JUDAH HALEVI.

Sweet as summer days that die when the months are in the bloom. — W. W. HARNEY.

Sweet as tropic winds at night. — P. H. HAYNE.

Sweet as the blossoms of the vine. — ROBERT HERRICK.

Sweet as vestry of the oracles. — IBID.

Sweet as the sweetest song of bird on summer's eve. — D. M. HERVEY.

As sweet as dewy turf to wayworn feet. — EMILY H. HICKEY.

Sweet as new-blown breath of opening flow'rs. — AARON HILL.

Sweet
As a meadow at noon.
— KATHERINE TYNAN HINKSON.

Sweet as the breath from an odalisque's fan. — O. W. HOLMES.

Sweet as the dawn star. — IBID.

Sweet as the first snow-drop, which the sunbeams greet. — IBID.

Sweet as honey. — HOMER (POPE).

Sweet as scarlet strawberry under wet leaves hidden. — NORA HOPPER.

Sweet as the hills. — RICHARD HOVEY.

Sweet as a rosebud crowned with moss. — HUGO.

Sweet as music. — IBID.

Sweet as the twilight notes of the thrush. — HELEN H. JACKSON.

Sweet as jasmine. — JAMI.

Sweet as the morning of life. — IBID.

Sweet as drops of balme. — BEN JONSON.

Sweet as a muskrose upon new-made hay. — KEATS.

Sweet as blue heavens o'er enchanted isles. — IBID.

Sweet as love. — IBID.

Sweeter than the rill
To its old channel. — IBID.

Sweet as a cat with syrup in its paws. — VAUGHAN KESTER.

Sweet as mountain honey. — KINGSLEY.

Sweet as the sigh of the spring gale. — MISS LANDON.

As sweet as a woman's flashing eye. — "LAYS OF ANCIENT INDIA."

Sweet . . . as the sad spirit of the evening breezes. — EMMA LAZARUS.

Sweet as the sound of bells at evening. — RICHARD LE GALLIENNE.

Sweet as a bell in the woods. — AMY LESLIE.

Sweet as morning dew upon a rose. — THOMAS LODGE.

Sweet as the cadence of a poet's song. — JOHN LOGAN.

Sweet was her breath as the breath of kine that feed in the meadows. — LONGFELLOW.

Sweet — *continued.*

Sweet as the songs of Sappho. — Charles B. Loomis.

Sweet as heaven's image in an unrippled lake. — George W. Lovell.

Sweet as over new-born son the croon of new-made mother. — Lowell.

Sweet as the sweet tooth of a calfe. — Lyly.

Sweet as the dew-drops of a wild rose. — Edward Lysaght.

Sweet as summer's showers. — George Mac-Henry.

Sweet as seraph's bliss. — Walter Malone.

Sweet as first love. — Gerald Massey.

Sweet as first spring violets. — Ibid.

Sweet as Eden. — George Meredith.

Sweet as victory half-revealed. — Ibid.

A secret sweet as songs of dawn
That linnets sing when mists are gone.
— R. M. Milnes.

Sweet as Angel accents. — James Montgomery.

Nothing half so sweet in life as Love's young dream. — Thomas Moore.

As sweet as the rose-scented zephyr those do meet who near the happy islands of the blest. — William Morris.

Sweet as every-day sunshine. — John Muir.

Sweet, like an angel's sigh. — Mary R. Murphy.

Sweet as the shepherd's pipe upon the mountains. — Otway.

Sweet, like a silver whistle. — Ouida.

Sweet as the morning air. — Benjamin F. Parker.

Sweet and white
As the most heretofore sin-spotted
Soul. — Coventry Patmore.

Sweet as violet-borders growing over fountains over-flowing. — Ambrose Philips.

As sweet as mown grass in the even. — Stephen Phillips.

Sweet as the melody of swans, that lave their nestling pinions in the silver wave. — Pratinas.

Music sweeter than the sweetest chime of magic bells by fairies set a-swinging. — T. Buchanan Read.

Sweet as blossoms after rain. — Lizette W. Reese.

Sweet as the dew's lip to the rose's. — James Whitcomb Riley.

As sweet as the life of the lily. — Ibid.

As sweet as the soul of a babe. — Ibid.

Sweet as smiles to the lips that are pale. — A. J. Ryan.

Sweet as the dew-drops that fall on the roses in May. — Ibid.

Sweet as the Summer's birds. — Ibid.

Sweet as the dreamings of the nightingales. — Charles Sangster.

Sweet as the note of a nightingale. — Sanskrit.

Sweet as Flora's favorite flower. — James Scadlock.

Sweet are the uses of adversity,
Which, like the toad, ugly and venomous,
Wears yet a precious jewel in his head.
— Shakespeare.

Sweet as balm. — Ibid.

Sweet, and musical,
As bright Apollo's lute. — Ibid.

Sweet as damask roses. — Ibid.

Sweet as ditties highly penn'd,
Sung by a fair queen in a summer's bower. — Ibid.

Sweet — *continued.*

Sweet as spring-time flowers. — Ibid.

Sweeter than the lids of Juno's
eyes,
Or Cytherea's breath. — Ibid.

Sweet as a summer night without a breath. — Shelley.

Sweet as if angels sang. — Ibid.

Her looks were sweet as Heaven's when loveliest in Autumn eves. — Ibid.

Sweet as the blossom is sweet. — F. D. Sherman.

More sweet than the honey of the Hybla bees. — Smollett.

Sweet as the songs of homestead birds. — E. C. Stedman.

Sweet-hearted as a bird that takes the
sun
With clear strong eyes and feels the
glad god run
Bright through his blood and wide
rejoicing wings,
And opens all himself to heaven and
sings. — Swinburne.

Sweet as April-clouded skies. — Ibid.

Sweet as a child's heart-lightening laugh to hear. — Ibid.

Sweet-souled as a dove. — Ibid.

Sweet as all the wide sweet south. — Ibid.

Sweet as death-annihilating song. — Ibid.

Sweet as dream's delight. — Ibid.

Sweet and comely as a dove's throat strained out to sing. — Ibid.

Sweet as early kisses of a mouth
Scented like honey. — Ibid.

Sweet as hope's first note of jubilation. — Ibid.

Sweet as life or death can be. — Ibid.

Sweet as rest. — Ibid.

Sweet
As running streams to men's way-
wearied feet. — Ibid.

Sweet as sleep on sorrow shed. — Ibid.

Sweet as sound the moving wings of night. — Ibid.

Sweet and good as summer air. — Ibid.

Sweet as forgiveness. — Ibid.

Sweet as night's dim dawn to weariness. — Ibid.

Sweet as the balm of sleep. — Ibid.

Sweet as the change that leaves the world in flower when spring laughs winter down to deathward. — Ibid.

Sweet as the dewfall. — Ibid.

Sweet as the flower that itself is May. — Ibid.

Sweet as the kiss wherewith sleep kisses pain. — Ibid.

Sweet as the spasm of erotic emotional error. — Ibid.

Sweet as the winds that beat
Round banks where Tyne is born.
— Ibid.

Sweet as when earth was new. — Ibid.

Sweet as when
Laughs a child of seven.
— Ibid.

A sound more sweet than April's flower-sweet rain. — Ibid.

Sweeter than joy-bells ringing. — Ibid.

Sweet as the voice of a mountain brook. — Arthur Symons.

Sweet as the blushing planet of the dawn. — Ibid.

Sweet as a vesper chime. — B. F Taylor.

Sweet — *continued.*

Songs of love are sweeter than Bassora's nightingales. — BAYARD TAYLOR.

Sweet as a morn of Paradise. — IBID.

Sweet as children's prattle. — PAMELA TENNANT.

Sweet as new buds in spring. — TENNYSON.

Sweet as honey. — NEW TESTAMENT.

Sweeter than honey to my mouth. — IBID.

Sweet as the apple-blossoms. — CELIA THAXTER.

Sweet and fresh
As the flower-skirted streams of Staffordshire. — IBID.

Sweet as the music of Apollo's lyre. — IBID.

Sweet, as when Venus and Love went hand in hand. — MAURICE THOMPSON.

Sweet as the early pipe along the dale. — WILLIAM THOMSON.

Sweeter than the waters of the Nile. — TUPPER.

Sweet as the dawn star. — WILBUR UNDERWOOD.

Sweet as regret. — MARIE VAN VORST.

Sweet is your strain to my ears, heavenly poet, as is sleep to tired limbs on the grass, as is the quenching of thirst in mid-day heat in the stream where sweet waters play. — VIRGIL.

Tinkling bell-notes falling sweet and cold as a stream's cadence, while a skylark sings high in the blue. — ROSAMUND MARRIOTT WATSON.

Sweet as the maiden's dream of love. — WHITTIER.

Music as sweet as the music which seems
Breathed softly and faint in the ear of our dreams. — IBID.

Sweeter than the song of birds,
Is the thankful voice. — IBID.

A voice sweet as an angel's. — N. P. WILLIS.

Sweet and joyful as the earliest note of the brown brilliant harbinger of spring. — C. P. WILSON.

Sweet as the faint, far-off, celestial tone of angel whispers, fluttering from on high. — WILLIAM WINTER.

Sweet as the lips that once you pressed. — IBID.

Sweet as morning fragrance shed
From flowers. — WORDSWORTH.

Sweet as the head of your cane. — WYCHERLEY.

Swell.

Swells as the poised ocean to the attracting moon obedient swells. — AKENSIDE.

Swells like an angry hen ruffling her feathers. — ANON.

Swelling like a tragic organ note. — IBID.

Swells like mushrooms. — IBID.

Swelled like the gourd. — IBID.

Voice swells up like mutter'd thunder. — BYRON.

Hearts swelling in presence of the Queen of Hearts ; like the sea swelling when once near its moon. — CARLYLE.

Swellynge like bubbles in a boillynge welle. — CHATTERTON.

His voice swelled like a sanctus rising from the choir of a cathedral. — DE QUINCEY.

Swell like a corporation which has been attached to a hose. — GEORGE FITCH.

Swelled like a sail by the sea-breeze. — FLAUBERT.

Swell — *continued.*

Swell like bubbles, shine and break. — John Gay.

Swells like a filthy toad with secret spite. — William Gifford.

Swelling like a torrent. — George Granville.

Swelled, like toad that meets disaster. — Lemuel Hopkins.

Swell like a boil. — Ben Jonson.

Swells like the chant of serenader or the chimes of silver bells. — A. B. Meek.

Swelling on
Like the waves of eternity.
— Thomas Moore.

Swell up like a stock company leading man. — George Jean Nathan.

Swelled like a psalm. — J. N. Paton.

Swell, like round and orient pearls. — Shakespeare.

Swells like a sail before a favouring breeze. — Shelley.

Swell like a shirt bleaching in high wind. — John Tobin.

Swells like the bosom of a man set free. — Wordsworth.

Swerve.

Swerved as from a blow. — Byron.

Swift.

As the breezes swift. — Thomas Aird.

Swift as the lightning flash. — Akenside.

Swift as a cannon ball. — Anon.

Swift as fate. — Ibid.

Swift as kindling flames arise. — Ibid.

Swift as the glance of a falling star. — Ibid.

Swifter than fleeing Daphne's twinkling feet. — Ibid.

Swift as the steed that feels the slackened rein. — Ibid.

Swift like a simoon of the desert. — Ibid.

Swifter than the falcon. — Max Beerbohm.

Swift as a sun-beam. — Thomas Blacklock.

Swift as the summer lightning. — R. D. Blackmore.

Swift as arrow. — William Blake.

Swift as the eye can mark. — H. H. Brownell.

Swift as Jove's lightning. — William Byrd.

Swift almost as a human smile may chase
A frown from some conciliated face.
— Calderon.

Swefte as descendeynge lemes [rays] of roddie lyghte plonged to the hulstred [secret] bedde of loveynge [washing] seas. — Chatterton.

Swefte as a feether'd takel [Arrow]. — Ibid.

Swefte as my wyshe. — Ibid.

Swift as the flying clouds distilling rain. — Ibid.

Swefte as the rayne-storme toe the erthe alyghtes. — Ibid.

Swefte, as the rayne uponne an Aprylle daie. — Ibid.

Swefte as the roareynge wyndes. — Ibid.

Swift as fowel in flight. — Chaucer.

As swifte as pelet out of gonne. — Ibid.

Swift as a spirit. — Coleridge.

Swift as dreams. — Ibid.

Swift as a sun ray. — Eliza Cook.

Swift as a lover's dreams. — Barry Cornwall.

Swift — *continued.*

Swift as Care. — NATHANIEL COTTON.

As swift and fierce as tempest from the north. — ABRAHAM COWLEY.

Swift as the wings of Morn. — IBID.

Swifter than a shadow flee. — COWPER.

Swift as a star falls through the night. — GEORGE DARLEY.

Swift as a sunshot dart of light. — IBID.

Swift as a whirlwind. — THOMAS DEKKER.

Swift as dead leaves by tempest borne. — AUBREY DE VERE.

Swift as the scattered clouds on high. — ALFRED DOMETT.

As swift as the glance of the arrowy
lance
That the storm spirit flings from high.
— JOSEPH R. DRAKE.

Swift as the wings of sound. — GEORGE ELIOT.

A swift movement, which was like a chained up resolution set free at last. — IBID.

Swift as fate. — PHILIP FRENEAU.

Swift as vision. — GOETHE.

Swift as the flight of lightning through the air. — WILLIAM HARBINGTON.

Swift as a flood of fire. — HOMER (POPE).

Swift as the vulture leaping on his prey. — IBID.

Swift as the wind. — IBID.

Swift as a swallow heading south. — LAURENCE HOPE.

Swifter than the rush of wind
That lifts the sea-gull off the lake.
— DOUGLAS HYDE.

Swift as a star. — SIR WILLIAM JONES.

Swift as a fathoming plummet down he fell. — KEATS.

As swift
As bird on wing to breast its eggs
again. — IBID.

Swift as fairy thought. — IBID.

Swifter than centaurs after rapine bent. — IBID.

Swifter than sight. — IBID.

Swift as the cloven tongues of Pentecost. — H. E. HAMILTON KING.

Flies as swift as shafts the bowmen pour. — ANDREW LANG.

Swift as the lightning's rapid flame darts on the unsuspecting sight. — JOHN LANGHORNE.

Swift as a flash. — LONGFELLOW.

Swift as the thunderbolt. — RICHARD LOVELACE.

Swift as the sea-bird's wing.—LOVER.

Swift as runs a wind-wave over grass. — GERALD MASSEY.

Swift as a blush in the cheeks of seventeen. — GEORGE MEREDITH.

Swift as the lightning glance. — MILTON.

Swift as the sparkle of a glancing star. — IBID.

Swift as Death's own arrows dart. — JAMES MONTGOMERY.

Swifter than the frighted dove. — IBID.

Fly swifter than light. — MISS MULOCK.

Swift as mercury. — THOMAS NASH.

Swift, like some fierce bird of prey. — ROBERT POLLOK.

Swift as an arrow soaring from the bow. — ALEXANDER POPE.

Swift as a cloud gust-driven from the sun. — T. BUCHANAN READ.

Swift as a shadow o'er the meadow grass chased by the sunshine. — IBID.

Swift — *continued.*

Swift as signal fires. — Ibid.

Swift as memory. — Edouard Rod.

Swift as the fleeting shades upon the golden corn. — Nicholas Rowe.

Swift as a hawk. — Charles Sangster.

Like a sunbeam, swift. — Sir Walter Scott.

Swift as a shadow. — Shakespeare.

Swift as breathed stags. — Ibid.

Swift as frenzy's thoughts. — Ibid.

Swift as lead. — Ibid.

As swift
As meditation, or the thoughts of love.
— Ibid.

Swift as quicksilver. — Ibid.

Swift as stones
Enforced from the old Assyrian slings.
— Ibid.

Swifter than arrow from the Tartar's bow. — Ibid.

Swift as thought. — Ibid.

Swift in motion as a ball. — Ibid.

Swifter than he that gibbets on the brewer's bucket. — Ibid.

Swifter than the moon's sphere. — Ibid.

Swift as a cloud between the sea and sky. — Shelley.

Swift as fire. — Ibid.

Swift as greyhounds. — Ibid.

Swift as leaves on autumn's tempest shed. — Ibid.

Swift as smoke from a volcano springs. — Ibid.

Swift as twinkling beams. — Ibid.

Swifter than summer's flight. — Ibid.

Swifter than youth's delight. — Ibid.

Swift as a beam of morning. — Elizabeth S. Sheppard.

Swift as an arrow in its flight. — Southey.

Swift as a falling meteor. — Ibid.

Swift as the bittern soars on spiral wing. — Ibid.

Swift away like fabrics in the summer's clouds. — Ibid.

Swift as any bucke in chace. — Spenser.

More swift than Myrrh' or Daphne in her race. — Ibid.

Swift as the flame devours the crackling wood. — Statius.

Swift as the headlong torrents of a flood. — Ibid.

Swift as a passing bird. — Robert Louis Stevenson.

Swift and steadfast as a sea-mew's wing. — Swinburne.

Swift as a shadow. — Ibid.

Swift as eternity. — Arthur Symons.

As swift as fiery lightning kindled new. — Tasso.

As swift as the eagle flieth. — Old Testament.

As swift as the roes upon the mountains. — Ibid.

Swift as the waters. — Ibid.

Swifter than a weaver's shuttle. — Ibid.

Swifter than the eagles of the heaven. — Ibid.

Now my days are swifter than a post: they flee away, they see no good. — Ibid.

Swift as desire. — Thomas Tickell.

Swift as the motions of desire. — Isaac Watts.

Swift as the Polar breeze. — H. K. White.

Swift as the eagle's glance of fire. — Whittier.

Swift — *continued.*

Swift as a rocketing woodcock. — HARRY LEON WILSON.

Swift as a Thracian Nymph o'er field and height. — WORDSWORTH.

Swift as darted flame. — YOUNG.

Swiftly.

As swiftly as a reach of still water is crisped by the wind. — ANON.

Swiftly like a cloud scud on a breezy day. — SIR A. CONAN DOYLE.

Swiftly as the explosion of a rifle cartridge follows the falling of the hammer. — ROBERT EDGREN.

Swiftly as smiles are caught in looks that meet. — GEORGE ELIOT.

Swiftly as the dolphins glide. — HOOD.

Swiftly as a bright Phœbean dart. — KEATS.

Swiftly, like birds that skim the air. — MAHABHARATA.

Swim.

Swim like a cork. — INCREASE MATHER.

Swims, like an eagle, in the eye of noon. — JAMES MONTGOMERY.

Swim like a duck. — SHAKESPEARE.

Swim like beams through floating clouds. — SHELLEY.

Swimmingly.

Go on as swimmingly as old Noah's Ark. — HOOD.

Swing.

Like rudder to the ripple veering,
When nobody on board is steering.
— HOOD.

Swinging like a reed in the air. — HUGO.

Swing like the compass in its brazen ring. — LONGFELLOW.

Swish.

Swished his tail,
As a gentleman swishes a cane.
— SOUTHEY.

Swollen.

Swollen as the cheeks of jubilant cherubim. — O. W. HOLMES.

Swollen immensely, like that of a man who has been drowned and lain under water for many weeks. — POE.

Swollen like a bladder. — R. B. SHERIDAN.

Swoon.

Sickly swoon, like lillies 'mid the blaze of noon. — SARA COLERIDGE.

Swoon like spring's daffodillies.
— ITALIAN LOVE SONG.

Swoon
Into the silence languidly
As a tune into a tune.
— D. G. ROSSETTI.

Made my blood burn and swoon
Like a flame rained upon.
— SWINBURNE.

Swoop.

Swooped down upon the kitchen, even as a vulture swoopeth upon carrion. — BOCCACCIO.

Swooped into the fray like a sea-eagle into a school of mackerel in a shallow. — MAURICE HEWLETT.

Sympathetic.

A sympathetic heart is like a spring of pure water bursting forth from the mountain side. — ANON.

Sympathetic as sentiment. — LAMARTINE.

Sympathetic as chameleons. — AMY LESLIE.

Symphony.

Delicious symphonies, like airy flowers,
Budded and swell'd, and, full-blown, shed full showers
Of light, soft, unseen leaves of sounds divine.
— KEATS.

Systematic.

Systematic as a country cemetery. — LOWELL.

T

Talent.

A man of great talents, but void of discretion, is like Polyphemus in the fable, strong and blind, endowed with an irresistible force, which for want of sight is of no use to him. — ADDISON.

Talent, like gout, sometimes skips two generations. — BALZAC.

Men of talents are variable as thermometers : genius alone is essentially good. — IBID.

Talent, like beauty, to be pardoned, must be obscure and unostentatious. — LADY BLESSINGTON.

Talk.

(*See also* CONVERSATION.)

Fish are talkative in comparison. — ANON.

Talkative as a magpie. — IBID.

Like a bagpipe, he never talks till his belly's full. — IBID.

All talking and no listening, after the manner of a Woman's Rights Convention. — J. R. BARTLETT'S "DICTIONARY OF AMERICANISMS."

Talk like poor Poll [Goldsmith]. — DAVID GARRICK.

Talking is like playing on the harp ; there is as much in laying the hand on the strings to stop a vibration as in twanging them to bring out their music. — O. W. HOLMES.

Writing or printing is like shooting with a rifle ; you may hit your reader's mind or miss it ; — but talking is like playing at a mark with the pipe of an engine ; if it is within reach, and you have time enough, you can't help hitting it. — IBID.

There are men of *esprit* who are excessively exhausting to some people. They are the talkers that have what may be called jerky minds. Their thoughts do not run in the natural order of sequence. They say bright things on all possible subjects, but their zigzags rack you to death. After a jolting half-hour with one of these jerky companions, talking with a dull friend affords great relief. It is like taking the cat in your lap after holding a squirrel. — IBID.

Talk without truth is hollow brass ; talk without love is like the tinkling cymbal, and when it does not tinkle it jingles, and when it does not jingle, it jars. — MRS. JAMESON.

He talks as a piano-organ grinds out music — steadily, strenuously, tirelessly. — J. K. JEROME.

Talking away like a mill-clapper. — SARAH ORNE JEWETT.

Talks like music set on fire. — RICHARD LE GALLIENNE.

His talk is like a stream which runs
With rapid change from rocks to roses ;
It slipped from politics to puns ;
It passed from Mahomet to Moses ;
Beginning with the laws that keep
The planets in their radiant courses,
And ending with some precept deep
For dressing eels or shoeing horses.
— PRAED.

Great talkers are like broken pitchers, everything runs out of them. — PERSIAN PROVERBS.

Talks like a knell, and his hum is a battery. — SHAKESPEARE.

A talkative person is like an English sparrow, — a bird that cannot sing, and will, and ought to be persuaded not to try to sing. — HENRY VAN DYKE.

Tall.

Tall and slender like an ode in quinary verses. — EDMONDO DE AMICIS.

Tall as a steeple. — ANON.

Tall as a May-pole. — SWIFT.

Tall — *continued.*

Tall as a figure lengthened on the sand. — TENNYSON.

Tall as a grenadier. — THACKERAY.

Tame.

Tame as a kitchen cat on a house-boat. — ANON.

Tame as tepid milk. — ARLO BATES.

Tame and humble, like a child that's whipp'd. — ROBERT BLAIR.

She lies in my hand as tame
As a pear late basking over a wall.
— ROBERT BROWNING.

Tame, as an lilye whyt. — CHAUCER.

Tame as a sheep. — THOMAS FROST.

Tame as a cat. — WILLIAM KING.

Tamer than sleep. — SHAKESPEARE.

Tangle.

Tangled in the Past, like a bird in a snare. — HUGO.

Tantalize.

The rattling of dice is as tantalizing to a penniless man as the sound of drums to a dethroned monarch. — SANSKRIT.

Tap.

Tapping like woodpeckers. — HOOD.

Taps light
As the hand of my heart's delight.
— SWINBURNE.

Taper.

Tapering, like an icicle. — ANON.

Tapering like a lizard's tail. — O. W. HOLMES.

Tarry.

Tarries . . . like quicksilver in a mould of lapis lazuli. — PILPAY.

Tart.

Tart and crisp . . . as the autumn butter that creams the sumac berry. — MARK TWAIN.

Taste (Noun).

As bad taste as a wig from the barber's on the head of a marble statue of Apollo. — BULWER-LYTTON.

Left a taste in his mouth like a tin-type factory. — IRVIN S. COBB.

A fastidious taste is like a squeamish appetite ; the one has its origin in some disease of the mind, as the other has in some ailment of the stomach. — SOUTHEY.

Taste (Verb).

Mouth tasted as if a Chinese family had just moved out. — ANON.

My mouth tastes like a rusty cent. — "KNICKERBOCKER MAGAZINE."

Taunts.

Taunts, like Vulcan out of heaven. — WORDSWORTH.

Taut.

Taut as a fiddle string. — ANON.

Taut as a forestay in a gale. — ALBERT EDWARDS.

Teacher.

The teacher is like the candle, it lights others in consuming itself. — HOSEA BALLOU.

Tear.

Tears of joy, like summer raindrops, are pierced by sunbeams. — HOSEA BALLOU.

Pearly tears, like rose's dew, wept she. — EMANUAL VON GEIBEL.

Sheds ceaseless tears, like dew on Hermon's hill. — JUDAH HALEVI.

Tearful and trembling as a dewy rose
The wind has shaken till it fills the air
With light and fragrance.
— O. W. HOLMES.

Tears like pears. — HUGO.

Tears herald smiles, as weeping April does this sunny May. — JAMES M. MORTON.

Tear — *continued.*

From his eyes a stream of tears descended like a broken necklace of pearls. — ORIENTAL.

Shining through tears, like April-suns in showers, that labor to o'ercome the cloud that loads them. — OTWAY.

Tears as big as ostrich's eggs. — RABELAIS.

Then fresh tears
Stood on her cheeks, as doth the honey-dew
Upon a gather'd lily almost wither'd.
— SHAKESPEARE.

Tears . . . shone as the dew on a lily, at the rising of the sun. — HERSART DE LA VILLEMARQUÉ.

Her tears, like drops of molten lead,
With torrents burn the passage to my heart.
—EDWARD YOUNG.

Tedious.

Tedious a task for the mind as oakum-picking or stone-breaking can be for the body. — ARTHUR ACHESON.

Tedious as a twice-told tale. — HOMER.

Tedious and dull as truth. — HENRY MACKENZIE.

Tedious as dull sorrows. — MASSINGER.

Tedious as a king. — SHAKESPEARE.

Tedious
As a tired horse, a railing wife.
— IBID.

So tedious is this day,
As is the night before some festival
To an impatient child, that hath new robes,
And may not wear them. — IBID.

As tedious as a guilty conscience. — CYRIL TOURNEUR.

Teeth.

Those cherries fairly do enclose
Of orient pearl a double row;
Which when her lovely laughter shows,
They look like rosebuds filled with snow.
— RICHARD ALISON.

Teeth, as the gourd's white seed. — ANON.

Teeth like string pearls in carceneto of gold. — ARABIAN NIGHTS.

Teeth like the tusks of jinni who frightened poultry in henhouses. — IBID.

Teeth
Like pearls a merchant picks to make a string. — EDWIN ARNOLD.

Her teeth were like pearls array'd in order. — SERVIAN BALLAD.

Her teeth are like a flock of sheep,
With fleeces newly washen clean,
That slowly mount the rising steep.
— BURNS.

Teeth like falling snow
For white, were placed in a double row. — COWLEY.

A girl with teeth like the pieces of broken glass people put on their walls. — EDMOND AND JULES DE GONCOURT.

White teeth showing like pearls dropped in a rose. — ADAMS S. HILL.

Thy teeth like rows of Kunda-petals. — JAYADEVA.

Red like lips disclosing
Twin rows of fairy pearl.
— LEWIS MORRIS.

Teeth serve as a fence to the mouth. — WEST AFRICAN PROVERB.

Teeth like ivory mixed with pearl. — CHARLES READE.

Thy teeth resemble stringed jewels; but how can I liken them to lifeless pearls? — "ROMANCE OF ANTAR."

Thy teeth are like a flock of sheep that are even shorn, which came up from the washing; whereof every one bear twins, and none is barren among them. — OLD TESTAMENT.

Teeth — *continued.*

Her teeth like pomegranate grains. — "VIKRAM AND THE VAMPIRE."

Tell-Tale.

Tell-tale as a register of birth. — BALZAC.

Temper.

Good temper, like a sunny day, sheds a brightness over everything; it is the sweetener of toil and the soother of disquietude. — WASHINGTON IRVING.

Temperate.

Temperate as the morn. — SHAKESPEARE.

Tempestuous.

Tempestuous as a hurricane out of heaven. — EDMOND SCHERER.

Temple.

Thy temples are like a piece of a pomegranate within thy locks. — OLD TESTAMENT.

Tempt.

And as a bird each fond endearment tries,
To tempt its new-pledg'd offspring to the skies,
He tried each art, reprov'd each dull delay,
Allur'd to brighter worlds, and led the way. — GOLDSMITH.

Temptations.

Temptations, when we meet them at first, are as the lion that roared upon Samson; but if we overcome them, the next time we see them we shall find a nest of honey within them.— BUNYAN.

Temptations, like misfortunes, are sent to test our moral strength. — MARGUERITE DE VALOIS.

Tempting.

Tempting as a barmaid. — ANON.

Tempting as a paradox. — IBID.

Tempting as a baked apple dumpling. — IBID.

Tempting as Eve without a fig leaf. — IBID.

Tempting as any fresh cowslip of spring. — ELIZA COOK.

Tenacious.

Grasp tenacious as a viper's. — SWINBURNE.

More tenacious than birdlime or than the pitch of Phrygian Ida. — VIRGIL.

Tender.

Tender as a bud. — ANON.

Tender as a capon. — IBID.

Tender as a woman. — IBID.

As tender as the murmur of the rain when great clouds gather. — EDWIN ARNOLD.

Tender as the midnight moon. — ALFRED AUSTIN.

Buds tenderly . . . Like a smile striving with a wrinkled face. — ROBERT BROWNING.

He is as tender of his clothes, as a coward is of his flesh, and as loath to have them disordered. — SAMUEL BUTLER.

Tender light, like the first moonrise of midnight. — BYRON.

Tender as April twilight. — BLISS CARMAN.

Tendre as dewe of flouer. — CHAUCER.

Tendre as is a chicke. — IBID.

Tender as a fond young lover's dream. — JOHN CUNNINGHAM.

Tender as a lamb. — DICKENS.

Tender as russet crimson dropt on snows. — JEAN INGELOW.

Tender as the breast of a mother. — R. G. INGERSOLL.

Tender as a summer night. — LONGFELLOW.

Tender — *continued.*

Tender, as if it twinned with sorrow. — HENRY MACKENZIE.

Tender as a summer heaven. — GERALD MASSEY.

Tender, like a mother's dream of her child. — GEORGE MEREDITH.

Tender as a woman when wounds should be staunched for the broken and ruined and routed. — RICHARD REALF.

Tender as dawn's first hill-fire. — C. G. ROSSETTI.

Tender as infancy and grace. — SHAKESPEARE.

Tender as a youthful mother's joy. — SOUTHEY.

Tender as a hurt bird's note. — SWINBURNE.

Tender as tears. — IBID.

Tender as sun-smitten dew. — IBID.

Tender as the inside of the eyelid. — IBID.

Tender as love's tear when youth and beauty die. — WILLIAM WINTER.

Tenderly.

Tenderly, as round the sleeping infant's feet,
We softly fold the cradle-sheet.
— WILLIAM CULLEN BRYANT.

Tenderly as lovers may
Who know the breaking dawn will be their wedding day.
— MARY A. DE VERE.

Tenderly as Robin Redbreast covered the dead babes with forest leaves. — HAWTHORNE.

Tenderly, as a mother might kiss a hot, impulsive child trying to still a restless spirit within. — ROBERT HERRICK (American).

Tenderly . . . like the song of the robin in the tree. — W. D. HOWELLS.

Tenderly, like one that leads the blind. — WILLIAM C. ROSCOE.

Tenderly be led by the nose,
As asses are. — SHAKESPEARE.

Tenderly as a bee that sips,
Your kisses settle on my lips,
— ARTHUR SYMONS.

Tense.

Tense as that cartilage which we have seen attaching the two Siamese. — EMERSON.

Fibres tense like a greyhound's sinews after a race. — CHARLES READE.

Tense as a war-steed girth. — SWINBURNE.

Tense as wire. — IBID.

Tensely

Tensely as the drawn wire rope of a suspension bridge. — KIPLING.

Terrible.

Terrible as a Cerberus. — ANON.

Terrible as the curse of a dead man's eye. — IBID.

Terrible as Jove. — IBID.

Terrible as the god of war. — FLAUBERT.

Terrible . . . something like the shriek of a giant in pain. — THOMAS A. JANVIER.

Terrible as a meteor of fire. — JAMES MACPHERSON.

Terrible as hell. — MILTON.

Terrible as torrents in their fall. — JAMES MONTGOMERY.

Terrible as war. — HANNAH MORE.

Terrible . . . like flames of death. — OSSIAN.

Terrible as the sea. — RUSKIN.

Terrible as fire. — SWINBURNE.

His countenance was like the countenance of an angel of God, very terrible. — OLD TESTAMENT.

Terrible as an army with banners. — IBID.

Terrifying.

Terrifying as the monologue of a storm. — HUGO.

Terror.

In terror . . . like a child that has lost its mother and sees a mastiff coming. — CARLYLE.

Testimony.

Testimony is like an arrow shot from a long bow; the force of it depends in the strength of the hand that draws it. Argument is like an arrow from a cross-bow, which has equal force though shot by a child. — DR. JOHNSON.

Theatre.

(*See also* STAGE).

A theatre, unfortunately, is like a stage-coach: empty or full, it starts at the same time. — BALZAC.

The stage is more beholding to love than the life of man; for as to the stage, love is ever matter of comedies, and now and then of tragedies; but in life it doth much mischief, sometimes like a siren, sometimes like a fury. — BACON.

Theatrical Favour, like Publick Commerce, will sometimes deceive the best Judgements by an unaccountable change of its Channel; the best Commodities are not always known to meet with the best Markets. — COLLEY CIBBER.

The Theatre is like a Turkish seraglio: the critics are the eunuchs. — FARQUHAR.

Thick.

Thick as ants. — ANON.

Thick as beans in a pod. — IBID.

Thick as blackberries in July. — IBID.

Thick as blanks in a lottery. — IBID.

Thick as Charon's ferry boat is with phantoms. — IBID.

Thick as dust in vacant chambers. — IBID.

Thick as gutter mud. — IBID.

Thick as hair on a dog's back. — IBID.

Thick as lichens on marble slab. — IBID.

Thick as molasses in December. — IBID.

Thick as peas in summer weather. — IBID.

Thick as pea soup. — IBID.

Thick as pitch. — IBID.

Thick as strings on a harp. — IBID.

Thick as the bark on a tree. — IBID.

Thick as the spawn of a fish. — IBID.

Thick as thistles. — IBID.

Thick as wax. — IBID.

Stars which stand out as thick as dewdrops on the field of heaven. — P. J. BAILEY.

Thick as burning stones that from the throat of some volcano foul the benighted sky. — IBID.

Stand thick as dewdrops on the bells of flowers. — ROBERT BLAIR.

Thick as starlings in a fen. — WILLIAM BROWNE.

Thick like a glory round the Stagirite. — ROBERT BROWNING.

Thick
As stars which storm the sky on
Autumn nights. — IBID.

Thick as hail. — BUNYAN.

As thikke as is a branched ook. — CHAUCER.

As thikke as motes in the sonne beem. — IBID.

Thick like two hungry torrents. — CHAPMAN.

Thick as spray. — H. F. CLARKE.

Thick, like wool. — ELIZABETH B. CUSTER.

Thick — *continued.*

Thick as scarecrows in England. — DICKENS.

His Pills as thick as Hand Granadoes flew,
And where they Fell, as Certainly they slew. — WENTWORTH DILLON.

Thick as bees. — AUSTIN DOBSON.

The air was as thick as the main deck in a close-fought action. — SIR A. CONAN DOYLE.

Thick as Egypt's locusts. — DRYDEN.

Thick as stars above. — GEORGE ELIOT.

Thick as stars that gem the Dolphin's brow. — SANSKRIT EPIC.

As thick as the sands of the wide wilderness. — F. W. FABER.

Thick as two body-snatchers. — O. HENRY.

Thick as autumn leaves or driving sand. — HOMER (POPE).

Thick as in spring the flow'rs adorn the land,
Or leaves the trees; or thick as insects play. — IBID.

Thick as London fog. — HOOD.

Thick as a swarm of bees. — JEAN INGELOW.

Thick as butter. — KIPLING.

Thick as swallows with the summer. — GEORGE W. LOVELL.

Thick as flakes of snow. — MACAULAY.

Thick
As starry mysteries written on the night. — GERALD MASSEY.

Thick as feathers. — GEORGE MEREDITH.

Thick as the gems on chalices
Kings keep for treasure.
— OWEN MEREDITH.

Thick as autumnal leaves that strow the brooks
In Vallombrosa. — MILTON.

Stood thick as stars. — IBID.

Thick as oatmeal. — THOMAS NASH.

Thick as the fleeces of the winter snows. — OUIDA.

Thick as the violets cluster round the spring. — JOHN PAYNE.

Thick as onions on a string. — J. R. PLANCHÉ.

Thick as hops. — "POOR ROBIN'S ALMANACK."

Thick as lotus flowers in Paradise. — J. HAMPDEN PORTER.

Thick as rain-drops. — PRESCOTT.

As thick as thieves. — OLD ENGLISH PROVERB.

Thick as the daisies blown in grasses fanned by odorous midsummer breezes. — JAMES WHITCOMB RILEY.

Thick as the schemes of human pride. — SIR WALTER SCOTT.

Thick as honeycomb. — SHAKESPEARE.

Thick as Tewksbury mustard. — IBID.

Thick as thought could make 'em. — IBID.

Thick as the snowflakes. — SOUTHEY.

Thick as the stars that stud the wintry sky. — IBID.

Thick as corn-blades in a field. — SPENSER.

Lay scattered over all the land,
As thicke as doth the seede after the sower's hand. — IBID.

Thick as swallows after storms. — E. C. STEDMAN.

Thick as a mob. — ROBERT LOUIS STEVENSON.

Thick as a snow fall. — IBID.

Thick as driving rain. — IBID.

Thick as the stars at night when the moon is down. — IBID.

Thick — *continued.*

Thick and silent like ants. — ROBERT LOUIS STEVENSON.

Thick as buds in April. — SWINBURNE.

Thick as the darkness of leaf-shadowed spring is encumbered with flowers. — IBID.

Lie thick as the blades of the grasses
The dead in their graves. — IBID.

Thick as grave-worms. — IBID.

Thick as Autumn rains. — TENNYSON.

Thick as dust in vacant chambers. — IBID.

Thick as hail. — THERSITES.

Thick as sparks above the rushing train. — J. T. TROWBRIDGE.

Thick as three rats in a little boy's stocking. — IBID.

The air is thick as incense-wreaths
That waver in the candles' gleam.
— G. S. VIERECK.

Thick as the hail with which the storm-clouds rattle on the roof. — VIRGIL.

Thick as seagulls. — VOLTAIRE.

Thicke, as shining lights, which we call starres. — SIR THOMAS WYATT.

Thick as hasty pudding. — "YANKEE DOODLE."

Thin.

Thin as a groat. — ANON.

Thin as a rail. — IBID.

Thin as a snake. — IBID.

Thin as a wafer. — IBID.

Thin as famished rats. — IBID.

Thin as gold leaf. — IBID.

Thin as wall paper. — IBID.

Thin as a reed. — IBID.

Thin as a spindle. — IBID.

Thin as a toothpick. — IBID.

Thin as the shadow of a hair. — IBID.

Thin as a pair of shears. — ARABIAN NIGHTS.

His poor body is as thin as a nail. — BALZAC.

Thin as the petal of the cotton blossom. — HENRY A. CLAPP.

Thin as a lath. — "FOUNDLING HOSPITAL FOR WIT," 1743.

So thin that he was obliged to put lead in his shoes so as to not be blown away by the wind. — HUGO.

Thin as a Ritz-Carlton sandwich. — STEPHEN LEACOCK.

Thin as a carriage painter's arm. — ABE MARTIN.

Thin as a weasel. — GEORGE MEREDITH.

Thin as mist. — IBID.

Thin as the shell of a sound. — IBID.

Thin as a brief forgotten dream. — R. M. MILNES.

A Spectre, thin as that dismal flame
That burns and beams, a moving lamp,
Where the dreary fogs of night encamp. — T. BUCHANAN READ.

Her body thin and bare as any bone. — SACKVILLE.

Thin as a skeleton. — THOMAS SHADWELL.

Thin of substance as the air. — SHAKESPEARE.

Thin as Fraud. — SHELLEY.

Thinned, as the shades in a vision of spirits that sinned. — SWINBURNE.

Thin as a costume worn by a Salome dancer. — WALTER TRUMBULL.

Thinly.

The early judicial circuits of Indiana. like the young gentleman's whiskers. — extensively laid out, but thinly settled. — SANFORD COX.

Thirst.

Thirst for them as Tantalus for inaccessible water, and the fruit that the wind blew away from him. — ANON.

My soul thirsteth after thee, as a thirsty land. — OLD TESTAMENT.

Thirsty.

Thirsty as a fish. — ANON.

Thirsty as a sponge. — IBID.

Thirsty as a dry road. — CYRIL HARCOURT.

Thirsty as Tantalus. — SYDNEY MUNDEN.

Thought.

Thoughts, like snowflakes on some far-off mountain side, go on accumulaing till some great truth is loosened, and falls like an avalanche on the waiting world. — ANON.

Great thoughts, like great deeds, need no trumpet. — P. J. BAILEY.

Dark wretched thoughts, like icesles in a stream, choke up my mind, and clash. — IBID.

Thoughts, like nuns, ought not to go abroad without a veil. — BULWER-LYTTON.

Thoughts, like waves that glide by night, are stillest when they shine. — IBID.

Thoughts are like persons met upon a journey ; I think them very agreeable at first but soon find, as a rule, that I am tired of them. — SAMUEL BUTLER (1835–1902).

Our thoughts, like the waters of the sea, when exhaled towards Heaven, will lose all their bitterness and saltness, and sweeten into an amiable humanity, until they descend in gentle showers of love and kindness upon our fellow-men. — C. C. COLTON.

Curran's airy thoughts, like purple birds that shine and soar. — C. G. DUFFY.

Human thought is like a monstrous pendulum : it keeps swinging from one extreme to the other. — EUGENE FIELD.

A thought would wander like a free bird over his features, flutter in his eyes, light on his parted lips, hide itself in the wrinkles of his brow, then utterly vanish away. — IVAN A. GONCHAROV.

Some kinds of thoughts breed in the dark of one's mind like the blind fishes in the Mammoth cave. We can't see them and they can't see us ; but sooner or later the daylight gets in and we find that some cold, fishy little negative has been sprawling all over our beliefs, and the brood of blind questions it has given birth to are burrowing round and under and butting their blunt notes against the pillars of faith we thought the whole world might lean on. — O. W. HOLMES.

A little thought in life is like salt upon rice. — KIPLING.

Thoughts, common as clay, and the trodden earth. — GEORGE MACDONALD.

My thoughts, like birds, were frightened from their nest.— OTWAY.

Beautiful thoughts that fall like rain
Are droughts for pleasure or balm for
pain. — D. G. ROSSETTI.

The presence of a thought is like the presence of a loved one. We deem that we shall never forget this thought and that the loved one can never become indifferent to us. But out of sight, out of mind ! The most beautiful thought runs the risk of being irrevocably forgotten if it is not written down, and the loved one to be torn from us if she has not been wedded. — SCHOPENHAUER.

A thought unknown is as a thought unacted. — SHAKESPEARE.

An old thought turns with the old
tune in my head
As a windmill turns in the wind on an
empty sky.
— ARTHUR SYMONS.

Thought. — *continued.*

Sweet thoughts, like honey-bees, have made their hive of her soft bosom cell, and cluster there. — AMELIA B. WELBY.

Thoughtful.

Thoughtful and dark, like the sun when he carries a cloud on his face. — JAMES MACPHERSON.

Thoughtless.

Thoughtless as a lark. — KEATS.

Thoughtless as if dead already. — "DHAMMAPADA."

Thrash.

Thrash invaders rash, like barley with a flail. — HOOD.

Thrashed him like a wheat-sheaf. — W. S. LANDOR.

Threadbare.

Threadbare as a lazzarone's velvet coat. — LEWIS ROSENTHAL.

Threatening.

Threatening as a porcupine. — ANON.

Threatening . . . like precipices. — BURNS.

Threatening, like a storm, just breaking on our heads. — DRYDEN.

Thrill.

Thrilling as the meteor's fall through the depths of lonely sky. — ANON.

Thrilled like the juice of the purple vine. — IBID.

Thrilled like the string of a lyre. — IBID.

Thrilled as was Rome when Cæsar returned laden with the spoils of conquest. — IBID.

Thrills in leafy tremblement,
Like a heart that after climbing
Beateth quickly though content.
— E. B. BROWNING.

Thrill like his lyre-strings. — BYRON.

Thrilled like a revelation. — JOSEPH CONRAD.

Thrilled in ecstasy, like an Oriental saint. — DAUDET.

Her timbers thrilled as nerves,
When through them passed the spirit of that shock.
— SIR FRANCIS H. DOYLE.

Thrilling her as with fire of rage divine
And battling energy.
— GEORGE ELIOT.

Thrill in your veins like shouts of victory. — IBID.

Thrill like the nightingale's song. — EDWARD OCTAVUS FLAGG.

Thrills . . . like a thing of song and gladness. — W. S. GILBERT.

Thrill with sound like a harp. — KENNETH GRAHAME.

Thrilled like witch-notes. — ARTHUR HENRY HALLAM.

Thrill like some fanciful land of romance. — BRET HARTE.

Thrills
As if the Enchanted Castle at the heart
Of the wood's dark wonderment
Swung wide his valves, and filled the dim sea-banks
With exquisite visitants.
— W. E. HENLEY.

Thrill like a battle shout. — MARY E. HEWITT.

Memories thrill,
Like a breath from the wood, like a breeze from the hill.
— O. W. HOLMES.

A leap and a thrill like the flash of a weaver's shuttle,
Swift and sudden and sure.
— RICHARD HOVEY.

Thrilling like the trump of battle. — WALTER MALONE.

Thrill,
Like sounds upon the wind-harp's chords when all the winds are still.
— GEORGE D. PRENTICE.

Thrill — *continued.*

My heart like a touched harp-string thrilled. — ALEXANDER SMITH.

Thrill as a theatre thronged at appeal of an actor's appalled agitation. — SWINBURNE.

Thrilled as by the clangorous call
Of storm's blown trumpets from the
core of night. — IBID.

Thrill,
Like the whole world's heart, with
warm new life and gladdening
flame. — IBID.

Thrilled . . . like Memnon waking from his marble dream. — SARAH H. WHITMAN.

Thrive.

Thrives like sin. — ANON.

Thrives like evil weeds. — ANDREW MARVELL.

Throat.

Her throat is like the swan. — WILLIAM DOUGLAS.

Throb.

Throbbed like some branch against some river swift. — AUBREY DE VERE.

Throbbed
As with some spiritual ecstasy.
— LEWIS MORRIS.

Throbbed, as by sudden fever stirred. — BAYARD TAYLOR.

Throbbing like a wounded bird. — FRANCIS THOMPSON.

Throng.

Thronged like a shower of gold king-cups in meadows sunny. — GERALD MASSEY.

Thronged, as to storm sweet heaven's triumphal gate. — SWINBURNE.

Through.

Through like a shot. — ANON.

Goes through 'em like the grace of heaven through a camp meeting. — IBID.

To go through me like water through a sieve. — ALEXANDER BARCLAY.

Through you, as through a breast of glass, I see. — ROBERT BROWNING.

Through me like a flash of lightning through a gooseberry bush. — BENJAMIN WEBSTER.

Throw.

He threw me from his breast, like a detested sin. — OTWAY.

Thunder.

Thunder like a whole sea overhead. — ROBERT BROWNING.

Thunder like the ocean when in strength and breadth and length it sets to shore. — C. G. ROSSETTI.

Thunder as Jove himself does. — SHAKESPEARE.

Thunder as of earthquake coming. — SHELLEY.

Thundering.

Thundering like ramping hosts of warrior horse. — GEORGE MEREDITH.

Thunderous.

Thunderous, like some Gregorian chant. — SARAH WILLIAMS.

Tick.

Tick,
Like the death-watch, within our ears
the ills
Past, present, and to come.
— BYRON.

Ticking like the love-making of a grasshopper. — THOMAS HARDY.

Tidy.

Tidy as a candy shop. — ANON.

Tied.

Mutual hate tied,
Like two dark serpents tangled in the
dust. — SHELLEY.

Tight.

Tight as a drum head. — ANON.

Tight — *continued.*

Locked tight as an oyster. — ANON.

Tight as a wad. — IBID.

Tight as Dick's hatband. — IBID.

Tight as the skin of a gooseberry. — IBID.

Tight as a bow-string. — BULWER-LYTTON.

Tight as a bottle. — JOSEPH CONRAD.

Tight as a gooseberry. — DICKENS.

Skin tight like a bursting vest. — AMY LOWELL.

Tight like teeth. — GEORGE MEREDITH.

Time.

Time is like a river made up of the events which happen, and a violent stream; for as soon as a thing has been seen, it is carried away, and another comes in its place, and this will be carried away too. — MARCUS AURELIUS.

Time is like money; the less we have of it to spare, the further we make it go. — JOSH BILLINGS.

Time, like a brilliant steed with seven rays, and with a thousand eyes, imperishable, full of fecundity, bears all things onward. — "HYMN TO TIME."

Time's shadows, like the shuttle, flee. — D. M. MOIR.

Time, like a seven-wheeled, seven-naved car, moves on. His rolling wheels are all the worlds, his axle is immortality. — FRIEDRICH RÜCKERT.

For time is like a fashionable host
That slightly shakes his parting guest
by the hand,
And with the arms outstretch'd, as he
would fly,
Grasps in the comer: welcome ever
smiles,
And farewell goes out sighing.
— SHAKESPEARE.

Time is like the peacefulness of grass, which clothes, as if with silence and deep sleep, deserted plains that once were loud with strife. — ALEXANDER SMITH.

Time is as wind, and as waves are we. — SWINBURNE.

Time, like the earth with flowers be-
spread
In youthful spring, is dark and
Dead when age and cares come on
And friends and pleasures are all
gone.
— WALTHER VON DER VOGELWEIDE.

Timid.

Timid as a child deserted by its nurse. — ANON.

Timid as a falling snowflake. — IBID.

Timid as a mouse. — IBID.

Timid voice, like a baby afraid of punishment. — HERMANN BAHR.

As timid, touching and inquiring, as she who charmed the gods from the threshold of Olympus. — DR. JOHN DORAN.

Timid as a youth can be. — MAHABHARATA.

Timid as a doe. — ROBERT NOEL.

Timid as a sheep. — OUIDA.

Timid as a fawn. — THACKERAY.

Timorous.

Timorous as a bird. — ANON.

Timorous . . . as the first chirrup of a callow bird. — OWEN MEREDITH.

Timorous as a truant child. — BAYARD TAYLOR.

Tinge.

Tinged like the face of the rainbow. — ANON.

The crimson stream, as if flowing from the dark-tinted rose, tinged her fair hand as with the purple current. — ADELBERT VON CHAMISSO.

Tingle.

Tingling, like cords of shaken lyres. — F. W. Faber.

Tingled in my veins like streams of liquid fire. — Adams S. Hill.

Tingled like a lute that is tuned too high. — J. H. McCarthy.

Tingle like fagots. — F. D. Sherman.

Tinkling.

Tinkling . . . like armourers at work upon their anvils. — Sir Walter Scott.

Tiny.

Tiny as the temple of Nike. — Anon.

Tipple.

Tippled like a fish. — Campbell.

Tip-tilted.

Tip-tilted, like a thirsty duckling's bill
After much guzzling in a pool.
— Oscar Fay Adams.

Her slender nose
Tip-tilted like the petal of a flower.
— Tennyson.

Tip-toe.

On tip-toe like escaping murderers. — E. B. Browning.

Tired.

Tired as old Nick. — Anon.

Tired as the dickens. — Ibid.

Tired as twilight. — Ibid.

Tired as tombstones. — Robert Browning.

Tiresome.

Tiresome as when poor Sisyphus reaches the top of the mountain vainly to feel his burden go rolling back from his shoulders. — Seneca.

Titter.

A titter
Like the skipping of rabbits by moonlight. — Robert Browning.

Title.

The title of knight, on the back of a knave, is like a saddle upon a sow. — Alexander Brown.

Titles of honor are like impressions on coin, which add no value to gold and silver, but only render brass current. — Sterne.

Titles and birth, like diamonds from the mine,
Must by your worth be polish'd ere they shine.
— William Whitehead.

Together.

Stick together like birds. — Anon.

Together like birds of prey watching a carcass. — Ibid.

Come in together like dinner and wax tapers. — Ibid.

We all live together like two wanton vines,
Circling our souls and loves in one another.
— Beaumont and Fletcher.

Grow together like tares and wheat. — E. B. Browning.

Hang together like bees or Scotchmen. — Bulwer-Lytton.

Cluttered together like so many pebbles in a tide. — Robert Burton.

Together unavoidably, like two ships becalmed near each other. — Joseph Conrad.

Together, like meeting rivers. — John Hughes.

Gathered herself together like a watch spring. — Kipling.

Paths now lie together, as our footprints on the strand. — T. Buchanan Read.

So we grew together,
Like to a double cherry, seeming parted,
But yet an union in partition;
Two lovely berries moulded on one stem;

Together — *continued.*

So, with two seeming bodies, but one heart,
Two of the first, like coats in heraldry,
Due but to one and crowned with one crest. — SHAKESPEARE.

Join they all together,
Like many clouds consulting for foul weather. — IBID.

Gathered together, as prisoners are gathered in the pit. — OLD TESTAMENT.

Together like the two kings of Brentford smelling at one nosegay. — BONNEL THORNTON.

Toil.

Toiled like a dog in a wheel.— ANON.

Toiled like branded slaves. — GERALD MASSEY.

Tolerant.

One who does his duty is tolerant like the earth . . . he is like a lake without mud. — BUDDHA.

Tolerate.

Tolerate as lions tolerate lice. — G. B. SHAW.

Toll.

Deep bells toll,
Like a last knell over the dead world's soul. — HOOD.

Tongue.

Your tongue is like a jaded nag. When the spurs prick its flanks it can only switch its tail. — LEONID ANDREYEFF.

His tongue is like any kind of carriage, the less weight it bears, the faster and easier it goes. — SAMUEL BUTLER.

His tongue is like a Bagpipe Drone, that has no Stop, but makes a continual ugly Noise, as long as he can squeeze any Wind out of himself. — IBID.

Their tongue was like a mellow turret bell
To toll hearts burning into wide-lipped hell. — LORD DE TABLEY.

All tongue, like the lily. — HAFIZ.

His tongue, like the tail of Samson's foxes, carries firebrands, and is enough to set the whole field of the world on a flame. — JOSEPH HALL.

The tongue of a louer should be like the poynt in the Diall, which though it go, none can see it going, or a young tree which though it growe, none can perceiue it growing, hauing alwayes the stone in their mouth which the Cranes vse when they flye ouer mountaines, least they make a noyse, but to be sylent, and lyghtly to esteeme of his Ladye, to shake hir off though he be secreat, to chaunge for euerything though he bewray nothing, is the onely thing that cutteth the heart in peeces of a true and constant louer, which deepely waying with my selfe, I preferred him that woulde neuer remoue, though he reueiled [reveal] all before him that woulde conceale all, and euer be slyding, thus wasting to [o] and fro, I appeale to you my good Violet, whether in loue be more required, secrecie, or constancy. — LYLY.

Whose tongue, like the dart of death, spares neither sex nor age. — CHARLES MACKLIN.

A fool's tongue is like the buye of an anchor, you will find his heart by it where soever it lyes. — SIR THOMAS OVERBURY.

His tongue is like a biscuit-seller's shovel — long tongued. — OSMANLI PROVERB.

Her tongue, which rosily
Peeped as a piercing bud between her lips. — D. G. ROSSETTI.

With tongue is like a sword's point. — SWINBURNE.

Thy tongue deviseth mischiefs ; like a sharp razor, working deceitfully. — OLD TESTAMENT.

Your tongue is like a scarlet snake that dances to fantastic tunes. — OSCAR WILDE.

Tongueless.

Tongueless as she whom a man-snake stung. — SWINBURNE.

Tooth.

The dentist pulled her tooth just like a serial, every day another piece. — BENJAMIN KOVNER.

Top.

Everything at the top and nothing at bottom, like a midshipman's chest. — W. C. RUSSELL.

Topple.

Toppled like a descending kite. — OWEN WISTER.

Tore.

Steamer . . .
Tore its way out like a savage sawfish.
— O. HENRY.

Torn.

Torn,
Like the remainder tatters of a dream.
— HOOD.

Torpid.

Torpid as a toad in marble. — DR. JOHNSON.

Tortuous.

Tortuous — like byways of despair. — JOSEPH CONRAD.

Tortuous as a labyrinth. — GUY DE MAUPASSANT.

Torture.

Torture . . . like poisoned sword. — ANCIENT BALLAD OF HINDUSTAN.

Torture, like a stoical fly on a pin. — ARNOLD BENNETT.

Toss.

Millions of grass blades that tossed like an emerald sea in the sunshine. — OSCAR FAY ADAMS.

Aside I'm tossed,
As an old sword whose scabbard's lost.
— ANON.

Tossing like an awakened conscience. —IBID.

Tossed like a peanut at sea. — IBID.

Tossed like a feather in a whirlwind. — IBID.

Tossed like a plebe in a blanket. — IBID.

I've been tossed like the driven foam. — EMERSON.

Tossed . . . like a cork on the waves. — THOMAS HARDY.

Tosses you about like cork crumbs in wine opened by an unfeed waiter. — O. HENRY.

Tossed it just like a haymaker at work. — HOOD.

Tossing like field-flowers in Spring. — GEORGE MEREDITH.

Tost like the bearded and billowy wheat by the winds of the mountain driven. — OWEN MEREDITH.

Tossing like a flower's head. — OUIDA.

Tossed like a fretted shallop-sail
Between ocean and the gale.
— T. BUCHANAN READ.

Like a frail bark thy weakened mind is tost. — RICHARD SAVAGE.

I am tossed up and down as the locust. — OLD TESTAMENT.

Tossed about like a few potatoes in a wheelbarrow. — MRS. TROLLOPE.

Toss like a ship at anchor, rocked by storms. — WORDSWORTH.

Totter.

Tottering like a man on a tight rope. — ANON.

Tottered away like a corpse set moving. — CHARLES READE.

Tottering . . . like lean herds pursued by gadflies. — SHELLEY.

Touch.

Her touch was as warm as the tinge of
the clover
Burnt brown as it reached to the kiss
of the sun. — JOAQUIN MILLER.

Tough.

Tough as any bough. — ANON.

Tough as leather. — IBID.

Tough as nails. — IBID.

Tough as shoe-leather. — IBID.

As tough as whit-leather. — IBID.

Tough as old hickory. — J. R. BARTLETT'S "DICTIONARY OF AMERICANISMS."

Tough as an India-rubber ball. — CHARLOTTE BRONTË.

Tough as a Cape Cod fisherman. — ROBERT EDGREN.

Tough as a telegraph wire. — RICHARD LE GALLIENNE.

Tower.

Towering above mortality, like Horace's swan. — ANON.

Towered above them as the eternal firmament above the ephemeral butterfly. — IBID.

Towers like another Saul. — IBID.

Towering, like the keel-compelling sail that takes the topmost tempest. — AUBREY DE VERE.

Towering above the common level of days, as cathedrals above houses. — J. J. JUSSERAND.

Towers like an ocean-cliff. — KEATS.

Towering like rocks of jet
Crowned with a diamond wreath.
— SHELLEY.

Traceless.

Traceless as a thaw of bygone snow. — C. G. ROSSETTI.

Trackless.

Trackless as the desert. — ANON.

Trackless as the sea. — IBID.

Trackless as a sound. — BALZAC.

Trackless as the immemorable hour
When birth's dark portal groaned and all was new.
— D. G. ROSSETTI

Tractable.

Tractable as a Sheepe. — LYLY.

Trailing.

Trailing like a wounded duck. — KIPLING.

Traitor.

Traitors in their fall are like the sun,
Who still looks fairest at his going down.
— OTWAY.

Trample.

Trample like dust under his feet. — ANON.

Trampled as the filth in the street. — JOHN W. WATSON.

Tranquil.

Tranquil as night. — ANON.

Tranquil as a star. — ALFRED AUSTIN.

As tranquil and unmoved as Fate. — AMBROSE BIERCE.

Tranquil like a summer cloud
Which, having rained itself to a tardy peace,
Stands still in heaven as if it ruled the day.
— E. B. BROWNING.

Tranquil as a child who goes to gather flowers. — FERNAN CABALLERO.

Tranquil as a marble statue. — THEODORE S. FAY.

Tranquil as the clear moonlight, that woos the palms on Orient shores. — P. H. HAYNE.

More tranquil than a musk-rose blowing in a green island. — KEATS.

Tranquil as a summer sea. — WORDSWORTH.

Tranquil as a dreamless sleep. — IBID.

Tranquilly.

Rest tranquilly like lilies under leaves. — ERNEST DOWSON.

Tranquilizing.

Tranquilizing, like oil in the water. — GAWAIN DOUGLAS.

Transform.

Transform like magic. — ANON.

The power of beauty will sooner transform honesty from what it is to a bawd, than the force of honesty can translate beauty into his likeness. — SHAKESPEARE.

Transformed as night or as day by the kindling year. — SWINBURNE.

Transforming.

Transforming sleep, like that of the chrysalis. — IBID.

Transient.

Transient as the summer storm. — ANON.

Transient as the inconstant sigh. — BYRON.

Transient . . . as is the fleeting hour. — COWPER.

Transient as breath shaking a flame. — GEORGE ELIOT.

Transient as lightning. — THOMAS HARDY.

Transient as vapours glimm'ring thro' the glades. — WALTER HARTE.

Transient as the dew. — RUSKIN.

Transient as faith or as terror that bows men's knees. — SWINBURNE.

Transient as the glance
Of flying sunbeams.
— WORDSWORTH.

Transitory.

Transitory as April showers. — ANON.

Translation.

Translations are like busy match-makers: they sing the praises of some half-veiled beauty and extol her charms, and arouse an irresistible longing for the original. — GOETHE.

Translucent.

Translucent as the pearly wave
Of that fair star that rules the night,
With an internal glory bright.
— JOHN PAYNE.

Translucent as pure crystal. — CHARLES SANGSTER.

Translucent, like a virgin's veil. — THEODORE WATTS-DUNTON.

Transmitted.

Transmitted, like the Lord Mayor's barge,
To the next comer. — BYRON.

Transparent.

Transparent as a veil. — HANS CHRISTIAN ANDERSEN.

Transparent as a young sardine. — ANON.

Transparent as crystal. — IBID.

Transparent as gossamer. — IBID.

Transparent as light. — IBID.

Transparent . . . as a ruby smitten by the sun. — DANTE.

Transparent as a rock of solid crystal. — DRYDEN.

Transparent as a rock-pool. — GEORGE ELIOT.

Transparent as mica. — O. HENRY.

Transparent as pure water. — SIGMUND KRASINSKI.

Transparent as glass. — GUY DE MAUPASSANT.

Transparent as air. — SAINT-PIERRE.

Transparent as barricadoes. — SHAKESPEARE.

Transparent as the soul of innocent youth. — WORDSWORTH.

Trapped.

Trapped like a rat. — ANON.

Trapped like bears in a pit. — HUGO.

Traveler.

I am of this minde with Homer, that as the Snayle that crept out of hir shell was turned eftsoones into a Toad, and thereby was forced to make a stoole to sit on, disdaining hir own house: so the Trauailer that stragleth from his own countrey, is in short tyme transformed into so monstrous a shape, that hee is faine to alter his mansion with his manners, and to liue where he canne, not where he would. — LYLY.

Treacherous.

Treacherous as the memory. — ANON.

Treading.

Treading warily, like one on the top of a tower. — HERBERT QUICK.

Treason.

Treason is like diamonds ; there is nothing to be made by the small trader. — DOUGLAS JERROLD.

Treason, like spiders weaving nets for
flies,
By her foul work is found, and in it
dies. — JOHN WEBSTER.

Tremble.

Trembled as though she were going to commit a wicked action. — HANS CHRISTIAN ANDERSEN.

Trembled as a flame blown by the wind. — ANON.

Trembled like a hymn. — IBID.

Trembling like needle to the pole. — IBID.

Trembled . . . like some high oak by a fierce tempest shaken. — IBID.

Tremble like the body of a guitar. — IBID.

Trembled like cold jelly. — IBID.

Trembled like the devil. — IBID.

Trembled like the strings of a violin. — IBID.

Trembles . . .
As the distracted herd, when they the
lion meet. — ARABIC.

She trembled, like the stem of a reed. — ASSYRIAN.

Trembling like a man with the palsy. — J. M. BARRIE.

Trembles like the luv-smitten harte ov a damsell. — JOSH BILLINGS.

Trembling, as sunshine comes through aspen-leaves. — R. D. BLACKMORE.

Trembled like a folded sheep at the bleating of her lamb. — IBID.

Tremble, like the trembling of an arch ere the key-stone is put in. — IBID.

Trembling, like water after sunset. — IBID.

Tremble . . . like a netted lioness. — E. B. BROWNING.

Trembling like a tub of size. — ROBERT BROWNING.

As a fish taken from his watery home and thrown in the dry ground, our thought trembles all over in order to escape the dominion of Mara [the tempter]. — BUDDHA.

Trembling like an ague. — BULWER-LYTTON.

Trembled as at an earthquake. — GIOSUÈ CARDUCCI.

Trembling like a frightened deer which is seeking a place of refuge. — LEWIS CARROLL.

Tremble like a fragile reed. — ELIZA COOK.

Tremble like dew on violet's leaves. — IBID.

Tremble,
Like the loose wrack in the sky,
When the four wild winds assemble.
— BARRY CORNWALL.

Trembling, as if eternity were hung
In balance on his conduct.
— COWPER.

Tremble, as the creatures of an hour
Ought at the view of almighty pow'r.
— IBID.

Trembling like an Eastern slave before the pasha. — WILLIAM E. CURTIS.

Tremble — *continued.*

Trembling like a bridal veil. — AUBREY DE VERE.

Trembling like a little child. — DUMAS, PÈRE.

Trembling as the dewy rose the wind has shaken. — O. W. HOLMES.

Tremble like the stars in the sky. — HOOD.

Trembles like a reed in flower. — HUGO.

Trembled in the social anxiety like leaves at the approach of the storm. — IBID.

Trembling, like Paris, on the brink of an obscure and formidable revolution. — IBID.

Trembled like a thing about to die. — JEAN INGELOW.

Tremble as a trembling leaf. — JAYADEVA.

Trembling like a falcon's game. — ROBERT U. JOHNSON.

Trembling like an aspen-bough. — KEATS.

Trembles like a harp full strung. — SIDNEY LANIER.

A-tremble like a new-born thing. — IBID.

Fell a-trembling like as the lips of lady that forth falter yes. — IBID.

Tremble like a shot pigeon. — ALFRED HENRY LEWIS.

Trembling . . . like beauty shining through a tear. — JOHN LEYDEN.

Trembling like a steed before the start. — LONGFELLOW.

Trembling, like a man that loves to be a soldier, yet is afraid of a gun. — CHARLES MACKLIN.

Lips trembled like those of a man caught in the act of doing wrong. — GUY DE MAUPASSANT.

Trembled as a man in fear. — WILLIAM MORRIS.

Trembling like a hunted prey. — OTWAY.

Trembling like a leaf in a hurricane. — OUIDA.

Trembling like a coward. — SAMUEL RICHARDSON.

Trembled like a frightened child. — C. G. ROSSETTI.

Trembled like a freezing man. — W. C. RUSSELL.

Tremble like aspen leaves. — SHAKESPEARE.

Trembled
Like ten thousand clouds which flow
With one wide wind. — SHELLEY.

Like a clipp'd guinea, trembles in the scale. — R. B. SHERIDAN.

Trembled like a lambe fled from prey. — SPENSER.

Tremble as with love that casts out fear. — SWINBURNE.

Trembled like a stricken thrall. — IBID.

Tremble like lute-strings. — IBID.

Trembling, like fiery light on crisped streams. — FREDERICK TENNYSON.

Tremble, like the light that strikes the zenith when the sun is down. — IBID.

Trembling, like those battlements of stone
That fell in fear when Joshua's horns were blown.
— HENRY VAN DYKE.

Trembling like a storm-struck tree. — THEODORE WATTS-DUNTON.

Trembles like a tender spark. — IBID.

Tremble in the sunny skies,
As if, from waving bough to bough,
Flitted the birds of paradise.
— WHITTIER.

Tremble — *continued.*

Tremble like a guilty thing surprised. — WORDSWORTH.

Trembling, as if with fear of some unconfessed peril, which she felt to be near at hand. — ZOLA.

Tremendous.

Tremendous, as that of trying to read the Universal Riddle. — LAFCADIO HEARN.

Tremor.

A slight tremor in thy tone,
Like that of some frail harp-string blown
By fitful breezes, faint and low.
— WHITTIER.

Tremulous.

Tremulous the voice . . . like any one's when jesting with a subject not a joke. — HOOD.

Tremulous as a nest. — HUGO.

Tremulous as the mimosa leaf. — LYDIA H. SIGOURNEY.

Tremulous like fire. — SWINBURNE.

Tremulous as brook-water. — OSCAR WILDE.

Tremulous as a leaf forsaken of the summer. — N. P. WILLIS.

Trepidation.

Eternal trepidation — like the ticking of a death watch to patients lying awake in the plague. — ANON.

Trickles.

Trickles down as from a wound. — EDWARD HAKE.

Tricky.

Tricky as a concierge. — ANON.

Tricky as a clown. — IBID.

Tricky as an ape. — IBID.

Tried.

Tried us as silver is tried. — OLD TESTAMENT.

Trifles.

Trifles light as air
Are to the jealous confirmations strong
As proofs of holy writ.
— SHAKESPEARE.

Trifling.

Trifling as hobby-horses. — ADDISON.

Empty and trifling, like little dogs biting one another, and little children quarreling, laughing, and straightway weeping. — MARCUS AURELIUS.

Trill.

Trilled at the rising sun almost like a stag which inhales the universal love and feels the April sap mounting and boiling in his veins. — HUGO.

Trim.

Trim as a lady of gentle degree. — JOANNA BAILLIE.

Trimmed like Alexandrine verses. — HUGO.

Trimm'd like a younker prancing to his love. — SHAKESPEARE.

Trip.

Tripping like winsome fairy through the woods at break of morn. — ANON.

Tripped . . . as light's a bird upon a thorn. — BURNS.

Tripping light as a sandpiper over the beach. — LOWELL.

Tripp'd, like a lamb playful and void of fear, through daisied grass and young leaves. — LEWIS MORRIS.

Trippingly.

As trippingly as a shepherdess's feet in a pastoral — OUIDA.

Trite.

Trite as Priam's tale, and twice as old. — WALTER HARTE.

Triumph.

Triumph like a king. — WILLIAM BYRD.

Triumph — *continued.*

Triumph like the bitterness of death. — SWINBURNE.

Triumphant.

Triumphant like a God. — SOUTHEY.

Triumphant as the sun. — SWINBURNE.

Triumphantly.

Triumphantly ride,
Like foam on the surges, the swans of
the tide. — JAMES MONTGOMERY.

Trivial.

Trivial as a parrot's prate.—COWPER.

Trivial as to attempt to blow out the stars. — GEORGE W. CURTIS.

As trivial as if a painter should put real gold upon his canvas instead of representing gold by means of paint. — IBID.

Trivial as the giggle of a housemaid. — HENRY JAMES.

Trivial as the tears of infancy. — JOHN RANDOLPH.

Trodden.

Trodden as grapes in the wine-press of lust. — SWINBURNE.

Shall be trodden down under him, even as straw is trodden down for the dunghill. — OLD TESTAMENT.

Trot.

Trot like a doe. — ANON.

Trot, like a servile footman, all day long. — SHAKESPEARE.

Trouble.

Troubles, like babies, grow larger by nursing. — LADY HOLLAND.

Troubles are like babies — they only grow by nursing. — DOUGLAS JERROLD.

Troubled, like a fountain stirr'd. — SHAKESPEARE.

Troubled, as Cretan seas when vext by warring winds. — EDMUND SMITH.

Troubled, as if with anger or pain. — TENNYSON.

Troublesome.

Troublesome as a wasp in one's ear. — THOMAS FULLER, M.D.

Troublesome as a monkey. — THOMAS SHADWELL.

Troublesome . . . as a young coxcomb-rhyming lover. — WYCHERLEY.

Trudge.

Trudge like a poor pedler. — ANON.

Trudge
Like a circuit-beast, plagu'd with a
gouty judge.
— HENRY VAUGHAN.

True.

True as that an apple is a fruit. — FRANKLIN P. ADAMS.

As true as God's own word is here. — GUSTAVUS ADOLPHUS.

True as the faithful watchdog of the fold. — ÆSCHYLUS.

True as the helm, the bark's protecting guide. — IBID.

True as a die. — ANON.

True as God is in heaven. — IBID.

True as gold. — IBID.

True as holy writ. — IBID.

As true as that nothing is but what is not. — IBID.

True as that a man who has shaved has lost his beard. — IBID.

True as that is is. — IBID.

About as true as that the cat crew, and the cock rocked the cradle. —IBID.

True as that the king has an egg in his pouch. — IBID.

True as that the world is turned upside down every twenty-four hours. — IBID.

True of his promise as a poor man of his eye. — IBID.

True — *continued.*

True as the gospel. — BEAUMONT AND FLETCHER.

True as written gospel. — ROBERT B. BROUGH.

True
And pauseless as the pulses.
— E. B. BROWNING.

True as that heaven and earth exist. — ROBERT BROWNING.

True as the dial to the sun. — SAMUEL BUTLER.

As true as a shepherd to his flock. — BYRON.

True as truth. — MADISON CAWEIN.

Trewe as any bonde. — CHAUCER.

Lovers be as trewe,
As eny metal that is forged newe.
— IBID.

True as turtill dove. — IBID.

As trewe as ever was any steel. — IBID.

True as a needle to the pole. — COWPER.

A clock so true, as might the sun control. — DONNE.

True as an arrow to its aim. — SIR FRANCIS H. DOYLE.

As true as Tristram and Isolde were. — DRYDEN.

True as the College clock's unvarying hand. — GEORGE ELLIS.

True as thy coat to thy back. — GEORGE GASCOIGNE.

True as the sun. — W. S. GILBERT.

True as swallow to the roadless blue. — EMILY H. HICKEY.

As true as God. — J. G. HOLLAND.

True as the dial's shadow to the beam. — O. W. HOLMES.

True as the watchman to his beat. — HOOD.

True as time. — JEAN INGELOW.

True as a gun. — BEN JONSON.

True as innocence. — KEATS.

True as the magnet is to iron. — W. S. LANDOR.

True as the Apocalypse. — AMY LESLIE.

True as death. — MARLOWE.

True to one as a beggar to his dish. — BRIAN MELBANCKE.

True as a barber's news on Saturday night. — MIDDLETON.

True as stars. — THOMAS MOORE.

True as the lute, that no sighing can waken. — IBID.

True as the homing-bird flies with its message. — JOHN BOYLE O'REILLY.

True as the Pentateuch. — POE.

True as Heaven. — EARL OF ROCHESTER.

She kept in time without a beat
As true as church-bell ringers.
— C. G. ROSSETTI.

True as steel, as plantage to the moon,
As sun to day, as turtle to her mate,
As iron to adamant, as earth to the centre. — SHAKESPEARE.

As true as truth's simplicity. — IBID.

As true as truest horse, that yet would never tire. — IBID.

Keep as true in soul
As doth that orbed continent the fire
That severs day from night. — IBID.

True as I live. — IBID.

Is as true as black is blue. — SKELTON.

Trewe as the gospell. — IBID.

True as truth's own heart. — SWINBURNE.

A friend as true as guardian-angels are. — WILLIAM THOMSON.

True it is, as cow chews cud. — THOMAS TUSSER.

True — *continued.*

True as the Stock-dove to her shallow
nest
And to the grove that holds it.
— WORDSWORTH.

Trumpet.

Trumpeted like figures of Fame. — HUGO.

Trustful.

Trustful as Don Juan's famous Monsieur Dimanche. — DAUDET.

Trustful as innocence. — W. S. GILBERT.

Truth.

Truth like a torch, the more it's shook, it shines. — ANON.

Truth and falsehood . . . are like the iron and clay in the toes of Nebuchadnezzar's image, they may cleave, but they will not incorporate. — BACON.

Moral truths, like human beings, change their aspect according to their surroundings, to the point of being unrecognizable. — BALZAC.

Truth, like the sun, submits to be obscured ; but, like the sun, only for a time. — C. N. BOVÉE.

Catch truth and wisdom unawares,
As men do health in wholesome airs.
— SAMUEL BUTLER.

The use of truth is like the use of words ; both truth and words depend greatly upon custom. — SAMUEL BUTLER (1835–1902).

Truth, like the juice of a poppy, in small quantities, calms men ; in large, heats and irritates them, and is attended by fatal circulation, because men have discovered that it is far more inconvenient to adulterate the truth than to refine themselves. — C. C. COLTON.

He who will tell the truth appears at times like a hen on a perch in windy weather. — OLOF VON DALIN.

Truth itself is sometimes like a ruddy apple which requires to be cut in halves before we can tell which portion contains the worm. — FRANCIS GRIERSON.

Truth, like beauty, varies in its fashions, and is best recommended by different dresses to different minds. — DR. JOHNSON.

The advent of truth, like the dawn of day, agitates the elements, while it disperses the gloom. — E. L. MAGOON.

Truth . . . shines like the sun, and like the sun it cannot perish. — NAPOLEON.

Truth, like a single point, escapes the
sight,
And claims attention to perceive it
right. — JOHN POMFRET.

Truth that has been merely learned is like an artificial limb, a false tooth, a waxen nose ; at best, like a nose made out of another's flesh ; it adheres to us only because it is put on. — SCHOPENHAUER.

Truthful.

Truthful as the genial spring. — NATHANIEL COTTON.

Truthful as a knight of old. — WENDELL PHILLIPS.

Tug.

Tug as a flag in the wind. — LOWELL.

Tumble.

Tumbled and jumbled, as in Titan wars. — LORD DE TABLEY.

"Squatter Sovereignty" squatted out of existence, tumbled down like a temporary scaffolding. — ABRAHAM LINCOLN.

Tumbling about in her head like a world in disruption. — GEORGE MEREDITH.

Time eftsoon will tumble
All of us together like leaves in a gust,
Humbled indeed down into the dust.
— JOAQUIN MILLER.

Tumbling . . . like rolling empty barrels down stairs. — MARK TWAIN.

Tuneful.

Tuneful as woods with the music of love. — WILLIAM MILLER.

Tuneless.

Tuneless as a bag of wool. — GEORGE ELIOT.

Tuneful, like a caged canary. — RICHARD BUTLER GLAENZER.

Turbid.

Turbid as passion. — WILLIAM WATSON.

Turbulent.

Turbulent as a children's ball at Christmas. — BULWER-LYTTON.

Turbulent as is the ocean. — HUGO.

Turn.

Turned upon me, as the lion turned upon the hunter's spear. — ANON.

Turn'd, as a vessel holds to sea, when near a Siren strand. — THOMAS ASHE.

Turn it, as a nose of wax, to their own ends. — ROBERT BURTON.

Doubling and turning like a hunted hare. — DRYDEN.

Turn, as upon pivots. — HUGO.

Turned like a weather cock with every wind. — GUY DE MAUPASSANT.

Turned me about as did Lot's wife. — RABELAIS.

Turns as a bucket turns in a well. — D. G. ROSSETTI.

Turn him off,
Like to the empty ass, to shake his ears,
And graze in commons.
— SHAKESPEARE.

Turn o' the toe like a parish-top. — IBID.

Turning as a turning wave
Against the land-wind.
— SWINBURNE.

Turned, like a panther in his lair. — WHITTIER.

Turning like a windmill sail. — IBID.

Turned, like Lot at Sodom. — IBID.

Turn
Like sunflowers to the pure and best.
— IBID.

Twilight.

Twilight is like death; the dark portal of night comes upon us, to open again in the glorious morning of immortality. — JAMES ELLIS.

Twine.

My thoughts twine and bud about thee, as with vines, about a tree. — E. B. BROWNING.

Twined in Memory's mystic hand,
Like pilgrim's withered wreath of flowers plucked in a far-off land.
— LEWIS CARROLL.

Twineth, like a lover's arm,
With sweet devotion.
— ELIZA COOK.

Twine, like pole ivy round the polished bark. — CUMBERLAND.

Sweet thoughts are twining in with bitter ones, as roses twine with rue. — JAMES M. MORTON.

Twines round it as the ivy does the ash. — MUNCHAUSEN.

Like the tendrils of the vine,
Do her auburn tresses twine.
— AMBROSE PHILIPS.

Twinge.

Twinged like a hollow tooth. — RICHARD LE GALLIENNE.

Twinkle.

Eyes twinkled like diamonds. — T. B. ALDRICH.

Twinkled like a candle flame where salt is sprinkled. — ANON.

Twinkling as the morning's tremulous gloss of balmy dew. — IBID.

Sharp eyes twinkled,
Like a candle-flame where salt is
sprinkled.
— ROBERT BROWNING.

Twinkle — *continued.*

Twinkling like the stars. — BUNYAN.

Twinkled
Like a smooth golden lake breeze-wrinkled. — F. W. FABER.

Twinkling like fireflies in the emerald grass. — FANNY FORESTER.

Lamps twinkled like stars along the water's edge. — CAMILLE LEMONNIER.

Twinkle like lanterns in a sepulchre. — SCHILLER.

Twinkling like a dawn out of a speckled cloud. — SHELLEY.

Twinkling . . . like a sullen star
Dimly reflected in a lonely pool.
— WORDSWORTH.

Twirl.

Twirling like a Dervish. — ANON.

Twirling like a weather cock in March. — IBID.

Twirling like a top. — CHARLES READE.

Twist.

Twisted as an Egyptian cripple. — ANON.

Twisted as Dick's hatband. — IBID.

Twisting like a mop. — IBID.

Twist like pearl white fire. — IBID.

Twisted like a house that has been enveloped and carried away by a waterspout.— BALZAC.

Twists like a whiskee phit. — JOSH BILLINGS.

Twisted like knotted snakes. — CHARLES HARPUR.

A writhing horror twisted itself across his features, like a snake gliding swiftly over them. — HAWTHORNE.

Twisted like an S. — HOOD.

Twisted like a rope. — HUGO.

Twisted in the maw of the wave like the angler's hook in the jaws of a pike. — IBID.

Twisted like an eel. — KINGSLEY.

Twisting like a serpent. — CHARLES LEVER.

Twist like fell ghosts that fear the light. — LEWIS MORRIS.

Twisted . . . like old olive branches. — RUSKIN.

Twists, like the curls of a bride. — SADI.

Twisting and twining like a conger eel. — MICHAEL SCOTT.

Twitter.

Twittering like a flock of angry sparrows. — ANON.

Twitter like the tuning of myriads of violins. — HELEN H. JACKSON.

Typical.

Typical as the sparrow is typical of London. — RICHARD LE GALLIENNE.

Tyrant.

Tyrants, like lep'rous kings, for public weal should be immured. — ANDREW MARVELL.

U

Ubiquitous.

Ubiquitous, like law's dread majesty. — F W. FABER.

Ugly.

Ugly as a scarecrow. — ANON.

Ugly as sin. — IBID.

As ugly as were ever born of mud. — CARLYLE.

Ugly as the devil. — FIELDING.

Ugly — *continued.*

Ugly as the devil's dam. — RICHARD FLECKNOE.

Ugly as a bear. — SHAKESPEARE.

Ugly as apes. — PAULUS SYLLOGUS.

Ugly as a worn-out cabhorse. — ANTON TCHEKHOV.

Ugly as the angel of a sign-board.
— THOMAS WADE.

Unabashed.

Unabashed as a little child. — GEORGE MOORE.

Unalterable.

His will is like the Persian law, unalterable. — THOMAS ADAMS.

Unalterable as the spots on a leopard. — ANON.

Unanswered.

Unanswered, like a vast sounding board gathering the uttered syllables and whispering them back in barren echoes. — CONDÈ B. PALLEN.

Unappetizing.

Unappetizing as the floor of a parrot's cage. — ANON.

Unappetizing as a cold sausage in the midst of its coagulated white grease. — GEORGE S. KAUFMAN.

Unappetizing as the remains of a feast. — EDITH WHARTON.

Unapproachable.

Unapproachable as a star. — O. HENRY.

Unarmed.

Unarm'd as bending angels.
— SHAKESPEARE.

Unasked.

Like Dian's kiss, unasked, unsought
Love gives itself, but is not bought.
— LONGFELLOW.

Unattractive.

Unattractive as a gargoyle. — ANON.

Unavailable.

As unavailable as for a man to whistle in the teeth of a gale, or to cast a jug of water against a tidal wave. — LI HUNG CHANG.

Unavailing.

Unavailing, as the cry of a spoiled child in its nurse's arms. — HENRY CLAY.

Unaware.

Catch Truth and Reason unawares,
As Men do Health in wholesome Airs.
— SAMUEL BUTLER.

Unawares, like the stroke of sudden death. — HAWTHORNE.

Great thoughts, great feelings come to them, like instincts, unawares. — R. M. MILNES.

Unbecoming.

Unbecoming as grace after meat. — FARQUHAR.

Unbidden.

Unbidden as the dews. — BULWER-LYTTON.

Unblemished.

Unblemished as the white-robed virgin choir. — WILLIAM LIVINGSTON.

Unbounded.

Unbounded, like infinity. — AUBREY DE VERE.

Unbounded as the ample air. — GOLDSMITH.

Unbridled.

Unbridled as the northern storm. — WILLIAM J. MICKLE.

Uncalled.

As light November snows to empty
nests,
As grass to graves, as moss to mildewed
stones,
As July suns to ruins, through the
rents,
As ministering spirits to mourners,
through a loss,

As Heaven itself to men, through
pangs of death,
He came uncalled wherever grief had
come. — E. B. BROWNING.

Uncared.

Uncared for, like a useless wayside stone. — T. BUCHANAN READ.

Uncaressable.

Uncaressable as puppets. — GEORGE MEREDITH.

Unceasing.

Unceasing as marriage. — ANON.

Unceasing as the murmur of the sea. — ROSAMUND MARRIOTT WATSON.

Unceasingly.

On — like a comet — on, unceasingly. — COSMO MONKHOUSE.

Unceasingly, like song in the time of birds. — N. P. WILLIS.

Unceremonious.

Unceremonious as a colony of flies. — ANON.

Uncertain.

Uncertain as a comet. — ANON.

Uncertain as horse flesh. — IBID.

Uncertain as weather. — IBID.

Uncertain as the wind. — C. C. COLTON.

Uncertain as the almanac. — "JACKE DRUM'S ENTERTAINMENT."

Uncertain in her temper as a morning in April. — SAM SLICK.

Uncertain as a child's swift moods. — ARTHUR SYMONS.

Uncertain as a vision or a dream. — TENNYSON.

Unchainable.

Unchainable as the dim tide. — WILLIAM B. YEATS.

Unchangeable.

Unchangeable as the past. — ANON.

Unchangeable as space. — P. J. BAILEY.

Unchanged.

Unchanged, like the cat which became blind, and still hankered after mice. — ARABIC.

Unchanging.

Unchanging as the belt Orion wears. — O. W. HOLMES.

Unchanging still from year to year,
Like stars returning in their sphere,
With undiminish'd rays.
— JAMES MONTGOMERY.

Unclean.

Unclean as sin. — RICHARD REALF.

Unclose.

Lids unclose
Like petals of a pearly rose
After the rain. — OLIVER HERFORD.

Uncoil.

Uncoiling, —
Like the rattlesnake's shrill warning
the reverberating drum.
— O. W. HOLMES.

Uncoiled itself like a huge boa about to engulf a tiny rabbit. — JAMES HUNEKER.

Uncomely.

Uncomely as a drove of pigs running down a lane. — GEORGE MOORE.

Uncomfortable.

Uncomfortable as a rooster in a pond. — ANON.

Uncomfortable as a girl sleeping with curl-papers. — IBID.

Uncomfortable as a raw oyster served with sweet pickles. — O. HENRY.

Uncomfortable as the Lilliputians made Gulliver with their arrows. — RUSKIN.

Uncommon.

Uncommon as common sense. — ANON.

Uncommon as pug noses in Jerusalem. — SYDNEY MUNDEN.

Uncomplaining.

Uncomplaining as a lamb. — EMILY BRONTË.

Uncompromising.

Uncompromising as justice. — WILLIAM LLOYD GARRISON.

Unconfined.

Unconfined as day. — AKENSIDE.

Unconfin'd as light. -- RICHARD DUKE.

Unconfined as air. — FRANCIS FAWKES.

Unconfin'd as our first parents in their Eden were. — OTWAY.

Unconfined, like some free port of trade. — POPE.

Unconquerable.

Unconquerable as chewing gum. — ARNOLD BENNETT.

Unconscious.

Unconscious as the sunshine. — LOWELL.

Unconscious as a statue. — SIR WALTER SCOTT.

Unconscious as a flower. — CELIA THAXTER.

Unconsciously.

Unconsciously as a flower exhales its perfume. — GEORGE MOORE.

Unconsciously as water drops over a coral reef in a tropical sea alive with the eyes of a thousand sharks. — THEODORE WATTS-DUNTON.

Unconstant.

Unconstant as the fashion. — "JACKE DRUM'S ENTERTAINMENT."

Uncontrollable.

Uncontrollable as the wave. — C. C. COLTON.

As uncontrollable as fate. — WILLIAM SOMERVILLE.

Uncorrected.

Uncorrected as outstretched swine. — GEORGE MEREDITH.

Uncouth.

I was as uncouth as a sea-fish upon the brae of a mountain. — ROBERT LOUIS STEVENSON.

Unctuous.

Unctuous as Sir Toby Belch. — ANON.

Unctuous as a hot-corn dodger slathered with sap. — W. C. BRANN.

Undefiled.

Undefiled like mountains made of snow. — ERIC MACKAY.

Understanding.

Understandings seem perfect Solids, as dead to Wit and as insensible of Reason as if their Souls and their Bodies (according to Hobbes's Philosophy) were both made of the same stuff and equally impenetrable. — ROBERT WOLSELEY.

Understood.

Harder to be understood than a piece of Egyptian antiquity, or an Irish manuscript. — CONGREVE.

Undimmed.

I have carried your glance within me undimmed, unaltered, as a lost boat, the compass some passing ship has lent her. — ARTHUR HUGH CLOUGH.

Undistinguishable.

Undistinguishable,
Like far-off mountains turned into clouds. — SHAKESPEARE.

Undisturbed.

Undisturb'd as Death. — COWLEY.

Undisturbed — *continued.*

Undisturbed as Justice. — SOUTHEY.

Undisturbed;
As on the pavement of a Gothic church
Walks a lone Monk, when service hath expired,
In peace and silence.
— WORDSWORTH.

Undone.

All undone,
As earth from her bright body casts off night. — SWINBURNE.

Undone, as we would undo an oyster. — CLEMENT WALKER.

Undulate.

Undulating like the sea. — BOCCACCIO.

Undulating like diluvian billows fixed into stone in the midst of their stormy swell. — BULWER-LYTTON.

Undulating, like the mane of a lion. — DUMAS, PÈRE.

Undulating like a snake rearing on its tail. — GAUTIER.

Long seaweed undulated beneath the water, like the waving of long tresses in the wind. — HUGO.

Unearthly.

Unearthly . . . like the remembered tone of a mute lyre. — BYRON.

Uneasy.

Uneasy as a pig in a parlor. — ANON.

Uneasy like a baffled thief. — JOSEPH CONRAD.

Unelastic.

Unelastic as a mathematical fact. — SYDNEY MUNDEN.

Unemotional.

Unemotional as a frozen flounder. — GEORGE BROADHURST.

Unending.

Unending as the river and the stars. — W. E. HENLEY.

Unerring.

Unerring as a logarithm. — ANON.

Unerring as light. — R. G. INGERSOLL.

Unerring as a leopard's leap. — OUIDA.

Unexciting.

Unexciting as the rain-sodden landscape. — FRANCES HODGSON BURNETT.

Unexpected.

Fortune came like Agag, unexpected. — ANON.

Unexpected as chastity at the bar of a tavern. — IBID.

Unexpected, like a thunderbolt. — IBID.

As unexpected as a serpent comes. — ROBERT BROWNING.

Unexpected as seeing a vision. — JOSEPH CONRAD.

Unexpected as a fifth ace in a poker deck. — ALFRED HENRY LEWIS.

Unexpectedly.

Unexpectedly, like a bolt out of the blue. — CARLYLE.

Unfaded.

Unfaded, as before it grew. — WILLIAM BROOME.

Unfading.

Unfading as the garden of kindness. — ANON.

Unfair.

Unfair to rest upon such decision, as it would be to ascribe wisdom to a judge, merely because he is dressed differently from other men. — WILLIAM COOKE.

Unfashioned.

Unfashioned, like a jewel in the mine. — ADDISON.

Unfathomable.

Unfathomable as the Pythagorean number. — ANON.

Unfathomable — *continued.*

Unfathomable as the heavens.— Wilkie Collins.

Unfeeling.

Like cold marble thou art all unfeeling. — Hood.

Unfeeling as rocks. — Smollett.

Unfelt.

Unfelt, like the release of death. — Southey.

Unfettered.

Unfetter'd as the windes. — Sir William Davenant.

Unfettered as the matin bird that cleaves the radiant sky. — W. B. O. Peabody.

Unfettered as bees that in gardens abide. — Wordsworth.

Unfit.

Unfit . . . as pure gold for circulation. — C. C. Colton.

Unfold.

Unfold themselves like flowers. — P. J. Bailey.

Unfolding, like the tree-tops of the forest, ever rising, rising. — Longfellow.

Ungracious.

Ungraciousness in rendering a benefit, like a hoarse voice, mars the music of the song. — Anon.

Unhappy.

Unhappy as King Lear. — Anon.

Unharmful.

Unharmful as the dove. — Ambrose Philips.

Unharmonious.

Unharmonious as a screech owl's serenade. — Anon.

Unhealthy.

Unhealthy as the liver of a goose intended for pâté. — Israel Zangwill.

Unheeded.

Unheeded as if life were o'er. — Byron.

Unheeded as a threshold brook. — Keats.

Unimaginative.

Unimaginative as a Chicago pig-sticking. — G. B. Shaw.

Unintelligible.

Unintelligible as any dream. — Dickens.

Unintentional.

Unintentional as the birth of a thought in the head. — Joseph Conrad.

United.

United, as flesh and soul in man. — P. J. Bailey.

United as the good thoughts that dwell in the same soul. — Maurice Maeterlinck.

United, like a hook and eye. — Sydney Munden.

In harmony united,
Like guests that meet, and some from far,
By cordial love invited.
— Wordsworth.

Unity.

Behold, how good and how pleasant it is for brethren to dwell together in unity! It is like the precious ointment upon the head, that ran down upon the beard, even Aaron's beard: that went down to the skirts of his garments. — Old Testament.

Universal.

Universal as the sun. — Beaumont and Fletcher.

The desire to pry into the future is as universal as the longing after immortal life. — William Dunlap.

Universal as seasickness. — G. B. Shaw.

Universal — *continued.*

Universal as the light. — SHELLEY.

Unjust.

Unjust, like the Jedburgh judges of Border history, it first hangs the prisoner and then tries him. — WILLIAM ARCHER.

Unkind.

Unkind as fate. — ANON.

Unkind as hail. — AMBROSE PHILIPS.

Blow, blow, thou winter wind,
Thou art not so unkind
As man's ingratitude. — SHAKESPEARE.

As winter's frost unkind. — SMOLLETT.

Unknown.

Unknown, like a seed in fallow ground. — T. B. ALDRICH.

Unknown as bells within a Turkish steeple. — BYRON.

Unknown as the Arimaspians. — GEORGE ELIOT.

Unlike.

Unlike as a wasp is to an ant. — ANON.

Unlike as intellect and body. — IBID.

Unlike as the pearl is unlike the mother shell-fish. — IBID.

Unlike as birth to death.
— ANTHONY BREWER.

As unlike as Luna is to a stage moon. — STEPHEN CHALMERS.

Unlike as diamond is to charcoal. — GEORGE ELIOT.

Unlike as an apple-dumpling and soda-cracker. — SEWELL FORD.

Unlike as British beer and sparkling Burgundy. — ARTHUR HORNBLOW.

Unlikely.

Unlikely as that a mouse should fall in love with a cat. — ANON.

Unlikely as that the wolf is to eat the moon. — IBID.

Unlikely as sweet fruit plucked from a dry tree, or sweet leaves on a dead stem. — IBID.

Unlikely . . . as to teach an alligator the polka. — IBID.

Unlikely as that a moth intends to be burnt when it flies into a candle flame. — IBID.

Unlikely as to see a hog fly. — IBID.

Unlovely.

Unlovely as the corpse of a man. — KIPLING.

Unlustrous.

Unlustrous as the smoky light
That's fed with stinking tallow.
— SHAKESPEARE.

Unmanageable.

Unmanageable as a ton of iron ore. — HAWTHORNE.

Unmanageable, like vicious horses of a charioteer. — KATHA UPANISHAD.

Unmeaning.

Unmeaning words, like some of those who call themselves physicians, but of the healing sciences nothing know. — LUCIAN.

Unmerciful.

Unmerciful as the billows. — JOHN GAY.

Unmerciful as the physician who with new arts keeps his miserable patient alive and in hopes, when he knows the disease is incurable. — WYCHERLEY.

Unmoved.

Stand unmoved, like a rock 'mid raging seas. — CALDERON.

Unmoved as a statue. — FLAUBERT.

Unmoved as death. — HOMER.

Unmusical.

A strain unmusical, like a dumb nightingale insatiate of song. — ÆSCHYLUS.

Unnatural.

Unnatural as the feverish life of the boulevard. — Israel Zangwill.

Unnoticed.

Unnoticed as a drop of water in a torrent. — Gaboriau.

They think they pass themselves off unnoticed, like the Irishman's bad guinea, in a handful of halfpences. — Julius C. Hare.

Unpitied.

Unpitied as fossils in a rock. — Charles Reade.

Unpredestinate.

Unpredestinate as the clouds over our heads. — Anon.

Unprofitable.

Unprofitable as picking feathers out of molasses. — Anon.

Unprofitable as smoke. — Alexander Barclay.

Unprofitably.

Our wasted oil unprofitably burns,
Like hidden lamps in old sepulchral urns. — Cowper.

Unquenched.

Unquenched . . . like Vesta's sacred fire. — Macaulay.

Unquiet.

Unquiet as noise shaken. — Anon.

Lay unquiet as absinth on a baby's stomach. — Richard Harding Davis.

Unreal.

Unreal as a dream. — F. W. Faber.

Unreal as the shell-heard sea. — Eugene Lee-Hamilton.

Half unreal, like music mingling with a dream. — John Kenyon.

Unreal as a painted city on a stage backdrop swayed by a wandering draft. — Louis Joseph Vance.

Unreasonable.

Unreasonable as to expect a hook to hold soft cheese. — Anon.

Unreconcilable.

Unreconcilable as cats and rats, as hounds and hares. — Anon.

Unremonstrant.

Unremonstrant as a fallen tree. — George Meredith.

Unresponsive.

Unresponsive to desire . . . as puppets in a peepshow. — Lord De Tabley.

Unripe.

Like fruit unripe, sticks on the tree. — Shakespeare.

Unruffled.

Unruffled as time. — Edgar Saltus.

Unruffled as a mirror. — Jules Sandeau.

Unsatiate.

Unsatiate as the barren womb or grave. — Dryden.

Unscrupulous.

Unscrupulous as Siegfried. — James Huneker.

Unseasonable.

Unseasonable as snow in summer. — Anon.

Unseasonable as long graces at a feast. — Thomas Killigrew.

Unseeing.

Unseeing stare, like that of a child who begins to see for the first time. — Balzac.

Unseen.

Not seen, like arrows shot by night. — Buddha.

Unseen, like the wind. — Edmund Gosse.

Unseen — *continued.*

Crept stealthily and unseen, like earth-worms to a carcase. — BULWER-LYTTON.

More unseen
Than Satan in his exile.
— KEATS.

Unseen as a disbanded rainbow. — SYDNEY MUNDEN.

Unseen, as lamps in sepulchres. — POPE.

Like a star of Heaven,
In the broad daylight,
Thou art unseen. — SHELLEY.

Unsettle.

As unsettling to us as a change of Government to Londoners. — J. M. BARRIE.

Unsettles
Like a bed of stinging nettles.
— W. S. GILBERT.

Unshaken.

Unshaken like a Thracian hill. — RICHARD GLOVER.

Like a rock in the sea, stands unshaken; like a rock in the sea before the rush and crash of waters, which, amid thousands of breaking waves, is fixed by its own weight; the crags and the spray-foamed stones roar about it in vain, and the lashed seaweed falls idly by its side. — VIRGIL.

Unshunnable.

'Tis destiny unshunnable, like death. — SHAKESPEARE.

Unsightly.

Unsightly as the Monster in the Tempest. — THOMAS RYMER.

Unsordid.

Unsordid as a bond of love. — ROBERT U. JOHNSON.

Unsparing.

Unsparing as the scourge of war. — ROBERT BLOOMFIELD.

Unspoken.

Unspoken,
Like daffodils that die with sheaths unbroken. — O. W. HOLMES.

Unstable.

Unstable as the wind. — ALEXANDER BARCLAY.

Unstable as the waves of the sea. — GEORGE BISHOP.

Unstable as water. — OLD TESTAMENT.

Unstaid.

Unstaid as rolling waves in ocean flood. — TASSO.

Unstained.

Unstained as snow. — JAMES LANE ALLEN.

Unstainèd as the sun. — EMERSON.

Unstained and pure as the lily or the mountain snow. — JAMES THOMSON.

Unsteady.

Unsteady as a shadow. — ANON.

Unsteady as the eye looking at the sun. — IBID.

Unsteady as the ocean. — GOLDSMITH.

Unsteady on his legs, like a young roe scared by a leaf. — HUGO.

Unsubstantial.

Unsubstantial as a ghost. — ANON.

Unsubstantial as a mirage. — BUDDHA.

Unsubstantial, like the teasing phantoms of a half-conscious slumber. — HAWTHORNE.

Unsubstantial as a bag of money in a looking-glass. — TELUGU PROVERB.

Unsubstantial as a dream. — THOMAS WADE.

Unsullied.

Unsullied in life and deed as a holy saint. — O. HENRY.

Unsullied — *continued.*

Unsullied as a cloistered nun. — WHITTIER.

Untasted.

My youth's dear sweets here spent
untasted,
Like a fair taper, with his own flame
wasted. — BEN JONSON.

Untenanted.

As untenanted of man
As a castle under ban
By a doom.
— ERASTUS W. ELLSWORTH.

Unthinkable.

Unthinkable as trees without roots. ALFRED AYRES.

Unthinkable as a mirror that would not reflect the objects before it. — FRANZ HARTMAN.

Unthrifty.

Our hedges like a wanton courtezan
Unthrifty of its beauty.
— OSCAR WILDE.

Untimely.

Like winter rose and summer ice,
Her joys are still untimely.
— ROBERT SOUTHWELL.

Untiring.

Untiring as the law of gravitation. — ANON.

Untiring as an Indian on trail. — OUIDA.

Untouched.

Like the lotus, which, although it grows in the water, yet remains untouched by the water. — BUDDHA.

Untouched as any islet
Shrined in an unknown sea.
— C. G. ROSSETTI.

Untrue.

It's as true as Biglam's cat crew, and the cock rock'd the cradle. — SCOTCH PROVERB.

Untwined.

Arms untwined, like some twin stream
That parts at last in hastening to the
sea. — EDMUND GOSSE.

Untwist.

Untwisted the fond links that bound us,
Like frost wreaths, that melt in the
morning's first beam.
— FRANCES ANNE KEMBLE.

Unuseful.

Unuseful, as if void of mind. — R. D. BLACKMORE.

Unusual.

Unusual as a sailor on horseback. — ANTHONY HAMILTON.

Unvaried.

The same unvaried tone,
Like the Scotch bagpipe's favorite
drone. — ROBERT LLOYD.

Unvexed.

Unvexed . . . like the candles round a shrine. — KIPLING.

Unwasted.

Like painted lamps they shine unwasted. — ABRAHAM COWLEY.

Unwatched.

Unwatched, unwept, as commonly a pauper sleeps. — HOOD.

Unwearied.

Unwearied as the heavens. — DE QUINCEY.

Unwelcome.

Unwelcome as snow in summer. — ANON.

Unwelcome as water in a leaking ship. — IBID.

Unwelcome as water in your shoe. — IBID.

Unwelcome to a woman as a looking-glass after the small-pox. — CONGREVE.

Unwelcome — *continued.*

Unwelcome and unasked, like Banquo's Ghost, in walked the long-lost Spouse. — Hood.

Unwelcome to any conceit as sluttish morsels, or wallowish potions to a nice stomach. — Sir Thomas Overbury.

Unwinding.

Unwinding themselves as so many clocks. — Robert Burton.

Unworthy.

As unworthy as to reject a comrade
In envy of his share of victory.
— Emerich Madách.

Unworthy of credence as an anonymous letter. — Brander Matthews.

Unyielding.

Unyielding as a rock. — Anon.

Up.

Up and down like a bucket in a well. — Anon.

Up like a lark in the air. — Richard Harvey.

Up and down like a milk punch in the shaker. — O. Henry.

Up and down, like a chicken drinking. — Leigh Hunt.

Went up as the smoke of a furnace. — Old Testament.

Upborne.

Upborne, like Aphrodite upon a meadowy swell of emerald sea. — Gerald Massey.

Uplift.

Uplifted like the everlasting dome
Which rises in the miracle sublime
over eternal Rome. — Anon.

Uplift as the hearts and the mouths of the singers, on the leaside and lawn. — Swinburne.

Uplifted like a quivering dart. — S. H. Thayer.

Uplifting as a jack-screw. — Daniel Webster.

Upright.

Upright as a ramrod. — Anon.

Upright as a sentinel. — Ibid.

As upright as a stake. — Ibid.

Upright as a young apple tree. — R. D. Blackmore.

Upright, like a taper. — Osmanli Proverb.

Upright as a tower. — Charles Reade.

Upright as a wooden sentinel at the door of a puppet-show. — Sir Walter Scott.

Upright as the cedar. — Shakespeare.

Upright as a wild Morisco. — Ibid.

Upright as a sheer cliff's wall. — Swinburne.

Upright as an heap. — Old Testament.

Uprise.

Uprisen as a prayer. — P. J. Bailey.

Uprising, like a bubble in a stream. — Gertrude Bloede.

Uprise like the islands of the Cyclades as seen from the mountains of Negroponte. — Paul Bourget.

Uprise, like a tempestuous ocean. — Shelley.

Uprising like the smoke wraith,
Blue ascending into heaven's blue.
— Ellen Burns Sherman.

Uproar.

An uproar like ten thousand Smithfield fairs. — Anon.

Upsoar.

Upsoaring like an eagle's wings. — Fitz-Greene Halleck.

Upstart.

Upstarting wild and haggard,
Like a man from dreams awakened.
— Longfellow.

Upward.

Upward tending although weak,
Like plants in mines which never saw the sun. — Robert Browning.

Upward, like the simulated pyramid of flame on a monumental urn. — George Eliot.

Upward flies;
Like holy thoughts to cloudless skies.
— William Motherwell.

Useful.

About as useful as a button on a hat. — Anon.

Useful as a shin of beef, which has a big bone for the big dog, a little bone for the little dog, and a sinew for the cat. — Ibid.

Useful as a cow. — Ibid.

Useful as daylight. — Ibid.

Useful as the useful. — Hugo.

Useless.

Useless as a chimney until you light your fire. — Anon.

Useless as a gun without a trigger. — Ibid.

Useless as a disabled pitcher. — Ibid.

As useless as a monkey's fat. — Ibid.

Useless as a sedan chair on a railway. — Ibid.

Useless as a shoulder of mutton to a sick horse. — Ibid.

Useless as whispering in the ear of a corpse. — Ibid.

Useless as a clock without wheels. — Ibid.

Useless as to stop up a rathole with an apple dumpling. — Ibid.

Useless as whistling psalms to a dead horse. — Bartlett's "Dictionary of Americanisms."

Useless as a candle in a skull. — Cowper.

Useless as a buttonhole without a button. — Henry Irving Dodge.

Useless as for her hand to try to grasp a shadow. — George Eliot.

Useless as to enlarge upon the obvious. — Epictetus.

Useless as the leg of a man with a sprained ankle. — Richard Le Gallienne.

Useless as a skyrocket without powder. — Charles Henderson.

Whose talk is as busily useless as the babble of a stream that hurries by a ruined mill. — R. G. Ingersoll.

Useless as the canal constructor without water. — G. B. Shaw.

Useless extra, like a sixth finger. — Anton Tchekhov.

Useless as perfumery to a hog. — Tolstoy.

Uselessly.

Uselessly and without any plan, just like ants crawling over bushes, which creep up to the top, and then down to the bottom again without gaining anything. Many men spend their lives in exactly the same fashion, which we may call a state of restless indolence. — Seneca.

Utility.

It is only the public situation which this gentleman holds which entitles me, or induces me to say a word about him. He is a fly in amber; nobody cares about the fly; the only question is, How the devil did it get there? Nor do I attack him for the love of the glory, but from the love of utility, as a burgomaster hunts a rat in a Dutch dyke, for fear it should flood a province. — Sydney Smith.

V

Vacant.

Vacant like air. — CHARLOTTE BRONTË.

Vacant as the beach from which the tide has receded. — HAMILTON WRIGHT MABIE.

Vacantly.

Vacantly
As ocean's moon looks on the moon in heaven. — SHELLEY.

Vagrant.

Vagrant as the wind. — JOHN FORD.

Vague.

Vague as a shadow. — ANON.

Vague like a suggestion of solid darkness. — JOSEPH CONRAD.

Vague . . . like feathers wafted backwards
From passage birds in flight.
— W. D. HOWELLS.

Vague and unmarked as desert sands. — MARY JOHNSTON.

Vague as solitary dove,
Nor knew that nests were built.
— KEATS.

Vague, like the thoughts of a child. — KINGSLEY.

A vague presentment of impending doom,
Like ghostly footsteps in a vacant room. — LONGFELLOW.

Vague surmise
Shines in the father's gentle eyes,
As firelight on a window-pane
Glimmers and vanishes away.
— IBID.

Vague as futurity. — OWEN MEREDITH.

Vague as the music of a moon-bathed brook. — FRANCIS S. SALTUS.

Vaguely.

Vaguely, like certain luminous scenes of the theatre back of those thin curtains which suddenly descend on the scenic stage, transporting the spectators from the tumult of a ballroom to the silence of a private house. — EDMONDO DE AMICIS.

Vaguely, as in a dream. — FITZ-JAMES O'BRIEN.

Vain.

Vain as a peacock. — ANON.

Vain as chasing a bug in the dark. — IBID.

Vain as the leaf upon the stream. — IBID.

Vain as the promises of a patent medicine advertisement. — IBID.

Vain as to water the plant when the root is dead. — IBID.

Vain as a rattle in a baby's clutch. — HENRY B. BINNS.

Vain as the passing gale. — CHARLOTTE BRONTË.

Vain
As for a brook to cope with ocean's flood.
— BYRON.

As organ plaiers, vnlesse some body blowe vnto them the windie bellowes, do make no sound at all: Euen so, vaine men, vnless they be pricked forward, with commendations and praises of others, haue neuer any minde, or purpose to lend themselves to any good action. — ANTHONIE FLETCHER'S "CERTAINE VERY PROPER AND MOST PROFITABLE SIMILES."

Vain as Niobe. — "FOUNDLING HOSPITAL FOR WIT," 1743.

Vain as the sick man's vow, or young man's sigh. — WALTER HARTE.

Vain as the summer's glowing spoils
Flung o'er an early bier.
— THOMAS KIBBLE HERVEY.

Vain — *continued.*

Vain your feeble cry,
As the babe's wailings to the thundering sky. — O. W. HOLMES.

Vain as a sick man's dream. — HORACE.

Vain as swords
Against the enchased crocodiles. — KEATS.

Vain . . . as to attempt to erase what Time has written with the Judgment Blood. — GEORGE MEREDITH.

Vain and unprofitable, as is the sunshine to a dead man's eyes. — H. H. MILMAN.

Vain as to strike an axe on a rock. — OSMANLI PROVERB.

Vain as a leaf from a tree,
As a fading day,
As veriest vanity,
As the froth and the spray
Of the hollow-billowed sea,
As what was and shall not be,
As what is and passes away. — C. G. ROSSETTI.

Vain as an idiot's dream. — CHRISTOPHER SMART.

Vain as to count the April drops of rain. — SMOLLETT.

Vain as a dead man's vision. — SWINBURNE.

Words as vain as wind. — FREDERICK TENNYSON.

Vain as a girl. — THACKERAY.

Troubles of this world are vain as billows in a tossing sea. — WORDSWORTH.

Vain as a Frenchman newly returned from a campaign. — WYCHERLEY.

Vain as a gaudy-minded man. — YOUNG.

Vainly.

Vainly spent, as dews on the sea. — CHARLOTTE BRONTË.

Vainly as the hydra bleeds. — SCHILLER.

Vainly given like rain upon the herbless sea poured down by too benignant heaven. — JOHN STERLING.

Valiant.

Valiant as the Cid. — ANTHONY HAMILTON.

Valiant as Mars. — HOMER.

Valiant as fire. — BEN JONSON.

Valiant as a lion. — SHAKESPEARE.

Valiant as the wrathful dove or most magnanimous mouse. — IBID.

Valiant as Hercules. — IBID.

As valiant a man as Mark Anthony. — IBID.

Less valiant than the virgin in the night. — IBID.

Valiant as Hector in every marciall nede. — SKELTON.

Valor.

True valor is like honesty; it enters into all that a man sees and does. — JOSH BILLINGS.

Valor higher than that which casts out fear. — SWINBURNE.

Valorless.

Valourless as a hare. — ANON.

Valorous.

Valorous as Cæsar. — ANON.

Valorous as Hector of Troy. — SHAKESPEARE.

Valuable.

Valuable as chiselled gold or facetted gems. — ANON.

About as valuable as the prayers for divine guidance in selecting a bishop. — APPLETON MORGAN.

Common sense is as inestimably valuable as the solar light. — WILLIAM WINTER.

Vanish.

Vanished like a trifling sigh.
— FRANKLIN P. ADAMS.

Vanished altogether, like the last spark on a burnt piece of paper. — HANS CHRISTIAN ANDERSEN.

Vanish like a bursted bubble. — ANON.

Vanished like a guilty thing. — IBID.

Vanished like a pantomime demon. — IBID.

Vanished like a pie. — IBID.

Vanished like a Titanic world of spectres. — IBID.

Like a vain dream . . . vanish'd hence, we know not how. — IBID.

Vanishing, like eerie bubbles, on the rough, tried sea of care. — IBID.

Vanishing like noxious exhalations. — IBID.

Vanish like the figments of a dream — IBID.

Vanish like the mist in the morning. — IBID.

Vanish like a ghost before the sun. — P. J. BAILEY.

Vanished like the furrow cut by a ship's keel in the sea. — BALZAC.

Vanished like dew before the morning sun. — GEORGE BEATTIE.

All vanished, like a vision vain. — EMILY BRONTË.

Vanished like a fairy. — E. B. BROWNING.

Vanished like a corpse-light from a grave. — BYRON.

Vanished like dawn to the daylight — GIOSUÈ CARDUCCI.

Vanishes, as is his wont, too like an *Ignis Fatuus*, leaving the dark still darker. — CARLYLE.

Vanished, like a ghost at cock-crowing. — IBID.

Vanish like a shot. — GIOVANNI BATTISTA CASTI.

Vanishing as flies a dream. — JOHN CLARE.

Vanish'd like dew-drops from the spray. — W. G. CLARK.

Passed away
As Fairies vanish at the break of day.
— HARTLEY COLERIDGE.

Vanished away, like spectres. — DICKENS.

Vanish like a breath. — IBID.

Vanished like a discontented fairy. — IBID.

Vanish . . . as easily as an eel into sand. — SIR A. CONAN DOYLE.

Gradually vanished like the receding hill-tops. — GEORGE ELIOT.

Vanish as mist before the sun. — FLAUBERT.

Colors, like the rainbow, ever vanished. — GILES FLETCHER.

Vanished like an empty shade. — PHINEAS FLETCHER.

Vanished like a beautiful evening cloud. — ARNE GARBORG.

Vanished like the shades of night upon the burst of a glorious morning in July. — WILLIAM GODWIN.

Vanish like an echo or a dream. — GOETHE.

Vanish, as by the waving of an enchanter's wand. — HAWTHORNE.

Vanish, like a glimmering light, that comes we know not whence, and goes we know not whither. — IBID.

Vanish like ephemeral things. — IBID.

Vanish out of life as completely as if . . . he lay at the bottom of the sea. — IBID.

Vanished like a baleful star. — P. H. HAYNE.

Vanish — *continued.*

Vanished like an empty dream. — Heinrich Heine.

Vanished . . . like the shadow of a cloud. — Hood.

Vanished like the enchanted castle on the approach of the conqueror. — Frank Horridge.

Vanished like the beautiful sparkling hoarfrost. — Hugo.

Vanish together, as a dream of morning flies. — Ibid.

Vanish like a fleeting dream,
The shadow of a chariot, or flash of sword. — Ibid.

Vanished like the fleeting forms drawn in an evening cloud. — Richard Jago.

All vanish as you shall vanish, like a bubble thrown up from the deep. — Louis Kossuth.

She vanished like the lightning's sudden gleam. — Lamartine.

Vanished like a fleet of cloud, like a passing trumpet-blast, are those splendors of the past. — Longfellow.

Vanish . . . like the mist of the lake. — James Macpherson.

Vanished . . . like the body in the tomb. — D. F. McCarthy.

Vanished . . . like the day branch in the fire. — Ibid.

Like the dreams of the Blind,
Vanish the glories and pomps of the earth in the wind.
— James Clarence Mangan.

Vanish like a dew-drop in a rose. — Gerald Massey.

Vanish like a view caught out of darkness by lightning. — George Meredith.

Vanished, like a blasted thing. — Donald G. Mitchell.

Vanish like gossamers of autumn eve. — Miss Mulock.

Vanished like the feathery snow in summer's running brooks. — Mrs. Norton.

Vanished like a mist that melts on the sunny hill. — Ossian.

Vanished like a scene of enchantment. — Jane Porter.

Vanished, like the airy fabric of an Eastern tale. — Prescott.

Vanished, like a shadow fled. — Edna D. Proctor.

He vanishes like a man who has caused his property to be snatched from a swindler. — Osmanli Proverb.

Vanished, like the writing from the sand. — T. Buchanan Read.

Like the swift shadows of Noon, like the dreams of the blind,
Vanish the glories and pomps of the earth in the wind.
— Friedrich Rückert.

Vanished from our eyes, like sunbeam on the billow cast. — Sir Walter Scott.

Vanisheth as smoke from Ætna.
— Shakespeare.

Vanish like hailstones. — Ibid.

Vanish, like smoke before the tempest's stream. — Shelley.

Vanished, like a star into a cloud. — Alexander Smith.

Vanish like a vision of the night. — Southey.

Beauty vanishes like a vapor. — Harriet P. Spofford.

Vanish like smoke of incense. — Richard H. Stoddard.

Vanish away like smoke. — Old Testament.

Vanish like a shooting star. — John Tobin.

Vanished like a mere soap-bubble. — Josef K. Tyl.

Vanish — *continued.*

Vanished . . . like a feathered shaft frae a yeoman's bow. — DAVID VEDDER.

Evanished like a blink
Of starlight ere the mind can think.
— FRANK WATERS.

Vanished, like a rush
Of self-consuming flame.
— ROBERT K. WEEKS.

Light as a sunbeam glides along the hills
She vanished. — WORDSWORTH.

Vanity.

Vanity acts like a woman — they both think they lose something when love or praise is accorded to another. — BALZAC.

Vaprous.

Vaprous as a witch's cauldron. — DICKENS.

Variable.

Variable as a shadow. — ANON.

Variable as color. — C. C. COLTON.

Variable as the weather. — FROUDE.

Variable as flickering flames. — JAMES MONTGOMERY.

O, woman! . . . variable as the shade,
By the light quivering aspen made.
— SIR WALTER SCOTT

Varied.

Varied as the day. — ANON.

Varied as nature. — IBID.

In France, political principles are as varied as a restaurant bill of fare. — BALZAC.

Varied as humanity. — DUMAS, FILS.

Varied as the shapes of nothingness. — JOSÉ ECHEGARAY.

Varied as varying Nature's ways. — WHITTIER.

Various.

Various as the words we speak. — ANON.

Their aims as various, as the roads they take in journeying thro' life. — ROBERT BLAIR.

Various as woman's will. — HENRY BROOKE.

Various as our palates. — ROBERT BURTON.

Various as the voices of the wind. — HARTLEY COLERIDGE.

Various as flowers on unfrequented plains. — CONGREVE.

Various as the hues of a rainbow. — POE.

Various as human life. — SAMUEL ROGERS.

Like nature various. — RICHARD SAVAGE.

Various as an April day. — JOHN SCOTT.

Various as the weather. — SIR RICHARD STEELE.

Various as the moon. — ISAAC WATTS.

Vary.

Ever varies, she can pass from gay to severe, from fancy to science — quick as thought passes from the dance of a leaf, from the tint of a rainbow, to the theory of motion, the problem of light. — BULWER-LYTTON.

The color also of this mixture varies in proportion to its degrees of heat and coldness ; as a burning coal, when it is hot, shines ; and when it is cold, looks black. — ROBERT BURTON.

Vary like the rainbow's hue. — BYRON.

Vast.

Vast as all heaven. — WILFRED S. BLUNT.

Vast as all space. — JOSEPH CONRAD.

Vast — *continued.*

Vast as cathedrals. — DAUDET.

Vast as Phœbus on his burning wheels. — O. W. HOLMES.

Vast as the mid bulk of a roof-tree's beam. — SWINBURNE.

Vaulted.

Vaulted like rebounding hail. — COLERIDGE.

Vaulted, like a balloon or kite. — JOHN TRUMBULL.

Veer.

Veers and swings,
Like an homing swallow with nightfall in her wings.
— BLISS CARMAN.

Veered like changing memories. — GEORGE ELIOT.

Veer
As the storm shifts of the tempestuous year.
— SWINBURNE.

Vehement.

Vehement as party spleen. — SYDNEY MUNDEN.

Veiled.

Veiled like noontide stars. — AUBREY DE VERE.

Thy beauty lies,
Veiled like a violet nestling in the moss.
— CLAYTON HAMILTON.

Veiled like a nun. — T. BUCHANAN READ.

Venice.

Venice is like a melancholy face of a former beauty who has ceased to rouge, or wipe away traces of her old arts. — GEORGE MEREDITH.

Venomous.

Venymous as a snake. — "BOKE OF MAYD EMLYN."

More venomous than the asp or the blue spider. — HUGO.

Venture.

I have ventur'd,
Like little wanton boys that swim on bladders,
This many summers in a sea of glory,
But far beyond my depth: my high-blown pride
At length broke under me; and now has left me,
Weary and old with service, to the mercy
Of a rude stream, that must forever hide me. — SHAKESPEARE.

Verse.

A sweete verse is that which, like a dish with a delicate Sauce, inuites the Reader to taste, euen against his will. — HENRY PEACHAM.

Vertical.

Vertical like a stake. — CHARLES NODIER.

Vexed.

Vexed like a morning eagle, lost and weary,
And purblind amid foggy midnight wolds. — KEATS.

Must I be vexed like the nightly bird,
Whose sight is loathsome to all winged fowls. — MARLOWE.

Vibrate.

Vibrated, like a coffee mill in operation. — ANON.

Vibrate like a soft musical note. — BALZAC.

Vibrating
Like some becalmed bark beneath the burst
Of Heaven's immediate thunder.
— COLERIDGE.

Felt all her being vibrate as if a violin bow were drawn over her nerves. — FLAUBERT.

Vice.

Vices, like beasts, are fond of none but those that feed them. — SAMUEL BUTLER.

Vice — *continued.*

Vice, like disease, floats in the atmosphere. — William Hazlitt.

The vices operate like age, — bring on disease before its time, and in the prime of youth, leave the character broken and exhausted. — Junius.

Vice leaves repentance in the soul like an ulcer in the flesh which is always scratching and lacerating itself. — Montaigne.

Every great vice is like a pike in a pond, that devours virtues and lesser vices. — Sir Thomas Overbury.

He that is deeply engaged in vice, is like a man laid fast in a bag, who, by a faint and lazy struggling to get out, does but spend his strength to no purpose, and sinks himself the deeper in it: the only way is, by a resolute and vigorous effort to spring out, if possible, at once. — John Tillotson.

Vice-President.

The Vice-President of the United States is like a man in a cataleptic state: he can not speak; he can not move; he suffers no pain, and yet he is perfectly conscious of everything that is going on about him. — Thomas Riley Marshall.

Vicious.

As vicious
As any feend that lith in helle adoun.
— Chaucer.

Victorious.

Victorious like the crest of Mars. — Anon.

Victory.

Triumphant in victories lyke the Palme tree, fruitfull in hir age lyke the Vyne, in all ages prosperous, to all men gratious, in all places glorious: so that there be no ende of hir praise, vntil the ende of all flesh. — Lyly.

Vigilant.

Vigilant as the stars. — Anon.

Vigilant as a cat to steal cream. — Shakespeare.

Vigorous.

Vigorous as fire. — John Pomfret.

Vile.

Wealth vile, as the dross upon the molten gold. — Akenside.

Vindictive.

Vindictive as Philip II. — Anon.

Vindictive as a parrot. — Bulwer-Lytton.

More vindictive than jealous love. — Shakespeare.

Violent.

Violent as a river, swollen with rain, rushes from the mountain. — Anon.

Violent as botel in the spence [store-room]. — Chaucer.

Violent as steam. — C. C. Colton.

Violent as hunger. — William Rowley.

Violent as poison. — Vance Thompson.

Virgin.

Virgins are like the fair flow'r in its lustre,
Which in the garden enamels the ground,
Near it the bees in play flutter and cluster,
And gaudy butterflies frolic around.
But when once plucked 'tis no longer alluring,
To Convent-garden 'tis sent (as yet sweet),
There fades and shrinks, and grows past all enduring,
Rots, stinks, and dies and is trod under feet.
— John Gay.

Virginity.

Virginity, like an old courtier, wears her cap out of fashion. — Shakespeare.

Virtue.

Virtue, like the sun, retains its resplendence, though frequently obscured by clouds. — ANON.

Virtue is like a rich stone, best plain set; and surely virtue is best in a body that is comely, though not of delicate features, and that hath rather dignity of presence than beauty of aspect. — BACON.

Virtue is like precious odors, most fragrant when they are incensed, or crushed; for prosperity doth best discover vice, but adversity doth best discover virtue. — IBID.

Virtue is like health, the harmony of the whole man. — CARLISLE.

Like other plants, virtue will not grow unless its roots be hidden, buried from the eye of the sun. — IBID.

Virtue and learning, like gold, have their intrinsic value; but if they are not polished, they certainly lose a great deal of their lustre; and even polished brass will pass upon more people than rough gold. — CHESTERFIELD.

The pleasure of a fine woman is like that of her own virtue — not so much in the thing, as the reputation of having it. — COLLEY CIBBER.

Virtue is like the polar star, which keeps its place, and all stars turn towards it. — CONFUCIUS.

My virtue, like a string, wound up by art
To the same sound, when yours was touched, took part,
At distance shook, and trembled at my heart. — DRYDEN.

The virtues, like the muses, are always seen in groups. A good principle was never found solitary in any breast. — JANE PORTER.

The virtues are lost in interest, as rivers are lost in the sea. — ROCHEFOUCAULD.

Virtue, like the clear heavens, is without clouds. — SIR PHILIP SIDNEY.

Virtues and discourses are like friends, necessary in all fortunes; but those are the best which are friends in our sadnesses, and support us in our sorrows and sad accidents: and in this sense, no man that is virtuous can be friendless. — JEREMY TAYLOR.

Virtuous.

Virtuous men . . . like some herbs and spices that give not out their sweet smell till they be broken or crushed. — BACON.

Virtuous as holy truth. — BEAUMONT AND FLETCHER.

Virtuous as a briar-rose. — EMERSON.

A truly virtuous person is like good metal, — the more he is fired, the more he is fined; the more he is opposed, the more he is approved. Wrongs may well try him and touch him, but they cannot imprint on him any false stamp. — RICHELIEU.

Visible.

Visible like evanescent grave-lights. — GEORGE MEREDITH.

Visitors.

(*See also* Guests.)

Fares with him as it does with a tranquil lake, which is generally disturbed by visitors. — R. R. MADDEN.

Visits.

Visits
Like those of angels, short and far between. — BLAIR.

Like angel visits, few and far between. — CAMPBELL.

Like angels' visits, short and bright. — JOHN NORRIS.

Vivid.

Vivid as a photograph. — ANON.

Vivid as a dream. — IBID.

Vivid — *continued.*

Vivid as from painted glass.—HOOD.

Vivid as light. — ADAM GOTTLOB OEHLENSCHLÄGER.

Vivid as a dream. — WORDSWORTH.

Vividness.

A vividness as of fire in dark night. — CARLYLE.

Vocal.

Vocal like a harpsichord touched in its ancient neglect by a master hand; its voice comes back and is eloquent again. — ANON.

Voice.

A voice like a broken phonograph. — ANON.

Her voice was like a bagpipe suffering from tonsillitis. — IBID.

For thy voice like an echo from Fairyland seems. — IBID.

A voice like the whistle of birds. — ARABIAN NIGHTS.

Her voice is like the harmony of angels. — BEAUMONT AND FLETCHER.

A voice like a concertina that has been left out in the rain. — MAX BEERBOHM.

A voice like the cry of an expiring mouse, shrill and thin. — ARTHUR C. BENSON.

Gruff voice, like the creaking of the gallows-chain. — R. D. BLACKMORE.

It was a voice so mellow, so bright and
  warm and round,
As if a beam of sunshine had been
  melted into sound.
— HJALMAR H. BOYESEN.

Voice like the music of rills. — WILLIAM CULLEN BRYANT.

Her voice is like the evening thrush
That sings in Cessnock banks unseen,
While his mate sits nestling in the
  bush. — BURNS.

His voice is like the rising storm.— BYRON.

Liquid voice resounded like the prelude of a flute. — D'ANNUNZIO.

Voice, as pure and sweet as if from heaven. — AUBREY DE VERE.

Voice . . . as sweet as the murmur of the brook and the rustle of the corn. — EMERSON.

A voice as sweet as the evening breeze of Boreas in the pleasant month of November. — FIELDING.

Delicate voices, like silver bells. — NIKOLAI V. GOGOL.

Voice like a coyote with bronchitis. — O. HENRY.

A voice like a strained foghorn. — W. W. JACOBS.

A voice like the fourth string of a violoncello. — LEVER.

Something like the voice of a frog with a quinsy. — IBID.

Voice like dish-water gurgling through a sink. — OCTAVE MIRBEAU.

Voice was like hollow wind in a cave. — OSSIAN.

Voice, low as the summer music of a brook. — T. BUCHANAN READ.

With full voice, pure and clear, uplifted, as some classic melody in sweetest legends of old minstrelsy. — JAMES WHITCOMB RILEY.

Voice, as hollow as the hollow sea. — C. G. ROSSETTI.

Thy voice like rills
Of silver, trills
Such sounds of liquid sweetness.
— CHARLES SANGSTER.

Voice . . . is soft like solitude's. — SHELLEY.

A voice like a north wind blowing over corn stubble in January. — CARL SANBURG.

Voice . . . like a peace-giving orison. — HERMANN SUDERMANN.

Voice — *continued.*

Voice like quiring waves. — SWINBURNE.

Voice . . .
That rings athwart the sea whence no man steers
Like joy-bells crossed with death-bells in our ears. — IBID.

Bernhardt's . . . voice is like a thing detachable from herself, a thing which she takes in her hands like a musical instrument, playing on the stops cunningly with her fingers. — ARTHUR SYMONS.

A great voice, as of a trumpet. — NEW TESTAMENT.

I have heard a voice as of a woman in travail, and the anguish as of her that bringeth forth her first child. — OLD TESTAMENT.

The tones of her voice, like the music which seems
Murmur'd low in our ears by the Angel of dreams. — WHITTIER.

A fall of voice,
Regretted like the nightingale's last note. — WORDSWORTH.

Voiceless.

Voiceless as silence. — ANON.

Voiceless as the sphinx. — IBID.

Voiceless as the tomb. — IBID.

Voiceless as a funeral train. — T. BUCHANAN READ.

Voiceless as the past. — THOMAS WATSON.

Void.

Void of pity as chased bears. — THOMAS HEYWOOD.

Void of sense as the movement of the trees and the sound of the winds. — HUGO.

Void of meaning as an oak wainscot. — HUNT.

Volatile.

Volatile as fragrance from a flower. — JAMES MONTGOMERY.

Volatile as a bell. — SYDNEY MUNDEN.

Volatile, like autumn leaves. — EUGENE FITCH WARE.

Voluptuous.

Voluptuous as the first approach of sleep. — BYRON.

Voluptuous as a tropical night. — AMY LESLIE.

Voluptuousness, like justice, is blind; but that is the only resemblance between them. — PASCAL.

Voracious.

Voracious as the monster of the Nile. — SAMUEL LOW.

Voracious as a camel, swallowing his leaven. — OSMANLI PROVERB.

Vulgar.

Vulgar as money. — ANON.

Vulgar as the face of Commerce. — BALZAC.

Vulgar as a church warden. — DONALD G. MITCHELL.

W

Waddle.

Waddle like a duck. — ANON.

Waddled to her with the graceless speed of a seal on land. — BETTINA VON HUTTEN.

Waddles like an Armenian bride. — OSMANLI PROVERB.

Wag.

Wags like a lamb's tail. — ANON.

Wagging, like a bed of clover-leaves in the morning. — R. D. BLACKMORE.

Wagging like bell-clappers. — EDWARD ROBINS.

Waggle.

Waggled like the hilt of a sword. — J. M. BARRIE.

Wail (Noun).

A lonely wail, like a lost child's cry. — ANON.

A wail, as of a babe new-born.
— GEORGE MEREDITH.

Continuous wail, like the moaning of a winter wind. — OUIDA.

Wail like echoes from the sea. — D. G. ROSSETTI.

A wail
Of impotent despair,
Like the sound that frightened marshes hear
From some leper in his lair.
— OSCAR WILDE.

Wail (Verb).

Wailed like starving infants. — ANON.

Wailing like a midnight wind. — AUBREY DE VERE.

Wailing like voices of woe. — ANNIE E. PRESTON.

Wailed as in some flooded cave
Sobs the strong broken spirit of a wave.
— SWINBURNE.

Wail . . . as one making moan for her child. — IBID.

Waist.

A waist, tapered as a well-twisted cord. — AMRIOLKAIS.

Her waist like the cup of a lily. — N. P. WILLIS.

Wait.

Wait,
Like trees fast rooted in the ground.
— ANON.

Wandering fires wait even on rottenness like a stray gleam of thought in an idiot's brain. — P. J. BAILEY.

Waiting, like a lamp-post. — R. D. BLACKMORE.

Thy pleasant youth, a little while withdrawn,
Waits on the horizon of a brighter sky;
Waits, like the morn, that folds her wings and hides
Till the slow stars bring back her dawning hour;
Waits, like the vanished spring, that slumbering bides
Her own sweet time to waken bud and flower.
— WILLIAM CULLEN BRYANT.

Idly wait
Like lovers at the swinging gate.
— O. W. HOLMES.

Waited with a frown,
Like some old champion of romance,
Who, having thrown his gauntlet down,
Expectant leans upon his lance.
— LONGFELLOW.

My love is waiting like corked soda-water to fly towards her. — BARRY PAIN.

Wake.

Was waked as by a bugle call. — T. BUCHANAN READ.

Memories waken, like golden strings 'neath the player's hand. — LADY WILDE.

Walk.

Walks like he had gravel in his shoes. — GEORGE ADE.

Walked like a chicken with frozen toes. — ANON.

She walked with a proud, defiant step, like a martyr to the Coliseum. — BALZAC.

She walks in beauty like the night
Of cloudless climes and starry skies.
— BYRON.

Walk like sprites
To countenance this horror.
— SHAKESPEARE.

Wallow.

Wallow like a boar. — BUNYAN.

Wallow. — *continued.*

Wallow . . . like a stalled cow. — KINGSLEY.

Wan.

Wan as moonlight. — T. B. ALDRICH.

Wan as a sea cliff. — ANON.

Wan as the watery beams of the moon. — IBID.

Wan and mute as vapor. — IBID.

Wan was her lip as the lily's petal. — IBID.

Wan,
Like a fat squab upon a Chinese fan.
— COWPER.

Wan as a wasted ember. — EDGAR FAWCETT.

Wan,
As a lily in the shade.
— JEAN INGELOW.

Wan
As snow at night when the moon is gone.
— IBID.

Wan as primroses gathered at midnight. — KEATS.

Wan
As shows an hour-old ghost.
— C. G. ROSSETTI.

Wan,
Like the head and the skin of a dying man.
— SHELLEY.

Wan as ashes. — SPENSER.

As a dead face wan and dun. — SWINBURNE.

Wan as foam blown up by the sunburnt sands. — IBID.

Wan as a withered flower. — GRAHAM R. TOMSON.

Wander.

Wandering like a passportless man. — ARTHUR ACHESON.

Wanderings as wild as those of the March-spirit. — CHARLOTTE BRONTË.

Wander — *continued.*

Wandering as the wind. — WILLIAM CULLEN BRYANT.

Wandered up and down there like an early Christian refugee in the catacombs. — JOSEPH CONRAD.

Wandering like a plaintive shadow about the places where I dwell. — GAUTIER.

Wanders like an unfettered stream. — HAWTHORNE.

Wander like a lost soul in a Sam Lloyd puzzle. — O. HENRY.

Wanders up and down the world like the noble Morninger. — ARCHIBALD MACMECHAN.

Wandering, like a leaf off the tree. — GEORGE MEREDITH.

Wander like streams through the snow. — MILES O'REILLY.

Wanderest
Like the world's rejected guest.
— SHELLEY.

Wander like a desert wind, without a place of rest. — ALEXANDER SMITH.

Wander from mistress to mistress, like a pilgrim from town to town, who every night must have a fresh lodging, and 's in haste to be gone in the morning. — VANBRUGH.

Wandered about at random, like dogs that have lost the scent. — VOLTAIRE.

I wander'd lonely as a cloud
That floats on high o'er vales and hills.
— WORDSWORTH.

Wanders like a gliding ghost. — IBID.

Wane.

Each with an aspect never twice the same,
Waxing and waning as the new-born host of fancies, like a single night's hoar-frost.
— ROBERT BROWNING.

Wane — *continued.*

Wane,
Like melodies upon a sandy plain,
Without an echo. — KEATS.

Wanes,
As a dream dies down and is dead.
— SWINBURNE.

Want.

Want's like an Irish bog, wherein who sticketh,
By striving to get out, still deeper sinketh. — MARTIAL.

Want is like the rack : it draws a man to endanger himself to the gallows rather than endure it. — CYRIL TOURNEUR.

Wanton.

Wanton as a calf with two dams. — ANON.

Wanton as a young widow. — CONGREVE.

Wanton . . . as a cat in a bowl of water. — MASSINGER.

Wanton as a child. — SHAKESPEARE.

Wanton as youthful goats. — IBID.

War.

A civil war, indeed, is like the heat of a fever ; but a foreign war is like the heat of exercise, and serveth to keep the body in health ; for, in a slothful peace, both courages will effeminate and manners corrupt. — BACON.

Warble.

Warbled like a bird in a sweet summer place. — ANON.

Warbled like a happy bird. — EDMUND GOSSE.

The spring of life warbled through her heart as a brook sometimes warbles through a pleasant dell. — HAWTHORNE.

Warble like the birds in June. — HOOD.

Wariest.

It is good to take the safest and wariest way in general, like the going softly by one that cannot well see. — BACON.

Warlike.

Warlike as the wolf. — SHAKESPEARE.

Warm.

Warm as a mouse in a churn. — ANON.

Warm as sunbeams. — IBID.

Warm as the glow of a topaz. — IBID.

Warm as Venus. — IBID.

Warm as a cricket. — R. D. BLACKMORE.

Warm as red sky's passing blush. — CHARLOTTE BRONTË.

Warm as the spark Prometheus stole. — ELIZA COOK.

Warm in affection as Phœbus at noon. — JOHN G. COOPER.

Warm as ecstasy. — COWPER.

Warm as a prayer in Paradise. — GEORGE DARLEY.

Warm as mead by May breezes fanned. — AUBREY DE VERE.

Warm as sun at noon's high hour. — PAUL LAURENCE DUNBAR.

Warms the soul,
Like the blushing bowl.
— FRANCIS M. FRENCH.

Warm as toast. — JOHN GAY.

Warm as the zeal of youth when first inspired. — IBID.

Warm as a sunned cat. — THOMAS HARDY.

Warmed, like a dove fledging in its downy nest. — CHARLES HARPUR.

Warm as if the brush
Of Titian or Velasquez brought the flush
Of life into their features.
— O. W. HOLMES.

Warm — *continued.*

Warm as young blood. — HOOD.

Warm as when Aurora rushes
Freshly from the god's embrace,
With all her shame upon her face.
— IBID.

Warm as a dove's nest among summer trees. — KEATS.

Warm as Cytherea. — GEORGE MACHENRY.

Her touch was as warm as the tinge of the clover
Burnt brown as it reached to the kiss of the sun. — JOAQUIN MILLER.

Warm and meek,
Like curls upon a rosy cheek.
— THOMAS MOORE.

Warm as life. — JOHN PAYNE.

Warm as wool. — JOHN PEELE.

Warm and cosy as a bird nest. — ALEXANDER SMITH.

Warm as a stove. — STERNE.

Warm and soft as the dome aloft. — SWINBURNE.

Glow warm as the thyme. — IBID.

Warm as a new-made bride. — BAYARD TAYLOR.

Warm as a love-sick poet's muse. — WILLIAM THOMSON.

Warm as sunshine. — WORDSWORTH.

Warn.

Warn, like the one drop of rain on your face, ere the storm. — GEORGE P. LATHROP.

Warrior.

Great warriors, like great earthquakes, are principally remembered for the mischief they have done. — C. N. BOVÉE.

Wary.

Wary as a fox. — ANON.

Wary as a blind horse. — THOMAS FULLER, M.D.

Wary as those that trade in poison. — JOHN WEBSTER.

Waste.

Wasted like the mountain snowe, before warme Phœbus' shine. — ENGLISH BALLAD.

Wasted, like a sermon for the dead. — AMBROSE BIERCE.

Wasted like well-streams. — ROBERT BROWNING.

Waste . . . like April snow in the warm noon. — WILLIAM CULLEN BRYANT.

Waste as fast as dyke water. — WILLIAM CARR'S "THE DIALECT OF CRAVEN."

As the drained fountain, filled with autumn leaves,
The field swept naked of its garnered sheaves;
So wastes at noon the promise of our dawn,
The springs all choking, and the harvest gone.
— O. W. HOLMES.

Waste like a wilderness. — LONGFELLOW.

Wasted, as the snow congealed
When the bright sunne his beams thereon doth beat. — SPENSER.

Wasted
Like an ember among the fallen ashes.
— SWINBURNE.

Waste like death. — IBID.

Wasteful.

Wasteful as a hen. — WELSH PROVERB.

Watch.

Watch, like a mourner. — H. C. KENDALL.

Watch, like terriers at a rat's hole. — KINGSLEY.

Watch, like one that fears robbing. — SHAKESPEARE.

Watchful.

Watchful as a sentinel. — ANON.

Watchful as the eye of a bird. — IBID.

Watchful as a bellman. — BEAUMONT AND FLETCHER.

Watchful as a spider sits in his web. — BULWER-LYTTON.

Watchful as the step of a mother by the couch of her sick child. — IBID.

Watching every glance of him like a British house-dog that will not be taken in with suspicious travelers if he can help it. — CARLYLE.

Watchful like owls awake. — G. K. CHESTERTON.

He was trying to see, with that watchful manner of a seaman who stares into the wind's eye, as if into the eye of an adversary. — JOSEPH CONRAD.

Watchful as spirits. — COWLEY.

Watchful as when fowlers their game will spring. — OTWAY.

Watchful, as a leopard is. — D. G. ROSSETTI.

Watchful as a wheeling eagle. — WORDSWORTH.

Watchfulness.

A soul without watchfulness is like a city without walls, exposed to the inroads of all its enemies. — THOMAS SECKER.

Wave.

Waving like mermaids' hair. — ANON.

Waving like the bosom of an Amazon. — IBID.

His fair hair waved backward like that of the angel upon his sombre car of stars. — HUGO.

Waving like a hand that beckons. — LONGFELLOW.

Waved like blessing hands. — GERALD MASSEY.

Waved like autumn-corn. — SIR WALTER SCOTT.

Fence . . . waved like cobweb in the gale. — IBID.

Waved like the enridged sea. — SHAKESPEARE.

Waved like a penon wyde dispred. — SPENSER.

Wave as with swing of the sea
When the mid tide sways at its height.
— SWINBURNE.

Her slender figure waved, like some light cypress when the merry winds carol midst the yielding boughs. — JOSEPH TURNLEY.

Waver.

Wavering as Hamlet. — ANON.

Wavers like a dry flame. — ARTHUR C. BENSON.

Wavers like a will-o-the-wisp. — WILLIAM BLACK.

He that wavereth is like a wave of the sea driven with the wind and tossed. — NEW TESTAMENT.

Wavered like a summer rill,
As her soft bosom rose and fell.
— WILLIAM B. YEATS.

Wax.

His face waxed like as sunburnt grass. — SWINBURNE.

Wayward.

Wayward as a flame. — ANON.

Wayward as the swallow overhead at set of sun. — GEORGE MEREDITH.

Wayward as wind. — WILLIAM MOTHERWELL.

Weak.

Weak as a cat. — ANON.

Weak as a lamb that can't stand the weight of its own wool. — IBID.

Weak — *continued.*

Weak as unfledged nestling in the falcon's grip. — THOMAS ASHE.

Weak as fear of shame. —HARTLEY COLERIDGE.

Weak as palsy. — LORD DE TABLEY.

Emanations weak as rain. — IBID.

Weak as the puny rillets of the hill. — IBID.

Weak as a reed. — DICKENS.

Weak as flesh. — IBID.

Weak as an eddy in the sandy wind. — EDMUND GOSSE.

Weak as a bled calf. — THOMAS HARDY.

Weak as spider's skein. — KEATS.

Weak as young corn withered, whereof no man may gather and make bread. — ANDREW LANG.

Weak as a poor straw upon a torrent's breast. — M. G. LEWIS.

Weake as sheepe. — LYLY.

Weaker than a woman's tear. — SHAKESPEARE.

Weaker than the wine. — IBID.

Small at first, and weak and frail
Like the vapor of a vale. — SHELLEY.

Weak as a flower that sways with every wind. — ALEXANDER SMITH.

Weak as foam on the sands. — SWINBURNE.

Weak as hearts made sick with hope deferred. — IBID.

Weak as snow. — IBID.

Repentance . . . weak as night devoured by day. — IBID.

Weaker than the worm. — IBID.

Weak as the Roman Chief, who strove to hide
His father's cot (and once his father's pride)
By casing a low shed of rural mould
With marble walls, and roof adorned with gold. — PAULUS SYLLOGUS.

Weak as water. — OLD TESTAMENT.

Weak as gruel. — LOUIS UNTERMEYER.

Weak as a lamb the hour that it is yeaned. — WORDSWORTH.

Wealth.

Wealth, like rheum, falls upon the weakest parts. — ANON.

Wealth is like a child's rattle, which pleases for a moment, and is enjoyed no more. — ROBERT BURTON.

His wealth increaseth, and the more he hath, the more he wants : like Pharaoh's lean kine, which devoured the fat, and were not satisfied. —IBID.

Wealth is like a viper, which is harmless if a man knows how to take hold of it ; but if he does not, it will twine round his hand and bite him. — SAINT CLEMENT.

Weary.

Wearied as a finch in a cage. — ANON.

Weary as a haystack-sleeper. — IBID.

Weary, with her hard embracing,
Like a wild bird being tamed with too much handling,
Or as the fleet-foot roe that's tired with chasing,
Or like the froward infant still'd with dandling. — SHAKESPEARE.

Wearily.

Wearily,
Like those whom living tires.
— THOMAS HARDY.

Weatherbeaten.

Weatherbeaten as a fisherman's oar. — THOMAS WADE.

Wedge.

Wedg'd in one body, like a flock of cranes. — HOMER (POPE).

Wedlock.

Wedlock, indeed, hath oft compared been
To public feasts, where meet the public rout.
Where they that are without would fain go in,
And they that are within would fain go out. — SIR JOHN DAVIES.

Wedlock's like wine, — not properly judged of till the second glass. — DOUGLAS JERROLD.

Honest wedlock
Is like a banqueting house built in a garden,
On which the spring's chaste flowers take delight
To cast their modest odours.
— THOMAS MIDDLETON.

Weep.

Weeps like a walrus o'er the waning moon. — ANON.

Wept like a lost child. — GEORGE W. BAGBY.

Weep like a cut vine-twig. — ROBERT BROWNING.

Wept like a baffled child. — BULWER-LYTTON.

Weep like a crocodile. — ROBERT BURTON.

Weepe as dooth a child that is ybete. — CHAUCER.

Weep . . . like a dear innocent child bitterly afflicted. — LA MOTTE FOUQUÉ.

I must seem like a hanging moon, a little waterish for a while. — THOMAS MIDDLETON.

Like a fair flower surcharged with dew, she weeps. — MILTON.

I'm weeping like a willow
That droops in leaf and bough.
— G. P. MORRIS.

Weep, like a young wench that had buried her grandam. — SHAKESPEARE.

Weeps like a wench that had shed her milk. — IBID.

Weigh.

Weigh like the shillings on a dead man's eyes. — O. W. HOLMES.

Weighs a man down like a hod of mortar. — N. P. WILLIS.

Weird.

Weird as the elfin lights that glimmer of frosty nights. — T. B. ALDRICH.

Weird as a witch's dream. — CHARLES KINGSLEY.

Weirdly.

Weirdly, like a dream. — LAFCADIO HEARN.

Welcome (Adjective).

Welcome as land to sailors long at sea. — ÆSCHYLUS.

About as welcome as a bullet. — ANON.

Welcome as water in a leaking ship. — IBID.

About as welcome as a coffin at a wooden wedding. — IBID.

Welcome as the clang of the dinner bell. — IBID.

Welcome as an engagement ring to an old maid. — IBID.

Welcome as a good-natured friend who makes short calls. — IBID.

Welcome as dew on parched flowers. — IBID.

As welcome as sunshine
In every place
Is the beaming approach
Of a good-natured face.
— IBID.

Welcome as a rainstorm in Hell. — GEORGE VAUX BACON.

Welcome as Eden. — BYRON.

Welcome — *continued.*

Welcome, like one tiny islet of Reality amid the shoreless sea of Phantasms, to the reflective mind, seriously loving and seeking what is worthy and memorable, seriously hating and avoiding what is the reverse, and intent not to play the dilettante in this world. — CARLYLE.

Welcome as water into one's shoes. — DENHAM'S "FOLK-LORE NORTH OF ENGLAND."

As welcome as the haven to the tempest-driven ship. — BARTHOLOMEW DOWLING.

Welcome as flowers that bloom in the spring. — W. S. GILBERT.

Welcome as a pole-cat at a picnic. — CHARLES HENDERSON.

Welcome as peace after destructive war. — ROBERT HERRICK.

Welcome as the bird to the elm-tree bough. — LOWELL.

Welcome as a boon long sought. — EVAN MACCOLL.

Welcome as stones in oats to horse. — "NEWS FROM CHELSMFORD."

Welcome as flowers in May. — JOHN RAY'S "HANDBOOK OF PROVERBS."

Welcome . . . as the deluge of early spring rain. — FRANCIS S. SALTUS.

Welcome . . . as dewy cherries to the
taste in June,
As shady lanes to travelers at noon.
— JOHN SCOTT.

Welcome hither
As is the spring to the earth.
— SHAKESPEARE.

The night to the owl and morn to the lark less welcome. — IBID.

Welcome as dogs unto a church they are. — JOHN TAYLOR.

Welcome! as beauty to the lovesick
swain,
For which he long had sigh'd in vain.
— WILLIAM THOMSON.

Welcome as the discovery of a five-dollar bill in an old coat to a salaried man the morning before pay day. — WALTER TRUMBULL.

Welcome as the rear view of a grizzly bear to a hunter who has left his fire-arms at home. — IBID.

Welcome to my tranced view,
As battle-yell to warrior's ear.
— WHITTIER.

Welcome as a star. — WORDSWORTH.

Welcome (Verb).

Welcome as a child left in the haunting dark welcomes the entrance of light. — BULWER-LYTTON.

Well.

Welled from out her happy heart like the carol of a bird. — SARAH JOSEPHA HALE.

Welter.

Weltering, shall I say, like an Egyptian pitcher of tamed vipers, each struggling to get its head above the others. — CARLYLE.

Poor Mugno! there he welters, like a toast at bottom of a tankard! — HORACE SMITH.

Wet.

Wet as a fish. — ANON.

Weet, as beest is in the reyn. — CHAUCER.

Her face with little drops was wet
Like pansy petals after rain.
— NORMAN GALE.

Wet as a drowned rat. — THOMAS HEYWOOD.

Wet as a dog in the rain. — JAMES HUNEKER.

Wet as the slush of a quagmire. — OUIDA.

Whang.

Whanged agin my ribs like a old-fashioned wheat Flale agin a barn door. — ARTEMUS WARD.

Wheeling.

Grenadiers continually wheeling, like so many reapers steady among wind-tossed grain. — Carlyle.

Wheeze.

Wheeze like a calliope with sore tonsils. — Anon.

Whelmed.

Whelmed me like a flood. — C. G. Rossetti.

Whelmed like the Egyptian tyrant's impetuous host. — Southey.

Whet.

Appetite whets, like the world-famous bark of Peru. — Bret Harte.

Whimper.

Whimper like a child for dread. — Bliss Carman.

Whimpers like a lowing cow. — John Gay.

Whimpered like a woman. — Longfellow.

Whimpers like a cur. — Arthur Symons.

Whine.

Whine like wind at a keyhole. — Anon.

Whyning like a Pigge halfe rosted. — Lyly.

Whined like a leashed wolf-pack. — Alfred Noyes.

He whines like a Jew whose house is burnt. — Osmanli Proverb.

Whip.

Whipped like a cur. — Anon.

Whipped like tops in Lent. — Ben Jonson.

Whipped like green rye. — Rabelais.

Whir.

Whir like the noise of an eagle's wings. — Ouida.

Whirl.

Whirl'd away like flakes of foam. — Æschylus.

Whirl like a scourge in the air. — Anon.

Whirl'd like a leaf. — G. F. S. Armstrong.

Blades whirled like spirited spray. — Laurence Binyon.

Whirling like dust. — Joseph Conrad.

Whirling . . . like the sand doth when the whirlwind breathes. — Dante.

Whirled like Ixion's wheel. — Euripides.

Whirling . . . as in jubilee of child-like sport. — E. T. A. Hoffmann.

Whirl along, like pebbles in a stream. O. W. Holmes.

Whirling like a windmill. — Kipling.

Whirled it round him like a rattler. — Longfellow.

Whirl, like maelstrom in the ocean. — Edwin Markham.

Whirled like a potter's wheel. — Shakespeare.

Whirl . . . like the leaves of a forest grown withered and dry. — Carmen Sylva.

Whirl as if a tempest flung them. — Bayard Taylor.

Whirled in a swift and cloudy turbulence, as when some star of Eblis downward hurled by Allah's bolt, sweeps with its burning hair the waste of darkness. — Ibid.

Whisker.

(*See also* Beard).

Fetlock whiskers, like that worn by a Percheron stallion. — Anon.

Whisper.

Whispers like the low wind's sighs. — Alice Cary.

Whisper — *continued.*

Whisper like the voice within the shell. — Lewis Morris.

Whispered like the restless brook. — C. G. Rossetti.

Whistle.

Whistling like the thrushes
With voice in silver gushes.
— Leigh Hunt.

Whistles like the jackal's scream. — Schiller.

Whistle, like a devil's baby. — Stephen Smith.

White.

White as a moonlit sail. — William Alexander.

White as the necks of swans. — James Lane Allen.

White as a bean. — Anon.

White as lime. — Ibid.

White as a baby's arm. — Ibid.

White as a diamond. — Ibid.

White as a doll. — Ibid.

White as a dove. — Ibid.

White as a fish. — Ibid.

White as a flock of sheep. — Ibid.

White as a ghost. — Ibid.

White as a live terrier. — Ibid.

White as a pillow. — Ibid.

White as arsenic. — Ibid.

White as a sheet. — Ibid.

White as a shroud. — Ibid.

White as a spirit. — Ibid.

White as a statue. — Ibid.

White as a sycamore. — Ibid.

White as a whale's tooth. — Ibid.

White as chastity. — Ibid.

White as his neck-cloth. — Ibid.

White as salt. — Ibid.

White as silver. — Ibid.

White as sin forgiven. — Ibid.

White as sunbeams. — Ibid.

White as the breakers' foam. — Ibid.

White as the breast of a gull. — Ibid.

White as the blossoms of the almond tree. — Ibid.

White as the foam that danced on the billow's height. — Ibid.

White as the gown of a bride. — Ibid.

White as the hand of Moses. — Ibid.

White as the snowy white rose that in the moonlight sighs. — Ibid.

White as white satin. — Ibid.

White like the inside of a shoulder of mutton. — Ibid.

White as the stem of a young palm. — Arabian.

White as paper of Syria. — Ibid.

White as camphor. — Arabian Nights.

Brow white as day. — Ibid.

White as morning. — Ibid.

White as the full moon when it mooneth on its fourteenth night. — Ibid.

White like egg of the pigeon hen. — Ibid.

White as bismuth. — William Archer.

White as frost on field. — W. E. Aytoun.

A maid as white as ivory bone. — English Ballad.

White as snow-drops. — Servian Ballad.

Purely white as the mountain snow. — Welsh Ballad.

White as porcelain. — Balzac.

White — *continued.*

White as soap. — R. H. Barham.

White as the hawthorn's crown. — Mary Barry.

White as a thread by hands of angels spun. — Francis Beaumont.

Whiter than mountain snow hath ever been. — Ibid.

White as swanne. — Sir Harry Beaumont.

Soul as white as heaven. — Beaumont and Fletcher.

White as innocence herself. — Ibid.

White as the foaming sea. — Park Benjamin.

White as snow. — Bion.

White as an angel. — William Blake.

White as foam-drift in the moony shimmer of starlit, wave-pavilioned dells. — Mathilde Blind.

White as the sun. — Emily Brontë.

White as candles against the altar's gold. — Katherine H. Brown.

White as foam thrown upon rocks from the old-spent wave. — E. B. Browning.

White as gulls. — Ibid.

White as moonshine. — Ibid.

White as wax. — Ibid.

White like a cloud at fall of snow. — Ibid.

White like a spirit's hand. — Ibid.

White with coming buds, like the bright side of a sorrow. — Robert Browning.

White as a curd. — Ibid.

White as the winding-sheet. — Robert Buchanan.

White as death. — Bulwer-Lytton.

White, as if she lived on blanched almonds. — Ibid.

White as a clout. — Bunyan.

As white's a daisy. — Burns.

White as the thoughts of an angel. — Mary Frances Butts.

White as a white sail on a dusky sea. — Byron.

White as fleece. — Alice Cary.

White as a cloth. — Bliss Carman.

White as the chaulkie clyffes of Brittaines isle. — Chatterton.

Whyte hys rade [neck] as the sommer snowe. — Ibid.

Whit as chalk. — Chaucer.

Whyte as floure. — Ibid.

Whit as is a lylie flour. — Ibid.

Whyte as lylye or rose in rys [twig]. — Ibid.

White as snowe falle newe. — Ibid.

White of hewe,
As snowe on braunche snawed newe.
— Ibid.

White was his berd as is the dayesie. — Ibid.

Whit was as the flour delys (Flower-de-luce). — Ibid.

White as a flock of egrets. — Chinese.

Gleaming white, like peach and plum blossoms. — Ibid.

Dressed in white — all white, like a bride or a bandaged thumb. — Irvin S. Cobb.

White as new-plucked cotton. — Frederick S. Cozzens.

White as an infant's spirit. — Aubrey De Vere.

White as ashes. — Dickens.

Hands . . . white, as if the blood began to chill there. — Dumas, père.

As white as teeth of twenty-five years old. — Ibid.

White — *continued.*

A sail as white as blossom upon spray. — WILLIAM DUNBAR.

The beautiful young lady, all in white, like a lily in the night, or the moon sweeping over a cloudless sky. — JOSEPH VON EICHENDORFF.

White as the canna upon the moor. — ANCIENT ERSE.

White as snow-wreath in the eye of spring. — F. W. FABER.

White as molten glass. — PHINEAS FLETCHER.

Breasts
As white as hedgeside May.
— NORMAN GALE.

White and awful as a shroud-enfolded ghost. — RICHARD GARNETT.

His beard was whiter than the feathers which veil the breast of the penguin. — GOLDSMITH.

Pure and white,
As some shy spirit in a haunted place.
— P. H. HAYNE.

White as the lips of passion. — IBID.

As white as bear's teeth. — THOMAS HEYWOOD.

As white as the pale ashes of a wasted coal. — J. G. HOLLAND.

White as sea-bleached shells. — HOLMES.

White as the sea-gull. — IBID.

White as Irish linen. — HOOD.

White as parading breeches. — IBID.

White as a chicken. — HUGO.

White as the gowan [daisy]. — JOHN IMLAH.

White,
Like ships in heaven full-sailed.
— JEAN INGELOW.

White as the snowy rose of Guelderland. — IBID.

White as flocks new-shorn. — KEATS.

Whiter than a star. — IBID.

White as the moon. — OMAR KHAYYÂM

White as the wonder undefiled of Eve just wakened in Paradise. — HARRIET MCEWEN KIMBALL.

White as an embodied hush. — IBID.

Thin-flanked woman, as white and as stale as a bone. — KIPLING.

White as an angel clad in light. — — J. S. KNOWLES.

White, like the apparition of a dead rainbow. — CHARLES LAMB.

White as maiden purity. — MISS LANDON.

White,
Like a gravestone seen in the pale
moonlight. — IBID.

White as Ketak's snow flower. — "LAYS OF ANCIENT INDIA."

White as a nun. — RICHARD LE GALLIENNE.

White as ivory. — IBID.

White as the face of the dead. — CAMILLE LEMONNIER.

Whiter than the downy spray. — JOHN LEYDEN.

White as a live terror.—GEORGE CABOT LODGE.

White as a cloud that floats and fades in the air. — LONGFELLOW.

White as a schoolboy's paper kite. — IBID.

White as seas' fog. — IBID.

White as the gleam of a receding sail. — IBID.

White as a dove. — LOVER.

White as thistle-down. — LOWELL.

White as alabaster. — LYLY.

White as driven snow. — IBID.

White — *continued.*

White as untrod snow. — Lewis Machin.

White as the foam of streams. — James Macpherson.

White as the whitest foam of the sea
That tosses its waves under fervent skies,
Or a feather dropped from an angel's wing
As it leant o'er the walls of Paradise.
— A. W. Marshall.

White and pure as any bridal veil. — Guy de Maupassant.

Sightless white, like eyes of lifeless stone. — William J. Mickle.

White as the bloom o' the pear. — — William Miller.

White as a sinner's shroud. — Miss Mulock.

White as virgin's pall. — Ibid.

Lilly-white as a lady's marrying smock. — Thomas Nash.

Venerable beard
White, hoary like the foam o' the sea.
— Enrico Nencioni.

White
Like girls for a first communion dight.
— Roden Noel.

White . . . like angels in their ascension clothes, waiting for those who prayed below. — Fitz-James O'Brien.

White as a winter home. — John Payne.

White as is the new blown bell
Of that frail flower that loves the wind.
— Ibid.

As white . . . as clay. — W. M. Praed.

White as the waxen petal of the flowers. — Helen C. Prince.

White like a young flock,
Coeval, newly shorn, from the clear brook recent, and branching on the sunny rock.
— Matthew Prior.

White as swans. — Rabelais.

White as fear. — Opie Read.

White as the living cheek opposed. — Charles Reade.

White as grit. — James Whitcomb Riley.

White as the cream-crested wave. — Ibid.

White as the gleam of her beckoning hand. — Ibid.

White a hand as lilies in the sunlight. — C. G. Rossetti.

White as the moon lies in the lap of night. — Ibid.

White like flame. — Ibid.

Whiter than sawn ivory. — Ruskin.

Wings as white as a dream of snow in love and light. — A. J. Ryan.

White as Dinlay's spotless snoe. — Sir Walter Scott.

White as a lily. — Shakespeare.

Soft as dove's down and as white. — Ibid.

White his shroud as the mountain snow. — Ibid.

Teeth as white as whale's bone. — Ibid.

Perfect white
Show'd like an April daisy on the grass.
— Ibid.

White as the foam o' the sea
That is driven o'er billows of azure agleam with sun-yellow.
— William Sharp.

White as isinglass. — G. B. Shaw.

Whitens like steel in a furnace. — Ibid.

White with the whiteness of what is dead,
Like troops of ghosts on the dry wind past.
— Shelley.

White as a swan's stray feather. — H. B. Smith.

White — *continued.*

White . . . like the flying cloud at noon. — SOUTHEY.

White as the swan's breast. — IBID.

White, withouten spot or pride, that seemed like silke and silver woven neare. — SPENSER.

White . . . like a dazie in a field of grass. — SIR JOHN SUCKLING.

White as a custard. — SWIFT.

White as dead stark-stricken dove. — SWINBURNE.

White as faith's and age's hue. — IBID.

White as moonlight snows. — IBID.

White as the live heart of light. — IBID.

White as the sparkle of snow-flowers in the sun. — IBID.

White as the unfruitful thorn-flower. — IBID.

White as mountain cotton-grass. — "IRISH EPIC TALES."

White as any flower. — TENNYSON.

White as privet. — IBID.

White as utter truth. — IBID.

White as the light. — NEW TESTAMENT.

It was like coriander seed, white. — OLD TESTAMENT.

Whiter than milk. — IBID.

White as a ceiling. — THACKERAY.

I turned as white as cold boil'd veal. — IBID.

White, and ghastly, like an army of tombstones by moonlight. — IBID.

Like the mists of spring, all silvery white. — "THE HAGOROMO."

More white than curds. — THEOCRITUS.

Slight and white as a peeled wand. — VANCE THOMPSON.

White as sculptured stone. — F. F. TIERNAN.

White as the down of angel's wings. — J. T. TROWBRIDGE.

White, like the Shah of Persia's diamond plume. — MARK TWAIN.

White as Carrara marble. — THEODORE WATTS-DUNTON.

White as evening clouds. — C. J. WELLS.

White as the wings of prayer. — WHITTIER.

Stainless white,
Like ivory bathed in still moonlight.
— IBID.

Whiter than a moony pearl. — OSCAR WILDE.

White as a charnel bone. — N. P. WILLIS.

White as flashing icicle. — IBID.

Whiz.

Whizzes like a hot iron. — FARQUHAR.

It whizzes like the waters from a mill. — CHRISTOPHER PITT.

Whole.

Whole as a fish. — SHAKESPEARE.

Whole as the marble. — IBID.

Wholesome.

Wholesome as ass's milk. — ANON.

Wholesome as the morning air. — CHAPMAN.

Wholesome as Heaven. — HAWTHORNE.

Whoop.

Whoop like boys, at Pounders. — KINGSLEY.

Whooped like a Bacchanal. — SIR WALTER SCOTT.

Whooping like artillery. — HENRY D. THOREAU.

Wicked (Adjective).

Wicked as a lie. — ZOLA.

Wicked (Noun).

The wicked, even whilst receiving favors, incline to their natural dispositions, as a dog's tail, after every part of anointing and chafing, to its natural bend. — HITOPADESA.

But the wicked are like the troubled sea, when it cannot rest, whose waters cast up mire and dirt. — OLD TESTAMENT.

Wide.

Wide as a barn door. — ANON.

Wide as the poles asunder. — IBID.

Wide stretching as the earth. — IBID.

As wide as land. — ALFRED AUSTIN.

Wide as the sea's perpetual flow. — HERBERT BATES.

Wide as night is wide. — WILFRED CAMPBELL.

Wide as the mouth of a wallet. — THOMAS DEKKER.

Wide as Shakespeare's soul. — SYDNEY DOBELL.

Wide-awake as mice. — DUMAS, PÈRE.

Wide as hope. — EMERSON.

Wide as the unbridged gulf that yawns between the rich man and the beggar. — J. G. HOLLAND.

As wide as the world is. — LANGLAND.

Wide as a church door. — SHAKESPEARE.

Wide as life. — SWINBURNE.

Wide as woe. — WILLIAM WATSON.

Wide as human thought. — WHITTIER.

Wide as the difference between death and life. — IBID.

Widespread.

Widespread as a tent at noon. — OSCAR WILDE.

Widow.

Widows, like ripe fruit, drop easily from their perch. — BRUYERE.

A widow is like a frigate of which the first captain has been shipwrecked. — ALPHONSE KARR.

Wife.

A cigar is like a wife!
Put it up to your lips, and light it;
When you've learned to do it right, it
Adds a certain zest to life.
Mind you keep on puffing it,
Or it's out, and can't be lit.
Ah, the aroma! Ah, the glow!
Will I have one? Thank you, No.
— ALEISTER CROWLEY.

Scolding wives, like bad clocks, are seldom in order. — S. DOWNEY.

A wife is like an unknown sea;
Least known to him who thinks he knows
Where all the Shores of Promise be,
Where lies the Island of Repose,
And where the rocks that he must flee.
— J. G. HOLLAND.

A wife, domestic, good, and pure,
Like snail, should keep within her door;
But not, like snail, with silver track,
Place all her wealth upon her back.
— WILLIAM W. HOW.

A good wife is like the ivy which beautifies the building to which it clings, twining its tendrils more lovingly as time converts the ancient edifice into a ruin. — DR. JOHNSON.

Our wives, like their writings, are never safe except when under lock and key. — WYCHERLEY.

Wiggle.

Wiggle like a knot of vipers. — HALL CAINE.

Wild.

Wild as vulture's cry. — ÆSCHYLUS.

Wild as the winds that tear the curled red leaf in the air. — T. B. ALDRICH.

Wild — *continued.*

Wild as a buck. — Anon.

Wild as a hawk. — Ibid.

Wild as a maniac's dream. — Ibid.

Wild as a mountain lion. — Ibid.

Wild as Scott's Macbriar. — Ibid.

Wild as Whiston's prophecies. — Ibid.

Wild as wild Arabs. — Arabian Nights.

Like a cowslip, growing wild. — Thomas Ashe.

As wild and as skeigh as muirland filly. — Joanna Baillie.

Wild as Winter. — Beaumont and Fletcher.

As wild as game in July. — Dion Boucicault.

Wild as one whom demons seize. — Charlotte Brontë.

Legends wild as those culled on shores licked by Hydaspes. — Bulwer-Lytton.

Wild as that hallow'd anthem sent to hail
Bethlehem's shepherds in the lonely vale,
When Jordan hush'd his waves, and midnight still
Watch'd on the holy towers of Zion hill. — Campbell.

Wild and capricious as the wind and wave. — James Cawthorn.

Wilde as chased deere. — Thomas Churchyard.

A landscape rose
More wild and waste and desolate than where
The white bear, drifting on a field of ice,
Howls to her sundered cubs with piteous rage
And savage agony. — Coleridge.

Wild as a maniac's mirth. — Eliza Cook.

Wild as the lightning. — Aubrey De Vere.

Wild as the waves. — Ibid.

Wild as dreams. — Emerson.

Wilder than the Adrain tides which form Calabrian bays. — Roswell M. Field.

As wild as the whirlwind. — Nikolai V. Gogol.

Wild as a sea-breeze. — Hawthorne.

Wild as if creation's ruins
Were heaped in one immeasurable chain
Of barren mountains, beaten by the storms
Of everlasting winter.
—James A. Hillhouse.

Wild as coursers with unsubdued neck. — Horace.

Wild as a tameless horse of Tartary. — Richard Hovey.

Wild as a fiend. — Sigmund Krasinski.

Wild as a burst of day-gold blown through the colors of morning. — George Cabot Lodge.

Wild and woful, like the cloud rack of a tempest. — Longfellow.

Wild as an unbroken horse. — Maria Lowell.

Wild as the heart of a bird. — Edwin Markham.

Wild as flowers upon a river's brink. — George Edgar Montgomery.

Wild as the changes of a dream. — James Montgomery.

Wild as mountain-breezes. — Thomas Moore.

Wild as the winds. — Pope.

Wild as ocean gale. — Sir Walter Scott.

Wild, like trumpet-jubilee. — Ibid.

Wildly as some vex'd and angry sea madly throws up its ancient firm foundation. — Anon.

Wild — *continued.*

Wild as young bulls. — IBID.

Wild as haggards of the rock. — IBID.

The other wild,
Like an unpractised swimmer plunging
still. — IBID.

Wild . . . as regret. — MARIE VAN VORST.

Wild as an errant fancy. — HELEN HAY WHITNEY.

Wild like the stormy wind. — WILLIAM WILKIE.

Wild as the tempests of the upper sky. — WILLIAM WINTER.

Wild and rude
As ever hue-and-cry pursued,
As ever ran a felon's race.
— WORDSWORTH.

Wilful.

Wilful as a pig that will neither lead nor drive. — ANON.

Wilful as the wind. — RICHARD HOVEY.

Wilful as a mule. — DANISH PROVERB.

Wilful as a prince. — SIR WALTER SCOTT.

Willing.

Willing as a turtle. — JOHN GAY.

With a heart as willing
As bondage e'er of freedom.
— SHAKESPEARE.

Willing as the springtide sea gives up
Her will to the eastern sea-wind's.
— SWINBURNE.

Willingly.

As willingly as any singing bird sets him to sing his morning roundelay, because he likes to sing and likes the song. — GEORGE ELIOT.

Willingly
As birds make ready for their bridal
time. — TENNYSON.

Wily.

Wily as an old fox. — SIR WALTER SCOTT.

Wind.

Winds about like a hare. — ANON.

Winds about like a snake in the grass. — IBID.

Winds like a lover's knot. — IBID.

Winding like the maze of love. — JOHN CUNNINGHAM.

Windy.

Windy as a dog-day in Kansas. — O. HENRY.

Wine.

Wine is like anger; for it makes us
strong,
Blind and impatient, and it leads us
wrong;
The strength is quickly lost; we feel
the error long.
— GEORGE CRABBE.

Wine is like rain: when it falls on the
mire it but makes it the fouler,
But when it strikes the good soil it
wakes it to beauty and bloom.
— JOHN HAY.

Winged.

Winged as Hermes' heels. — ANON.

Wink.

Winks like the stars. — HOOD.

Wink with one eye like a gunner. — WILLIAM ROWLEY.

Winning.

As winning as the Queen of Love. — RICHARD SAVAGE.

Winter.

Winter, like a felon ghost, that with its viewless presence chills the blood. — EDMUND GOSSE.

Wintry.

Wintry as despair. — LORD DE TABLEY.

Wipe.

Wipe
My life away like a vast sponge of
fate. — KEATS.

I will wipe Jerusalem as a man wipeth a dish, wiping it, and turning it upside down. — OLD TESTAMENT.

Wisdom.

Wisdom is like electricity. There is no permanently wise man, but men capable of wisdom, who, being put into certain company, or other favorable conditions, become wise for a short time, as glasses rubbed acquire electric power for a while. — EMERSON.

Wisdom which is only theoretical and never put into practise is like a double rose ; its color and its perfume are delightful, but it withers away and leaves no seed. — SCHOPENHAUER.

Wisdom excelleth folly, as far as light excelleth darkness. — OLD TESTAMENT.

Wise.

Wise as Minerva. — ANON.

Wise as Solomon. — IBID.

As wise as the men of Gotham, who went to build a wall about the wood to keep out the cuckoo. — IBID.

Wise as Time and Silence are. — ALFRED AUSTIN.

Looking wise,
As men find woodcocks by their eyes.
— SAMUEL BUTLER.

Wise as Thurlow looks. — C. J. FOX.

As wise as a woodcock. — JOHN HEYWOOD.

Wise as an owl. — KEATS

Wise as the Mayor of Banbury, who would prove that Henry III was before Henry II. — LEAN'S "COLLECTANEA."

Wise as age. — W. J. LINTON.

Wise as nature. — POPE.

Wise as Waltom's calfe. — JOHN SKELTON.

Wise as serpents. — NEW TESTAMENT.

Wiser than the children of light. — IBID.

Wise as Shakespeare. — THOREAU.

Wise as her mother's apron string. — NICHOLAS UDALL.

Wish.

Wishes, like castles in the air, are inexpensive and not taxable. — SAM SLICK.

Wishes, like painted landscapes, best
delight,
Whilst distance recommends them to
the sight.
Placed far off, they beautiful appear ;
But show their coarse and nauseous
colours, near.
— THOMAS YALDEN.

Wistfully.

Wistfully,
Like to some maiden spirit pausing
pale,
New-wing'd, yet fain to sail
Above the serene gulf to where a
bridegroom soul
Calls o'er the soft horizon.
— SIDNEY LANIER.

Wit.

Wit is like a ghost, much more often talked of than seen. — ANON.

Wit kills the soul, as argument kills reason. — BALZAC.

Full of wit as a ginger-bottle is of pop. — J. R. BARTLETT'S "DICTIONARY OF AMERICANISMS."

Wits, like Physicians, never can agree,
When of a different Society.
— APHRA BEHN.

His wit is like fire in a flint, that is nothing while it is in, and nothing again as soon as it is out. — SAMUEL BUTLER.

Wit — *continued.*

All wit and fancy, like a diamond,
The more exact and curious 'tis ground,
Is forc'd for every carat to abate,
As much in value as it wants in weight.
— IBID.

Wit's like a luxuriant vine ;
Unless to virtue's prop it join,
Firm and erect toward Heaven bound,
Though it with beauteous leaves and pleasant fruit be crown'd
It lies, deformed and rotting, on the ground. — COWLEY.

Wit, like fierce-claret, when't begins to pall,
Neglected lies, as 'f of no use at all ;
But, in its full perfection of decay,
Turns vinegar, and comes again in play. — EARL OF DORSET.

Wit, like hunger, will be with great difficulty restrained from falling into vice and ignorance, where is great plenty and variety of food. — HENRY FIELDING.

True wit is like the brilliant stone,
Dug from the Indian mine,
Which boasts two different powers in one,
To cut as well as shine.
— "GRUB-STREET JOURNAL," 1730.

Homebred wits are like home-made wines, sweet, luscious, spiritless, without body, and ill to keep. — JULIUS C. HARE.

Wit, like an insect clamb'ring up a wall,
Mounts to one point, and then of course must fall,
No wiser, if its pains proceed, than end,
And all its journey to descend.
— WALTER HARTE.

Wits, like misers, always covet more. — IBID.

Wit is like love — the softest is the best. — AARON HILL.

Wits, like drunken men with swords, are apt to draw their steel upon their best acquaintances. — DOUGLAS JERROLD.

Wit, like money, bears an extra value when rung down immediately it is wanted. Men pay severely who require credit. — IBID.

Wit, like every other power, has its boundaries. Its success depends on the aptitude of others to receive impressions ; and that as some bodies, indissolute by heat, can set the furnace and crucible at defiance, there are minds upon which the rays of fancy may be pointed without effect, and which no fire of sentiment can agitate or exalt. — DR. JOHNSON.

Bring all wits to the Rack, whose Noses are euer like Swine spoyling and rooting vp the Muses Gardens, and their whole Bodies like Moles, as blindly working vnder Earth to cast any, the least, hilles vpon Vertue. — BEN JONSON.

For wits, like adjectives, are known to cling to that which stands alone. — ROBERT LLOYD.

Nor make to dangerous wit a vain pretense,
But wisely rest content with modest sense ;
For wit, like wine, intoxicates the brain,
Too strong for feeble women to sustain :
Of those who claim it more than half have none ;
And half of those who have it are undone. — LORD LYTTELTON.

Wit and wisdom differ ; Wit is upon the sudden turn, Wisdom is in bringing about ends. Nature must be the ground-work of Wit and Art ; otherwise whatever is done will prove but Jack-Pudding's work. Wit must grow like Fingers. If it be taken from others, 'tis like Plums stuck upon black Thorns ; there they are for a while, but they come to nothing. — SELDEN.

Wit . . . blunt as the fencer's foils. — SHAKESPEARE.

Wit — *continued.*

One wit, like a knuckle of ham in soup, gives a zest and flavor to the dish; but more than one serves only to spoil the pottage. — SMOLLETT.

Some men's wit is like a dark lantern, which serves their own turn and guides them their own way, but is never known (according to the Scripture phrase) either to shine forth before men or to glorify their Father in heaven. — POPE.

As in smooth oil the razor best is whet,
So wit is by politeness keenest set.
— YOUNG.

Wither.

Withered like a Normandy pippin. — ANON.

Withered like a rose without light. — IBID.

Like the rainbow in a summer shower,
Or gaudy poppy, of fugacious bloom,
'Tis thine to flourish for a transient hour,
Then, withered, sink in dark oblivious tomb. — ALEXANDER BALFOUR.

Her white soul withered in the mire
As paper shrivels in the fire.
— STEPHEN VINCENT BENÉT.

Wither away like a flower ungathered in a garden. — ROBERT BURTON.

Withered as an autumn leaf. — WILKIE COLLINS.

Withered like a plucked flower ready to be flung on some rotting heap of rubbish. — JOSEPH CONRAD.

Withered and pale as an old pauper. — DICKENS.

Withers like debauchery. — DUMAS, PÈRE.

Withers, like a palm
Cut by an Indian for its juicy balm.
— KEATS.

Withered like a leaf in the breath of an oven. — FRITZ H. LUDLOW.

Withered like some short-lived flower. — MARLOWE.

Withered like an old apple-john. — SHAKESPEARE.

Like a blasted sapling, withered up. — IBID.

Withered like green corn under the hot winds of the unirrigated American desert. — JOHN R. SPEARS.

Withered like hay. — SPENSER.

Wither like a dying rose. — FRANK L. STANTON.

Withered like stars in the morning. — ROBERT LOUIS STEVENSON.

Withered all our strength like flame. — SWINBURNE.

My heart is smitten, and withered like grass. — OLD TESTAMENT.

Wither as the green herb. — IBID.

Withered like an apple that the snow
Finds still upon the bough.
— L. FRANK TOOKER.

Withered, as in death congealed. — TUPPER.

The egoist withers like a solitary barren tree. — IVAN S. TURGENEV.

Withered as if struck by a blight. — VOLTAIRE.

Wither like a thing of earth. — ALARIC A. WATTS.

Withheld.

Withheld as things forbidden. — SWINBURNE.

Within.

Within another, like the ivory balls in a Chinese carving. — DICKENS.

Witless.

Witless as a jackdaw. — THOMAS SHADWELL.

Witness.

Witnesses, like watches, go
Just as they're set, too fast or slow.
— SAMUEL BUTLER

See also Wit.) **Witty.**

Witty as a Frenchman. — ANON.

Witty as a roll of ten dollar bills. — IBID.

Witty as Diana. — IBID.

Witty as two fools and a madman. — IBID.

Witty men commit the most fatal errors, as the strongest horses make the most dangerous stumbles. — IBID.

Wizen.

An old man, wizened as a dried plaice. — CAMILLE LEMONNIER.

Wizen, like a small dry tree. — SWINBURNE.

Woman.

A painted woman is like a gilded pill; fools admire the former, and children the latter, for the disguise. — ANON.

A woman, like a melon, is hard to choose. — IBID.

Women are like melons: it is only after having tasted them that we know whether they are good or not. — IBID.

Pretty women are like sovereigns: one flatters them only through interest. — IBID.

Woman, like good wine, is a sweet poison. — IBID.

Women, like the plants in woods, derive their softness and tenderness from the shade. — IBID.

Most women proceed like the flea, — by leaps and jumps. — BALZAC.

Women, like birds, are shy of a single spring; perplex them by a choice, their heads become giddy, they flutter, and drop into the trap. — ROBERT M. BELL.

Women, like conjurers' tricks, are miracles to the ignorant. — IBID.

Women, like loadstones, lose their attraction, when they suffer the rust of a fretful temper to eat away their brightness. — IBID.

Women are like wasps in their anger. Not so, for wasps leave their stings, but women never leave their tongues behind them. — NICHOLAS BRETON.

Pleasant at first she is, like Dioscorides' Rhododaphne, that fair plant to the eye, but poison to the taste, the rest as bitter as wormwood in the end and sharp as a two-edged sword. — ROBERT BURTON.

Your women
Are like new plays, which self-complacent authors
Offer at some eight hundred royals each,
But which, when once they're tried, you purchase dear
Eight hundred for a royal.
— CALDERON.

Women, and men who are like women, mind the binding more than the book. — CHESTERFIELD.

Women are like tricks by sleight of hand,
Which to admire, we should not understand. — CONGREVE.

Women are like medlars, no sooner ripe than rotten. — THOMAS DEKKER.

Beautiful peaches are not always the best flavored; neither are handsome women the most amiable. — W. S. DOWNEY.

The happiest women, like the happiest nations, have no history. — GEORGE ELIOT.

Women are like pictures; of no value in the hands of a fool, till he hears men of sense bid high for the purchase. — FARQUHAR.

The womenfolk are like the books, — most pleasing to the eye,
Whereon if anybody looks he feels disposed to buy.
— EUGENE FIELD.

Woman — *continued.*

Woman is like a pot of oil, and a man a burning coal. A wise man will not put the oil and the fire together. — Hitopadesa.

Women, with their tongues,
like polar needles, ever on the jar.
— O. W. Holmes.

You look at a star from two motives, because it is luminous — and because it is impenetrable. You have at your side a softer radiance and a greater mystery — woman. — Hugo.

A fine woman, like a fortified town . . . demands a regular siege; and we must even allow her the honors of war, to magnify the greatness of our victory. — Hugh Kelly.

I have been servitor in a college at Salamanca, and read philosophy with the doctors; where I found that a woman, in all times, has been observed to be an animal hard to understand, and much inclined to mischief. Now as an animal is always an animal, and a captain is always a captain, so a woman is always a woman; whence it is that a certain Greek says, her head is like a bank of sand; or, as another, a solid rock; or, according to a third, a dark lanthorn: and so, as the head is the head of the body; and that body without a head, is like a head without a tail; and that where there is neither head nor tail, 'tis a very strange body; so, I say, a woman is, by comparison, do you see? (for nothing explains things like comparisons). I say by comparison, as Aristotle has often said before me, one may compare her to the raging sea; for as the sea, when the wind rises, knits its brows like an angry bull, and that waves mount upon rocks, rocks mount upon waves, that porpoises leap like trouts, and whale skip about like gudgeons; that ships roll like beer-barrels, and mariners pray like saints; just so, I say, a woman — a woman, I say, just so, when her reason is ship-wrecked upon her passion, and the hulk of her understanding lies thumping against the rock of her fury; then it is, I say, that by certain emotions, which — um — cause, as one may suppose, a sort of convulsive — yes — hurricanes — um — like — in short, a woman is the devil. — Thomas King.

Hard is the fortune that your sex attends;
Women, like princes, find few real friends:
And who approach them their own ends pursue;
Lovers and ministers are seldom true.
— Lord Lyttelton.

A woman is like the ivy, which grows luxuriantly whilst it clings to some sturdy tree, but never thrives if it is separated from it. — Molière.

A woman who loves to be at the window is like a bunch of grapes at the wayside. — Italian Proverb.

A woman possessing nothing but outward advantages is like a flower without fragrance, a tree without fruit. — Regnier.

Women are like thermometers, which, on a sudden application of heat, sink at first a few degrees, as preliminary to rising a good many. — Richter.

Women, like summer storms, awhile are cloudy,
Burst out in thunder and impetuous show'rs;
But straight the sun of beauty dawns abroad,
And all the fair horizon is serene.
— Nicholas Rowe.

Women, like things, at second hand
Do half their value lose;
But, whilst all courtship they withstand,
May at their pleasure choose.
— Sir Charles Sedley.

Woman — *continued.*

Women use lovers as they do cards; they play with them awhile, and, when they have got all they can of them, throw them away, call for new ones, and then perhaps lose by the new ones all they got by the old ones. — POPE.

Women are as roses, whose fair flower
Being once displayed, doth fall that very hour. — SHAKESPEARE.

A woman that is like a German clock,
Still a-repairing, ever out of frame,
And never going right, being a watch,
But being watch'd that it may still go right! — IBID.

A woman mov'd is like a fountain troubled,
Muddy, ill-seeming, thick, bereft of beauty;
And while it is so, none so dry and thirsty
Will deign to sip or touch one drop of it. — IBID.

Woman the other world resembles well,
In whose looks Heav'n is, in whose breast is Hell.
— SIR EDWARD SHERBURNE.

A continual dropping in a very rainy day and a contentious woman are alike. — OLD TESTAMENT.

Women are like curst dogs: civility keeps them tied all day-time, but they are let loose at midnight; then they do most good, or most mischief. — JOHN WEBSTER.

Woman is like the reed that bends to every breeze, but breaks not in the tempest. — WHATELY.

You say, sir, once a wit allow'd a woman to be like a cloud, accept a simile as soon between a woman and the moon; for let mankind say what they will, the sex are heavenly bodies still. — JAMES C. WHYTE.

Women are like minors; they live on their expectations. — OSCAR WILDE.

Women, like old soldiers, more nimbly execute than they resolve. — WYCHERLEY.

Wonderful.

As wonderful as calves with five legs. — BEAUMONT AND FLETCHER.

Wonderful as a starlit sky. — RICHARD LE GALLIENNE.

Wondrous.

Wondrous as a dream. — FRANCES ANNE KEMBLE.

Wooden.

As wooden as the shoe on a Dutch peasant. — ANON.

Words.

Words . . . as sweet as founts that murmur low,
To one who in the deserts drear,
With parched tongue moves faint and slow.
— ANCIENT BALLAD OF HINDUSTAN.

Sweet words are like honey; a little may refresh, but too much gluts the stomach. — ANNE BRADSTREET.

Words are like money; there is nothing so useless, unless when in actual use. — SAMUEL BUTLER (1835-1902).

Burning Words, like so many full-formed Minervas, issuing amid flame and splendor from Jove's head. — CARLYLE.

Words, like glass, darken whatever they do not help us to see. — JOSEPH JOUBERT.

There comes Emerson first, whose rich words, every one,
Are like gold nails in temples to hang trophies on. — LOWELL.

His words, like so many nimble and airy servitors, trip about him at command. — MILTON.

Words are like leaves; and where they most abound,
Much fruit of sense beneath is rarely found. — POPE.

Words — *continued.*

But obscene Words, too grosse to move Desire,
Like heaps of Fuel do but choak the Fire.
That Author's Name has undeserved Praise
Who pall'd the Appetite he meant to raise. — LORD ROCHESTER.

These words, like daggers, enter in mine ears. — SHAKESPEARE.

My words hang together like feathers in the wind. — SKELTON.

Thy words, like genial showers to the parch'd earth, refresh my languid soul. — SMOLLETT.

With words as with sunbeams, — the more they are condensed, the deeper they burn. — SOUTHEY.

My words are like spoken roses. — SWINBURNE.

With all the rhymes like stars above you,
And all the words like flowers.
— IBID.

Words like swords and thunder-clouded creeds. — IBID.

A word fitly spoken is like apples of gold in pictures of silver. — OLD TESTAMENT.

Pleasant words are as an honeycomb, sweet to the soul, and health to the bones. — IBID.

The words of a talebearer are as wounds, and they go down into the innermost parts of the belly. — IBID.

Work.

Work like a horse. — ANON.

Worked like a fury. — IBID.

Worked like a Trojan. — IBID.

Worked like a miner in a landslide. — IBID.

Work like beavers. — IBID.

Working like the gills of a fish. — O. HENRY.

Work like a galley slave. — LEAN'S "COLLECTANEA."

Work like a brick. — LYLY.

World.

The world is like yon children's merry-go-round; what men admire are carriages and hobbies. — P. J. BAILEY.

The world is like the shifting scenes of a panorama: ten years convert the population of the schools into men and women, and make and mar fortunes; twenty years converts infants into lovers, fathers, and mothers, and decide men's fortunes; thirty years turn fascinating beauties into bearable old women, and convert lovers into grandfathers; forty years change the face of all society; and fifty years will, alas! find us in a world of which we know nothing, and to which we are unknown. — FROUDE.

The world is like a great staircase, some go up and others go down. — HIPPONAX.

This world is like carrion, round which are thousands of vultures: this one strikes that one with his claws, that one darts at this one with his beak, till at length they all fly away, and all that remains is the carcass. — PILPAY.

The world is like a tree trunk full of ants; he who comes into it knows nothing; he who goes from it, comes not again. — OSMANLI PROVERB.

Everything in the world is like a hollow nut; there is little kernel anywhere, and when it does exist, it is still more rare to find it in the shell. — SCHOPENHAUER.

Worlds on worlds are rolling ever
From creation to decay,
Like the bubbles on a river,
Sparkling, bursting, borne away.
— SHELLEY.

World — *continued.*

The World is not unfitly compared to a fishing-net, the end of the world to be the drawing up of the nets. While the nets are down, there is nothing said to be caught; for the nets may break, and the fish escape: But at the end of the world, when the nets are drawn up, it will then evidently appear, what every man hath caught. — JOHN SPENCER'S "THINGS NEW AND OLD; OR, A STORE-HOUSE OF SIMILES," 1658.

Worn.

Worn down . . . like a shape in a shroud. — ARABIAN NIGHTS.

Worn like a cloth
Gnawn into rags by the devouring
moth. — GEORGE SANDYS.

Worried.

Worried as a toad under a harrow. — ANON.

Worried,
Like a tempest-driven bark.
— T. BUCHANAN READ.

Worry.

Worry as a wolf a lamb. — ANON.

Worship.

Worship me like an Idol. — ROBERT BURTON.

Worthless.

Worthless as withered weeds, or idlest froth amid the boundless main. — EMILY BRONTË.

Worthless all as sands. — SWINBURNE.

Worthless as the lightest falling leaf. — CELIA THAXTER.

Wound.

Wounds . . . show
Like graves i' the holy church-yard.
— SHAKESPEARE.

Woven.

Woven like winter serpents in a pit. — AMBROSE BIERCE.

Woven as raiment. — SWINBURNE.

Woven . . . like bubbles in a frozen pond. — WILLIAM B. YEATS.

Wrap.

Wrapped, as in a mist. — ANON.

All wrapped up in flannel, like a race horse. — EUGÈNE BRIEUX.

Wrathful.

Wrathy as a militia officer on a training day. — J. R. BARTLETT'S "DICTIONARY OF AMERICANISMS."

Wrathful as Justice in her earnest mood. — W. J. LINTON.

Wriggle.

Wriggles, as though she had the itch. — BEAUMONT AND FLETCHER.

Wriggle, like a screw. — SAMUEL BUTLER.

Wriggle in and out like an eel in a sandbag. — MIDDLETON.

Wriggling about like a mouse in the middle of a wall. — PLAUTUS.

Wriggle . . . like sleep struggling to wake up. — RABINDRANATH TAGORE.

Wrinkle.

Wrinkled as a raisin. — ANON.

His face wrinkled like an old parchment. — GEORGES EEKHOUD.

Wrinkled like a baked apple. — NOKOLAI V. GOGOL.

Wrinkled like a fresh-blown poppy. — ALFRED HAYES.

Wrinkled like a last year's apple. — GUY DE MAUPASSANT.

Wrinkles, like a Book
Of Vellam, at a fire.
— "MUSES RECREATION."

Writ.

Writs like wild-fowl, fly abroad,
And then return o'er cities, towns,
and hills,
With clients, like dried straws, between
their bills.
— THOMAS MIDDLETON.

Write.

A witty writer is like a porcupine; his quill makes no distinction between friend and foe. — JOSH BILLINGS.

Our writings are as so many dishes, our readers guests, our books like beauty, that which one admires, another rejects; so are we approved as men's fancies are inclined. — ROBERT BURTON.

The writer, like the priest, must be exempted from secular labor. His work needs a frolic health: he must be at the top of his condition. — EMERSON.

Write like an angel (Goldsmith). — DAVID GARRICK.

Writing or printing is like shooting with a rifle; you may hit your reader's mind, or miss it; — but talking is like playing at a mark with the pipe of an engine; if it is within reach, and you have time enough, you can't help hitting it. — O. W. HOLMES.

Clear writers, like clear fountains, do not seem so deep as they are; the turbid looks most profound. — W. S. LANDOR.

Witty Writings, when directed to serve the good ends of Virtue and Religion, are like the Lights hung out in a Pharos, to guide the Mariners safe through dangerous Seas; but the Brightness of those, that are impious or immoral, shines only to betray, and lead Men to Destruction. — LORD LYTTELTON.

This much I have discovered, that it is in writing as in building, where, after all our schemes and calculations, we are mightily deceived in our accounts, and often forced to make use of any materials we can find that the works may be kept a-going. — SWIFT.

Writhe.

Writhes like Saint Laurent on the gridiron. — ANON.

Writhed like twisted locks. — IBID.

Writhe like the Pythian. — E. B. BROWNING.

Writhing o'er its task,
As heart-sick jesters weep behind the mask. — HOOD.

Writhed like a feather on the fire. — GUY DE MAUPASSANT.

Writhed like a worm on a hook. — CHARLES READE.

Writhe as a dragon by some great spell curbed and foiled. — WILLIAM WATSON.

Y

Yawn.

Yawned much as a bored tiger does in the face of a philosophical student of savage manners in the zoölogical gardens. — BULWER-LYTTON.

Yawns like a grave in a cemetery. — HUGO.

Yawn'd like a gash on warrior's breast. — SIR WALTER SCOTT.

Yawn and stretch like a greyhound by the fireside. — VANBRUGH.

Yawning.

Yawning wide like the mouth of a cavern. — JOHN DENNIS.

Yawning destruction, deep as the grave. — CHARLES KISFALUDY.

Yawning, like some old crater rent anew. — THOMAS MOORE.

Yawning — *continued.*

Yawning silently like an image. — Octave Uzanne.

Yearn.

Yearned as the parched land for summer's rain. — Anon.

Yearn'd as the captive toiling at escape. — Byron.

Yearning, like the first fierce impulse into crime. — Hood.

Yearning, like a swallow in the void. — Trumbull Stickney.

Yearning as with child of death. — Swinburne.

Yell.

Yelling like savages. — Anon.

Yolleden, as fendes doon in helle. — Chaucer.

Yelling like a maniac. — Dumas, père.

A discordant universal yell, like house-dogs howling at a dinner-bell. — John H. Frere.

Yell like a wronged panther. — Alfred Henry Lewis.

A yell as of wild beasts in their famine. — Ouida.

Yelled like incarnate fiends. — Michael Scott.

Dire yell,
As when, by night and negligence, the fire
Is spied in populous cities.
— Shakespeare.

Yell'd out
Like syllable of dolour. — Ibid.

Yelled like all-possessed. — Sam Slick.

Yelled as beasts of ravin. — Swinburne.

Yellow.

Yellow as a cat's eye. — Anon.

Yellow as a corpse. — Ibid.

Yellow as a guinea. — Ibid.

Yellow as a hopeless lover. — Arabian Nights.

She was as yellow as a quince. — Balzac.

Yellow as gamboge. — R. D. Blackmore.

Yellow like to fire. — E. B. Browning.

Yellow, like April bees. — C. S. Calverley.

As yelowe of hewe
As ony basyn scoured newe.
— Chaucer.

Yellow as liquid honey. — D'Annunzio.

Yellow as jealousy. — Anthony Hamilton.

Yellow as saffron. — Bret Harte.

Yellow as a Chinaman. — O. Henry.

Yellow as cowslips. — James Hogg.

Yellow as the amber. — Hood.

Yellow as Nature, abetted by time. — Bettina von Hutten.

Yellow and ill-fitting as the shuck on a dried cob. — Kipling.

Yellow, like a lion's mane. — Henry Luttrel.

Yellow as jaundice. — George Meredith.

Yellow as corn in the sun. — Ouida.

Yellow as wood ashes. — Henry M. Rideout.

Yaller — like you've saw custard-pie with no crust. — James Whitcomb Riley.

Yellow, like ripe corn. — D. G. Rossetti.

His face grew yellow as gamboge. — Horace Smith.

Yellow as sulphur. — Robert Louis Stevenson.

Yellow as pestilence. — Swinburne.

As yellow as the blossom of the broom. — "Mabinogion."

Yellow — *continued.*

Yellow like canned corn. — CAROLYN WELLS.

Yield.

Yielded like melted snow. — J. FENIMORE COOPER.

Yielded like the mist
Which eagles cleave, upmounting from their nests. — KEATS.

Yielded, like bruised limb to leech. — GEORGE MEREDITH.

Yielding as light. — JOHN G. NEIHARDT.

Young.

Young as the hour of birth. — MATHILDE BLIND.

Young as Eve with nature's daybreak in her face. — E. B. BROWNING.

Young as old Homer's song is young. — GEORGE MEREDITH.

Young as morn. — MEREDITH NICHOLSON.

Young as Truth. — D. G. ROSSETTI.

Young as dawn. — SWINBURNE.

Youth.

Youth, like white paper, will take any impression. — ANON.

Youth is like green corn, all sap and promise. — IBID.

The rose, like ready youth, enticing stands,
And would be cropt if it might choose the hands.
— WILLIAM BROWNE.

Youth like genius gives its best at first. — CHARLOTTE BRONTË.

Youth, like spring-time, light and nimble,
Evanescent in its glee.
— HARTLEY COLERIDGE.

Youth is not like a new garment which we can keep fresh and fair by wearing sparingly ; youth, while we have it, we must wear daily ; and it will fast wear away. — JOHN FOSTER.

Youth is like those verdant forests tormented by winds : it agitates on every side the abundant gifts of nature, and some profound murmur always reigns in its foliage. — M. DE GUERIN.

Youth, like the aloe, blossoms but once, and its flower springs from the midst of thorns: but see with what strength and to what height the aloe-flower rises over them. — W. S. LANDOR.

Blithe youth is like a smile,
So mirthful, and so brief.
— ROBERT NICHOLL.

Youth passes like the odour
From the white rose's cup
When the hot sun drinks up
The dew that overflowed her.
— C. G. ROSSETTI.

Youth like summer morn, age like winter weather,
Youth like summer brave, age like winter bare. — SHAKESPEARE.

Youthful.

Youthful as the month of May. — ANON.

Z

Zeal.

Zealous, like a Quaker railing at lace. — ANON.

Zeal without humanity is like ship without a rudder, liable to be stranded at any moment. — OWEN FELTHAM.

Zeal without knowledge is like expedition to a man in the dark. — NEWTON.

Zigzag.

Zigzag like lightning. — SOUTHEY.

ADDENDA

A

Abandonment.

A final abandonment of pride that was like changing at the end of a dreadful day from tight boots to slippers. — Henry James.

Ability.

Some persons have ability enough, but it is like goods in the pieces ; they never make it up into anything. — George Hembert Wesley.

Abnormal.

Abnormal as an eight-heart hand. — Ibid.

Abominable.

Abominable as the man who is surly and sulky and snappish with a woman who is trying to please him. — Anon.

Abrupt.

Abrupt as cock-crow. — G. K. Chesterton.

Absorb.

Able to absorb punishment as open buds absorb the dew. — Grantland Rice.

Absurd.

Absurd as a Hottentot marooned on an iceberg. — Anon.

Absurd as an Esquimau pretending the desert is a sea of ice. — Ibid.

Absurd as for a doctor to ask whether to give the ether before or after cutting off a man's leg. — Ibid.

Absurd as mathematics without numbers. — Ibid.

Absurd as to clap spurs into a wooden horse and expect him to gallop. — Ibid.

Absurd as to say that a fox is the son of a gander. — Ibid.

Absurd as to try to drive a windmill with a pair of bellows. — Ibid.

Absurd as to try to keep the sea back with a pitchfork. — Ibid.

Absurd as to give a boy some mystic treatise of the Middle Ages on alchemy to serve as a text-book in chemistry. — Charles Anthon.

Absurd as to instruct a rooster in the laying of eggs. — Henry L. Mencken.

For a man beyond forty to be daffy with love seems quite as absurd to me as for an archbishop to die of cholera morbus. — Ibid.

Absurd as to expect harvest in the dead of winter. — Robert South.

Abuse.

Abuse, like other poisons, when administered in too strong a dose, is thrown off by the intended victim, and often relieves where it is intended to destroy. — Anon.

Acrimonious.

Acrimonious as post-mortems of the bridge table. — Anon.

Act.

To see Kean act was like reading Shakespeare by flashes of lightning. — S. T. Coleridge.

He acted [Hamlet] like a suffering plumber suicidal over his troubles with the I. W. W. — Amy Leslie.

Acting, like playwriting, is lowering buckets into empty wells and drawing nothing up. — Alice Gerstenburg.

Action.

This play has no more action than a snake has hips. — ANON.

Active.

About as active as a left-over fly in January. — ANON.

Actors.

The public behaves to actors like love to warriors : it has no consideration for an old soldier. — SOPHIE ARNOULD.

Adapted.

About as well adapted to the purpose as a one-pronged fork for pitching hay. — HERMAN MELVILLE.

Adroit.

Adroit as a rhinoceros. — FRANKLIN P. ADAMS.

Advancing.

Advancing and receding like an automatic pistol. — VINCENTE BLASCO-IBÁÑEZ.

Adversity.

Adversity, like winter weather, is of use to kill those vermin which the summer of prosperity is apt to produce and nourish. — JOHN ARROWSMITH.

Advice.

Advice is like castor oil, — easy enough to give, but dreadful uneasy to take. — J. R. BARTLETT'S "DICTIONARY OF AMERICANISMS," 1877.

Gives her excellent advice, but it is a good deal like giving a child a dictionary to learn a language with. — HENRY JAMES.

Advice, like water, takes the form of the vessel it is poured into. — PUNCH, August 1, 1857.

Good advice is like a tight glove ; it fits the circumstances, and it does not fit other circumstances. — CHARLES READE.

Affections.

Affections are like slippers ; they will wear out. — EDGAR SALTUS.

Affluence.

A man in time of affluence is like unto a tree,
Round which the folk collect as fruit thereon they see,
Till, when its burden it hath cast, they turn from it away,
Leave it to suffer heat and dust and all inclemency.
— "ARABIAN NIGHTS" (PAYNE).

Aggressive.

Aggressive as an elbow in the side. — HENRY JAMES.

Agitation.

Producing the same violent agitation in the public mind that was excited in the proverbial ox when the fly lighted on its off horn. — HENRY MORFORD.

Aglow.

Aglow like the dream of a lover. — NEWMAN HOWARD.

Agreeable.

Agreeable as an uninvited guest. — ABE MARTIN.

Alike.

No more alike than an elephant and a giraffe. — ANON.

Allies.

Allies . . . are of the description of twins joined by a membrane. — GEORGE MEREDITH.

Aloof.

Aloof as in prayer. — CAROLINE HAZARD.

Alternately.

Alternately, like the layers of bread and meat in a plate of sandwiches. — DICKENS.

Ambition.

Ambition is like a treadmill ; it knows no limits ; you no sooner get to the end of it than you begin again. — JOSH BILLINGS.

American.

American as corn on the cob. — ANON.

American as Yankee nutmegs or the Pilgrim Fathers. — GEORGE AGNEW CHAMBERLAIN.

American as a catcher's mit. — GEORGE JEAN NATHAN.

Amorous.

Amorous as Emma Bovary. — JAMES G. HUNEKER.

Amorous, as the first of May. — TENNYSON.

Anachronistic.

Anachronistic as a Watteau shepherdess at a clambake. — LAWRENCE GILMAN.

Anarchist.

An anarchist is like a man who throws an egg in an electric fan. He doesn't stop the fan, but he smears the place up some. — ANON.

Anarchy.

Anarchy reigning is like stagnation stirring, cold burning, or heat freezing. — PUNCH, 1856.

Anger.

Anger, like grief, is a mark of weakness ; both mean being wounded and wincing. — MARCUS AURELIUS.

Wise anger is like fire from the flint ; there is a great ado to bring it out ; and when it does come, it is out again immediately. — MATTHEW HENRY.

Angling.

You will find angling to be like the virtue of humility, which has a calmness of spirit and a world of other blessings attending upon it. — IZAAK WALTON.

Angry.

Angry and choleric men are as ungrateful and unsociable as thunder and lightning, being in themselves all storms and tempests ; but quiet and easy natures are like fair weather, welcome to all, and acceptable to all men : they gather together what the others disperse, and reconcile all whom the others incense : as they have the good will and the good wishes of all other men, so they have the full possession of themselves, have all their own thoughts at peace, and enjoy quiet and ease in their own fortune, how strait soever it may be. — EARL OF CLARENDON.

Animated.

About as animated as a dummy. — ANON.

Ankles.

The young lady has a pair of ankles like chianti bottles. — GEORGE JEAN NATHAN.

Annoying.

Annoying as a fly speck in a column of figures. — ANON.

Antique.

Antique as the clown at the circus. — JAMES G. HUNEKER.

True antique as family heirlooms. — CHARLES WAGNER.

Apart.

As far apart as the atheists who claim there is no soul, and the Christian Scientists who declare that there is no body. — ANON.

Appalling.

Appalling as a great fat mother-in-law. — R. S. SURTEES.

Apparent.

About as apparent as a microbe's eyebrow. — ANON.

Apparent to the naked eye as the Woolworth Building. — ROBERT CORTES HOLLIDAY.

Appetizing.

Appetizing as a boiled cocktail. — HENRY L. MENCKEN.

Appropriate.

Appropriate as a country dance in a private vault. — DICKENS.

Arbitrary.

Arbitrary as a cyclone. — ANON.

Argument.

Entering upon an argument with a metaphysician is like getting into an omnibus : you know where you start from, but it is impossible to tell where it will carry you. — PUNCH, 1854.

Aristocracy.

Aristocracy, Hinnissy, is like rale estate, a matter iv location. I'm aristocracy to th' poor O'Briens back in the alley, th' brewery agent's aristocracy to me, his boss is aristocracy to him, an' so it goes, up to the Czar of Rooshia. — FINLEY PETER DUNNE.

Arms.

Arms like legs of mutton. — W. SOMERSET MAUGHAM.

Thine arms are as a young sapling under the bark. — EZRA POUND.

Army.

An army is like an old maid : it lives on rumors. — ANON.

Sending men to that army is like shoveling fleas across a barnyard. — ABRAHAM LINCOLN.

The German army moved into Brussels as smoothly and as compactly as an Empire State Express. — RICHARD HARDING DAVIS.

Art.

Art in America is like a patent medicine or a vacuum cleaner. It can hope for no success until 90,000,000 people know what it is. — MARSDEN HARTLEY.

Art, like the universe, said they, exists for itself alone. — HEINRICH HEINE.

Art, like nature, has her monsters, things of bestial shape and with hideous voices. — OSCAR WILDE.

Naïveté in art is like zero in a number : its importance depends on the figure it is united with. — HENRY JAMES.

Art, like the microscope, reveals many things that the naked eye does not see. — GEORGE MOORE.

Art is like a charming woman who once had her age of innocence in the nursery, when she was beautiful without knowing it, being wholly intent on what she was making or telling or imagining. — GEORGE SANTAYANA.

Artists.

The mood of an artist, his exultations and depressions . . . were like the pen-flourishes a writing master makes in the air when he begins to set his copy. — HENRY JAMES.

Ascends.

Thought ascends, and buds from the brain, as the fruit from the root. — VICTOR HUGO.

Ascends like the spiral smoke of perishing flame. — WILLIAM SHARP.

Ashamed.

Ashamed as a fox caught in a trap. — ANON.

Askew.

All askew like a hat on one ear. — ROMAIN ROLLAND.

Athwart.

Athwart it like the dagger in a contadina's hair. — HENRY JAMES.

Attention.

The attention is like a narrow mouthed vessel ; pour into it what you have to say cautiously, and, as it were, drop by drop. — JOSEPH JOUBERT.

Attracted as little attention as a dirty finger nail in the third grade. — RING LARDNER.

Auctioneer.

An auctioneer like a man with an ugly countenance . . . is always forbidding. — PUNCH, 1841.

Avaricious.

An avaricious man is like a pig, which seeks its food in the mud, without caring where it comes from. — JEAN B. M. VIANNEY.

Avarice is like a grave yard : it takes all that it can get, and gives nothing back. — JOSH BILLINGS.

Awkwardly.

Splashes . . . a little awkwardly, like an elephant in a bathtub. — MALCOLM COWLEY.

B

Baby.

A baby is like a sheaf of wheat : first it is cradled, then thrashed, and then it becomes the flower of the family. — ANON.

Bachelor.

A bachelor is a nondescript in human society, like the odd end of a pair of shears, of little use till it's joined to its mate. — BENJAMIN FRANKLIN.

The town bull is as much a bachelor as he. — THOMAS FULLER'S "GNOMOLOGIA," 1731.

Backbone.

Some men have so little backbone that you might as well undertake to help them as to stand an angleworm on end and ask him to dance a jig. — JOSH BILLINGS.

Backwards.

To bang compliments backwards and forwards, like two asses scrubbing one another. — JONATHAN SWIFT.

Like a Witch's Prayer, to be said backwards. — SAMUEL BUTLER, 1612–1680.

As bears go down hill, backwards. — WILLIAM GURNALL.

Bad.

Bad as beating a crippled child with a mallet. — GEORGE ADE.

Bad as cheating the devil in the dark. — THOMAS FULLER'S "GNOMOLOGIA," 1731.

Bad as plowing with dogs. — GENTLEMAN'S MAGAZINE, 1795.

Baffling.

Baffling as a blizzard. — ANON.

Bald.

Bald as a bat. — ANON.

Bald as a watermelon. — IBID.

Bald as an orange. — THOMAS BAILEY ALDRICH.

Bald as time. — RICHARD BROME.

Bald as a Mussulman in the morning. — DICKENS.

Balmy.

Balmy as the dew which sheds on the roses' cheek. — HENRY GLAPTHORNE.

Kisses balmier than half-opening buds of April. — TENNYSON.

Bandy.

Bandy like a racket ball. — John Davies.

Bandied about, like bullets in a battle. — Balzac.

Bare.

Bare, as a wild wave in the wide North Sea. — Anon.

Bare as a new-born Venus rising from the sea. — Colley Cibber.

Bare as an anatomy. — John Marston.

Lay bare, as lies the mirrored moon in silver sleeping seas. — Gerald Massey.

Bare as the sides of a living volcano. — Frederick O'Brien.

Bare, like a carcass picked by crows. — Swift.

Barren.

Barren as an iceberg of vegetation. — Anon.

Barren as a draught-struck sky. — Henry C. Bunner.

Barren as the ground around a cabin door. — William Allen White.

Bashful.

Bashful as a clock, which always has its hands before its face. — Anon.

Bashful as a shrapnel shell. — Ibid.

Battering.

Battering down meanings like a man that drives palings. — Charles Edward Russell.

Beat.

His heart beat like a hopper of a mill. — Maurice Hewlett.

He will beat at me like the rainy west wind on a lily. — George Meredith.

Beaten . . . like dirty linen on the washing-board. — R. L. Stevenson.

Beautiful.

Beautiful as a rich orphan. — Gelett Burgess.

Beautiful as a martyr's visions. — Mrs. Centlivre.

Beautiful as a flower in a seed catalogue. — Robert H. Davis.

Beautiful as the sun going into the sea. — Giacomo Greber.

Beautiful as Liberty. — Heinrich Heine.

Beautiful as is the gorgeous palace of the sun. — Thomas Heywood.

Beautiful as flame. — John Sterling.

Beautiful as a child's dream of a star. — Henry Christeen Warnack.

Beautiful as nature in the spring. — O. S. Wondersford.

Beauty.

For beauty, like white powder, makes
 no noise,
And yet the silent hypocrite destroys.
 — Dryden.

Her faded beauty was like summer twilight. — Henry James.

It is a great comfort for timid men, that beauty, like the elephant, doesn't know its strength. Otherwise, how it would trample upon us. — "Joe Miller's Jests," 1739.

The beam of her beauty was as the constant bite of a serpent, poisoning his blood. — George Meredith.

Beauty without virtue is like a flower without perfume. — Giovanni Ruffini.

Belch.

Belch like popguns. — John Fletcher.

Belong.

He didn't belong any more than a white poodle on a coal barge. — Arthur Baer.

Benefactor.

A true benefactor is like a vine which is satisfied by being fruitful in its kind and bears a bunch of grapes without expecting anything for it. — MARCUS ANTONINUS.

Benefits.

Benefits, like bread, soon become stale. — CAROLINE FORNE.

Bible.

The truths of the Bible are like gold in the soil. Whole generations walk over it and know not what treasures are hidden beneath. So centuries of men pass over the Scriptures and know not what truths be under the feet of their interpretation. — HENRY WARD BEECHER.

The Bible itself is like an old Cremona; it has been played upon by the devotion of thousands of years, until every word and particle is public and tunable. — R. W. EMERSON.

But the way in which common people read their Bibles is just like the way that the old monks thought hedgehogs ate grapes. They rolled themselves (it was said) over and over, where the grapes lay on the ground. What fruit stuck to their spines, they carried off, and ate. So your hedgehoggy readers roll themselves over and over their Bibles, and declare that whatever sticks to their own spines is Scripture, and that nothing else is. But you can only get the skins of the texts that way. If you want their juice, you must press them in cluster. — RUSKIN.

Bills.

Bills are like dram-drinking . . . when one once begins, it is very hard to leave off. — ANTHONY TROLLOPE.

Biting.

Biting as nitric acid in an etcher's copper plate. — ANON.

Bitter.

Bitter as a disappointed Democrat. — ABE MARTIN.

Black.

Black as if cast from the shadow of a fallen angel's wing. — ANON.

Black as the ace of spades. — IBID.

Black as the back alley in Chelsea village. — IBID.

Black as the inside of a fountain pen. — IBID.

Black as perjury. — IBID.

Black as murder. — THOMAS DEKKER.

Black as the ninth plague of Egypt. — THOMAS HARDY.

Black as an honorary pallbearer's hat. — HENRY L. MENCKEN.

Black as sorrow. — SIR PHILIP SIDNEY.

Blank.

Blank of subjects as the white canvas before the stereopticon picture is thrown upon it. — ARLO BATES.

Blazed.

Blazed up like one universal soda bottle. — CARLYLE.

Blind.

Blind as a stone. — CHAUCER.

Blind as a heathen. — GEORGE ELIOT.

Blind as the waves of the sea. — EVA GORE-BOOTH.

Blind as death. — BEAUMONT AND FLETCHER.

Blind as ignorance. — IBID.

Blind as Hell. — WILLIAM HABBINGTON.

Blind as a flame of fire. — SWINBURNE.

Blinking.

Blinking as a revolving coast-light. — THOMAS HARDY.

Blithe.

Blithe as five-and-twenty. — John Collins.

Blithesome.

Blithesome as the sun. — James Grainger.

Blonde.

Thy hair is as blonde as a sheaf of wheat. — Pierre Louys.

Blooming.

Blooming as a bride. — Anon.

Blooming as spring. — Dryden.

Blooming like Eden. — James Montgomery.

Blue.

Blue as the sky in April. — Sir William Jones.

Eyes as blue as cornflowers. — Celia Thaxter.

Blue as the cholera. — James Thomson.

Blunt.

Blunt as ignorance. — Samuel Rowley.

Blush.

Blushed like a brick. — Samuel Hopkins Adams.

Blush like a geranium. — Harry Graham.

Blushing like a tomato. — E. V. Lucas.

Bluster.

Bluster like the north wind. — Mrs. Centlivre.

Boasts.

Boasts like a quack doctor. — Anon.

Bobbing.

Bobbing up and down like a barometer on an April morning. — Clifford Mills.

Bobbing up and down, . . . like an apple in a bowl of toddy. — Edgar Allan Poe.

Body.

The body is like a vase or a receptacle for the soul. — Cicero.

Her body was like a white satin stove. — James G. Huneker.

A doctor knows the human body as a cabman knows the town ; he is well acquainted with all the great thoroughfares and small turnings ; he's intimate with all the principal edifices, but he cannot tell you what is going on inside of any one of them. — Punch, 1856.

My body, like a leather sack, is full of joy and sorrow, spite and good-humor, wisdom and folly, hay and straw, figs and grapes, fruit ripe and unripe, roses and haws — what I have seen, felt and known, owned and lived, all jumbled together in the game bag, and what fun to dive into it. — Romain Rolland.

A man's body and his mind, with the utmost reverence to both I speak it, are exactly like a jerkin and a jerkin's lining ; rumple the one, you rumple the other. — Laurence Sterne.

Bold.

Coming boldly to the Bait as if it were a Mastiff dog at a Bear. — Joseph Blagrave.

Bold as Paul in the presence of Agrippa. — Cowper.

Bold as love. — Edmund Gosse.

Bold as Mars. — Nathaniel Lee.

Bold as the piercing shriek of the God of Gold. — Kenneth L. Roberts.

Bold as a dying saint. — Elkanah Settle.

Bold as a miller's shirt, which takes a rogue by the throat every morning. — "Marriage of Wit and Science."

Books.

Books, like Madeira, much improve at sea. — Bernard Blackmantle.

Books — *continued.*

What is a great love of books? It is something like a personal introduction to the great and good men of all past time. Books, it is true, are silent as you see them on their shelves; but, silent as they are, when I enter a library I feel as if almost the dead were present, and I know if I put questions to these books they will answer me. — JOHN BRIGHT.

Some books, like the city of London, fare the better for being burnt. — THOMAS BROWN.

A room without books is like a body without a soul. — CICERO.

Books, like friends, should be few and well chosen. — THOMAS FULLER.

A book, to meet with its proper desert, should be gone through like a bag of filberts . . . you throw away the bad ones, of course, and crack only the good ones; these you enjoy with all the greater relish after the bad specimens, and you do not condemn the whole lot because there happens to be one or two among them not quite so sound as the rest. — HORACE MAYHEW.

As good almost kill a man as kill a good book: who kills a man kills a reasonable creature, God's image; but he who destroys a good book, kills reason itself, kills the image of God, as it were, in the eye. — MILTON.

Alfred Naquet once said to me with true French flavor: "A book without an index is as incomplete as an eunuch." — THEODORE STANTON.

A new book, like a young man, has a reputation to acquire; and on the other hand, an old book, like an old man, is bound to have a good character already established, and must expect to be looked upon with suspicion, if it has not. — CLARENCE WALWORTH.

Boom.

Boomed out like a dinner-gong. — SIR A. CONAN DOYLE.

Boomed, like the big bell in the Kremlin at Moscow. — CARL VAN VECHTEN.

Bores.

Bores are not to be got rid of except by rough means. They are to be scraped off like the scales from a fish. — C. N. BOVÉE.

Bothered.

Bothered, like a novel reader when the third volume's missing. — ANON.

Bottomless.

Bottomless as Hell. — BEN JONSON.

Bounce.

Bounce right back like an anvil dropped in a swamp. — ARTHUR BAER.

Bound.

Bounded like a rate exchange when some one has trodden on the tail of a Foreign Minister. — PHILIP GUEDALLA.

Bow.

He bows to the Court like a mandarin before the Emperor of China. — RICHARD LAYLOR SHEIL.

Bowed.

Bowed down like barley. — WALTER DE LA MARE.

Bowed like a broken flower. — SWINBURNE.

Brain.

His brain felt like the ashes of a bonfire. — GERTRUDE ATHERTON.

Branching.

Branchin' out like the genealogical tree of a ducal family. — R. S. SURTEES.

Brays.

Brays, like a gong. — WILLIAM LISLE BOWLES.

Breaking.

The German lines [1918] are breaking like the river ice, — rapidly in some places, slowly in others, but everywhere breaking. — Frank H. Simonds.

Breasts.

Breasts, like kettledrums of brass. — Henry Fielding.

Breasts like giant cabbages. — W. Somerset Maugham.

Her breasts, like ivory globes circled with blue. — Shakespeare.

Her breasts are like white birds. — Swinburne.

Breath.

Thy breath is like the steam of apple-pies. — Robert Greene.

Her breath is like the gentle air of Spring. — Longfellow.

Breathing.

Breathing like an escape valve. — Joseph C. Lincoln.

Bridesmaid.

A very stout bridesmaid like a first-rate bottle of claret — she's all body and bouquet. — Punch, 1863.

Brief.

Brief as a sinner's prayer. — Anon.

Brief as a monarch's audience. — Ibid.

Brief as the flutter of a star in flight. — Dana Burnet.

Brief as the Z column in a pocket dictionary. — Irvin S. Cobb.

Brief as a drop of dew. — Cale Young Rice.

Brief . . . as woman's love. — Shakespeare.

Bright.

Bright as a ten-cent shine. — Anon.

Bright as the world was in its infant years. — John Banks.

Bright as the Lord Mayor's coach. — Bulwer-Lytton.

Bright as the blushes of the roseate morn. — Luiz Vaz de Camoëns.

Bright as bullion unalloyed. — William Cowper.

Bright as new-in-the-store. — Zona Gale.

Bright as the wings of angels. — James Hervey.

Bright as the lamp of night, or orb of day. — Homer.

Bright as those gold candles fixed in heaven's air. — Shakespeare.

Bright as the path to a beloved home. — Shelley.

Brisk.

Brisk as a dancing master. — Thomas Durfey.

Brisk as Cupid. — George Lyttelton.

Brogue.

A brogue that sounded like ripping a sheet. — Sewell Ford.

Brown.

Brown as a roasted coffee berry. — John Galsworthy.

Brown as old unbaked leather. — W. H. Hudson.

Brows.

A great deal of brow in a face is like a great deal of horizon in a view. — Victor Hugo.

The brows, which were likewise very projecting, like two long promontories thickly wooded on top. — Herman Melville.

Flung up her brows like a fortress lifted by gunpowder. — George Meredith.

Bruise.

Bruised like a half-back in a football game. — Francis W. Crowninshield.

Brunette.

Brunette as a brigand. — ANON.

Bubble.

Bubble like a Seidlitz Powder. — ANON.

Bulged.

Bulged out like a Thornton squash. — GEORGE ADE.

Bunched.

Bunched and jammed together as solidly as the bristles in a brush. — MARK TWAIN.

Burn.

Burned up with the glad spontaneous alacrity of a celluloid comb. — IRVIN S. COBB.

My insides burned like pipes in a boiler. — GOUVERNEUR MORRIS.

Burst.

Bursts upon me like a shower of shrapnel. — ANON.

Burst like a pent-up flood. — IBID.

Bursting with poetry like a young bud. — DICKENS.

Burst upon him with an effect almost like that of the Pacific upon Balboa's gaze. — THOMAS HARDY.

Business.

Business, after all, is very much like Religion : it is founded on Faith. — WILLIAM McFEE.

Busy.

About as busy as a Swiss Admiral. — ANON.

Busy as a barber on Saturday night. — IBID.

Busy as a dog with fleas. — IBID.

Busy as a one-eyed sky terrier in a sausage shop. — IBID.

Busier than a one-eared telephone operator. — ARTHUR BAER.

Busy as the interpreter at the gates of heaven. — BURNS MANTLE.

Busy as a telephone line. — DON MARQUIS.

Busy as an east-bound tramp. — ABE MARTIN.

Busy as an undertaker in Arizona. — WALT MASON.

Busy as an innkeeper in a comic opera. — F. BERKELEY SMITH.

Busy as a set of dice in a negro camp. — H. C. WITWER.

Busy as a hydraulic drill. — IBID.

C

Callous.

Heart as callous as that of an army surgeon. — HERMAN MELVILLE.

Calm.

Calm as a sister's kiss. — P. J. BAILEY.

Calm as a knitting party. — SAMUEL G. BLYTHE.

Calmly as Monte Cristo picking his victims. — HEYWOOD BROUN.

Calm as an iceberg. — GELETT BURGESS.

Stretched his limbs calmly and lazily, like a good man awaiting a sermon. — A. W. KINGLAKE.

Calm as a good player with a royal straight flush. — ARTHUR B. REEVE.

Calmly as a child that falls asleep upon its mother's breast to wake in paradise. — JAMES E. SMITH.

Doing it as calmly as if he were attending a funeral and weren't related to the corpse. — MARK TWAIN.

Capacious.

Capacious as the mouth of Hell. — ANON.

Capacious as the sea. — HARTLEY COLERIDGE.

Capacious as the porches of cathedrals. — HERMAN MELVILLE.

Carefully.

Carefully as a rider does a water-jump. — RICHARD HARDING DAVIS.

Careless.

Careless as a wad in a window. — W. M. LETTS.

Careless as a flower glassed in a greenhouse. — WORDSWORTH.

Caresses.

Caressing as the arms of night. — ANON.

Caresses as a flower accepts the evening rain. — REMY DE GOURMONT.

A derisive caress which was like the strike of a snake. — JULIAN STREET.

Catching.

Catching as the baseball fever when you're in the mob watching the scores posted. — SEWELL FORD.

Catching as drowsy yawning. — EDWARD WARD.

Cautiously.

Unfolds as cautiously as Sir Humphry Davy would a manuscript of Herculaneum. — RICHARD LALOR SHEIL.

Cautiously as a tight-rope dancer. — C. H. SPURGEON.

Ceased.

Ceased like a dropped watch. — HENRY JAMES.

Ceremoniously.

Salute as ceremoniously as lawyers when they meet after a long vacation. — THOMAS MIDDLETON.

Certain.

Certain as that one hand washes another. — ANON.

Certain as the bands of matrimony all around, at the end of a comedy. — IBID.

Certainly as the cross of St. George means English patriotism. — G. K. CHESTERTON.

Certain as smoke is a proof of fire. — CICERO.

Imbecile breeds imbecility as certainly as white hens breed white chickens. — NEW REPUBLIC, March 16, 1916.

Chance.

About as much chance as a chicken at a camp-meeting. — GEORGE ADE.

About as much chance as a bow-legged girl in her home town. — ANON.

About as much chance as a feather boa in a blast furnace. — IBID.

About as much chance as a snowball in hell. — IBID.

About as much chance as a stump-tailed cow in fly time. — IBID.

About as much chance of recognition as would the breathing of a lute under an elevated train. — IBID.

About as much chance as to sell a British flag in Ireland. — IBID.

About as much chance as a woodpecker making a nest in a concrete telephone pole. — IBID.

About as much chance as a blind man who falls into the sea has of coming up with a fish in his mouth. — IBID.

About as much chance as a bar-fixture salesman in Zion City. — IBID.

He has about as much chance as one apple in an orphan asylum. — ARTHUR BAER.

About as much chance as a dish-faced chimpanzee in a beauty contest. — IBID.

Chance — *continued.*

About as much chance as a woodpecker in a hardwood forest with a rubber bill. — IBID.

No more chance than a hothouse in a hail-storm. — IBID.

About as much chance as a silk shirt in a steam laundry. — IBID.

About as much chance as a nickel in a two-bit crap game. — OCTAVUS ROY COHEN.

As much chance as a monocle at a teamsters' ball. — LAWRENCE GILMAN.

About as much chance as a peashooter in an air raid. — IBID.

About as much chance as a quart o' whisky on an Indian reservation. — PETER B. KYNE.

About as much chance as Shenandoah [airship] in a cloudburst of pitchforks. — NEAL O'HARA.

About as much chance of being recognized as a skunk in a hay fever colony. — BOSTON POST, February 10, 1921.

No more chance than a barber on an Indian reservation. — JOHN D. WELLS.

Chaotic.

Chaotic as the mind of a photo-play director. — DON MARQUIS.

Character.

The fragrance of her rich and delightful character still lingered about the place where she had lived, as a dried rosebud scents the drawer where it has withered and perished. — NATHANIEL HAWTHORNE.

Charged.

The angry rhinoceros charged like a demented express train. — ANON.

Chaste.

Chaste as when she was new born. — DAVID GARRICK.

Chaste as untrodden snow. — V. S. LEAN'S "COLLECTANEA," 1903.

Chastity.

Chastity is like unto a bright mirror, that is bedimmed and troubled not only by the touch of filthy things, but also by the breath of man. — "THE LITTLE FLOWERS OF ST. FRANCIS," circa 1390.

Chastity is like an isikel. If it onse melts that's the last ov it. — JOSH BILLINGS.

Chatter.

Chattered like a shipload of monkeys in a storm. — ANON.

Chattered like a Chinese when you have lost your laundry ticket and want your washing. — ELBERT HUBBARD.

Cheek.

Her cheeks are like the blushing clouds. — ANON.

He blew out his cheeks like a capital O. — IBID.

Her cheeks like lilies dipt in wine. — ROBERT BURNS.

His cheek was like a rose in the snow. — O. W. HOLMES.

Hollow cherry cheeks ; she looks like an old coach new painted. — WILLIAM WYCHERLEY.

Cheerful.

Cheerful as birds that welcome the day. — APHRA BEHN.

Cheerful as cold boiled potatoes on a foggy night. — THOMAS BURKE.

Cheerful as a new oak upright piano — SINCLAIR LEWIS.

Cheerless.

Cheerless as the Arctic. — ANON.

Child.

It is a groundless fallacy to suppose that a child is like a carpet, that requires to be instantly pulled up, and thoroughly well beaten, before it can be put down. — PUNCH, 1859.

Christian.

A true Christian is like the ripening corn; the riper he grows the more lowly he bends his head. — ANON.

Some Christians are like soiled bank notes: while we acknowledge their value we wish them changed. — WILLIAM LEWIS.

Chummy.

About as chummy as a pair of panthers. — JAMES FORBES.

Cigar.

A cigar is like some people: jest as soon as it gits pop'lar it begins to deterirate. — ABE MARTIN.

Circle.

He started going around in circles like a glass-eyed zebra on a Coney Island carrousel. — ARTHUR BAER.

Circled like a clasping arm. — JAMES A. GARFIELD.

In a circle like a horse tethered to an iron pin. — RICHARD JEFFERIES.

Cities.

Cities, like cats, will reveal themselves at night. — RUPERT BROOKE.

Cities are like woman in respect of the evanescent and impressionistic quality that is suggested by the word charm; they have it or they have it not; one does not know why if one seeks to define or to analyse it, it is quite apt to vanish away. — BRAND WHITLOCK.

Clamorous.

Clamorous as the boys of a district school just let out to play at lunch-time. — JOSH BILLINGS.

Clang.

Clanged like fifty fire-engines. — HERMAN MELVILLE.

Clatter.

Clattered like a dropped tray of tin things. — FANNIE HURST.

Clean.

Clean as a New England kitchen. — ANON.

Clean as a cold winter morning. — ELLIS PARKER BUTLER.

Clean as the deck of a yacht. — RICHARD HARDING DAVIS.

Clean as a pint of filtered spring-water in a non-fillable bottle. — WILLIAM SLAVENS MCNUTT.

Clean as a pearl. — PLAY, "JACOB AND ESAU," 1586.

Cleverness.

Little clevernesses are like half-ripened plums, only good eating on the side that has had a glimpse of the sun. — HENRY JAMES.

Cling.

Clings like an impecunious school friend. — ANON.

Clung, like an iron ring. — BARRY CORNWALL.

Cling like a long hair to a wet hand. — WILLIAM GEORGE JORDAN.

Close.

Close as the gum on a postage stamp. — IBID.

Close as the cu's in cucumbers. — IBID.

Close as a dead heat. — IBID.

The game was closer than a carriage dog's spots. — ARTHUR BAER.

Close as any true lovers in the spring. — EDWARD BLUNDEN.

Close as my lady's shoe to her foot. — GEORGE CHAPMAN.

Close as the report follows the powder. — JOHN FLETCHER.

Close as beggary to a prodigal. — JOHN KIRK.

Close together as the two shells of an oyster. — LEONARD MCNALLY.

Close — *continued.*

Close as the skin to the flesh, or as the flesh to the bone. — THOMAS RAWLINS.

Close as the bark to the tree. — SIR CHARLES SEDLEY.

Close as an uncracked nut. — PLAY, "ALL VOWS KEPT," 1733.

Closed.

Closed — like banks on Sunday. — ANON.

Clothes.

A suit iv clothes that looked like a stained-glass window in th' house iv a Dutch brewer. — FINLEY P. DUNNE.

A suit iv clothes that looks like a tablecloth in a section house. — IBID.

Clouds.

Clouds, like Alps in the sky. — KENELM H. DIGBY.

Large puffed clouds like deliberate loads of hay. — RICHARD JEFFERIES.

Little white clouds like cushions of cotton. — EUGÉNIE DE GUÉRIN.

Large black clouds, like chimney-sweepers' feather-beds. — PUNCH, 1841.

The summer clouds lay pitched like tents. — JOHN R. THOMPSON.

Coarse.

Coarse as a turnip field. — HENRY JAMES.

Coarse as horse hair. — EUGENE SUE.

Coiled.

Coiled up like a spiral spring. — DAMON RUNYON.

Coiled up like the letter S. — IBID.

Cold.

Cold as a white rose waking at day-break. — ANON.

Her nature was as cold as the reflection of the moon in a boghole. — IBID.

Cold as a six-card poker hand. — ARTHUR BAER.

Cold as the obit of a Pope. — BALZAC.

Cold as an egg in a deserted bird's nest. — SIR JAMES M. BARRIE.

Cold as a stepmother's kiss. — ZELDA SEARS.

Cold as a corpse after the spirit's flight. — SHELLEY.

Cold as Presbyterian charity. — SAM SLICK.

Cold as the new-sprung girlhood of the moon. — FRANCES THOMPSON.

Cold as unsunned snow. — ROSAMUND MARRIOTT WATSON.

Cold as a pawnbroker's smile. — H. C. WITWER.

Collapse.

Collapsed like a concertina. — ANON.

Collapses like a financial system with no cash basis whatever. — WILLIAM JAMES.

Colorless.

Colorless as a Scotch lowland in a fog. — ANON.

Colorless as the entries of a log-book. — J. HAMPDEN PORTER.

Come.

Always comin' and goin', like Mulligan's blanket (i. e. to the pawnbroker). — V. S. LEAN'S "COLLECTANEA," 1903.

Come as country gentlemen do into the fashion ; that is, in the tail end or latter end on't. — EDWARD SHARPHAM.

Comfort.

Creature comforts are like the soft morning dews which, while they water the branches of the trees, leave the roots dry. — WILLIAM SECKER.

A man's comfort is like a cigar, — if he cannot get it at home, he will go in search of it elsewhere. — PUNCH, 1859.

Comfortable.

About as comfortable as a roller-coaster. — ANON.

Comfortable as a litter of pups sleeping under a stove. — IBID.

Comfortable as a farmer with his Sunday shoes under his arm. — ARTHUR BAER.

About as comfortable as a hairbrush in bed. — W. L. GEORGE.

Comfortable as the melting wax to the impress of the seal. — JAMES HERVEY.

Comforting as a good old-fashioned murder. — EDGAR SALTUS.

Comfortable as a toothache. — MARK TWAIN.

'Bout as comfortable as a rooster in a pond. — EDWARD NOYES WESTCOTT.

Comfortless.

Comfortless as frozen water to a starved snake. — ANON.

Common.

Common as pump water. — JOSEPH G. BALDWIN.

Common as gas-posts and telegraph posts. — HENRY ARTHUR JONES.

Common as spots upon doves, moles upon faces, caterpillars upon sweet apples, cobwebs upon fair windows. — LYLY.

Common as the way between St. Alban's and London. — SHAKESPEARE.

Common as public houses in an English slum. — NEW YORK WORLD, August 19, 1922.

Compact.

Compact as a watch. — ANON.

Compact as a Greek temple. — HENRY JAMES.

Compact as a thatch. — R. L. STEVENSON.

Compact as the shape of chestnuts and oranges. — WALT WHITMAN.

Company.

Bad company is like a nail driven into a post, which after the first or second blow may be drawn out with little difficulty ; but being once driven up to the head, the pinchers cannot take hold to draw it out, but which can only be done by the destruction of the wood. — ST. AUGUSTINE.

Compelling.

Compelling as gunpowder. — ANON.

Complete.

Exquisitely complete as a nocturne by Chopin. — WILLIAM SHARP.

Complexion.

Complexion like the Sunset Blush on a Snow Bank. — GEORGE ADE.

Complexion like the blushy side of a peach. — ANON.

A complexion like a brick. — W. L. GEORGE.

A complexion like the skin of a raw fowl. — JOHN OLIVER HOBBES.

A complexion like a Holland cheese. — WILLIAM WYCHERLEY.

Compliments.

Compliments to me [an old man] are like strawberries in winter time, deuced cloying, and a good deal out of season. — EDWARD LAMAN BLANCHARD.

Conceited.

Conceited as a negro bishop. — HENRY L. MENCKEN.

Concise.

Concise as a king's declaration of love. — LAURENCE STERNE.

Concrete.

Concrete as a bird in a cage, a bait on a hook, a piece of cheese in a mouse-trap. — HENRY JAMES.

Conduct.

Wind up your conduct, like your watch, once every day, examining minutely whether you are "fast" or "slow." — PUNCH, 1857.

Conquerors.

Conquerors are like fires — the greater their brilliancy, the larger the ruin they leave behind them. — PUNCH, 1857.

Conscience.

Conscience is like a sun-dial ; if you let truth shine upon it, it will put you right ; but you may cover it over so that no truth can fall upon it, or you may let false light gleam upon it and then it will lead you astray. — HAMILTON BOWER.

Conscience, in many souls, is like an English sovereign ; it reigns but it does not govern ; its function is merely to give a formal assent to the bills passed by the passions. — W. H. MALLOCK.

No more conscience than a fox in a poultry farm. — G. B. SHAW.

Conscience, like every other judge, may be misled, and there is no advocate so eloquent as self-interest, before that high, but infallible tribunal. — RICHARD LALOR SHEIL.

Considerate.

Considerate as the Fiji islander was of the missionary, when he asked him if he would rather be cooked *à la maître d'hôtel* or *en papillote*. — PAUL LEICESTER FORD.

Conspicuous.

Conspicuous as a sore thumb at an amateur piano contest. — ANON.

Conspicuous as a man at The Capitol without a badge. — NEW YORK TRIBUNE, February 14, 1917.

Constant.

A pipe in his mouth as constant as his front teeth. — DOUGLAS JERROLD.

Constitutions.

Constitutions are like virgins ; they never bear fruit till they have been violated. — PEARSON'S MAGAZINE, November, 1920.

Consulted.

Consulted as you would run over the leaves of a dictionary. — FRANCISQUE SARCEY.

Contagious.

Contagious as the sympathy of a smile. — JACINTO BENAVENTE.

Contemporary.

Contemporary as a newspaper. — WILLIAM LYON PHELPS.

Contemptible.

Contemptible as an apoplectic dancing-master. — PUNCH, 1841.

Contented.

Contented as a clam at sea. — ANON.

Contented as kittens before the fire. — IBID.

Contented as the debutante on receiving her first basket of orchids. — FRANCIS W. CROWNINSHIELD.

Contented as a cobra full of warm milk. — RUPERT HUGHES.

Conversation.

My conversation, it is like the Sun's, with all men, and with a friendly aspect to good and bad. — SIR THOMAS BROWNE.

Conversation is like a boot. When damped it loses its polish. — SIR FRANCIS C. BURNAND.

The conversation of Sir James Mackintosh has the effect of reading a well-written book ; that of his friend is like hearing a bewildering dream. — WILLIAM HAZLITT.

Conversation — *continued.*

The conversation of Burke must have been like the procession of a Roman triumph, exhibiting power and riches at every step, — occasionally, perhaps, mingling the low Fescennine jest with the lofty music of its march, but glittering all over with the spoils of the whole ransacked world. — THOMAS MOORE.

Conversation should be like a salad, composed of various ingredients, and well stirred with salt, oil and vinegar. — JOQUIN SETANTI.

Lettuce is like conversation : it must be fresh and crisp, so sparkling that you scarcely notice the bitter in it. Lettuce, like most talkers, is however, apt to run rapidly to seed. Blessed is that sort which comes to a head, and so remains — like few I know — growing more solid and satisfactory and tender at the same time, and whiter at the centre, and crisp in its maturity. Lettuce, like conversation, requires a good deal of oil, to avoid friction, and keep the company smooth ; a pinch of Attic salt, a dash of pepper, a quantity of mustard and vinegar, by all means — but so mixed that you will notice no sharp contact — and a trifle of sugar. You can put anything — and the more things the better — into salad, as into conversation ; but everything depends upon the skill in mixing. — CHARLES DUDLEY WARNER.

Convincing.

Convincing as a proposition in Euclid. — ANON.

Cook.

She cooked like the mother of all the Delmonicos. — HAROLD FREDERIC.

Coquette.

Coquettes are like hunters who are fond of hunting, but do not eat the game. — BALZAC.

A coquette is like your shadow ; chase her and she flees from you, flee from her and she chases you. — HINDU PROVERB.

Coquetry whets the appetite ; flirtation depraves it. Coquetry is the thorn that guards the rose — easily trimmed off when once plucked. Flirtation is like the slime on water-plants, making them hard to handle, and when caught, only to be cherished in slimy waters. — DONALD G. MITCHELL.

Cordial.

Cordial as an open door. — OWEN JOHNSON.

Corrupt.

Corrupt as a political boss. — ANON.

Cosy.

About as cosy as he would be standing on a bull's horns. — HERMAN MELVILLE.

Courage.

As a cur that goes through a Village, if he clap his tail between his legs, and run away, every cur will insult over him, but if he bristle up himself, and stand to it, give but a counter-snarl, there's not a dog dares meddle with him. Much is in a man's courage and discreet carriage of himself. — ROBERT BURTON.

Courtesy.

Courtesy is a science of the highest importance. It is like grace and beauty in the body, which charm at first sight, and lead on to further intimacy and friendship, opening a door that we may derive instruction from the example of others, and at the same time enabling us to benefit them by our example, if there be anything in our character worthy of imitation. — MONTAIGNE.

Courtship.

Courtship is something like stag hunting, of which few care to see the finish. — R. S. SURTEES.

Covetous.

A covetous man is like a camel with a great hunch on his back ; heaven's gate must be made higher and broader, or he will hardly get in. — THOMAS ADAMS.

Coy.

Coy as an alderman's eldest daughter. — THOMAS NABBES.

Cracks.

Cracks like the firing of pistols in dead of night. — KATHLEEN NORRIS.

Cramped.

Cramped like malefactors with the chain and ball. — HERMAN MELVILLE.

Crash.

A crash like the combined force of all the battering rams of Titus Flavius Vespasianus on one of the gates of Jerusalem. — CHARLES FAIRBANKS.

Creamy.

Creamy as a charlotte russe. — ANON.

Critic.

The critic has the same relation to literature that a flea has to a dog — he infests it, lives off it without either advancing or adorning it. — ANON.

The mule is like the critic of the drama. He can kick, but he cannot produce. — HARRY B. SMITH.

The critics are a race of scholars I am very little acquainted with ; having always esteemed them but like brokers, who, having no stock of their own, set up a trade with that of other men ; buying here, and selling there, and commonly abusing both sides, to make out a paltry gain, either of money or of credit, for themselves, and care not at whose cost. — SIR WILLIAM TEMPLE.

Crooked.

Crooked as a hair in a gale of wind. — ANON.

Crooked as an Arab street. — CHANNING POLLOCK.

Cropped.

Cropped as close as Time at Greenwich. — EDITH SITWELL.

Cross.

Cross as a capital X. — ANON.

Cross as a bag of cats. — P. W. JOYCE'S "ENGLISH AS WE SPEAK IT IN IRELAND," 1910.

Crowded.

Crowded as the Presbyterian hell for babies. — HENRY L. MENCKEN.

Cruel.

Cruel as the Holy. — GEORGE ELIOT.

Cruel as loneliness. — W. L. GEORGE.

Cruel as love or life. — SWINBURNE.

Crumpled.

Crumpled as a Palm Beach suit which has passed through a torrid afternoon. — ARTHUR BAER.

Crush.

Crush his neighbor's interest under foot, like a horse-roller over a daisy. — RICHARD JEFFERIES.

Crushed in the bottom of Stubb's boat, like one trodden underfoot of herds of elephants. — HERMAN MELVILLE.

Crushed like rotten apples. — SHAKESPEARE.

Crying.

Crying before people is just like taking off all your clothes before people. — MARGARET DELAND.

Culture.

As the soil, however rich it may be, cannot be productive without culture, so the mind without cultivation can never produce good fruit. — SENECA.

Curiosity.

Unconquerable curiosity, like that of our mother Eve. — BALZAC.

Curled.

They hurled the Javelins into him until he curled up like a Rubber Band. — GEORGE ADE.

Curled up like gummed labels. — ARTHUR BAER.

His backbone curled up like two broken sofa springs. — IBID.

Curled like an ocean wave. — LAWRENCE HOPE.

D

Dainty.

Dainty as a chorus man. — ANON.

Dance.

Danced like a man in a swarm of hornets. — ANON.

Danced as though he had two left feet. — IBID.

Dancing . . . like nothing so much as the jerking of a wooden monkey on a pole in the hands of a small boy. — ARLO BATES.

I don't think much of a dance where th' girl looks like she wuz bein' carried out of a burnin' buildin'. — ABE MARTIN.

She dances like a cattle stampede. — ALBERT PAYSON TERHUNE.

Dangle.

As the exhausted prize fighter sat on his second's knee, his head dangled about like a poppy in a shower. — H. S. CANBY'S "ENGLISH COMPOSITION IN THEORY AND PRACTICE," 1909.

Dark.

Dark as a club flush.—H. C. WITWER.

Daughter-in-Law.

A daughter-in-law is not like a shoe, you can't kick her off. — LEO TOLSTOY.

Dazzling.

Dazzling as a pawnbroker's wife. — ANON.

Dead.

Deader than a moosehead hatrack. — ARTHUR BAER.

Jack Dempsey will knock him deader than a two-hour old street-car transfer. — IBID.

Dead as last year's sand grass. — IDA M. EVANS.

Dead as a fern-leaf in a lump of coal. — THOMAS HARDY.

Dead as charity. — ROBERT HERRICK.

Dead as the eye of the fish served at a 60-cent table d'hôte. — DON MARQUIS.

Dead as the *beau monde* of Pompeii, or as the remains of Etruscan leaders of the ton. — GRACE AND PHILIP WHARTON.

Dear.

Dear as radium. — LEONARD MERRICK.

Debts.

Small debts are like small shot ; they are rattling on every side and can scarcely be escaped without a wound. Great debts are like cannons of loud noise but little danger. — DOCTOR JOHNSON.

Decorated.

The ring was decorated like a canary bird's cage on Audubon's birthday. — ARTHUR BAER.

Decorous.

Walked as decorously as Mr. Rockefeller would enter a Baptist church. — St. John G. Ervine.

Decorous, as a superannuated coquette. — Washington Irving.

Definite.

Definite and enduring as Hamlet or Micawber. — Frederic Taber Cooper.

Definite as a map for a townsite. — Benjamin De Casseres.

Definite as the colour red. — Henry James.

Delicate.

Delicate as the play of moonbeams on a field of snow. — Robert P. Downs.

Delicate as the hands of the almond-white daughter of the Emperor of Pekin. — Harris Merton Lyon.

Delicate as a fairy's sigh. — Frances Sargent Osgood.

Delicious.

Delicious as an Apricot. — Captain John Smith, 1580–1631.

Delightful.

Delightful as the recovery of lost sight. — Apollonius Rhodius.

Delusion.

Delusion and a snare, like the paint on a second-handed flivver. — Arthur Baer.

Demoralizing.

Demoralizing as a holiday. — Abe Martin.

Demure.

Demure as a bawd at a christening. — James Kelly's "Scottish Proverbs," 1721.

Dense.

Dense as a Scotchman at a Charity bazaar. — Anon.

Dependable.

Dependable as the sun. — Anon.

About as dependable as a woman's wrist watch. — Ibid.

Descends.

Descends like mining stock. — Bert Leston Taylor.

Desolate.

Desolate looking as a summer resort in midwinter. — Richard Harding Davis.

Destitute.

Destitute of relations as Melchisedec. — Dr. John Brown.

Destructive.

Destructive as a sledge hammer in a jewelry store. — Anon.

Determined.

Determined as a cook to make a beefsteak tender. — Baudelaire.

Developed.

Developed like a bottle from the neck down. — Anon.

Dictionaries.

Dictionaries are like watches; the worst is better than none, and the best cannot be expected to go quite true. — Doctor Johnson.

Differ.

Differ as a cuckatoo and an elephant. — Ibid.

Differ as a holocaust and a hollyhock. — Ibid.

Differ as a mountain range and a grain of sand. — Ibid.

Differ as a mouse and an elephant. — Ibid.

Differ as an eagle and an ant. — Ibid.

Differ as the dusk does from the day. — Harry Kemp.

Difference.

The difference between vivacity and wit is the same as the difference between the lightning-bug and lightning. — Josh Billings.

A difference surely as great as between the bottle and the wine. — Edgar Saltus.

Different.

Different as Piers Plowman and Mr. Pickwick. — Ibid.

Different as orchids' breath from grocery garlic. — William Beebe.

Different as three men singing the same chorus from three men playing three tunes on the same piano. — G. K. Chesterton.

Different . . . as grape-juice from vodka. — Katharine Fullerton Gerould.

Difficult.

Difficult as putting a blister on a porcupine. — Anon.

Difficult as to collect loose feathers in a hurricane. — Arthur Baer.

Difficult as virtue and almost as unreasonable. — Arlo Bates.

Difficult as to catch an eel in a bucket of oil. — Ibid.

Difficult as to remember a wheeze devised in a dream. — Ibid.

Difficult as to sell a ham at Long Branch. — Ibid.

Difficult as to sell needles in the blacksmith's street. — Ibid.

It would be scarcely more difficult to push a stone out from the Pyramids with the bare hand than to alter a word, or the position of a word, in Milton or Shakespeare (in their most important works at least), without making the poet say something else, or something worse, than he does say. — S. T. Coleridge.

Difficult as finding a fifty-dollar bill on the floor of a poorhouse. — Joseph C. Lincoln.

Difficult as getting a concession to put a merry-go-round on the front lawn of the White House. — Kenneth L. Roberts.

Dignified.

Dignified as Julius Caesar. — Anon.

Dignified as the electoral college. — Albert E. Hoyt.

More dignified than a whitewashed negro. — Herman Melville.

Direct.

Direct as a torpedo. — Wallace Irwin.

A directness in the argument was like the ache of old pinchers. — Henry James.

Disappear.

Disappear like one apple in an orphan asylum. — Arthur Baer.

Disappeared as though behind the curtain of a theatre. — Victor Hugo.

Disappeared like a rabbit down a boa-constrictor's throat. — R. S. Surtees.

Disappointing.

Disappointing as a honeymoon. — Henry L. Mencken.

Disarrayed.

Disarrayed as a woman's top dresser drawer. — Burton Rascoe.

Disconnected.

Disconnected like the buzzing song of a swarm of gnats. — May Sinclair.

Disconsolate.

Disconsolate as a bee that has lost its sting. — Thomas Shadwell.

Discords.

As many discords as bullets in a battle. — Anon.

Discouraged.

Discouraged as a frog catcher in the Desert of Sahara. — DON MARQUIS.

Discourse.

His discourse was like a fire, which, instead of enlightening, obscured everything with its smoke. — ABELARD.

Discreet.

About as discreet as streetwalkers. — GERTRUDE ATHERTON.

Disgusting.

Disgusting, like mediocrity in verse. — HILAIRE BELLOC.

Disgusting az the opening ov Rockway clams with a shoe-hammer. — JOSH BILLINGS.

Dismal.

Dismal as a bowling alley without beer. — JAMES G. HUNEKER.

Dismal as a cypress swamp on a rainy Sunday. — CORNÉLIS DE W. WILCOX.

Dispersed.

Dispersed, as fiends before rebuking saints. — SIR AUBREY DE VERE.

Distinct.

Distinct as in a line engraving. — THOMAS HARDY.

Distinctive.

Distinctive as a nigger in a snowstorm. — THOMAS BURKE.

Distressing.

Distressing as an amateur cocktail. — ANON.

Divorce.

Divorce is like matrimony, a fellow has got to go through it three or four times before he knows how. — EDGAR SALTUS.

Do.

Do as beggars do, go away when you have got enough. — JONATHAN SWIFT.

Doctor.

A doctor, be he never so clever and delightful, who doesn't cure, is like a mole-catcher who can't câtch moles, or a watchmaker who can do everything but make your watch go. — DR. JOHN BROWN.

Dog.

A good dog, like a good candidate, cannot be of a bad colour. — PETER BECKFORD.

Dogma.

Without dogma a religion is like a body without skeleton. It can't stand. — JAMES G. HUNEKER.

Domestic.

Domestic as a doughnut. — ANON.

Down.

Down like a sledge hammer. — ANON.

He went down like a clothing-store dummy. — CLARENCE L. CULLEN.

The barometer went down like sands in an hourglass. — GOUVERNEUR MORRIS.

Came down on him like a new Republican President on a Democratic postmaster. — GEORGE W. PECK.

Drastic.

Drastic as surgery. — ANON.

Draws.

Draws like a dog fight. — MARK TWAIN.

Dreaming.

A certain amount of dreaming is good, like a narcotic in discreet doses. — VICTOR HUGO.

Dreary.

Dreary as pyramid under the stars. — G. K. CHESTERTON.

Dreary as chaos ere creation's reign. — VOLTAIRE.

Dressed.

Dressed like a Christmas tree. — ANON.

Dressed like an Easter egg. — IBID.

Dressed up like a sore thumb. — IBID.

All his body was dressed like a May-pole. — JOHN EVELYN.

Drink.

Drink like a suction hose. — THOMAS BURKE.

My drooping soul drinks up your words as the parched earth does a refreshing shower. — EDWARD RAVENSCROFT.

Drip.

Dripping like a leaky watering-cart. — GELETT BURGESS.

On we went, dripping, and sloshing, and looking very like men that had been turned back by the Royal Humane Society as being incurably drowned. — A. W. KINGLAKE.

Dripping like sea deities after an elemental Waterloo. — HOWARD PAUL.

Droop.

Droop like flowers when evening shuts her eyes. — SIR WILLIAM DAVENANT.

Mouth drooped as in the mask which the ancients sculptured on tombs. — VICTOR HUGO.

Drooping like the boughs of a weeping ash. — RICHARD JEFFERIES.

Drooped like birch-boughs. — DINAH MARIA MULOCK.

Dropped.

Men dropped, like brown leaves from autumn trees. — SIR PHILIP GIBBS.

Drops like the released pile-driver. — MARK TWAIN.

Drowsy.

Drowsed like so many hibernating bears. — GEORGE ADE.

Drowsy as watchers at a death bed. — ANON.

Drunk.

Drunk as Pluto, who drinks lightning and never gets scorched. — ANON.

Drunk as a bacchanal. — THOMAS DURFEY.

Drunk as nurses at a christening. — "LONDON CHANTICLEERS," 1659.

Drunken as our swine. — EDWARD MORE.

Drunk as an M. P. (Can't stand up). — G. F. NORTHALL'S "FOLK PHRASES," 1894.

Drunk as a prohibition enforcement agent. — BERT LESTON TAYLOR.

Dry.

Dry as the tonsils that thought their master was taking in washing. — ANON.

Her throat was as dry as if it had been swabbed with blotting paper. — IBID.

Dry as a covered bridge. — ARTHUR BAER.

Dry as the clerk of a lime-kiln. — J. R. BARTLETT'S "DICTIONARY OF AMERICANISMS," 1877.

More dry than a fever. — RICHARD BROME.

Dry as a prohibitionist lost in the Sahara Desert. — BENJAMIN DE CASSERES.

Dry as corn fodder in March. — DAVID GRAYSON.

Dry — *continued.*

Dry as sawdust. — HENRY HIGDEN.

Dry as a parliamentary blue-book. — JAMES G. HUNEKER.

Dry as noon. — RICHARD JEFFERIES.

Dry as seasoned fish. — PATRICK MACGILL.

Dry as the Congressional Record. — JAMES J. MONTAGUE.

Dry as the crop report. — H. C. WITWER.

Dry as an author's pocket. — EDMUND YATES.

Dull.

Dull as a Philadelphia Sunday. — ANON.

Dull as books in a guest room. — IBID.

Dull as the man who thought Scotland Yard a place where they hung out kilts. — IBID.

Dull as a banker. — BALZAC.

Throb dull as the measured beat of the steam-engine. — KENNETH GRAHAME.

Dull as a flower without the sun. — THOMAS HARDY.

Dull as an obsolete almanac. — JOHN HAY.

Dull as a London fog. — JAMES G HUNEKER.

Dull as duty. — DON MARQUIS.

Dull as oysters. — HENRY L. MENCKEN.

Dull as a Trinity Sunday sermon. — JONATHAN SWIFT.

Dull as a lecture at the Royal Society. — OSCAR WILDE.

Dumb.

Dumb as a stage doorkeeper. — ANON.

Dumb as the man who thinks a baseball fan is run by electricity. — IBID.

He is as dumb as the man who thought a football coach has four wheels. — IBID.

Dumb as the ninnyhammer who thought the Mann act a quartette. — IBID.

Durable.

Durable as a pig's nose. — WARREN LEWIS.

Durable as the stars. — DANIEL WEBSTER.

Duration.

No more duration than a blaze of straw. — JOSEPH E. CONRAD.

E

Eager.

Eager as an understudy. — L. MONTA BELL.

Eager as fire horses, heads lifted to the gong. — MARY ROBERTS RINEHART.

Eager as the dinner gong to make himself heard. — RUFUS E. SHAPLEY.

Ears.

Ears like mangled doughnuts. — ANON.

Pricked up his ears like two railroad signals. — LEWIS CARROLL.

Earth.

The earth is like a broad leaf floating in the air. — ANAXIMENES.

Easy.

Easy as falling out of a canoe. — ANON.

Easy as getting the hat privilege in a synagogue. — IBID.

Easy as to bite a dentist. — IBID.

He's as easy to spot as a fawn-colored vest at a soup banquet. — ARTHUR BAER.

Easy — *continued.*

Easy as a fire chief in an asbestos village. — Ibid.

Easy as selling beer at a picnic. — Guy Bolton.

Easy as sucking a fresh egg. — Benvenuto Cellini.

Easy as spitting. — Anton T. Chekhov.

Gallop easy as an iceboat's rush before the wind. — R. B. Cunningham Graham.

Easy as falling off a cable-car. — Cutcliffe Hyne.

To swim in the open ocean is as easy to the practised swimmer as to ride in a spring-carriage ashore. — Herman Melville.

Easy as ordering a drink. — Leonard Merrick.

About as easy as to do up an elephant in a shawl strap. — Channing Pollock.

Easy as for a cat to have twins. — Mark Twain.

Editors.

Editors are like the people who bought and sold in the book of Revelation ; there is not one but has the mark of the beast upon them. — Samuel Butler, 1835–1902.

Education.

Education, like politics, is a rough affair, and every instructor has to shut his eyes and hold his tongue as though he were a priest. — Henry Adams.

Your education, like . . . carrots, is not a manufactured article, but just a seed which has grown up largely under nature's friendly influence. — William J. Long.

Effect.

The blows rattled off Jack Dempsey's chin with no more effect than a tack hammer against a statue of bronze. — New York Tribune, July 3, 1921.

Effective.

Effective as a bullet. — Edgar Saltus.

Efficacious.

About as efficacious as mustard plaster on a wooden leg. — Washington Post, October 5, 1918.

Efficient.

Efficient, like the hero in a cinema play. — Edward S. Martin.

Elastic.

Elastic as a steel spring. — Anon.

Elegant.

Elegant as the Claypool Hotel in Indianapolis. — George Ade.

Eloquence.

His eloquence [Bishop Joseph Butler] was like a chain of gold. — London Magazine, 1752.

As the shadow runs over the field, so the impression of his [Daniel O'Connell] varying eloquence ran over the assemblage. — Justin McCarthy.

Eloquent.

Eloquent as a bushel of alphabets. — John Brougham.

Elusive.

Elusive as a wet fish. — Anon.

Empty.

Empty as a contribution box. — Anon.

Empty as an author's pocket. — Ibid.

Empty as a poorhouse's boarder's pocket. — Joseph C. Lincoln.

Enemy.

An enemy as much as the fox is the enemy of the poultry-yard, and the hound is the enemy of the fox. — George Meredith.

English.

English as Piccadilly. — ANON.

Enigmatic.

Her smile as enigmatic as a gambler's thinking. — MARION STROBEL.

Entangled.

I would not take any risk of being entangled upon the river, like an ox jumped halfway over a fence and liable to be torn by dogs front and rear without a fair chance to gore one way or kick the other. — ABRAHAM LINCOLN.

Enthusiasm.

Enthusiasm, like a match, must be held down, to burn well. — LIFE, December 9, 1920.

Enthusiastic.

Enthusiastic as a bride buying her trousseau. — ANON.

About as enthusiastic as a guy going to the chair. — H. C. WITWER.

Enthusiastic as a three-headed cat in a creamery. — IBID.

Envious.

Envious as a dropsical man looking at the Mississippi River. — ANON.

Essays.

His [Emerson] Essays are like a plot of ground sown with lilies and other white flowers, without perfume. — FRANCIS GRIERSON.

His [Montaigne] Essays are like a mythological landscape — you hear the pipe of Pan in the distance, the naked goddess moves past, the satyr leers from the thicket. — ALEXANDER SMITH.

Eternal.

Eternal as mediocrity. — JAMES G. HUNEKER.

Etiquette.

As good-breeding is an expedient to make fools and wise men equals, so etiquette is the invention of wise men to keep fools at a distance. — SIR RICHARD STEELE.

Even.

Even as a set of false teeth. — ARTHUR BAER.

Even as a row of West Point cadets on parade. — IBID.

Evident.

Evident as a wooden leg. — ANON.

Exact.

Exact as a blue print. — ANON.

Exact as the technical jargon of a trade. — ALDOUS HUXLEY.

Exasperated.

The American mind exasperated the European as a buzz-saw might exasperate a pine forest. — HENRY ADAMS.

Excel.

Excel as much as diamond does glass. — PLAY, "LIFE AND DEATH OF LORD CROMWELL," 1602.

Excel, as the sun with beams most clear and bright excels the stars. — JOHN LYDGATE.

Exciting.

About as exciting as a ride on a stone camel. — ANON.

Excited as if Rockefeller had asked her to get married. — GELETT BURGESS.

Exciting as war. — RT. HON. WINSTON CHURCHILL.

Exciting as a sudden gallop. — HENRY JAMES.

Excited as a cop making his first pinch. — H. C. WITWER.

Exclusive.

Exclusive as a Turkish Bath on Saturday night. — GEORGE ADE.

About as exclusive as the Grand Central Station. — ANON.

Exhilarating.

Exhilarating as love. — BALZAC.

Exhilarating as iced champagne. — MARION HARLAND.

Exhilarating as a fanfare of bugles. — HENRY L. MENCKEN.

About as exhilarating as the morning after the celebration of New Year's resolutions. — EDWIN L. SABIN.

Expect.

As well expect a hook to hold soft cheese. — ANON.

As well expect an experimental physiologist to bless the Anti-vivisection Society, or a saloon keeper to uphold a temperance lecturer as a model of all the virtues. — IBID.

As well expect a tempest in a saucer. — IBID.

As well expect bird lime in a cuckoo clock. — IBID.

As well expect the King of England to be a Nonconformist, or to find a statue of Voltaire in the Vatican. — IBID.

As well expect to saddle and bridle an eagle. — IBID.

Expensive.

Expensive as a mistress. — ANON.

Expensive and exclusive as millinery masterpieces. — WILL LEVINGTON COMFORT.

Experience.

Experience is like medicine; some persons require larger doses of it than others, and do not like to take it pure, but a little disguised and better adapted to the taste; like medicine, also, it is a cure for many ills to which we are liable. — "ACTON; or, THE CIRCLE OF LIFE," 1849.

Expressionless.

Expressionless as the grin of letter boxes. — BALZAC.

Extinct.

Extinct, like the Harlem goat. — GRANT M. OVERTON.

Eyebrows.

The eyebrow polished and dark as though the brush had drawn it. — DANTE.

Eyebrows arched like skipping ropes. — HENRY JAMES.

Eyes.

His eyes looking like the frosting on an angel cake. — ARTHUR BAER.

Her eyes were like bright blots of ink. — MAX BEERBOHM.

Eyes like acetylene headlights. — ALEXANDER BLACK.

The eyes, like sentinels, occupy the highest place in the body. — CICERO.

Eyes like the lakes of Killarney for clarity. — RICHARD HOVEY.

Her eyes looked like two rainy autumn moons. — HENRY JAMES.

His eyes [Edwin Booth] shone out like gleaming jets of grief. — AMY LESLIE.

Had an eye like a loose button on an ulster. — MARK TWAIN.

His [Captain Anson] eyes were like twin pansies in a bucket of blood. — LEONARD WASHBURNE.

F

Face.

He had a face like a bottle of warts. — ANON.

He has a face like a busted sofa. — IBID.

Your face looks like a Chinese lantern after a wet lawn fête. — IBID.

A face like an open book. — IBID.

A face like a wet holiday. — IBID.

A face that looks like it had worn out four bodies. — IBID.

A face like the battlefields of France. — IBID.

A face that looked like a sucked lemon. — JOSH BILLINGS.

A face like a drowning horse. — GELETT BURGESS.

His face was afire with intelligence as a flannel pincushion. — STEPHEN CRANE.

Faces like the backs of cabs. — W. H. T. CROSLAND.

His face like a shout on a sunny morning. — A. S. M. HUTCHINSON.

Face like a three-parts deflated football. — IBID.

It was an oddity of Mrs. Lowder's that her face in speech was like a lighted window at night, but that silence immediately drew the curtain. — HENRY JAMES.

Face like a sea-monster. — BEN JONSON.

A sad face like a salt fish. — DON MARQUIS.

A great red face like a leg of mutton. — W. SOMERSET MAUGHAM.

A face like the abdomen of a tenpin. — HENRY L. MENCKEN.

A face like a sea boot. — CLIFFORD MILLS.

A face like a pug-dog. — CARL VAN VECHTEN.

A face like a sallow bust on a bracket in a university library. — EDITH WHARTON.

Fade.

Faded as a fashionable beauty at the end of a London season. — J. STERLING COYNE.

Fading away like a mist from Killarney of a fine morning. — RUPERT HUGHES.

You are beautiful and faded,
Like an old opera tune
Played upon a harpsichord ;
Or like the sun-flooded silks
Of an eighteenth-century boudoir.
— AMY LOWELL.

Faded, like a cloud which has outwept its rain. — SHELLEY.

Faint.

Faint as a chicken's note that has the pip. — WILLIAM COWPER.

Faint as far-off bugles blowing. — WILLIAM WALLACE HARNEY.

Fair.

Fair as milk. — LORD BYRON.

Fair as the maiden spring. — JOHN CARTER.

Fair as day in its first birth. — SIR WILLIAM DAVENANT.

Fairer than the bud unfolding in a shower. — JOHN LOGAN.

Fair as Cupid's mother. — MOSES MENDES.

Fair as faith. — JOAQUIN MILLER.

Fair as the inhabitants of heaven. — MARY PIX.

Fair and fresh as flowers in May. — EDMUND SPENSER.

Fair as heaven or freedom won. — SWINBURNE.

Fair as Paradise. — WORDSWORTH.

Faith.

Our faith is too often like the mercury in the weather-glass; it gets up high in fine weather; in rough weather it sinks proportionally low. — ANON.

Faithful.

Faithful as angel guardians. — PLAY, "EMILIA," 1672.

Faithless.

Faithless as Don Giovanni in love. — PIERCE EGAN.

Faithless as the Muses' oaths. — EDMUND GOSSE.

Fall.

Fall like a bullet spent. — CLINTON SCOLLARD.

Fallacious.

Fallacious as the harlot's kiss. — STEPHEN DUCK.

False.

False as a dentist's smile. — ANON.

Falser than the weeping crocodile. — DRYDEN.

False as harlot's tears. — THOMAS DURFEY.

False as the loose coquet's inveigling airs. — JOHN GAY.

Falser than malice in the mouth of envy. — MARY PIX.

False as the fowler's artful snare. — TOBIAS SMOLLETT.

Fame.

Men's fame is like their hair, which grows after they are dead, and with just as little use to them. — GEORGE VILLIERS.

Familiar.

Familiar as a town clock. — ANON.

Familiar as an old mistake. — EDWIN ARLINGTON ROBINSON.

Fancy.

Fancy is like a butterfly, which must be delicately handled; if rude fingers tamper with it, the bloom is rubbed off, and the gay insect perishes. — FREDERICK BOUTERWEK.

Fantastic.

It would be as fantastic for a housekeeper to comment upon a gentleman's absence as for a clock to remark upon not being wound up. — HENRY JAMES.

Fascinating.

Fascinating as a seed catalogue. — ANON.

Fascinating as the scene of the murder. — IBID.

Fascinating as a hanging or a dog-fight. — HENRY L. MENCKEN.

Fashion.

Fashion is like a shadow — fly from it and it follows you; follow it and it flies from you. You can point your finger at it, but you can't put your finger on it. It is as much an affair of carriage as of clothes, and more an affair of the wearer, than of the tailor, haberdasher or bootmaker. — ANON.

Fast.

Fast as Jehu drove for a crown. — CHARLES CHURCHILL.

Fast as a clinched nail. — DOUGLAS JERROLD.

Fast as a cook cracks eggs. — THOMAS NASH.

Fast as a musical professor's fingers travel over the keys of a piano. — MARK TWAIN.

Fat.

Fat as a balloon. — MARK TWAIN.

Fat as plenty. — HUGH WARD.

Fearful.

Fearful as degradation. — ANON.

Fearless.

Fearless as valour. — Barbara Hoole.

Feeble.

Feeble as a winter's fly. — Evelyn Scott.

Feeling.

About as much feeling as a milk trust has for babies. — Anon.

Feet.

His feet were like icicles in refrigerating stockings. — Sir Francis C. Burnand.

Felicity.

Many in this world run after felicity like an absent-minded man hunting for his hat while all the time it is on his head or in his hand. — Sydney Smith.

Felt.

He felt like the symptoms on a medicine bottle. — George Ade.

Fermenting.

Fermenting like bungalow brew. — Arthur Baer.

Fettered.

Fettered to a pack of useless memories like a living person, to a corpse. — Ouida.

Fictitious.

Fictitious as a sick man's dream. — Horace.

Fidgety.

Fidgety, like a rabbit's nose — or a commuter. — Don Marquis.

Fierce.

Fierce as a shark. — Anon.

Fierce as a rat-catcher's dog at a sink-hole. — Alfred Crowquil.

Look as fierce as if he took Gunpowder Snuff. — Samuel [Maggoty or Fiddler] Johnson.

Fierce as Frenzy's fevered blood. — Sir Walter Scott.

Fierce as a pacifist in a passion. — H. G. Wells.

Fiercer.

Fiercer than famine, war, or spotted pestilence. — Nicholas Rowe.

Figure.

A woman with a figure like a pouter pigeon. — Julian Street.

A figure like a beer barrel. — Oscar Wilde.

Fire.

The Irish . . . they will stand fire like a mutton chop. — Punch, 1850.

Firm.

Firm as Plymouth Rock. — Anon.

Planted firm like castles. — Richard Jefferies.

Stand firm as the foot of resolution. — Thomas Southerne.

Firm as the pillars of the earth, and lasting. — William Thompson.

Fit.

Fits as a hollow fits its circle. — Anon.

Fits like a duck's foot in the mud. — Ibid.

Fits like a glass eye. — Ibid.

Fits like the skin on a sausage. — Ibid.

Fits him as easily as his skin. — Thomas Hughes.

Fitted.

He was no more fitted to rule than a sea-serpent is competent to be an apothecary. — Edgar Saltus.

Fixed.

Fixed as the sun. — Erasmus.

Fixed and unchangeable, as the pole star in heaven. — Friedrich von Schiller.

Fizzle.

The usual fizzle, like a mattoid blonde attempting to express emotion in a moving picture. — ANON.

Flabbergasting.

Flabbergasting as the amorous glance of a lady embalmer. — HENRY L. MENCKEN.

Flapped.

Flapped like a loose top-sail in a gale of wind. — JOSEPH C. LINCOLN.

Flashed.

Flashed like long pear earrings. — GEORGE W. BAGBY.

Flashed like a mirror played at the face of the sun. — HENRY JAMES.

Flash like a live wire flopping against an iron rail. — EDISON MARSHALL.

Flash'd like Gun-Powder. — COTTON MATHER.

Flat.

Flat as if an English tank had happened along and sat down on him. — ANON.

Flat as a waiter's feet. — ARTHUR BAER.

Flat as last night's beer. — LOUIS UNTERMEYER.

Flattery.

Flattery is like the smoke of incense; it defiles the object it pretends to adore. — ANON.

Flattery is like champagne, it soon gets into the head. — WILLIAM BROWNE.

Flattery is like wine, which exhilarates a man for a moment, but usually ends by going to his head and making him act foolish. — HELEN ROWLAND.

I was not accustomed to flattery. I was rather like the Hoosier with the gingerbread — who reckoned he loved it better than any man, and got less of it. — ABRAHAM LINCOLN.

Fleeting.

Fleeting as a ferryboat shoe-shine. — F. P. ADAMS.

Flexible.

Flexible as a diplomat's conscience. — ANON.

Flickered.

Flickered like a candle in a wind. — HENRY JAMES.

Flippant.

Flippant as a man-milliner. — WILLIAM CHARLES MACREADY.

Flippant as a Court Coquet in Tragedy. — JAMES RALPH.

Flopped.

Fluent as a rill that wanders silver-footed down a hill. — ANON.

Flopped like the ears of a dog. — — EDGAR ALLAN POE.

Fluttered.

Fluttered on her lips like a drop of dew on a flower. — VICTOR HUGO.

Fluttering down like a hooded hawk. SIR PHILIP SIDNEY.

Fly.

Fly like a thief from the gallows. — TOBIAS SMOLLETT.

Foamed.

Foaming at the mouth like a cream-puff. — ANON.

The sea foamed like the mouth of madness. — GEORGE MEREDITH.

Foggy.

Foggy . . . as the wraith of a jelly fish dipped in ink. — ANON.

Foggy as Blackfriar's bridge on Lord Mayor's day. — LEIGH HUNT.

Folded.

He folded up like a Pocket Camera. — GEORGE ADE.

The handsome immigrant [Georges Carpentier, pugilist] folded up like a violin stand. — ARTHUR BAER.

Folds.

Full of folds as a sleeping boa-constrictor. — WILLIAM MATHEWS.

Folly.

A woman to be suspected of folly is as a bracelet of gold upon the wrist; but to be convicted of wrong-doing is a handcuff whereof the grip is iron. — GELETT BURGESS.

Fool.

A Fool in an elevated position is like a man in a ballroom — everybody appears little to him, and he appears little to everybody. — PUNCH, 1856.

Foolish.

Foolish as the fly that mistook a spider's web for a full set of whiskers. — ANON.

Foolish as to cut off the head to preserve the hair. — IBID.

Foolish as to expect a snake to hatch out a rope. — IBID.

Foolish as to judge a horse by its harness. — IBID.

Foolish as to cast missiles at a rat in the vicinity of a priceless piece of porcelain. — LI HUNG CHANG.

Forlorn.

Forlorn as an unmated coon. — J. R. BARTLETT'S "DICTIONARY OF AMERICANISMS," 1877.

Fortune.

Fortune is like a coquette; if you don't run after her, she will run after you. — JOSH BILLINGS.

We treat fortune like a mistress; the more she yields, the more we demand. — MME. ROLAND.

Freckles.

Freckles, like rust spots. — WILLA CATHER.

Free.

Free as the grace of God and twice as plentiful. — ANON.

Free as the butterfly. — W. H. HUDSON.

A hand as free as that of a compositor scattering type. — HENRY JAMES.

Free as fish that glide through the deep. — THOMAS KILLIGREW.

Free as the birds among the flowers and sunshine. — AUGUST STRINDBERG.

Free as Nature is. — JAMES THOMSON.

The diplomatists at Vienna . . . thought themselves as free to carve up the world as one is free to carve up such a boneless structure as a cheese. — H. G. WELLS.

Freedom.

Freedom is like drink. If you take anny at all ye might as well take enough to make you happy f'r awhile. — FINLEY PETER DUNNE.

Fresh.

Fresh as English bowling-green. — BALZAC.

Fresh as to-morrow. — JAMES G. HUNEKER.

Fresh as an unveiled statue. — HENRY JAMES.

Fresh as in the month of May. — LYLY.

Freshened.

She freshened up like a wilted violet in water. — FRANK R. ADAMS.

Friend.

A bad friend is like a smith, who if he does not burn you with fire will injure you with smoke. — ANON.

A cheerful friend is like a sunny day, which sheds its brightness on all

Friend — *continued.*

around ; and most of us can, as we choose, make of this world either a palace or a prison. — SIR JOHN LUBBOCK.

Friendship

Friendship is a good deal like China ; it is very beautiful and durable as long as it is quite whole ; break it and all the cement in the world will never quite repair the damage. — ANON.

Friendship, like the immortality of the soul, is too good to be believed. — R. W. EMERSON.

An old friendship is like old wine ; the longer it lasts the stronger it grows. — ANTONIO PEREZ.

A hollow friendship is like a hollow tooth — it's always best to have it out at once. — PUNCH, 1862.

Many men that pretend friendship, they are like the shadow of the bodie, they follow a man while the sun of prosperitie shines : but if a cloud of adversity hide that sun, those shadows are gone. — THOMAS SHELTON'S "A CENTURIE OF SIMILES," 1640.

Frightful.

Frightful, like funerals. — MAY SINCLAIR.

Frigid.

Frigid and academic as a painted nude in a blizzard. — JAMES G. HUNEKER.

Frivolous.

Frivolous as polished idleness. — ANON.

Frowning.

Frowning as if they'd swallow forks. — RABELAIS, THE YOUNGER.

Full.

Full of wisdom as a tree of leaves. — WILLIAM ROSE BENÉT.

Full of Germans as a brass band. — FINLEY PETER DUNNE.

Full of poetry as a lily is of dew. — ANATOLE FRANCE.

Full as a bus on a wet Sunday. — AUGUSTUS MAYHEW.

Full of money as a miser's stocking. — IBID.

Fun.

Fun is like life insurance, the older you git the more it costs. — ABE MARTIN.

Funny.

Funny as a high hat. — ANON.

Futile.

Futile as to attempt to dust cobwebs off the moon. — ANON.

Futile as to oppose an earthquake with argument. — IBID.

Futile as for a traffic policeman to ask passers-by where they come from and why. — DOROTHY SCARBOROUGH.

Futile as the philandering of a chorus man. — SIDNEY C. WILLIAMS.

G

Gallant.

Gallant and gay as Lover to the Altar. — GERALD MASSEY.

Gasp.

Gasp as if in the chamber of a diving-bell. — JAMES G. HUNEKER.

Gathered.

Gathered like female idlers around a bonnet-shop. — THOMAS HARDY.

Gay.

Gay as a Spring bonnet. — ANON.

Gay — *continued.*

Fiction as gay as a Cancer Week Circular. — BERTON BRALEY.

Gay as a parade. — HILDA CONKLING.

Gay as paradise, when first its sweetness bloomed. — EDWARD HOWARD.

Gay as a tea-store chromo. — JOSEPH C. LINCOLN.

Gay as a frigate's pennant. — HERMAN MELVILLE.

Gazing.

Gazing at me in a way in which the damned gaze out of their cauldrons of boiling pitch at some soul walking scot free in the place of torment. — JOSEPH CONRAD.

Generous.

Generous as the man who would give you the sleeves out of his vest. — ANON.

Genial.

About as genial and communicative as a maiden aunt over a married sister's new dress. — A. S. M. HUTCHINSON.

Genius.

A genius without vices is like a race horse without a good jockey. — BENJAMIN DE CASSERES.

Genius, in one respect, is like gold; numbers of persons are constantly writing about both, who have neither. — C. C. COLTON.

Gentle.

Gentle as the falling tear. — THOMAS CHATTERTON.

Gentle as a glove. — CONGREVE.

Gentle as bridal smiles. — SIR WILLIAM DAVENANT.

Gentle as an apostle. — EDMOND ROSTAND.

Gently.

Gently as if she were lifting a veil from the face of the dead. — HENRY JAMES.

Girl.

A girl like a flaming rose. — HEINE.

Glad.

Glad as youth. — BRIAN HOOKER.

Glad as brook that through a meadow strays. — JOHN L. SPAULDING.

Glimmer.

Glimmer like dying tapers. — MARY PIX.

Glimpse.

A rare glimpse like the rabbit in the conjurer's sleeve. — HENRY JAMES.

Glitter.

Glittering as Phoebus. — HENRY BRADSHAW.

Glittering like a morning star, full of life and splendor and joy [of Marie Antoinette]. — EDMUND BURKE.

Glittered and glared like a glacier. — HERMAN MELVILLE.

Glitters like burnished gold. — GILBERT WHITE.

Gloomy.

Gloomy . . . like an undertaker out of employment. — T. B. ALDRICH.

Gloomy as an old man by a fireless hearth. — ANON.

Gloomy as a wet holiday. — IBID.

Gloomy as a mute at a funeral, or an Englishman at a party of pleasure. — BULWER-LYTTON.

He wears an habitual expression of gloom, like a dissenting clergyman who is a chronic sufferer from hay fever and whose salary is a year and a half in arrears. — EDWARD E. PRICE.

Glow.

Glow like a rosebud. — HEINE.

Eyes glowed like yellow wine when the sun shines through it. — SELMA LAGERLÖF.

Glow — *continued.*

Glowed like the initials of an illuminated manuscript. — EDMUND L. PEARSON.

Glow'd like a torch when shaken in the wind. — TASSO.

Glum.

Glum as a tongue-tied parrot. — JOSEPH C. LINCOLN.

Gnaw.

Gnaws like a silent poison. — GEORGE SANTAYANA.

Go.

Go as if nine men pulled you and ten men held you. — JOHN WITHAL'S "DICTIONARY IN ENGLISH AND LATIN," 1521.

Goading.

Goading him like an untractable donkey. — GEORGE CRUIKSHANK'S "COMIC ALMANACK," 1847.

Golden.

Kinder golden, like the hair o' them British Blondes that was here in the Variety Show. — BRET HARTE.

Gone.

Gone, like the life from a busted balloon;
Gone, like the soul from a ruptured bassoon;
Gone, like the sheen of a pock-pitted cheek;
Gone, like our change at the close of the week.

— PALMER COX.

Gone as a dream is gone from a dreamer waked with a shout. — LORD DUNSANY.

Good.

Good as a glass of sherry in front of a wood fire. — WILLIAM ROSE BENÉT.

Good out of the world, as out of fashion. — THOMAS FULLER, M. D., "GNOMOLOGIA," 1732.

Gorgeous.

Gorgeous as the gold of sunset. — CHARLES EDWARD RUSSELL.

Gossip.

Confirmed gossips are like connoisseurs of cheese: the stuff they relish must be stout. — HOLMAN DAY.

Governments.

Governments are like men, more or less suspicious according to their temperament. — PUNCH, 1844.

Government is not reason, it is not eloquence, it is force; like fire, a troublesome servant and a fearful master. Never for a moment should it be left to irresponsible action. — GEORGE WASHINGTON.

Graceful.

Graceful as Diana when she draws her bow. — LORD BYRON.

Graceful as the swallow's flight. — JULIAN GRENFELL.

About as graceful as a hippopotamus. — W. CAREW HAZLITT.

Graceful as a butterfly. — F. BERKELEY SMITH.

Graceful as a matron's bosom heaving. — THOMAS WADE.

Gracious.

Gracious as a traffic cop. — F. P. ADAMS.

Gracious as the morning star of heaven. — ROBERT GREENE.

Grateful.

Grateful as the rosy month of May. — WILLIAM THOMPSON.

Grating.

Grating as an harmonica. — BALZAC.

Grave.

Grave as a German soldier marching to battle. — BALZAC.

Grave — *continued.*

Grave as a proctor. — GEORGE CRUIKSHANK'S "COMIC ALMANACK," 1838.

Grave as an old abbess. — SIR WILLIAM DAVENANT.

Grave as Spain. — JOHN GAY.

Grave as a wintry sea. — JOHN OLIVER HOBBS.

Grave, but satisfied, like a widower. — GORDON ARTHUR SMITH.

Grave as a society of bearers. — WESTMINSTER REVIEW, January, 1856.

Gravity.

There is a false gravity that is a very ill symptom; and it may be said that as rivers, which run very slowly, have always the most mud at the bottom, so a solid stiffness in the constant course of a man's life is a sign of a thick bed of mud at the bottom of his brain. — SIR GEORGE SAVILE.

Greedily.

Greedily as a puritan hunting vice. — LAWRENCE GILMAN.

Green.

Green as a Sinn Feiner's conception of heaven. — WASHINGTON STAR, September, 1919.

Grim.

Grim . . . like monks awaiting a massacre. — A. W. KINGLAKE.

Grinning.

A lop-sided grin, like he had a lemon in his mouth. — JOSEPH C. LINCOLN.

Grinnin' like a toothpick advertisement. — H. C. WITWER.

Gripped.

Gripped him like an empty belly. — CUTCLIFFE HYNE.

Groan.

Groan like the cholera. — PUNCH, 1858.

Grotesque.

Grotesque as a gargoyle. — RAFAEL SABATINI.

Growl.

The growl of Chapel Organs, like prayer by machinery; proclaiming, as in a kind of horrid diabolic horse-laughter, Vanity of Vanities, all is Vanity. — THOMAS CARLYLE.

Guarded.

Guarded as the wind guards the ash, as the wolf guards the flock of sheep. — SELMA LAGERLÖF.

Gun.

A machine gun made a noise like a giant tearing calico. — IAN HAY BEITH.

Gurgling.

Gurgling like the last pint of suds in a sink. — IRVIN S. COBB.

H

Hair.

Gray hairs are like the light of a soft moon, silvering the evening of life. — ANON.

Hair that looked like an exploded can of tomato soup. — IBID.

Her hair is like the sunlight on a field when the grain is ripe. — JENS PETER JACOBSEN.

Her hair clustered round her face like dark leaves round a pale rose. — OSCAR WILDE.

Hand.

Hands like three-times-a-day-in-the-dishpan. — ANON.

His hands like pitchforks. — "ARABIAN NIGHTS" (PAYNE).

Hand — *continued.*

His hands looked like elephant's ears. — ARTHUR BAER.

He ironed him out again with a right meathook that looked like a bale of cotton with knuckles. — IBID.

A hand like twenty cents' worth of bananas. — GELETT BURGESS.

Hand like weather-stained ivory. — ROBERT ROE.

Hang.

Hang on like a summer cold. — ANON.

Happy.

Happy as a boy with a sling shot in a heaven full of greenhouses. — ANON.

Happy as a poker player reaching for chips. — ARTHUR BAER.

Happy as the king who dreams himself twelve hours a chimney sweep. — CALDERON.

Happy as a girl with her dance card full. — RICHARD HARDING DAVIS.

Happy as a brewer with a brand-new baronetcy. — CUTCLIFFE HYNE.

Happy-lookin' as if he'd just heard the foreman say "Not Guilty." — WILLIAM SLAVENS McNUTT.

Happy as a three-year-old kid who has got hold of a bottle of mucilage. — DON MARQUIS.

Happy like a naked star. — GEORGE SANTAYANA.

Happy as any hero in the *Ladies' Home Journal.* — ASHTON STEVENS.

Happy as trees that find a wind to sway them. — SARA TEASDALE.

Happy as a traffic policeman with flat feet. — CHARLES HANSON TOWNE.

Hard.

Hard to procure as a left-handed mustache cup. — WALTER PRITCHARD EATON.

Hard as to read "Science and Health" while down with lumbago. — H. L. MENCKEN.

Hard as to think o' a name when you get caught in a raid. — ABE MARTIN.

Hard as Pharaoh's heart. — CHARLES E. VAN LOAN.

Harmless.

Harmless and without effect, as is the echo of a cannon's crack discharged against the battlements of heaven. — ANON.

Harmless as a steeryopticon letcher. — FINLEY PETER DUNNE.

Harmless, like a rubber rabbit. — NINA WILCOX PUTNAM.

Harsh.

Harsh as iron falling on iron. — ANON.

Hate.

Hates publicity like Polly hates crackers. — ARTHUR BAER.

Head.

A rangy Person with a Head the shape of a Rocky Ford Cantaloupe. — GEORGE ADE.

Head like a peeled onion. — ANON.

A head on him like a lima bean. — IBID.

A Chinaman is a vastly conservative person, and his head is constructed after the manner of certain fish — traps, into which, now and again, something may stray, but out of which nothing that has once entered can ever pass. — SIR HUGH CLIFFORD.

A head shaped like a alligator pear. — FINLEY PETER DUNNE.

A round bald head, like the egg of an ostrich. — WASHINGTON IRVING.

Heart.

The heart of man is like a creeping plant, which withers unless it has something around which it can entwine. — CHARLES JAMES APPERLEY.

The heart of a young woman in love is like a golden sanctuary which often

Heart — *continued.*

enshrines an idol of clay. — PAULIN LIMAYRAC.

The human heart is like a millstone in a mill : when you put wheat under it, it turns and grinds and bruises the wheat to flour ; if you put no wheat, it still grinds on, but then 'tis itself it grinds and wears away. — MARTIN LUTHER.

A man's heart, like an automobile, is always apt to skid and ditch him just at the psychological moment when he thinks he has it under perfect control. — HELEN ROWLAND.

A man's heart is like a sponge, just soaked with emotions and sentiment of which he can squeeze a little bit out for every pretty woman. — IBID.

Heaving.

Heaving like a counterpane upon a restless sleeper. — THOMAS HARDY.

Helpless.

Helpless as a Sultana made ready for the Bosphorus. — MAX BEERBOHM.

Helpless . . . as a hooked fish swinging to land. — THOMAS HARDY.

Helpless as a plant without water. — F. HOPKINSON SMITH.

Helter-Skelter.

Piled helter-skelter like packages from a bundle chute. — DIAL, August, 1920.

Here and there.

Here and there, like teeth in an old man's mouth. — MAXIM GORKY.

Hide.

Hiding like bootleggers in a police raid. — ARTHUR BAER.

Hide it like a disgrace. — GEORGE GISSING.

The bright shining clearness thereof I am forced to hide under this shadow of dissimulation, as the sun doth hir beams under some great cloud, when the wether in sommer time overcasteth. — "THE HYSTORIE OF HAMPLET," 1608.

Hills.

The hills, like elephants, shoulder noiseless through the clouds. — JOSEPHINE PINCKNEY.

Hips.

Hips like hills of sand. — "ARABIAN NIGHTS" (PAYNE).

Holds.

It seems like next t' a bull terrier nothin' holds on like a feller with a damp hand. — ABE MARTIN.

Hollow.

Hollow as the soul of an echo. — J. R. BARTLETT'S "DICTIONARY OF AMERICANISMS," 1877.

Hollow as the ghastly amiabilities of a college reunion. — RAYMOND M. WEAVER.

Hollow as a [Russian] refugee's stomach. — N. Y. WORLD, September 6, 1921.

Homeless.

Homeless as a small-town man in house-cleaning time. — ANON.

Homely.

Homely as Mrs. Devil. — ANON.

Homely as a basket of chips. — MASSACHUSETTS SPY, November 28, 1827.

Honesty.

Honesty is like an icicle — if once it melts that is the end of it. — ANON.

Hope.

Hope is to man as a bladder to a learning swimmer, — it keeps him from sinking in the bosom of the waves, and by that help he may attain the exercise ; but yet it many times makes him

Hope — *continued*.

venture beyond his height, and then, if that breaks, or a storm rises, he drowns without recovery. — OWEN FELTHAM.

Hopeful.

Hopeful as a playwright. — DON MARQUIS.

Hospitable.

Hospitable as a hungry shark to a swimming missionary. — FREDERICK O'BRIEN.

Hot.

Hot as a blister. — SIR FRANCIS C. BURNAND.

Hot as the glass windows of a conservatory. — FLAUBERT.

Hot as Satan's hoof. — HERMAN MELVILLE.

Feet as hot as an iron pump-handle on a July noon. — FREDERICK O'BRIEN.

Hot as a four-alarm fire. — H. C. WITWER.

Humble.

Humble as a street crossing sweeper. — ANON.

Humble as a button. — STEPHEN CRANE.

Humor.

Humor, like history and married women, repeats itself, and like well-bred detectives it assumes many disguises. — STUART W. KNIGHT.

Humorist.

The humorist's like a man firin' at a target — he doesna ken whether he hits or no till them at the target tells 'im. — SIR JAMES M. BARRIE.

Husbands.

Husbands, like governments, must never admit that they are in the wrong. — BALZAC.

The husband, like a loaded ass, must drag on the heavy burthen, till death alone relieves him. — FIELDING.

Husbands are like motor cars : All are good the first year. — CHANNING POLLOCK.

An husband, like unto religion and medicine, must be taken with blind faith. — HELEN ROWLAND.

Hush.

An immense hush, like a dusky silence in a cathedral aisle. — DOROTHY CANFIELD.

Hushed as when the Host is lifted. — EDITH WHARTON.

I

Ideals.

Ideals, like comets, revisit the earth periodically after a long cycle of years — always excepting the enormous ideas that so many sublime donkeys entertain of themselves. — PUNCH, 1859.

Ideals are like stars ; you will not succeed in touching them with your hands, but like the seafaring man on the desert of waters, if you choose them as your guides and follow them you reach your destiny. — CARL SCHURZ.

Ideas.

Ideas of your own are like babies. They are all right if you can keep them quiet. — ANON.

An idea, like a ghost (according to the common notion of ghosts), must be spoken to a little before it will explain itself. — DICKENS.

Old ideas, like old clothes, put carefully away, come out again after a time almost as good as new. — PUNCH, 1856.

Identical.

Identical . . . as two reproductions of the same cinema film. — WILLIAM J. LOCKE.

Idiotic.

Idiotic as a Zulu's notion of therapeutics. — HENRY L. MENCKEN.

Idle.

Idle as a December wind in a dumb-waiter shaft. — DON MARQUIS.

Idleness.

Idleness, like kisses, to be sweet must be stolen. — JEROME K. JEROME.

Idleness is like the nightmare — the moment you begin to stir yourself you shake it off. — PUNCH, 1853.

Ignorant.

Ignorant as a war news editor back home. — STARS AND STRIPES, Paris, 1918.

Immoral.

Immoral as a tomcat. — ANON.

Immutable.

Immutable as the eighteenth amendment. — N. Y. TRIBUNE, July 31, 1921.

Impact.

An impact like an automatic riveter. — ANON.

Impassioned.

Impassioned as a German rendition of the Marseillaise. — GEORGE JEAN NATHAN.

Impassive.

Impassive as an Anglican congregation. — ANON.

Impassive as blanks. — ALDOUS HUXLEY.

Imperceptible.

Imperceptible as a hotel detective's sign to his pal on duty. — F. BERKELEY SMITH.

Impersonal.

Impersonal as a cyclone. — ANON.

Impervious.

Impervious to the projectiles and torpedoes of invective as the sides of a man-of-war are to a pop-gun. — ANON.

Important.

About as important as a game of golf to an astronomer. — ANON.

Important as mathematics to an engineer. — IBID.

About as important as a flea in a Bowery lodging house. — ARTHUR BAER.

Impossible.

Impossible as to make nutmegs out of pine-knots. — ANON.

Impossible as to paddle a coffin across the ocean with a tea-spoon. — IBID.

Impossible as to pull hair from a bald man's head. — IBID.

Impossible as to refute a sneer. — IBID.

Impossible as to rivet a nail in a custard pie. — IBID.

Impossible as to straighten a dog's tail. — IBID.

Impossible as to imagine a man without a head. — FRANCISQUE SARCEY.

Impossible as a secret Fourth of July celebration. — JOHN T. MCCUTCHEON.

Impractical.

Impractical as a market garden on the lava streams of Vesuvius. — ANON.

Inaffective.

Inaffective as a coroner's physician at a Christian Science revival. — HENRY L. MENCKEN.

Incapable.

Incapable of taint as gold of rust. — ÆSCHYLUS.

Inclusive.

Inclusive as a news stand that carries the *Bookman*. — FRANKLIN P. ADAMS.

Incoherent.

Incoherent as a musical show. — ANON.

Incongruous.

Incongruous as a mouse doing a one-step with an elephant. — ANON.

Incongruous as a *faux pas* of the grave and comely damsel called Discretion, who answered the bell at the door of the house Beautiful. — LORD MACAULAY.

Incredible.

Incredible as a mythological deity. — MARCEL PROUST.

Independent.

Independent as a gypsy in his caravan. — ANON.

Independent as a hog on ice. — ANON.

Independent as an electric clock. — ANON.

Independent as an ostrich. — BALZAC.

Indiscreet.

An indiscreet man is like an unsealed letter — everybody can read it. — SEBASTIEN SHAMFORT.

Indiscreet as a valet who betrays the fact that his master wears a wig. — GEORGE MOORE.

Inefficient.

Inefficient as a belled cat. — ANON.

Inevitable.

Inevitable as the income tax. — ANON.

Inexorable.

Inexorable as fat. — ANON.

Inexperienced.

Inexperienced as a young swallow flying south. — CHARLES READE.

Infatuation.

Infatuation, like paralysis, is often all on one side. — HELEN ROWLAND.

Influential.

About as influential as the p in pneumonia. — ANON.

Innocent.

Innocent as bed-time stories for children. — ANON.

Inquisitive

Inquisitive as an X-ray. — ANON.

Insignificant.

As insignificant to ask, whether a man's will be free, as to ask whether his sleep be swift, or his virtue square. — JOHN LOCKE.

Intelligent.

About as intelligent as a bundle of shawls. — HENRY JAMES.

Intimate.

Intimate as two sardines in a can. — ANON.

Intolerant.

Intolerant as a sinner newly turned saint. — ANON.

Intolerant of others as Great Britain is of Tierra del Fuego. — ANON.

Intricate.

Intricate as a raveled skein of silk. — ALEXANDER DUMAS, PÈRE.

Invisible.

About as invisible as red elephants in snow. — ARTHUR BAER.

Invulnerable.

Invulnerable as old-fashioned pincushions. — E. P. ROE.

Inwards.

Leaned inwards like a train going round a curve. — RICHARD JEFFERIES.

Irreconcilable.

Irreconcilable as a jazz band and a symphony orchestra. — PAUL MOURAND.

Irresistible.

Irresistible as a ton of coal going down a chute into a cellar.—KEBLE HOWARD.

Irritable.

An irritable man is like a hedgehog rolled up the wrong way, tormenting himself with his own prickles. — THOMAS HOOD.

Irritating.

Irritating to the nerves like the pitiless clamor of a pneumatic drill. — W. SOMERSET MAUGHAM.

J

Jangling.

Jangling like a belfry bell under a thrust of thunder. — ARCHIBALD MACLEISH.

Jar.

Jar you like an Anarchist banner. — LEONARD MERRICK.

Jealous.

Jealous as newly-married women at a ball. — CHARLES JAMES APPERLEY.

Jingle.

Makes me jingle all over like my tambourine. — HERMAN MELVILLE.

Joke.

A huge joke, like robbing a man of his clothes and compelling him to run about ludicrously. — MARY AUSTIN.

The smutty joke is like the denudation of a person of the opposite sex to whom the joke is directed. — SIGMUND FREUD.

Joy.

Joy is like the ague ; one good day between two bad ones. — GERARD DUDOYER DE GASTELS.

Juggle.

Juggled like a shuttle. — EDWIN MEADE ROBINSON.

Jumps.

He jumped at the chance like a sardine leaps for a can. — ANON.

Jumps like a lioness stung by a wasp. — BALZAC.

K

Kind.

Kind as a kiss. — LAURENCE HOPE.

Kind as love. — RICHARD LALOR SHEIL.

Kiss (Noun).

Kisses are like confidences, one follows the other. — DENIS DIDEROT.

His kiss was like a flash of lightning. — HENRY JAMES.

Kiss (Verb).

Kissing her is like tasting a sherbet. — JOSEPH HERGESHEIMER.

Kittens.

Kittens, like Japanese and Negro babies, may lose some of their charm when they grow older, but as kittens they are paramount. — CARL VAN VECHTEN.

Knocked.

His heart knocked like a Ford car trying to climb the roof of a Methodist church. — GELETT BURGESS.

Know.

He knew about as much about navigation as a fly in a milk pan. — MARTHA BAKER DUNN.

Knowledge.

Many people think of knowledge as of money. They would like knowledge, but cannot face the perseverance and self-denial that go to the acquisition of it. — JOHN VISCOUNT MORLEY.

L

Laborious.

Laborious as idleness. — LOUIS IV.

Lakes.

Lakes in a beautiful country are like silver ornaments on a lovely dress, like liquid gems in a beautiful setting, or bright eyes in a lovely face. — SIR JOHN LUBBECK.

Language.

Their language . . . was like the sweepings of the cow barns. — JOSEPH HERGESHEIMER.

Lashes.

Her lashes lay like fans upon her cheek. — LAURENCE HOPE.

Laugh (Noun).

A little laugh, like the sudden gurgle of water poured from a jug. — ANON.

A laugh like a fog-horn. — E. PHILLIPS OPPENHEIM.

Laugh (Verb).

Laughed like the explosion of a blunderbuss. — JAMES STEPHENS.

Laughter.

His laughter was like the creaking of a rusty barn door. — SHERWOOD ANDERSON.

A roar of laughter, like the bursting of a mortar. — BALZAC.

Laughter, like love, is an expression of man's vehement revolt against reason. — WILLIAM J. LOCKE.

Lazy.

Lazy as the man who smoked a clay pipe, so that when it fell it would break and he wouldn't have to stoop to pick it up. — ANON.

Lazy as a village clock. — MARCEL PROUST.

Lean.

Lean as a vegetarian's cat. — ANON.

Learning.

Learning, like a river, beginneth in a little stream. — ANON.

Legs.

She had legs like an hour-glass. — ANON.

Letter.

An elegant letter is like a meadow enameled with flowers. — IBN AL BAWWAB.

Librarian.

The Librarian may be just compared with him who keeps an Armoury of Weapons ; for as the Keeper doth neither forge the implements of War, nor employ them in the field of Battle, so neither doth the Librarian compose the learn'd Works which are under his charge, nor use their wisdom in his own special interest. But like that Keeper,

Librarian — *continued.*

it is his Duty to see that his Armoury (which is the Library) be well stock'd with the fittest Weapons, and that they be put into the hands of such as can use them at proper time. — EDMUND L. PEARSON'S "THE OLD LIBRARIAN'S ALMANAC," 1774.[1]

Lie (Verb).

Lie like a dentist. — ANON.

Lies like an affidavit. — IBID.

Lies like a gas-meter. — "NOTES AND QUERIES," VIII, XII. 5.

Life.

Life is more like wrestling than dancing ; it must be ready to keep its feet against all onsets, however unexpected. — MARCUS AURELIUS.

Life is like playing a violin solo in public and learning the instrument as one goes on. — SAMUEL BUTLER, 1835–1902.

Life is like an onion — you peel off layer after layer and then you find there is nothing in it. — JAMES G. HUNEKER.

Life often seems like a long shipwreck, of which the débris are friendship, glory, and love ; the shores of existence are strewn with them. — MME. DE STAËL.

Light.

Light as morning cobwebs on the grass. — AUSTIN DOBSON.

Lightly.

Responsibilities rested upon him as lightly as the freckles on his nose. — ALICE CALDWELL HEGAN.

Like.

Much like another as one print of a mimeograph is like its original. — ANON.

My playing is no more like hers than a lamp is like sunshine. — JANE AUSTEN.

So like to one another that we can less discern an egg from an egg or a fig from a fig. — THOMAS BECON.

Like as star to star. — ANTHONY BREWER.

He is like him as if he were spit out of his mouth. — THOMAS DRAXE'S "TREASURIE OF ANCIENT ADAGES," 1633.

About as much like a water-fall as a canvas-covered ham is like a cataract. — MARK TWAIN.

Like as two drops of water. — JAMES MILLER.

Likeness.

The same manifest likeness between Tailings, the father, and Tailings, the son, as there is between Her Most Gracious Majesty's profile on a half-crown, and Her Most Gracious Majesty's profile on a half-penny ; the same square Tailings face, the same Tailings pug nose, the same little ferrety eye, the same sly mouth, above all, the same beautiful bow-legs, so inviting to a headstrong run-a-way pig to pop through. — R. S. SURTEES.

Limber.

Limber as a yard of tripe. — IRVIN S. COBB.

Limp.

Limp as a cold storage chicken. — ALINE KILMER.

Limped.

Limped like a Percheron with a stone in its hoof. — DAMON RUNYON.

Linked.

Linked like Alpine climbers. — STUART P. SHERMAN.

[1] This Almanac was a hoax, published in 1909.

Lips.

Lips like pinks. — T. B. ALDRICH.

Lips like twilight water. — ANON.

Lips like Maraschino cherries. — IBID.

Lips curved like a slice of melon. — IBID.

Lips like a red morocco pocket-book. — THOMAS JOHN DIBDEN.

Her lips curving like scorched paper. — HENRY JAMES.

Lips like cherries crimson — juicy. — SIR C. HANBURY WILLIAMS.

Lithe.

She was as lithe as a skein of spaghetti. — RUPERT HUGHES.

Littered.

Littered with . . . débris as a picnic train. — GERTRUDE ATHERTON.

Lively.

Lively as a galvanized corpse. — SISLEY HUDDLESTON.

Lonely.

Lonely as a bachelor looking at Niagara Falls in June. — ARTHUR BAER.

More lonely than the Eddystone Lighthouse. — HERMAN MELVILLE.

Lonely and ineffectual as two left-hand gloves. — HELEN ROWLAND.

Lonesome.

Lonesome as a bachelor's tooth-brush. — ANON.

Lonesome as a freckle in Pittsburgh. — IBID.

Lonesome as a guardhouse without a rat. — STARS AND STRIPES, Paris, 1918.

Long.

Long as a bootlegger's calling list. — ANON.

Long as a Lenten sermon. — JAMES PETER JACOBSON.

Long (Verb).

I long as Gama [Portuguese navigator, Vasco da Gama, 1469?–1524] longed for land. — HERMAN MELVILLE.

Look.

He looks like the third man in a quartette. — ANON.

She looks like the third page of the Old Testament. — IBID.

Looking like a dirty deuce in a new deck. — BILLY BAXTER.

She looked like a fire in a pawnshop, fair covered with dimons an' goold watches an' chains. — FINLEY PETER DUNNE.

He looks like one of those fellows who would go on the stage if a magician asked him to. — ABE MARTIN.

She looked like a garden after an early frost. — ALICE DUER MILLER.

Loose.

Loose as ashes. — ANON.

Lopsided.

Lopsided as a fighter's nose. — ARTHUR BEAR.

Lost.

Lost as a handful of salt spilt in the sea. — EDGAR SALTUS.

Lost as a sob in the midst of cheering. — SARA TEASDALE.

Love.

Love is like a cold. Easy to catch but hard to cure. — ANON.

Love is like soup — it cools when the fire dies out. — IBID.

Love is like the devil ; he whom it has in its clutches it surrounds with flames. — BALZAC.

In love, regardless of the soul, a woman is like a lyre that only yields its secrets to him who is a skillful player. — IBID.

Love — *continued.*

Falling in love is like being thrown from a horse ; if you let yourself go it doesn't hurt as badly as if you try to save yourself. — EDWIN L. BLANCHARD.

Love is like a lounge cushion — it has to be stuffed with illusions and patched with laughter before one can rest on it. — BENJAMIN DE CASSERES.

His love is like unto a tapster's glasse that is broken with every touch. — ROBERT GREENE.

Love is like the measles ; we all have to go through it. — J. K. JEROME.

Love is like a cigar — the longer it burns the less it becomes. — PUNCH, 1855.

Love, like a chicken salad or restaurant hash, must be taken with blind faith or it loses all its flavor. — HELEN ROWLAND.

Going through life without love is like going through a good dinner without an appetite — everything seems flat and tasteless. — IBID.

Love is like a painter, who in drawing the picture of a friend having a blemish in one eye, would picture only the other side of the face. — ROBERT SOUTH.

Love is exactly like war in this — that a soldier, though he has escaped three weeks complete on Saturday night, may nevertheless be shot through his heart on Sunday morning. — LAURENCE STERNE.

Love is like what is called the Milky Way in Heaven, a brilliant mass formed by thousands of little stars, of which each perhaps is nebulous. — STENDHAL.

Love hit Elmer like a hod of bricks dropped on a plug hat from the top of the Woolworth Building. — HUGH WILEY.

Lovely.

Lovely as a dream in marble. — BAUDELAIRE.

Lovely as a violin. — JOSEPHINE PRESTON PEABODY.

Lover.

An old lover is as winter without flowers. — THOMAS DRAXE'S "TREASURIE OF ANCIENT ADAGES," 1633.

Luminous.

Golden fire in a porcelain vase would not be more luminous than the soul of that actress [Adelaide Neilson] as it shone through her ideal of Juliet. — WILLIAM WINTER.

M

Man.

Some men are like the Einstein Theory ; nobody at home understands them. — ANON.

Some men, like modern shops, hang everything in their show windows ; when one goes inside, nothing is to be found. — BERTHOLD AUERBACH.

Man is like a napkin, the more neatly the housewife doubles him, the more carefully she lays him on the shelf. Neither can a man once doubled know how often he may be doubled. Not only his wife folds him in two, but every child quarters him into a new double, till what was a wife and handsome substance, large enough for anything in reason, dwindles into a pitiful square that will not cover one platter — all puckers and creases — smaller and smaller with every double — with every double a new crease. — BULWER-LYTTON.

Most men are like eggs, too full of themselves to hold anything else. — JOSH BILLINGS.

Man — *continued.*

Great men are like mountains ; we do not appreciate their magnitude while we are still close to them. — JOSEPH CHAMBERLAIN.

Man is like a bit of Labrador spar, which has no lustre as you turn it in your hand, until you come to a particular angle, then it shows deep and beautiful colors. — RALPH WALDO EMERSON.

Men are like strange dogs . . . Walk right up to them, bold as life, and they're as gentle as ducks. — OWEN JOHNSON.

Men, like pictures, must be viewed on a favorable day. — NAPOLEON I.

Men, like jewels, require a setting. A clerk on a high stool, poring over a ledger, is not unimpressive, or a cook over her stove. But place the cook on the stool, poring over the ledger! — MARY ROBERTS RINEHART.

A man is like a cat ; chase him and he'll run ; sit still and ignore him and he'll come purring at your feet. — HELEN ROWLAND.

A man is like a pigeon. Give him plenty to eat, a comfortable house and the freedom of the whole wide world to fly about in and he will never desert you — for long. — IBID.

Men are like the earth and we are the moon ; we turn always one side to them, and they think there is no other, because they don't see it — but there is. — OLIVE SCHREINER.

Some men are like rifles with plenty of powder but no bullet ; they have a great flow of language but no thought. — SYLVANIUS STALL.

It is with men as with horses : those who do the most prancing make the least progress. — BARON DE STASSART.

Man in this life is like one who stands with one foot on a board and with the other on the ground. As soon as reason awakens in him, he sees that the board on which he all but stepped hangs over a precipice, and is not only bending and cracking, but is already falling down ; he then shifts his weight to the other leg, which is on the ground. How then can one help being afraid, if one is standing on that which is bending, cracking and falling down, and what can one fear if one stands on that onto which everything falls and below which one cannot fall? — LEO TOLSTOY.

Men are like bricks, alike, but placed high or low by chance. — JOHN WEBSTER.

Manners.

The kind, generous souls, who are rough and almost insulting in their manners, are like the rich man, who, when solicited to relieve his poor relations, used to fling his old clothes at them, taking good care to secrete money in the pockets. — PUNCH, 1856.

Many.

Although there may be as many divils in Worms as there are tiles on the housetops, I will go. — MARTIN LUTHER.

As many lies as will lie in thy sheet of paper, although this sheet were big enough for the bed of Ware in England. — SHAKESPEARE.

Marriage.

Marriage is like a besieged fortress ; those without want to get in and those within want to get out. — ANON.

Marriage is like a department store. It is all over when you buy. — IBID.

Marriage is like a Paris gown. The more you pay for it the less there's to it. — IBID.

Marriage is like a river. It is easier to fall in than out. — IBID.

A bad marriage is like consumption. It is better to prevent it because later you can't cure it. — IBID.

Marriage — *continued.*

Marriage is like twirling a baton, turning handsprings or eating with chopsticks ; it looks so easy till you try it. — Helen Rowland.

Marriage resembles a pair of shears, so joined that they cannot be separated ; often moving in opposite directions, yet always punishing any one who comes between them. — Sydney Smith.

Marry.

For an old man to marry a young girl is like buying a new book for somebody else to read. — Anon.

Marrying.

Marrying a woman for her munny is vera mutch like setting a rat-trap, and baiting it with yure own finger. — Josh Billings.

To marry a woman merely for her person is buying an empty vessel : and a woman is a vessel which a man will grow cursed weary of in a long voyage. — Henry Fielding.

Massive.

The building looked as massive as a large woman in a one-piece bathing suit. — Anon.

Matrimony.

Matrimony, like a dip in the sea, first stimulates, then chills. But once out of the water the call of the ocean lures the bather to another plunge. — Anon.

Matrimony is like motoring, because it's really travelling by means of a series of explosions. — Arthur Stringer.

Mean.

So mean he'd make dice out of the knuckle-bones of his aunt. — Anon.

So mean that he would rob a cuspidor. — Ibid.

So mean he would steal a dead fly from a blind spider. — Ibid.

Mean as the man who skimmed his milk on the top, and, turning it over, skimmed it on the bottom. — Ibid.

Mean as the man who told his children that Santa Claus is dead. — Ibid.

Mean as the man who insisted on getting sleeves with his vests. — Arthur Baer.

Mean enough to steal acorns from a blind hog. — J. R. Bartlett's "Dictionary of Americanisms," 1877.

Mechanical.

Mechanical as a levee at St. James's Palace. — Henry Adams.

Meek.

Meek as a Quaker. — Punch, 1863.

Melancholy.

Melancholy as a bass viol in a concert. — Robert Green.

Melancholy as a fiddle with one string. — Thomas Holcroft.

Melancholy as a hairpin on a tombstone. — James G. Huneker.

Melancholy as a sick monkey. — John Leanerd.

Melancholy as a discarded statesman. — William Mountford.

Memory.

Memory is a delicate instrument. Like an old musical box it will lie silent for long years ; then a mere nothing, a jerk, a tremor, will start the spring, and from beneath its decent covering of dust it will talk to us of forgotten passion and desire. — Thomas Burke.

Memory is like the Moon ; it hath its new, its full, and its wane. — Duchess of Newcastle.

Menacing.

Menacing as metal. — Vance Thompson.

Mendacious.

Mendacious as a real estate agent. — DON MARQUIS.

Merry.

Merry as bees in clover. — ANON.

Merry as a Christmas tree. — JOSEPH C. LINCOLN.

Methodical.

Methodical as a policeman on his beat. — ANON.

Methodical as a tailor. — EDWARD HOWARD.

Mexican.

A Mexican must look like a toadstool t' a aviator. — ABE MARTIN.

Mild.

Mild as Mercy looking on Repentance's tear. — ROBERT POLLOK.

Mild as the star-beam on the silent wave. — ANNA A. SEWARD.

Mild as the angelic guardian of the blest. — JANE WEST.

Milk.

Modern milk is like a bank-note, — not current without a water mark. — SKETCH (London), January 11, 1922.

Milky Way.

The Milky Way — which I think looks exactly like a torn wreath of tulle with diamonds. — SIR HARRY JOHNSTON.

Mind.

He had a mind like the face of a great Cathedral clock, — but with a Waterbury movement. — ANON.

Your mind is like a sun-dial. It records only pleasantness. — IBID.

The mind is like a merchant's ledger; it requires to be continually posted up to the latest date. — PHILIP GILBERT HAMERTON.

My mind is like a flogged horse — it won't give another kick. — HENRY JAMES.

Some minds are like trunks — packed tight with knowledge, no air and plenty of moths. — LIFE, January 31, 1918.

The human mind, both in persons and societies, is like a pendulum, which, the moment it has reached the limit of its swing in one direction, goes inevitably back as far as the other side and so on forever. — J. R. LOWELL.

My mind is like the Panama Canal.
Great ocean-going ideas
Lie moored in the locks
Until my thoughts rise to the level
Where they can proceed.
Every now and then
There is a brainslide
In the Culebra cut.
And all the traffic is haulted.
— CHRISTOPHER MORLEY.

The human mind should be like a good hotel — open the year round. — WILLIAM LYON PHELPS.

Many minds are like low-grade ores — there is gold in them, but it takes a vast deal of labor to get it out. — JOHN ALFRED SPENDER.

The mind is like a slate, — one thing gets rubbed out for another. — SAM SLICK.

Mirth.

Mirth, and even cheerfulness, when employed as remedies in low spirits, are like hot water to a frozen limb. — DR. BENJAMIN RUSH.

Miserable.

Miserable as a wet dog shivering dejectedly in a rain-swept alley. — E. D. PRICE.

Missed.

Missed more chances than a farmer at a circus raffle. — ARTHUR BAER.

Mistake.

A mistake is like a mule, not always distinguishable from a horse in front, but known beyond doubt by acquaintance with its kicking qualities. — New York Sun, 1918.

Modesty.

Modesty, in a woman, is like the angel's flaming sword, to keep vile men out of the paradise of their chastity. — Owen Feltham.

Modesty is like virtue ; suspected only when it is advertised. — Douglas Malloch.

Money.

Money is in some respects like fire ; it is a very excellent servant, but a terrible master. — P. T. Barnum.

Money is shaped like a wheel ; it rolls to some, from others ; but seldom is at rest. — Edward Parsons Day.

Money, like a boot, when it's tight, is extremely trying. — Punch, 1864.

Monotonous.

Monotonous as an animated electric sign. — Anon.

Monotonous as a London suburb. — Ibid.

Monotonous as a metronome. — George Jean Nathan.

Monotonous as a million one-dollar bills. — Robert Roe.

Moon.

The moon drowsed between the trees like a great yellow moth. — Anon.

The moon, like a gardenia in the night's buttonhole. — Max Beerbohm.

The moon like a big goldfish bowl. — Grace Hazard Conklin.

This resplendent luminary, like a youth on the Fourth of July, has its first quarter ; like a ruined spendthrift, its last quarter ; and, like an omnibus, is occasionally full and new. The evenings on which it appears between these last stages are beautifully illumined by its clear, mellow light. — John Phoenix.

O yellow moon,
Drifting across the night,
As a rakish pirate brig
Tattered of rig
And ghostly white
Goes floating down the black lagoon
Of a dead sea.

— Lew Sarett.

Mothers-in-law.

Mothers-in-law, like cats, show a great attachment to the houses they inhabit, without caring much for the persons who inhabit them. — Punch, 1859.

Motives.

Motives are like harlequins ; there is always a second dress beneath the first. — Jacob Jan Artevold.

More.

More money than the telephone company's got wrong numbers. — Sam Hellman.

Motionless.

Motionless as a stone above a grave. — William Wetmore Storey.

Mountains.

Mountains like frozen wrinkles on a sea. — Anon.

The mountains are like crouching camels. — Milton Raison.

Mouth.

He has a mouth like a slit in the sidewalk. — Anon.

Her mouth opened like a folding bed. — Ibid.

His mouth, thin and straight, like a cut in his face. — Balzac.

What a hideous, odd-looking man Sydney Smith is! With a mouth like

Mouth — *continued.*

an oyster, and three double chins. — Mrs. W. H. Brookfield.

A mouth like a vent in an oysterman's cantern. — "Cruikshank at Home," 1845.

A mouth like a crack in the pavement. — Sewell Ford.

A mouth cut like a scallop in a pie. — Edgar Lee Masters.

Mouth like a rent in an old, battered purse. — Frederick O'Brien.

The curve of her mouth was like blood upon snow. — Arthur Train.

A mouth as open as the North Atlantic. — H. C. Witwer.

Music.

Music is like soft hands stealing into ours in the dark, and holding us fast without a spoken word. — Anon.

Musik, after all, is sumthing like vittels, the more cooking and seasoning we use, the more we have to hav, till after a while we kant enjoy annything ov the vittels but the pepper. — Opera don't have enny more loosening effeck on me, than caster ile wud on a graven image. — Josh Billings.

It is like eating vanilla cream in Paradise, listening to beautiful music. — Camille Lemonnier.

Musical.

Musical as a pumpkin rolling down a barn floor. — Anon.

Musical as the air whistling through a maiden's teeth at the end of a long adhesive kiss. — Henry L. Mencken.

Mustache.

A mustache like a walrus. — Abe Martin.

A mustache like a pump with two handles. — Ibid.

A little black mustache like an eyebrow. — George du Maurier.

A white mustache, cut short like a worn-out brush. — Henry James.

N

Naked.

Naked as an egg. — Anon.

Naked as Eve ere she the apple ate. — Alfred de Musset.

Naked as a soul for judgment. — Sir Aubrey de Vere.

Naked as a cornet solo. — James G. Huneker.

Naked as a poulterer's capon. — Punch, 1842.

Naked as the moon. — George Sterling.

Naked as the sun at noon. — James Thomson.

Naked as Adam. — Thomas Ward.

Naked as a fish. — Hugh Wiley.

Names.

Some people have names like pitchforks, some people have names like cakes,
Names full of sizzling esses like a family quarrel of snakes,
Names black as a cat, vermilion as the cockscomb of a fool,
But your name is a green small garden, a rush asleep in a pool.

— Stephen Vincent Benét.

A German with a name like a lady's sneeze. — William McFee.

Natural.

It's just as natural for lawyers tu lie, as it is for a white-hared young one's nose tu run. — Josh Billings.

Natural — *continued.*

Natural . . . as the passion for air, or food, or drink. — STEPHEN MCKENNA.

Near.

Near as twilight is to darkness. — THOMAS PAINE.

Near now as June is to May. — SWINBURNE.

Near as death to life. — SIR AUBREY DE VERE.

Neat.

Neat as a bandbox. — ANON.

Neat as a coffin. — IBID.

About as neat as a coal-heaver's nails. — PHILADELPHIA LEDGER, October 9, 1922.

Neatly.

Picked up as neatly as if he had been prodded by a fork, swallowed down straight, and ground into small pieces. — HENRY JAMES.

Necessary.

Necessary as a handsaw to a carpenter. — ANON.

Necessary for man's life as water, air and fire. — RICHARD R. EDWARDS.

Necessary to me as honey to the bee or hell to the Christians. — HENRY L. MENCKEN.

Necessity.

As much a necessity as poverty is to incompetents. — BEN HECHT.

Need.

Doesn't need it any more than a dog needs a pocket handkerchief. — ANON.

Nervous.

Nervous as a high-school valedictorian. — ARTHUR BAER.

Nervous as a commuter in the third act of Parsifal. — ORSON LOWELL.

New.

New as dollar bills. — PADRAIC COLUM.

New as a morning. — D. H. LAWRENCE.

Newspaper.

An off-colored newspaper is like that kind of a woman. A man might not care to be seen in a café with it, but taking it home is something else again. — ANON.

Nimbly.

Nimbly as a woman to a dance. — E. BARRINGTON.

Noiseless.

Noiseless as the fall of snow. — ANON.

Noiseless as the tread of a kitten in a molasses factory. — BENJAMIN DE CASSERES.

Noisy.

Noisy as a trunkmaker. — ANON.

Noisy as iron waves splashing and dashing on an iron ocean. — IBID.

Noisy as the prompter at the opera. — IBID.

Noisy as the testing room of a base-drum factory. — IBID.

Noisy as two skeletons having a wrestling match on a tin roof. — IBID.

Noisy as the Stock Exchange. — AUGUSTINE BIRELL.

Noisy as a barracks on pay-day night. — STARS AND STRIPES, Paris, 1918.

Nose.

A nose like a sponge. — MAXIM GORKY.

Blows his nose with a noise like the falling of a tree. — DAVID GRAYSON.

A large nose like a trumpet. — EDWARD LEAR.

His nose stuck out like the first joint of a thumb. — FREDERICK O'BRIEN.

Nose — *continued.*

A nose like a Bartlett pear. — JAMES WHITCOMB RILEY.

His nose sprang out of the big face like an ejaculation. — H. M. TOMLINSON.

Novel.

The charm of a novel is like the charm of a woman reserved for special sympathies and beings. — JOSEPH HERGESHEIMER.

A novel is like a bow — the violin which gives out the sound is the soul of the reader. — STENDHAL.

Nude.

Nude as a star. — FRANCES S. SALTUS.

Numerous.

Numerous as a bank or trust company's vice-presidents. — NEW YORK TRIBUNE, January 6, 1921.

O

Obstinacy.

Obstinacy is like red hair : there is no cure for it but to die. — JOSH BILLINGS.

Obvious.

Obvious as gestures. — STEPHEN CRANE.

Odorless.

Odorless as a Congressional investigation. — GEORGE ADE.

One-sided.

One-sided as a tramp's heels. — ARTHUR BAER.

Open.

Open as the brain of a maiden the day after her marriage. — BALZAC.

Open to observation as the coops at a dog show. — SINCLAIR LEWIS.

Firpo was as open as an umbrella. — NEAL O'HARA.

Opposite.

Opposite as yea and nay. — FRANCIS QUARLES.

Opposition.

A fierce, turbulent opposition, like the north wind, only serves to make a man wrap his notions about him. — SAMUEL CROXALL.

Tremendous opposition . . . taking a paving stone to crush a fly ; or raising a whirlwind to blow out a farthing candle. — PUNCH, 1849.

Out of Place.

Felt as out of place as an Elk at Oxford. — PERCY HAMMOND.

Overdone.

Everything was as overdone as a soubrette taking supper at Rector's. — GEORGE HORACE LORIMER.

Overloaded.

Overloaded as a Ford on Sunday. — ANON.

P

Padded.

The catcher is padded like an arm chair. — LONDON TIMES, 1918.

Painful.

Painful as kicking a burglar with your bare foot. — ABE MARTIN.

Pale.

Pale like white wine. — SIR KENELM DIGBY.

Pale as Christmas roses. — NORA HOPPFR.

She turned as pale as if she had heard of the landing, there on her coast, of a foreign army. — HENRY JAMES.

Passed.

Passed like a flivver in a Vanderbilt Cup race. — ARTHUR BAER.

Passionate.

About as passionate as shredded wheat. — LAWRENCE GILMAN.

Passionless.

Passionless as a clam. — GERTRUDE ATHERTON.

Passionless as algebra. — EDGAR SALTUS.

Passions.

Passions are like the trout in my pond : one devours another until only one fat old trout is left. — PRINCE HERBERT BISMARCK.

Our wild passions are like so many lawyers wrangling and bawling at a bar ; discretion is the lord-keeper of man that sits as judge, and moderates their contestations. — OWEN FELTHAM.

The passions, like the managers of a playhouse, often force men upon parts without consulting their judgment, and sometimes without any regard to their talents. — FIELDING.

Passive.

Passive as a bronze Buddha! — ANON.

Pathetic.

Pathetic as an octogenarian messenger boy. — CHARLOTTE LEBEAU.

Patient.

Patient as hat-racks. — ANON.

Patient as a prostitute. — JAMES G. HUNEKER.

Peaceful.

Peaceful as Socrates. — ANON.

Peaceful as a London suburb on bank holiday. — LONDON CHRONICLE, 1917.

Peacefully.

Rested as peacefully as a night nurse on duty. — ANON.

Pedants.

Pedants who prescribe pleasantry are like cripples who decry dancing. — PUNCH, 1856.

Penmanship.

His penmanship looks like the autograph of a dying spider which has paid a surreptitious visit to the ink bottle. — ANON.

His penmanship looks like the lid of a Chinese tea chest. — IBID.

His penmanship looks like the marks that might be made by a kangaroo jumping out of a mud puddle and splashing a pillow sham with its tail. — IBID.

Pep.

Full of pep as an electric fan. — ANON.

Perfect.

Perfect as a sonnet. — JAMES G. HUNEKER.

Perfunctory.

Perfunctory as an officer's return salute to a Y. M. man. — STARS AND STRIPES, Paris, 1918.

Perilous.

Perilous as T N T. — ANON.

Personal.

About as personal as an amputated limb. — GERTRUDE ATHERTON.

Personality.

He had no more physical personality than a consulted thermometer. — HENRY JAMES.

Persons.

Some persons, like certain paintings, appear to advantage at a distance. — MARY G. HORSFORD.

Persons extremely difficult are like old enameled watches, which had painted covers that hindered your seeing what o'clock it was. — HORACE WALPOLE.

Phantasmagoric.

Phantasmagoric, like a prismatic reflection or a serial novel. — HENRY JAMES.

Pieces.

He went to pieces like a fifty-cent umbrella in a gale. — ANON.

Pinch.

Pinch like a new shoe. — ANON.

Pinch like a painless dentist. — IBID.

Pit-a-pat.

His heart going pit-a-pat, like a duck's foot in mud. — GEORGE MOORE.

Place.

Out of place as gasoline in a fire extinguisher. — H. C. WITWER.

Plain.

Plain as a famous beauty before breakfast. — ANON.

Plain as the chalk marks on the schoolhouse fence. — DON MARQUIS.

Plain as a sheep's nose. — F. BERKELEY SMITH.

Plainly.

Plainly as the man of science finds evolution in the physical universe. — "A GENTLEMAN WITH A DUSTER."

Plays.

Plays are like trees, which will not grow without nourishment; but like mushrooms, they shoot up spontaneously, as it were, in a rich soil. — FIELDING.

Plays, like motor-engines, must be running when one locates trouble. — CHANNING POLLOCK.

Pleasant.

About as pleasant as to have an umbrella jammed down your throat — and opened there — and pulled out open, so that the broken ribs lacerate your lungs, and beaten over the head with the handle. — DON MARQUIS.

Pleasures.

Pleasures are much like mushrooms. The right kind are fine, but you have to be on the lookout for toadstools. — BOSTON TRANSCRIPT, May 21, 1921.

Plenty.

Plenty as frogs in a Dutch inundation. — THOMAS MOORE.

Pliable.

Pliable as cloth. — EUGENE SUE.

Plunge.

Plunges like a hangman's trap. — ANON.

Poets.

Poets are like birds; they sing best when they are half starved. — HORACE WALPOLE.

Poignant.

Poignant as a bell for fire. — WITTER BYNNER.

Poor.

Poor as the family that could wash its dishes with a tear. — ANON.

Popular.

About as popular as a mouse at a suffragette meeting. — ANON.

Popular as a safety razor at a darkey picnic. — ROBERT H. DAVIS.

Popular as a munition stock before peace talk. — LAWRENCE GILMAN.

Popular, like reform. — ARTHUR B. REEVES.

Possible.

No more possible than the development of an orchid in the middle of a crowded street. — W. H. MALLOCK.

Practical.

Practical as a razor. — COSMO HAMILTON.

Praising.

The practice of praising children is like opium . . . because it's laudanum. — PUNCH, 1853.

Preacher.

A preacher that will speak everything that comes into his mind is like a maid that goes to market, and, meeting another maid, makes a stand, and they hold together a goose-market. — MARTIN LUTHER.

Precious.

Precious as a bundle of love letters in a breach of promise case. — ARTHUR BAER.

Precise.

Precise, like rooms which we enter and leave, not those in which we settle and dwell. — BULWER-LYTTON.

Presbyterianism.

Presbyterianism without infant damnation would be like the dog on the train that couldn't be identified because it has lost its tag. — MARK TWAIN.

Pride.

Pride, like all ringmasters in all circuses, is always in evening dress and wears a high hat, even in the morning. — BENJAMIN DE CASSERES.

Prim.

Prim as a peeled pine pole. — ANON.

Principles.

Principles are like mountains ; they rise very near heaven, but when they stand in our way, we drive a tunnel through them. — CARDINAL RAMPOLLA.

Privacy.

About as much privacy as a statue in a park. — ANON.

No more privacy than a traffic cop. — IBID.

Probable.

About as probable as that Napoleon the Third should have forbidden the polka. — HILAIRE BELLOC.

Profound.

Profound and illuminating as the discovery that children are born, not hatched. — LITTLE REVIEW, December, 1919.

Profusion.

Comets are scattered through the heavens with as much profusion as fishes in the ocean. — JOHANN KEPLER.

Prologue.

Prologues precede the piece in mournful verse,
As undertakers walk before the hearse.
— DAVID GARRICK.

Prominent.

Prominent, like a fried egg stain on a full dress vest. — ARTHUR BAER.

Promotes.

It promotes conviviality, just as a pack of foxhounds promotes sport. — R. S. SURTEES.

Prose.

Prose is like music, — every word, every letter must be placed for sound, color, nuance. — JAMES G. HUNEKER.

Prosperity.

Prosperity is like perfume, it often makes the head ache. — DUCHESS OF NEWCASTLE.

Prosperitie and abundance are like long garments to a man that walkes; they will trip up his heales if he take not heed. — THOMAS SHELTON'S "A CENTURIE OF SIMILES," 1640.

Proud.

Proud as a hen that got a duck for a chicken. — DION BOUCICAULT.

Jerry in his new clothes is as proud as a whitewashed pig. — P. W. JOYCE.

Prudent.

A prudent man is like a pin, — his head prevents him from going too far. — ANON.

Publishing.

Publishing a book of verse is like dropping a rose leaf down the Grand Cañon of the Colorado and waiting to hear the echo. — DON MARQUIS.

Puffed.

His lordship [Lord Norbury, 1745–1831] it should be noted, always puffed like an asthmatic locomotive, before uttering a joke. — R. SHELTON MACKENZIE.

Punctually.

Punctually, as the Tax gatherer. — PUNCH, 1862.

Punctually as a cuckoo in a Swiss clock. — EDITH WHARTON.

Pure.

Pure as a bishop's bathroom. — ANON.

Pure as a naked flame. — SARA TEASDALE.

Puzzled.

Puzzled like a roach trying to crawl downstairs on an escalator. — ARTHUR BAER.

Q

Quake.

Quake like mice when the cat is mentioned. — BALZAC.

Quickly.

Quickly as the effervescence on a bottle of ginger beer. — HENRY VAN DYKE.

Quiet.

Quiet as an eel swimming in oil. — ARTHUR BAER.

Quiet as far-away waters. — SAMUEL HOFFENSTEIN.

Quiet as a street of tombs in a buried city. — JOHN RUSKIN.

Quiet as a Sunday morning in an Ohio village. — BRAND WHITLOCK.

Quietly.

Quietly as a stout lady accumulates her fat — by the daily satisfaction of her appetite. — GILBERT HAMERTON.

Quiver.

Quivered like a sob. — CONRAD AIKEN.

Quivering like a taxicab. — ANON.

Quivered like a dish of marmalade in an earthquake. — ARTHUR BAER.

Quiver like a naked Russian in the snow. — SIR WILLIAM DAVENANT.

R

Racked.

Racked his ears like an explosion of steam-whistles. — ANON.

Radiant.

Radiant as a tiara of celestial diamonds. — VICTOR HUGO.

Radiant as ice. — EVELYN SCOTT.

Ragged.

Ragged as a scarecrow. — THOMAS HEYWOOD.

Ran.

He ran the bases as if he were hauling William H. Taft in a rickshaw. — HEYWOOD BROUN.

Rang.

Rang like a golden jewel down a golden stair. — SYDNEY DOBELL.

Rapid.

Rapid as the fragmentary images of the cinema. — RÉMY DE GOURMONT.

Rapid as the wing of time. — JOHN HAMILTON.

Rare.

Rare as holy water in an Orange lodge. — ANON.

Rare as snowflakes in a well-regulated August. — IBID.

Rare as the rose in December, a bird in an arctic clime. — IBID.

Rare, as a mind that's chaste. — FITZ-GREENE HALLECK.

Rare in life as black lightning on a blue sky. — JAMES G. HUNEKER.

Rare as a fat man in a clothing advertisement. — GEORGE S. KAUFMAN.

Rare as humility in a grizzly bear. — JULIAN RALPH.

Rattle.

Rattle like a taxicab. — ANON.

Rattling like a crockery shop in a earthquake. — ARTHUR BAER.

Rattled like dried scales. — GEORGE CRUIKSHANK'S "TABLE-BOOK," 1845.

Raved.

Raved like a ravished virgin. — BAUDELAIRE.

Ravishing.

Ravishing as the returning sun to Greenland. — FIELDING.

Ravishing like the music of the spheres. — LODOWICK CARLELL.

Read.

A person who cannot read is something like a blind man walking through a pleasant meadow, where there are flowers and fruit trees ; there are many pleasant things and many wise and good things printed in books, but we cannot get them unless we read. — TIMOTHY DWIGHT.

Readers.

The first class of readers may be compared to an hourglass, their reading being as the sand ; it runs in and runs out, and leaves not a vestige behind. A second class resembles a sponge, which imbibes everything, and returns it in nearly the same state, only a little dirtier. A third class is like a jelly-bag, which allows all that is pure to pass away, and retains only the refuse and dregs. The fourth class may be compared to the slave of Golconda, who, casting aside all that is worthless, preserves only the pure gems. — S. T. COLERIDGE.

Reading.

Reading is to the mind what exercise is to the body. As by the one, health is preserved, strengthened and invigorated ; by the other, virtue, which is the health of the mind, is kept alive,

Reading — *continued.*

cherished and confirmed. But as exercise becomes tedious and painful, when we make use of it only as a means of health, so reading is apt to grow uneasy and burdensome, when we apply ourselves to it only for our improvement in virtue. For this reason, the virtue which we gather from a fable, or an allegory, is like the health we get from hunting ; as we are engaged in an agreeable pursuit that draws us on with pleasure, and makes us insensible of the fatigues that accompany it. — SIR RICHARD STEELE.

Reading Milton is like dining off gold plate in a company of kings ; very splendid, very ceremonious, and not a little appalling. — ALEXANDER SMITH.

Real.

Real as hunger. — ANON.

Real as George Washington and Valley Forge. — ALICE BROWN.

Realistic.

Realistic as a kinematogram. — WILLIAM ARCHER.

Red.

Red as a radish. — ANON.

Red as Robin's breast. — IBID.

Red as Rob Roy's beard. — DR. JOHN BROWN.

Red as Charlemagne's knightly blood. — E. B. BROWNING.

It is red as the flame where it springs from the molten metal, as red as the beating heart of a Red Indian, as the famous sport coat of little Miss R. Riding Hood, as a red herring's tongue, as a clown's nose, as Mme. Bernhardt's painted finger nails. — HOWARD BRADY MULLIN.

Red as the face of shame. — JOHN O'KEEFFE.

Red as an auction flag. — BERT LESTON TAYLOR.

Refused.

Being refused by a woman is like being turned down in an election ; the unlucky candidate's first sensation is soreness, but after that he spends years of amiable amusement in watching the struggles of the successful party. — MARGUERITE MOOERS MARSHALL.

Regular.

Regular as the moon makes the tides. — HENRY JAMES.

Regularly.

Regularly as the clock strikes nine in the morning. — MARK TWAIN.

Relatives.

Poor relatives, that have been flung aside, often turn up and prove of value when least expected — like banknotes that have been found, before now, in a waste-paper basket. — PUNCH, 1866.

Reliable.

Reliable as a plain wife's smile. — ANON.

Reliable as a salary. — FRANK R. STOCKTON.

Religion.

Religion is like love ; it plays the devil with clear thinking. — ROSE MACAULAY.

Some people are afraid of anything like joy in religion . . . Their religion is something like the stars, very high, and very clear, but very cold. — ROBERT MURRAY McCHEYNE.

Alteration of religion is dangerous. because we know not where it will stay. 'Tis like a millstone that lies upon the top of a pair of stairs : 'tis hard to remove it, but if once it be thrust off the first stair, it never stays till it comes to the bottom. — JOHN SELDEN.

Religion is like the breath of heaven ; if it goes abroad into the open air, it scatters and dissolves. — JEREMY TAYLOR.

Remorseless.

Remorseless as a mad Pasha. — ANON.

Remorseless as an alarm-clock. — ANON.

Remote.

Remote as a nightmare. — WALTER DE LA MARE.

Rend.

Rend and tear like an arrant Turk. — "STRANGE METAMORPHOSES OF MAN," 1634.

Renews.

Renews itself like a classic. — PERCY HAMMOND.

Repentance.

Repentance without amendment is like continually pumping without mending the leak. — ANON.

Repentant.

Repentant as Magdalen. — FRANCIS MERES.

Reproachful.

Reproachful as a curate's eye. — OSBERT SITWELL.

Reputation.

The reputation of a woman is like that chaste flower amaranthus, which is no sooner touched but withers. — CHRISTOPHER BULLOCK.

A good reputation is like the cypress ; once cut, it never puts forth leaf again. — FRANCESCO GUICCIARDINI.

Resembled.

Resembled each other like two drops of water. — DUKE OF SAINT SIMON.

Fedor resembled his father as a fawn resembles a boa-constrictor. — EDGAR SALTUS.

Resembles.

Clara Morris resembles Joe Jefferson to the same extent that an April thunder storm resembles a pastoral symphony. — NYM CRINKLE.

Reserved.

Reserved ladies are like ice, Egad no sooner begin to soften when they melt. — HANNAH COWLEY.

Resolutions.

Sudden resolutions, like the sudden rise of the mercury in the barometer, indicate little else than the changeableness of the weather. — JULIUS CHARLES HARE.

Resonant.

Resonant as a bugle-note. — DOROTHY CANFIELD.

Respect.

About as much respect for women as a tomcat has for a marriage license. — ANON.

Respond.

Could Respond to a Dinner Invitation like a Fireman going to a Fire. — GEORGE ADE.

Restful.

Restful as the Firing Line. — GEORGE ADE.

Restful as a bowling alley. — ANON.

Restful as a Rembrandt background. — IBID.

Restless.

Restless as a bluebottle fly on a warm summer's day. — ANON.

Restless as a man with the itch. — IBID.

Restless as sharp desire. — ARTHUR C. BENSON.

He [E. A. Sothern] is wiry ; elastic, as restless as a bundle of nerves under galvanic influence. — T. EDGAR PEMBERTON.

Restrain.

Restrain as in a corset. — Edmond Rostand.

Retreat.

This force retreated through Germany, as a man might retreat who had ventured into a cageful of drugged lions and found that the effects of the drug were evaporating. — H. G. Wells.

Rhythmical.

Rhythmical as a pianola. — Percy Hammond.

Rich.

Rich as a munition maker. — Anon.

Ridiculous.

Ridiculous as any theatrical wigs in the world. — Dickens.

It would be as ridiculous as the owl pairing with the sprightly lark. — William Heard.

Ridiculous as the British public in one of its periodical fits of morality. — T. B. Macaulay.

Right.

The right of every man to judge on every question for himself is like the right of every man who possesses a balance at his bankers to require its immediate payment in sovereigns. — Arthur James Balfour.

Ripened.

For love and charity ripened in that nature [Charles Lamb] as peaches ripen on the wall that fronts the sun. — Alexander Smith.

Risque.

About as risque as a bed in a hospital. — George Jean Nathan.

Roared.

Roared, as if stabbed. — Stephen Crane.

Roar like an army of Fenians. — Brick Pomeroy.

Romantic.

About as romantic as the Chicago stockyards. — Will Irwin.

Rooms.

A flat with rooms like a string of buttons. — Clyde Fitch.

Round (Adjective).

Round as a German sausage. — Peter C. Asbjornsen.

Round (Adverb).

Round and round like a woodpecker climbing a tree. — Richard Jefferies.

Rove.

Rove like a searchlight. — New York Times, August 29, 1920.

Ruddy.

Complexion ruddy as a pail of lard. — Anon.

Rules.

Rules, like Clocks and Watches, were all made for Fools. — John Byron.

Rustled.

Rustled like a mouse in a waste-paper basket. — David Graham Phillips.

Ruthless.

Ruthless as the old devil gods of the world's first darkness. — Sir Philip Gibbs.

Ruthlessly.

Ruthlessly as the hoof of a horse tramples on a rose. — Anon.

S

Sad.

Sad as a Government mule hauling a load of pig iron. — ANON.

Safe.

About as safe as a cow in the stock-yards. — ANON.

Safe as porch-rockers. — ANON.

Safe from harm as a baby with a bucketful of nitroglycerine. — ANON.

Safe as little birds
Busy behind leaves.
— LOUISE REDFIELD.

Sank.

Sank like thermometer mercury plunged into ice. — WILLIAM J. LOCKE.

Satiated.

Satiated, as a lion glutted with slaughter. — PLUTARCH.

Savage.

Savage as a meat axe. — J. G. HOLLAND.

Scandal.

Scandal, like a kite, to fly well, depends greatly on the length of the tale it has to carry. — PUNCH, 1854.

Scarce.

Scarce as wireless telegraph poles. — ANON.

Scarce as tips in an automat. — ARTHUR BAER.

Scarcer than Democrat's in a Vermont town meeting. — JOSEPH C. LINCOLN.

Scarce as corsets in a gypsy camp. — ABE MARTIN.

Scatter.

Scattered like storm-lashed birds. — JOHAN BOYER.

The field got scattered over the pasture, as a shop-keeper scatters his change on the counter, or as an old stage coachman used to scatter his passengers on the road with an upset. — R. S. SURTEES.

Scrape.

Began to scrape his feet on the floor like a cock before a fight. — MAXIM GORKY.

Scream.

Scream like a child born with neuralgia. — ANON.

Scream like the devil's baby. — IBID.

Screaming like an impaled madman. — MARK TWAIN.

Sea.

Of all the things I have ever seen, only the sea is like a human being; the sky is not, nor the earth. But the sea is always moving; always something deep in itself is stirring it. It never rests; it is always wanting, wanting, wanting. It hurries on; and then it creeps back slowly without having reached, moaning. It is always asking a question, and it never gets the answer. — OLIVE SCHREINER.

Searching.

Searching as the Röntgen ray. — AUGUSTA EVANS WILSON.

Secret (Noun).

Secrets are like the measles; they take easy and spread easy. — BARTLETT'S "DICTIONARY OF AMERICANISMS," 1877.

Secret (Adjective.)

Secret as a Black Hand conference. — ANON.

Secret as the fading of the breath. — ELLEN GLASGOW.

Secret as a fish. — JOHN O'KEEFFE.

Seditious.

Seditious as a hollow stomach. — Anon.

Selected.

Personally selected as a sweetheart. — Lawrence Gilman.

Self-conscious.

Self-conscious as a young man walking up the aisle in a girls' school. — Don Marquis.

Self-effacing.

Self-effacing as an auctioneer. — John Peter Toohey.

Sensitive.

Sensitive as a barometer. — Thomas Bailey Aldrich.

Sensitive as the money-market. — Thomas Hardy.

Sensitive as the leaves of a silver birch. — Joseph Hergesheimer.

Sensitive as a wireless receiving apparatus. — Keble Howard.

Sentences.

Burke's sentences are pointed at the end, — instinct with pungent sense to the last syllable. They are like a charioteer's whip, which not only has a long and effective lash, but cracks, and inflicts a still smarter sensation at the end. They are like some serpents of which I have heard it vulgarly said, their life is the fiercest in the tail. — John Foster.

Long sentences in a short composition are like large rooms in a little house. — William Shenstone.

Serious.

Serious as a white mouse in a wire trap. — Josh Billings.

Serious as a shortage of gas in a balloon. — Guy Bolton.

Serious as an English adaptation of a French farce. — Leonard Merrick.

Serious as the Ten Commandments. — W. B. Yeats.

Servants.

Female servants are like dogs of the same gender ; both are nuisances or account of the excess of company. — Anon.

Servility.

Servility is like a golden pill, which outwardly giveth pleasure, but inwardly is full of bitterness. — Nahum Tate.

Set.

Set in his ways as a chunk of concrete. — F. Hopkinson Smith.

Shaking.

Shaking like an old-time bartender mixing a drink. — Anon.

Shaking the bars like an ourang-outang enraged by exile. — Baudelaire.

Shamefaced.

Shamefaced as a blind man's dog. — Balzac.

Shaped.

In the days of "Evangeline" the most admired girl in the chorus was shaped like a bass viol. Now she has all the variations of a flagpole. — George Ade.

Sharp.

Sharp as Shylock's knife. — Douglas Jerrold.

Sharp as an apparition's nails. — Play, "Honest Lawyer," 1616.

Shells.

The German shells were coming down like rice at a wedding. — Charles W. Baker.

Shine.

Shine like a sweet lyric in a page of prose. — Francis G. Walrond.

Shoes.

Green cloth shoes, very like Chinese junks with the sails down. — LOUISA M. ALCOTT.

Short.

Short and sweet like an old woman's dance. — ABRAHAM LINCOLN.

Short and sharp like a donkey's gallop. — SAMUEL PEGGE'S "ANONYMIANA," 1776.

Shoulders.

Shoulders like the Parthenon. — HENRY L. MENCKEN.

With shoulders projecting like a Swiss châlet. — RUFUS E. SHAPLEY.

Shoulders like a pair of walking beams. — H. C. WITWER.

Shrieked.

Shrieked like a member of the musical union asked to play at a cripple's benefit. — JAMES L. FORD.

Shrill.

Shrill like newspaper headlines. — ROBERT MORSE LOVETT.

Shrunk.

A dollar has shrunk like a Hester Street all-wool suit. — ARTHUR BAER.

Sigh (Verb).

Sighing like a punctured tire. — GUY BOLTON.

Sigh (Noun).

A sigh like cutting out an airbrake. — SEWELL FORD.

Silent.

Silent as the sheeted dead. — ANON.

Silent as a bagpipe without wind. — THOMAS HOLCROFT.

Silly.

Silly as tying strings to soap bubbles and passing them off as balloons. — ANON.

Silly as a souse trying to open a Yale lock with his thumb. — ARTHUR BAER.

Silly as a young widower. — ABE MARTIN.

Simile.

Very unlike the usual Homeric simile which generally is like a comet, a small nucleus with a long tail. — J. H. V. MACBETH.

Similes are a good deal like Ford cars : you can get a good one second-hand and fix it up so you can't recognize it yourself, — but everybody else can. — NEW YORK POST, January 9, 1924.

Simple.

Simple as living in a barrel. — ANON.

Simple as the golden rule. — IBID.

Simple as the intercourse of a child with its mother. — IBID.

Simple as rain. — THEODORE DREISER.

Sin.

Sin is a sort of bog ; the farther you go in, the more swampy it gets. — MAXIM GORKY.

Sincere.

Sincere as a twenty-dollar gold piece. — STUART RIVERS.

Sinister.

Sinister as the morgue at Nôtre Dame. — JULES DE GONCOURT.

Sizzling.

Sizzling . . . like a family quarrel of snakes. — STEPHEN VINCENT BENÉT.

Skin.

Skin like a fading rose leaf. — ELLEN GLASGOW.

Skirts.

A woman's skirts should be like an after-dinner speech, — long enough to cover the subject, but short enough to be interesting. — ANON.

Slacker.

A slacker is just like a custard pie, yellow all through and without crust enough to go over the top. — Don Marquis.

Slanderers.

Slanderers are like flies, they leap all over a man's good parts to light upon his sores. — John Tillotson.

Sleepy.

Sleepy as a minister's horse. — Joseph C. Lincoln.

Slender.

Slender as a flower's stem. — Arthur Sherburne Hardy.

Slide.

Threw himself on his stomach to slide to his base ; it was like an iron-clad coming into port. — Mark Twain.

Slipped.

Spring slipped into summer like a hussy into some one's arms. — Ida M. Evans.

Slippery.

Slippery as an eel in a kettle of soft soap. — Anon.

Slits.

Eye slits, like wise, smiling old buttonholes. — Fannie Hurst.

Slow.

Slow as an agony. — Leconte de Lisle.

Slump.

Slump, like waiting soldiers. — Babette Deutsch.

Small.

Small as the little end of nothing. — John S. Farmer's "Americanisms," 1889.

Smell.

She had on so much perfume she smelt like a chemical laboratory. — Anon.

He smelled like a box of Cashmere Bouquet. — George Ade.

Smells like a G string burning up. — Abe Martin.

Smells like a buzzard's breath. — Mark Twain.

Smile (Noun).

Smile like a benediction. — Anon.

A sickly smile, like Calais to Dover. — Ibid.

Is there anything more like the sea than the smile of a woman? You say the sea smiles ; and you sail on its bosom. You say a woman smiles ; you would discover her heart ; and the smile of the sea is not more uncertain than her smile. — Jacinto Benavente.

There was something in the smile of this girl in his dream that was cool and far-off, like the shine of the stars. — Floyd Dell.

Smile like a dentifrice advertisement. — Peter B. Kyne.

A smile like an airy pat on the arm. — Sinclair Lewis.

His smile [Sir Robert Peel's] is like a silver plate upon a coffin. — Daniel O'Connell.

Smile like a tooth-powder advertisement. — Helen Rowland.

Smile (Verb).

Smiled like a swordfish. — Anon.

Smiling as the face of a Buddha. — Lafcadio Hearn.

Smile like a brewer's horse. — James Howell's "Paroimiologia," 1659.

Smoking.

Smoking like a flivver radiator. — Arthur Baer.

Smooth.

Smooth as an automobile salesman. — ANON.

Smooth as a schoolmarm's thigh. — IBID.

Smooth as the road to ruin. — IBID.

Smouldering.

Smouldering like inside the door of a banked-up furnace; smouldering like if you touched him he'd burst out into roaring flame and sparks. — A. S. M. HUTCHINSON.

Snicker.

A rustling snicker, as of a bead curtain pushed swiftly aside. — HARRIS MERTON LYON.

Snorting.

Snorting like a mad battle steed that has lost its rider. — HERMAN MELVILLE.

Snorting like an exasperated crocodile. — R. S. SURTEES.

Snug.

Snug as the yolk in an egg. — HENRIK IBSEN.

Sober.

Sober as a coroner inspecting a corpse. — AMELIE RIVES.

Soft.

Soft, like a gelatine pudding. — DOROTHY CANFIELD.

Soft as the hoof of a horse. — RICHARD EDWARDS.

Soft as the zephyr's kiss. — DAVID GARRICK.

Soft as the organ stop ere the bass grumbles. — DAVID GRAY.

Soft as winnowing plumes of Sleep. — GEORGE MEREDITH.

Soft as bird alights on bough. — SWINBURNE.

Soft as a sweetheart's hair. — JOHN D. WELLS.

Softly.

Softly, as a butterfly alighting on a flower. — FRANCIS GRIERSON.

Soggy.

Soggy, like a paper bag full of sour milk. — REX BEACH.

Solemn.

Solemn as if he was on a coroner's jury in the presence of the remains. — SEWELL FORD.

Solemn as a minstrel show. — LOUISE CLOSSER HALE.

Solid.

Solid as the skull of a Congressman. — HENRY L. MENCKEN.

Solitary.

Solitary as an oyster. — DICKENS.

A solitary figure, like the king on a playing card. — MARCEL PROUST.

Soothing.

Soothing as the hum of a spinning wheel. — LUCAS MALET.

Sophisticated.

Sophisticated as an ambulance doctor. — RUPERT HUGHES.

Sore.

Sore as a porcupine with ingrown quills. — ARTHUR BAER.

Sought.

Much sought after, like a man who breaks out of jail. — ANON.

Soul.

Did'st thou ever see a lark in a cage? Such is the soul in the body: this world is like her little turfe of grass; and the heaven o'er our heads, like her looking-glass, only gives us a miserable knowledge of the small compass of our prison. — JOHN WEBSTER.

Sound.

Sound as a fish in the water. — BENVENUTO CELLINI.

Soundless.

Soundless as ghost's intended tread. — LEWIS CARROLL.

Sparkle.

Sparkled like a gold chain on an embroidered vest. — ANON.

Sparkling as fire. — SIR JOHN MANDEVILLE.

Speculates.

A man who speculates is like an animal upon a barren waste, chased round by an ill spirit, whilst all about him fair green pastures stretch. — JOHANN W. VON GOETHE.

Speculations.

Speculations are like snapdragons. A cool hand may sometimes pick a plum, where a hasty one but burns his fingers. — PUNCH, 1853.

Spinning.

Spinning around like car wheels on a soaped track. — ARTHUR BAER.

Spirited.

Spirited as a choir of heroic tenors. — VICENTE BLASCO IBANEZ.

Spiritless.

Spiritless as corked champagne. — JAMES G. HUNEKER.

Splendid.

Splendid, as your morning bath is splendid. — HENRY JAMES.

Spontaneous.

Spontaneous like the combustion in a grain elevator. — ARTHUR BAER.

Spontaneous as the wordless note of a bird in song. — MAX BEERBOHM.

Spontaneous as the song of a bird. — W. H. HUDSON.

Sports.

He that spends his time in sports is like him whose garment is all made of fringes, and his meat nothing but sauces : they are healthless, chargeable, and useless. — JEREMY TAYLOR.

Spotless.

Spotless as naked innocence. — JOHN SMITH, 1662–1717.

Spotted.

Spotted like a pair of dice. — ANON.

Spouts.

He spouts it out, like a Chinaman sprinkling wash. — GEORGE JEAN NATHAN.

Sprawling.

Sprawling like a wet mosquito. — WILL IRWIN.

Spry.

Spry as a two-year-old colt behind a band of music. — ANON.

Spun.

Spun around like the indicator on a leaky gas meter. — ARTHUR BAER.

Sputtering.

Sputtering like a leaky valve. — JOHN PETER TOOHEY.

Square.

Square as a dry-goods box. — MARK TWAIN.

Squat.

Squat . . . like a dumpling set a-walking. — WILLIAM COOMBE.

Squawk.

Squawk like a Comanche college yell. — ANON.

Stagger.

Jess Willard was staggering around like a farmer's wife in the old days of Peruna and Dr. Pierce's Golden Remedy. — ARTHUR BAER.

Staggered as if her feet were numb. — HARVEY J. O'HIGGINS.

Stale.

Stale, like the butt of a dead cigar. — KIPLING.

Smelling stale as a plush dress on which a goblet of champagne has been upset. — JULIAN STREET.

Star.

The evening star hung like a jewel on blue velvet. — E. F. BENSON.

One twilight star shone like a blissful tear unshed. — PAUL H. HAYNE.

One star, serene and still,
Hangs like an altar light.
— MAURICE MORRIS.

The stars came out like lamps in windows. — CHARLES P. PHILLIPS.

The stars swam like goldfish across the midnight blue. — A. SAFRONI-MIDDLETON.

Staring.

Staring like a wooden saint. — GEORGE ELIOT.

Startling.

Startling like the first handful of mould cast on the coffined dead. — P. J. BAILEY.

Stationary.

Stationary as a letter carrier's wages. — ARTHUR BAER.

Steadfast.

Steadfast as earth's solid base. — WILLIAM RICHARDSON.

Steady.

Steady as the throb of an engine. — ANON.

Steady as the stare of a glass eye. — ARTHUR BAER.

Steady as water flowing from a hydrant. — JAMES G. HUNEKER.

Stick.

Stick as close to a man as a cast-off mistress. — JOHN GAY.

Stiff.

Stiff as a frozen statue. — ANON.

Stiff as Paddy's father when he was nine days dead. — IBID.

Stiff as if she had been six years in a museum. — CHARLES JAMES APPERLEY.

Stiff as an infanta in her jewels. — ELIZABETH T. COASTWORTH.

Stiffly.

Stiffly, like a toy tree. — MAY SINCLAIR.

Still.

Still as a mask. — JOSEPH CONRAD.

Still as a churchyard at midnight. — THOMAS CROFTON CROKER.

Still as a mummy in a case. — HENRY JAMES.

Still as a frozen mill-wheel. — ROBERT DWYER JOYCE.

Stingy.

Stingy as the man who crawled under the fence to save the wear and tear on the hinges. — ANON.

Stir.

A little love stirs up my heart, as tides stir up the ocean. — CHARLES GODFREY LELAND.

Stir that town up like the first night of a Billy Sunday season. — JOHN PETER TOOHEY.

Stirring.

Stirring as the cry of fox hounds in chase. — ANON.

Stomach.

The stomach is like a crucible, for it has a chemical kind of virtue to transmute one body into another, to transubstantiate fish and fruits into flesh within and about us. — JAMES HOWELL.

Stout.

Stout as miller's waistcoat, that takes a thief by the neck every day. — JOHN RAY'S PROVERBS, 1670.

Straight.

That fellow walks as straight up and stiff as if he took a breakfast of ramrods. — J. W. JOYCE'S "ENGLISH AS WE SPEAK IT IN IRELAND," 1910.

Stranded.

Stranded like an Uncle Tom Show in a Kansas tank town. — ANON.

Strangeness.

The strangeness was like a tooth gone from a well-known face. — WILL LEVINGTON COMFORT.

Stratified.

Stratified, like a chocolate layer-cake. — BRANDER MATTHEWS.

Stray.

Stray down the wind like a gentleman's hat. — BARRY PAIN.

Strict.

Strict as Lent. — SIR WALTER SCOTT.

Stripping.

They go on stripping like the Gravedigger in Hamlet. — R. S. SURTEES.

Stupid.

Look as stupid as a poet in search of a simile. — THOMAS HOLCROFT.

Stupid as oysters. — AUGUST E. F. VON KOTZEBUE.

Stutters.

Stutters like a Ford starter. — ARTHUR BAER.

Style.

To praise the style of an author more than his thoughts, is like commending a woman for her dress more than for her person ; style, like dress, should be appropriate, and not detract attention from what it was meant to adorn. — LADY BLESSINGTON.

She had style — like the prose of Thèophile Gautier, the Venus of Milo, the Petit Trianon. — WILLIAM J. LOCKE.

No more style, — literary style, — than my Chinaman's laundry-bill. — CHARLES FREDERIC NIRDLINGER.

The energetic style will resemble an impetuous torrent, which carries away rocks, disdains a bridge, and makes banks for itself ; it will impel the judge, even though he strive against it, whithersoever it pleases, and oblige him to take the course into which it hurries him. — QUINTILIAN (WATSON).

Style in painting is the same as in writing, — a power over materials, whether words or colors, by which conceptions or sentiments are conveyed. — SIR JOSHUA REYNOLDS.

Subsided.

Subsided like a water-tap turned off. — KENNETH GRAHAME.

Substantial.

Substantial as a George Grey Barnard statue. — FRANK VREELAND.

Subtle.

She is as subtle as a coal scuttle and as refined as a cabbage. — ANON.

About as subtle as the tapping of a pile-driver. — CHANNING POLLOCK.

Sudden.

Sudden as a dislocated joint slipping back into place. — ANON.

Suddenly.

Opened her eyes as suddenly as a mechanical doll that is patted on the back. — ANON.

Started as suddenly as a nickel piano. — ARTHUR BAER.

Suddenly — *continued.*

Suddenly and mysteriously, as a demon bolts through a trap in a Christmas pantomime. — HOWARD PAUL.

Suffocating.

Suffocating as the interior of a sepulchre. — ANON.

Suffrage.

We are going to find out that universal suffrage is like the appendix — useful at the early stage of the race's evolution, but to-day merely a threat to life. — OWEN WISTER.

Suitable.

Suitable to the mouth of the speaker as a tobacco pipe would be in the lips of the Venus de Medici. — LEIGH HUNT.

Suited.

Suited to her as a piano is to a kitchen. — EDGAR SALTUS.

Sun.

The red sun was pasted on the sky like a wafer. — ANON.

Regards the sun as a rather enervating institution, like central heating in a house. — MAX BEERBOHM.

The sun was setting like a disc of glowing metal. — EUGENE LEE-HAMILTON.

She watched the splendid sun go down like some great sailing ship on fire. — JOAQUIN MILLER.

The rising sun is like a ball of blood. — ROBERT W. SERVICE.

Superfluous.

An appendix is as superfluous at the end of the human cæcum as at the end of a volume of light literature. — REV. WILLIAM RALPH INGE.

Superfluous as to light a candle to the sun. — ROBERT SOUTH.

Superior.

Superior . . . as a horse is superior to a donkey. — HENRY KINGSLEY.

Supple.

Supple as a buggy whip. — GEORGE JEAN NATHAN.

Supple as a glove. — PLAY, "MISTAKEN BEAUTY," 1661.

Sure.

That was as sure as amen in church. — ANON.

Sure as Sundays appear. — THOMAS HOOD.

Sure of it as I am that I have a nose to my face. — SIR ROBERT HOWARD.

Sure as to hold an eel by the tail. — V. S. LEAN'S "COLLECTANEA," 1903.

Sure as every throng is of a pickpocket. — THOMAS MIDDLETON.

Sure as there is a hip on a goat. — "NOTES AND QUERIES," IX, IV. 461.

Surely.

Surely as water follows the curve of a basin. — ANON.

Surely as the harvest comes after the seedtime. — DR. JOHN BROWN.

Surely as the moon is bound to the earth. — ALFRED THAYER MAHAN.

As surely as the tree becomes bulky when it stands alone, and slender if one of a group ; as surely as a blacksmith's arm grows large, and the skin of a labourer's hand thick ; as surely as the eye tends to become long-sighted in the sailor, and short-sighted in the student ; as surely as a clerk acquires rapidity in writing and calculation ; as surely as the musician learns to detect an error of a semitone amidst what seems to others a very babel of sounds ; as surely as a passion grows by indulgence and diminishes when restrained ; as surely as a disregarded conscience becomes inert, and one that

Surely — *continued.*

is obeyed active ; as surely as there is any meaning on such terms as habit, custom, practice ; so surely must the human faculties be moulded unto complete fitness for the social state ; so surely must evil and immorality disappear ; so surely must man become perfect. — HERBERT SPENCER.

Surely as that two ends of a seesaw cannot both be elevated at the same time. — ALEXANDER WOOLLCOTT.

Surprise (Noun).

A surprise, like that of the chicken coming forth from its shell. — EUGÉNIE DE GUÉRIN.

Surprised.

Looks as surprised as a sardine that went to sleep in the ocean and woke up in a delicatessen store. — ARTHUR BAER.

Surprising.

Surprising as to see a stone statue walking. — ANON.

Suspicious.

Suspicious as a hairpin in a bachelor's bed. — ANON.

Sway.

Sway like an elephant. — ANON.

Swear.

Swear like the army in Flanders. — STERNE.

Sweet.

Sweet as the breath of love. — ANNA LETITIA AIKIN.

Sweet as a gumdrop to an Eskimo. — ANON.

Sweet as a June breeze in a hay field. — ANON.

Sweet as angel's dreams. — IBID.

Sweet as the smile of Spring. — IBID.

Sweet as the blush of bashfulness. — LORD BYRON.

Life is as sweet as nitrous oxide. — R. W. EMERSON.

Nothing's so dainty sweet as lovely melancholy. — JOHN FLETCHER.

Sweet as the weaving of sleep. — GERVAIS GAGE.

Sweeter than pardon's voice, or angels' songs. — ABRAHAM PORTAL.

Her face is sweet as blossoms after rain. — LIZETTE WOODWORTH REESE.

Sweet as stops of planetary music heard in trance. — SHELLEY.

Sweet as the tune of morn-saluting lark. — LOUIS THEOBALD.

Sweet as blushing rose-buds dipped in morning dew. — EDWARD YOUNG.

Swells.

Swells in me like a tide. — RICHARD JEFFERIES.

Swells, as Samson's chest in his sleep. — HERMAN MELVILLE.

Swells with emotion of the soul, like glass in a furnace. — ARTHUR MURPHY.

Swift.

Swift as unbridled rage. — HENRY ABBEY.

Swift as light. — BARRY CORNWALL.

Swift as a swallow sweeps the liquid way. — HOMER.

Swift as fear. — THOMAS PARNELL.

Swift as desire. — MARY PIX.

Swift as the telegraph. — PUNCH, 1847.

Swirl.

Swirling about like boiling milk in a saucepan. — H. G. WELLS.

Swoon.

Swoon like a couple of billiard balls about to kiss. — ANON.

Swoon — *continued.*

Swoons like a flower in the embrace of spring. — Ibid.

The vast park swoons beneath the burning eye of the sun, as youth beneath the lordship of love. — Charles Baudelaire.

Sympathetic.

About as sympathetic as a masculine stepmother. — Anon.

T

Talk (Noun).

His talk is like an incessant play of fireworks. — Anon.

Their talk, like a C Major chord introduced into Debussy nuances. — Dorothy Canfield.

His talk was like the tinkling of glass. — Henry James.

Talking with him was like skating on thin ice, and his companions had a constant mental vision of spots designated "Dangerous." — Ibid.

A good talk is like a good dinner: one assimilates it. — Jerome K. Jerome.

His talk was like a charge of horse. — John Masefield.

Natural talk, like ploughing, should turn up a large surface of life, rather than dig mines into geological strata. — Robert Louis Stevenson.

Talk (Verb).

Talked like a disordered soda fountain. — Anon.

Dr. Birch [1652–1710] dreaded a pen as he did a torpedo; but he could talk like running water. — A. W. Chambers.

Talks like a fog-horn. — Holman Day.

Talking away like a soda-water bottle just uncorked. — A. S. M. Hutchinson.

Talk like an American novel. — Henry James.

Talking like a tract. — Leonard Merrick.

Talkative.

Talkative persons are like barrels, the less there is in them, the more noise they make. — John Gideon Mulligan.

Talker.

A tremendous talker is like a greedy eater at an ordinary dinner, keeping to himself an entire dish of which every one present would like to have partaken. — Punch, 1857.

Tame.

Tame as parlor rabbits. — Anon.

Tame as fear. — Beaumont and Fletcher.

Tame as patience. — Ibid.

Taste.

Taste in his mouth like a bird-and-animal store. — Irvin S. Cobb.

Teaches.

He who teaches a child is like one who writes on clean paper; but he who teaches old people is like to one who writes on blotted paper. — The Talmud (Barclay).

Tear.

A stealing shower of tears rolled down her cheeks, like dew-drops trickling o'er the bloom of roses. — Colley Cibber.

Tears hang upon his cheeks like morning dews on roses. — Nathaniel Lee.

Bursting forth tears like springs out of a banke. — Edmund Spenser.

Teased.

Teased in her head like a secret. — DOROTHY RICHARDSON.

Tedious.

Tedious as waiting for a train. — ANON.

Teeth.

Teeth like saws. — ROBERT BUCHANAN.

Locked teeth like the tight edges of a sprung trap. — IRVIN S. COBB.

Two big teeth in front like the double blank at dominos. — GEORGE DU MAURIER.

Teeth like rakes. — FRANÇOIS VILLON.

Had teeth each larger than the monument. — SAMUEL WESLEY.

Temporary.

Temporary as a wave. — ANON.

Temporary looking, as a mining-camp street in the motion pictures. — SINCLAIR LEWIS.

Tenacious.

Tenacious as remorse. — VICENTE BLASCO-IBÁÑEZ.

Tender.

New married folk upon their honeymoon are as tender as poached eggs. — H. FIELDING-HALL.

Terms.

Technical terms, you know, are like red, white, and blue poker chips. They stand for whatever the players agree upon. The outsider can't tell whether the game is pennyante or a million a minute. And often enough, when the players come to cash in, the bank is broke. — JOHN B. KERFOOT.

Terrible.

Terrible like the love of a woman of forty years. — BALZAC.

Terrible as Milton's devils. — DENIS DIDEROT.

Thick.

Thick as fiddlers in hell. — ANON.

Thick as leaves. — ABRAHAM COWLEY.

Thick as oil. — MAXIM GORKY.

Thick as the green leaves of a garden. — HENRY JAMES.

Thick as buttercups in June. — IBID.

As thick and numberless as the gay motes that people the sunbeams. — MILTON.

Thickly as fireflies burn in a tropic night. — PUNCH, 1850.

Thin.

She is as thin as a whisper. — ANON.

Thin as the girl who didn't have enough to her to itch. — IBID.

Thin as the girl who swallowed the pit of an olive and was rushed to a maternity hospital. — IBID.

Thin like an exclamation mark. — IBID.

So thin that she could fall through a flute and never strike a note. — IBID.

Thin as boarding house consommé. — ARTHUR BAER.

Thin as a movie plot. — BENJAMIN DE CASSERES.

Thin as the homeopathic soup that was made by boiling the shadow of a pigeon that had starved to death. — ABRAHAM LINCOLN.

Thin as poorhouse gruel. — JOSEPH C. LINCOLN.

Thin as a thermometer. — ALBERT L. WEEKS.

Thoughts.

My very thoughts were like a ghostly rustle of dead leaves. — JOSEPH CONRAD.

Her thoughts are like a flock of butterflies. — BRIAN HOOKER.

Every thought is like dough ; you have only to knead it well — you can make anything you like out of it. — TURGENEV.

Thrashed.

Thrashed like clothes at wash. — François Villon.

Thrill.

Thrilled as a debutante at her first ball. — Anon.

Thrilled like throbbing violins. — Ibid.

Thrilling.

Thrilling as an account of a flower show. — Gertrude Atherton.

About as thrilling as a lesson in swimming would be to a middle-aged goldfish. — H. C. Witwer.

Through.

He went through it like a clown through a paper hoop. — Temple Scott.

Thumping.

Thumping like ramping host of warrior horse. — George Meredith.

Tiara.

A tiara like a tin lamp reflector. — Dickens.

Ticking.

I heard my watch ticking its little tick on the mantelpiece by the side of the clock, like a pony trotting by a big horse. — George du Maurier.

Tight.

Tight as the skin on a sausage. — Anon.

Tight as the bark of a tree. — J. R. Bartlett's "Dictionary of Americanisms," 1877.

Tight as the lining of a refrigerator. — Gelett Burgess.

Tight as wadding in a gun.— Palmer Cox.

Tilted.

Tilted her graceful head as a bird does when it listens. — Mark Twain.

Tired.

Tired as the leaves that are drooping and brown on the trees in the Tuilleries. — Sir Philip Gibbs.

Tiresome.

Tiresome as musical parties. — Countess of Blessington.

Tiresome as virtue. — Edith Wharton.

Tiresome as a woman without imagination. — Edgar Saltus.

Together.

My belly is grown together like an empty satchel. — John Fletcher.

Packed together like dried figs in a wooden drum. — T. Edgar Pemberton.

Held it together as a backbone holds together the ribs and limbs and head to a body. — H. G. Wells.

Tongue.

The Tongue is like a Race-Horse, which runs the faster the lesser Weight it carries. — Joseph Addison.

His tongue hangs out like a pump-handle. — Arthur Baer.

Tongue like a pink dart. — Joseph Conrad.

Her tongue hung out like a yard of red hall carpet. — Wilson Mizner.

His tongue ran on like a millstream. — Lloyd Osbourne.

A woman without a tongue is as a soldier without his weapon. — George Peele.

A tongue which felt like a freshly painted shingle. — Edwin L. Sabin.

Her tongue ; it was like an inner cut of watermelon. — Edgar Saltus.

Torment.

I will be a greater torment to him than a beadle to a beggar, a cat to a rat, or a candle to a moth. — Thomas Holcroft.

Tough.

Tough as bull beef. — ANON.

Tough as Job's Turkey. — IBID.

Touzled.

A shock of hair, as touzled as a sparrow taking a bath. — BALZAC.

Towers.

Towers like a stovepipe above a thimble. — W. C. BRANN.

Town.

That town looks like a cluster of chicken coops along a bankrupt trolley line. — EDWARD CHILDS CARPENTER.

The town, like a peevish child, knows not what it desires, and is always best pleased with a rattle. — FIELDING.

Tranquil.

About as tranquil as a Texas cyclone. — ANON.

Tranquil as a shape of stone. — WINTHROP M. PRAED.

Tranquilly.

Tranquilly and contentedly, like a quiet ghost with a clean conscience sitting inside the bars of a snug family vault. — HERMAN MELVILLE.

Treasure.

Treasure like one's mother's portrait or like one's father's sword. — FRANCIS W. CROWNINSHIELD.

Trees.

The trees looked like leaping animals in a photograph. — J. WASSERMANN.

Tremble.

Tremble like a frosty Russian on a hill. — SIR WILLIAM DAVENANT.

Tremble like a lamb snatched from the fangs of some fell wolf. — GEORGE SAND.

Trembling.

Trembling like a blancmange. — HORACE MAYHEW.

Tremulous.

Lord Downes [1752–1825] was tremulous as if he were composed of calves'-foot jelly. — R. SHELTON MACKENZIE.

Tried.

Even as gold is tried with a touch stone : So is man tried with gold . . . There is no touch stone in all the world, that doth more truly touch and trie, than gold, wealth, and abundance of riches. — ANTHONIE FLETCHER.

Troublesome.

Troublesome as a stage mother. — ANON.

Troublesome as a law-suit. — COLLEY CIBBER.

True.

True as the compass. — ANON.

True as a blade to hilt. — THOMAS DIBDEN.

True as the town time. — THOMAS HARDY.

True as The Voyage of Pantagruel. — THOMAS LODGE.

Truth.

Truth is like a mother-in-law. Nobody likes it. — ANON.

Truth, like a gentle shower, soaks through the ears and moistens the intellect. — SOUTHGATE'S "MANY THOUGHTS ON MANY THINGS," 1858.

Tugged.

Tugged like the tackle of a sail. — STEPHEN CRANE.

Tune.

As much out of tune as a cornstalk fiddle is in the hands of a ploughboy. — ELDRIDGE G. PAGE.

Tunes like flowers that dreaming lips have kissed. — BARBARA YOUNG.

Twangs.

Twang like a wet guitar. — JAMES WHITCOMB RILEY.

Twinkled.

Twinkled as if a rainbow had explored in the room. — GELETT BURGESS.

The man twinkled all over with impudence like a piece of sham jewelry. — R. L. STEVENSON.

Twist.

Twisted as an old paint tube. — FANNIE HURST.

He twisted from side to side like a coin partly spun round by the finger and thumb. — RICHARD JEFFERIES.

Twisting like a nest of anacondas. — HERMAN MELVILLE.

Twisted like a lie. — EDGAR SALTUS.

Typewriter.

A typewriter which makes a sound like some one having a fit in a tin-can factory. — ANON.

Tyranny.

Tyranny, like hell, is not easily conquered. — THOMAS PAINE.

U

Ugly.

Ugly as a baboon. — MRS. CENTLIVRE.

Umbrella.

An umbrella is like a Scotch shower . . . the moment it rains it's missed. — PUNCH, 1850.

Unalterable.

Unalterable as the little paper flowers permanently visible inside the lumpy glass paperweights. — EZRA POUND.

Unbearable.

Unbearable as a five-act, unactable, intractable tragedy. — ANON.

Uncanny.

Uncanny, like death on a mop-stick. — ANON.

Uncanny as the thought of immortality. — BENJAMIN DE CASSERES.

Unchanging.

Unchanging as a nation's flag. — GEORGE JEAN NATHAN.

Uncomfortable.

Uncomfortable as the garden of Eden during the mosquito season. — ANON

Unconscious.

Unconscious as an oak tree of its growth. — ANON.

Unconscious as the loyalty of bees to their queen. — LAFCADIO HEARN.

Unconscious as a face of stone. — W. H. HUDSON.

Unconscious of being indecent as our mythical first parents. — SIR HARRY JOHNSTON.

Unconsciously as you grow your finger nails. — G. B. SHAW.

Undefiled.

Undefiled as heaven. — SHAKERLEY MARMION.

Undistinguishable.

Undistinguishable as the effect of a particular drop when the meadows are floated by a summer shower. — DR. JOHNSON.

Undone.

I am undone! like an oyster. — JOHN FLETCHER.

Undulated.

Undulated to this side and that, even as a wave receding and advancing. — DANTE.

Unearthly.

Unearthly — like half articulated wailings of the ghosts of all Herod's murdered innocents. — HERMAN MELVILLE.

Unexpected.

It fell out unexpected — pop, on a sudden ; like the going off of a field-piece, or an alderman in an apoplexy. — GEORGE COLMAN (The Younger).

Unexpected as a hymn tune in a cent-in-the-slot talking machine. — JOSEPH C. LINCOLN.

Unfit.

Unfit for it as a pig's mouth for whistling. — ANON.

Unfit for it as an ass at the lyre. — AULUS GELIGS.

Uniform.

Uniform as so many buttons or brass pins. — NEW YORK POST, September 3, 1921.

Unintelligent.

Unintelligent as grapeshot. — GEORGE MACFARREN.

Uninteresting.

Uninterestin' as a disciplined husband. — ABE MARTIN.

Unlike.

Unlike as a yacht and a coal barge. — ANON.

Unlike real life as a clown's red nose. — ROSE MACAULAY.

Unlikely.

Unlikely as that you could mount upward on the shadow of a staircase. — ANON.

Unmistakable.

Unmistakable as foreign clothes. — HENRY JAMES.

Unnatural.

Unnatural as mirth at a funeral. — EDWARD YOUNG.

Unobtrusive.

Unobtrusive as a pawnbroker. — F. BERKELEY SMITH.

Unquestioned.

Unquestioned as the rights of a thunderbolt to explode into whoever's roof it chooses. — JAMES STEPHENS.

Unreadable.

Unreadable as a vacuum. — DENIS DIDEROT.

Unreal.

Unreal . . . as the eleven thousand virgins of Cologne, who were but a couple. — CHARLES READE.

Unreasonable.

Unreasonable as an amateur leading woman on a first night. — SINCLAIR LEWIS.

Unremembered.

Unremembered as old rain. — EDNA ST. VINCENT MILLAY.

Unreservedly.

He spoke to me unreservedly, as a poet to his muse. — BULWER-LYTTON.

Unrestricted.

Unrestricted like the rain. — MARK TWAIN.

Unromantic.

Unromantic as physic. — ANON.

Unsatisfying.

Unsatisfying as a set compliment. — HEYWOOD BROUN.

Unshaken.

Unshaken, like his Grace the Duke of Wellington, amid the red-hot cannon balls. — PUNCH, 1842.

Unsportsmanlike.

Unsportsmanlike as gunning in a hennery. — Heywood Broun.

Unsubstantial.

Unsubstantial like a pyramid of eggs. — Matthew Arnold.

Unsubstantial, like the glorified dreams of an alchemist. — Nathaniel Hawthorne.

Unsullied.

Unsullied as the rectitude of Addison. — Dr. John Brown.

Unsullied as new fallen snow.— J. G. Cooper.

Unthinkable.

Unthinkable as an honest burglar or a virtuous harlot. — Henry L. Mencken.

Untidy.

Untidy as a bohemian. — Alphonse Daudet.

Unused.

Unused, like miser's gold. — Anon.

Unusual.

Unusual as snow at the equator or mango trees at the North Pole. — Anon.

Unvarying.

Unvarying as the course of a homing bird. — Anon.

Unwelcome.

Unwelcome as an early morning telephone call for a friend next door. — Anon.

Unyielding.

Unyielding — like the Puritan moral code. — Anon.

Up.

The prices went up like putting your thermometer out in the Rio Grande sun. — Owen Wister.

Up and Down.

Up and down . . . like a kettle-drum stick. — Thomas Hardy.

Jump up and down like a pair of fiddle-bows in a finale of one of Verdi's noisiest operas. — Howard Paul.

Up and down, as a yard of pump water. — W. C. Russell's "Sailors' Language."

Up and down with her head like a boat in a storm. — Sir Philip Sidney.

Up and down by turns, like a well with two buckets. — James Thomson.

Upright.

Upright as a ninepin. — Balzac.

Upright as any Briton who owes not a penny. — George Gissing.

Upright as a candle standeth in a socket. — John Heywood.

Use.

About as much use for him as a duck has for a life preserver. — Anon.

I got about as much use for Magruder as a skinned eel has for a haircut and a shoeshine. — Sam Hellman.

Binjamin's of no more use with a pack of 'ounds than a hopera-box would be to a cow, or a frilled shirt to a pig. — R. S. Surtees.

Useful.

Useful as a bale of hay in a garage. — Anon.

About as useful as an umbrella to a fish. — Ibid.

About as useful as a wooden ship in a bottle. — Ibid.

Useful as a balance at the bank. — Harold Begbie.

Useless.

Useless as a broken feather. — Anon.

Useless as a comb to a baldhead. — Ibid.

Useless — *continued.*

Useless as a fan to an Esquimo. — IBID.

Useless as a lamp without a wick. — IBID.

Useless as an alarm clock on Sunday morning. — IBID.

Useless as an icebox to an Eskimau. — IBID.

Useless as an umbrella to a hippopotamus. — IBID.

Useless as an umbrella to a fish. — IBID.

Useless as a pair of shoes to a sherry cobbler. — IBID.

Useless as a pop-gun on the Somme. — IBID.

Useless as a sheriff at Herrin [Ill.]. — IBID.

Useless as a tassel on an umbrella. — IBID.

Useless as the vermiform appendix.— IBID.

Useless as a euchre prize. — ARTHUR BAER.

Useless as a glass eye at a keyhole. — L. MONTA BELL.

Useless as a dead actor. — BRANDER MATTHEWS.

Useless as the fifth wheel to a waggon. — V. S. LEAN'S "COLLECTANEA," 1903.

Useless as a pilot to persons on shore. — PLATO.

Useless as Monsieur Jourdain's fencing lessons, which failed to defend him against the housemaid. — G. B. SHAW.

Useless as a handful of ashes. — MARK TWAIN.

V

Vacant.

A face as vacant as an untenanted house. — MARCEL PROUST.

Vague.

Vague as a wood gazed in at dusk. — AMY LOWELL.

Vain.

To look for gratitude from a money-dealer is as vain as to try to touch the heart of the wolves of the Ukraine in winter. — BALZAC.

Vain as a flea on a bishop's cranium. — JAMES G. HUNEKER.

Vain a thing as to attempt weighing a Dutch barn in jewellers' scales. — HERMAN MELVILLE.

Vain as bottling up of wind. — JONATHAN SWIFT.

Vainglorious.

Vainglorious, like a Shanghai rooster on a gatepost. — GEORGE RANDOLPH CHESTER.

Vainly.

Vainly as one strikes at water with a sword. — WITTER BYNNER.

Valuable.

About as valuable as a railway ticket when there is a permanent block on the line. — G. K. CHESTERTON.

Valueless.

Valueless as sea shells. — KATHERINE FULLERTON GEROULD.

Vanish.

Vanish like a cocktail before dinner. — ANON.

Vanish as raindrops which fall in the sea. — SUSAN COOLIDGE.

Vanished . . . like the forms that the infant's finger traced upon the beach ; the next tide erases them, and confounds them with the barren undistinguished strand. — JOHN P. CURREN.

Vanish — *continued.*

Vanished away like the smoke of tobacco. — BEN JONSON.

Vanish like plunging stars. — DON MARQUIS.

Vanish like a paper dollar on Saturday night. — ABE MARTIN.

Vanish like a breath off a razor blade. — P. G. WODEHOUSE.

Vanity.

Vanity is to a man what the oily secretion is to a bird, with which it sleeks and adjusts the plumage ruffled by whatever causes. — ALEXANDER SMITH.

Variable.

Variable as thermometers. — BALZAC.

Varied.

Varied as the expression of the human face. — GEORGE H. ELLWANGER.

Varied in his choice as was the Sultan before he met with Scheherazade. — SIR HARRY JOHNSON.

Various.

Various As the Fancies of Men in the Pursuit of a Wife. — JAMES RALPH.

Vast.

Vast as the orb that circles in its breast the world of stars. — GEORGE TOWNSEND.

Vers Libre.

Most of our native vers libre sounds like a ton of coal falling through too small an aperture in the sidewalk. — JAMES G. HUNEKER.

Vibrant.

Vibrant as an E string. — CARL VAN VECHTEN.

Vicious.

Vicious, like an eating chemical. — HARRIS MERTON LYON.

Vigorous.

Vigorous as the sun. — JAMES THOMSON.

Virginal.

Virginal as Eve before she knew Adam. — ANON.

A simile should be as virginal as a toothbrush. — LAWRENCE GILMAN.

Virtue.

Virtue is like an enemy avoided. — DANTE.

Virtue, like a dowerless beauty, has more admirers than followers. — LADY BLESSINGTON.

Virtue within a woman's heart
By nature's hand is rammed in,
There must be kept by steady art,
Like water when it's dammed in ;
But if once broken
Past all revoking,
Virtue flies off in a minute ;
Like a river left,
Of waters bereft,
Each man may venture in.
— FIELDING.

A virtue is like a city set upon a hill, it cannot be hid. — ROBERT HICHENS.

Virtue, like hops, must wait the time of the market, or virtue itself becomes a very drug. — PUNCH, 1843.

The virtue of a wife is like the merit of a poet, never justly valued until after death. — SIR RICHARD STEELE.

Virtuous.

Virtuous as a convict in the death house. — HENRY L. MENCKEN.

Visible.

Visible as fever. — HENRY JAMES.

Visible as a nose on a man's face. — SHAKESPEARE.

Vital.

Vital as seed warm-nestled in the sod. — FLORENCE EARLE COATES.

Vivid.

Vivid as a nerve. — ANON.

Voice.

Her voice was like the carol of a bird. — HENRY ABBEY.

She [Ouida] had a voice like a carving knife. — ANON.

Her voice is like a whistle on a peanut stand. — IBID.

A voice like the grumbling of a wagon on a corduroy road. — IBID.

Her voice was rich and vibrant, like the middle notes of a 'cello. — IBID.

A voice like the notes of a harp played on by a hammer. — IBID.

Her voice is like the tinkling flow of tiny mountain waters dropping into the concave heart of an avalanche. — IBID.

Her voice was like the voice the stars had when they sang together. — IBID.

A voice like roaring Aetna. — IBID.

His voice was like the fall of stones in the bottom of a mine. — R. D. BLACKMORE.

A voice like a trombone. — FINLEY PETER DUNNE.

His voice was like a buzz saw striking a rusty nail. — ARTHUR FOLWELL.

A voice like a brass cornet, and she was using it too. — SEWELL FORD.

That magical voice like the bugle-call of a Highland chief. — PARKE GODWIN.

His voice was like a sword swinging. — BEN HECHT.

A voice like the faint jangle of an old thin piano. — JOSEPH HERGESHEIMER.

His voice came like a stone from a catapult. — ROBERT HICHENS.

He had a high, quavering voice like a bagpipe with the wind failing in it. — RUPERT HUGHES.

Her [Bernhardt] voice was soft as chartreuse and had a glisten in it like the shine upon pearls. — AMY LESLIE.

She has a voice just like one of them air whistles that the flagman keeps pullin' when they're backin' the Limited in. — RING W. LARDNER.

A voice like a decrepit old melodeon. — E. V. LUCAS.

He has a deep thick voice like a bumble bee in a jug. — ABE MARTIN.

Voice like the bursting of a rocket. — HERMAN MELVILLE.

Voice like an old worn-out coffee mill. — IBID.

Voices like clarion trumpets. — JOHN, VISCOUNT MORLEY.

A voice like a pair of cymbals. — HENRI MURGER.

Voice . . . like a bass string of a damaged guitar. — PUNCH, 1843.

A voice like a steam siren. — CARL VAN VECHTEN.

His [Edwin Forrest] voice surged and roared like an angry sea lashed into fury by a storm, till, as it reached its boiling, seething climax, in which the serpent hiss of hate was heard at intervals amidst its louder, deeper, coarser tone, it was like the falls of Niagara, in its tremendous, down-sweeping cadence : it was a whirlwind, a tornado, a cataract of illimitable rage. — GEORGE VANDENHOFF.

Her voice was like water bubbling from a silver jar. — OSCAR WILDE.

W

Waddled.

Waddles like a childless spinster's pet dog. — DON MARQUIS.

A Tank waddled over the ruts and sandbags like a walrus on a broken ice-floe. — ELLIOTT H. PAUL.

Waggled.

Waggled about in his saddle, like a diadem upon the head of a cow. — BALZAC.

Waist.

She had a waist like an hourglass. — ANON.

Waiting.

Waiting like a hired girl waits for Thursday afternoon. — SEWELL FORD.

Walk.

Walk like a stage-struck queen. — BIRCH ARNOLD.

He walks up and down like a charged musket. — BEN JONSON.

She walked like one blown against. — GEORGE MEREDITH.

Wallowed.

Wallowed like trodden sandbags. — SIEGFRIED SASSON.

Wanted.

Always wanted, like the last novel. — JAMES THOMSON.

Wanton.

Wanton as summer breezes. — APHRA BEHN.

Wanton as a monkey. — NICHOLS BRETON.

Wanton as a calf. — THEOCRITUS.

Warm.

Warm as a mouse in cotton. — ANON.

Warm as love. — JAMES THOMSON.

Warm them up like a camp-meeting revival. — MARK TWAIN.

Wave.

Waved to and fro like the topknot on some old Pottawattamie Sachem's head. — HERMAN MELVILLE.

Weak.

Weak as cambric tea. — ANON.

Weak as tears. — ALEXANDER SMITH.

Weeping.

Weeping like a fountain. — A. GUSTAVE DROZ.

Welcome.

Welcome as a box of rattlesnakes. — ANON.

About as welcome as a criticism of one's club. — IBID.

About as welcome as a gas attack. — IBID.

Welcome as a sharp steel file in a prison. — IBID.

Welcome as a snow-flake in hell. — IBID.

Welcome as a wild deuce to a bob-tail flush. — IBID.

About as welcome as diphtheria. — IBID.

Welcome as moistening showers unto the parched ground. — IBID.

Welcome as the postman's whistle on remittance day. — IBID.

Welcome as four aces. — ARTHUR BAER.

Welcome as a storm. — THOMAS FULLER'S "GNOMOLOGIA," 1732.

About as welcome as a coal bill in father's Christmas mail. — FRANK WARD O'MALLEY.

Welcome as a thief. — JOHN TAYLOR.

Went.

He went through his money like the cannon-ball express through Schenectady. — ANON.

Wept.

She wept like a gutter on a rainy day. — GUY DE MAUPASSANT.

Whirl.

Whirling like acrobatic witches. — ZONA GALE.

Whirl like the fly-wheel in a power house. — BERT LESTON TAYLOR.

Whirring.

Whirring, as a scythe goes through the stem of a single flower. — LORD DUNSANY.

Whiskers.

My butler is the kind you see on the stage, with little side whiskers on each side of his face, like brackets inclosing a blank space; so [ ]. — IRVIN S. COBB.

His whiskers resembled the cylinder of a Swiss music box. — O. HENRY.

Horribly hirsute with sable whiskers stretching out like the prongs of a pitchfork. — FRANK RICHARDSON.

Whisper (Noun).

A whisper like a locomotive letting off steam. — ANON.

Whispers (Verb).

Each fan whispers like a lion paging some food. — ARTHUR BAER.

White.

White as naked innocence. — ANON.

White as the soul of Keats in Paradise. — T. B. ALDRICH.

White as Albian rocks. — MICHAEL DRAYTON.

White as your handkerchief. — HENRY JAMES.

White as a Sunday shirt. — JOSEPH C. LINCOLN.

Whizzed.

Whizzed like a skyrocket. — MARK TWAIN.

Whoop.

Whoop like an evangelist dragging the damned out of hell. — ANON.

Whooping.

Whooping like red Indians. — JOSEPH CONRAD.

Whoop and halloo like a troup of Don Cossacks. — WASHINGTON IRVING.

Wicked.

Wicked as the left bank of the Seine. — ANON.

Wife.

A wife is like a diamond pin: Always a catch to it. — ANON.

A wife is like heart disease: You can't cure it. — IBID.

A wife is like the toothache: sooner or later you have to have it. — IBID.

Good wives, like filberts, will remain good for a long time. It depends upon the care you take of them, and how you husband them. — PUNCH, 1857.

A man's wife is something like the Equator; in a subconscious way, he knows she's there, of course, but he can look right at her without seeing her. — HELEN ROWLAND.

Wild.

Wild as primeval chaos. — ANON.

Wild as accents of lovers' farewell. — LORD BYRON.

Winces.

Winces like a touched nerve. — HENRY JAMES.

Wise.

Wise as a bishop. — COLLEY CIBBER.

Wise as . . . the astute Arabian who put his hand into the bag of serpents and drew forth the one and only eel. — FRANCIS W. CROWNINSHIELD.

Wistful.

Wistful as a letter lying unclaimed. — SARA SAPER.

Wit.

Wit without learning is like a tree which bears no fruit. — ARISTIPPUS.

Sharp wits, like sharp knives, do often cut their owner's fingers. — JOHN ARROWSMITH.

Wit, without wisdom, is like a song without sense ; it does not please long. — JOSH BILLINGS.

Wit resembles a coquette ; those who the most eagerly run after it are the least favored. — MARIE JOSEPH CHENIER.

Gibbon had a low wit like that which defaces outbuildings. — R. W. EMERSON.

Wit and wisdom are like the seven stars, seldom seen together. — THOMAS FULLER'S "GNOMOLOGIA," 1732.

His wit was like that of a quick-flashing blade. — HENRY JAMES.

Wit and humor are like those volatile essences, which, being too delicate to bear the open air, evaporate almost as soon as they are exposed to it. — S. P. NEWMAN'S "RHETORIC," 1835.

Wit is like a Chinese lady's foot . . . brevity is the sole of it. — PUNCH, 1841.

Wit is brushwood : judgment, timber ; the one gives greatest flame, the other yields the most durable heat; and both meeting make the best fire. — SIR THOMAS OVERBURY.

Great wits, like great beauties, look upon mere esteem as a flat insipid thing ; nothing less than admiration will content them. — JEREMIAH SEED.

Woman.

A woman is like a gun. Don't fool with it. — ANON.

A woman is like a salad : much depends on the dressing. — IBID.

Women are like dogs, — they need a little fighting now and again. — IBID.

Women are like sheep in a storm : they huddle together. — IBID.

A gasoline engine is like a woman, when she will, she will ; and when she won't, she won't. — IBID.

Wimmin are like flowers, a little dust ov squeezing makes them the more fragrant. — JOSH BILLINGS.

Women are like those calculations in arithmetic, which one can never bring to an exact account. — BULWER-LYTTON.

Woman is like your shadow ; follow her, she flies ; fly from her, she follows. — SEBASTIAN R. N. CHAMFORT.

Women are like hounds, most kind, being beaten and abused. — GEORGE CHAPMAN.

Women are like Egyptian temples, beautiful without, but with idols inside. — GEORGE CHAPMAN.

Woman is like a gun. Her range is limited. But in the home she hits a man like ten thousands of brick. — G. K. CHESTERTON.

Women are very like religion ; we must take them on faith, or go without. — F. MARION CRAWFORD.

Women, like quicksilver, are never fixed till they are dead. . . . Egad, they are more like gold, I think ; for they are never fixed but by dross. — FIELDING.

A white horse and a beautiful woman are akin, and two troublesome things to manage : the first is difficult to be kept clean ; and the second, honest. — SAMUEL FOOTE.

Woman — *continued.*

A woman who won't flatter is like a piano that won't play. It may be an imposing piece of furniture, but it isn't a piano. — Ellen T. Fowler.

A big woman . . . like a cantaloupe melon. — Gilbert Frankau.

Women are like cats. If you move toward them they run away, but if you sit there and say, "Puss, puss, puss," and put a saucer of milk on the floor, in due course they will be moved by curiosity to come and see what there is in the saucer. Then, click! you've got the cat by the back of the neck, so that it can't scratch you. When the cat has struggled enough and discovered that she can't get away, and been tickled behind the ear, she'll sit on your lap and purr. And then, ah, then you no longer need say, "Puss, puss, puss!" You can say, "You damn cat!" and she'll go on sitting there, purring. — W. L. George.

Women are like Bradshaw — a guide and a puzzle. — Sydney Grundy.

Women as compared to men are like point lace to canvas. — Charles H. Hoyt.

Witches cannot shed tears, though women in general are, like the crocodile, ready to weep upon every light occasion. — King James.

Lone women, like to empty houses, perish. — Christopher Marlowe.

Cantaloupes are jest like women — we kin themp 'em, an' lift 'em, an' squeeze 'em, but we can't tell a blamed thing about 'em till it's too late. — Abe Martin.

Women are just like elephants t' me. I like t' look at 'em, but I wouldn't want one. — Ibid.

Women, . . . are like the sawdust put in cases containing chinaware; it is counted for naught, and still, without it, everything would be wrecked. — Madame Necker.

A woman, like the Koh-i-noor,
Mounts to the price that's put on her.
— Coventry Patmore.

Woman's like a looking glass
That when its owner goes,
Will flatter any other face
As much as it doth his.
— Lope de Vega.

It's kindness that brings everything that's best out of us women. We're terribly like sliced pineapple in that respect: give us just a sprinkling of sugar, and out come all the juices. — Arthur Stringer.

Words.

His words tumbling, crashing, slithering over each other like coals down a steel chute. — Fannie Hurst.

Slowly pronouncing and delivering his words like a man pitching quoits. — D. H. Lawrence.

Their words, like stage processions, stalk along. — Robert Lloyd.

Arranging words like the parts of a tessellated pavement, or mosaic work. — Gaius Lucilius (Watson).

Long words, like long dresses, frequently hide something wrong about the understanding. — Punch, 1853.

The words are like a cloud of winged snakes. — Shelley.

Words are like money; and when the current value of them is generally understood, no man is cheated by them. — Sir Richard Steele.

Her words fell like rain on a waterproof umbrella; they made a noise, but they could not reach the head which they seemed destined to deluge. — Frances Trollope.

Words are, like money, a medium of exchange, and the sureness with which they can be used varies not only with the character of the coins themselves, but also with the character of the things they buy, and that of the men who tender and receive them. — Allen Upward.

World.

The world is a great book, of which they that never stir from home read only a page. — SAINT AUGUSTINE.

The face of the world looks as though it had shaved itself with a broken beer bottle while standing on a barrel in a cyclone. — BENJAMIN DE CASSERES.

The world is like an inn : a rider comes at night
Is fed and lodged, and then jogs on at morning light.
— WISDOM OF THE BRAHMIN.

The world is like a beautiful book, but of little use to him who cannot read it. — CARLO GOLDONI.

The world is like an old coquette, who conceals her age. — VOLTAIRE.

Worries.

Worries as a hen under a shower bath. — ARTHUR BAER.

Wrinkle.

Wrinkled like a mud-bank drying in the sun. — ANON.

Her face was wrinkled like a roll-top desk. — ARTHUR BAER.

Wrinkled like a newly plowed field. — JULES VERNE.

Writer.

An unpractised writer will sometimes send a beautiful and powerful phrase jostling along in the midst of a clumsy sentence — like a crowned king escorted by a mob. — SIR WALTER RALEIGH, 1860–1922.

Writhing.

I could see the man's very soul writhing in his body like an impaled worm. — JOSEPH CONRAD.

Writing.

Dislocated writing that looks like a Profile Drawing of the Sierra Nevadas. — GEORGE ADE.

Writing is like pulling the trigger of a gun : if you are not loaded, nothing happens. — HENRY SEIDEL CANBY.

She confesses [George Sand] that her writing was like the turning on of a water-tap, the stream always flowed, a literary hydrant. — JAMES G. HUNEKER.

Method in writing is like ceremony in living too often us'd to supply the want of better things. — THOMAS KILLIGREW.

I find by experience that writing is like building ; wherein the undertaker, to supply some defect or serve some convenience which at first he saw not, is usually forced to exceed his first model and proposal, and many times to double the charge and expense of it. — JOHN SCOTT.

Wrong.

Wrong as two left shoes. — ARTHUR BAER.

You thought wrong, like Hob's hog (who fancied that the butcher who came to kill him had brought his breakfast). — A. B. EVANS'S "PROVERBS," 1848.

Y

Yacht.

A yacht like a great moth with folded wings. — WILLIAM MCFEE.

Yawn.

Yawned like a menagerie lion. — GELETT BURGESS.

Yell.

Yell as if caught in a trap. — DR. JOHN BROWN.

Yelled like the mate on a tramp steamer. — JOSEPH C. LINCOLN.

Yellow.

Yellow . . . like a bilious brunette. — DICKENS.

Yellow as the Missouri river. — WILLIAM SLAVENS MCNUTT.

Young.

Young as the slip of the new moon. — GEORGE MEREDITH.

Young as our streams after rain. — EDWARD THOMAS.

Youth.

At almost every step in life we meet with young men from whom we anticipate wonderful things, but of whom, after careful inquiry, we never hear another word ; like certain chintzes, calicoes, and ginghams, they show finely in their first newness, but cannot stand the sun and rain, and assume a very sober aspect after washing day. — NATHANIEL HAWTHORNE.

Z

Zeal.

Zeal without knowledge is like a fire without a grate to contain it, like a sword without a hilt to wield it by, like a high-bred horse without a bridle to guide him ; zeal without knowledge speaks without thinking, acts without planning, seeks to accomplish a good end without the adoption of becoming means ; it goes about seeking to establish its own righteousness, not having submitted to the righteousness of God. — JOHN BATE.

As a cancer is to a man's body, so is party zeal to his soul. — WILLIAM SCOTT DOWNEY'S "PROVERBS," 1854.

Zeal without judgment is like gunpowder in the hands of a child. — BEN JONSON.

Zeal without knowledge is like expedition to a man in the dark. — JOHN NEWTON.

Zigzag.

Zigzag like a snipe. — ANON.

Zigzagged like a lady's vandyked petticoat. — R. S. SURTEES.